READINGS IN STRATEGY
AND STRATEGIC
PLANNING

READINGS IN STRATEGY AND STRATEGIC PLANNING

— edited by —

HARRY COSTIN

THE DRYDEN PRESS

HARCOURT BRACE COLLEGE PUBLISHERS

FORT WORTH   PHILADELPHIA   SAN DIEGO   NEW YORK   ORLANDO   AUSTIN   SAN ANTONIO
TORONTO   MONTREAL   LONDON   SYDNEY   TOKYO

Publisher: George Provol
Acquisitions Editor: John Weimeister
Product Manager: Lisé Johnson
Developmental Editor: Steve Schoen
Project Editor: Andrea Wright
Art Director: Linda Wooton
Production Manager: Lois West
Cover Image: Marc Brown

ISBN: 0-03-017983-1
Library of Congress Catalog Card Number: 97-77740

Address for orders:
The Dryden Press
6277 Sea Harbor Drive
Orlando, FL 32887-6777
1-800-782-4479

Address for editorial correspondence:
The Dryden Press
301 Commerce Street, Suite 3700
Fort Worth, TX 76102

Web site address:
http://www.hbcollege.com

THE DRYDEN PRESS, DRYDEN, and the DP Logo are registered trademarks of Harcourt Brace & Company.

Printed in the United States of America

7 8 9 0 1 2 3 4 5 6 066 9 8 7 6 5 4 3 2 1

The Dryden Press
Harcourt Brace College Publishers

Dedicated to Liam Fahey, John Mahon, and Noel McGinn
Three of the greatest teachers I've ever met

The Dryden Press Series in Management

Preface

The readings included in *Readings in Strategy and Strategic Planning* describe and illustrate diverse ways to conceptualize and apply strategy. The premise in the selection of the readings was that, given the rich literature on strategy in fields as diverse as military history, public policy, and business, important opportunities for conceptual cross-fertilization exist.

The ways in which we conceptualize and operationalize strategy are functions of the specific field of application and of personal choice based on an individual worldview. However, an exposure to the ways different intellectual traditions have conceived strategy may enrich our own conceptions and augment the repertoire from which we make our choices, usually for specific purposes. For example, political conceptions of the role of strategy as consensus building are useful when many stakeholders play a direct role in the formulation of strategy. And strategy conceived as a logical choice among options, through the analysis of organizational strengths and weaknesses and environmental opportunities and threats, remains a useful model to guide strategy formulation in profit and nonprofit organizations, although it may not fully reflect the political reality of organizations.

ORIGINS OF STRATEGY

Strategy as a field of human inquiry and concern may be as old as civilization itself. However, our understanding of early strategic thinking is limited for reasons such as the lack of written sources, our own prejudices that attribute the beginnings of "rational" thinking to the Greeks, and a fragmentary, nonsystemic worldview that makes it difficult for us to "walk in our ancestors' sandals."

Some of the few Oriental, Greek, and Roman classics that have survived deal to some extent with what we might commonly term *strategy* (conceived as rational decision making and selection of the best course of action under a given set of circumstances). Among these classics are the *I Ching*, one of the Confucionist treaties; the writings of Sun Tzu; Thucydides' *Pelopponisian War*; Plutarch's *Parallel Lives*; and Caesar's *Gallic Wars*.

More recent writings include those of Machiavelli and the rich military literature published since the 18th century, when the science of strategy attempted to replace the art of strategy. This trend reached its peak after World War II with the introduction of operations analysis, which employed computer technology that attempted to model reality using a large but finite number of variables.

Currently, a more intuitive view of human behavior is contributing insight to strategic thinking. A view of human nature and interactions that is both intuitive and rational may well lead us to a deeper understanding of the complex whole entity of reality. Intuitive and rational thought is implicit in models such as the learning organization. The reintroduction of systemic thought in the social sciences reminds us that we cannot understand the whole as a simple linear sum of its parts. It may also signal the return of the concept of strategy as an art.

THE ETYMOLOGICAL DEFINITION

Etymologically, the word *strategy* can be traced back to the Greek word *strategos*, defined as the commander in chief of the ancient Greek city-states. Further, *strategos* is composed of two other words: *stratos* (the army) and *agein* (to lead). By extension, the concept of strategy came to imply "the art of the general in the conduct of war."

The etymological meaning of *strategy* relates this concept to that of leadership. One of the leader's (or leaders') main roles is to formulate and implement strategy. This function of leadership implies a continuous flow of decisions, often made under conditions of high stress and with incomplete and ambiguous information. Such a decision-making process is an art that integrates experience with analytical and intuitive capabilities. The next step is to implement these decisions. Strategy implementation then relies on another set of leadership skills that includes the ability to communicate clearly and to mobilize the necessary people and resources to translate decisions into actions. This early conception of strategy has strongly influenced the strategy literature throughout the ages.

NORMATIVE VERSUS DESCRIPTIVE PERSPECTIVES

A fundamental difference exists between the normative and descriptive literature on strategy. At one end of the continuum are complex, detailed analytical-logical models that tell us what strategists ought to do. The planning school and Ansoff (1965) offer examples of the normative perspective. At the other end are thick descriptions of the messy process of strategy formulation and implementation, usually in the form of case studies. Authors such as Mintzberg (1994) have criticized the normative literature and argued that its detailed prescriptions of what strategists should do have little resemblance to observable reality.

Most of the strategy literature combines normative and descriptive elements (such as descriptions of successful strategies, commonplace in the rich military literature), but it remains useful to ask to which extent a particular piece is normative or descriptive.

STRATEGY: DEFINITIONS AND CONCEPTS

A taxonomy of strategy definitions and schools of strategic thinking will always remain incomplete. Therefore, we do not attempt to fully map the field of strategy considered as a conceptual subset of military thought, public policy formulation, or business planning. Nevertheless it is useful to highlight some of the most common definitions of strategy, schools of strategic thinking, and other related concepts.

In the reading included in this book, Mintzberg offers five possible definitions of strategy that embrace the leading concepts of the field: strategy as a plan, a pattern, a position, a perspective, or a ploy.

Strategy as a plan implies a deliberate set of objectives and the means selected to achieve those objectives. This may be the most common definition of strategy and relates to the process of strategy formulation.

Strategy as a pattern focuses less on intentions and more on the pattern emerging from actions and choices, whether deliberate or not. This definition focuses on strategy implementation. A strategy may be said to exist whether it is deliberate and formulated a priori or not.

Strategy as a position is a definition particularly appropriate to the business field. Products and services are positioned in specific competitive markets to address the needs of defined segments of consumers. This definition of strategy has achieved prominence as a natural outgrowth of the sophisticated marketing techniques of segmentation. A prominent example of strategy conceived as a position is Porter's model for the generic strategies of product differentiation and niches.

Strategy as a perspective implies an organization's ingrained way of seeing the world. This perspective, which we may interpret as a key element of the organizational culture, is a shared worldview, a paradigm that influences decision making and behavior.

Strategy as a ploy to outsmart the enemy or competitor is a definition closely linked to the military field and can be traced as far back as Sun Tzu. In the military writings one of the main objectives of the strategist is to infer the true intentions of the enemy.

Closely related to different definitions of strategy are different schools of strategy. Mintzberg (1994, pp. 3–5) offered the useful taxonomy of "ten schools of strategy formation":

> Three [schools] are prescriptive, seeking to explain the "proper" ways of going about the making of strategy. The first I call the "design school," which considers strategy making as an informal process of conception, typically in a leader's conscious mind. The design school model, sometimes called SWOT (for internal strengths and weaknesses to be compared with external opportunities and threats), also underlies the second, which I call the "planning school" and which accepts the premise of the former, save two—that the process be informal and the chief executive be the key actor. . . . The third, which I call the "positioning school," focuses on the content of strategies (differentiation, diversification, etc.) more than on the processes by which they are prescribed to be made (which are generally assumed, often implicitly, to be those of the planning school). In other words, the positioning school simply extrapolates the messages of the planning school into the domain of actual strategy content.

The other seven schools Mintzberg mentioned are briefly described as follows:

> The "cognitive school" considers what happens in a human head that tries to cope with strategy; the "entreprenurial school" depicts strategy making as a visionary process of a strong leader; the "learning school" finds strategy to emerge in a process of collective learning; the "political school" focuses on conflict and the exploitation of power in the process; the "environmental school" sees strategy making as a passive response to external forces; and the "configurational school" seeks to put all the other schools into the contexts of specific episodes in the process.

In synthesis, according to Mintzberg, each school has a particular view of the process of strategy formation as shown in Table 1.

TABLE 1
School View of Process

Design	Conceptual
Planning	Formal
Positioning	Analytical
Cognitive	Mental
Entreprenurial	Visionary
Learning	Emergent
Political	Power
Cultural	Ideological
Environmental	Passive
Configurational	Episodic

STRATEGY FORMULATION AS A LEFT-BRAIN, RIGHT-BRAIN, OR GROUP PROCESS

An implicit disagreement between the normative and descriptive perspectives on strategy is whether the process of strategy formulation is, or should be, essentially analytical and rational or intuitive and synthetic. Further, because strategy formulation seldom involves a single actor, to what extent do group dynamics and politics play a role in real-life strategy formulation? Formulated in the abstract, these positions may appear irreconcilable and historically often have been so. Advocates of formal planning or strategy formulation as rigorous analytical information processing have had little sympathy for the need of inclusive decision making and the use of intuition and other such "fuzzy" skills as valid instruments for complex information processing.

USE OF STRATEGIC SCENARIOS

A potential solution to the controversy may lie in the differentiation of scenarios. Diverse ways of formulating strategy may be appropriate (that is, most efficient) and possible under different scenarios.

Several variables will define the various strategic scenarios. Among these are the following:

1. The *number of actors* directly involved in the process of strategy formulation and the number of stakeholders. It may also be useful to differentiate internal and external stakeholders. Internal stakeholders are defined as those on "our" side, that is, those who share most of our goals. External stakeholders are affected by our decisions but do not share our goals and may include our current or potential competitors. We should remember that unholy alliances may transform external stakeholders into internal ones (for example, a joint venture between competitors in other fields).

2. The *information available* to those involved in strategy formulation, in terms of the number of variables to be considered, the completeness of the information, accuracy, and timeliness.

3. The *time* available to make a decision and the potential impact of the decision made.

A variety of strategic scenarios are possible.

SINGLE ACTOR, RATIONAL DECISION MAKING

Much of the business literature, particularly that of strategic positioning, implicitly describes a single-actor, rational decision-making scenario. A specific course of action, such as the decision to introduce a new product line targeted to a specific customer segment, is taken based on the analysis of specific variables (such as market segmentation, customer preferences, cost, or actual and anticipated competitor moves). The quality of the outcome will depend largely on the quality of the information available for the analysis and accurate assessment of the future (for example, critical inputs such as the cost of oil over a given period) or the definition of worst-case, best-case, or most-likely future scenarios.

We term this scenario *single actor* because the role of group dynamics is minimized. There is either a single final decision maker (for example, the CEO) or a belief that given similar information and assumptions the result of the analysis will be the same for all actors/stakeholders. Under this scenario, disagreement concerning assumptions about the future may be bounded rationally by deciding that "if A happens we will do B, and if C happens we will do D."

A further assumption under this scenario is that there is no important gap between strategy formulation and strategy implementation. A decision based on a rational assessment of existing information can be translated into action. Also, the time to implement a decision does not affect its quality.

In summary, this scenario assumes the following:

- *Actors/stakeholders.* Single or can be viewed as single because the consensus is a function of logical analysis. Given the same information, each actor will arrive at the same conclusion.
- *Goals.* Common to all actors and internal stakeholders (those on "our" side as opposed to other stakeholders, such as competitors). These common goals can be referred to as the "quest for the organizational good."
- *Decision-making process.* Rational/analytical. Given a finite number of factors considered for decision making, a "right" answer can be determined under specific conditions.
- *Decision-making factors.* Finite and few. Amenable to be understood by a single human mind.
- *Information.* Relatively complete and accurate (at least for the purposes of the analysis) and available (potentially at a cost).
- *Assumptions about the future.* The future may be unknown but can be articulated as input variables in the form of likely or best/worst-case scenarios.

SINGLE ACTOR, RATIONAL DECISION MAKING, AND COMPLEX INFORMATION

This second scenario is a variation of the first. The only difference is that there are many variables to be considered for decision making and more information is available. Such information overload can be addressed "rationally" using sophisticated information processing technology. However, such technology may be costly and therefore not available to all. Information processing capability becomes a barrier to entry. As an example, the oil industry relied early on supercomputers to find prospective oil fields.

MULTIPLE ACTORS, POLITICAL DECISION MAKING

Under this scenario, commonly found in descriptions of the development of public policy, the actors are many and the process shifts from rational/analytical to political. A minimum common denominator may or may not exist among the goals of the different actors and stakeholders. Further, even assuming that there is common ground (the key assumption of modern negotiation models), group dynamics play a significant role in the process of strategy formulation, understood as the attempt to find politically acceptable common ground.

This scenario assumes the following:

- *Actors/stakeholders.* The more actors there are, the more likely it is that coalitions will form among those with common goals.
- *Goals.* At least some degree of real or perceived commonality of goals exists among the members of a coalition.
- *Decision-making process.* Political. Also, group dynamics plays an important role in the effort to find common ground and reach consensus.
- *Decision-making factors.* Not only the few or many variables of the task at hand (such as in the formulation of public policy) but also group process factors (such as asymmetries of power within or between coalitions). The importance of factors such as animosity among specific coalitions may obscure and replace the objective analysis of task-related variables.
- *Information.* Includes not only what is related to the task but also perceptions about the position of other coalitions.
- *Assumptions about the future.* Can vary widely across and within coalitions.

IMPORTANCE OF THE SCENARIOS

These strategic scenarios are but a few among many possible options. They integrate what we have called *normative* versus *descriptive* perspectives on strategy. They are descriptive because they do exist; that is, they correspond to observable reality. They are normative because there is an implicit assumption that given certain variables, such as the involvement of one or many actors in decision making, certain decision-making processes make more sense than others. For example, if critical information for decision making is widely available, time to make a decision abundant, and internal stakeholders many, an involved consensus-building process may be appropriate. However, in the case of an emergency, when only scarce and ambiguous information is available and the urgency of the situation allows little time to make a decision, the appropriate decision-making process is likely to be more centralized. It is also interesting to note that an inverse relationship exists between the availability of critical information and the use of "fuzzy" skills such as intuition.

These scenarios support the fundamental premise of this book: no one strategic approach is all-encompassing. Diverse models can provide useful complementary insights into the complex processes of strategy formulation and implementation and are therefore appropriate to specific scenarios. Further, experts from different fields have excelled in analyzing different scenarios. Military historians have provided rich descriptions of decision making under conditions of uncertainty, public policy analysts have offered insights into goal integration and consensus building, and business scholars have shed light on the analytical uses of data and rational decision making.

STRUCTURE OF THE BOOK

Any selection of readings remains by definition only a selection. We hope that the appetizers provided in this book, however substantial they may be, will serve as only an introduction to the many topics available for study. A full follow-up dinner may include some of the original texts from which excerpts were taken or an exotic adventure into the Oriental or Graeco-Roman strategic cuisine.

Part 1 includes excerpts from the well-known strategic classics by Sun Tzu and Clausewitz. The essay on Oriental strategy illustrates the classic concern about the development of the strategos, who has to make life and death decisions under conditions of high uncertainty and pressure.

Part 2 introduces representative selections from some of the best-known business strategy authors and scholars. A useful recommended exercise is to highlight the different definitions of strategy provided by these authors. It is also recommended that readers who are completely unfamiliar with the classics included in Part 1 read Part 2 first.

Part 3 introduces the reader to the implementation of the process of strategic planning and to concepts that help us understand (describe) and frame (influence) the process. It should be noted that the ongoing tension between normative and descriptive approaches to strategy may not necessarily be bad; in fact, it may actually be a creative process in itself.

Part 4 builds on the political dimension of strategic planning introduced in some of the readings in Part 3. The authors included are practitioners who have worked with the large-scale implementation of strategic planning processes. Their perspectives integrate profound conceptual thinking illuminated by the insights gained from actually implementing strategic planning in complex environments.

Part 5 introduces tools and models widely used in the process strategy formulation. Some of the most creative processes useful to consensus building have emerged from disciplines such as anthropology and manufacturing, which traditionally have not been termed strategic.

Part 6 focuses on strategic resources. Over the past two decades our understanding of these resources has become increasingly sophisticated as software, rather than hardware, has emerged as the key source of competitive advantage in many industries. Today it is commonplace to speak of time, design capabilities, and people as key strategic resources. We deeply regret not having been able to include a selection from Pfeffer (1994), who has highlighted the importance of people as the key source of competitive advantage.

Part 7 explores international business strategies, impact of globalization, and attempts to speculate about likely future trends and their impact on businesses and individuals.

REFERENCES

Ansoff, H. I. 1965. *Corporate strategy.* New York: McGraw-Hill.
Mintzberg, Henry. 1994. *The rise and fall of strategic planning.* New York: The Daily Free Press.
Pfeffer, Jeffrey. 1994. *Competitive advantage through people.* Boston: Harvard Business School Press.

Contents

PART 4:   Political Strategy   171

PART 5:   Tools for Strategic Analysis and Planning   201

PART 6:   Sources of Competitive Advantage   289

PART 7:   Global Strategies and the Future   327

READINGS IN STRATEGY AND STRATEGIC PLANNING

PART 1

Classics on Strategy

The Art of War:
Strategic Assessment*

SUN TZU

1. War is a matter of vital importance to the State; the province of life or death; the road to survival or ruin.[1] It is mandatory that it be thoroughly studied.

> *Li Ch'üan*: 'Weapons are tools of ill omen.' War is a grave matter; one is apprehensive lest men embark upon it without due reflection.

2. Therefore, appraise it in terms of the five fundamental factors and make comparisons of the seven elements later named.[2] So you may assess its essentials.
3. The first of these factors is moral influence; the second, weather; the third, terrain; the fourth, command; and the fifth, doctrine.[3]

> *Chang Yü*: The systematic order above is perfectly clear. When troops are raised to chastise transgressors, the temple council first considers the adequacy of the rulers' benevolence and the confidence of their peoples; next, the appropriateness of nature's seasons, and finally the difficulties of the topography. After thorough deliberation of these three matters a general

---

[1] Or 'for [the field of battle] is the place of life and death [and war] the road to survival or ruin'.

[2] Sun Hsing-yen follows the *T'ung T'ien* here and drops the character *shih* (📦): 'matters', 'factors', or 'affairs'. Without it the verse does not make much sense.

[3] Here *Tao* (法) is translated 'moral influence'. It is usually rendered as 'The Way', or 'The Right Way'. Here it refers to the morality of government; specifically to that of the sovereign. If the sovereign governs justly, benevolently, and righteously, he follows the Right Path or the Right Way, and thus exerts a superior degree of moral influence. The character *fa* (法), here rendered 'doctrine', has as a primary meaning 'law' or 'method'. In the title of the work it is translated 'Art'. But in v. 8 Sun Tzu makes it clear that here he is talking about what we call doctrine.

is appointed to launch the attack.[4] After troops have crossed the borders, responsibility for laws and orders devolves upon the general.

4. By moral influence I mean that which causes the people to be in harmony with their leaders, so that they will accompany them in life and unto death without fear of mortal peril.[5]

> *Chang Yü:* When one treats people with benevolence, justice, and righteousness, and reposes confidence in them, the army will be united in mind and all will be happy to serve their leaders. The Book of Changes says: 'In happiness at overcoming difficulties, people forget the danger of death.'

5. By weather I mean the interaction of natural forces; the effects of winter's cold and summer's heat and the conduct of military operations in accordance with the seasons.[6]

6. By terrain I mean distances, whether the ground is traversed with ease or difficulty, whether it is open or constricted, and the chances of life or death.

> *Mei Yao-ch'en:* . . . When employing troops it is essential to know beforehand the conditions of the terrain. Knowing the distances, one can make use of an indirect or a direct plan. If he knows the degree of ease or difficulty of traversing the ground he can estimate the advantages of using infantry or cavalry. If he knows where the ground is constricted and where open he can calculate the size of force appropriate. If he knows where he will give battle he knows when to concentrate or divide his forces.[7]

7. By command I mean the general's qualities of wisdom, sincerity, humanity, courage, and strictness.

> *Li Ch'üan:* These five are the virtues of the general. Hence the army refers to him as 'The Respected One'.
> *Tu Mu:* . . . If wise, a commander is able to recognize changing circumstances and to act expediently. If sincere, his men will have no doubt of the certainty of rewards and punishments. If humane, he loves mankind, sympathizes with others, and appreciates their industry and toil. If courageous, he gains victory by seizing opportunity without hesitation. If strict, his troops are disciplined because they are in awe of him and are afraid of punishment.
> Shen Pao-hsu . . . said: 'If a general is not courageous he will be unable to conquer doubts or to create great plans.'

---

[4]There are precise terms in Chinese which cannot be uniformly rendered by our word 'attack'. Chang Yü here uses a phrase which literally means 'to chastise criminals', an expression applied to attack of rebels. Other characters have such precise meanings as 'to attack by stealth', 'to attack suddenly', 'to suppress the rebellious', 'to reduce to submission', &c.

[5]Or 'Moral influence is that which causes the people to be in accord with their superiors. . . .' Ts'ao Ts'ao says the people are guided in the right way (of conduct) by 'instructing' them.

[6]It is clear that the character *t'ien* (法) (Heaven) is used in this verse in the sense of 'weather', as it is today.

[7]'Knowing the ground of life and death . . .' is here rendered 'If he knows where he will give battle'.

8. By doctrine I mean organization, control, assignment of appropriate ranks to officers, regulation of supply routes, and the provision of principal items used by the army.

9. There is no general who has not heard of these five matters. Those who master them win; those who do not are defeated.

10. Therefore in laying plans compare the following elements, appraising them with the utmost care.

11. If you say which ruler possesses moral influence, which commander is the more able, which army obtains the advantages of nature and the terrain, in which regulations and instructions are better carried out, which troops are the stronger;[8]

> *Chang Yü:* Chariots strong, horses fast, troops valiant, weapons sharp—so that when they hear the drums beat the attack they are happy, and when they hear the gongs sound the retirement they are enraged. He who is like this is strong.

12. Which has the better trained officers and men;

> *Tu Yü:* . . . Therefore Master Wang said: 'If officers are unaccustomed to rigorous drilling they will be worried and hesitant in battle; if generals are not thoroughly trained they will inwardly quail when they face the enemy.'

13. And which administers rewards and punishments in a more enlightened manner;

> *Tu Mu:* Neither should be excessive.

14. I will be able to forecast which side will be victorious and which defeated.

15. If a general who heeds my strategy is employed he is certain to win. Retain him! When one who refuses to listen to my strategy is employed, he is certain to be defeated. Dismiss him!

16. Having paid heed to the advantages of my plans, the general must create situations which will contribute to their accomplishment.[9] By 'situations' I mean that he should act expediently in accordance with what is advantageous and so control the balance.

17. All warfare is based on deception.

18. Therefore, when capable, feign incapacity; when active, inactivity.

19. When near, make it appear that you are far away; when far away, that you are near.

20. Offer the enemy a bait to lure him; feign disorder and strike him.

> *Tu Mu:* The Chao general Li Mu released herds of cattle with their shepherds; when the Hsiung Nu had advanced a short distance he feigned a retirement, leaving behind several thousand men as if abandoning them. When the Khan heard this news he was delighted, and at the head of a strong force marched to the place. Li Mu put most of his troops into formations on the right and left wings, made a horning attack, crushed the Huns and slaughtered over one hundred thousand of their horsemen.[10]

---

[8]In this and the following two verses the seven elements referred to in v. 2 are named.

[9]Emending *i* (法) to *i* (已). The commentators do not agree on an interpretation of this verse.

[10]The Hsiung Nu were nomads who caused the Chinese trouble for centuries. The Great Wall was constructed to protect China from their incursions.

21. When he concentrates, prepare against him; where he is strong, avoid him.

22. Anger his general and confuse him.

Li Ch'uan: If the general is choleric his authority can easily be upset. His character is not firm.

Chang Yü: If the enemy general is obstinate and prone to anger, insult and enrage him, so that he will be irritated and confused, and without a plan will recklessly advance against you.

23. Pretend inferiority and encourage his arrogance.

Tu Mu: Toward the end of the Ch'in dynasty, Mo Tun of the Hsiung Nu first established his power. The Eastern Hu were strong and sent ambassadors to parley. They said: 'We wish to obtain T'ou Ma's thousand-*li* horse.' Mo Tun consulted his advisers, who all exclaimed: 'The thousand-*li* horse! The most precious thing in this country! Do not give them that!' Mo Tun replied: 'Why begrudge a horse to a neighbour?' So he sent the horse.[11]

Shortly after, the Eastern Hu sent envoys who said: 'We wish one of the Khan's princesses.' Mo Tun asked advice of his ministers who all angrily said: 'The Eastern Hu are unrighteous! Now they even ask for a princess! We implore you to attack them!' Mo Tun said: 'How can one begrudge his neighbour a young woman?' So he gave the woman.

A short time later, the Eastern Hu returned and said: 'You have a thousand *li* of unused land which we want.' Mo Tun consulted his advisers. Some said it would be reasonable to cede the land, others that it would not. Mo Tun was enraged and said: 'Land is the foundation of the State. How could one give it away?' All those who had advised doing so were beheaded.

Mo Tun then sprang on his horse, ordered that all who remained behind were to be beheaded, and made a surprise attack on the Eastern Hu. The Eastern Hu were contemptuous of him and had made no preparations. When he attacked he annihilated them. Mo Tun then turned westward and attacked the Yueh Ti. To the south he annexed Lou Fan…and invaded Yen. He completely recovered the ancestral lands of the Hsiung Nu previously conquered by the Ch'in general Meng T'ien.[12]

Ch'en Hao: Give the enemy young boys and women to infatuate him, and jades and silks to excite his ambitions.

24. Keep him under a strain and wear him down.

Li Ch'üan: When the enemy is at ease, tire him.

Tu Mu: …Toward the end of the Later Han, after Ts'ao Ts'ao had defeated Liu Pei, Pei fled to Yuan Shao, who then led out his troops intending to engage Ts'ao Ts'ao. T'ien Fang, one of

---

[11]Mo Tun, or T'ou Ma or T'ouman, was the first leader to unite the Hsiung Nu. The thousand-*li* horse was a stallion reputedly able to travel a thousand *li* (about three hundred miles) without grass or water. The term indicates a horse of exceptional quality, undoubtedly reserved for breeding.

[12]Meng T'ien subdued the border nomads during the Ch'in, and began the construction of the Great Wall. It is said that he invented the writing-brush. This is probably not correct, but he may have improved the existing brush in some way.

Yuan Shao's staff officers, said: 'Ts'ao Ts'ao is expert at employing troops; one cannot go against him heedlessly. Nothing is better than to protract things and keep him at a distance. You, General, should fortify along the mountains and rivers and hold the four prefectures. Externally, make alliances with powerful leaders; internally, pursue an agro-military policy.[13] Later, select crack troops and form them into extraordinary units. Taking advantage of spots where he is unprepared, make repeated sorties and disturb the country south of the river. When he comes to aid the right, attack his left; when he goes to succour the left, attack the right; exhaust him by causing him continually to run about. . . . Now if you reject this victorious strategy and decide instead to risk all on one battle, it will be too late for regrets.' Yuan Shao did not follow this advice and therefore was defeated.[14]

25. When he is united, divide him.

Chang Yü: Sometimes drive a wedge between a sovereign and his ministers; on other occasions separate his allies from him. Make them mutually suspicious so that they drift apart. Then you can plot against them.

26. Attack where he is unprepared; sally out when he does not expect you.

Ho Yen-hsi: . . . Li Ching of the T'ang proposed ten plans to be used against Hsiao Hsieh, and the entire responsibility of commanding the armies was entrusted to him. In the eighth month he collected his forces at K'uei Chou.[15]

As it was the season of the autumn floods the waters of the Yangtze were overflowing and the roads by the three gorges were perilous, Hsiao Hsieh thought it certain that Li Ching would not advance against him. Consequently he made no preparations.

In the ninth month Li Ching took command of the troops and addressed them as follows: 'What is of the greatest importance in war is extraordinary speed; one cannot afford to neglect opportunity. Now we are concentrated and Hsiao Hsieh does not yet know of it. Taking advantage of the fact that the river is in flood, we will appear unexpectedly under the walls of his capital. As is said: "When the thunder-clap comes, there is no time to cover the ears." Even if he should discover us, he cannot on the spur of the moment devise a plan to counter us, and surely we can capture him.'

He advanced to I Ling and Hsiao Hsieh began to be afraid and summoned reinforcements from south of the river, but these were unable to arrive in time. Li Ching laid siege to the city and Hsieh surrendered.

'To sally forth where he does not expect you' means as when, toward its close, the Wei dynasty sent Generals Chung Hui and Teng Ai to attack Shu[16] . . . In winter, in the tenth month,

---

[13]This refers to agricultural military colonies in remote areas in which soldiers and their families were settled. A portion of the time was spent cultivating the land, the remainder in drilling, training, and fighting when necessary. The Russians used this policy in colonizing Siberia. And it is in effect now in Chinese borderlands.

[14]During the period known as 'The Three Kingdoms', Wei in the north and west, Shu in the southwest, and Wu in the Yangtze valley contested for empire.

[15]K'uei Chou is in Ssu Ch'uan.

[16]This campaign was conducted *c.* A.D. 255.

Ai left Yin P'ing and marched through uninhabited country for over seven hundred *li*, chiselling roads through the mountains and building suspension bridges. The mountains were high, the valleys deep, and this task was extremely difficult and dangerous. Also, the army, about to run out of provisions, was on the verge of perishing. Teng Ai wrapped himself in felt carpets and rolled down the steep mountain slopes; generals and officers clambered up by grasping limbs of trees. Scaling the precipices like strings of fish, the army advanced.

Teng Ai appeared first at Chiang Yu in Shu, and Ma Mou, the general charged with its defence, surrendered. Teng Ai beheaded Chu-ko Chan, who resisted at Mien-chu, and marched on Ch'eng Tu. The King of Shu, Liu Shan, surrendered.

27. These are the strategist's keys to victory. It is not possible to discuss them beforehand.

Mei Yao-ch'en: When confronted by the enemy respond to changing circumstances and devise expedients. How can these be discussed beforehand?

28. Now if the estimates made in the temple before hostilities indicate victory it is because calculations show one's strength to be superior to that of his enemy; if they indicate defeat, it is because calculations show that one is inferior. With many calculations, one can win; with few one cannot. How much less chance of victory has one who makes none at all! By this means I examine the situation and the outcome will be clearly apparent.[17]

---

[17]A confusing verse difficult to render into English. In the preliminary calculations some sort of counting devices were used. The operative character represents such a device, possibly a primitive abacus. We do not know how the various 'factors' and 'elements' named were weighted, but obviously the process of comparison of relative strengths was a rational one. It appears also that two separate calculations were made, the first on a national level, the second on a strategic level. In the former the five basic elements named in v. 3 were compared; we may suppose that if the results of this were favorable the military experts compared strengths, training, equity in administering rewards and punishments, and so on (the seven factors).

EDITOR'S INTRODUCTORY NOTE: ORIENTAL STRATEGY

This editor presented the authors of this paper with a daunting task: to translate and describe key concepts of Oriental classics on strategy for Western readers *without fundamentally changing the spirit and language* of the original texts. This may seem like a paradox to those familiar with the style of ancient Oriental classics. One may ask, "How does one make clear what is intentionally vague?" Because Oriental strategic thinking is unencumbered by Western intellectual conventions, which include a demand for focus, clarity, and a clearly defined issue to be analyzed, readings on Oriental strategy may at first seem more poetic and less straightforward than readers expect. Let me simply say that the authors have risen to the challenge and provided us with an essay that will appeal both to our analytical and intuitive capacities.

It can be argued that the main interest of Oriental strategic thinking is not conceptual clarity but the development of the strategist himself, as he is the one who will have to face the challenges of decision making and leadership under extreme and ambiguous situations. According to traditional Oriental strategic thinking, this requires a particular *state of mind* rather than a set of rules or scenarios with associated appropriate behaviors. Such a state of mind needs to be conquered gradually by the aspiring *strategos* (the Greek etymological root of *strategy*, which also refers to an individual endowed with the skills of strategic thinking and leadership). The Oriental classics on strategy, which include, among others, the *I Ching* and the works of Sun Tzu and Musashi Miyamoto, are intended as *food for thought and meditation*, not as rigid behavioral guidelines.

It may be useful for the reader to explore the selection of the classic *The Art of War* by Sun Tzu, also included in this part, before reading this paper, which is based on a large selection of Oriental classics on strategy. Also, a copy of the *I Ching* (available in many different editions and translations) will allow the reader to further explore Oriental strategic thinking according to the suggestions presented by the authors at the end of this paper.

Some Codes of Behavior Applicable to the Business World Taken from Ancient Oriental Texts on Strategy

HORACIO LABAT AND JUAN MANUEL DE FARAMIÑAN

The mechanistic logic of people in the West tends to make us emphasize the external aspect of things and, to some extent, to neglect their inner principles. It may therefore be helpful to look at certain Eastern approaches to behavior, in particular those of Taoism, in order to balance this deficiency. In drawing on these ancient works on strategy from the Far East, then, our intention has been not so much to add more ideas to a field where little remains to be said but to discover modes of conduct that can be useful for the Western world, whether in everyday life or in business. Life is indeed a battlefield.

If we were looking for permanent codes of conduct, we would do well to listen to the words of the *Tao-Te-Ching* on its *VIII Poem:*

> The highest benevolence is like water. The benevolence of water is to benefit all beings without strife. It dwells in places which man despises. Therefore it stands close to DAO. In dwelling benevolence shows itself in place. In thinking benevolence shows itself in depth. In giving benevolence shows itself in love. In speech benevolence shows itself in truth. In ruling benevolence shows itself in order. In working benevolence shows itself in competence. In movement benevolence shows itself in timing. He who does not assert himself thereby remains free of blame.[1]

Being natural is the first principle of all possible codes of conduct, in particular remaining calm and balanced about results whether they are favorable or unfavorable. This natural simplicity, which is adaptable like water as it flows over different spaces and which can equally be ruffled by the wind or become a mirror when in repose, is the wisdom of equilibrium, or balance. Equilibrium, however, is by its very nature unstable and can only be maintained when we are in a state of serene attention. It needs two opposite but complementary attitudes: serenity, which implies peace, and attention, which implies tension. A deficiency in either of these attitudes breaks the equilibrium. It is broken by an excess of peace or by an excess of tension, and its nature, which is in a permanent state of change, lies in its equinoctial point.

For an understanding of this unstable but permanent equilibrium and its point of natural simplicity, the clearest of the Eastern sources to which we have access is the *I Ching*, or Book of Changes. In it, we learn how the various combinations of two antagonistic but complementary elements, called *liang i*, give rise to all the possible relationships in nature. All those possibilities imply the intervention of unlike forces, and from their combinations arise a number of possible states of equilibrium. In that harmonious and unstable, yet at the same time permanent whole, lies the essence of the Tao.

These two forces, *liang i*, are the *yang* and the *yin*, which constitute the permanent dialectical duality that moves all things. The two basic forces allow things to be combined and to change into one another as they arise from a positive principle (the *yang*) and a negative principle (the *yin*). They are also two elemental or primary forms, whose possible configurations give rise to secondary forms. It has been said that from the struggle of these two elements arises the temperament of all things, including that of human beings.

In the search for a code of conduct, we must take as our starting point the *I Ching*, in particular the *liang i*. Thus, we could speak of "visible strategies" within *yang* behavior and of "hidden strategies" within *yin* behavior. Without forgetting that the best strategy, the peak of perfection as Sun Tzu reminds us in *The Art of War (Sun Zi Bingfa)*, is to "win without fighting."[2]

In the Chinese compendium called the *Thirty-Six Stratagems*, we find a veritable source of ways in which difficult situations can be faced. From these we have selected twelve— six of which will refer to *yang* behavior and the other six to *yin* behavior—plus a further six types, which can be used as a basis for conduct in life.

However, none of these strategies is absolutely *yang* (i.e., implying a wholly active behavior) or absolutely *yin* (i.e., wholly passive), for in the Tao every white space contains a black dot and every black space has a white dot, which implies that there are no pure strategies. In other words, in spite of the tendency of some strategies toward activity and others toward passivity, all of them are in fact complementary; otherwise they would lack the flexibility any action needs if it is to lead to victory. An excess of activity is recklessness, just as an excess of passivity leaves the field to the adversary. It is the combination of the two in each strategy that makes them brilliant and allows them to succeed.

YANG BEHAVIOR: THE VISIBLE STRATEGIES

WINNING WITHOUT FIGHTING

Following Sun Tzu's theory, we find the same idea again in the *Thirty-Six Stratagems* in the rule "Beat the grass to startle the snake" (*Da cao jing se*).[3] This refers to deterrent actions that restrict the action of the enemy and give the impression of possessing greater strength than we actually have. This often depends on our own self-confidence. Confidence and serenity about our own values generally discourage the opponent, thus avoiding unnecessary confrontations.

LOOKING FOR THE MOST FAVORABLE TERRAIN

This is what the *Thirty-Six Stratagems* refers to as "luring the tiger out of the mountains" (*Diao hu li shan*).[4] It is a behavior that uses cunning to attract the adversary onto a terrain that the adversary does not control. By bringing the opponent onto a terrain that is favorable to us, we strengthen our qualities and increase our opportunities.

We move more easily on familiar ground, and in addition there are certain *a priori* advantages: first, we do not have to waste time studying the characteristics of the field, and, second, we can use arguments or strengths that are part of our everyday activity. That is to say, on our own ground we already have the use of familiar instruments from the first encounter, and this implies an additional gain from the outset.

ALLOWING THE OPPONENT TO BECOME WEAKENED

Another of the stratagems is to "Watch the fires burning across the river" (*Ge an guan huo*),[5] meaning that on certain occasions no action should be taken. It is a matter of sitting and waiting for good news. As the opponent is being weakened by internal struggles, our victory draws closer: "This stratagem doesn't mean one should wait passively. When the time is ripe, one should strike and destroy the economy."[6]

This idea is condensed in a Chinese fable:

> A clam was basking in the sun with its shell open, when a crane came along and picked at its flesh. The clam closed its shell instantly, trapping the crane's long beak. Neither of them would admit defeat. In the end, a fisherman who was passing by caught both the clam and the crane.

This idea is similarly illustrated in the Chinese proverb "sit down on the top of the mountain, and watch how the tigers fight among themselves."

In short, our action in this case consists of waiting—not in a passive attitude but as a strategy, as a way of acting and observing while the enemy engages in actions that weaken and distract him or her—and waiting for the opportunity.

WAITING FOR THE RIGHT MOMENT

It has always been said that a good strategy is based on being able to recognize the right place and time to launch the offensive. The *Thirty-Six Stratagems* states "Lead away a goat in passing" (*Shun shou qian yang*),[7] which implies that one should pay permanent attention and observe the enemy's behavior in order to take advantage of any mistake the opponent may make.

This is the art of small details, of supplying deficiencies. In a way, strategy plays with spaces, and our counters gradually cover the empty spaces. As with any living being, when our adversary moves, this movement produces free spaces in the adversary's area and that is where we should penetrate. In doing so, we take advantage of those opportunities that are generated by overconfidence, loss of concentration, exhaustion, or a miscalculation of our strength.

This strategy was implemented by Mao Tse Tung in his "Long March," as he states in his *Red Book*: "When the enemy attacks, I draw back. When he stops, I attack. When he rests, I march. When he deploys his forces, I wait."[8] It could be summed up as the strategy of permanent attention, since we modify our behavior to adapt to the movements of others, following the principle of covering the void that others have left behind.

SACRIFICING A PART IN ORDER TO OBTAIN THE WHOLE

This idea appears in the *Thirty-Six Stratagems* as "Sacrificing the plum-tree for the peach-tree" (*Li dai tao jiang*),[9] in accordance with a popular Chinese song which goes: "A peach-tree grows beside the well; a plum-tree takes root beside it. When the worm comes to gnaw the peach-tree, the plum-tree offers itself as a sacrifice."

This indicates that certain sacrifices of a partial nature have to be made in order to preserve the whole. This idea is commonly applied in medicine as when cutting out the diseased part in a patient's body prevents the infection from spreading to the rest of the body and endangering the patient's life. This strategy implies an attitude of detachment and clarity of vision with regard to the importance of the whole, because attachments make us dependent on the superfluous as if it were the essential. When this happens, attachment to a part can endanger or cause the loss of the whole.

GIVING YOUR ENEMY AN ESCAPE ROUTE

This appears in the stratagems as "letting the enemy off in order to ensnare him" *(Yu qin gu zong)*.[10] It implies great skill on the part of the strategist, who has to calculate the right moment—when he or she is in the dominant position—to present the enemy with the opportunity to escape. This brings victory closer and also avoids unnecessary waste when the result is almost certain anyway. But above all, this strategy prevents any unforeseen change of circumstances that might go against the strategist. For example, an enemy who is completely trapped might take desperate action, which could alter the course of events to the enemy's advantage.

For this reason, enemies who already consider themselves to be defeated should be offered an opportunity to retreat. The field will then be ours, and we will not need to invest any further effort in the contest.

YIN BEHAVIOR: THE HIDDEN STRATEGIES

SECRETS ARE CONCEALED IN OPEN SPACES

The idea contained in this strategy is that if we want something to pass unnoticed, it is advisable to do it naturally and obviously. In the *Thirty-Six Stratagems* this appears in the phrase "Cross the sea under camouflage" *(Man tian guo hai)*.[11] It implies the idea that not arousing any concern will lull our opponent into thinking that we are not dangerous. Instead of using all forces against us, our opponent will leave open spaces where we can penetrate without the slightest effort.

Furthermore, if we make something appear familiar, then our opponent will allow it unimpeded movement. Therefore, if our aim is to penetrate the adversary's defenses, we should employ an open strategy that displays movements other than those that are really being concealed.

USING THE OPPONENT'S STRENGTH TO OUR ADVANTAGE

This strategy is contained in the aphorism of the *Thirty-Six Stratagems*, which states, "to kill with a borrowed knife" *(Jie dao sha ren)*.[12] It is what the Master Morihei Ueshiba, the founder of *Aikido*, called *Aiki*: "the power of harmony, of all beings, of all things working together,"[13] whereby we can make use of our opponent's strength with techniques of spherical rotation, thereby overcoming our opponent without opposition.

If we are able to tune into the energy of the universe, following the idea of *Ki*—which is the essential harmony associated with the dual activity of the *yang* and the *yin*—the opposition becomes harmonized because opposites complement one another. Thus, the strategist who is able to tune into the waves of nature, by consciously observing how they operate and without opposing antagonistic forces, will not waste any energy but will be able to take advantage of the flow of those forces. As a proverb of Chinese strategy states, "If you want to do something, get your opponent to do it for you."

THE ART OF INDIRECT CONFRONTATION

This strategy appears in the *Stratagems* as "laying siege to the kingdom of Wei to save the kingdom of Zhao" (*Wei wei jiu Zhao*).[14] It implies not attacking directly but employing stratagems that succeed in confusing the enemy.

The aphorism derives from an ancient tradition that tells how Sun Bin—a descendant of Sun Tzu and probably the person responsible for preserving the *Sun Zi Bingfa*—used it to outwit an enemy general. For, when the king of Wei sent his general to besiege the kingdom of Zhao, instead of defending the besieged kingdom, Sun Bin attacked the kingdom of Wei, forcing its king to recall the besieging troops immediately. As they were returning, they were trapped in an ambush that Sun Bin had previously prepared.

The idea here is that the best form of defense is attack, but to do so from a completely different point than expected using consequential logic. In this case the confrontation will never be head-on, but indirect and even in a different area from where the main confrontation is taking place. All of this confusion causes the opponent to act distractedly or carelessly and to open up vulnerable points.

PRETENDING TO TAKE ANOTHER ROUTE

This is contained in the proverb of the *Thirty-Six Stratagems* that says, "Repair the plank road openly while advancing to Chencang by a hidden path" (*An du chen cang*).[15] As in other cases, this is a way of distracting the enemy. By our deploying false movements that conceal our real intention, our opponent neglects his or her defense.

The adversary should not be aware of what we are thinking, yet we must make him or her believe what in fact we have no intention of doing. As Miyamoto Musashi says, "do not let others see into your mind"[16] or "the science of martial arts involves the presence of mind to act as the sea when the enemy is like a mountain, and act as a mountain when the enemy is like a sea."[17]

TAKING ADVANTAGE OF THE ENEMY'S WEAKNESS

This strategy is closely linked with that of *Ge an guan huo*, which proposed "watching the fires" of the enemy,[18] letting him grow weak, and awaiting the opportunity for a strategy of action. In the situation we are analyzing now, the behavior, which is *yin*, is not just about watching but is also about waiting for the right moment to enter our enemy's house, without effort or waste of energy, once the enemy's internal struggles have completely worn him or her out. The maxim of the *Thirty-Six Stratagems* calls it "looting a burning house" (*Chen huo da jie*),[19] because in this case there is obviously no confrontation at all. No one is going to put up any opposition, and the paradox may even arise whereby our totally weakened opponent sees our arrival as a way to escape these growing difficulties. When the enemy has internal problems, he is ready to be conquered.

KNOWING HOW TO WAIT AND TO ADAPT LIKE WATER

This is an art that Sun Tzu refers to when he states "when opponents are at ease, it is possible to tire them; when they are well fed, it is possible to starve them; when they are at rest, it is possible to move them."[20] It is the same as the advice given in the *Thirty-Six Stratagems:* "Wait at ease for the fatigued enemy" *(Yi yi dai lao).*[21]

With this strategy we are to act like water, which adapts to all circumstances and gains from them or which, when the time comes, can gather all its strength and rush down in a raging torrent or with the patience of the drop can make holes in the hardest rock. In the same spirit, Miyamoto Musashi said in the *Gorin-no-Sho* or *The Book of Five Rings:* "Taking water as the basic point of reference, one makes the mind fluid. Water conforms to the shape of the vessel, square or round, it can be a drop, and it can be an ocean."[22] Using this strategy reduces our enemy by wearing him or her out while waiting for the time when our enemy has no energy left.

STRATEGIES FOR EXTREME SITUATIONS

There are times when all strategies fail, whether they are visible or hidden. We then need to use our cunning to combine the forces of the *yang* and the *yin* into a single strategic effect. Although everything is relative and mutable, as we have said, the visible strategies include *yin* elements and the hidden strategies include *yang* elements. In extreme situations, the order of the Tao reorganizes chaos, and the two *Liang i* forces are combined so that the extreme type of strategy is visible in its tactics but invisible in the desperation from which it stems.

The *Thirty-Six Stratagems* presents six strategies that are designed for use in desperate situations. The first, *Mei ren ji,* literally means "beauty trap,"[23] which implies making our opponent fall into an irresistible temptation in order to weaken his or her will. The second, *Kong cheng ji,* is the "empty city ploy."[24] This implies that we surrender, apparently. The objective is to cause mistrust in the enemy by giving him or her so many facilities that our enemy is fearful of a trap; instead of entering the city, our enemy withdraws. The third, *Fan jian ji,* implies "sow discord in the enemy's camp"[25] by manipulating the adversary's spies so as to provide them with false information. It is interesting that Sun Tzu dedicates the last chapter of the *Sun Zi Bingfa* to the use of spies and, along the lines we mentioned, he states, "The enemy agents that have come to spy on you must be found. Bribe them and induce them to change sides, so as to use them as double agents."[26]

The fourth strategy for extreme situations, *Ku rou ji,* is "to inflict injury on oneself to win the enemy's confidence"[27]; it implies inflicting a self-laceration in order to arouse the sympathy of the indifferent. There are times when a hunger strike is more effective than an armored division. The fifth strategy is *Lian huan ji,* which means to tie the enemy's boats together, that is, to apply "interlocking stratagems."[28] This implies converting our enemy's strength into his or her greatest hindrance—trying to turn a strength into a weakness. This is effectively what is achieved by guerrilla warfare or skirmishing, where the weak has greater speed of movement than the strong who is then obliged to deploy large forces. Of the sixth strategy, a Chinese proverb says, "Of the Thirty-Six Stratagems, the definitive one is the last," and indeed this last one is *Zou wei shang ji*, "When retreat is the best option."[29] When there are no other ways out, a timely retreat is a victory, provided that the retreat does not imply abandonment but is a way of following the course of water, which adapts to all circumstances and retreats now, only to return later. Retreat is not to be confused with surrender, which implies giving up. Retreat, on the other hand, is a tactic that one can use until better opportunities arise or can be found. As Lao Tzu enigmatically reminds us, *Tao Te Ching*, *LXIX Poem*, "Among soldiers there is a saying: I dare not advance an inch, I'd rather withdraw a foot."[30]

RULES FOR THE DEVELOPMENT OF CHARACTER

1. Difficult circumstances are generally the norm in human life, for even at the best of times we are always in danger of losing what we have. Nothing in nature is permanent; everything is changeable and transitory. Good strategists assume these conditions in the environment and make use of them. Far from weakening us, difficulties—if we know how to take advantage of the circumstances—can make us stronger. A Chinese proverb says that "difficult times create heroes," and the philosopher Jorge Angel Livraga said that "when the march is hard, only the hard keep marching" and that "effort makes the bones crack but illuminates the face."[31]

2. In the different strategies we have considered, the good strategist is like water, which adapts to all circumstances without losing its nature. Water is water, whether in the torrent or in the lake, in ice or in the clouds. Another Chinese proverb says that "the truly wise man does not usually give the appearance of being very clever," and indeed, in the strategies we make use of every day, it is advisable to be discreet; otherwise we arouse mistrust and envy. The *Thirty-Six Stratagems* discusses *Jia chi bu diam*, "feigning foolishness,"[32] which means pretending to be stupid without being unintelligent, thus reminding us of the need for modesty and discretion.

   To pass unnoticed is one of the idiosyncratic characteristics of the East which is not very well suited to the Western way of being. However, as a mode of behavior, it is in the West that it may be most useful in the development of character.

3. Another moral rule that we can extract from the use of Eastern strategies is losing the fear of defeat, because those who face their enemy with fear have already lost, which is why it is said that the coward dies twice.

   Calmness of mind is one of the most essential rules of conduct for a good strategist. Imperturbability is one of the fundamental conditions for dealing with any conflict, without forgetting that there is no such thing as a total defeat or a final victory. Therefore every contest needs to be approached with equanimity. As Miyamoto Musashi states, "In my military science, it is essential that the physical aspect and the mental state both be simple and direct, gaining victory by causing opponents to strain distortedly and go off kilter, causing the hearts ad adversaries to do the twisting and twirling."[33] In order to obtain victory, it is necessary to obey reason.

4. In life, strategy should be an amusement. Therefore, when we are facing our enemy, we should not do so inspired by hatred but—even if it may appear paradoxical—by love. The contest is a didactic exercise: in a way, we are trying to teach our opponent about what we consider to be an approximation to the truth or what is most right. Therefore, no teacher acts out of resentment, for this would cause the teacher to fail in his or her objective.

The best teaching for the development of character that we can extract from the reading and practice of the *Stratagems* is that hate is a good strategist's worst adviser. Truly, life is an act of love in conflict. Generation occurs through a meeting of opposite sexes, and from that amorous combat comes life.

Therefore, as strategists hatred is a bad path for us to follow. Instead, love should inspire our actions as strategists, even when facing our enemies. In fact, strategy aims to persuade the opponent through different tricks, and in the game of life, which war is that, we have to accept victory and defeat with equal indifference. If we are to win today, in the game of opposites tomorrow it will be our turn to lose.

We can learn lessons from all of this and gain wisdom too. Sometimes our enemies teach us more than our friends, and on many occasions throughout history great enemies have been seen to feel a mutual admiration for one another. Life is a game.

5. None of the strategies we have studied constitutes a fixed rule. We must become familiar with them, make them part of ourselves, so that when the time comes to apply them they will emerge naturally, without our having to think about them. We should respond as we do when a branch falls on us from above and we automatically raise our arm to protect our head.

The key to a strategy lies in the spontaneity of its application. If a strategy is overrefined and overcomplicated, and if when designing it we are inspired by anger, it will turn against us. If, on the other hand, a strategy arises spontaneously and our attitude toward our enemies is one of understanding and is inspired in the pedagogy of our resolution and our convictions, success is assured.

No student of the Eastern martial arts knows exactly what techniques he or she will use against an opponent in a contest, only that these techniques will arise of their own accord from his or her inner source, as the combat unfolds. That is why the strategies must be known on paper and on the GO board, as the martial artist knows the *Katas* and the movements then arise of their own accord.

This has been the reason for reconstructing the three hexagrams of the visible strategies, the hidden strategies, and the desperate strategies. We have not used them all, only a didactic selection which in our opinion are best suited to the Western mentality. These can help to build a more eclectic and holistic character, in tune with the times that are approaching with the coming third millennium. Our intention has been to make these strategies better known in the West, in the hope that, once they have been harmoniously integrated, they can arise naturally in the game of everyday life.

In the field of personal development, the main adversary we have is ourselves, our faults and our weaknesses. In this sense, Lao Tzu's phrase in the *Tao Te Ching, XXXIII Poem,* is very suggestive: "Whosoever conquers others has force, whosoever conquers himself is the force."[34]

COMPLEMENTARY ASSOCIATIONS WITH THE *I CHING*

In the hexagrams of the *I Ching* we can find further connections with the strategies we selected from the *Thirty-Six Stratagems* which, by following the possible correspondences, can be more fully interpreted and understood.

Without implying that the connections we are making have to be exact, anyone using the *I Ching* can find others, the writers have found them useful, especially the Commentaries made by Confucius (*Kung Tze*). We are therefore presenting the following extracts, as a guide for each of the strategies contained in this work.

Thus, in the case of the visible strategies, we can relate (1) *Winning without fighting* to hexagram 11 (*T'ai*, Peace). In the Commentaries, which says, "bearing with the uncultured in gentleness . . . the wall falls back into the moat. Use no army now. Make your commands known within your own town."[35] (2) *Looking for the favorable terrain* relates to hexagram 39 (*Chien*, Obstruction). In the Commentaries, which says, "The obstruction is overcome not by pressing forward into danger nor by idly keeping still, but by retreating, yielding."[36] (3) *Allowing the opponent to become weakened* relates to hexagram 14 (*Ta Yu*, Possession in Great Measure). In the Commentaries, which says, "The yielding receives the honored place in the great middle, and upper and lower correspond with it. Through fellowship with men, things are sure to fall to one's lot."[37] (4) *Waiting for the right moment* relates to hexagram 5 (*Hsü*, Waiting). In the Commentaries, which says, "All transactions require patient waiting. Waiting means not advancing."[38] (5) *Sacrificing a part in order to obtain the whole* relates to hexagram 41 (*Sun*, Decrease). In the Commentaries, which says, "The hexagram is based on the idea that the top line of the lower trigram is descreased in order to increase the top line of the upper trigram. The ruler is the one who is enriched through decrease of what is below and increase of what is above."[39] (6) *Giving your enemy an escape route* relates to hexagram 8 (*Pi*, Holding Together). In the Commentaries, which says, "Holding together brings good fortune; thus, the kings of antiquity bestowed the different states as fiefs and cultivated friendly relations with the feudal lords. In the hunt the king uses beaters on three sides only and foregoes game that runs off in front."[40]

With regard to the hidden strategies, *we can relate (1) secrets are concealed in open spaces* to hexagram 25 (*Wu Wang*, Innocence). In the Commentaries, which says, "The unexpected means misfortune from without. Under heaven thunder rolls: all things attain the natural state of innocence. If one does not count on the harvest while plowing, nor on the use of the ground while clearing it, it furthers one to undertake something."[41] (2) *Using the opponent's strength to our own advantage* relates to hexagram 26 (*Ta ch'u*, The Taming Power of the Great). In the Commentaries, which says, "When innocence is present, it is possible to tame. The taming power of the great depends upon the time. The upper trigram, Keeping Still, is able to hold fast the lower, the Strong."[42] (3) *The art of indirect confrontation* relates to hexagram 57 (*Sun*, The Gentle). In the Commentaries, which says, "The Gentle means crouching. The dark line is below, it crouches down beneath the light lines, and through this gentle crouching succeeds in penetrating among the strong lines. Penetration is under the bed."[43] (4) *Pretending to take another route* relates to hexagram 44 (*Kou*, Coming to Meet). In the Commentaries, which says, "so that the dark principle thus unexpectedly encounters the light. The movement is initiated by the dark principle, the feminine, which advances to meet the light principle, the masculine, and the weak advances to meet the firm."[44] (5) *Taking advantage of the enemy's weakness* relates to hexagram 18 (*Ku*, Work on What Has Been Spoiled). In the Commentaries, which says, "Work on what has been spoiled means undertakings. Work on what has been spoiled. Afterward there is order. At the same time, however, something thus spoiled imposes the task of working on it, with expectation of success. Work on what has been spoiled has supreme success, and order comes into the world."[45] (6) *Knowing how to wait and to adapt like water* relates to hexagram 29 (*K'an*, The Abysmal, Water). In the Commentaries, which says, "Water flows on without piling up anywhere, and even in dangerous places it does not lose its dependable character. In this way the danger is overcome. Water flows on uninterruptedly and reaches its goal."[46]

For the extreme strategies we can relate (1) *Beauty trap* to hexagram 21 (*Shih Ho,* Biting Through). In the Commentaries, which says, "When there is something that can be contemplated, there is something that creates union. Biting through means consuming. The sun is high above, while the turmoil of the market is below."[47] (2) *Empty city ploy* relates to hexagram 46 (*Sheng,* Pushing Upward). In the Commentaries, which says, "The yielding pushes upward with the time. The favorableness of the conditions comes from the invisible world; we must make the most of them, however, through work. From the first line, the pushing upward proceeds step by step. The first line meets with confidence, the second needs small sacrifices only, the third pushes up into a deserted city, and the fourth finally gains admittance even to realms beyond."[48] (3) *Sow discord in the enemy's camp* relates to hexagram 6 (*Sung,* conflict). In the Commentaries, which says, "If one does not perpetuate the affair, there is a little gossip. In the end, good fortune comes. Although there is a little gossip, the matter is finally decided clearly. Although there is a brief altercation with the neighboring nine, which comes from without, the conflict cannot continue. One cannot engage in conflict; one returns home, gives way."[49] (4) *Injure yourself in order to win the enemy's confidence* relates to hexagram 47 (*K'un,* Oppression). In the Commentaries, which says, "Oppression is the test of character. Oppression leads to perplexity and thereby to success. Through oppression one learns to lessen one's rancor. The superior man alone is capable of being oppressed without losing the power to succeed. He who considers the mouth important falls into perplexity. Thus the superior man stakes his life on following his will."[50] (5) *Interlocking stratagems* relates to hexagram 60 (*Chieh,* Limitation). In the Commentaries, which says, "Establish measure and mean for holding the world within bounds. Limitation means stopping. Joyous in passing through danger; in the appropriate place, in order to limit; central and correct, in order to unite."[51] (6) *When retreat is the best option* relates to hexagram 33 (*Tun,* Retreat). In the Commentaries, which says, "Retreat means withdrawing. This means that success lies in retreating. Great indeed is the meaning of the time of Retreat. Success lies in being able to retreat at the right moment and in the right manner. This success is made possible by the fact that the retreat is not the forced flight of a weak person but the voluntary withdrawal of a strong one."[52]

In conclusion, it should be borne in mind, as Chuang-Tzu would say, that everything in manifestation is relative and mutable: "Destruction is construction, construction is destruction. There is no destruction and construction; both are only one and the same";[53] and the strategies are no exception.

Notes

[1] *Tao Te Ching,* trans. Richard Wilhelm (London: Penguin Classics, 1976), 64.

[2] Sun Tzu, *The Art of War,* trans. Thomas Cleary (Boston and London: Shambhala Dragon Editions, 1988), 67.

[3] Liu Yi, *Secret Art of War: Thirty-Six Stratagems* (Singapore: Asiapac Books, 1992), 90.

[4] Ibid., 102.

[5] Ibid., 64.

[6] Ibid., 70.

[7] Ibid., 83.

[8] Lluis Racionero, ed., *Textos de estetica taoista* (*Texts of Taoist Aesthetics;* Madrid: Alianza, 1983), 10.

[9] Yi, *Secret Art of War,* 78.

[10] Ibid., 107.

[11] Ibid., 6.

[12] Ibid., 20.

[13] Kisshomaru Ueshiba, *The Spirit of Aikido*, trans. Taitetsu Unno (Tokyo, New York, and London: Kodhansha International, 1987), 31.

[14] Yi, *Secret Art of War*, 13.

[15] Ibid., 57.

[16] Miyamoto Musashi, *The Book of Five Rings*, trans. Thomas Cleary (Boston and London: Shambhala Dragon Editions, 1993), 18.

[17] Ibid., 46.

[18] Yi, *Secret Art of War*, 64.

[19] Ibid., 34.

[20] Tzu, *The Art of War*, 101.

[21] Yi, *Secret Art of War*, 27.

[22] Musashi, *Book of Five Rings*, 9.

[23] Yi, *Secret Art of War*, 198.

[24] Ibid., 203.

[25] Ibid., 208.

[26] Tzu, *The Art of War*, 171.

[27] Yi, *Secret Art of War*, 213.

[28] Ibid., 218.

[29] Ibid., 225.

[30] *Tao Te Ching*, 131.

[31] Jorge Angel Livraga Rizzi, ed. N.A., *Cartas a Delia y Fernando* (*Letters to Delia and Fernand,* Madrid 1981), 250.

[32] Yi, *Secret Art of War*, 172.

[33] Musashi, *Book of Five Rings*, 53.

[34] *Tao Te Ching*, 92.

[35] *I Ching* or *Book of Changes*, trans. Richard Wilhelm (London: Arkana, Penguin Group, 1989), 445.

[36] Ibid., 579.

[37] Ibid., 456.

[38] Ibid., 410, 411.

[39] Ibid., 589.

[40] Ibid., 425, 429.

[41] Ibid., 510, 512.

[42] Ibid., 515, 516.

[43] Ibid., 680, 682.

[44] Ibid., 608, 609.

[45] Ibid., 476, 477.

[46] Ibid., 532.

[47] Ibid., 489, 490.

[48] Ibid., 619, 621, 623.

[49] Ibid., 417, 418.

[50] Ibid., 624, 625.

[51] Ibid., 694, 695.

[52] Ibid., 550, 551.

[53] Rancionero, *Textos de estetica taoista*, 13.

The authors wish to thank Maria Dolores Fernandez-Figares and Yolando Calvo for their suggestions in regard to the above references and Julian Scott for his English translation.

On War: Strategy*

Carl von Clausewitz

Chapter I
Strategy

In the second chapter of the second book, Strategy has been defined as *'the employment of the battle as the means towards the attainment of the object of the War'*. Properly speaking it has to do with nothing but the battle, but its theory must include in this consideration the instrument of this real activity—the armed force—in itself and in its principal relations, for the battle is fought by it, and shows its effects upon it in turn. It must be well acquainted with the battle itself as far as relates to its possible results, and those mental and moral powers which are the most important in the use of the same.

Strategy is the employment of the battle to gain the end of the War; it must therefore give an aim to the whole military action, which must be in accordance with the object of the War; in other words, Strategy forms the plan of the War; and to this end it links together the series of acts which are to lead to the final decision, that is to say, it makes the plans for the separate campaigns and regulates the combats to be fought in each. As these are all things which to a great extent can only be determined on conjectures some of which turn out incorrect, while a number of other arrangements pertaining to details cannot be made at all beforehand, it follows, as a matter of course, that Strategy must go with the Army to the field in order to arrange particulars on the spot, and to make the modifications in the general plan which incessantly become necessary in War. Strategy can therefore never take its hand from the work for a moment.

That this, however, has not always been the view taken is evident from the former custom of keeping Strategy in the cabinet and not with the Army, a thing only allowable if the cabinet is so near to the Army that it can be taken for the chief headquarters of the Army.

Theory will therefore attend on Strategy in the determination of its plans, or, as we may more properly say, it will throw a light on things in themselves, and on their relations to each other, and bring out prominently the little that there is of principle or rule.

If we recall to mind from the first chapter how many things of the highest importance War touches upon, we may conceive that a consideration of all requires a rare grasp of mind.

A Prince or General who knows exactly how to organize his War according to his object and means, who does neither too little nor too much, gives by that the greatest proof of his

---

*"Strategy" from *On War* by Carl Von Clausewitz. Reprinted by permission of Routledge Ltd.

genius. But the effects of this talent are exhibited not so much by the invention of new modes of action, which might strike the eye immediately, as in the successful final result of the whole. It is the exact fulfilment of silent suppositions, it is the noiseless harmony of the whole action which we should admire, and which only makes itself known in the total result.

The inquirer who, tracing back from the final result, does not perceive the signs of that harmony is one who is apt to seek for genius where it is not, and where it cannot be found.

The means and forms which Strategy uses are in fact so extremely simple, so well known by their constant repetition, that it only appears ridiculous to sound common sense when it hears critics so frequently speaking of them with high-flown emphasis. Turning a flank, which has been done a thousand times, is regarded here as a proof of the most brilliant genius, there as a proof of the most profound penetration, indeed even of the most comprehensive knowledge. Can there be in the bookworld more absurd productions?

It is still more ridiculous if, in addition to this, we reflect that the same critic, in accordance with prevalent opinion, excludes all moral forces from theory, and will not allow it to be concerned with anything but the material forces, so that all must be confined to a few mathematical relations of equilibrium and preponderance, of time and space, and a few lines and angles. If it were nothing more than this, then out of such a miserable business there would not be a scientific problem for even a schoolboy.

But let us admit: there is no question here about scientific formulas and problems; the relations of material things are all very simple; the right comprehension of the moral forces which come into play is more difficult. Still, even in respect to them, it is only in the highest branches of Strategy that moral complications and a great diversity of quantities and relations are to be looked for, only at that point where Strategy borders on political science, or rather where the two become one, and there, as we have before observed, they have more influence on the 'how much' and 'how little' is to be done than on the form of execution. Where the latter is the principal question, as in the single acts both great and small in War, the moral quantities are already reduced to a very small number.

Thus, then, in Strategy everything is very simple, but not on that account very easy. Once it is determined from the relations of the State what should and may be done by War, then the way to it is easy to find; but to follow that way straightforwardly, to carry out the plan without being obliged to deviate from it a thousand times by a thousand varying influences, requires, besides great strength of character, great clearness and steadiness of mind, and out of a thousand men who are remarkable, some for mind, others for penetration, others again for boldness or strength of will, perhaps not one will combine in himself all those qualities which are required to raise a man above mediocrity in the career of a general.

It may sound strange, but for all who know War in this respect it is a fact beyond doubt, that much more strength of will is required to make an important decision in Strategy than in tactics. In the latter we are hurried on with the moment; a Commander feels himself borne along in a strong current, against which he durst not contend without the most destructive consequences, he suppresses the rising fears, and boldly ventures farther. In Strategy, where all goes on at a slower rate, there is more room allowed for our own apprehensions and those of others, for objections and remonstrances, consequently also for unseasonable regrets; and as we do not see things in Strategy as we do at least half of them in tactics, with the living eye, but everything must be conjectured and assumed, the convictions produced are less powerful. The consequence is that most Generals, when they should act, remain stuck fast in bewildering doubts.

Now let us cast a glance at history—upon Frederick the Great's campaign of 1760, celebrated for its fine marches and manoeuvres: a perfect masterpiece of Strategic skill as critics tell us. Is there really anything to drive us out of our wits with admiration in the King's first trying to turn Daun's right flank, then his left, then again his right, etc.? Are we to see profound wisdom in this? No, that we cannot, if we are to decide naturally and without affectation. What we rather admire above all is the sagacity of the King in this respect, that while pursuing a great object with very limited means, he undertook nothing beyond his powers, and *just enough* to gain his object. This sagacity of the General is visible not only in this campaign, but throughout all the three Wars of the Great King!

To bring Silesia into the safe harbour of a well-guaranteed peace was his object.

At the head of a small State, which was like other States in most things, and only ahead of them in some branches of administration; he could not be an Alexander, and, as Charles XII, he would only, like him, have broken his head. We find, therefore, in the whole of his conduct of War, a controlled power, always well balanced, and never wanting in energy, which in the most critical moments rises to astonishing deeds, and the next moment oscillates quietly on again in subordination to the play of the most subtil political influences. Neither vanity, thirst for glory, nor vengeance could make him deviate from his course, and this course alone it is which brought him to a fortunate termination of the contest.

These few words do but scant justice to this phase of the genius of the great General; the eyes must be fixed carefully on the extraordinary issue of the struggle, and the causes which brought about that issue must be traced out, in order thoroughly to understand that nothing but the King's penetrating eye brought him safely out of all his dangers.

This is one feature in this great Commander which we admire in the campaign of 1760—and in all others, but in this especially—because in none did he keep the balance even against such a superior hostile force, with such a small sacrifice.

Another feature relates to the difficulty of execution. Marches to turn a flank, right or left, are easily combined; the idea of keeping a small force always well concentrated to be able to meet the enemy on equal terms at any point, to multiply a force by rapid movement, is as easily conceived as expressed; the mere contrivance in these points, therefore, cannot excite our admiration, and with respect to such simple things, there is nothing further than to admit that they are simple.

But let a General try to do these things like Frederick the Great. Long afterwards authors, who were eye-witnesses, have spoken of the danger, indeed of the imprudence, of the King's camps, and doubtless, at the time he pitched them, the danger appeared three times as great as afterwards.

It was the same with his marches, under the eyes, nay, often under the cannon of the enemy's Army; these camps were taken up, these marches made, not from want of prudence, but because in Daun's system, in his mode of drawing up his Army, in the responsibility which pressed upon him, and in his character, Frederick found that security which justified his camps and marches. But it required the King's boldness, determination, and strength of will to see things in this light, and not to be led astray and intimidated by the danger of which thirty years after people still wrote and spoke. Few Generals in this situation would have believed these simple strategic means to be practicable.

Again, another difficulty in execution lay in this, that the King's Army in this campaign was constantly in motion. Twice it marched by wretched cross-roads, from the Elbe into Silesia, in rear of Daun and pursued by Lascy (beginning of July, beginning of August). It required to be always ready for battle, and its marches had to be organized with a degree of skill which necessarily called forth a proportionate amount of exertion. Although attended and delayed by thousands of waggons, still its subsistence was extremely difficult. In Silesia, for eight days before the battle of Leignitz, it had constantly to march, defiling alternately right and left in front of the enemy: this costs great fatigue, and entails great privations.

Is it to be supposed that all this could have been done without producing great friction in this machine? Can the mind of a Commander elaborate such movements with the same ease as the hand of a land surveyor uses the astrolabe? Does not the sight of the sufferings of their hungry, thirsty comrades pierce the hearts of the Commander and his Generals a thousand times? Must not the murmurs and doubts which these cause reach his ear? Has an ordinary man the courage to demand such sacrifices, and would not such efforts most certainly demoralize the Army, break up the bands of discipline, and, in short, undermine its military virtue, if firm reliance on the greatness and infallibility of the Commander did not compensate for all? Here, therefore, it is that we should pay respect; it is these miracles of execution which we should admire. But it is impossible to realize all this in its full force without a foretaste of it by experience. He who only knows War from books or the drill-ground cannot realize the whole effect of this counterpoise in action; *we beg him, therefore, to accept from us on faith and trust all that he is unable to supply from any personal experience of his own.*

This illustration is intended to give more clearness to the course of our ideas, and in closing this chapter we will only briefly observe that in our exposition of Strategy we shall describe those separate subjects which appear to us the most important, whether of a moral or material nature; then proceed from the simple to the complex, and conclude with the inner connexion of the whole act of War, in other words, with the plan for a War or campaign.

OBSERVATION

In an earlier manuscript of the second book are the following passages endorsed by the author himself to be used for the first Chapter of the second Book: *the projected revision of that chapter not having been made, the passages referred to are introduced here in full.*

By the mere assemblage of armed forces at a particular point, a battle there becomes possible, but does not always take place. Is that possibility now to be regarded as a reality and therefore an effective thing? Certainly, it is so by its results, and these effects, whatever they may be, can never fail.

1. Possible combats are on account of their results to be looked upon as real ones.

If a detachment is sent away to cut off the retreat of a flying enemy, and the enemy surrenders in consequence without further resistance, still it is through the combat which is offered to him by this detachment sent after him that he is brought to his decision.

If a part of our Army occupies an enemy's province which was undefended, and thus deprives the enemy of very considerable means of keeping up the strength of his Army, it is entirely through the battle which our detached body gives the enemy to expect, in case he seeks to recover the lost province, that we remain in possession of the same.

In both cases, therefore, the mere possibility of a battle has produced results, and is therefore to be classed amongst actual events. Suppose that in these cases the enemy has opposed our troops with others superior in force, and thus forced ours to give up their object without a combat, then certainly our plan has failed, but the battle which we offered at (either of) these points has not on that account been without effect, for it attracted the enemy's forces to that point. And in case our whole undertaking has done us harm, it cannot be said that these positions, these possible battles, have been attended with no results; their effects, then, are similar to those of a lost battle.

In this manner we see that the destruction of the enemy's military forces, the overthrow of the enemy's power, is only to be done through the effect of a battle, whether it be that it actually takes place, or that it is merely offered, and not accepted.

2. Twofold object of the combat

But these effects are of two kinds, direct and indirect; they are of the latter, if other things intrude themselves and become the object of the combat—things which cannot be regarded as the destruction of the enemy's force, but only leading up to it, certainly by a circuitous road, but with so much the greater effect. The possession of provinces, towns, fortresses, roads, bridges, magazines, etc., may be the *immediate* object of a battle, but never the ultimate one. Things of this description can never be looked upon otherwise than as means of gaining greater superiority, so as at last to offer battle to the enemy in such a way that it will be impossible for him to accept it. Therefore all these things must only be regarded as intermediate links, steps, as it were, leading up to the effectual principle, but never as that principle itself.

3. Examples

In 1814, by the capture of Buonaparte's capital the object of the War was attained. The political divisions which had their roots in Paris came into active operation, and an enormous split left the power of the Emperor to collapse of itself. Nevertheless the point of view from which we must look at all this is, that through these causes the forces and defensive means of Buonaparte were suddenly very much diminished, the superiority of the Allies, therefore, just in the same measure increased, and any further resistance then became *impossible*. It was this impossibility which produced the peace with France. If we suppose the forces of the Allies at that moment diminished to a like extent through external causes; if the superiority vanishes, then at the same time vanishes also all the effect and importance of the taking of Paris.

We have gone through this chain of argument in order to show that this is the natural and only true view of the thing from which it derives its importance. It leads always back to the question, What at any given moment of the War or campaign will be the probable result of the great or small combats which the two sides might offer to each other? In the consideration of a plan for a campaign, this question only is decisive as to the measures which are to be taken all through from the very commencement.

4. When this view is not taken, then a false value is given to other things.

If we do not accustom ourselves to look upon War, and the single campaigns in a War, as a chain which is all composed of battles strung together, one of which always brings on another; if we adopt the idea that the taking of a certain geographical point, the occupation of an undefended province, is in itself anything; then we are very likely to regard it as an acquisition which we may retain; and if we look at it so, and not as a term in the whole series of events, we do not ask ourselves whether this possession may not lead to greater disadvantages hereafter. How often we find this mistake recurring in military history.

We might say that, just as in commerce the merchant cannot set apart and place in security gains from one single transaction by itself, so in War a single advantage cannot be separated from the result of the whole. Just as the former must always operate with the whole bulk of his means, just so in War, only the sum total will decide on the advantage or disadvantage of each item.

If the mind's eye is always directed upon the series of combats, so far as they can be seen beforehand, then it is always looking in the right direction, and thereby the motion of the force acquires that rapidity, that is to say, willing and doing acquire that energy which is suitable to the matter, and which is not to be thwarted or turned aside by extraneous influences.

CHAPTER II
ELEMENTS OF STRATEGY

The causes which condition the use of the combat in Strategy may be easily divided into elements of different kinds, such as the moral, physical, mathematical, geographical, and statistical elements.

The first class includes all that can be called forth by moral qualities and effects; to the second belong the whole mass of the military force, its organization, the proportion of the three arms, etc., etc.; to the third, the angle of the lines of operation, the concentric and eccentric movements in as far as their geometrical nature has any value in the calculation; to the fourth, the influences of country, such as commanding points, hills, rivers, woods, roads, etc., etc.; lastly, to the fifth, all the means of supply. The separation of these things once for all in the mind does good in giving clearness and helping us to estimate at once, at a higher or lower value, the different classes as we pass onwards. For, in considering them separately, many lose of themselves their borrowed importance; one feels, for instance, quite plainly that the value of a base of operations, even if we look at nothing in it but its relative position to the line of operations, depends much less in that simple form on the geometrical element of the angle which they form with one another, than on the nature of the roads and the country through which they pass.

But to treat upon Strategy according to these elements would be the most unfortunate idea that could be conceived, for these elements are generally manifold, and intimately connected with each other in every single operation of War. We should lose ourselves in the most soulless analysis, and as if in a horrid dream, we should be for ever trying in vain to build up an arch to connect this base of abstractions with facts belonging to the real world. Heaven preserve every theorist from such an undertaking! We shall keep to the world of things in their totality, and not pursue our analysis further than is necessary from time to time to give distinctness to the idea which we wish to impart, and which has come to us, not by a speculative investigation, but through the impression made by the realities of War in their entirety.

CHAPTER III
MORAL FORCES

We must return again to this subject, which is touched upon in the third chapter of the second book, because the moral forces are amongst the most important subjects in War. They form the spirit which permeates the whole being of War. These forces fasten themselves soonest and with the greatest affinity on to the Will which puts in motion and guides the whole mass of powers, uniting with it as it were in one stream, because this is a moral force itself. Unfortunately they will escape from all book-analysis, for they will neither be brought into numbers nor into classes, and require to be both seen and felt.

The spirit and other moral qualities which animate an Army, a General, or Governments, public opinion in provinces in which a War is raging, the moral effect of a victory or of a defeat are things which in themselves vary very much in their nature, and which also, according as they stand with regard to our object and our relations, may have an influence in different ways.

Although little or nothing can be said about these things in books, still they belong to the theory of the Art of War, as much as everything else which constitutes War. For I must here once more repeat that it is a miserable philosophy if, according to the old plan, we establish rules and principles wholly regardless of all moral forces, and then, as soon as these forces make their appearance, we begin to count exceptions which we thereby establish as it were theoretically, that is, make into rules; or if we resort to an appeal to genius, which is above all rules, thus giving out by implication, not only that rules were only made for fools, but also that they themselves are no better than folly.

Even if the theory of the Art of War does no more in reality than recall these things to remembrance, showing the necessity of allowing to the moral forces their full value, and of always taking them into consideration, by so doing it extends its borders over the region of immaterial forces, and by establishing that point of view, condemns beforehand every one who would endeavour to justify himself before its judgement seat by the mere physical relations of forces.

Further out of regard to all other so-called rules, theory cannot banish the moral forces beyond its frontier, because the effects of the physical forces and the moral are completely fused, and are not to be decomposed like a metal alloy by a chemical process. In every rule relating to the physical forces, theory must present to the mind at the same time the share which the moral powers will have in it, if it would not be led to categorical propositions, at one time too timid and contracted, at another too dogmatical and wide. Even the most matter-of-fact theories have, without knowing it, strayed over into this moral kingdom; for, as an example, the effects of a victory cannot in any way be explained without taking into consideration the moral impressions. And therefore the most of the subjects which we shall go through in this book are composed half of physical, half of moral causes and effects, and we might say the physical are almost no more than the wooden handle, whilst the moral are the noble metal, the real bright-polished weapon.

The value of the moral powers, and their frequently incredible influence, are best exemplified by history, and this is the most generous and the purest nourishment which the mind of the General can extract from it. At the same time it is to be observed, that it is less demonstrations, critical examinations, and learned treatises, than sentiments, general impressions, and single flashing sparks of truth, which yield the seeds of knowledge that are to fertilize the mind.

We might go through the most important moral phenomena in War, and with all the care of a diligent professor try what we could impart about each, either good or bad. But as in such a method one slides too much into the commonplace and trite, whilst real mind quickly makes its escape in analysis, the end is that one gets imperceptibly to the relation of things which everybody knows. We prefer, therefore, to remain here more than usually incomplete and rhapsodical, content to have drawn attention to the importance of the subject in a general way, and to have pointed out the spirit in which the views given in this book have been conceived.

CHAPTER IV
THE CHIEF MORAL POWERS

These are *The Talents of the Commander; The Military Virtue of the Army; Its National feeling*. Which of these is the most important no one can tell in a general way, for it is very difficult to say anything in general of their strength, and still more difficult to compare the strength of one with that of another. The best plan is not to undervalue any of them, a fault which human judgement is prone to, sometimes on one side, sometimes on another, in its whimsical oscillations. It is better to satisfy ourselves of the undeniable efficacy of these three things by sufficient evidence from history.

It is true, however, that in modern times the Armies of European states have arrived very much at a par as regards discipline and fitness for service, and that the conduct of War has—as philosophers would say—naturally developed itself, thereby become a method, common as it were to all Armies, so that even from Commanders there is nothing further to be expected in the way of application of special means of Art, in the limited sense (such as Frederick the Second's oblique order). Hence it cannot be denied that, as matters now stand, greater scope is afforded for the influence of National spirit and habituation of an army to War. A long peace may again alter all this.

The national spirit of an Army (enthusiasm, fanatical zeal, faith, opinion) displays itself most in mountain warfare, where every one down to the common soldier is left to himself. On this account, a mountainous country is the best campaigning ground for popular levies.

Expertness of an Army through training, and that well-tempered courage which holds the ranks together as if they had been cast in a mould, show their superiority in an open country.

The talent of a General has most room to display itself in a closely intersected, undulating country. In mountains he has too little command over the separate parts, and the direction of all is beyond his powers; in open plains it is simple and does not exceed those powers.

According to these undeniable elective affinities, plans should be regulated.

PART 2

Defining Strategy

The Strategy Concept I: Five Ps for Strategy*

HENRY MINTZBERG

Human nature insists on a definition for every concept. The field of strategic management cannot afford to rely on a single definition of strategy, indeed the word has long been used implicitly in different ways even if it has traditionally been defined formally in only one. Explicit recognition of multiple definitions can help practitioners and researchers alike to maneuver through this difficult field. Accordingly, this article presents five definitions of strategy—as plan, ploy, pattern, position, and perspective—and considers some of their interrelationships.

STRATEGY AS PLAN

To almost anyone you care to ask, *strategy is a plan*—some sort of *consciously intended* course of action, a guideline (or set of guidelines) to deal with a situation. A kid has a "strategy" to get over a fence, a corporation has one to capture a market. By this definition, strategies have two essential characteristics: they are made in advance of the actions to which they apply, and they are developed consciously and purposefully. (They may, in addition, be stated explicitly, sometimes in formal documents known as "plans," although it need not be taken here as a necessary condition for "strategy as plan.") To Drucker, strategy is "purposeful action"[1], to Moore "design for action," in essence, "conception preceding action."[2] A host of definitions in a variety of fields reinforce this view. For example:

- in the military: Strategy is concerned with "draft[ing] the plan of war...shap[ing] the individual campaigns and within these, decid[ing] on the individual engagements."[3]
- in Game Theory: Strategy is "a complete plan: a plan which specifies what choices [the player] will make in every possible situation."[4]
- in management: "Strategy is a unified, comprehensive, and integrated plan...designed to ensure that the basic objectives of the enterprise are achieved."[5]
- and in the dictionary: strategy is (among other things) "a plan, method, or series of maneuvers or stratagems for obtaining a specific goal or result."[6]

As plans, strategies may be general or they can be specific. There is one use of the word in the specific sense that should be identified here. As plan, *a strategy can be a ploy, too, really* just a specific "maneuver" intended to outwit an opponent or competitor. The kid may use the fence as a ploy to draw a bully into his yard, where his Doberman Pincher awaits intruders. Likewise, a corporation may threaten to expand plant capacity to discourage a competitor from building a new plant. Here the real strategy (as plan, that is, the real intention) is the threat, not the expansion itself, and as such is a ploy.

In fact, there is a growing literature in the field of strategic management, as well as on the general process of bargaining, that views strategy in this way and so focusses attention on its most dynamic and competitive aspects. For example, in his popular book, *Competitive Strategy*, Porter devotes one chapter to "Market Signals" (including discussion of the effects of announcing moves, the use of "the fighting brand," and the use of threats of private antitrust suits) and another to "Competitive Moves" (including actions to preempt competitive response).[7] Likewise in his subsequent book, *Competitive Advantage*, there is a chapter on "Defensive Strategy" that discusses a variety of ploys for reducing the probability of competitor retaliation (or increasing his perception of your own).[8] And Schelling devotes much of his famous book, *The Strategy of Conflict*, to the topic of ploys to outwit rivals in a competitive or bargaining situation.[9]

STRATEGY AS PATTERN

But if strategies can be intended (whether as general plans or specific ploys), surely they can also be realized. In other words, defining strategy as a plan is not sufficient; we also need a definition that encompasses the resulting behavior. Thus a third definition is proposed: *strategy is a pattern*—specifically, a pattern in a stream of actions.[10] By this definition, when Picasso painted blue for a time, that was a strategy, just as was the behavior of the Ford Motor Company when Henry Ford offered his Model T only in black. In other words, by this definition, strategy is *consistency* in behavior, *whether or not* intended.

This may sound like a strange definition for a word that has been so bound up with free will ("strategos" in Greek, the art of the army general[11]). But the fact of the matter is that while hardly anyone defines strategy in this way,[12] many people seem at one time or another to so use it. Consider this quotation from a business executive:

> Gradually the successful approaches merge into a pattern of action that becomes our strategy. We certainly don't have an overall strategy on this.[13]

This comment is inconsistent only if we restrict ourselves to one definition of strategy: what this man seems to be saying is that his firm has strategy as pattern, but not as plan. Or consider this comment in *Business Week* on a joint venture between General Motors and Toyota:

> The tentative Toyota deal may be most significant because it is another example of how GM's strategy boils down to doing a little bit of everything until the market decides where it is going.[14]

A journalist has inferred a pattern in the behavior of a corporation, and labelled it strategy.

The point is that every time a journalist imputes a strategy to a corporation or to a government, and every time a manager does the same thing to a competitor or even to the senior management of his own firm, they are implicitly defining strategy as pattern in action—that is, inferring consistency in behavior and labelling it strategy. They may, of course, go further and impute intention to that consistency—that is, assume there is a plan behind the pattern. But that is an assumption, which may prove false.

Thus, the definitions of strategy as plan and pattern can be quite independent of each other: plans may go unrealized, while patterns may appear without preconception. To paraphrase Hume, strategies may result from human actions but not human designs.[15] If we label the first definition *intended* strategy and the second *realized* strategy, as shown in Figure 1, then we can distinguish *deliberate* strategies, where patterns developed in the absence of intentions, or despite them (which went *unrealized*).

STRATEGIES ABOUT WHAT?

Labelling strategies as plans or patterns still begs one basic question: *strategies about what?* Many writers respond by discussing the deployment of resources (e.g., Chandler, in one of the best known definitions[16]), but the question remains: which resources and for what purposes? An army may plan to reduce the number of nails in its shoes, or a corporation may realize a pattern of marketing only products painted black, but these hardly meet the lofty label "strategy." Or do they?

As the word has been handed down from the military, "strategy" refers to the important things, "tactics" to the details (more formally, "tactics teaches the use of armed forces in the engagement, strategy the use of engagements for the object of the war"[17]). Nails in shoes, colors of cars: these are certainly details. The problem is that in retrospect details can sometimes prove "strategic." Even in the military: "For want of a Nail, the Shoe was lost: for want of a Shoe the Horse was lost…" and so on through the rider and general to the battle, "all for want of Care about a Horseshoe Nail."[18] Indeed one of the reasons Henry Ford lost his war with General Motors was that he refused to paint his cars anything but black.

Rumelt notes that "one person's strategies are another's tactics—that what is strategic depends on where you sit."[19] It also depends on *when you sit*: what seems tactical today may prove strategic tomorrow. The point is that these sorts of distinctions can be arbitrary and misleading, that labels should not be used to imply that some issues are *inevitably* more important than others. There are times when it pays to manage the details and let the strategies emerge for themselves. Thus there is good reason to drop the word "tactics" altogether and simply refer to issues as more or less "strategic," in other words, more or less "important" in some context, whether as intended before acting or as realized after it.[20] Accordingly, the answer to the question, strategy about what, is: potentially about anything. About products and processes, customers and citizens, social responsibilities and self interests, control and color.

Two aspects of the content of strategies must, however, be singled out because they are of particular importance and, accordingly, play major roles in the literature.

external

STRATEGY AS POSITION

The fourth definition is that *strategy is a position*—specifically, a means of locating an organization in what organization theorists like to call an "environment." By this definition, strategy becomes the mediating force—or "match," according to Hofer and Schendel[21]—

FIGURE 1

Deliberate and Emergent Strategies

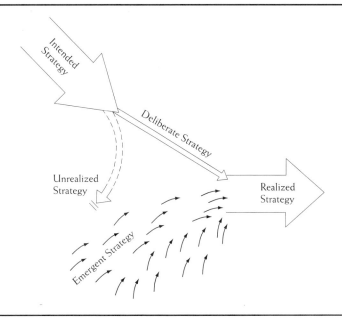

between organization and environment, that is, between the internal and the external context. In ecological terms, strategy becomes a "niche"; in economic terms, a place that generates "rent" (that is "returns to [being] in a 'unique' place"[22]); in management terms,
formally, a product-market "domain,"[23] the place in the environment where resources are
concentrated (leading McNichols to call this "root strategy"[24])

   Note that this definition of strategy can be compatible with either (or all) of the preceding ones: a position can be preselected and aspired to through a plan (or ploy) and/or
it can be reached, perhaps even found, through a pattern of behavior ("the concept of strategy need not be tied to rational planning or even conscious decision-making assumptions.
Strategy is essentially a descriptive idea that includes an organization's choice of niche and
its primary decision rules...for coping with that niche"[25]).

   In military and game theory views of strategy, it is generally used in the context of what
is called a "two-person game," better known in business as head-on competition (where ploys
are especially common). The definition of strategy as position, however, implicitly allows
us to open up the concept, to so-called n-person games (that is, many players), and
beyond. In other words, while position can always be defined with respect to a single competitor (literally so in the military, where position becomes the site of battle), it can also
be considered in the context of a number of competitors or simply with respect to markets or an environment at large.[26] Since head-on competition is not the usual case in business, management theorists have generally focussed on the n-person situation, although
they have tended to retain the notion of economic competition.[27] But strategy as position
can extend beyond competition too, economic and otherwise. Indeed, what is the meaning of the word "niche" but a position that is occupied to *avoid* competition.

Thus, we can move from the definition employed by General Ulysses Grant in the 1860s, "Strategy [is] the deployment of one's resources in a manner which is most likely to defeat the enemy," to that of Professor Rumelt in the 1980s, "Strategy is creating situations for economic rents and finding ways to sustain them,"[28] that is, any viable position, whether or not directly competitive.

Astley and Fombrun, in fact, take the next logical step by introducing the notion of "collective" strategy, that is, strategy pursued to promote cooperation between organizations, even would-be competitors (equivalent in biology to animals herding together for protection).[29] Such strategies can range "from informal arrangements and discussions to formal devices such as interlocking directorates, joint ventures, and mergers."[30] In fact, considered from a slightly different angle, these can sometimes be described as *political* strategies, that is strategies to subvert the legitimate forces of competition.

STRATEGY AS PERSPECTIVE

While the fourth definition of strategy looks out, seeking to locate the organization in the external environment, the fifth looks inside the organization, indeed inside the heads of the collective strategist. Here, *strategy is a perspective*, its content consisting not just of a chosen position, but of an ingrained way of perceiving the world. Some organizations, for example, are aggressive pacesetters, creating new technologies and exploiting new markets; others perceive the world as set and stable, and so sit back in long established markets and build protective shells around themselves, relying more on political influence than economic efficiency. There are organizations that favor marketing and build a whole ideology around that (an IBM); others treat engineering in this way (a Hewlett-Packard); and then there are those that concentrate on sheer productive efficiency (a McDonald's).

Strategy in this respect is to the organization what personality is to the individual. Indeed, one of the earliest and most influential writers on strategy (at least as his ideas have been reflected in more popular writings) was Philip Selznick, who wrote about the "character" of an organization—distinct and integrated "commitments to ways of acting and responding" that are build right into it.[31] A variety of concepts from other fields also capture this notion: psychologists refer to an individual's mental frame, cognitive structure, and a variety of other expressions for "relatively fixed patterns for experiencing [the] world"[32]; anthropologists refer to the "culture" of a society and sociologists to its "ideology"; military theorists write of the "grand strategy" of armies; while management theorists have used terms such as the "theory of the business"[33] and its "driving force"[34]; behavioral scientists who have read Kuhn[35] on the philosophy of science refer to the "paradigm" of a community of scholars; and Germans perhaps capture it best with their word "Weltanschauung," literally "worldview," meaning collective intuition about how the world works.

This fifth definition suggests above all that strategy is a *concept*. This has one important implication, namely, that all strategies are abstractions which exist only in the minds of interested parties—those who pursue them, are influenced by that pursuit, or care to observe others doing so. It is important to remember that no-one has ever seen a strategy or touched one; every strategy is an invention, a figment of someone's imagination, whether conceived of as intentions to regulate behavior before it takes place or inferred as patterns to describe behavior that has already occurred.

What is of key importance about this fifth definition, however, is that the perspective is *shared*. As implied in the words Weltanschauung, culture, and ideology (with respect to a society) or paradigm (with respect to a community of scholars), but not the word personality, strategy is a perspective shared by the members of an organization, through their intentions and/or by their actions. In effect, when we are talking of strategy in this context, we are entering the realm of the *collective mind*—individuals united by common thinking and/or behavior. A major issue in the study of strategy formation becomes, therefore, how to read that collective mind—to understand how intentions diffuse through the system called organization to become shared and how actions come to be exercised on a collective yet consistent basis.

INTERRELATING THE Ps

As suggested above, strategy as both position and perspective can be compatible with strategy as plan and/or pattern. But, in fact, the relationships between these different definitions can be more involved than that. For example, while some consider perspective to be a plan (Lapierre writes of strategies as "dreams in search of reality"[36]; Summer, more prosaically, as "a comprehensive, holistic, gestalt, logical vision of some future alignment"[37]), others describe it as *giving rise* to plans (for example, as positions and/or patterns in some kind of implicit hierarchy). This is shown in Figure 2a. Thus, Majone writes of "basic principles, commitments, and norms" that form the "policy core," while "plans, programs, and decisions" serve as the "protective belt."[38] Likewise, Hedberg and Jonsson claim that strategies, by which they mean "more or less well integrated sets of ideas and constructs" (in our terms, perspectives) are "the causes that mold streams of decisions into patterns."[39] This is similar to Tregoe and Zimmerman who define strategy as "vision directed"—"the framework which guides those choices that determine the nature and direction of an organization."[40] Note in the second and third of these quotations that, strictly speaking, the hierarchy can skip a step, with perspective dictating pattern, not necessarily through formally intended plans.

Consider the example of the Honda Company, which has been described in one highly publicized consulting report[41] as parlaying a particular perspective (being a low cost producer, seeking to attack new markets in aggressive ways) into a plan, in the form of an intended position (to capture the traditional motorcycle market in the United States and create a new one for small family motorcycles), which was in turn realized through an integrated set of patterns (lining up distributorships, developing the appropriate advertising campaign of "You meet the nicest people on a Honda," etc.). All of this matches the conventional prescriptive view of how strategies are supposed to get made.[42]

But a closer look at Honda's actual behavior suggests a very different story: it did not go to America with the main intention of selling small, family motorcycles at all; rather, the company seemed to fall into that market almost inadvertently.[43] But once it was clear to the Honda executives that they had wandered into such a lucrative strategic position, that presumably became their plan. In other words, their strategy emerged, step by step, but once recognized, was made deliberate. Honda, if you like, developed its intentions through its actions, another way of saying that pattern evoked plan. This is shown in Figure 2b.

Of course, an overall strategic perspective (Honda's way of doing things) seems to have underlaid all this, as shown in the figure as well. But we may still ask how that perspective

FIGURE 2

Some Possible Relationships between Strategy as Plan, Pattern, Position, Perspective

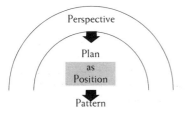

(a) Conventional hierarchy

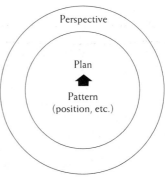

(b) Formalizing on emergent strategy
within a perspective

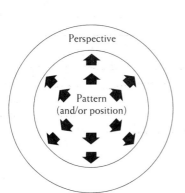

(c) Pattern (or position) producing perspective

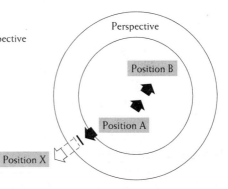

(d) Perspective constraining shift in position
("Egg McMuffin" syndrome)

arose in the first place. The answer seems to be that it did so in a similar way, through earlier experiences: the organization tried various things in its formative years and gradually consolidated a perspective around what worked.[44] In other words, organizations would appear to develop "character"—much as people develop personality—by interacting with the world as they find it through the use of their innate skills and natural propensities. Thus pattern can give rise to perspective too, as shown in Figure 2c. And so can position. Witness Perrow's discussion of the "wool men" and "silk men" of the textile trade, people who developed an almost religious dedication to the fibers they produced.[45]

No matter how they appear, however, there is reason to believe that while plans and positions may be dispensable, perspectives are immutable.[46] In other words, once they are established, perspectives become difficult to change. Indeed, a perspective may become so deeply ingrained in the behavior of an organization that the associated beliefs can become subconscious in the minds of its members. When that happens, perspective can come to look more like pattern than like plan—in other words, it can be found more in the consistency of behaviors than in the articulation of intentions.

Of course, if perspective is immutable, then change in plan and position is difficult unless compatible with the existing perspective. As shown in Figure 2d, the organization can shift easily from Position A to Position B but not to Position X. In this regard, it is interesting to take up the case of Egg McMuffin. Was this product when new—the American breakfast in a bun—a strategic change for the McDonald's fast food chain? Posed in MBA classes, this earth-shattering (or at least stomach-shattering) question inevitably evokes heated debate. Proponents (usually people sympathetic to fast food) argue that of course it was: it brought McDonald's into a new market, the breakfast one, extending the use of existing facilities. Opponents retort that this is nonsense, nothing changed but a few ingredients: this was the same old pap in a new package. Both sides are, of course, right—and wrong. It simply depends on how you define strategy. Position changed; perspective remained the same. Indeed—and this is the point—the position could be changed so easily because it was compatible with the existing perspective. Egg McMuffin is pure McDonald's, not only in product and package, but also in production and propagation. But imagine a change of position at McDonald's that would require a change of perspective—say, to introduce candlelight dining with personal service (your McDuckling à l'Orange cooked to order) to capture the late evening market. We needn't say more, except perhaps to label this the "Egg McMuffin syndrome."

THE NEED FOR ECLECTICISM IN DEFINITION

While various relationships exist among the different definitions, no one relationship, nor any single definition for that matter, takes precedence over the others. In some ways, these definitions compete (in that they can substitute for each other), but in perhaps more important ways, they complement. Not all plans become patterns nor are all patterns that develop planned; some ploys are less than positions, while other strategies are more than positions yet less than perspectives. Each definition adds important elements to our understanding of strategy, indeed encourages us to address fundamental questions about organizations in general.

As plan, strategy deals with how leaders try to establish direction for organizations, to set them on predetermined courses of action. Strategy as plan also raises the fundamental issue of cognition—how intentions are conceived in the human brain in the first place, indeed, what intentions really mean. Are we, for example, to take statements of intentions at face value? Do people always say what they mean, or mean what they say? Ostensible strategies as ploys can be stated just to fool competitors; sometimes, however, those who state them fool themselves. Thus, the road to hell in this field can be paved with those who take all stated intentions at face value. In studying strategy as plan, we must somehow get into the mind of the strategist, to find out what is really intended.

As ploy, strategy takes us into the realm of direct competition, where threats and feints and various other maneuvers are employed to gain advantage. This places the process of strategy formation in its most dynamic setting, with moves provoking countermoves and so on. Yet ironically, strategy itself is a concept rooted not in change but in stability—in set plans and established patterns. How then to reconcile the dynamic notions of strategy as ploy with the static ones of strategy as pattern and other forms of plan?

As pattern, strategy focusses on action, reminding us that the concept is an empty one if it does not take behavior into account. Strategy as pattern also introduces another important phenomenon in organizations, that of convergence, the achievement of consistency in behavior. How does this consistency form, where does it come from? Realized strategy is an important means of conceiving and describing the direction actually pursued by organizations, and when considered alongside strategy as plan, encourages us to consider the notion that strategies can emerge as well as be deliberately imposed.

As position, strategy encourages us to look at organizations in context, specifically in their competitive environments—how they find their positions and protect them in order to meet competition, avoid it, or subvert it. This enables us to think of organizations in ecological terms, as organisms in niches that struggle for survival in a world of hostility and uncertainty as well as symbiosis. How much choice do organizations have, how much room for maneuver?

And finally as perspective, strategy raises intriguing questions about intention and behavior in a collective context. If we define organization as collective action in the pursuit of common mission (a fancy way of saying that a group of people under a common label—whether an IBM or a United Nations or a Luigi's Body Shop—somehow find the means to cooperate in the production of specific goods and services), then strategy as perspective focusses our attention on the reflections and actions of the collectivity—how intentions diffuse through a group of people to become shared as norms and values, and how patterns of behavior become deeply ingrained in the group. Ultimately, it is this view of strategy that offers us the best hope of coming to grips with the most fascinating issue of all, that of the "organizational mind."

Thus, strategy is not just a notion of how to deal with an enemy or a set of competitors or a market, as it is treated in so much of the literature and in its popular usage. It also draws us into some of the most fundamental issues about organizations as instruments for collective perception and action.

To conclude, a good deal of the confusion in this field stems from contradictory and ill-defined uses of the term strategy, as we saw in the Egg McMuffin syndrome. By explicating and using five definitions, we may be able to remove some of this confusion, and thereby enrich our ability to understand and manage the processes by which strategies form.

REFERENCES

[1] P.F. Drucker, *Management: Tasks, Responsibilities, Practices* (New York, NY: Harper & Row, 1974), p. 104.

[2] Moore, in fact, prefers not to associate the word strategy with the word plan per se: "The term *plan* is much too static for our purposes unless qualified. There is not enough of the idea of scheming or calculation with an end in view in it to satisfy us. Plans are used to build ships. Strategies are used to achieve ends among people. You simply do not deal strategically with inanimate objects." But Moore certainly supports the characteristics of intentionality. D.G. Moore, "Managerial Strategies," in W.L. Warner and N.H. Martin, eds., *Industrial Man: Businessmen and Business Organizations* (New York, NY: Harper & Row, 1959), pp. 220, 226.

[3] C. Von Clausewitz, *On War,* translated by M. Howard and P. Paret (Princeton, NJ: Princeton University Press, 1976), p. 177.

[4] J. Von Newmann and O. Morgenstern, *Theory of Games and Economic Behavior* (Princeton, NJ: Princeton University Press, 1944), p. 79.

[5] W. F. Glueck, *Business Policy and Strategic Management,* 3rd Edition (New York, NY: McGraw-Hill, 1980), p. 9.

[6] *Random House Dictionary.*

[7] M.E. Porter, *Competitive Strategy: Techniques for Analyzing Industries and Competitors* (New York, NY: The Free Press, 1980).

[8] M.E. Porter, *Competitive Advantage: Creating and Sustaining Superior Performance* (New York, NY: The Free Press, 1985).

[9] T.C. Schelling, *The Strategy of Conflict,* 2nd Edition (Cambridge, MA: Harvard University Press, 1980).

[10] H. Mintzberg, "Research on Strategy-Making," *Proceedings after the 32nd Annual Meeting of the Academy of Management,* Minneapolis, 1972, pp. 90–94; M. Mintzberg, "Patterns in Strategy Formation," *Management Science,* 24/9 (1978):934–948; H. Mintzberg and J.A. Waters, "Of Strategies, Deliberate and Emergent," *Strategic Management Journal,* 6/3 (1985):257–272.

[11] Evered discusses the Greek origins of the word and traces its entry into contemporary Western vocabulary through the military. R. Evered, "So What Is Strategy," *Long Range Planning,* 16/3 (1983):57–72.

[12] As suggested in the results of a questionnaire by Ragab and Paterson; M. Ragab and W.E. Paterson, "An Exploratory Study of the Strategy Construct," Proceedings of the Administrative Sciences Association of Canada Conference, 1981. Two notable exceptions are Herbert Simon and Jerome Bruner and his colleagues; H.A. Simon, *Administrative Behavior,* 2nd Edition (New York, NY: Macmillan, 1957); J.S. Bruner, J.J. Goodnow, and G.A. Austin, *A Study of Thinking* (New York, NY: Wiley, 1956), pp. 54–55.

[13] Quoted in J.B. Quinn, *Strategies for Change: Logical Incrementalism* (Homewood, IL: Richard D. Irwin, 1980), p. 35.

[14] *Business Week,* October 31, 1983.

[15] Via G. Majone, "The Uses of Policy Analysis," in *The Future and the Past: Essays on Programs,* Russell Sage Foundation Annual Report, 1976–1977, pp. 201–220.

[16] A.D. Chandler, *Strategy and Structure: Chapters in the History of the Industrial Enterprise* (Cambridge, MA: M.I.T. Press, 1962), p. 13.

[17] Von Clausewitz, op. cit., p. 128.

[18] B. Franklin, *Poor Richard's Almanac* (New York, NY: Ballatine Books, 1977), p. 280.

[19] R.P. Rumelt, "Evaluation of Strategy: Theory and Models," in D.E. Schendel and C.W. Hofer, eds., *Strategic Management: A New View of Business Policy and Planning* (Boston, MA: Little Brown, 1979), pp. 196–212.

[20] We might note a similar problem with "policy," a word whose usage is terribly confused. In the military, the word has traditionally served one notch in the hierarchy above strategy, in business one notch below, and in public administration in general as a substitute. In the military, policy deals with the purposes for which wars are fought, which is supposed to be the responsibility of the politicians. In other words, the politicians make policy, the generals, strategy. But modern warfare has confused this usage (see Summers), so that today strategy in the military context has somehow come to be associated with the acquisition of nuclear weapons and their use against non-military targets. In business, while "policy" has been the label for the entire field of study of general management (at least until "strategic management" gained currency in the 1970s), its technical use was as a general rule to dictate decisions in a specific case, usually a standard and recurring situation, as in "Our policy is to require long-range forecasts every fourth months." Accordingly, management planning theorists, such as George Steiner, describe policies as deriving from strategies although some textbook writers (such as Leontiades, Chang and Campo-Flores, and Peter Drucker) have used the two words in exactly the opposite way, as in the military. This reflects the fact that "policy" was the common word in the management literature before "strategy" replaced it in the 1960s (see, for example, Jamison, and Gross and Gross). But in the public sector today, the words "policy" and "policymaking" correspond roughly to "strategy" and "strategy making." H.G. Summers, *On Strategy: The Vietnam War in Context* (Carlisle Barracks, PA: Strategic Studies Institute, U.S. Army War College, 1981); G.A. Steiner, *Top Management Planning* (New York, NY: MacMillian, 1969), p. 264 ff; M. Leontiades, *Management Policy, Strategy and Plans* (Boston, MA: Little Brown, 1982), p. 4; Y.N.A. Chang and F. Campo-Flores, *Business Policy and Strategy* (Goodyear, 1980), p. 7; Drucker, op. cit., p. 104; C.L. Jamison, *Business Policy* (Englewood Cliffs, NJ: Prentice-Hall, 1953); A. Gross and W. Gross, eds., *Business Policy: Selected Readings and Editorial Commentaries* (New York, NY: Ronald Press, 1967).

[21] C.W. Hofer and D. Schendel, *Strategy Formulation: Analytical Concepts* (St. Paul, MN: West Publishing, 1978), p. 4.

[22] E.H. Bowman, "Epistomology, Corporate Strategy, and Academe," *Sloan Management Review,* 15/2 (1974):47.

[23] J.D. Thompson, *Organizations in Action* (New York, NY: McGraw-Hill, 1967).

[24] T.J. McNichols, *Policy-Making and Executive Action* (New York, NY: McGraw-Hill, 1983), p. 257.

[25] Rumelt, op. cit., p. 4.

[26] R.P. Rumelt, "The Evaluation of Business Strategy," in W.F. Glueck, *Business Policy and Strategic Management,* 3rd Edition (New York, NY: McGraw-Hill, 1980), p. 361.

[27] E.g., Porter, op. cit. (1980, 1985), except for his chapters noted earlier, which tend to have a 2-person competitive focus.

[28] Expressed at the Strategic Management Society Conference, Paris, October 1982.

[29] W.G. Astley and C.J. Fombrun, "Collective Strategy: Social Ecology of Organizational Environments," *Academy of Management Review,* 8/4 (1983):576–587.

[30] Ibid., p. 577.

[31] P. Selznick, *Leadership in Administration: A Sociological Interpretation* (New York, NY: Harper & Row, 1957), p. 47. A subsequent paper by the author (in process) on the "design school" of strategy formation shows the link of Selznick's early work to the writings of Kenneth Andrews in the Harvard policy textbook. K.R. Andrews, *The Concept of Corporate Strategy,* Revised Edition (Homewood, IL: Dow Jones-Irwin, 1987).

[32] J. Bieri, "Cognitive Structures in Personality," in H.M. Schroder and P. Suedfeld, eds., *Personality: Theory and Information Processing* (New York, NY: Ronald Press, 1971), p. 178. By the same token, Bieri (p. 179) uses the word "strategy" in the context of psychology.

[33] Drucker, op. cit.

[34] B.B. Tregoe and J.W. Zimmerman, *Top Management Strategy* (New York, NY: Simon & Schuster, 1980).

[35] T.S. Kuhn, *The Structure of Scientific Revolutions*, 2nd Edition (Chicago, IL: University of Chicago Press, 1970).

[36] My own translation of "un reve ou un bouquet de reves en quete de realite." L. Lapierre, "Le changement strategique: Un reve en quete de reel," Ph.D. Management Policy course paper, McGill University, Canada, 1980.

[37] Summer, op. cit., p. 18.

[38] G. Majone, op. cit.

[39] B. Hedberg and S.A. Jonsson, "Strategy Formulation as a Discontinuous Process," *International Studies of Management and Organization*, 7/2 (1977):90.

[40] Tregoe and Zimmerman, op. cit., p. 17.

[41] Boston Consulting Group, *Strategy Alternatives for the British Motorcycle Industry* (London: Her Majesty's Stationery Office, 1975).

[42] E.g., H.I. Ansoff, *Corporate Strategy* (New York, NY: McGraw-Hill, 1965); Andrews, op. cit.; Steiner, op. cit.; D.E. Schendel and C.H. Hofer, eds., *Strategic Management: A New View of Business Policy and Planning* (Boston, MA: Little Brown, 1979), p. 15.

[43] R.T. Pascale, "Perspectives on Strategy: The Real Story Behind Honda's Success," *California Management Review*, 26/3 (Spring 1984):47–72.

[44] J.B. Quinn, "Honda Motor Company Case," in J.B. Quinn, H. Mintzberg, and B.G. James, *The Strategy Process: Concepts, Contexts, Cases* (Englewood Cliffs, NJ: Prentice-Hall, 1988).

[45] C. Perrow, *Organizational Analysis: A Sociological View* (Belmont, CA: Wadsworth, 1970), p. 161.

[46] E.g., N. Brunsson, "The Irrationality of Action and Action Rationality: Decisions, Ideologies, and Organizational Actions," *Journal of Management Studies*, 19/1 (1982):29–44.

The Strategy Concept II:
Another Look at Why
Organizations Need Strategies*

HENRY MINTZBERG

In the preceding article, I proposed five definitions of strategy—as a plan, ploy, pattern, position, and perspective. Drawing on these, I wish to investigate here the question of why organizations really do need strategies. In discussing some of the conventional reasons as well as other ones—to set direction, focus effort, define the organization, provide consistency—I will consider how these may suggest not only why organizations *do* need strategies, but also why they *don't*.

SETTING DIRECTION

Most commentators, focussing on the notions of strategy as deliberate plan and market position, argue that *organizations need strategy to set direction for themselves and to outsmart competitors, or at least enable themselves to maneuver through threatening environments*. In its boldest (and baldest) form: "the main role of strategy is to evolve a trajectory or flight path toward that bull's eye."[1] If its strategy is good, such commentators argue, then the organization can make various mistakes, indeed can sometimes even start from a weaker position, and still come out on top. Chandler quotes one of the men responsible for Sears Roebuck's great success: "Business is like war in one respect—if its grand strategy is correct . . . any number of tactical errors can be made and yet the enterprise proves successful."[2] In a similar vein, Tilles explains that:

> When Hannibal inflicted the humiliating defeat on the Roman army at Cannae in 216 B.C., he led a ragged band against soldiers who were in possession of superior arms, better training, and competent 'noncoms.' His strategy, however, was so superior that all of those advantages proved to be relatively insignificant.[3]

The assumption here is that the competitor with the better strategy will win, or, as a corollary, that the competitor with a clear strategy will beat the one that has none. Strategy, it

*"The Strategy Concept II: Another Look at Why Organizations Need Strategies" by Henry Mintzberg. Copyright © 1987 by The Regents of the University of California. Reprinted from the California Management Review, Vol. 30, No. 1. Fall 1987. By permission of The Regents.

is suggested, counts for more than operations: what really matters is *thinking* it through; *seeing* it through, while hardly incidental, is nonetheless secondary. "Doing the right thing" beats "doing things right" is the expression for such strategic thinking, or to take the favorite example of the opposite, "rearranging the deck chairs on the Titanic."

Sound strategic thinking can certainly explain a good deal of success, in fact, more success than it should, since it is always easy, after the fact, to impute a brilliant strategy (and, behind it, a brilliant strategist) to every great victory. But no shortage of failure can probably be attributed to organizations that got their strategy right while messing up their operations. Indeed, an overdose of strategic thinking can impede effectiveness in the operations, which is exactly what happened on the Titanic. The ship did not go down because they were rearranging the deck chairs at all, but for exactly the opposite reason: they were so busy glorying in the strategy of it all—that boat as a brilliant conception—that they neglected to look out for icebergs.

As for the assumption that any strategy is always better than none, consider an oil company executive in 1973, just as the price of oil went up by a factor of four. What strategy (as plan) should he have pursued when his whole world was suddenly upset. Setting oneself on a predetermined course in unknown waters is the perfect way to sail straight into an iceberg. Sometimes it is better to move slowly, a little bit at a time, looking not too far ahead but very carefully, so that behavior can be shifted on a moment's notice.

The point is not that organizations don't need direction, it is that they don't need homilies. It stands to reason that it is better to have a good strategy, all things being equal. But all things are never equal. The Titanic experience shows how a good strategy can blind an organization to the need to manage its operations. Besides, it is not always clear what a good strategy is, or indeed if it is not better at times to proceed without what amounts to the straitjacket of a clear intended strategy.

FOCUSSING EFFORT

A second major claim, looking inside the organization, is that *strategy is needed to focus effort and promote coordination of activity.* Without strategy, an organization is a collection of individuals, each going his or her own way, or else looking for something to do. The essence of organization is *collective action,* and one thing that knits individual actors together is strategy—again, through providing a sense of direction. Alfred Sloan notes in his memoirs a justification of the consolidated product line strategy developed at General Motors under his leadership: "some kind of rational policy was called for . . . it was necessary to know what one was trying to do," especially with regard to duplication across certain product lines.[4] Of course, by so focussing effort and directing the attention of each part within the integrated whole, the organization runs the risk of being unable to change its strategy when it has to.

DEFINING THE ORGANIZATION

Third, *strategy is needed to define the organization.* Strategy serves not only to direct the attention of the people working within an organization, but also to give the organization meaning for them as well as for outsiders. As plan or pattern, but especially as position or perspective, its strategy defines the organization, providing people with a shorthand way to understand it and to differentiate it from others. Christensen et al. discuss "the power of strategy as a simplifying concept" that enables certain outsiders (they are referring here to independent directors, but the point applies to any interested outsider) "to *know* the business (in a sense) without being *in* the business."[5] Of course, that "little knowledge" can be "a dangerous thing." But there is no denying that strategy does provide a convenient way to understand an organization.

In the early 1980s, the business press was very enthusiastic about General Electric. A reading of the reports of journalists and financial analysts suggests that what really impressed them was not what General Electric had done up to that point but that its new chief executive had articulated a clear, intended strategy for the firm. Thus Kidder, Peabody opened a December 21, 1983 newsletter with the statement: "General Electric is in the process of becoming a somewhat simpler company to understand," the result of the CEO's statement that it would focus on three major segments—core businesses, high technology, and services. Later they explained that "one of the main reasons we have been recommending General Electric for the past three years is the dynamic, creative, motivational leadership that the youthful Jack Welch . . . has provided. . . . His energy, enthusiasm, and ability to articulate a tight and viable corporate strategy are very impressive." No analyst can ever hope to understand much about a company so diversified and complex as General Electric, hence a clear, articulated strategy becomes a surrogate for that understanding.

The important question is whether a simplified strategy for such a complex system helps or hinders its performance—and the question is not meant to be rhetorical. On one hand, such a strategy cannot help but violate the immense complexity of the system, encouraging various dysfunctional pressures from outsiders (directors, for example, who may try to act on their "little knowledge") or even from insiders (chief executives, for example, who try to exercise control over divisions remote from their understanding by putting them into the simplistic categories of "dog" or "cash cow"). On the other hand, the enthusiasm generated by a clear strategy—a clear sense of mission—can produce a host of positive benefits. Those stock analysts not only helped to raise General Electric's stock price, they also helped to fire up the enthusiasm of the company's suppliers and customers, as well as the employees themselves, thereby promoting commitment which can improve performance. Thus, strategy may be of help, not only technically, through the coordination of work, but also emotionally, through the development of beliefs.

Imagine an organization without a name. We would not even be able to discuss it. For all purposes—practical and otherwise—it would not exist. Now imagine an organization with a name but with no strategy, in any sense—no position, no perspective, no plan (or ploy), not even any pattern consistent in its behaviors. How would we describe it or deal with it? An organization without a strategy would be like an individual without a personality—unknown, and unknowable. Of course, we cannot imagine such an organization. But some do come close. Just as we all know bland people with hardly any personality, so too do we know organizations with hardly any sense of strategy (which Rhenman labels "marginal organizations"[6]).

Most people think of such organizations as purely opportunistic, flitting from one opportunity to another,[7] or else as lethargic, with little energy to do anything but allow inertia to take its course (which may suggest strategy as pattern but not as plan). But we need not be so negative about this. Sometimes, lack of strategy is temporary and even necessary. It may, for example, simply represent a stage in the transition from an outdated strategy to a new, more viable one. Or it may reflect the fact that an environment has turned so dynamic that it would be folly to settle on any consistency for a time (as in the oil companies in 1973).

In one study,[8] a film company that began with a very clear direction lost it over time. It never really had formal plans; at best there existed broad leadership intentions in the earliest years. But it did have a very clear position and a very distinct perspective, as well as rather focussed patterns, the latter at least at certain periods in its history. But over time, the position eroded, the perspective clouded, and the patterns multiplied, so that diffusion replaced definition. The insiders become increasingly frustrated, coming to treat their organization more like a shell under which they worked than a system of which they were an integral part. As for the outside influences, lacking any convenient means to define the organization, they attacked it increasingly for irrelevance. Ironically, the organization turned out a number of brilliant films throughout all this, but—contrary to General Electric yet reinforcing the same conclusion—what it did do proved less important than what it did not exhibit, namely, strategy as a clear sense of direction.

PROVIDING CONSISTENCY

A return to the notion of strategy as a "simplifying concept" may provide the clearest reason as to why organizations seem to need strategies. *Strategy is needed to reduce uncertainty and provide consistency (however arbitrary that may be), in order to aid cognition, to satisfy intrinsic needs for order, and to promote efficiency under conditions of stability (by concentrating resources and exploiting past learning).*

Psychologist William James once described the experiences of the infant as a "blooming, buzzing confusion." According to Ornstein, who so quotes him, that is due to "the lack of a suitable categorizing scheme in which to sort experiences consistently."[9] An organization without a strategy experiences the same confusion; its collective cognition can become overloaded, its members having no way to deal with experiences consistently. Thus, strategy is a categorizing scheme by which incoming stimuli can be ordered and dispatched.

In this sense, a strategy is like a theory, indeed, it *is* a theory (as in Drucker's "theory of the business"[10])—a cognitive structure (and filter) to simplify and explain the world, and thereby to facilitate action. Rumelt captures the notion well with the comment that "the function of strategy is not to 'solve a problem,' but to so structure a situation that the emergent problems are solvable."[11] Or, as Spender puts it (and so specifies how ambitious is research on the process of strategy making): "Because strategy-making is a type of theory building, a theory of strategy-making is a theory of theory-building."[12]

But, like every theory, strategy is a simplification that necessarily distorts the reality. Strategies and theories are not reality themselves, only representations (that is, abstractions) of reality in the minds of people. Thus, every strategy must misrepresent and mistreat at least some stimuli; that is the price of having a strategy. Good strategies, like good theories, simply minimize the amount of distortion.

"Strategy," notes James Brian Quinn, "deals…with the unknowable."[13] But it might perhaps be more accurate to write that strategy assumes the unknowable can be made knowable, or at least controllable. As such, it is important to emphasize that strategy is a concept rooted in *stability*.[14] No one should be fooled by all the attention to change and flexibility. When Miller and Friesen write that "strategy is essentially a dynamic concept, it describes a modus operandi more than a posture, a process more than a state,"[15] they are not talking about strategy at all but about the process of making strategy. Strategy is not about adaptability in behavior but about regularity in behavior, not about discontinuity but about consistency. Organizations have strategies to reduce uncertainty, to block out the unexpected, and, as shown here, to *set* direction, *focus* effort, *define* the organization. Strategy is a force that *resists* change, not one that encourages it.

Why then do organizations seem to have such an overwhelming need for consistency? In other words, why the obsession with strategy? To some extent, this is a human need per se. Consistency provides us with a sense of being in control (and nowhere is this better illustrated than in the prescriptive literature of strategic management, although those of us who feel compelled to study strategy as pattern in behavior may be accused of the same thing). That is presumably why some psychologists have found that people claim to discover patterns even in streams of random numbers.[16] Moore makes this point well: strategy is "a relief from the anxiety created by complexity, unpredictability, and incomplete knowledge. As such, it has an element of compulsion about it."[17]

But there is more to the need for consistency than that. Above all, consistency is an efficient response to an environment that is stable, or at least a niche that remains lucrative.

For one thing, strategy enables the organization to concentrate its resources and exploit its opportunities and its own existing skills and knowledge to the very fullest. Strategies reflect the results of organizational learning, the patterns that have formed around those initiatives that have worked best. They help to ensure that these remain fully exploited.

Moreover, once established, strategies reduce the need to keep learning in a broad sense.[18] In this respect, strategy works for an organization much like instinct works for an animal: it facilitates fast, almost automatic response to known stimuli. To be efficient, at least in a stable environment, means to get on with things without the need to think them through each time. As Jonsson notes about "myth," his equivalent to what we call strategy as perspective:

> The myth provides the organization with a stable basis for action. It eliminates uncertainty about what has gone wrong, and it substitutes certainty: we can do it, it is up to us…the riskiness disappears when you 'know' what has to be done. If there is much at stake and you are uncertain as to what is wrong, action is inhibited. If you are certain about what should be done, action is precipitated.[19]

To rethink everything all the time, as Jonsson implies, is unproductive. The person who gets up every morning and asks, "Do I really want to remain married?" or even, "I wonder if it is better today to wash before I brush my teeth," will eventually drive themselves crazy, or at least work themselves into inaction. The same will be true of the organization that is constantly putting its strategies into question. That will impede its ability to get on with things. (A colleague makes this point best with his proposed epitaph: "Here lies RR: he kept his options open.")

We function best when we can take some things for granted, at least for a time. And that is a major role of strategy in organizations: it resolves the big issues so that people can get on with the little details—targeting and serving customers instead of debating which markets are best, buying and operating machines instead of wondering about different technologies, rearranging deck chairs and looking for icebergs. This applies not only at the bottom of the hierarchy, but all along it, right to the very top. Most of the time, the chief executive, too, must get on with managing the organization in a given context; he cannot continually put that context into question.

There is a tendency to picture the chief executive as a strategist, conceiving the big ideas while everyone else gets on with the little details. But his job is not like that at all. A great deal of it has to do with its own little details—reinforcing the existing perspective ("culture" is the currently popular word now) through all kinds of mundane figurehead duties, maintaining the flow of information by developing contacts and disseminating the resulting information, negotiating agreements to reinforce existing positions, and so on.[20]

The problem with all this, of course, is that eventually situations change, environments destabilize, niches disappear. Then all that is constructive and efficient about an established strategy becomes a liability. That is why even though the concept of strategy is rooted in stability, so much of the study of strategy making focusses on change. But while prescription for strategic change in the literature may come easy, management of the change itself, in practice, especially when it involves perspective, comes hard. The very encouragement of strategy to get on with it—its very role in protecting the organization against distraction[21]—impedes the organization's capacity to respond to change in the environment. As Kuhn notes, in discussing the paradigms of communities of scholars, "retooling is expensive."[22] This is especially true when it is not just machines that have to be retooled, but human minds as well. Strategy, as mental set, can blind the organization to its own outdatedness. Thus we conclude that strategies are to organizations what blinders are to horses: they keep them going in a straight line, but impede the use of peripheral vision.

And this leads to our final conclusion, which is that strategies (and the strategic management process) can be vital to organizations, both by their presence *and* by their absence.

REFERENCES

[1] B. Yavitz and W.H. Newman, *Strategy in Action: The Execution, Politics, and Payoff of Business Planning* (New York, NY: The Free Press, 1982), p. 7.

[2] A.D. Chandler, *Strategy and Structure: Chapters in the History of the Industrial Enterprise* (Cambridge, MA: M.I.T. Press, 1962), p. 235.

[3] S. Tilles, "How to Evaluate Corporate Strategy," *Harvard Business Review* (July/August 1963), p. 111.

[4] A.P. Sloan, *My Years at General Motors* (New York, NY: Doubleday, 1963), p. 267.

[5] C.R. Christensen, D.R. Andrews, J.L. Bower, R.G. Hamermesh, and M.E. Porter, *Business Policy: Text and Cases*, 5th Edition (Homewood, IL: Richard D. Irwin, 1982), p. 834.

[6] E. Rhenman, *Organization Theory for Long-Range Planning* (New York, NY: Wiley, 1973).

[7] H.I. Ansoff, *Corporate Strategy* (New York, NY: McGraw-Hill, 1965), p. 113.

[8] H. Mintzberg and A. McHugh, "Strategy Formation in an Adhocracy," *Administrative Science Quarterly*, 30 (June 1985):160–197.

[9] R.E. Ornstein, *The Psychology of Consciousness* (New York, NY: Freeman, 1972), p. 74.

[10] P.F. Drucker, *Management: Tasks, Responsibilities, Practices* (New York, NY: Harper and Row, 1974).

[11] R.P. Rumelt, "Evaluation of Strategy: Theory and Models," in D.E. Schendel and W.C. Hofer, eds., *Strategic Management: A New View of Business Policy and Planning* (Boston, MA: Little Brown, 1979), p. 199.

[12] J.C. Spender, "Commentary," in D.E. Schendel and C.W. Hofer, eds., *Strategic Management: A New View of Business Policy and Planning* (Boston, MA: Little Brown, 1979), p. 396.

[13] J. B. Quinn, *Strategies for Change: Logical Incrementalism* (Homewood, IL: Richard D. Irwin, 1980), p. 163.

[14] D.J. Teece, "Economic Analysis and Strategic Management," *California Management Review*, 26/3 (Spring 1984):88; R.E. Caves, "Economic Analysis and the Quest for Competitive Advantage," *AEA Papers and Proceedings*, 74/2 (May 1984):127–128.

[15] D. Miller and P.H. Friesen, "The Longitudinal Analysis of Organizations: A Methodological Perspective," *Management Science*, 28/9 (1982):1020.

[16] R.N. Taylor, "Psychological Aspects of Planning," *Long Range Planning*, 9/2 (1976):70.

[17] D.G. Moore, *Managerial Strategies and Organization Dynamics in Sears Retailing*, Ph.D. Thesis, University of Chicago, 1954, p.34.

[18] J.S. Bruner, J.J. Goodnow, and G.A. Austin, *A Study of Thinking* (New York, NY: Wiley, 1956), p. 12.

[19] S.A. Jonsson and R.A. Lundin, "Myths and Wishful Thinking as Management Tools," in P.C. Nystrom and W.H. Starbuck, eds., *Perspective Models of Organization* (New York, NY: North Holland Publishing, 1977), p. 43.

[20] H. Mintzberg, *The Nature of Managerial Work* (New York, NY: Harper and Row, 1973).

[21] Christensen et al., op. cit.

[22] T.S. Kuhn, *The Structure of Scientific Revolutions*, 2nd Edition (Chicago, IL: University of Chicago Press, 1970), p. 76.

How Competitive Forces Shape Strategy*

MICHAEL E. PORTER

The essence of strategy formulation is coping with competition. Yet it is easy to view competition too narrowly and too pessimistically. While one sometimes hears executives complaining to the contrary, intense competition in an industry is neither coincidence nor bad luck.

Moreover, in the fight for market share, competition is not manifested only in the other players. Rather, competition in an industry is rooted in its underlying economics, and competitive forces exist that go well beyond the established combatants in a particular industry. Customers, suppliers, potential entrants, and substitute products are all competitors that may be more or less prominent or active depending on the industry.

The state of competition in an industry depends on five basic forces. . . . The collective strength of these forces determines the ultimate profit potential of an industry. It ranges from *intense* in industries like tires, metal cans, and steel, where no company earns spectacular returns on investment, to *mild* in industries like oil field services and equipment, soft drinks, and toiletries, where there is room for quite high returns.

In the economists' "perfectly competitive" industry, jockeying for position is unbridled and entry to the industry very easy. This kind of industry structure, of course, offers the worst prospect for long-run profitability. The weaker the forces collectively, however, the greater the opportunity for superior performance.

Whatever their collective strength, the corporate strategist's goal is to find a position in the industry where his or her company can best defend itself against these forces or can influence them in its favor. The collective strength of the forces may be painfully apparent to all the antagonists, but to cope with them, the strategist must delve below the surface and analyze the sources of each. For example, what makes the industry vulnerable to entry? What determines the bargaining power of suppliers?

Knowledge of these underlying sources of competitive pressure provides the groundwork for a strategic agenda of action. They highlight the critical strengths and weaknesses of the company, animate the positioning of the company in its industry, clarify the areas where strategic changes may yield the greatest payoff, and highlight the places where industry trends promise to hold the greatest significance as either opportunities or threats. Understanding these sources also proves to be of help in considering areas for diversification.

CONTENDING FORCES

The strongest competitive force or forces determine the profitability of an industry and so are of greatest importance in strategy formulation. For example, even a company with a strong position in an industry unthreatened by potential entrants will earn low returns if it faces a superior or a lower-cost substitute product—as the leading manufacturers of vacuum tubes and coffee percolators have learned to their sorrow. In such a situation, coping with the substitute product becomes the number one strategic priority.

Different forces take on prominence, of course, in shaping competition in each industry. In the ocean-going tanker industry the key force is probably the buyers (the major oil companies), while in tires it is powerful OEM buyers coupled with tough competitors. In the steel industry the key forces are foreign competitors and substitute materials.

Every industry has an underlying structure, or a set of fundamental economic and technical characteristics, that gives rise to these competitive forces. The strategist, wanting to position his or her company to cope best with its industry environment or to influence that environment in the company's favor, must learn what makes the environment tick.

This view of competition pertains equally to industries dealing in services and to those selling products. To avoid monotony in this article, I refer to both products and services as "products." The same general principles apply to all types of business.

A few characteristics are critical to the strength of each competitive force. I shall discuss them in this section.

THREAT OF ENTRY

New entrants to an industry bring new capacity, the desire to gain market share, and often substantial resources. Companies diversifying through acquisition into the industry from other markets often leverage their resources to cause a shake-up, as Philip Morris did with Miller beer.

The seriousness of the threat of entry depends on the barriers present and on the reaction from existing competitors that entrants can expect. If barriers to entry are high and newcomers can expect sharp retaliation from the entrenched competitors, obviously the newcomers will not pose a serious threat of entering.

There are six major sources of barriers to entry:

1. *Economies of scale*—These economies deter entry by forcing the aspirant either to come in on a large scale or to accept a cost disadvantage. Scale economies in production, research, marketing, and service are probably the key barriers to entry in the mainframe computer industry, as Xerox and GE sadly discovered. Economies of scale can also act as hurdles in distribution, utilization of the sales force, financing, and nearly any other part of a business.

2. *Product differentiation*—Brand identification creates a barrier by forcing entrants to spend heavily to overcome customer loyalty. Advertising, customer service, being first in the industry, and product differences are among the factors fostering brand identification. It is perhaps the most important entry barrier in soft drinks, over-the-counter drugs, cosmetics, investment banking, and public accounting. To create high fences around their businesses, brewers couple brand identification with economies of scale in production, distribution, and marketing.

THE EXPERIENCE CURVE AS AN ENTRY BARRIER

In recent years, the experience curve has become widely discussed as a key element of industry structure. According to this concept, unit costs in many manufacturing industries (some dogmatic adherents say in *all* manufacturing industries) as well as in some service industries decline with "experience," or a particular company's cumulative volume of production. (The experience curve, which encompasses many factors, is a broader concept than the better-known learning curve, which refers to the efficiency achieved over a period of time by workers through much repetition.)

The causes of the decline in unit costs are a combination of elements, including economies of scale, the learning curve for labor, and capital-labor substitution. The cost decline creates a barrier to entry because new competitors with no "experience" face higher costs than established ones, particularly the producer with the largest market share, and have difficulty catching up with the entrenched competitors.

Adherents of the experience curve concept stress the importance of achieving market leadership to maximize this barrier to entry, and they recommend aggressive action to achieve it, such as price cutting in anticipation of falling costs in order to build volume. For the combatant that cannot achieve a healthy market share, the prescription is usually, "Get out."

Is the experience curve an entry barrier on which strategies should be built? The answer is: not in every industry. In fact, in some industries, building a strategy on the experience curve can be potentially disastrous. That costs decline with experience in some industries is not news to corporate executives. The significance of the experience curve for strategy depends on what factors are causing the decline.

If costs are falling because a growing company can reap economies of scale through more efficient, automated facilities and vertical integration, then the cumulative volume of production is unimportant to its relative cost position. Here the lowest-cost producer is the one with the largest, most efficient facilities.

A new entrant may well be more efficient than the more experienced competitors; if it has built the newest plant, it will face no disadvantage in having to catch up. The strategic prescription, "You must have the largest, most efficient plant," is a lot different from, "You must produce the greatest cumulative output of the item to get your costs down."

Whether a drop in costs with cumulative (not absolute) volume erects an entry barrier also depends on the sources of the decline. If costs go down because of technical advances known generally in the industry or because of the development of improved equipment that can be copied or purchased from equipment suppliers, the experience curve is no entry barrier at all—in fact, new or less experienced competitors may actually enjoy a cost *advantage* over the leaders. Free of the legacy of heavy past investments, the newcomer or less experienced competitor can purchase or copy the newest and lowest-cost equipment and technology.

If, however, experience can be kept proprietary, the leaders will maintain a cost advantage. But new entrants may require less experience to reduce their costs than the leaders needed. All this suggests that the experience curve can be a shaky entry barrier on which to build a strategy.

While space does not permit a complete treatment here, I want to mention a few other crucial elements in determining the appropriateness of a strategy built on the entry barrier provided by the experience curve:

- The height of the barrier depends on how important costs are to competition compared with other areas like marketing, selling, and innovation.
- The barrier can be nullified by product or process innovations leading to a substantially new technology and thereby creating an entirely new experience curve.* New entrants can leapfrog the industry leaders and alight on the new experience curve, to which those leaders may be poorly positioned to jump.
- If more than one strong company is building its strategy on the experience curve, the consequences can be nearly fatal. By the time only one rival is left pursuing such a strategy, industry growth may have stopped and the prospects of reaping the spoils of victory long since evaporated.

---

* For an example drawn from the history of the automobile industry, see William J. Abernathy and Kenneth Wayne, "The Limits of the Learning Curve," HBR September–October 1974, p. 109.

---

3. *Capital requirements*—The need to invest large financial resources in order to compete creates a barrier to entry, particularly if the capital is required for unrecoverable expenditures in up-front advertising or R&D. Capital is necessary not only for fixed facilities but also for customer credit, inventories, and absorbing start-up losses. While major corporations have the financial resources to invade almost any industry, the huge capital requirements in certain fields, such as computer manufacturing and mineral extraction, limit the pool of likely entrants.
4. *Cost disadvantages independent of size*—Entrenched companies may have cost advantages not available to potential rivals, no matter what their size and attainable economies of scale. These advantages can stem from the effects of the learning curve (and of its first cousin, the experience curve), proprietary technology, access to the best raw materials sources, assets purchased at preinflation prices, government subsidies, or favorable locations. Sometimes cost advantages are legally enforceable, as they are through patents. (For an analysis of the much-discussed experience curve as a barrier to entry, see the ruled insert.)
5. *Access to distribution channels*—The newcomer on the block must, of course, secure distribution of its product or service. A new food product, for example, must displace others from the supermarket shelf via price breaks, promotions, intense selling efforts, or some other means. The more limited the wholesale or retail channels are and the more that existing competitors have these tied up, obviously the tougher that entry into the industry will be. Sometimes this barrier is so high that, to surmount it, a new contestant must create its own distribution channels, as Timex did in the watch industry in the 1950s.
6. *Government policy*—The government can limit or even foreclose entry to industries with such controls as license requirements and limits on access to raw materials. Regulated industries like trucking, liquor retailing, and freight forwarding are noticeable examples; more subtle government restrictions operate in fields like ski-area development and coal mining. The government also can play a major indirect role by affecting entry barriers through controls such as air and water pollution standards and safety regulations.

The potential rival's expectations about the reaction of existing competitors also will influence its decision on whether to enter. The company is likely to have second thoughts if incumbents have previously lashed out at new entrants or if:

- The incumbents possess substantial resources to fight back, including excess cash and unused borrowing power, productive capacity, or clout with distribution channels and customers.
- The incumbents seem likely to cut prices because of a desire to keep market shares or because of industrywide excess capacity.
- Industry growth is slow, affecting its ability to absorb the new arrival and probably causing the financial performance of all the parties involved to decline.

Changing Conditions

From a strategic standpoint there are two important additional points to note about the threat of entry.

First, it changes, of course, as these conditions change. The expiration of Polaroid's basic patents on instant photography, for instance, greatly reduced its absolute cost entry barrier built by proprietary technology. It is not surprising that Kodak plunged into the market. Product differentiation in printing has all but disappeared. Conversely, in the auto industry economies of scale increased enormously with post–World War II automation and vertical integration—virtually stopping successful new entry.

Second, strategic decisions involving a large segment of an industry can have a major impact on the conditions determining the threat of entry. For example, the actions of many U.S. wine producers in the 1960s to step up product introductions, raise advertising levels, and expand distribution nationally surely strengthened the entry roadblocks by raising economies of scale and making access to distribution channels more difficult. Similarly, decisions by members of the recreational vehicle industry to vertically integrate in order to lower costs have greatly increased the economies of scale and raised the capital cost barriers.

POWERFUL SUPPLIERS & BUYERS

Suppliers can exert bargaining power on participants in an industry by raising prices or reducing the quality of purchased goods and services. Powerful suppliers can thereby squeeze profitability out of an industry unable to recover cost increases in its own prices. By raising their prices, soft drink concentrate producers have contributed to the erosion of profitability of bottling companies because the bottlers, facing intense competition from powdered mixes, fruit drinks, and other beverages, have limited freedom to raise *their* prices accordingly. Customers likewise can force down prices, demand higher quality or more service, and play competitors off against each other—all at the expense of industry profits.

The power of each important supplier or buyer group depends on a number of characteristics of its market situation and on the relative importance of its sales or purchases to the industry compared with its overall business.

A *supplier* group is powerful if:

- It is dominated by a few companies and is more concentrated than the industry it sells to.

- Its product is unique or at least differentiated, or if it has built up switching costs. Switching costs are fixed costs buyers face in changing suppliers. These arise because, among other things, a buyer's product specifications tie it to particular suppliers, it has invested heavily in specialized ancillary equipment or in learning how to operate a supplier's equipment (as in computer software), or its production lines are connected to the supplier's manufacturing facilities (as in some manufacture of beverage containers).
- It is not obliged to contend with other products for sale to the industry. For instance, the competition between the steel companies and the aluminum companies to sell to the can industry checks the power of each supplier.
- It poses a credible threat of integrating forward into the industry's business. This provides a check against the industry's ability to improve the terms on which it purchases.
- The industry is not an important customer of the supplier group. If the industry *is* an important customer, suppliers' fortunes will be closely tied to the industry, and they will want to protect the industry through reasonable pricing and assistance in activities like R&D and lobbying.

   A *buyer* group is powerful if:
- It is concentrated or purchases in large volumes. Large-volume buyers are particularly potent forces if heavy fixed costs characterize the industry—as they do in metal containers, corn refining, and bulk chemicals, for example—which raise the stakes to keep capacity filled.
- The products it purchases from the industry are standard or undifferentiated. The buyers, sure that they can always find alternative suppliers, may play one company against another, as they do in aluminum extrusion.
- The products it purchases from the industry form a component of its product and represent a significant fraction of its cost. The buyers are likely to shop for a favorable price and purchase selectively. Where the product sold by the industry in question is a small fraction of buyers' costs, buyers are usually much less price sensitive.
- It earns low profits, which create great incentive to lower its purchasing costs. Highly profitable buyers, however, are generally less price sensitive (that is, of course, if the item does not represent a large fraction of their costs).
- The industry's product is unimportant to the quality of the buyers' products or services. Where the quality of the buyers' products is very much affected by the industry's product, buyers are generally less price sensitive. Industries in which this situation obtains include oil field equipment, where a malfunction can lead to large losses, and enclosures for electronic medical and test instruments, where the quality of the enclosure can influence the user's impression about the quality of the equipment inside.
- The industry's product does not save the buyer money. Where the industry's product or service can pay for itself many times over, the buyer is rarely price sensitive; rather, he is interested in quality. This is true in services like investment banking and public accounting, where errors in judgment can be costly and embarrassing, and in businesses like the logging of oil wells, where an accurate survey can save thousands of dollars in drilling costs.
- The buyers pose a credible threat of integrating backward to make the industry's product. The Big Three auto producers and major buyers of cars have often used the threat of self-manufacture as a bargaining lever. But sometimes an industry engenders a threat to buyers that its members may integrate forward.

Exhibit 1

Forces Governing Competition in an Industry

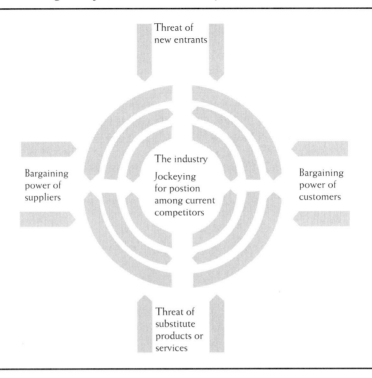

Threat of
new entrants

The industry

Jockeying
for postion
among current
competitors

Bargaining
power of
suppliers

Bargaining
power of
customers

Threat of
substitute
products or
services

Most of these sources of buyer power can be attributed to consumers as a group as well as to industrial and commercial buyers; only a modification of the frame of reference is necessary. Consumers tend to be more price sensitive if they are purchasing products that are undifferentiated, expensive relative to their incomes, and of a sort where quality is not particularly important.

The buying power of retailers is determined by the same rules, with one important addition. Retailers can gain significant bargaining power over manufacturers when they can influence consumers' purchasing decisions, as they do in audio components, jewelry, appliances, sporting goods, and other goods.

Strategic Action

A company's choice of suppliers to buy from or buyer groups to sell to should be viewed as a crucial strategic decision. A company can improve its strategic posture by finding suppliers or buyers who possess the least power to influence it adversely.

Most common is the situation of a company being able to choose whom it will sell to—in other words, buyer selection. Rarely do all the buyer groups a company sells to enjoy equal power. Even if a company sells to a single industry, segments usually exist within that industry that exercise less power (and that are therefore less price sensitive) than others.

For example, the replacement market for most products is less price sensitive than the overall market.

As a rule, a company can sell to powerful buyers and still come away with above-average profitability only if it is a low-cost producer in its industry or if its product enjoys some unusual, if not unique, features. In supplying large customers with electric motors, Emerson Electric earns high returns because its low cost position permits the company to meet or undercut competitors' prices.

If the company lacks a low cost position or a unique product, selling to everyone is self-defeating because the more sales it achieves, the more vulnerable it becomes. The company may have to muster the courage to turn away business and sell only to less potent customers.

Buyer selection has been a key to the success of National Can and Crown Cork & Seal. They focus on the segments of the can industry where they can create product differentiation, minimize the threat of backward integration, and otherwise mitigate the awesome power of their customers. Of course, some industries do not enjoy the luxury of selecting "good" buyers.

As the factors creating supplier and buyer power change with time or as a result of a company's strategic decisions, naturally the power of these groups rises or declines. In the ready-to-wear clothing industry, as the buyers (department stores and clothing stores) have become more concentrated and control has passed to large chains, the industry has come under increasing pressure and suffered falling margins. The industry has been unable to differentiate its product or engender switching costs that lock in its buyers enough to neutralize these trends.

SUBSTITUTE PRODUCTS

By placing a ceiling on prices it can charge, substitute products or services limit the potential of an industry. Unless it can upgrade the quality of the product or differentiate it somehow (as via marketing), the industry will suffer in earnings and possibly in growth.

Manifestly, the more attractive the price-performance trade-off offered by substitute products, the firmer the lid placed on the industry's profit potential. Sugar producers confronted with the large-scale commercialization of high-fructose corn syrup, a sugar substitute, are learning this lesson today.

Substitutes not only limit profits in normal times; they also reduce the bonanza an industry can reap in boom times. In 1978 the producers of fiberglass insulation enjoyed unprecedented demand as a result of high energy costs and severe winter weather. But the industry's ability to raise prices was tempered by the plethora of insulation substitutes, including cellulose, rock wool, and styrofoam. These substitutes are bound to become an even stronger force once the current round of plant additions by fiberglass insulation producers has boosted capacity enough to meet demand (and then some).

Substitute products that deserve the most attention strategically are those that (a) are subject to trends improving their price-performance trade-off with the industry's product, or (b) are produced by industries earning high profits. Substitutes often come rapidly into play if some development increases competition in their industries and causes price reduction or performance improvement.

JOCKEYING FOR POSITION

Rivalry among existing competitors takes the familiar form of jockeying for position—using tactics like price competition, product introduction, and advertising slugfests. Intense rivalry is related to the presence of a number of factors:

- Competitors are numerous or are roughly equal in size and power. In many U.S. industries in recent years foreign contenders, of course, have become part of the competitive picture.
- Industry growth is slow, precipitating fights for market share that involve expansion-minded members.
- The product or service lacks differentiation or switching costs, which lock in buyers and protect one combatant from raids on its customers by another.
- Fixed costs are high or the product is perishable, creating strong temptation to cut prices. Many basic materials businesses, like paper and aluminum, suffer from this problem when demand slackens.
- Capacity is normally augmented in large increments. Such additions, as in the chlorine and vinyl chloride businesses, disrupt the industry's supply-demand balance and often lead to periods of overcapacity and price cutting.
- Exit barriers are high. Exit barriers, like very specialized assets or management's loyalty to a particular business, keep companies competing even though they may be earning low or even negative returns on investment. Excess capacity remains functioning, and the profitability of the healthy competitors suffers as the sick ones hang on.[1] If the entire industry suffers from overcapacity, it may seek government help—particularly if foreign competition is present.
- The rivals are diverse in strategies, origins, and "personalities." They have different ideas about how to compete and continually run head-on into each other in the process.

As an industry matures, its growth rate changes, resulting in declining profits and (often) a shakeout. In the booming recreational vehicle industry of the early 1970s, nearly every producer did well; but slow growth since then has eliminated the high returns, except for the strongest members, not to mention many of the weaker companies. The same profit story has been played out in industry after industry—snowmobiles, aerosol packaging, and sports equipment are just a few examples.

An acquisition can introduce a very different personality to an industry, as has been the case with Black & Decker's takeover of McCullough, the producer of chain saws. Technological innovation can boost the level of fixed costs in the production process, as it did in the shift from batch to continuous-line photo finishing in the 1960s.

While a company must live with many of these factors—because they are built into industry economics—it may have some latitude for improving matters through strategic shifts. For example, it may try to raise buyers' switching costs or increase product differentiation. A focus on selling efforts in the fastest-growing segments of the industry or on market areas with the lowest fixed costs can reduce the impact of industry rivalry. If it is feasible, a com-

---

[1]For a more complete discussion of exit barriers and their implications for strategy, see my article, "Please Note Location of Nearest Exit," *California Management Review,* Winter 1976, p. 21.

pany can try to avoid confrontation with competitors having high exit barriers and can thus sidestep involvement in bitter price cutting.

FORMULATION OF STRATEGY

Once having assessed the forces affecting competition in an industry and their underlying causes, the corporate strategist can identify the company's strengths and weaknesses. The crucial strengths and weaknesses from a strategic standpoint are the company's posture vis-à-vis the underlying causes of each force. Where does it stand against substitutes? Against the sources of entry barriers?

Then the strategist can devise a plan of action that may include (1) positioning the company so that its capabilities provide the best defense against the competitive force; and/or (2) influencing the balance of the forces through strategic moves, thereby improving the company's position; and/or (3) anticipating shifts in the factors underlying the forces and responding to them, with the hope of exploiting change by choosing a strategy appropriate for the new competitive balance before opponents recognize it. I shall consider each strategic approach in turn.

POSITIONING THE COMPANY

The first approach takes the structure of the industry as given and matches the company's strengths and weaknesses to it. Strategy can be viewed as building defenses against the competitive forces or as finding positions in the industry where the forces are weakest.

Knowledge of the company's capabilities and of the causes of the competitive forces will highlight the areas where the company should confront competition and where avoid it. If the company is a low-cost producer, it may choose to confront powerful buyers while it takes care to sell them only products not vulnerable to competition from substitutes.

The success of Dr Pepper in the soft drink industry illustrates the coupling of realistic knowledge of corporate strengths with sound industry analysis to yield a superior strategy. Coca-Cola and Pepsi-Cola dominate Dr Pepper's industry, where many small concentrate producers compete for a piece of the action. Dr Pepper chose a strategy of avoiding the largest-selling drink segment, maintaining a narrow flavor line, forgoing the development of a captive bottler network, and marketing heavily. The company positioned itself so as to be least vulnerable to its competitive forces while it exploited its small size.

In the $11.5 billion soft drink industry, barriers to entry in the form of brand identification, large-scale marketing, and access to a bottler network are enormous. Rather than accept the formidable costs and scale economies in having its own bottler network—that is, following the lead of the Big Two and of Seven-Up—Dr Pepper took advantage of the different flavor of its drink to "piggyback" on Coke and Pepsi bottlers who wanted a full line to sell to customers. Dr Pepper coped with the power of these buyers through extraordinary service and other efforts to distinguish its treatment of them from that of Coke and Pepsi.

Many small companies in the soft drink business offer cola drinks that thrust them into head-to-head competition against the majors. Dr Pepper, however, maximized product differentiation by maintaining a narrow line of beverages built around an unusual flavor.

Finally, Dr Pepper met Coke and Pepsi with an advertising onslaught emphasizing the alleged uniqueness of its single flavor. This campaign built strong brand identification and great customer loyalty. Helping its efforts was the fact that Dr Pepper's formula involved lower raw materials cost, which gave the company an absolute cost advantage over its major competitors.

There are no economies of scale in soft drink concentrate production, so Dr Pepper could prosper despite its small share of the business (6%). Thus Dr Pepper confronted competition in marketing but avoided it in product line and in distribution. This artful positioning combined with good implementation has led to an enviable record in earnings and in the stock market.

INFLUENCING THE BALANCE

When dealing with the forces that drive industry competition, a company can devise a strategy that takes the offensive. This posture is designed to do more than merely cope with the forces themselves; it is meant to alter their causes.

Innovations in marketing can raise brand identification or otherwise differentiate the product. Capital investments in large-scale facilities or vertical integration affect entry barriers. The balance of forces is partly a result of external factors and partly in the company's control.

EXPLOITING INDUSTRY CHANGE

Industry evolution is important strategically because evolution, of course, brings with it changes in the sources of competition I have identified. In the familiar product life-cycle pattern, for example, growth rates change, product differentiation is said to decline as the business becomes more mature, and the companies tend to integrate vertically.

These trends are not so important in themselves; what is critical is whether they affect the sources of competition. Consider vertical integration. In the maturing minicomputer industry, extensive vertical integration, both in manufacturing and in software development, is taking place. This very significant trend is greatly raising economies of scale as well as the amount of capital necessary to compete in the industry. This in turn is raising barriers to entry and may drive some smaller competitors out of the industry once growth levels off.

Obviously, the trends carrying the highest priority from a strategic standpoint are those that affect the most important sources of competition in the industry and those that elevate new causes to the forefront. In contract aerosol packaging, for example, the trend toward less product differentiation is now dominant. It has increased buyers' power, lowered the barriers to entry, and intensified competition.

The framework for analyzing competition that I have described can also be used to predict the eventual profitability of an industry. In long-range planning the task is to examine each competitive force, forecast the magnitude of each underlying cause, and then construct a composite picture of the likely profit potential of the industry.

The outcome of such an exercise may differ a great deal from the existing industry structure. Today, for example, the solar heating business is populated by dozens and perhaps hundreds of companies, none with a major market position. Entry is easy, and competitors are battling to establish solar heating as a superior substitute for conventional methods.

The potential of this industry will depend largely on the shape of future barriers to entry, the improvement of the industry's position relative to substitutes, the ultimate intensity of competition, and the power captured by buyers and suppliers. These characteristics will in turn be influenced by such factors as the establishment of brand identities, significant economies of scale or experience curves in equipment manufacture wrought by technological change, the ultimate capital costs to compete, and the extent of overhead in production facilities.

The framework for analyzing industry competition has direct benefits in setting diversification strategy. It provides a road map for answering the extremely difficult question inherent in diversification decisions: "What is the potential of this business?" Combining the framework with judgment in its application, a company may be able to spot an industry with a good future before this good future is reflected in the prices of acquisition candidates.

MULTIFACETED RIVALRY

Corporate managers have directed a great deal of attention to defining their businesses as a crucial step in strategy formulation. Theodore Levitt, in his classic 1960 article in HBR, argued strongly for avoiding the myopia of narrow, product-oriented industry definition.[2] Numerous other authorities have also stressed the need to look beyond product to function in defining a business, beyond national boundaries to potential international competition, and beyond the ranks of one's competitors today to those that may become competitors tomorrow. As a result of these urgings, the proper definition of a company's industry or industries has become an endlessly debated subject.

One motive behind this debate is the desire to exploit new markets. Another, perhaps more important motive is the fear of overlooking latent sources of competition that someday may threaten the industry. Many managers concentrate so single-mindedly on their direct antagonists in the fight for market share that they fail to realize that they are also competing with their customers and their suppliers for bargaining power. Meanwhile, they also neglect to keep a wary eye out for new entrants to the contest or fail to recognize the subtle threat of substitute products.

The key to growth—even survival—is to stake out a position that is less vulnerable to attack from head-to-head opponents, whether established or new, and less vulnerable to erosion from the direction of buyers, suppliers, and substitute goods. Establishing such a position can take many forms—solidifying relationships with favorable customers, differentiating the product either substantively or psychologically through marketing, integrating forward or backward, establishing technological leadership.

---

[2]Theodore Levitt, "Marketing Myopia," reprinted as an HBR Classic, September–October 1975, p. 26.

READING 7

Market Driven Strategy: Managing in Turbulent Markets*

George Day

There is no resting place for an enterprise in a competitive society.
Alfred Sloan, Jr.

Unless we change our direction we are likely to end up where we are headed.
Ancient Chinese Wisdom

Benetton and Sears, Roebuck both compete for a piece of the retail apparel market. Otherwise there are few similarities. The differences between these two firms are more interesting for they illustrate the richness and complexity of competitive strategies, as well as the adverse consequences for performance when a strategy drifts out of touch with the market. Their stories are also apt metaphors for some of the forces that will be sweeping the markets of the 1990s.

Sears is a classic example of what happens when a firm becomes complacent in its market.[1] Until 1986 Sears was the dominant retailer in the United States, before being challenged by Kmart and Wal-Mart. By 1989 it was struggling to reverse a decade-long decline in its share of general merchandise sales from 18 percent to 13 percent, overcome bloated selling and administrative costs of 30 percent of sales, and raise pretax margins from 3.7 percent to a level closer to the 7 percent of their competitors.

The problems with apparel were symptomatic of Sears's difficulties. The traditional key success factors in this department were quality of presentation and assortment. Both were major problems to manage because of the number of stores and diversity of product lines in each store. Many suppliers of branded apparel didn't like Sears's sloppy presentation or considered a mass market outlet inappropriate. Changes to overcome these problems proved difficult to make. One proposal was to create "neighborhood stores" that would sell only apparel and home furnishings. However, the executives representing "hard goods" such as appliances, electronics, and automotive products argued they shouldn't be left out of the stores, and killed the proposal.

Despite Sears's problems, its standing with consumers remained strong. Consistently it was picked as a company associated with high quality, and 75 percent of Americans visited a Sears store at least once a year. Unfortunately, this reservoir of goodwill was being dissipated by a ponderous and noncompetitive culture, antiquated systems, and excessive in-fighting. Customers were being siphoned off by trendier specialty retailers, such as The Gap or The Limited, or superdiscounters such as Circuit City or Toys 'R' Us who dominated specific merchandise types.

Benetton was anything but complacent. In just 10 years this Italian-based fashion retailer opened 5,000 shops in 79 countries. Each shop offered brightly colored sportswear with a distinctive flair, presented in basic color and design configurations, with lots of excitement and ever-changing variety.

The contrasts with Sears were telling; Benetton was focused, global. It competed with a distinct strategy that provided a stable platform for managing in a turbulent fashion market where life cycles were often less than a season. Not surprisingly, their net profit margins were also three times those of Sears.

The most noticeable difference was their "customer draw" system[2] that electronically tied the 5,000 stores directly to their factories—so closely that turnaround from order to deliver was only two to six weeks. Store managers didn't have to guess in advance what to order, they could monitor what was selling and reorder the "hot" items. The highly automated factories produced only to order. If a new style or fabric emerged unexpectedly, a sophisticated computer-aided design (CAD) system could compress the time from design to production of a full range of sizes and colors. Not only had they broken the traditional constraints of time with this system, they were also able to avoid being penalized by costs that typically rise with increasing variety (see Figure 1). This gave them a distinct competitive advantage.

While it is tempting to dismiss Sears as a dinosaur ill-equipped to match fleet-footed competitors in fast-changing global markets, and celebrate Benetton as a prototype of innovative winners in the future, that would be terribly misleading. Their respective positions reflect past strategic choices and intentions, but their future performance hinges on how well they adapt to the future environment. If Sears management can shake loose from their

FIGURE 1

Traditional versus Fast-Response Systems: Why Benetton Prevails

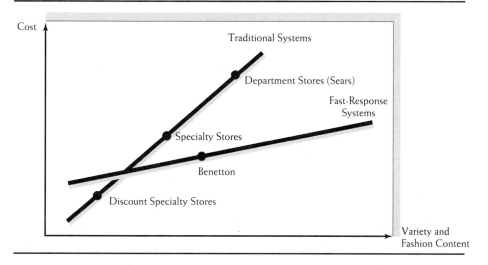

bad habits, they have enormous strengths to exploit. Conversely Benetton must keep innovating or be surpassed by eager emulators. Their futures are very much in their hands, depending on the wisdom and commitment their management brings to the critical choices any business must make to successfully manage its markets. This reading introduces the strategic choices that collectively determine whether the rules of their competitive games are defined to their advantage and not preempted by their rivals.

CHOICES AND CHALLENGES IN TURBULENT MARKETS

A competitive strategy specifies how a business intends to compete in the markets it chooses to serve. This strategy provides a conceptual glue that gives shared meaning to all the separate functional activities and programs. Effective strategies are straightforward in their intent and direction. Too much subtlety and complexity, and the essential ingredients won't be consistently understood or acted upon by the organization. This is damaging to performance in the market because it sends erratic and confusing signals to customers.

Strategies are directional statements, rather than detailed step-by-step plans of action. The direction is set by four choices:

Arena: the markets to serve and customer segments to target

Advantage: the positioning theme that differentiates the business from competitors

Access: the communication and distribution channels used to reach the market

Activities: the appropriate scale and scope of activities to be performed

These choices are highly interdependent—change one and all the other elements of the strategy have to be changed. The result of these choices is an integrated pattern that collectively specifies the strategy in Figure 2.

A fifth and final set of choices deals with the adaptation of the strategy to impending threats and emerging opportunities. Winning strategies don't change every year or at the whim of new management, because if they did the customers and the organization would soon become confused. This doesn't mean a sound strategy can be static, for that would stifle innovation and lead to stagnation. Successful adaptation requires a clear sense of the growth direction to pursue that will best capitalize on the competencies of the business.

The choice of the best direction depends on making sense of a myriad of events, trends, and cross-currents, and placing bets on how the environment will unfold. If the bets are wrong, and the business can't change course quickly, the penalty is below par performance and foreclosure from future opportunities. Each of the critical strategic choices will be more difficult in the future because of the challenges posed by an accelerating rate of change and competition of unprecedented intensity.

ARENA: CHOOSING MARKETS AND TARGET SEGMENTS

As soon as the market arena is chosen management loses many of their degrees of freedom. This single choice largely dictates the customers to be served, the rivals to surpass, and the key success factors (KSFs) they must master. These KSFs are the functions and activities that must be managed well for the business to outperform the rivals.

FIGURE 2
Strategy as an Integrated Pattern of Choices

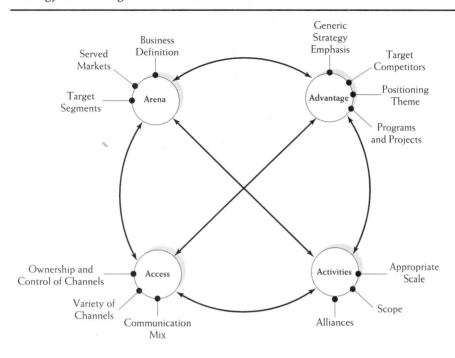

Conversely if these are done badly then failure is almost assured. Each market has a distinctive profile of KSFs, shaped by the attributes of the market. In mature industrial markets, for example, the defining attributes are technology—whether it is small or large batch or continuous processing—and transaction complexity, which reflects the frequency of purchase, risk of failure, and size of the decision-making unit.[3]

Despite the importance of choosing target segments, this is often done by default; a failing attributable to the misguided logic that says that since we make hydraulic hoses, semiconductors, or frozen food, we serve all the customers for these products. Serving every segment with a common strategy is seldom the best choice. Alternatively, the business may serve the broad market with distinct, tailored strategies for each segment, or limit coverage to a single segment to the exclusion of the others. . . .

Challenges

Firms are reconsidering their choice of market arena under pressure from three trends that cannot be ignored.

First, there is increasing market fragmentation. New segments with distinct needs and requirements are emerging and being served by specialist competitors with tailored offerings. In markets from soup to cars, sweeping demographic and life-style changes are rendering mass marketing obsolete and eroding brand loyalties. This trend breeds product diversity that encourages further fragmentation. The automobile market, for example, is rapidly becoming a collection of niche markets in which customers can personalize their choice with specific models, designs, and features, rather than take a standard design and add accessories and options.

Second, traditional market boundaries are blurring as a result of a barrage of substitutes that result from new technologies. Today there are auto springs from plastic, telephone lines of glass with awesome channel capacity, engines made of ceramics that promise to run efficiently at high temperatures, minerals mined by microbes, and holes being drilled cheaply and accurately by pinpoint, high-pressure jets of water. Worse, these changing market structures usually bring new competitors. To name a few: telecommunication companies have entered the computer industry and vice versa; more management and technical education is done within companies than by universities and some of these companies grant academic degrees; and some churches own television stations.

The third and most compelling market-shaping trend is the transformation of previously self-contained national markets into linked global markets. Many forces underlie this trend: increasing homogenization of buying patterns for products from sweaters to audio-disc players; the challenge from global competitors who gain scale or skill advantages from coordinated country strategies; the emerging economic prowess of the Pacific Rim countries; the upheavals triggered by Europe 1992 and the opening of the Communist block of countries; and technology change that makes it feasible to coordinate far-flung operations and easily communicate with customers across national boundaries.

The challenge for management is to find the right balance of global reach and standardization of activities, versus local adaptation. For example, Nabisco is unlikely to launch their Grey Poupon family of Dijon mustards, which leads the premium segment in the United States, into other markets where tastes may differ or competitors are already solidly entrenched. Their challenge is to use the skills and scale gained in the U.S. market to develop products suited to the unique needs of other markets....

ADVANTAGE: POSITIONING FOR COMPETITIVE SUPERIORITY

When a new management team inherits or acquires a business, the market arena has already been chosen for them by the actions and commitments of their predecessors. Initially their emphasis has to be on strengthening their competitive advantages within that arena. This involves achieving demonstrably superior performance on attributes that are important to the target customers at a competitive cost. Points of superiority that cost more than the customer is willing to pay are a profit sink that can't be endured for long.

The essence of competitive advantage is a positioning theme that sets a business apart from its rivals in ways that are meaningful to the target customers. The most successful themes are built on some combination of three thrusts: better (through superior quality or service), faster (by being able to sense and satisfy shifting customer requirements faster than competitors), and closer (with the creation of durable relationships). The task for management is to simultaneously find a compelling theme and ensure continuing superiority in the skills, resources, and controls that will be the source of this advantage over target competitors....

Successful businesses can't afford to stop and celebrate their current advantages. They have to be paranoid about competitors and move aggressively to defend their position. As important as a strong defense might be, it can only delay the inevitable erosion. This means continuously innovating to build new sources of advantage before rivals overtake. Thus

Kodak reasserted itself in the film market by introducing its best film ever, Ektar, just two years after introducing another world-class product, Kodacolor Gold film. Kodak management has pledged to keep making these improvements ahead of their arch-rival Fuji.

Challenges

During the eighties it became increasingly difficult for firms to be complacent about the durability of their advantages. By one estimate 70 percent of all product innovations were matched within a year.[4] Process knowledge was easier to protect, but 60 to 90 percent eventually diffused to competitors. Price and advertising moves could be readily matched because they are so visible.

The trends that have quickened the rate of erosion of advantages will continue to intensify. Overshadowing everything is the compression of product life cycles which puts a premium on getting to market first, or imitating quickly to avoid missing a short-lived profit window. This trend can be appreciated only by looking back to markets like refrigerators that took 30 years to fully mature, and comparing them to the market for microwaves that took only 10 years to get to the same place, or compact disc players that matured in three years.

Further pressure on advantages will come from supply gluts. Markets as diverse as commodity petrochemicals, automobiles, and electronics presently suffer chronic global overcapacity of 15 to 40 percent. Why?

- There are too many firms competing. Besides traditionally established firms there are new players from other geographic areas, including the newly industrialized countries, and others that are subsidized by their host government.
- Customers may back integrate by making their requirements rather than buying them. This first reduces the volume of market demand relative to supply. Then these customers may sell their excess capacity in competition with their one-time supplier.
- All firms are increasingly productive as technology improvements diffuse rapidly. The ubiquity of the experience curve is evidence of the extent of productivity improvements.[5]
- Because of significant legal, physical, technological, and financial barriers that block their exit, not enough firms are leaving.

Customer bargaining power also works to narrow the differences between competitors— or at least, to erase the possibility of capturing superior profits for long periods. This is particularly evident in industrial markets, where large customers are bent on eliminating all but a few of their suppliers by raising the acceptable quality and performance requirements even as they demand price concessions.

ACCESS: SELECTING CHANNELS TO REACH THE ARENA

Until recently, channels were not seen as a matter of strategic choice—they were a fact of life that came with the market. A propensity for inertia was reinforced by a perceived absence of good alternatives, and the justified fear of the conflicts that would be unleashed by any changes.

A great deal of attention has been devoted to managing the channel to keep costs in line, motivating the sales force to improve their productivity, and instituting tighter controls over key channel relationships. But basic choices over the form of the channel have seldom been confronted by most firms; they have elected to go directly to their markets with their own sales force if tight control was essential, or opted for intermediaries such as distributors when they could benefit from their superior efficiency and coverage. Seldom was there any debate, for example, over whether to appoint only an exclusive handful of dealers versus pushing for intensive distribution. These issues were not viewed as important, as they were largely ordained by the characteristics of the product or service.

This view of channels obscures the contribution the choice of a channel makes to the firm's competitive advantage. In most markets, distribution strength (coverage, cost, and closeness of relationships) plays a distinct role in reinforcing superior product performance and maintaining a strong position in end-user markets. Industrial firms in particular cannot maintain market leadership without having a strong distribution system. This applies equally to consumer goods firms, as Procter & Gamble found in the soft drink market. After nine frustrating years in which the U.S. market share of their subsidiary Crush International declined from 1.3 to 0.8 percent in 1989, they finally gave up and sold the brand. They were crippled by not being able to get adequate access to the local bottlers who buy concentrate from the marketers, such as Coke and Pepsi, and then bottle the product and stock the shelves. The overwhelming presence of the two soft drink giants eventually forced P&G to try an alternative store-to-warehouse distribution system. This move not only cut them out of nongrocery store outlets—such as vending machines—but so angered their remaining bottlers that they retaliated.

Challenges

Passive acceptance of existing channel arrangements will be increasingly risky for a number of reasons.[6] Companies in all markets are facing greatly increased direct sales costs with little evidence of improved productivity to offset these costs. Meanwhile, customer demands for closer relationships and information technologies that permit direct order-entry links and rapid information flows from buyer to seller and back are forcing companies to reconsider traditional channels.

Companies that use intermediaries are encountering an unwelcome shift in the balance of power. In consumer markets, the retail trade is forcing major concessions on their national brand suppliers. The pressure for trade allowances, deals, and discounts has substantially reduced the funds available for franchise-building advertising. Many industrial markets are seeing rapid concentration among previously fragmented distributors, who bring unprecedented purchasing power, sophistication, and new forms of value-adding services to their dialogue with their suppliers. In response there is an increasing tendency for firms to create hybrid arrangements, and use a variety of channels to reach distinct segments. This escalation in the complexity and scale of channel arrangements has certainly raised the strategic visibility of this area. . . .

ACTIVITIES: CHOOSING THE APPROPRIATE SCALE AND SCOPE

The next set of strategic choices is the selection of the strategically central and distinct activities to be performed to convert inputs into outputs that customers will value. Among the potential activities are purchasing, manufacturing or processing, design, sales, distribution, and service. When these activities are assembled together, with the necessary organizational structures, controls, and technology linkages, they establish the value chain for the business.

Few businesses choose to be fully "integrated," that is, to carry out all possible activities starting with raw materials and culminating in a finished product sold and delivered to the end user. Instead, their value chain is limited to only those activities that have to be done very well in order to achieve a competitive advantage—the key success factors. Surrounding this value chain is a set of value chains that links suppliers at one end to the channels and end users at the other end.

Challenges

Until recently the choice of appropriate scale and scope was guided by two rules of thumb: bigger is better, and keep as many activities as possible under one roof to maintain control. Adherence to these beliefs led to big companies characterized by sprawling plants, extensive vertical integration, a continuous striving for economies of scale, hierarchical and functional organizations, and mass marketing with a strong volume orientation.[7]

A wrenching era of global competition, resulting in restructuring and cost control to generate cash flow, and market share losses to more agile, entrepreneurial specialists, is changing the rules. Today, large corporations are behaving as though the old organization structures are obsolete. The benefits of specialization, scale, and the control they promised have been nullified by inefficiencies and lack of flexibility. Meanwhile, the imaginative use of information technologies is overcoming the control problem. A company that once might have acquired a key supplier to get more control over component quality may now feel it can do better simply by tracking the supplier's performance by computer. Increasingly, large companies are trying to create autonomous, small, entrepreneurial units to find responsive solutions to customer problems in well-defined market niches.[8] Long-term advantages are sustained by simultaneously investing heavily in core competencies, such as microprocessor controls or digital imaging, that are common to families of business units. Other activities, such as public relations or managing the computer system that are not central to the strategy are increasingly farmed out to independent contractors.

Structures are also changing to accommodate long-term alliances that come in many guises: joint ventures for co-development of technology or entering new markets, supply and service agreements, and sundry licensing agreements. Even IBM, which once felt strong enough to go it alone, had arranged more than 40 active alliances by 1990, including several major partnerships with Japanese firms. They created links with Ricoh in the distribution of low-end computers, with Nippon Steel in systems integration, and NTT in value-added networks.

The move to alliances reminds us that the same forces are often working on several strategic choices at the same time. Globalization has already presented a challenge to thinking about the choice of arena and the directions for growth. But this force puts equally insistent pressure on the need to form alliances. Their appeal lies in the way they help defray the immense fixed costs that must be borne because of the broadened market base.[9] Few companies can afford the costs of building and maintaining a brand name, while investing in automated factories, distribution networks, and communications networks to serve a global market at a pace that will keep them ahead of their rivals. But alliances are only one of a number of means to this end. The essence of strategy is knowing which choices to make, and then making sure they happen.

ADAPTATION AND RENEWAL: GROWTH DIRECTIONS TO PURSUE

Sooner or later all market arenas lose their luster, as sales growth stagnates, profit margins are squeezed, and competition intensifies. Management can't wait until this has happened before taking action, for then they will surely be too late to capitalize on emerging market opportunities. Delay means attractive positions will already be staked out by competitors, and the best opportunities for alliances and acquisitions are likely to have been preempted.

Vigilant companies constantly seek new opportunities in related markets, products, and services, where their distinctive competencies can be effectively utilized. When senior management is committed to finding new sources of growth, the rest of the organization is energized to innovate and propose new directions with some confidence they will be heeded. However, unmanaged growth can be just as dangerous as complacency and inertia, if it leads the business into diverse markets that management doesn't understand, where the available competencies can't be used, and unanticipated competitors are better situated. Such unproductive directions distract management and diffuse their scarce resources. Thus, the choices of where to look for new opportunities, and how aggressively to move, have to be made very carefully. These choices are specified by a growth strategy that...specifies the growth paths worth pursuing, the purpose of new products and markets, the size of the risks to be taken, and the alternative entry strategies to be used to reduce the risks of internal development.

Challenges[10]

Managers will find that charting new directions for their business will be increasingly difficult. Each market has its own sources of uncertainty and opportunity—but few will be exempt from the three megaforces of demographic and life-style changes, technology change, and environmental concerns.

At the heart of demographic and life-style changes are population aging, and seemingly insatiable demands for convenience and service. By the year 2000, the baby boom generation will be 36 to 54 years old, and their households include more than half the U.S. population. Japan and Germany will have even older populations, all with tastes that will be difficult for youth-oriented firms to satisfy. Whole new markets are being created to satisfy the fastest growing of all demographic groups that is over 85 years old.

Technological change will be the main impetus behind new market opportunities. The possibilities range from so-called "super" technologies such as superconductors, fusion power, and robotics, to "appropriate" technologies including micro refineries and photovoltaics, "bio" technologies that promise designer genes, and "information" technologies that are being created by advanced generations of lightning-fast microprocessors coupled to modern computer networks.

The least predictable influence on new market directions is environmentalism. Escalating concerns about acid rain, ozone depletion, water quality, and waste disposal foreshadow the future. The global plastics and petrochemical industry is one of the most likely to bear the brunt of these concerns. West German chemical companies are already devoting about half of their capital spending to the environment and safety. While few industries will be as exposed as this, it is also unlikely that many will entirely escape the growing social and political forces at work to deal with the public consequences of private consumption.[11]

SUCCESSFUL MARKET MANAGEMENT

There are three kinds of companies: those that make things happen, those who watch things happen, and the rest who wonder what happened.

ANONYMOUS

Strategic choices have wide-ranging ripple effects through the organization. They determine the key success factors, dictate the programs and projects to initiate and continue, define the skills and resources to mobilize or acquire, and shape expectations for profit and growth performance. In short, they give meaning and direction to the myriad activities of the business. Yet without effective implementation the clearest strategic thinking will be for nought—mired in functional conflicts, ill-conceived programs, budget overruns, missed schedules, and poor follow-through. The penalties are loss of confidence, missed opportunities, diminished capabilities, and poor performance.

While strategy guides implementation, it is equally true that implementation has a steering effect on the strategic choices. No strategy is so prescient that it can anticipate all eventualities and opportunities. Instead, there must be enough latitude to permit wide-ranging adaptation and learning at the operating level where the changing market reality is continually encountered. These bottom-up experiments, initiatives, and adjustments, continuously made by informal problem-solving groups and ad hoc task forces, go a long way toward deciding the future strategic choices.... These inputs are a crucial ingredient to a robust planning process.

Some firms are consistently better at managing the process, making the right strategic choices, and ensuring superior execution. They can be contrasted with their lagging peers along two critical dimensions. . . . Winners are:

- guided by a shared strategic vision,
- driven to be responsive to market requirements and continuously strive to satisfy their customers.

THE ROLE OF STRATEGIC VISION

A vision is a guiding theme that articulates the nature of the business and its intentions for the future. These intentions are based on how management collectively believes the environment will unfold, and what the business can and should become in the future. Visions are not vague expressions of goodwill, but explicit systems about what it takes to succeed in the future.

Without a vision, and the leadership to rally others around the vision, the organization is likely to be reactive in its present arena and aimless in pursuit of new directions. One well-known strategy typology[12] calls them "Reactors" to highlight an organizational mind-set that dwells solely on how to protect past gains. A reactor's world is full of threats, while opportunities are filtered through a haze that is like glaucoma. New directions are pursued with little relish by individual contributors responding to customer requests, new findings in the lab, or preemptive moves by competitors. Broad-based encouragement for initiatives is hard to find since the organization lacks guiding principles to help distinguish between sensible moves that might support a future direction versus tangential undertakings that dissipate effort.

While there is abundant evidence that successful businesses are guided by a meaning-ful vision, it is unclear whether the losers suffered because they simply lacked a vision or were following a misguided vision. To avoid being misguided, however, there are four defin-ing characteristics of meaningful visions: they are informed, shared, competitive, and enabling.

Informed

A vision must be grounded in a solid understanding of the business, and the ability to fore-see how the forces operating in the market will change in the future. Here vision is equated with insight, of the sort that distinguishes Perrier from its competitors. Perrier has become almost a generic term for mineral water, by understanding that their business was neither water nor soft drinks, but natural beverages. This may seem a subtle distinction, but is has a profound impact on how the market is approached, and was missed by some for-midable competitors including Anheuser-Busch and Nestlé, who have largely abandoned the market.

Shared

Visions will motivate organizations when they are created through collaboration, with the leader serving as the articulator and sponsor of the vision that emerges from the team's col-laboration. The vision must reflect the leader's view of opportunities, values, and impor-tant trade-offs. However, as one CEO put it,

> Visions are more powerful when they are inspired by strong personal conviction and moti-vation. They are richer when they flow from an internal source that can constantly respond with different aspects of the vision as new and changing circumstances arise. And yet visions are powerless unless they are derived from and embraced by those individuals in the orga-nization who will collectively achieve them.[13]

If the leader's vision is not accepted, the price is likely to be high. In fact, Charles Parry, who became CEO of Alcoa in 1983, was deposed because his vision was rejected by a deep-seated, conservative company culture.[14] For years Alcoa, the largest U.S. producer of alu-minum, had suffered through boom-bust cycles in the industry. By the early eighties the combination of chronic excess capacity to produce ingots, and several state-owned com-petitors who were more concerned with job protection than profits reduced profits to a break-even level. In response, Parry articulated a vision of Alcoa as the preeminent producer of highly engineered alloys, using ceramics, composites, and plastics. His eventual aim was to derive 50 percent of revenues from nonaluminum markets. Unfortunately, Parry had already alienated most of his management with a series of shutdowns to cut costs and they were in no mood to fund diversification adventures with aluminum profits. Meanwhile the board, which generally endorsed the need to reduce dependency on primary aluminum, were uneasy with the 50 percent goal which had never been explicitly justified. They were further disenchanted with the logic of the acquisitions being proposed, and by 1987 withdrew their support.

Competitive

Powerful visions are also statements of intent that create an obsession with winning throughout the organization. By focusing attention on a desired leadership position, measuring progress against that achievement, and continually searching for new ways to gain competitive advantage, the actions and aspirations of the organization are given meaning.

Audacious intentions can be powerful, in light of evidence that they are often realized even when they outrun the current capabilities and resources. It is unlikely that so many Japanese firms like Honda, Matsushita, and NEC would have achieved global leadership had they been content to tailor their intentions to their resources of 10 to 15 years ago.[15]

Aggressive intentions are most likely to be realized when the target competitor has low aspirations, and is willing to concede its leadership position under pressure. This nearly happened to Caterpillar, when they suffered global losses of shares to Komatsu who had an avowed intent of "encircling Caterpillar." By 1986 Komatsu had gained 12 percent of the U.S. market, despite starting in 1970 with revenues that were only 35 percent of Caterpillar's and mostly from the sales of small bulldozers within Japan. But unlike many of its American peers Caterpillar intended to do everything possible to protect market share.[16] When Komatsu began underselling it by as much as 40 percent in the early 1980s the company cut prices heavily in markets around the world. Although some market share was lost, the company would have fared far worse had they not stood their ground. Their intention to maintain leadership by beating back Komatsu also benefited from the high quality of their product. By comparison with U.S. automakers, their machines had set the world standard for workmanship for decades.

Visions that merely strive to catch up to the competition and match "best" practices that are visible in the market are usually flawed and unproductive. The flaw lies in the transparency of the resulting strategic moves to competitors that have already mastered them, and are already preparing the next generation of moves that will continue to keep them ahead. Imitative moves are also unproductive because they won't create competitive advantages. This is not to say that efforts to rationalize product lines to improve global economies of scale, institute quality circles to improve quality, or follow the lead of other banks to institute "relationship" banking programs, are not worthwhile. But if all the energy of management is expended to reproduce the cost and quality advantages their competitors have already achieved, there won't be much energy left to devote to finding meaningful ways to be different.

Enabling

Visions flourish within organizations where individual managers have enough latitude to make meaningful decisions about strategies and tactics. These individuals are empowered to use the general framework articulated by the vision to decide which opportunities or threats to respond to, and which to ignore. They have confidence that they will not be second-guessed by their superiors, who realize they are unable to anticipate every twist and turn in the market environment and must delegate downwards.

MARKET-DRIVEN MANAGEMENT

Compelling visions are best nourished in market-driven organizations. While there are many views on what this means, all start with Drucker's original formulation[17] of the marketing concept as a general management responsibility. This concept holds that, "There is only one valid definition of a business purpose: to create a satisfied customer. . . . It is the customer who determines what the business is." While being customer-oriented is an essential condition it is not sufficient, for there has to be an equally intense emphasis on outperforming the competition. This keeps the business focused on well-defined market segments and the continual enhancement of their competitive advantages. Thus it pervades all the strategic choices made by the business.

The rewards that come from being market-driven are an integrating theme. Responsiveness to customers is a prerequisite to superior performance. Yet many firms continue to behave otherwise, by emphasizing internal concerns and short-term financial performance rather than long-run customer satisfaction.

Recently there has been a "rediscovery" of the marketing concept as firms wrestle with new or intensifying environmental challenges.[18] The growing acceptance of the need to be market-driven closely parallels the evolving role of the marketing function:

- Until the mid-1950s marketing was equated with sales. The marketer's job was to convince prospects to want what the firm could most readily produce.
- The 1960s and early 1970s was the golden era of acceptance of the marketing concept as the driving philosophy for a business. Volume, production, or sales orientations toward the market were seen as less profitable than satisfying the needs of attractive customer segments with appropriately tailored products. The role of marketing was seen as persuading the firm to have what the customer wanted—not the other way round.
- Throughout the 1970s the commitment to a customer-orientation waned, as strategic planning ascended in the favor of top management. Only retrospectively was it realized that these approaches to setting strategic direction were overweighted with top-down financial imperatives, and analyses of industry structures as guidelines to action. The main emphasis was on managing share, and allocating cash flows to conserve scarce financial resources. Even firms that had been market-driven lost their focus on the customer, and marketing was relegated to short-run tactical concerns.[19]

An unfortunate and costly side effect of the enthusiasm for strategic planning was a deflection of attention away from customer satisfaction as the main source of long-run competitive advantage and profitability. This lapse was adroitly exploited by off-shore competitors who invested heavily to bring new products and processes to segments that had been smugly underserved by domestic competitors. Indeed, much of the economic history of the eighties was shaped by the successful global conquests of Japanese and European firms and the efforts of American firms to redress their shortcomings and become market-driven. There are many manifestations of American resurgence, including greater emphasis on customer value through quality enhancement, leaner and more flexible organizations that are closer to their markets, a search for innovative strategies to combat competitive incursions—and ultimately the recognition that marketing is everyone's job.

SUMMARY: WHEN STRATEGY MATTERS

The need for a forward-looking competitive strategy, that specifies how a business intends to compete in its chosen markets wasn't always as pressing as it is today. When markets are stable or slowly evolving in predictable ways, and the rules of competition are accepted by all the players, it is possible to prosper with a trial-and-error approach. This puts a premium on maintaining programs and activities that seem to be working and dropping those that have stopped working. In effect, the business is reacting to events, and the strategy is only understood after the fact by looking for consistent patterns in the stream of decisions taken piecemeal through the year.

The implicit assumption of a reactive strategy is that the organization can adapt faster than the environment is changing. This was never a very good assumption, but is increasingly dangerous in light of the intensifying forces impinging on competitive markets:

- markets are fragmenting, and traditional boundaries are blurring,
- previously self-contained national markets are being transformed into linked global markets,
- competitive advantages are harder to sustain as product life cycles shorten, and global competitors contest more markets,
- supply gluts further intensify competitive pressures by giving customers more bargaining power,
- customer relationships are changing as customers reduce the number of suppliers and information technologies permit closer links,
- new market opportunities are being created from demographic and life-style changes, technological changes, and rising environmental concerns,
- old organization arrangements are suffering at the hands of more agile, entrepreneurial specialists.

Three ingredients are necessary for a business to successfully steer a strategic course through market turbulence and become proactive in shaping events and competitive behavior to its advantage. The first is a strategic vision or theme that articulates the nature of the business and focuses the energies of all parts of the organization toward the task of outperforming the competition. The second ingredient is a market orientation in which the beliefs and values that pervade the organization emphasize the need to put the customer first. Finally, a successful business needs a robust process for formulating and choosing the best strategy in light of the issues facing the business. . . .

NOTES

[1] Patricia Sellers, "Why Bigger Is Badder at Sears," *Fortune* (December 5, 1988), 79–84.

[2] Alan Zakon and Richard Winger, "Consumer Draw: From Mass Markets to Variety," *Management Review* (April 1987), 20–27.

[3] J.A. Sousa De Vasconcellos e Sá and D.C. Hambrick, "Key Success Factors: Test of a General Theory in the Mature Industrial–Product Sector," *Strategic Management Journal* 10 (July–August 1989), 367–383.

[4] Pankaj Ghemawat, "Sustainable Advantage," *Harvard Business Review* 64 (September–October 1986), 55–58.

[5] George S. Day and David B. Montgomery, "Diagnosing the Experience Curve," *Journal of Marketing* 47 (Spring 1983), 44–58.

[6] Frank V. Cespedes, "Channel Management Is General Management," *California Management Review* 31 (Fall 1988), 98–120.

[7] "Is Your Company Too Big?" *Business Week* (March 27, 1989).

[8] Frederick E. Webster, Jr., *It's 1990—Do You Know Where Your Marketing Is?* (Cambridge, Mass.: Marketing Science Institute, 1989).

[9] Kenichi Ohmae, "The Global Logic of Strategic Alliances," *Harvard Business Review* 67 (March–April 1989), 143–154.

[10] "Managing Now for the 1990s," *Fortune* (September 26, 1988), 44–94.

[11] Amitai Etzioni, *The Moral Dimension* (New York: Free Press, 1988).

[12] The typology is described in R. E. Miles and Charles C. Snow, *Organizational Strategy, Structure and Process* (New York: McGraw-Hill, 1978).

[13] Roy Stata, "The Role of the Chief Executive Officer in Articulating the Vision," *Interfaces* 18 (May–June 1988), 3–9.

[14] "The Quiet Coup at Alcoa," *Business Week* (June 27, 1988), 58–65.

[15] The notion of strategic intent as an active management process that starts with a vision of a desired leadership position, and establishes the criterion the organization will use to assess progress is developed further in Gary Hamel and C.K. Prahalad, "Strategic Intent," *Harvard Business Review* 67 (May–June 1989), 63–76.

[16] Ronald Henkoff, "This Cat Is Acting Like a Tiger," *Fortune* (December 19, 1988), 71–76.

[17] Peter F. Drucker, *The Practice of Management* (New York: Harper and Row, 1954).

[18] This section draws on Frederick E. Webster, Jr., *Rediscovering the Marketing Concept* (Cambridge, Mass.: Marketing Science Institute, 1988).

[19] George S. Day and Robin Wensley, "Marketing Theory with a Strategic Orientation," *Journal of Marketing* 47 (Fall 1983).

READING 8

Managing on the Edge: The Fit/Split Paradox*

RICHARD TANNER PASCALE

STAGNATION AND RENEWAL

The past ten years have provided me with the opportunity to study, and in several instances, consult extensively with, the top management of a dozen of America's largest companies. The list includes AT&T, GE, GM, Ford, IBM, Apple, Chrysler, Coca-Cola, Hewlett-Packard, American Medical International (the third largest for-profit health care company), HEB Stores (the nation's twelfth largest supermarket chain), The New York Times, Marriott, Intel, General Motors, McKinsey (the consulting firm), British Petroleum and J. P. Morgan Bank. In addition, having a long-standing interest in Japan, I have engaged in research at Honda, Mazda, Sony, and Matsushita.

There was a quality common to all of the firms in the study. Each had a tradition of success. Yet each was struggling with the task of revitalization. The challenge in each case was for management to capitalize on their market position and reinvigorate their institution. The unseen hindrances were subtle, underlying beliefs about management, closed-loop organizational habits, and, in some instances, an appetite for quick fixes. In Chrysler's case, with urgency self-evident, it was imperative that it unshackle itself from the past. For Coca-Cola, the challenge was more subtle because Pepsi's encroachment occurred gradually. In the instances of General Electric, Hewlett-Packard, and Marriott, the competitive threats were not life-threatening, but there was evidence of each institution drifting off target, looking too much inward and losing competitiveness, or being far too internally oriented. Studying the predicament of top management in each of the latter three examples, I participated in, and observed, success and failure in the task of revitalization.

The twenty-two previously mentioned companies provided extensive interview opportunities and permitted me to observe the cycle of stagnation and renewal over many months—often over years. In many instances, circumstances permitted exposure to behind-the-scenes management issues not generally visible. As a means of broadening reach, a second, and much larger, sample of eighty-eight firms was tracked over the past five years.** (See Box 1.) This effort relied primarily on a literature review and structured interviews of managers at each of these companies.

---

*"The Fit/Split Paradox" reprinted with the permission of Simon & Schuster from *Managing on the Edge* by Richard Tanner Pascale. Copyright © 1990 by Richard Pascale.

**The firms listed were not selected to be representative of U.S. industry. Rather, the bias was toward "the action"—in particular, toward companies reported to be doing extremely well or very poorly.

BOX 1
RESEARCH BASE

A. Adidas
Allen Bradley
AMD
Amdahl
Amoco
Anheuser-Busch
Apple*
Atari*
AT&T*

B. Bank of America*
Bechtel
Black & Decker
Boeing
Bristol-Myers
British Leyland
British Steel
Bulova
Burroughs

C. Campbell Soup
Canon
Chesebrough Pond's
Chrysler*
Coca-Cola*
Continental Illinois Bank

F. Fairchild
Federal Express*
Firestone/Michelin
Fluor
Ford*
Frito-Lay*

G. Genentech
General Electric*
General Foods*
General Motors*
Gerber
Goldman, Sachs*
Goodyear

H. Hallmark
Harley-Davidson
Harvard Business School*
Head Ski/Prince
Hewlett-Packard*
Hilton
Hitachi
Honda*
Howard Johnson
Hughes

L. Levi Strauss
Lockheed
Lucasfilm*

M. Macy's*
Marriott*
Mars
Martin Marietta*
Mary Kay
Matsushita*
Maytag
Mazda*
McDonald's*
McDonnell Douglas
McKinsey*
Merck
Merrill Lynch
Microsoft
Miller Lite

J.P. Morgan*
Motorola

N. National Semiconductor
NCR
Nike
Nissan
Nordstrom's*

Sears
Selectron
Shearson Lehman
Sony*
Sun Microsystems*
Supermarkets (HEB,*
   Safeway)
Syntex*

T. Tandem
Tandy
Texas Instruments
Time Warner
Timken
Toyota*
Toys "R" Us
TRW*
Tupperware*
TWA

U. United Airlines*
United Technologies
UPS
USX

Control Data
Cummins Diesel

D. Dana
Dart & Kraft
Data General
DEC*
Delta
Disney
Dow
Dun & Bradstreet
DuPont

E. EDS*
Emerson Electric
Esprit
Exxon

EF Hutton
Hyatt
Hyundai

I. IBM*
Indian Head Mills
Intel*
International Harvester
ITT*

J. Johnson & Johnson
Joseph Magnin

K. Kentucky Fried Chicken
K mart
Kodak
Kyowa Hakku

P. Pan Am
J.C. Penney*
Pepsi-Cola
Polaroid
Procter & Gamble*

Q. Quaker Oats

R. Raychem
Reebok
Rent-A-Wreck
Revlon
Rockwell*
ROLM*

S. Sainsbury's*
Schlumberger

W. Wang
Wells Fargo*
Western Union
Westinghouse
Weyerhaeuser*

X. Xerox

Y. YKK*

Z. Zales*
Zenith

*First tier research sites

Finally, this work has been deeply influenced by my prior research on Japanese management. The original efforts, 1972–1978, entailed an in-depth study of fourteen Japanese firms with major facilities in the United States. Each was paired with a closely matched (and high performing) American competitor. This research shed considerable light on the management practices of Japanese firms, and on the ways in which they exported their practices to their facilities here. This work culminated with the book *The Art of Japanese Management*, written with Anthony Athos. The central thrust of this work was to identify the practices and subtle assumptions that characterize Japanese management, and to explore their relevance to the West.[1]

As noted earlier, this book is based on thousands of hours of interviews and observation. Interviews focused broadly on the competitive environment, on the organizations' purposes and internal functioning, and on the process through which continuous improvement was attained. The most difficult aspect of the work emerged when I began to focus on the important domains of contention, whether, and how, conflict served the cause of renewal and, most difficult of all, how organizations dealt with contention within their own ranks. Organizations often conceal or avoid conflicts. Fine-grained questioning and observation was necessary to penetrate the veil.

THE SEVEN S FRAMEWORK REVISITED

I was assisted in these interviews by the Seven S Framework.[†] The framework (see Figure 1) is nothing more than seven important categories that managers pay attention to—strategy, structure, systems, style and shared values, skills (an organization's distinctive competence)

FIGURE 1

The Seven S Framework

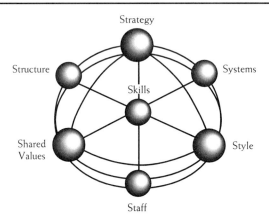

[†] I had a hand in developing this model as a consulting tool for the firm McKinsey & Co. in 1979—along with Anthony Athos, then at Harvard Business School, and Robert Waterman and Tom Peters, both then at McKinsey.

and people (to maintain the alliteration, we called the people category "staff"). There is nothing sacred about the number seven. There could be six or eight S's. The value of a framework such as the Seven S's is that it imposes an interviewing discipline on the researcher. It forces one to audit an organization from all perspectives, both "hard" (strategy, structure, and systems) and "soft" (style, staff, and shared values).[2] Behind each of the dimensions is a history that is important to understand—strategies that have been tried, organizational structures that have been imposed and cast aside, shared values that have been announced and then abandoned, and so on. Above all, it is a superb vehicle for assessing fit. Learning as much as one can about each of the seven dimensions and *assembling* what one has collected invariably reveals a lot. Readers wishing a quick refresher on the Seven S's may wish to glance at Box 2.

PLUSES AND MINUSES OF FIT

When an organization hangs together, when its strategy is reinforced by its organizational structure, and this, in turn, is supported by its measurement and reward systems, its style, its values, and so on, then the gears mesh. The resulting coherence contributes mightily to focus. If the company's strategy is sound, the result is usually success in the marketplace.

McDonald's illustrates the point. The fast-food chain assigns its success to a strategy that emphasizes quality control and efficiency. (McDonald's doesn't just sell hamburgers, it sells a predictable experience.) Anywhere you go, you can count on McDonald's to provide you with a Big Mac, and French fries that look and taste like they're supposed to. In support of McDonald's strategy are (1) disciplined management control systems, (2) stringent standards of cleanliness and equipment maintenance, and (3) a complementary set of values and personnel systems. When all of these elements are in sync, exceptional organizational performance is possible. That's what fit is all about.

But the 1980s witnessed changes in consumer tastes that impacted the fast-food industry. Americans stopped eating as many meats, sweets, and fried foods. Parents learned that a hamburger and French fries contained the equivalent of ten tablespoonfuls of grease. A new factor entered the equation—namely, to innovate. McDonald's response was the Egg McMuffin, Chicken McNuggets, and the salad bar. It appears straightforward because they responded appropriately, and it worked. But, as will be seen, history demonstrates how easily fit could have caused McDonald's to narrowly stick to "hamburgers."[3]

It may seem an exaggeration to imagine McDonald's defining their business so narrowly as to have gotten fixated on hamburgers. Yet UPS defined its business as "moving parcels by trucks"—resisting for over a decade the inroads of Federal Express (which moved parcels by air). I could cite a dozen, similar examples. The reason it happens so frequently is that what appears to be a minor adaptation (from hamburgers to a range of breakfast, chicken, and salad offerings; from a parcel delivery system reliant primarily on trucks to one dependent primarily on airplanes) requires fundamental shifts in an organization's skills. After the fact we are wont to say that an organization made a "bad decision" or was "too slow" to decide to do things differently. But underlying this superficial explanation is the tendency for organizations to do what they best know how to do. Decisions are largely determined by existing skills. As noted in Box 2, skills are the product of the other six S's. When an organization is *exceptionally* skilled, it is, in a sense, overadaptive. In the short run,

Box 2
The Seven S Framework

Strategy Plan or course of action leading to the allocation of a firm's scarce resources, over time, to reach identified goals

Structure Salient features of the organization chart (i.e., functional, decentralized, etc.) and how the separate entities of an organization are tied together

Systems Proceduralized reports and routinized processes (such as meeting formats), etc.

Staff "Demographics" description of important personnel categories within the firm (i.e., engineers, entrepreneurs, MBA's, etc.). "Staff" is not meant in line-staff terms

Style Characterization of how key managers behave in achieving the organization's goals; also the cultural style of the organization

Shared Values The significant meanings or guiding concepts that an organization imbues in its members

Skills Distinctive capabilities of key personnel and the firm as a whole

Strategy pertains to a firm's plan of action that causes it to allocate its scarce resources over time to get from where it is to where it wants to go. **Structure** refers to the way a firm is organized—whether it emphasizes line of staff—in short, how the "boxes" are arranged. **Systems** refers to how information moves around within the organization. Some systems are the "hard copy" variety—computer printouts and other ink-on-paper formats that are used to keep track of what's going on. Other systems are more informal—such as meetings. These three elements—*strategy, structure, and systems*—are probably quite familiar to most readers.

The next three factors are what we call the "soft" S's. **Staff** pertains not to staff in the line/staff sense, but to demographics characterizations of the kind of people who collectively comprise "the organization." In some instances we encounter an "engineering culture" (Hewlett-Packard). In other cases we note that a company is dominated by a cadre of current and former salesmen (Tupperware), governed by flinty-eyed MBA's (Goldman, Sachs), or populated by computer jocks (Microsoft).

Style refers to the patterns of behavior of the top executive and the senior management team. For example, ITT's Harold Geneen and his team had a tough, facts-oriented style. *Style* also refers to distinct traits of an organization as a whole. Clearly, General Motors has a different style than Apple Computer.

Shared values pertains to the overarching purposes to which an organization and its members dedicate themselves. These are never bottom-line secular goals (such as growing 10 percent a year or obtaining a 20-percent return on investment). *Shared values* tend to "move men's hearts" and knit individual and organization purposes together.

The last of the Seven S's, **skills**, is both "hard" and "soft." *Skills* refers to those things which the organization and its key personnel do particularly well—the distinctive capabilities that truly set a company apart from competition. For example, at the *organizational* level, Apple is skilled at marketing computers. At the *individual* level, at least historically, it has had one of the most skilled cadre of software developers in the business.

The most significant aspect of *skills* (and the reason it is always listed last) is that it is the *dependent* variable. In other words, *skills* is the derivative of the other six S's. More often than not, managers are charged with the task of improving a skill (such as building a marketing capability, upgrading quality or reinvigorating customer service). The Seven S framework reminds us that to achieve these ends we must systematically fine-tune the other six S's to get the dependent variable, *skills*, to shift accordingly.

---

this may provide superb performance, but concomitantly, fit magnifies the difficulty of any type of change. UPS's inability to compete successfully against Federal Express stemmed from its lack of key skills.

Consider what UPS lacked. It needed a "real time" information system to deal with much shorter delivery cycles. It needed a higher-caliber workforce geared to faster response times. The easiest part was purchasing a fleet of airplanes and the linear programs necessary to route them efficiently. What UPS couldn't overcome was the massive overhaul of virtually all aspects of its organization that would have been necessary to match the courtesy, service levels, and response times that Federal Express provides.[4] UPS was a trained marathoner in a world of sprinters.

It is of interest to study how McDonald's escaped the perils of too much fit. Somewhere amongst the cost accountants and kitchen operations experts at McDonald's headquarters there was a new-product-development function with adequate capability to rise to the challenge. Most significantly, McDonald's 7,907 independently owned franchises comprise a high-quality cadre of successful entrepreneurs. They represent a powerful voice in the McDonald's system—indeed, they are often an irritant and source of tension to corporate staff. The franchisees' identification of shifting consumer tastes was communicated forcefully enough to pierce complacency at the corporate level. It broke through attachment to the status quo. In short, contention came to the rescue; it challenged the smug comfort of fit. Contention prodded the chain to life once the market began to change.[5]

SPLIT

Simply put, when things get too big or too homogeneous, it is generally helpful to break organizations into smaller units. Multidisciplinary task forces, subsidiaries, or decentralized profit centers are often best suited for addressing special customer needs, niche market segments, or difficult technological challenges. . . . IBM utilized split when it established its personal computer subsidiary, Entry Systems, in 1980. In so doing, it cut the new entity free from the overhead, red tape, and operating assumptions that had prevented IBM from gaining a foothold in this rapidly growing market. The new cross-disciplinary team violated IBM norms, borrowed components from outside, and delivered a 63-percent market share within three years.[6]

IBM reorganizes frequently, using split to stir things up, refocus the organization in a changing marketplace, and reenergize employees to rethink their jobs. This was the rationale behind the massive decentralization effort in 1988 that split the company into seven loosely autonomous businesses and four worldwide regions. IBM maintains that a reorganization of this scope is not so disruptive that the costs outweigh the gains. It takes at least six months—often much longer—for essential informal networks to be rebuilt, and before a new entity starts to really work effectively. IBM gets away with frequent, and large-scale, reorganizations (split) because it is working from a solid foundation of fit (e.g., IBMers often identify themselves with statements such as "I work for IBM and am currently in the XYZ division"). This identification with *the company* generates coherence. Each "card" knows it belongs to a common "deck," even though the deck is continually reshuffled. Results tend to reaffirm IBM's view. Since the reorganization, IBM has reduced overhead by 20 percent, launched a vastly improved networking product, and reduced its development time for mainframes from three years to eighteen months.[7]

The idea of decentralization, or splitting off self-contained units from their monolithic parents, was pioneered by General Motors and DuPont in the early decades of this century.[8] It has long since entered the mainstream of management thinking. The concept reached its apogee in the 1960s when dissatisfaction with large, bureaucratic organizations spawned a wave of decentralization. Sometimes it worked—many times it did not.[9] The breakdowns occurred when the separated units became so far removed from the parent culture that necessary levels of connectedness and synergy were lost. There has been a resurgence of this decentralization wave in the past decade. Over a dozen best-sellers have championed the virtues of split. These include E. F. Schumacher's *Small Is Beautiful*,[10] and a variety of books on innovation, including Gifford Pinchot's *Intrapreneuring.*[11]

A variety of factors make split an attractive recourse: economists point out competitive and market necessities; technologists remind us that discontinuities in technology require it; behaviorists have shown that people are more motivated and productive in small clusters. There is even an ideological argument built on the premise that society would be more humane if our organizations were on more of a human scale.[12]

A compelling case for split is provided by Michael J. Piore and Charles Sabel in *The Second Industrial Divide*.[13] They argue for "flexible specialization" (i.e., having the organizational capability to remain agile and to focus on niche markets). They document how the world's industrial economies have generated every-increasing demands for more specialized goods. Concomitantly, technological advances in information management have made it feasible to produce specialty products economically. Robotics enable us to customize products that formerly had to be mass produced. Apple Computer, for example, carries near-zero inventory, and routinely manufactures computers and workstations to order in less than five days. Clearly, high degrees of market segmentation do not necessarily require organizational decentralization (i.e., split), but smaller market niches combined with technology have placed small manufacturers on an equal footing with larger ones. Piore and Sabel trace the inroads of small, flexible producers in industries such as steel, chemicals, textiles, and computers that a mere decade ago were regarded as impervious to small-scale competition. Ironically, in almost all cases, the smaller players are the most profitable.

We would not do justice to the rationale for split without addressing its role in coping with technological discontinuity. Peter Drucker's book *The Age of Discontinuity* describes the commercial era in which we live.[14] Under steady-state conditions, large, monolithic units can perform well, but when a technological breakthrough comes along, it is often better to be small. Consider the electronics industry. In twenty-five years there have been eight step-function shifts in technology—in almost every case pioneered by a small spin-off. Some of these units operated at least initially under the umbrella of larger companies. Most were start-ups.[15]

It is not nearly as surprising that the new entrants did well as it is that the former leaders almost always fell out of the race. Across the past two and a half decades there has been an almost complete turnover of leadership. The leader in the earlier generation of technology failed to provide the next era with the resources and autonomy required to execute a meta-shift into the new technology.

The organizational rationale for split is not hard to grasp. First, a dedicated entity can focus on the key success factors of a new market or technology. Second, new expertise often requires different people (e.g., electrical instead of mechanical engineers). New units that start from scratch can staff themselves more easily to meet such needs. Third, the cross-disciplinary nature of new markets or technology often requires talent from several functional disciplines. In established firms, individuals are often *borrowed* from preexisting departments on a part-time basis. This seldom works. Full-time commitment to the new stand-alone entity is the preferred approach. Finally, smaller, more manageable entities perform better as innovators. A National Science Foundation survey found that small firms produced about four times as many innovations per research and development dollar as medium-sized firms, and about twenty-four times as many as large firms.[16]

BEING BIG, ACTING SMALL

The case for split might lead us to conclude that small entities are good at almost all things, and that large companies, like the dinosaurs of ages past, are candidates for extinction. Yet a little reflection suggests that this is a vast oversimplification. We see examples of companies such as McDonald's, IBM, or Honda for whom size, deep pockets, and market clout represent a major competitive advantage. The trick is to combine advantages of size with an ability to generate focus and commitment at the subunit level. Throughout this decade, we have witnessed dedicated efforts by companies to be big, and yet to act small. Success turns, in large measure, on rather subtle organizational arrangements. Dana, for example, redefined its plant executives as "store managers," and instituted systems and incentives toward creating a sense of entrepreneurship at the plant level.[17] 3M does similar things with its venture teams,[18] as does Texas Instruments with over ninety Product Customer Centers.[19] New words have been coined to capture the informal processes that go hand in hand with these arrangements. Our everyday business vocabulary includes terms such as *champions*, *performance shoot-outs* (among rival teams), and *skunkworks*.

IDEOLOGICAL UNDERTOW?

A cautionary note is in order. Split is a valuable link in the renewal chain, but it is not a panacea. In particular, be on the watch for the ideological undercurrent that submerges the thoughtful application of split in a sea of indiscriminate euphoria. Illustrative of the phenomenon is this quote from Thomas J. Peters' and Nancy Austin's *A Passion for Excellence*:

> When it comes to innovation, small, as we have seen, is more beautiful than even we had ever imagined. Virtually all successful innovation comes from or is markedly enhanced by decentralization and disrespect.[20]

TABLE 1
Technological Transitions and Leadership Shifts from Vacuum Tubes to Microprocessors

TECHNOLOGY	INVENTING COMPANY	YEAR OF INNOVATION	MARKET LEADERS (RANKED BY 1988 MARKET SHARE*)				
			#1	#2	#3	#4	#5
Vacuum Tube	Bell Labs (AT&T)	1915	RCA	Sylvania	GE	Raytheon	Westinghouse
Transistor	Bell Labs (AT&T)	1950	Hughes	Transitron	Philco	Sylvania	Texas Instruments
Semiconductor	Texas Instruments	1960	Texas Instruments	Motorola	Fairchild	RCA	GE
Static Random Access Memory (RAM)	Intel	1969	Hitachi	NEC	Toshiba	Fujitsu	Mitsubishi
Dynamic RAMs (DRAM)	Intel	1970	Toshiba	NEC	Mitsubishi	Texas Instruments	Hitachi
EPROM	Intel	1971	Intel	Fujitsu	Hitachi	Mitsubishi	Toshiba
8- and 16-Bit Microprocessors	Intel	1971–1974	Intel	NEC	Motorola	Hitachi	Mitsubishi
Microcontroller	Intel	1976	Mitsubishi	Hitachi	Motorola	NCR	NEC
32-Bit Microprocessor	National Semiconductor	1982	Motorola	Intel	National Semiconductor	INMOS	AT&T

*Market share rankings by revenues for 1987, with the exception of vacuum tubes, transistors, and semiconductors. (*Courtesy Dataquest*)

The populist appeal of such quotes is almost irresistible. It champions the little guy against the system. It is macho, and it resonates with American ideals. Many of the terms used interchangeably with split (*autonomy, profit centers, entrepreneurship,* and so on), have an ideological undertow—especially in America, where constitution and custom hold these values dear. The result: our ideological affinity for split fuels a great number of ill-thought through decentralization efforts. Most of us have experienced the disruption that occurs when such blind leaps of faith lack substance.

THE PERILS OF SPLIT

Hewlett-Packard is an enthusiastic proponent of split. Size and "bureaucratization" have been historically regarded as grave threats to HP's entrepreneurial spirit. Policy dictates that every time a head count in a parent division exceeds 1,200, a new division is created. But too much split, like too much fit, causes trouble. HP's tradition of hiving off divisions works well when each unit is dedicated to a distinct market segment, but in the 1980s HP found itself designing and manufacturing computers. Excessive decentralization proved crippling in this new area. Hewlett-Packard has repeatedly taken too long to move its products from the design stage to the market.[21]

Computers are made of microprocessors, memory units, disk drives, keyboards, CRT screens, and software. All must integrate into a coherent system that constitutes the final offering. At HP, each of these components was made by a separate entity, each jealously guarding its prerogatives. In due course, a consensus can be hammered out among these stakeholders, but almost always after arduous negotiation. The price paid is a long product development cycle, and sometimes not the best results (some HP computers have had awkward interfaces, which might have been avoided had the original design been driven by one, powerful guiding vision).

The costs of overdifferentiation have been significant. HP was ideally positioned to pioneer, and to be the dominant participant in, the sixteen-billion-dollar workstation market. Instead, they came to market five years late—long after Sun, Apollo, and a host of competitors had grabbed the lead.

Hewlett-Packard's response has been to somewhat hesitantly reverse course. Through several reorganizations, HP has tried to loosely couple the errant divisions into a "Systems Group." So doing, it has sought to restore fit and deemphasize split. Such rebalancing is usually a necessary, but insufficient, remedy. It can result in the worst of both worlds—burdening formerly independent units with what feels like onerous bureaucracy, sacrificing their entrepreneurial spirit and sense of ownership. HP's remedies to date have not been particularly effective. As will be seen, striking the right tension between fit and split takes more than a compromise between the two factors.[22]

THE CONTEND FACTOR

Fit contributes to coherence—but too much of it risks overadaptation. Split helps instill vitality and focus—but too much of it diffuses energy. That's where the third factor, contend, enters the equation. Contention management is essential to orchestrate tensions that arise. Why? Because you can never engineer just the right blend of fit and split without deal-ing with the human element. Making an organization tick isn't like wiring a circuit board. Recourse to the hard levers—strategy, structure, and systems—takes you only so far. Inevitably, one must deal with the passion and perspiration of human interaction. Organizations are, in the last analysis, interactions among people. These interactions often generate disagreements of one type or another. At HP these disagreements arose when-ever the key divisions convened to hammer out a final computer design. Each sought to optimize at the other's expense. The software designers imposed hardships on hardware, an elegant innovation by the storage technology division fouled up the microprocessor unit. Trade-offs had to be made, and could only be made effectively by facing the contention and channeling it constructively. Unfortunately, Hewlett-Packard's emphasis on congeniality at all costs tended to "smooth and avoid."

Hewlett-Packard's inability to "engineer" the perfect blend of fit and split confirms what we know intuitively—namely, that there are no static prescriptions that will keep organi-zations vital. Problems of administration are never "solved" the way things dissolve in water or are resolved in mathematics. The problem you solve today creates the opportunity to solve the next problem that your last solution created.

NOTES

[1] Pascale and Athos, *The Art of Japanese Management.* Underlying the more general treatment of Japanese management in this book are a considerable number of technical papers written by Richard Pascale and his coauthors over several years. Listed in chronological order, these are:

"Made in America (Under Japanese Management)," with William Ouchi, *Harvard Business Review,* Sept.–Oct. 1974.

"The Adaptation of Japanese Subsidiaries in the United States," *Columbia Journal of World Business,* Vol. 12, No. 7 (Spring 1977).

"Communication and Decision Making across Cultures: Japanese and American Comparisons," *Administrative Science Quarterly,* April 1978.

"Personnel Practices and Employee Attitudes: A Study of Japanese and American Managed Firms in the United States," *Human Relations,* Vol. 31, No. 7 (1978).

"Zen and the Art of Management," *Harvard Business Review,* March-April 1978.

"Communication, Decision Making and Implementation among Managers in Japanese and American Managed Companies in the United States," with Mary Ann Maguire, *Sociology and Social Research,* Vol. 63 No. 1, (1978).

"Comparison of Selected Work Factors in Japan and the United States," with Mary Ann Maguire, *Human Relations,* Vol. 31, No. 7 (July 1980).

[2] For a discussion of the Seven S's see Pascale and Athos, *The Art,* pp. 80–82; also Robert H. Waterman, *The Renewal Factor* (New York: Bantam Books, 1987), p. 57.

[3] Robert Johnson, "Fast-Food Chains Draw Criticism for Marketing Fare as Nutritional," *Wall Street Journal,* April 6, 1987, p. 27.

[4] Interviews at Federal Express (internal competitive analysis of UPS), Memphis, Tenn., Feb. 14, 1989. Also see Kenneth Labich, "Big Changes at Big Brown," *Fortune,* Jan. 18, 1988, pp. 56–64; also Daniel Machalaba, "United Parcel Service Gets Deliveries Done by Driving Its Workers: But Its Vaunted Efficiency's Now to Be Challenged by an Automated Rival," *Wall Street Journal,* April 22, 1986, pp. 1 and 26.

[5] Interviews of McDonald's franchisees, February–March 1987; also Robert Johnson, "McDonald's Combines a Dead Man's Advice with Lively Strategy," *Wall Street Journal*, Dec. 18, 1987, pp. 1 and 13; also see Penny Moser, "The McDonald's Mystique," *Fortune*, July 4, 1988, pp. 112–16.

[6] Chposky and Leonis, *Blue Magic*, p. 209. For a broader discussion of the pros of split, see Michael Tushman and David Nadler, "Organizing for Innovation," *California Management Review*, Vol. 28, Nov. 3 (Spring 1986), pp. 74–92; also Bill Saporito, "Companies that Compete Best," *Fortune*, May 22, 1989, p. 39, and Robert B. Reich, "Entrepreneurship Reconsidered: The Team as Hero," *Harvard Business Review*, May–June 1987, pp. 77–83.

[7] Jeremy Main, "The Winning Organization," *Fortune*, Sept. 26, 1988, p. 50, and Joel Dreyfuss, "Reinventing IBM," *Fortune*, Aug. 19, 1988, pp. 30–39.

[8] Alfred Chandler, *Strategy and Structure*.

[9] E.L. Ginzberg and George Vojta, *Beyond Human Scale: The Large Corporation at Risk* (New York: Basic Books, 1985). Also anon., "Centralization vs. Decentralization," unpublished internal study of 26 companies. (McKinsey Organizational Practice, Yountville, Calif., Organizational Effectiveness Workshop, Nov. 16–21, 1980.) McKinsey tracked 18 client companies in the aftermath of decentralization; two thirds recentralized within five years and did not feel that they realized major benefits from decentralization. For a discussion of how split led to overreliance on financial reporting, see Kim B. Clark and Robert H. Heyes, "Recapturing America's Manufacturing Heritage," *California Management Review*, Vol. 30, No. 4 (Summer 1988), pp. 27–31.

[10] E.F. Schumacher, *Small Is Beautiful* (New York: Harper & Row, 1973).

[11] Gifford Pinchot III, *Intrapreneuring* (New York: Harper & Row, 1985).

[12] Ginzberg and Vojta, *Beyond Human Scale.*

[13] Michael J. Piore and Charles F. Sabel, *The Second Industrial Divide* (New York: Basic Books, 1984).

[14] Peter F. Drucker, *The Age of Discontinuity*, pp. 54–57 and 188–211.

[15] Table 1 is based on three sources: Intel internal data; SIA Public Information: "Crisis in a Critical Industry," Washington, D.C., Sept. 28, 1988; and Data Quest, March 7, 1989. Also see Richard Foster, *Innovation* (New York: Summit Books, 1986), p. 133.

[16] National Science Foundation, "International Science and Technical Data Update" (Washington, D.C., National Science Foundation, 1984).

[17] Telephonc interviews at Dana, May 27, 1987.

[18] Interviews at 3M, St. Paul, Minn., Jan. 24, 1986. Also see Russell Mitchell, "Masters of Innovation," *Business Week*, April 10, 1989; anon., *Our Story So Far* (St. Paul: Minnesota Mining and Manufacturing Co., 1977); and Virginia Huck, *Brand of the Tartan: The 3M Story* (New York: Appleton-Crofts, 1955).

[19] Interview with Dean Tombs, former VP at Texas Instruments, March 10, 1987; also see "Texas Instruments Show U.S. Business How to Survive in the Eighties," *Business Week*, Sept. 18, 1978; and Eugene W. Helms, "The OST System for Managing Innovation at Texas Instruments," an address to the Armed Forces Management Association, April 7, 1971.

[20] Peters and Austin, *A Passion*, p. 187.

[21] Interviews at Hewlett-Packard, July 1985, December 1985, January–February 1986, and April 1988.

[22] Interviews at HP, 1985, 1986, 1988. Also see Bro Uttal, "Delays and Defections at Hewlett-Packard," *Fortune*, Oct. 29, 1984, p. 62; Bro Uttal, "Mettle Test Time for John Young," *Fortune*, April 29, 1985, pp. 242–48; and Peter Waldman, "Hewlett-Packard, Citing Software Snag, Will Delay New Computer Six Months," *Wall Street Journal*, Sept. 26, 1986, p. 2.

PART 3

Strategic Planning

Six Theories of Planning:
Myths and Realities*

Guy Benveniste

Let me repeat again: Planning is a relatively new activity. Planners or analysts belong to relatively young professions. New roles emerge from needs, but as new roles emerge many theories or myths are used to explain, justify, and differentiate what is done by these new actors from what is done by others. These theories may be normative in the sense that they define what planning should be, or they may derive from careful analysis of the behavior of planners. These latter theories can be useful in understanding why practice differs from the normative order.

But as new roles are played, new experience is also acquired. As experience is acquired, theories are altered to conform to reality. Ideas about planning have therefore evolved over time. What I intend to do in the next few pages is to rapidly review and summarize some of the principal theories of planning of the last decades. My purpose is twofold:

First, I wish to explain why certain assumptions dominate our thinking about planning. For example, much current legislation assumes that comprehensive planning is desirable. But as we will discuss at greater length later, the degree of comprehensiveness of a plan depends on the interplay of technical and political factors and on the way these impact on the perceived credibility of the plan to be implemented. Thus, even if comprehensive planning is a myth, it is a myth that has utility.

Second, I wish to be able to place this discussion of planning—the idea that planners are managers with a limited but very real involvement in the operational aspects of decision making and implementation—in the context of a general discussion of planning theory.

We will focus on six main theories: (1) the comprehensive rational approach, (2) advocacy planning, (3) apolitical politics, (4) critical planning theory, (5) strategic planning, and (6) incrementalism. All these theories deal with planning, but they differ for various reasons. It will be our purpose here to understand why these six theories emerged, why they differ from one another, and why they continue to serve as the prevailing myths of planning.

THE COMPREHENSIVE RATIONAL APPROACH

The comprehensive rational approach, which dominated early planning thought (Altshuler, 1965; Waterston, 1965), is a set of procedures whereby the planner clarifies goals, conducts systematic analysis to generate a set of policy alternatives, establishes criteria to choose among these alternatives, and, once choices have been made and implemented, monitors results.

This definition implies a systems view and a systems approach: The planner clarifies the goals of the system and then conducts a thoroughgoing analysis of alternatives. The analysis must be comprehensive if it is to be rational since all elements of the system contribute to the goals. Once the analyst is able to define a system and once the relations among the components of the system are understood, it is possible to ascertain the best means to achieve given objectives.

A TYPICAL COMPREHENSIVE PLAN

Some years ago I was a member of a World Bank team that undertook a long-term study of the future demand and supply of electric power in the central Mexican plateau where Mexico City is located. This was a technical assistance project designed to assist the Mexican government in elaborating a coordinated sectorial plan for expanding the generation, transmission, and distribution of electricity in that country. At the time of the study, electric power in Mexico was provided by several foreign companies and by the government's own Federal Power Commission. One of the foreign companies operating in the central plateau was the Mexican Light and Power Company (Mexlight). Mexlight operated hydroelectric plants in the state of Puebla at Necaxa and had other hydro- and thermal-generating capability. The Federal Power Commission generated power and sold some of it to Mexlight to distribute in the central plateau area. There were also smaller privately owned systems in that area. Other foreign companies, such as American Foreign Power, operated elsewhere in the country.

The political conflict centered on the continued ownership of the electric power companies by foreign interests. The government had nationalized the foreign petroleum companies in the late thirties, and as economic growth accelerated in the postwar period, there were increasing calls for placing the foreign electric companies under direct government control and ownership. As a result, the government, as regulator of electric rates, had tended to resist Mexlight's request for rate increases in an effort to delay the expansion of the private companies while at the same time keeping electric rates as low as possible. But the company argued that it needed rate increases to be able to pay dividends to its shareholders sufficient to attract new capital and obtain foreign loans to expand the electric system. The company could not stand still and meet the rising demand for electricity, which had been doubling every ten years. But the government postponed rate increases on the grounds that the projected future growth of the system did not warrant such capital expansion.

The study we undertook was to be the first comprehensive review of electricity requirements in the central plateau. The World Bank provided a well-known and accomplished international expert—a very distinguished English specialist in electric power systems—to guarantee the impartiality of the study. As Mexlight saw the situation, the study was needed to demonstrate that the expansion of the Mexican economy, especially around the central plateau of the country, would require continued expansion of the electric system during the next twenty years. The study was to demonstrate once and for all that the growth of demand would require large investments in generation, transmission, and distribution facilities. The Mexican government would then come to its senses. Obviously, it could not attempt to nationalize Mexlight at a time when the company needed fresh infusions of foreign capital and new loans. The study would lead to one of two results: Either Mexlight would obtain rate increases sufficient to attract new capital and loans, or the Mexican economy would suffer because neither the company nor the government would be able to meet the increased energy demand.

Our role was purely technical. The bank was concerned about maintaining or accelerating the rate of growth of the Mexican economy and hoped the study would provide a basis for action, one way or another. As technicians, we knew that, at the time, Mexican statistics were not very accurate, but we believed that we could arrive at fairly accurate projections of future electricity demand. We had relatively good historical data for the electric systems, and we had sufficient demographic and economic data to make forecasts about the future. We were encouraged by the apparent constancy of worldwide demand for electricity, which, at that time, seemed to grow at 7 percent a year, thus doubling every ten years. We were also encouraged by the comprehensiveness of the undertaking. We thought our projections would be influential because we would be able, for the first time, to look at the entire interconnected electric system serving the area. We went beyond the confines of each company and agency and brought together information that, until then, had not been generally available.

Subsequent events confirmed our high expectations. The Mexican government received the report, studied it, and acted. But it did not raise Mexlight's electric rates. Clearly, the study had an impact, and subsequent events showed that the impact was different from Mexlight's expectations. The government realized it could not continue to allow the company to stagnate. The Federal Power Commission would not be able to handle the distribution needs we were forecasting even if it were to expand its generating capacity. Squeezed between a nationalistic clamor for Mexican ownership of the company and the evident need to expand the system, the government opted for a novel alternative: It kept the electric rates low and, when the price of Mexlight stock fell, the government bought a controlling interest and took the company over. Good technical planners that we were, we had presented a comprehensive view of the problem. But the Mexican government responded in a way that took us somewhat by surprise, as we had expected the government to raise Mexlight's rates. But, as technicians, we had paid little attention to the political implications of the problem. It was not something we felt we should concern ourselves with. Not only had we defined our role narrowly, but we were working for the World Bank and could not appear to be interfering in internal Mexican politics.

Comprehensiveness was important for the legitimacy of the study because it allowed us to inform both Mexlight and the Federal Power Commission that their data and estimates of on-line generating and transmission capabilities had been taken into account in our study. In that perspective, our study was superior to the independent studies each of them had conducted in the past. Moreover, we extended the time horizon of our projections far beyond previous studies, giving us an advantage over these studies because our time horizon included periods for which no planned expansion of the system was scheduled. This allowed us to demonstrate the rapid increases in investments that the additional expansion would require.

Our study resulted in major changes regarding the way electric service was to be provided in Mexico. But although we thought we were comprehensive, we were really only "partially comprehensive." There was a huge reality out there that we did not even take into account. We had defined the problem in our own way and completely neglected political issues. Thus the outcome of the study had not been what some of the participants had expected and they were taken by surprise. This is the first lesson to learn about comprehensive planning. A plan can never be truly comprehensive, even if it aims to be, because reality is always more complex. As a result, planning misjudgments happen, and they illustrate that too much confidence is placed in this planning myth.

USEFULNESS OF THE COMPREHENSIVE APPROACH

In general, the comprehensive approach to problem solving gives planners needed legitimacy to provide expert advice. There are several reasons for this:

First, the comprehensive approach provides a systems view that yields far more information than a piecemeal approach would. For example, in national economic planning the comprehensive approach is thought to be "conceptually superior" to partial planning (Waterston, 1965, p. 66) because it permits use of macroeconomic models that provide far more information than would otherwise be available. Estimates can be made of the aggregate levels of savings, investments, imports, exports, and other economic variables required to achieve a desired rate of growth in real per-capita income.

Second, the comprehensive approach makes it possible to obtain information from parties that might not provide it otherwise. The comprehensive approach gives planners authority to acquire information about the activities of many agencies accustomed to protecting their turf and desirous of maintaining secrecy. Our study had access to Mexlight and Federal Power Commission data that had not been readily available before. Our arguments were therefore new and created interest both within those agencies and outside them. By providing planners with the right to seek and obtain data, the comprehensive approach gives them access to information that they can to use to influence decisions.

Third, it allows issues faced by the entire system to be addressed. Therefore, it is more concerned with the public good than with parochial interests. For example, those of us on the World Bank team felt that we were serving the general public interest because it seemed clear to us that shortages of electric power would inevitably slow down economic growth and therefore result in a lower standard of living for the Mexican people.

The comprehensive approach suits a young profession seeking to establish itself in a complex political arena. Why should anyone listen to planners? One argument is that they are agents of rationality: "In one sense PPB (Program Planning and Budgeting) [an organizational planning technique that became fashionable in the late 1960s] can be viewed as introducing a new set of participants into the decision process [who], for want of a better term, I have labeled partisan efficiency advocates. At each level of the decision process these participants become particular champions of efficiency and effectiveness as criteria in decision making" (Shultze, 1968, p. 101).

But rationality is not enough. After all, the Prince is not irrational, and even if he does not have the time to conduct detailed studies, his lieutenants do. The lieutenants of the Prince know their own agencies or departments inside out. To differentiate themselves, therefore, the planners need a claim that goes beyond expertise. Comprehensiveness provides this claim. As Sarfatti Larson points out in a detailed analysis of the emergence of professions, the main instrument of professional advancement is a claim to expertise that cannot be easily disregarded. This claim is used to obtain social recognition and sufficient prestige to allow the new profession to "assert authority and demand respect." Comprehensiveness provided such a claim for the young profession of planning.

DYSFUNCTIONS OF THE COMPREHENSIVE APPROACH

But systemwide claims of expertise can also be dysfunctional. By separating themselves from those who manage or implement in the field, planners can come to disregard practical reality. For example, in the days when the comprehensive approach dominated the educational planning movement, most educational planners tended to be economists who did not have too high an opinion of educators or of politicians. At a seminar some years ago, a leading comprehensive educational planner asserted that the "main bottleneck to educational planning is political" (Benveniste, 1965, p. 110). He argued that there were too many ephemeral politicians working in education, who sought only prestige and had short-term interests. There were not enough planners to counteract their influence. He thought that planners should have more influence. In his view, which was widely shared, planning would succeed only when technicians trained in planning could begin to convince the general public and permanent administrators of the utility of their craft and thus undo the bad influence that politicians who do not understand technical issues have when they impose their will on policy and planning decisions. Basically, he was arguing that control be given to the technicians. He obviously had a very narrow and parochial view of planning, even though he espoused the notion of comprehensiveness.

More importantly, claims of expertise are dysfunctional when they are not met. While some comprehensive planning was and still is successful, it also very quickly became evident that many planning problems did not lend themselves to a comprehensive technical solution. For example, a major study of planning for public housing in Chicago in the late forties and early fifties already indicated that the ideology of the comprehensive approach could not readily be put into practice. Plans were not readily implemented even if they were rational and comprehensive (Meyerson and Banfield, 1955). Observing the complexities of the city of Chicago, where a major public housing program was under way, the two authors showed that the Plan Commission was simply unable to muster enough authority: "There were good reasons why the Plan Commission could not readily make a comprehensive plan of the kind described in the ideology of the city planning government. Power to make fundamental decisions affecting city development . . . was widely dispersed" (p. 274).

Meyerson and Banfield emphasize that there were too many decision makers over whom the planners had no control: "To make a comprehensive plan which would be achieved—if not achievable, we would not term it a 'plan'—would mean subordinating all of these decision makers, public and private, to a single intention—an impossibility so long as power is widely dispersed and power holders have conflicting ends" (p. 274). The result was that the planners could not decide where industry should locate, whether or not the "Negro" ghetto (as it was referred to at the time) of Chicago should be preserved, and so on.

Moreover, the planners were not inheriting a clean slate. Many previous decisions had already set the stage for what was to follow. Congress had enacted the Housing Act of 1919, and the Illinois legislature, the city council, and numerous other actors were already in motion.

For example, it was decided to go ahead with large slum clearance projects without examining other promising alternatives because these projects were already under way. The planners could not alter the course of events, and it was, therefore, difficult to label their intervention as "comprehensive." To be sure, they were able to inject minimal technical considerations into the selection of sites, but even then political considerations prevailed: "Was the site in the ward of an alderman who would support the project or oppose it?" (Banfield, 1959, p. 365).

The comprehensive rational approach provides the basis for a normative definition of planning: Planning should be rational and comprehensive. This normative ideology served and still serves the planning movement well. It was highly useful in the sixties, at a time of rapid worldwide expansion of planning activity. For example, it provided legitimacy for a vast expansion of town and city planning, including the many planned new towns that were created in England in the decade of the sixties (Hall, 1979). It provided legitimacy for the rapid growth of planning in developing countries and in some Western European countries. It provided legitimacy for—and is incorporated into many statutes mandating—comprehensive planning, including land-use legislation. It still provides legitimacy for planning in corporate organizations (Branch, 1983; Brickner and Cope, 1977). Moreover, as one keen observer points out, it even provides legitimacy for the teaching of planning in the academy (Dalton, 1986). Some authors have loudly denied its utility, arguing that comprehensive planning has little impact and that if such planning is "everything," maybe it is "nothing" (Wildavsky, 1973; Caiden and Wildavsky, 1974). But even if planning can never become comprehensive, striving for comprehensiveness is not necessarily a useless exercise. The degree of comprehensiveness that is achieved depends on the leverage that planners are able to achieve, and that is what matters in the final analysis. Meanwhile, the concept of a comprehensive, rational approach to problem solving opened many doors for a new and emerging profession.

ADVOCACY PLANNING

If comprehensive planning gave the planning movement a professional identity distinct from that of stakeholders or lieutenants of the Prince, advocacy planning gave public-sector planners another professional characteristic: a concern for their clients, that is, for the beneficiaries of the plans they elaborate. Advocacy planning emerged in the mid sixties when planners began to argue that the very complexity of the decisions they had to make meant that ordinary citizens could not participate in the decision process. The choices faced by city planners, as well as by educational and economic planners, reflected the increasing complexity and uncertainty of the world. The ordinary political process had come to seem inadequate and not suitable for debates on complex issues. The antibureaucratic revolts of the sixties—for example, the events of May 1968, in France, or the earlier free speech movement in Berkeley—were indicative of a general malaise. People felt overwhelmed by the impersonal bureaucratic apparatus.

Advocacy planners argued that existing plans reflected the distribution of power in society. So, for example, they called for planners to take to heart the needs of low-income communities. Davidoff (1965) wrote that there were partisan ways of looking at problems, that one could design various alternative designs for the future, and that advocacy planners should propose designs that were sympathetic to the needs of the poor.

ADVOCACY PLANNING AND PARTICIPATION

Advocacy planning parallels the enactment of legislation mandating citizen participation in federal and state programs (Barber, 1984; Spiegel, 1968). For example, the Economic Opportunity Act of 1964 calls for "maximum feasible participation" of the poor in the War on Poverty. Title II-A, section 202, authorizes the creation of community action programs that "were to be developed, conducted, and administered with the maximum feasible participation of residents of the areas and members of the groups served" (Kramer, 1969, p. 1). Similar language appears in the Demonstration City Act of 1966 (the Model Cities program).

For planners imbued with the vision of a comprehensive rational approach, the role of the advocate planner was to facilitate the participation of the poor and to ensure that their input was taken into account in the selection of alternatives. They viewed the poor as quite incapable of planning for themselves since they did not have the necessary expertise or the time and energy to do so (Edelston and Kolodner, 1968). These planners set out to help the underprivileged with the same assumptions and dedication that other professions have adopted. Lawyers, for instance, have institutionalized pro bono service as part of their code of professional responsibilities. The 1981 code of ethics of the American Institute of Certified Planners directs planners to "strive to give citizens the opportunity to have a meaningful impact on the development of plans and programs. Participation should be broad enough to include people who lack formal organization and influence . . . . A planner must strive to expand choice and opportunity for all persons, recognizing a special responsibility to plan for the needs of the disadvantaged groups or persons" (Wachs, 1985, p. 336).

Advocacy practice is not easily achieved. Funding for advocacy planning is not always available, and volunteers have a limited amount of time to give to this work. More importantly, the client-expert relationship needed for advocacy planning is not easily achieved because the profession is not yet well known. The poor may come to ask for pro bono service from lawyers because individuals understand this function. But planning issues require collective action, which means that the poor have to be organized, and this requirement is not always understood even by the planners who want their participation. Moreover, planning issues are couched in a complex and abstract language that does not facilitate participation. Therefore, it is common for advocacy planners working as volunteers to select the causes they fight for, and advocacy planning can easily become the name of an activity guided by the political interests of some planners (Peattie, 1968; Funnye, 1970; Furner, 1975). When communities and other local interest groups are organized, these may use the services of planners. But this then becomes the more conventional client-expert relationship, and the term *advocacy* no longer applies.

Conceptually, advocacy planning is a perfected form of bottom-up comprehensive rational planning. The advocate planner ensures that the plan takes into account the goals and options of the underprivileged that might otherwise be neglected. In that perspective, advocacy planning involves the ability to learn about the needs of clients; it becomes a humanized form of design (Perin, 1970; Burke, 1979; Jenkins-Smith, 1982).

Advocacy planning can be interpreted as a form of organizing whereby the planner becomes an agent of change who raises the consciousness of the underprivileged. This function can have some impact on the distribution of power in society if the planners also happen to be good at community organizing—which is not always the case.

Alternatively, advocacy planning may show concern for the poor but have little power to achieve its goals. Young or inexperienced planners may like to believe that planning can serve an adjudicative function whereby planners use the mantle of their technical and professional capability to redistribute power, protect the underprivileged, and reallocate resources. One purpose of this reading is to make clear the very real limitations planners face in implementing such dreamy visions of their own role in society.

Likewise, one might believe that participation will, of itself, increase the power of the poor. But as Mulder (1971) has shown, power equalization does not come automatically with participation. In fact, participation, per se, reduces the power of the weak by making them more dependent on the expertise of those who have access to knowledge. Power equalization depends more on organizing than on advocacy, and to the extent that advocacy hampers organizing by providing the illusion of help, advocacy planning and participation do not help.

IMPACT ON PLANNING THOUGHT

Advocacy planning had an important impact on the development of planning thought. It forced planners to explore their own assumptions about those whom they were planning for. It made it clear that the poor and underprivileged had valid opinions about the kind of help they needed. Planners had no right to disregard these opinions. Advocacy planning forced planners to stop hiding behind data reports and computer spreadsheets and instead pay attention to some of the potential outcomes of their own planning decisions. It made them far more aware of the importance of field reality and of the experience of those who could translate what was happening in the new towns or the complexes that the planners had designed. In short, it made them aware of one of the political dimensions of the planning process, and provided an opportunity for them to become involved in the politics of planning. It was the first step toward converting technicians into managers.

APOLITICAL POLITICS

"Of course, planning is a technical activity, but it is not only technical. One cannot disregard political considerations. Young planners just out of school have dreams. They think they can convince with their arguments. Seasoned planners have learned from experience. They pay attention to political reality." My informant is French, a national planner who has been the *rapporteur* of one of the French planning commissions. (The *rapporteur*, while not chairing the commission, has the responsibility for formulating the consensus decisions of the commission and therefore plays an important facilitating role.) This man, a pioneer French planner, was very forthright in saying that political considerations have to be taken into account in planning.

Apolitical politics is a theory of planning that tells us that since planners are seen as technicians, they must therefore appear to play the role of technicians. It follows that in attending to the political issues that inevitably arise, they have to do so discreetly (Benveniste, 1977). Planners might attend to political issues because they are partisan actors or advocacy planners, as just mentioned. But this is not all my French informant is talking about. Planners try to invent solutions to problems and must, therefore, pay attention to all relevant political interests. They cannot disregard stakeholders. My French informant explains how the planning commissions operate: The relevant and organized groups that have an interest—a stake—in the sector plan participate in the working commission.

They come up with proposals. It is the function of the *rapporteur* to collect and integrate these proposals. Some proposals are based on careful analysis and some are not. At times, more studies have to be conducted. Negotiations are also undertaken and agreements are sought. In due time, the commission comes out with the sector plan: "My function is to seek the political compromise that makes sense technically," he asserts, "but I do not act too visibly. That is the function of the chairman. I work quietly with the other experts and make sure we have a solid technical basis for our proposed solutions."

Apolitical politics defines planning as the use of technical knowledge to achieve political or managerial compromises. Therefore, the role of the planner remains distinct from that of the politician or manager. The fact that planners play an apolitical role helps them to avoid conflicts. As several authors put it, planners should trust politicians and vice versa. More importantly, planners should not hesitate to act as apolitical politicians or as covert activists (Catanese, 1974, 1984; Beyle and Lathrop, 1970).

Apolitical politics does not recognize a managerial role for planning. No budget is allocated for essential managerial activities. If planners have to play politics, organize support, and become advocates, they will have to do so on their own time. Apolitical politics recognizes a political dimension to planning and asks planners to attend to it, but does no more than that. It does not tell us what resources to use nor provide time to attend to the political dimension. It is, therefore, dysfunctional. But it is one further step in the evolution of our concept of planning.

The apolitical stance of planners has considerable political utility: it lessens the visibility of the influence that technocrats have in the political system. Since planners are not given a mandate for whatever power they happen to exercise, they need the legitimacy provided by the technical dimension of their role to influence decisions. To be sure, there is a paradox here. The apolitical, technical definition of the planning role allows planners to influence political choices. Therefore, it has the opposite effect of what it is supposed to have, and the term *apolitical politics* reflects that paradox.

But apolitical politics also results in confusion. Some planners see themselves, or prefer to see themselves, as technicians serving the Prince. They prefer to keep their distance from politics. Others feel uncomfortable with the prospect of becoming involved in politics. In a sense, apolitical politics provides a basis for rapid retreat. Since it asks planners to act covertly, it also opens the door for those who prefer to think that planners should stick to technical issues. It is no surprise, therefore, to find a leading planning theoretician arguing that planners should simply help decision makers make better decisions and not get involved beyond that point (Faludi, 1987).

Over the years, planners have become somewhat more reconciled to the political facts of life. In the fifties and early sixties, it was still uncommon to view planning as apolitical politics. For example, a study conducted in the mid sixties interviewed thirty-three mid-career economic development planners from eighteen different developing countries who were attending a training program. The study documented a strong hostility to politics. These technocrats saw politics as an evil to be avoided. Thirty-three percent of the interviewees felt that politics and politicians were the cause of the economic problems of their countries, and they were, therefore, not at all inclined to see themselves as political actors. They were committed to technocratic approaches and felt that political considerations should be avoided as much as possible (Ilchman, Stone-Ilchman, and Hastings, 1968). More recent studies also report similar normative attitudes. For example, Baum (1980, 1983), in his studies of fifty city planners in the Baltimore region, reports a strong desire for professional autonomy. These planners would prefer to play a technical role, and they resent having to become bureaucrats or negotiators. Playing multiple and ambiguous roles is not easy, and the problem is not limited to economic or city planning. Knott (1986) points out the dilemmas faced by policy analysts who enter the political arena. Whose interest do they pursue? He calls them "paradoxical" politicians and suspects that they are concerned less with the rights and wrongs of issues than with their own pocketbooks (Knott, 1986).

Yet the empirical data confirm the fact that planners play a political role. Vasu (1979), who surveyed the 1974 roster of members of the American Institute of Planners, found that 87.7 percent of the respondents to his questionnaire agreed that a plan cannot be politically neutral and 78.3 percent thought that the planning process was value oriented. Regarding the role of the planner, 48.3 percent of the sample thought the role was technical, 32.0 percent that of a moderator, and 19.7 percent that of an advocate.

More recent research has focused on three roles for the planner: political actor, technician, and a hybrid of both (Howe, 1980; Howe and Kaufman, 1979; Kaufman, 1985). Data collected in 1978 and 1982 in the United States indicate that the prevalent perception of the role of city planner is that he or she has both a political and a technical role. Using a random sample of the membership of the American Institute of Planners, Howe and Kaufman found in 1978 that 27 percent thought the role technical, 17 percent political, and 51 percent a hybrid of both. By 1982 the figures had shifted to 26 percent technical, 17 percent political, and 54 percent a hybrid of both. Data from Israel were more revealing still: 22 percent of a sample of Israeli city and regional planners in 1983 saw their role as technical, only 8 percent saw it as political, and 70 percent thought it was a hybrid of both. Meltsner's (1976) earlier study of 116 policy analysts, in which he focused on skills rather than attitudes, seems to provide an explanation for these data. Looking at the political and technical skills of the analysts in his sample, he found 27 "entrepreneurs" who had both high political and technical skills, 41 "politicians" who were high on political skills and low on technical skills, and 48 "technicians" whose high technical skills were matched by low political ones. In other words, nearly 60 percent of those sampled were politically adroit and might have tended to see policy analysis in that light.

Apolitical politics is dysfunctional, and these data suggest why. It creates confusion, and this confusion has the following consequences:

- *Planning is perceived as mystification.* The fact that planners have to act as political actors while pretending to be technicians implies that they are pursuing agendas other than the announced ones. As we shall see shortly, this is the assumption of critical planning theory.
- *Planners are not prepared, and are not given the necessary resources, to play a political role.* Essentially, planners are not given much training in management, bureaucratic politics, or intervention techniques. Moreover, since they act informally in these areas, their formal time and resource budgets are inadequate to the task, and they tend to fail because they are not sufficiently staffed.
- *Managers or politicians distrust them.* The Prince who hires the planners does not expect them to become involved in political or managerial action. He may perceive the planner's interventions as a threat to his own authority and may, therefore, attempt to curb the planner's ability to act. This seems to have occurred in many instances of both corporate and public planning.
- *Planners tend to disregard implementation.* Since implementation is not part of their official responsibility, planners seldom have the authority or the time and resources to pay sufficient

attention to implementation issues. It is difficult for them to focus on client needs because they are too far removed from line responsibilities, and they do not have enough funding and access to information to pay sufficient attention to field realities.
- *Planners blame their failures on politics and management.* Since politics and management are not part of their official responsibilities, unsuccessful planners are quick to blame politicians or managers for their failure. Correspondingly, politicians and managers are quick to point out that planners are unrealistic, do not address relevant issues, or overemphasize models and data that do not capture what the managers and politicians think is important.
- *Planners are not clear as to their professional role.* Last, but not least, apolitical politics appears as a distortion of the ideal or normative professional role. It seems to be a form of expediency, or unethical behavior, that inevitably makes the profession suspect.

On the positive side, apolitical politics provides a new image of planning that recognizes the real-world limitations of both technical and static methodologies. Since it does not confront the problem head on, however, this theory creates a paradox and makes the planning role an uncomfortable one. Therefore, there is instability: Either planning retreats into its technical shell (Faludi, 1987), or it proceeds into the open and becomes a recognized and accepted managerial function.

CRITICAL PLANNING THEORY

The term *critical planning theory* is used to refer to a number of writings and activities critical of current planning practice. Stated succinctly, critical planning theory is concerned with the distribution of power in society and the extent to which planning reflects this distribution of power. The argument is made that planning is not a professional or technical activity, but simply a front, the mask under which powerful interests are able to maintain and justify their power. Thus a typical critical planner might criticize the way in which narrow economic interests dominate land-use patterns in an urban area and urge that different values and criteria be used to allocate urban resources. Some, but by no means all, critical planning theorists use Marxist assumptions as a starting point. Many of these writers focus on problems of urbanization in capitalist societies (Castells, 1977, 1978; Cox, 1978; Scott and Dear, 1981; Harvey, 1985). Some of these authors believe that planners have a special responsibility to act militantly and not to accept the status quo. In their view planners should redefine problems and learn to work as political actors in close partnership with those political and economic organizations that represent the interests of the disfranchised (Kraushaar, 1988). A comprehensive review of the field is provided in Friedmann's (1987) history of ideas in planning.

A REACTION TO APOLITICAL POLITICS

For our purposes here, we want to discuss critical planning theory as a reaction to apolitical politics. Critical planning theory always asks whose interests are being served by a given plan, and it argues that the professional mantle used by social scientists engaged in policy work is often very thin indeed. Who pays the salary of these experts? One cannot disregard the fact that planners depend on the Prince, both for sustenance and for access to power.

It follows, therefore, that they must often serve power instead of talking truth to power (Silva and Slaughter, 1984). Apolitical politics reinforces this perception. Critical theory questions the tendency toward mystification in planning. Why does the planner pretend to be a technician and then admit that politics are involved? Does overt technical planning hide a covert political agenda? As a result of this questioning, planners suddenly feel unsure of their own mission. They thought they were working for the public interest, but now they are uncertain. They thought they were serving the firm, but now they have to ask themselves whether they really know which way to go.

It is a moment of revelation. Planners realize that maybe they are not really planners but just hired lackeys ready to crank out facts and figures that will please this or that lieutenant in the entourage of the Prince (Torgerson, 1986). In the meantime, critical theorists are calling for greater awareness on the part of planners. The naive technicians who assume that they are not affecting political interests are enjoined to become aware of their impact, to develop a political philosophy that allows them to understand their role in society (Beatley, 1987; Dunn, 1982; Marcuse, 1976). There is also a call for openness, for demystification of the planning role. Some theorists find promise in certain aspects of Jurgen Habermas's approach (de Neufville, 1983; Forester, 1985; Paris, 1982). Habermas argues that technocracy hides the latent contradictions and conflicts of the capitalist state. Technical decisions are made, but the general public is unaware of their political content and of the political forces at work behind the scene. Technocracy provides legitimacy for a state apparatus controlled by the owners of the means of production. For Habermas, demystification requires the use of ideal forms of communication. Ideal forms of speech are devoid of hidden agendas. There are no hidden agendas when people speak to each other outside of the context of power relations. Demystification encourages the use of ideal forms of speech—speech that is understandable, sincere, and true. Once true knowledge is available, it can be used to revitalize the political process. Demystification finally results in participation in politics and the building of a genuine consensus (Habermas, 1974, 1976, 1979).

As pointed out earlier, critical planning theory does not necessarily take its point of departure from a Marxist view of the world. But it focuses on unequal power relations and on the importance of true communications in the search for consensus. Consequently, critical planning theory rejects the notion of an apolitical political approach to planning. It highlights Habermas's concept of the importance of demystification in the search for political consensus. It presents an idealized vision in which planners provide the communication channels that allow all participants in the planning process to express themselves without fear and with equal chances of being heard. To accomplish this, critical planners begin by questioning the assumptions that technical or apolitical political planners take for granted. Critical planners want to understand how their actions can impinge on the status quo, and they seek to speak "comprehensively," "sincerely," and "legitimately" and thus to achieve the "truth" (Forester, 1985, p. 209).

CRITICAL PLANNING THEORY AND PHENOMENOLOGY

There is a close relationship between critical planning theory and phenomenology. Phenomenology attempts to understand a phenomenon on its own terms. A phenomenological approach in the social sciences starts from an understanding of the assumptions, views of the world, explanations, feelings, desires, and values of the individuals being studied. When we comprehend how people approach problems or opportunities, when we perceive how they think and act, we can begin to understand what information or knowledge may cause them to act differently (Berger and Luckmann, 1966; Giorgi, 1985; Luckmann, 1978; Thines, 1977). But if planning is not to result in mystification, if apolitical politics is to be avoided, what are planners to depend on? The logical answer is that they need to depend on useful knowledge, that is, on knowledge that moves individuals to action (de Neufville, 1987). Since phenomenology appears to be a promising approach to the search for such knowledge and since it emphasizes an understanding of values and assumptions, it is not surprising that a phenomenological approach to planning occupies the attention of some planning theorists (Bolan, 1980; Comfort, 1985).

Critical planning theory and phenomenology provide new conceptualizations of planning. At one level, these concepts can be viewed as normative, namely, as arguments for a new role for planners. They can also be viewed as too idealistic. But the conceptualizations have a practical component. If we can better understand how citizens, clients, or members of organizations infer how to act—if we can place ourselves in their shoes—we may be in a better position to help them correct their errors. If we come to understand the strategies that groups pursue, we may be in a better position to find solutions that have a chance of being adopted.

Whether ideal forms of speech can be achieved is another matter. Habermassian thought would like to eliminate power relations as a prelude to creating a new political structure in which power would still be exercised but truth would reign supreme. Such a philosophical ideal may not be very practical in a world where power relations continue to exist and where secrecy has distinct functions. I am reminded of an old saying about not telling the truth to one's mother-in-law if one seeks happiness in marriage. The paradox of planning is that communicating the truth does not automatically lead to desirable solutions. It can easily lead to protracted conflicts, to the erosion of authority, and to other unforeseen and unhappy consequences.

LESSONS FROM CRITICAL THEORY

Critical theory provides important lessons to planning thought. It emphasizes the pursuit of knowledge—the kind of knowledge that can become a catalyst for action. It encourages planners to take an active role in bringing about change. It asks them not to hide behind the mask of technocracy but rather to actively search for, and then hold fast to, the truth.

We would carry the same ideas to a different outcome by suggesting that planners are rarely mere technicians and that they often have the opportunity to play political and managerial roles. But whether they are conservatives or progressives is not for us to decide. They obviously come to their tasks with their own inclinations and preferences. We would concur with critical planning theory that the apolitical approach to playing a political and managerial role is dysfunctional. We would certainly place much less faith in Habermassian ideals and ideologies than critical theorists do, but we would emphasize the potential value of using a phenomenological approach to understand why people act the way they do. We would concur that planners need to be aware of their own values and of the purposes they pursue, just as politicians and managers do. We would argue that secrecy can be useful to planners in the same ways that secrecy plays a role in politics or management, not all of which are evil. In short, we would suggest that effective planning requires planners to drop the assumption that they are mere technicians playing an apolitical political role. They are not only staff but also line managers in their own right.

STRATEGIC PLANNING

Strategic planning emerged in the corporate world and differs markedly from comprehensive planning. Strategic planning asks broad questions such as what stage of development are we in? What should we do if this event happens? How can we cope with this problem? What are our goals? But strategic planning does not assume that it can achieve comprehensiveness nor does it assume that there exist best solutions. Strategic planners may have a systems view, but they are not deterred if they do not. One school of thought (the Harvard Policy Model) focuses on SWOT analysis, that is, on the study of the *strengths* and *weaknesses* of the organization together with the study of the *opportunities* and *threats* in the environment of the organization (Andrews, 1980; Christensen and others, 1983). SWOT analysis is less concerned with defining the entire system of the organization in relation to its environment than with making a partial approximation of the situation in which the organization finds itself. It seeks to define what might or could happen and to present alternative courses of action under different scenarios. A good review of this field is provided by a recent text on strategic planning (Bryson, 1988).

Much of strategic planning reflects a strong distrust of our ability to predict the future. So much cannot be predicted that it is necessary to be able to move rapidly when particular events occur. In contrast to comprehensive planning, strategic planning is never finished and is always partial and selective. It often attempts to answer such questions as what impact would this event have? How probable is it? How will we know if it happens? Who will alert us? What consequences will it have? What will we do next? (O'Conner, 1978).

Concern with the environment translates into a concern with markets and market shares. For example, the Boston Consulting Group Matrix is an analytical technique that contrasts the potential growth and decline of overall markets with the potential share of a particular market that might be captured or lost (Sharplin, 1985). Portfolio Analysis provides a means of classifying the potential markets of a set of firms to determine resource allocation on the basis of a competitive strategy that takes into account the growth and revenue potential of all these firms (Bicksler and Samuelson, 1974; Elton and Gruber, 1987; Hamermesh, 1986). Planners using this technique do their best to select the "stars," "cash cows," "question marks," and "dogs" (Bogue and Buffa, 1986).

The scope of strategic planning varies. For example, the focus of strategic planning activities might be on plant closings, international marketing, mergers and acquisitions, product redesign, or other domains. While planners may center on a firm's environment, they may also be concerned with internal human resource planning, including necessary steps to replace key corporate executives, with reorganization, or with the impact of technological innovations on productivity.

The key initial concerns are: What is crucial here? What has "make" or "break" consequences? What are the leverage points for action? Once the overall picture of the environment is clearer, one can ask more pointed questions. What form of integration and coordination does the organization use to cope with its problems? Which issues are most important? Strategic issue management seeks to determine priorities for action (Ansoff, 1980; Below, Morrisey, and Acomb, 1987).

Responsibilities for planning may be centralized or dispersed. There may be an overall strategic effort to integrate divisional planning exercises, and longer-term planning may provide a framework for operational plans. Issue or sector plans may complement other planning endeavors.

Taken in perspective, we find that most corporate planning is of the "what do we do if . . . ?" variety (Naylor and Mann, 1982). Conditions in the environment or the technology of the industry do not often lend themselves to answering and therefore asking such questions as how do we reach these targets? or what is best for us? And while integration and coordination are important in strategic planning, comprehensiveness is not.

The claims to expertise of strategic planners differ from those of comprehensive long-range planners. Where the latter can claim the attention of the Prince, his lieutenants, and the stakeholders because they have an overall systems view that can provide a rational basis for selecting the best course of action, the former do not have such a view. Strategic planners rarely attempt a comprehensive, long-term view. Their contribution relies on their presentation of eventualities and their ability to point to the need for organizational integration and coordination to cope with these eventualities. If comprehensive long-range planning tends toward a unitary plan and specified set of objectives, strategic planning is far more concerned with opportunities and contingencies.

The sources of influence and legitimate authority of strategic planners differ from those of comprehensive planners. Of course, one has to take into account differences in the authority structures of the organizations where planning takes place. While most strategic planning takes place in corporations, attempts have also been made to introduce the concept in the public sector (Bryson and Einsweiler, 1987; Kaufman and Jacobs, 1987). Corporations tend to be more highly centralized and their authority structure tends to be more closely linked than in the public sector. It is, therefore, not surprising to find that most of the literature emphasizes that the CEO is the most important planner and that planners should work closely with him or her and the top management team. But in these writings, the managerial role of the planner and the importance of creating support for positions, using persuasion, and finding allies are rarely alluded to. Nevertheless, some authors emphasize the importance of stakeholders while others tell us that planners need to learn how to persuade or cajole management (Freeman, 1984). Conflicts between planners and management are rarely alluded to. In the view of some, there can be no significant conflicts and problems because the CEO always has sufficient authority to act (Amey, 1986). When conflicts are alluded to, this is done delicately, and it is made clear that planners must be careful not to make too many waves (Colley, 1984).

In short, the literature on corporate strategic planning emphasizes that the CEO plays a crucial role, that planning should concern itself with coordination and integration, and that planners are to act as facilitators or as team coaches who make it possible for the top management team to do its task. In this view planners are seen as a competent secretariat that establishes and maintains the planning calendar, prepares formal documents for planning meetings, briefs the CEO and top management teams, integrates information, and is very careful to keep a low profile and not go beyond the narrow scope of its role.

But as you already know, I argue that effective planning is not a limited staff function. Strategic planning staffs in corporations share similar problems with planners and policy analysts in the public arena. Corporate planners are inevitably involved in line action, and their role would be greatly facilitated if this were better understood. We would not be surprised to find that there is considerable suspicion of planning in the corporate world. No manager wants to lose authority to staff professionals even if these professionals have their uses. The fad era of strategic planning came and went, but the problems remain. It is our task to understand how the line functions of planners differ from the line responsibilities of other managers so that the suspicions and doubts that surround strategic planners can be allayed.

INCREMENTALISM

How do decision makers deal with difficult choices? Charles Lindblom argues in a series of books and papers that decision making is incremental, a matter of mutual adjustment. It is based on successive yet limited comparisons among a few alternatives. This he calls the "science of muddling through" (Lindblom, 1959, 1965, 1979, 1980; Braybrooke and Lindblom, 1963).

A first argument of Lindblom is that we do not need to agree about goals to set policy, we simply need to agree about policy. In an uncertain environment, when we find ourselves pressured by many interest groups and serve fickle consumers, we will act when we agree to act, even if our goals are not clear. Moreover, our agreement to act will be easiest when we find ourselves choosing among slightly different alternatives that do not depart too far from past practice. Lindblom tells us that effective decision making consists of small steps taken one at a time.

VALUE OF INCREMENTALISM

But why take small steps? Because coordination of our actions with the actions of others will be facilitated if we do not innovate too rapidly. For example, if you and I are crossing the street from opposite directions, I adjust my path to miss yours, and I also respond to your adjustments. You do the same and we manage to adjust mutually to each other and we do not collide. Mutual adjustment does not necessitate central coordination, but it does require that the involved parties be able to predict one another's behavior. Sometimes the cues are insufficient. We all experience situations where we misunderstand the cues of the other pedestrian and suddenly seem on a collision course. At that point, we stop, smile, say excuse me, and begin afresh, passing by each other. To predict the behavior of others requires knowledge of past behavior. In other words, mutual adjustment requires consistency and does not allow us to invent too fast or too rapidly. Mutual adjustment requires that we act incrementally; if we depart too quickly from accepted norms, we will collide. Lindblom's imagery is powerful. In an uncertain environment, groups or individuals are only able to adjust to each other, that is, to avoid serious errors by making small incremental changes that allow each party to learn how to respond to the others.

It is not that Lindblom is against policy analysis or planning. On the contrary, he simply wants to stress that the knowledge and time needed to search for solutions are limited by our ability to play new roles. Moreover, if policy is often incremental, so, in Lindblom's view, is policy analysis. It is bound to be fragmented or disjointed. But granted that Lindblom is against the dogma of comprehensiveness, why does he think that disjointed incremental analysis is a preferable strategy for policy analysis? Because there can never be enough time and resources to be comprehensive. Pragmatism reigns here too. Those who aspire to an overall vision or those who want a synopsis are tackling problems that are too big: "An aspiration to synopsis does not help an analyst choose manageable tasks, while an aspiration to develop improved strategies does" (Lindblom, 1979, p. 518).

USES AND MISUSES OF INCREMENTALISM

Critics of Lindblom were quick to point out that incrementalism might be suitable for situations where changes are slow and mutual adjustment is feasible but that more centralized efforts would be necessary if changes involving numerous units had to be carried out rapidly. For example, one could not expect a military campaign to rely exclusively on mutual adjustment and fragmented incrementalism. One of these critics went even further. He charged that incrementalism would reinforce the natural inertia and anti-innovation forces in any organization and argued that Lindblom provided ample justification for refusing to plan and for simply accepting the status quo (Dror, 1969).

But Lindblom never asserts that planning is not useful. He simply reminds us that the political process depends on transactions. To change the way business is transacted takes time. There are always interests at stake. If one tackles projects that are too vast, one will fail. Therefore, it is necessary to proceed step by step and to take on as much as possible, but no more. Incrementalism has an action component because it justifies individual or small-group action. It is not necessary to change the entire university to modify arrangements in one department. We can begin somewhere and proceed gradually. Similarly, it is not necessary to be in charge to take responsibility for change. Anyone can begin to make incremental changes to improve performance.

Incrementalism opens the door to informal processes. Rules and regulations may exist, but if they do not work well, we will have to bend them. Maybe we should not change them yet because we do not know for sure whether what we are trying to do will work. Meanwhile, let us bend the rules and see if we can do things differently. The official structure was designed to fit past realities. It fit the way problems were formulated in earlier times. As changes take place, as people invent new ways of doing things, the structures change. At some point there may be confrontations between those who uphold the present authority structure and those who no longer see the utility of the existing arrangements. But long before the rules are changed, incremental modifications take place. People talk about the need for change and they begin to behave differently.

For example, many educators are concerned with the need to debureaucratize American public education (Wise, 1979; Benveniste, 1987). Many educational leaders have urged that teaching become more professionalized (Carnegie Task Force on Teaching as a Profession, 1986; Holmes Group, 1986). But changes also start at the bottom in the form of small incremental innovations. Thus, "entrepreneurial" teachers emerge from the ranks of their profession, and these lead teachers may decide to assume responsibility for tasks that they have not undertaken before. For example, they may decide to run a summer training institute on their own, without the help of the central district office. They decide what kinds of training are needed, what form the program will take, and what experts to bring in. What we have here is a nucleus of change agents at work. What they are doing is significant to them. If we want to help them, if we want to do some planning to improve the professionalization of teaching, we will have to start with these individuals and go on from there. Lindblom (1969) argues that "logically speaking, one can make change in the social structure as rapidly through a sequence of incremental steps as through drastic—hence, less frequent—alterations. Psychologically and sociologically speaking, decision makers can sometimes bring themselves to make changes easily and quickly only because the changes are incremental and are not fraught with great risk of error or of political conflict" (p. 157).

Although effective planning is often incremental, it is not always preferable to take small steps. It depends on the issue, the cultural and historical context, the participants, and the nature of the possible solutions. There clearly are situations where bold departures are the only way to proceed. But incrementalism is important on two major counts: It clearly places responsibility for action on the planner, and it gives weight to both formal and informal approaches. And, as I like to emphasize, many of the subtleties of networking and coalition formation that lead to triggering the multiplier depend very much on informal processes.

CONCLUSION

This review of the main lines of thought in planning theory allows us to place our view of planning as a managerial activity in an intellectual context. Several points that we have made in this chapter need to be given more emphasis:

- *Planning as a new role.* Planning and policy analysis are new roles, and we are still attempting to understand these roles. It is to be expected that we would arrive at different versions of what these roles are, as these different versions are tested and experience is acquired.
- *Planning deals with various kinds of situations.* The words *planning* and *policy analysis* are used to describe very different problem-solving activities. In some situations the problems arise from uncertainties associated with the environment in which organizations operate. In other situations it is a problem of coordination and integration of the policies of many disparate and independent decision makers. In some cases the problem has no known solution and the solution must still be invented; at other times the real issue is finding a solution that engenders less opposition. In still other cases the problem is understanding what clients can live with, or it may reside in the lack of information reaching decision makers. It is normal that different theories would reflect these and other situational differences.
- *Planning takes place in different organizational settings.* Theories of planning or policy analysis reflect organizational realities. When the Prince is all-powerful and has his planners on a short leash, opportunities for apolitical politics may be limited. In other organizational contexts, however, power may be diffused and apolitical politics may take on considerable importance. The emphasis of different planning theories reflects these differences.
- *Knowledge of the technology impacts on planning.* In some situations we happen to understand the technology, we know how the system works, and we can even produce fairly reliable statements about the probable consequences of different decisions. In other situations, there is disagreement among experts, and the technology is perceived in different ways. Planning is affected by such differences, and the various planning theories reflect these differences.
- *Historical and cultural variables affect planning.* Individuals, groups, regions, and nations vary. Different attitudes, different styles of living, and different institutions affect planning and policy analysis. The quality and care taken in designing a plan, what is designed and what is improvised, what is done ahead of time and what is attempted at the last minute are also matters of taste, of sensibility. It is not surprising that different individuals or different countries would evolve planning theories that reflect historical and cultural differences.
- *Yet there is a common thread in all these theories.* Planning and policy analysis deal with the future. All theories of planning or policy analysis deal with a set of roles that address problems or opportunities *ahead of time.* The main question, therefore, is how does one address issues about the future? And more specifically, what kind of issues are individuals in organizations and society concerned with? How is consensus avoided or resolved? How is action initiated? These are the issues that effective planners are concerned with.

REFERENCES

Altshuler, A. A. *The City Planning Process: A Political Analysis.* Ithaca, N.Y.: Cornell University Press, 1965.
Amey, L. R. *Corporate Planning: A Systems View.* New York: Praeger, 1986.

Andrews, K. *The Concept of Corporate Strategy.* (Rev. ed.) Homewood, Ill.: Irwin, 1980.

Ansoff, I. "Strategic Issue Management." *Strategic Management Journal,* 1980, *1,* 131–142.

Banfield, E. C. "End and Means in Planning." *International Social Science Journal,* 1959, *11,* 361–368.

Barber, B. *Strong Democracy: Participatory Politics for a New Age.* Berkeley: University of California Press, 1984.

Baum, H. S. "Analysts and Planners Must Think Organizationally." *Policy Analysis,* 1980, *6,* 479–494.

Baum, H. S. *Planners and Public Expectations.* Cambridge, Mass.: Schenkman, 1983.

Beatley, T. "Planners and Political Philosophy." *Journal of the American Planning Association,* 1987, *53,* 235–236.

Below, P. J., Morrisey, G. L., and Acomb, B. L. *The Executive Guide to Strategic Planning.* San Francisco: Jossey-Bass, 1987.

Benveniste, G. "Highlights of the Seminar." In R. Lyons (ed.), *Problems and Strategies of Educational Planning: Lessons from Latin America.* Paris: UNESCO, 1965.

Benveniste, G. *The Politics of Expertise.* (2nd ed.) San Francisco: Boyd & Fraser, 1977.

Benveniste, G. *Professionalizing the Organization: Reducing Bureaucracy to Enhance Effectiveness.* San Francisco: Jossey-Bass, 1987.

Berger, P. L., and Luckmann, T. *The Social Construction of Reality.* New York: Anchor, 1966.

Beyle, T. L., and Lathrop, G. T. (eds.). *Planning and Politics: Uneasy Partnership.* New York: Odyssey, 1970.

Bicksler, J. L., and Samuelson, P. A. (eds.). *Investment Portfolio Decision Making.* Lexington, Mass.: Heath, 1974.

Bogue, M. C., III, and Buffa, E. S. *Corporate Strategic Analysis.* New York: Free Press, 1986.

Bolan, R. S. "The Practitioner as Theorist: The Phenomenology of the Professional Episode." *Journal of the American Planning Association,* 1980, *46,* 261–274.

Branch, M. C. *Comprehensive Planning: General Theory and Principles.* Palisades, Calif.: Palisades Publishers, 1983.

Braybrooke, D., and Lindblom, C. E. *A Strategy of Decision: Policy Evaluation as a Social Process.* New York: Free Press, 1963.

Brickner, W. H., and Cope, D. M. *The Planning Process.* Cambridge, Mass.: Winthrop, 1977.

Bryson, J. M. *Strategic Planning for Public and Nonprofit Organizations: A Guide to Strengthening and Sustaining Organizational Achievement.* San Francisco: Jossey-Bass, 1988.

Bryson, J. M., and Einsweiler, R. C. "Introduction to Symposium on Strategic Planning." *Journal of the American Planning Association,* 1987, *53,* 6–8.

Burke, E. M. *A Participatory Approach to Urban Planning.* New York: Human Sciences Press, 1979.

Caiden, N., and Wildavsky, A. *Planning and Budgeting in Poor Countries.* New York: Wiley, 1974.

Carnegie Task Force on Teaching as a Profession. *A Nation Prepared: Teachers for the 21st Century. Report of the Task Force on Teaching as a Profession.* New York: Carnegie Forum on Education and the Economy, 1986.

Castells, M. *The Urban Question.* Cambridge, Mass.: MIT Press, 1977.

Castells, M. *City, Class, and Power.* New York: St. Martin's Press, 1978.

Catanese, A. J. *Planners and Local Politics.* Beverly Hills, Calif.: Sage, 1974.

Christensen, R., and others. *Business Policy: Text and Cases.* Homewood, Ill.: Irwin, 1983.

Colley, J. *Corporate and Divisional Planning.* Reston, Va.: Reston Publishing, 1984.

Comfort, L. K. "Action Research: A Model for Organizational Learning." *Journal of Policy Analysis and Management,* 1985, *5,* 100–118.

Cox, K. R. (ed.). *Urbanization and Conflict in Market Societies.* Chicago: Maaroufa, 1978.

Dalton, L. C. "Why the Rational Paradigm Persists: The Resistance of Professional Education to Alternative Forms of Planning." *Journal of Planning Education and Research,* 1986, *5,* 147–153.

Davidoff, P. "Advocacy and Pluralism in Planning." *Journal of the American Institute of Planners,* 1965, *31,* 331–338.

de Neufville, J. I. "Planning Theory and Practice: Bridging the Gap." *Journal of Planning Education and Research,* 1983, *3,* 35–45.

de Neufville, J. I. "Knowledge and Action: Making the Link." *Journal of Planning Education and Research,* 1987, *6*, 86–92.

Dror, Y. "Muddling Through—'Science' or Inertia?" *Public Administration Review,* 1969, *29*, 153–157.

Dunn, W. N. (ed.). *Values, Ethics, and the Practice of Policy Analysis.* Lexington, Mass.: Lexington Books, 1982.

Edelston, H., and Kolodner, F. K. "Are the Poor Capable of Planning for Themselves?" In H. B. Spiegel (ed.), *Citizen Participation in Urban Development.* Vol. I: *Concepts and Issues.* Washington, D.C.: National Training Laboratories Institute for Applied Behavioral Science, 1968.

Elton, E. I., and Gruber, M. J. *Modern Portfolio Theory and Investment Analysis.* (3rd ed.) New York: Wiley, 1987.

Faludi, A. *A Decision-Centered View of Environmental Planning.* Elmsford, N.Y.: Pergamon Press, 1987.

Forester, J. "Critical Theory and Planning Practice." In J. Forester (ed.), *Critical Theory and Public Life.* Cambridge, Mass.: MIT Press, 1985.

Freeman, R. E. *Strategic Management: A Stakeholder Approach.* Boston: Pittman, 1984.

Friedmann, J. *Planning in the Public Domain: From Knowledge to Action.* Princeton, N.J.: Princeton University Press, 1987.

Funnye, C. "The Advocate Planner as Urban Hustler." *Social Policy,* 1970, *1*, 35–37.

Furner, M. O. *Advocacy and Objectivity: A Crisis in the Professionalization of American Social Science, 1865-1905.* Lexington: University Press of Kentucky, 1975.

Giorgi, A. (ed.). *Phenomenology and Psychological Research.* Atlantic Highlands, N.J.: Humanities Press International, 1985.

Habermas, J. *Theory and Practice.* London: Heinemann, 1974.

Habermas, J. *Legitimation Crisis.* London: Heinemann, 1976.

Habermas, J. *Communication and the Evolution of Society.* Boston: Beacon Press, 1979.

Hall, P. "Planning: A Geographer's View." In B. Goodall and A. Kirby (eds.), *Resources and Planning.* Elmsford, N.Y.: Pergamon Press, 1979.

Hamermesh, R. G. *Making Strategy Work: How Senior Managers Produce Results.* New York: Wiley, 1986.

Harvey, D. *Consciousness and the Urban Experience: Studies in the History and Theory of Capitalist Urbanization.* Baltimore, Md.: Johns Hopkins University Press, 1985.

Holmes Group. *Tomorrow's Teachers.* Lansing, Mich.: Holmes Group, 1986.

Howe, E. "Role Choices of Urban Planners." *Journal of the American Planning Association,* 1980, *46*, 399–409.

Howe, E., and Kaufman, J. "The Ethics of Contemporary Planners." *Journal of the American Planning Association,* 1979, *45*, 243–255.

Ilchman, W. F., Stone-Ilchman, A., and Hastings, P. K. *The New Men of Knowledge and the Developing Nations; Planners and the Polity: A Preliminary Survey.* Berkeley: Institute of Governmental Studies, University of California, 1968.

Jenkins-Smith, H. C. "Professional Roles for Policy Analysts: A Critical Assessment." *Journal of Policy Analysis and Management,* 1982, *2*, 88–100.

Kaufman, J. L. "American and Israel Planners: A Cross-Cultural Comparison." *Journal of the American Planning Association,* 1985, *51*, 352–364.

Kaufman, J. L., and Jacobs, H. M. "A Public Planning Perspective on Strategic Planning." *Journal of the American Planning Association,* 1987, *53*, 23–33.

Knott, J. H. "The Multiple and Ambiguous Roles of Professionals in Public Policy Making." *Knowledge: Creation, Diffusion, Utilization,* 1986, *8*, 131–153.

Kramer, R. M. *Participation of the Poor: Comparative Community Case Studies in the War on Poverty.* Englewood Cliffs, N.J.: Prentice-Hall, 1969.

Kraushaar, R. "Outside the Whale: Progressive Planning and the Dilemmas of Radical Reform." *Journal of the American Planning Association,* 1988, *54*, 91–100.

Lindblom, C. E. "The Science of Muddling Through." *Public Administration Review,* 1959, *19*, 79–88.

Lindblom, C. E. *The Intelligence of Democracy: Decision Making Through Mutual Adjustment.* New York: Free Press, 1965.

Lindblom, C . E. "Contexts for Change and Strategy: A Reply." *Public Administration Review,* 1969, *29,* 157–159.

Lindblom, C. E. "Still Muddling, Not Yet Through." *Public Administration Review,* 1979, *39,* 517–525.

Lindblom, C. E. *The Policy-Making Process.* (2nd ed.) Englewood Cliffs, N.J.: Prentice-Hall, 1980.

Luckmann, T. (ed.). *Phenomenology and Sociology: Selected Readings.* New York: Penguin, 1978.

Marcuse, P. "Professional Ethics and Beyond: Values in Planning." *Journal of the American Institute of Planners,* 1976, *42,* 264–274.

Meltsner, A. J. *Policy Analysts in the Bureaucracy.* Berkeley: University of California Press, 1976.

Meyerson, M., and Banfield, E. C. *Politics, Planning, and the Public Interest: The Case of Public Housing in Chicago.* New York: Free Press, 1955.

Mulder, M. "Power Equalization Through Participation." *Administrative Science Quarterly,* 1971, *16,* 31–39.

Naylor, T. N., and Mann, M. H. *Computer-Based Planning Systems.* Oxford, Ohio: Planning Executives Institute, 1982.

O'Connor, R. *Planning Under Uncertainty: Multiple Scenarios and Contingency Planning.* New York: Conference Board, 1978.

Paris, C. (ed.). *Critical Readings in Planning Theory.* Elmsford, N.Y.: Pergamon Press, 1982.

Peattie, L. R. "Reflections on Advocacy Planning." *Journal of the American Institute of Planners,* 1968, *34,* 80–88.

Perin, C. *With Man in Mind: An Interdisciplinary Prospectus for Environmental Design.* Cambridge, Mass.: MIT Press, 1970.

Schultze, C. L. *The Politics and Economics of Public Spending.* Washington, D.C.: Brookings Institution, 1968.

Scott, A. J., and Dear, M. *Urbanization and Urban Planning in Capitalist Society.* London: Methuen, 1981.

Sharplin, A. *Strategic Management.* New York: McGraw-Hill, 1985.

Silva, E. T., and Slaughter, S. A. *Serving Power: The Making of the Social Science Expert.* Westport, Conn.: Glenwood, 1984.

Spiegel, H. B. (ed.). *Citizen Participation in Urban Development.* Vol. I: *Concepts and Issues.* Washington, D.C.: National Training Laboratories Institute for Applied Behavioral Science, 1968.

Thines, G. *Phenomenology and the Science of Behavior: A Historical and Epistemological Approach.* London: Allen & Unwin, 1977.

Torgerson, D. "Between Knowledge and Politics: Three Faces of Policy Analysis." *Policy Sciences,* 1986, *19,* 33–59.

Vasu, M. L. *Politics and Planning: A National Study of American Planners.* Chapel Hill: University of North Carolina Press, 1979.

Wachs, M. (ed.). *Ethics in Planning.* New Brunswick: Center for Urban Policy Research, Rutgers, State University of New Jersey, 1985.

Waterston, A. *Development Planning: Lessons of Experience.* Baltimore: Johns Hopkins University Press, 1965.

Wildavsky, A. "If Planning Is Everything, Maybe It's Nothing." *Policy Sciences,* 1973, *4,* 127–153.

Wise, A. E. *Legislated Learning: The Bureaucratization of the American Classroom.* Berkeley: University of California Press, 1979.

The Art of Strategic Thinking—
Analysis: The Starting Point*

KENICHI OHMAE

Some weeks ago I received a brochure from a Japanese travel agency inviting me to "enjoy sport amid fantastic scenic beauty." The eye-catching headline advertised "golf, tennis, archery, bicycling, sailing—the sport of your choice" in an "ideal vacation spot," the heart of Ise-Shima National Park, famous for its intricate shoreline and its production of cultured pearls.

Having once worked as a tour guide, I knew how exhausting an all-day trip from Tokyo to the Shima Peninsula can be; but the pamphlet intrigued me.

The schedule was strenuous. The bus was to leave Tokyo at 9 A.M. on Saturday, arriving at the vacation hotel at 5 P.M. after a journey of more than 200 miles. The next morning, there would be time for the sports the pamphlet touted. Then, at 2:30 P.M., the bus would leave for Tokyo, arriving at 10:30 P.M. Sunday night.

It looked to me as if the time available for enjoying the beauties of nature described in the brochure—"majestic green ridges linking mountain to mountain," "clear cobalt-blue skies," "the azure sea," and "picturesque small bays dotted with pearl rafts"—was likely to be rather short. My pocket calculator confirmed that nearly 43 percent of the excursion period would be spent riding in the bus. Sleeping, eating, bathing, dressing, and so on, which one can (and will) do at home anyway, would take up another 40 percent. That would leave 6½ hours, or a mere 17 percent, for the sports which were supposed to be the object of the trip. The cost quoted was $125, which would work out to approximately $19.25 per hour of sport. If it was tennis I had in mind, I would clearly do a lot better to take a half-hour drive out to some public tennis club in a Tokyo suburb, pay a fee of $12, and enjoy myself there for the day.

What the travel agency was selling, of course, was a package consisting of a number of different elements, including "atmosphere," integrated into a whole. Customers normally pay their $125 for the package without trying to identify precisely how much they are paying for each element and whether it is all really worth the cost. To do this, one has to probe into what is actually being offered, disentangling the various components of the package and understanding how each element contributes to the whole.

Returning to my example, it is clear that as far as the sport alone is concerned, a tennis player would get 10 times the value by staying in the city and playing on a local court.

---

*"Analysis: The Starting Point" from *The Mind of the Strategist: The Art of Japanese Business* by Kenichi Ohmae. Reprinted with permission of McGraw-Hill Companies.

But having recognized that, suppose you love to play tennis in a spectacular scenic setting, and you've been longing to see the well-advertised beauties of Ise-Shima National Park. In that case, do these secondary considerations justify the expense after all? They might, or they might not. The point is that analysis has enabled you to substitute your own *self-directed* judgment for the *other-directed* way of accepting the package—paying for an atmosphere you haven't even tried to define.

Analysis is the critical starting point of strategic thinking. Faced with problems, trends, events, or situations that appear to constitute a harmonious whole or come packaged as a whole by the common sense of the day, the strategic thinker dissects them into their constituent parts. Then, having discovered the significance of these constituents, he reassembles them in a way calculated to maximize his advantage.

In business as on the battlefield, the object of strategy is to bring about the conditions most favorable to one's own side, judging precisely the right moment to attack or withdraw and always assessing the limits of compromise correctly. Besides the habit of analysis, what marks the mind of the strategist is an intellectual elasticity or flexibility that enables him to come up with realistic responses to changing situations, not simply to discriminate with great precision among different shades of gray.

In strategic thinking, one first seeks a clear understanding of the particular character of each element of a situation and then makes the fullest possible use of human brainpower to restructure the elements in the most advantageous way. Phenomena and events in the real world do not always fit a linear model. Hence the most reliable means of dissecting a situation into its constituent parts and reassembling them in the desired pattern is not a step-by-step methodology such as systems analysis. Rather, it is that ultimate nonlinear thinking tool, the human brain. True strategic thinking thus contrasts sharply with the conventional mechanical systems approach based on linear thinking. But it also contrasts with the approach that stakes everything on intuition, reaching conclusions without any real breakdown or analysis (Figure 1).

No matter how difficult or unprecedented the problem, a breakthrough to the best possible solution can come only from a combination of rational analysis, based on the real nature of things, and imaginative reintegration of all the different items into a new pattern, using nonlinear brainpower. This is always the most effective approach to devising strategies for dealing successfully with challenges and opportunities, in the market arena as on the battlefield.

DETERMINING THE CRITICAL ISSUE

The first stage in strategic thinking is to pinpoint the critical issue in the situation. Everyone facing a problem naturally tries in his or her own way to penetrate to the key issue. Some may think that one way is as good as another and that whether their efforts hit the mark is largely a matter of luck. I believe it is not a question of luck at all but of attitude and method. In problem solving, it is vital at the start to formulate the question in a way that will facilitate the discovery of a solution.

Suppose, for example, that overtime work has become chronic in a company, dragging down profitability. If we frame the question as: What should be done to reduce overtime? many answers will suggest themselves:

FIGURE 1

Three Kinds of Thinking Process

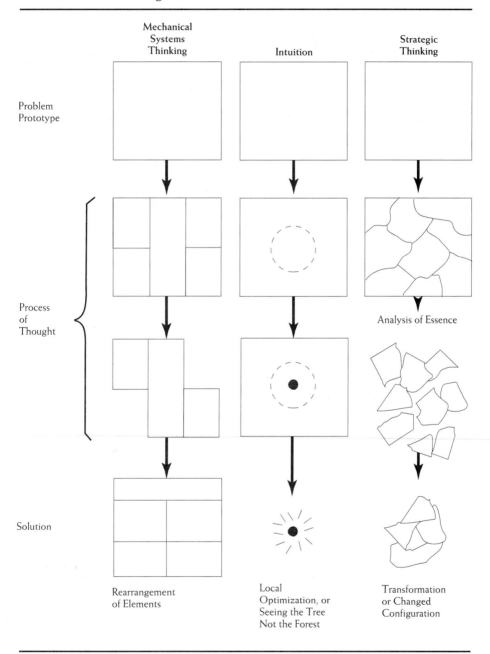

- Work harder during the regular working hours
- Shorten the lunch period and coffee breaks
- Forbid long private telephone conversations

Such questioning is often employed by companies trying to lower costs and improve product quality by using zero defect campaigns and quality control (QC) circles that involve the participation of all employees. Ideas are gathered, screened, and later incorporated in the improvement program. But the approach has an intrinsic limitation. *The questions are not framed to point toward a solution; rather, they are directed toward finding remedies to symptoms.*

Returning to our overtime problem, suppose we frame the question in a more solution-oriented way: Is this company's workforce large enough to do all the work required?

To this question there can be only one of two answers—yes or no. To arrive at the answer yes, a great deal of analysis would be needed, probably including a comparison with other companies in the same industries, the historical trend of workload per employee, and the degree of automation and computerization and their economic effectiveness. On the other hand, if—after careful perusal of the sales record, profit per employee, ratio between direct and indirect labor, comparison with other companies, and so on—the answer should turn out to be no (i.e., the company is currently understaffed), this in itself would be tantamount to a solution of the original problem. This solution—an increase in personnel—will be validated by all the usual management indicators. And if the company adopts this solution, the probability increases that the desired outcome will actually follow. This way, objective analysis can supplant emotional discussions.

That is not the only way the question could have been formulated, however. We might have asked it this way: Do the capabilities of the employees match the nature of the work?

This formulation, like the previous one, is oriented toward deriving a possible solution. Here too, a negative answer would imply a shortage of suitable personnel, which would in turn suggest that the solution should be sought either in staff training or in recruiting capable staff from elsewhere. On the other hand, if the answer is yes, this indicates that the problem of chronic overtime lies not in the nature of the work but in the amount of the workload. Thus, not training but adding to the workforce would then be the crucial factor in the solution.

If the right questions are asked in a solution-oriented manner, and if the proper analyses are carried out, the final answer is likely to be the same, even though it may have started from a differently phrased question and may have been arrived at by a different route. In either case, a question concerning the nature and amount of work brings the real issue into focus and makes it easy to arrive at a clear-cut verdict.

It is hard to overstate the importance of formulating the question correctly. People who are trained and motivated to formulate the right questions will not offer vague proposals for "improvements," as are seen in many suggestion boxes. They will come up with concrete, practical ideas.

By failing to grasp the critical issues, too many senior managers today impose great anxiety on themselves and their subordinates, whose efforts end in failure and frustration. Solution-oriented questions can be formulated only if the critical issue is localized and grasped accurately in the first place. A clear common understanding of the nature of a problem that has already been localized provides a critical pressure to come up with creative solutions. When problems are poorly defined or vaguely comprehended, one's creative mind does not work sharply. The greater one's tolerance for lukewarm solutions, half measures, and what the British used to call muddling through, the more loosely the issue is likely to be defined. For this reason, isolating the crucial points of the problem—in other words, determining the critical issue—is most important to the discovery of a solution. The key at this initial stage is to *narrow down the issue by studying the observed phenomena closely.*

Figure 2 illustrates one method often used by strategists in the process of *abstraction,* showing how it might work in the case of a large, established company faced with the problem of declining competitive vigor.

The first step in the abstraction process is to use such means as brainstorming and opinion polls to assemble and itemize the respects in which the company is at a disadvantage vis-à-vis its competitors. These points can then be classified under a smaller number of headings (shown in the exhibit as Concrete Phenomena) according to their common factors.

Next, phenomena sharing some common denominator are themselves combined into groups. Having done this, we look once again at each group as a unit and ask ourselves what crucial issue each unit poses. The source of the problem must be understood before any real solution can be found, and the process of abstraction enables us to bring the crucial issues to light without the risk of overlooking anything important.

Once the abstraction process has been completed, we must next decide on the right approach to finding a solution. Once we have determined the solution in principle, there remains the task of working out implementation programs and then compiling detailed action plans. No solution, however perfectly it may address the critical issue, can be of the slightest use until it is implemented. Too many companies try to short-circuit the necessary steps between identification of critical issues and line implementation of solutions by skipping the intermediate steps: planning for operational improvement and organizing for concrete actions. Even the most brilliant line manager cannot translate an abstract plan into action in a single step.

Later we shall look at examples of the intermediate steps in more detail. For the time being it will suffice to remember that the process pictured in Figure 3 [p. 122]—abstraction followed by movement toward a concrete plan for improvement—is characteristic of the method of solution finding that focuses on critical issues.

FAIL-SAFE METHODOLOGY

Suppose we have only a general idea of what the critical issue may be in a problem. How can we pinpoint it without wasting time? People with a genius for ferreting out the critical issue by instinct are rare. Fortunately for the rest of us, it can also be done by method.

The issue diagram is a device familiar to those with experience in computer programming or using decision trees for decision making. The overall problem or issue is divided into two or more mutually exclusive and collectively exhaustive subissues; then the process is repeated for emergent subissues, and so on, until a level is reached at which the subitems are individually manageable. In this way, even a problem that originally seemed too large to cope with will gradually be broken down into a whole series of smaller issues. The secret here is that each of the final items must be something that can be managed by human effort, and the results should be definite and measurable.

Consider the case of a company whose Product A has been showing a steep decline in competitiveness because of high costs. Costs must be lowered, but how? Historical devel-

FIGURE 2

F I G U R E   2

Narrowing Down the Issue

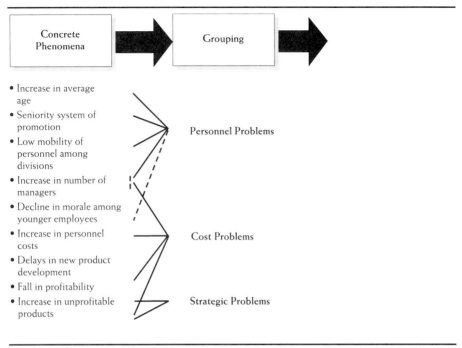

• Increase in average age
• Seniority system of promotion
• Low mobility of personnel among divisions
• Increase in number of managers
• Decline in morale among younger employees
• Increase in personnel costs
• Delays in new product development
• Fall in profitability
• Increase in unprofitable products

Concrete Phenomena

Grouping

Personnel Problems

Cost Problems

Strategic Problems

opments and changes in the environment of the company and in Product A will determine the answer to that question.

THE ISSUE DIAGRAM

Rather than recklessly attempting to come up with a solution simply on the basis of experience or intuition, without analyzing these objective factors, the strategic thinker would take a blank sheet of paper and draw up an issue diagram (Figure 4). The reasoning would go something like this:

When the manufacturing costs of Product A are too high, the first thing to look at is its design. If the product is manufactured to existing specifications and is already too costly to be competitive, it is obviously overdesigned. But this does not necessarily mean that we ought to alter the design without further ado. Before doing that, we must study the basic needs and tastes of our customers and then estimate how much market share we would be likely to lose to the competition and what the net impact on our profits would be if we were to sell the overdesigned Product A at a higher price, reflecting its actual manufacturing cost.

If we are confident that Product A can earn more than enough to break even in such a contracted market, our next move is likely to be in the marketing area. For example, we might launch a major advertising campaign to persuade the pertinent customer segment that Product A represents premium quality at a premium price. (Volvo, Porsche, and

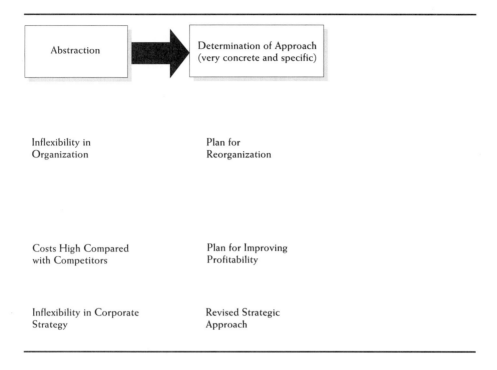

Mercedes-Benz price and sell their cars in this manner, successfully passing on the "high" element of their production costs to the customers.)

But suppose that for reasons of consistent pricing policy or smaller market size we cannot pass the high cost of Product A on to the customer. In this case, the appropriate move would probably be to have recourse to value analysis (VA) and value engineering (VE). The purpose of these techniques, which are now employed by practically every Japanese manufacturer as a part of the routine control of business operations, is to investigate and analyze purchased materials or components from the point of view of price so that the results can be incorporated into planning in such areas as cost reduction and development of new products. Studies of purchased goods are carried out to examine whether their quality and reliability are right for a particular product design and function (value engineering) and whether their costs are reasonable for the product price (value analysis). Production processes, cost structure, and suppliers are examined similarly.

Returning to our example, assume that a thorough study of the trade-off between design costs and the market requirements leads us to conclude that Product A cannot be profitable on the basis of current design. In this situation, VA and VE can help us bring about the conditions necessary to enable Product A to compete in the market.

Remember that the market is formed by Product A and its competition. No product is sold in the desert or on the moon; manufacturers' prices and the various customer segments they serve are determined in a competitive environment. What if *all* manufacturers in the market are producing similar high-quality products and offering them to the market at a

FIGURE 3

Stages of Strategic Thinking

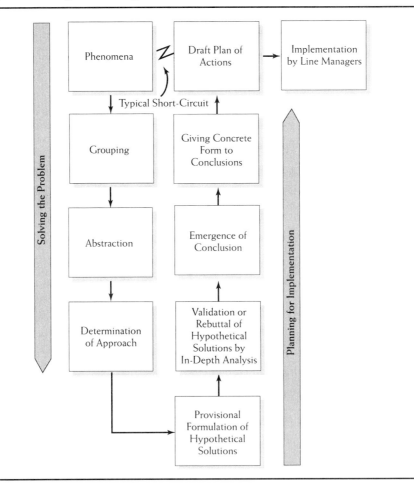

relatively low price (i.e., with narrow profit margins)? In this case, it would be disastrous for the company to modify Product A's design in order to reduce costs—even if, for example, it proved technically feasible to substitute plastic for metal housing—because the resulting seemingly lower quality product would be driven out of the market by the low-priced, high-quality products already competing for the customer's favor.

VA and VE techniques, then, cannot be employed safely in a vacuum. By the same token, designers can't afford to withdraw to an ivory tower and dream up cost-saving design modifications without reference to what is going on in the marketplace. In the situation I have described, the best way to come up with an effective competitive move would be to set the most successful competing product beside Product A, dismantle it completely, and meticulously compare the two in every aspect: construction method, number of parts, quality of materials and components, and so forth. This would enable the company to discover what

FIGURE 4

A Sample Issue Diagram

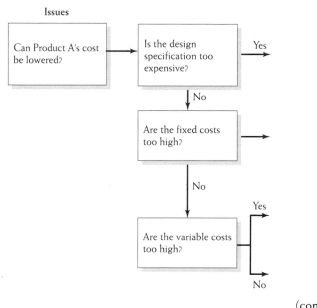

(continued)

part or aspect of Product A is responsible for its higher costs. Through the application of VE, we could then bring down the cost of this part or aspect relative to that of its competitor without imposing any competitive handicap on Product A in the marketplace (Figure 5).

At the same time, however, our investigation might have shown that even though the costs of Product A are higher overall, the competing product was made from better-quality materials or had a better finish. In that case, we might need to improve the materials specification or design of Product A and accept the higher costs.

I have digressed somewhat, but for a reason. In many companies today, functional activities such as design, manufacturing, and sales, which are usually divided from one another organizationally, devote more energy to guarding their own territories than to looking for ways to cooperate. As a result the full potential for major profit improvement that typically lies in the interfunctional border areas tends to be overlooked. VA and VE are cited here as examples of forcing devices for analyzing these border areas. VA and VE are normally used by a group of engineers as an internal device to streamline design, but if used in the broader sense as described above, they become a powerful tool to reduce product cost.

In recent years, some advanced companies in Japan pushed this concept even further, challenging the status quo by designing both product and production facility from a zero base, given a specified concept of a product for a well-defined target customer group. This kind of approach—zero-based production and value design (or design from scratch to the standard the user is willing to accept)—is the basis of the success of Honda's Civic and Ricoh's copiers, to name two representative examples.

FIGURE 4 — continued

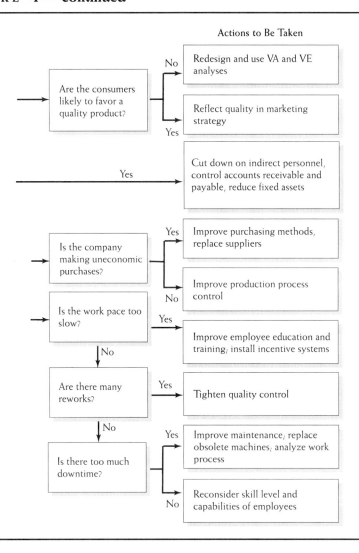

Let us look once again at Figure 4. When we suspect that variable costs are too high and carry our analysis further on the issue diagram, we see that the action required could be either shop-floor training or improved purchasing methods. Jumping from the symptom "variable costs" to a diagnosis of "high cost of goods purchased" and then implementing measures based on that diagnosis would only lower our chances of correcting the problem.

As I mentioned earlier, this process of narrowing a problem down by means of an issue diagram resembles the methods used in computer programming and decision trees. Alternatively, we can compare it to the process by which a doctor questions a patient in order to arrive at a diagnosis, sequentially eliminating certain areas of irrelevance. A business enterprise is an organic, living entity. When disease attacks some part of it, the malfunction is bound to be reflected in a reduction of the profit (or future profit potential) that

FIGURE 5

Product-Change Options after Competitive Tear-Down

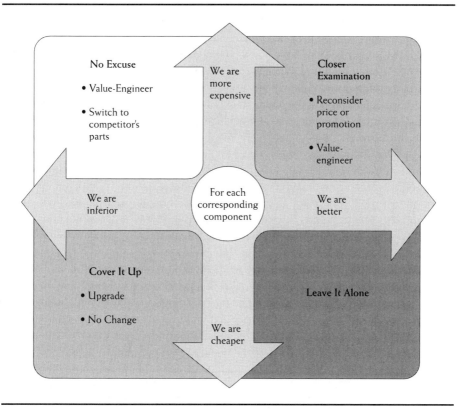

is the energy source of the organism's growth. If they recognize the gravity of the symptoms, the company's top management, either on their own or with the aid of outside consultants, will naturally want to probe for the cause of the problem, just as a doctor questions a patient to find out what is wrong.

THE PROFIT DIAGRAM

Starting from the assumption that the costs of a given product are too high, the issue diagram gives us, as we have just seen, a tool for analyzing the possible reasons. But suppose it has not yet been established that high product costs are in fact the problem; all we know for certain is that selling Product A in the existing market by present sales methods is proving unprofitable. To diagnose this phenomenon, we must move back slightly closer to fundamentals.

This time we start from the question, To what extent can Product A's profitability be improved? Since profit is determined by selling price, cost, and sales volume, all three variables must be given equal weight in the initial stages of a diagnosis aimed at improving profitability.

FIGURE 6

The Starting Point of a Profit Diagram

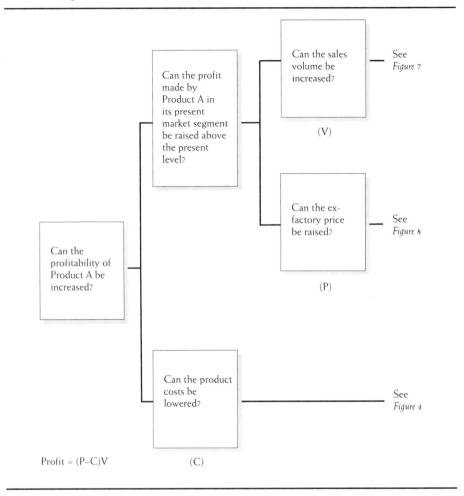

Not long ago a machine-tool company sought my advice on how to improve the profitability of certain products in its line. As the initial step in the project, I drew up the diagrams set out in Figures 6 to 8. Because these diagrams apply to most products and are directly related to profit, which is the basis of all business, I call them profit diagrams. We can use them to advantage in the case of Product A.

Two basic issues are involved in increasing the profitability of Product A.

- Can more profit be gained *externally* (i.e., from the market)?
- Can product profitability be improved at the present selling price by raising efficiency *internally* (i.e., through cost reduction)?

The first issue can be further divided, as Figure 6 shows, into two subissues.

- Can sales volume be increased?
- Can the price be raised?

In order to find the answers to these questions, more detailed analysis is needed, as shown in Figures 7 and 8. On the right-hand side of both these exhibits I have given some examples of the analyses required by the issues as posed.

Each type of analysis requires considerable skill and experience and can be undertaken seriously only when there is constant access to accurate market information. Companies that are strong in marketing gather market information at regular intervals so that they can carry out these analyses routinely. Companies that are less marketing-minded and tend to collect information haphazardly are not so fortunate. If they are to carry out each analysis with any prospect of reliable results, they will need to make an extra effort to fill the gaps in the flow of market data they receive.

No proper business strategy can be built on fragmentary knowledge or analysis. If such a strategy happens to produce good results, this is due to luck or inspiration. The true strategist depends on neither the one nor the other. He has a more reliable recipe for success: the combination of analytical method and mental elasticity that I call strategic thinking.

In my opinion, these two are complementary. For the strategic mind to work creatively, it needs the stimulus of a good, insightful analysis. In order to conduct a good analysis, it takes a strategic and inquisitive mind to come up with the right questions and phrase them as solution-oriented issues. Analyses done for the sake of vindicating one's own preconceived notions do not lead to creative solutions. Intuition or gut-feel alone does not ensure secure business plans. It takes a good balance between the two to come up with a successful strategy.

FIGURE 7 ─────────────────────────────
Profit Diagram for Increasing Market Share

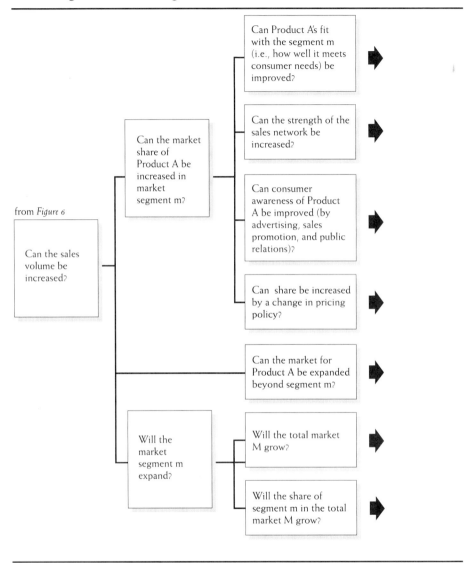

Sample Items Requiring Analysis

- Basic consumer needs
- Analysis of value (real and perceived) offered by competing products

- Trends in sales channel and geographical coverage
- Comparison of servicing capability, delivery time

- Survey of customer awareness in brand and product
- Analysis of purchasing decision-making process

- Price elasticity
- Influence of payment terms and trade-in conditions

- Possibility of geographical expansion
- Possibility of expansion in final customers outside the segment
- Cost-benefit analysis of expansion

- Anticipated demand (3–5 years ahead) for product constituting the total market M

- Factors determining the size of segment m within the market M
- Trends and forecasts of factors above

F I G U R E   8

Profit Diagram for Analyzing Pricing Flexibility

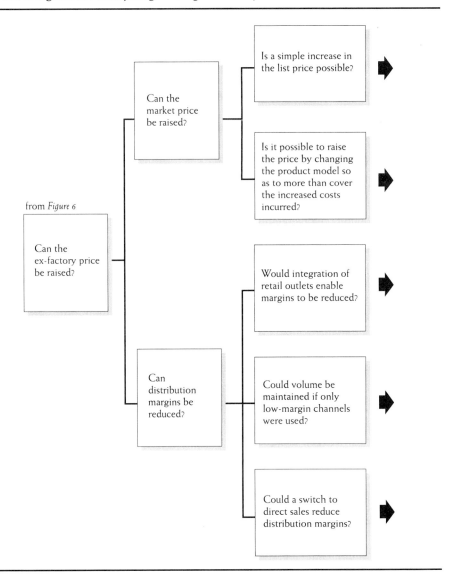

- Price elasticity
- Possibility of price rises differentiated by geographical areas, models, or by distribution channels
- Results achieved by competitors (possibility of "follow-the-leader" price increase)

- Basic consumer needs in each market segment
- Price elasticity
- Cost-benefit analysis

- Basic economic analysis of distribution system
- Analysis on economies of scale
- Correlation between number of sales outlets and market coverage

- Flexibility in physical flow of goods by distribution channels
- Degree of motivation and sales efforts exerted by different channels

- Analysis of long-term strategic effect
- Analysis of short-term cost-benefit
- Possibility of maintenance of sales skills

Strategic Change: "Logical Incrementalism"*

JAMES BRIAN QUINN

When I was younger I always conceived of a room where all these [strategic] concepts were worked out for the whole company. Later I didn't find any such room . . . . The strategy [of the company] may not even exist in the mind of one man. I certainly don't know where it is written down. It is simply transmitted in the series of decisions made.

INTERVIEW QUOTE

When well-managed major organizations make significant changes in strategy, the approaches they use frequently bear little resemblance to the rational-analytical systems so often touted in the planning literature. The full strategy is rarely written down in any one place. The processes used to arrive at the total strategy are typically fragmented, evolutionary, and largely intuitive. Although one can usually find embedded in these fragments some very refined *pieces* of formal strategic analysis, the real strategy tends to *evolve* as internal decisions and external events flow together to create a new, widely shared consensus for action among key members of the top management team. Far from being an abrogation of good management practice, the rationale behind this kind of strategy formulation is so powerful that it perhaps provides the normative model for strategic decision making— rather than the step-by-step "formal systems planning" approach so often espoused.

- *The Formal Systems Planning Approach.* A strong normative literature states what factors *should* be included in a systematically planned strategy[1] and how to analyze and relate these factors step by step.[2] The main elements of this "formal planning approach" include: analyzing one's own *internal situation:* strengths, weaknesses, competencies, and problems; *projecting* current product lines, profits, sales, and investment needs into the future; analyzing selected *external environments* and opponents' actions for opportunities and threats; establishing *broad goals* as targets for subordinate groups' plans; *identifying the gap* between expected and desired results; communicating *planning assumptions* to the divisions; requesting *proposed plans* from subordinate groups with more specific target goals, resource needs, and supporting action plans; occasionally asking for *special studies of alternatives,*

---

contingencies, or *longer-term opportunities; reviewing and approving* divisional plans and *summing* these for corporate needs; developing *long-term budgets* presumably related to plans; *implementing* plans; and *monitoring and evaluating* performance (presumably against plans, but usually against budgets).

While this approach is excellent for some purposes, it tends to focus unduly on measurable quantitative factors and to underemphasize the vital qualitative, organizational, and power-behavioral factors that so often determine strategic success in one situation versus another. In practice, such planning is just one building block in a continuous stream of events that really determines corporate strategy.

- *The Power-Behavioral Approach.* Other investigators have provided important insights on the crucial psychological, power, and behavioral relationships in strategy formulation. Among other things, these have enhanced understanding about the *multiple goal structures* of organizations;[3] the *politics* of strategic decisions;[4] executive *bargaining* and *negotiation* processes;[5] *satisficing* (as opposed to maximizing) in decision making;[6] the role of *coalitions* in strategic management;[7] and the practice of *"muddling"* in the public sphere.[8] Unfortunately, however, many power-behavioral studies have been conducted in settings far removed from the realities of strategy formulation. Others have concentrated solely on human dynamics, power relationships, and organizational processes and ignored the ways in which systematic data analysis shapes and often dominates crucial aspects of strategic decisions. Finally, few have offered much normative guidance for the strategist.
- *The Study.* Recognizing the contributions and limitations of both approaches, I attempted to document the dynamics of actual strategic change processes in some ten major companies as perceived by those most knowledgeably and intimately involved in them. These companies varied with respect to products, markets, time horizons, technological complexities, and national versus international dimensions.[9] While the problems of this kind of research are well recognized,[10] many precautions were taken to ensure accuracy.[11]

SUMMARY FINDINGS

Several important findings have begun to emerge from these investigations.

- Neither the "power-behavioral" nor the "formal systems planning" paradigm adequately characterizes the way successful strategic processes operate.
- Effective strategies tend to emerge from a series of "strategic subsystems," each of which attacks a specific class of strategic issues, (e.g., acquisitions, divestitures, or major reorganizations) in a disciplined way, but which is blended incrementally and opportunistically into a cohesive pattern that becomes the company's strategy.
- The logic behind each "subsystem" is so powerful that, to some extent, it may serve as a normative approach for formulating these key elements of strategy in large companies.
- Because of cognitive and process limits, almost all of these subsystems—and the formal planning activity itself—must be managed and linked together by an approach best described as "logical incrementalism."
- Such incrementalism is not "muddling." It is a purposeful, effective, proactive management technique for improving and integrating *both* the analytical and behavioral aspects of strategy formulation.

This article will document these findings, suggest the logic behind several important "subsystems" for strategy formulation, and outline some of the management and thought processes executives in large organizations use to synthesize them into effective corporate strategies. Such strategies embrace those patterns of high leverage decisions (on major goals, policies, and action sequences) which affect the viability and direction of the entire enterprise or determine its competitive posture for an extended time period.

CRITICAL STRATEGIC ISSUES

Although certain "hard data" decisions (e.g., on product market position or resource allocations) tend to dominate the analytical literature,[12] executives identified other "soft" changes that have at least as much importance in shaping their concern's strategic posture. Most often cited were changes in the company's:

- overall organizational structure or its basic management style;
- relationships with the government or other external interest groups;
- acquisition, divestiture, or divisional control practices;
- international posture and relationships;
- innovative capabilities or personnel motivations as affected by growth;
- worker and professional relationships reflecting changed social expectations and values; and
- past or anticipated technological environments.

When executives were asked to "describe the processes through which their company arrived at its new posture" vis-à-vis each of these critical domains, several important points emerged. First, few of these issues lent themselves to quantitative modeling techniques or perhaps even formal financial analyses. Second, successful companies used a different "subsystem" to formulate strategy for each major class of strategic issues, yet these "subsystems" were quite similar among companies even in very different industries. Finally, no single formal analytical process could handle all strategic variables simultaneously on a planned basis. Why?

PRECIPITATING EVENTS

Often external or internal events, over which managements had essentially no control, would precipitate urgent, piecemeal, interim decisions that inexorably shaped the company's future strategic posture. One clearly observes this phenomenon in the decisions forced on General Motors by the 1973–1974 oil crisis;[13] the shift in posture pressed upon Exxon by sudden nationalizations; or the dramatic opportunities allowed for Haloid Corporation[14] and Pilkington Brothers, Ltd.,[15] by the unexpected inventions of xerography and float glass.

In these cases, analyses from earlier formal planning cycles did contribute greatly, as long as the general nature of the contingency had been anticipated. They broadened the information base available (as in Exxon's case), extended the options considered (Haloid-Xerox), created shared values to guide decisions about precipitating events in consistent directions (Pilkington), or built up resource bases, management flexibilities, or active search routines for opportunities whose specific nature could not be defined in advance (General Mills, Pillsbury).[16] But no organization—no matter how brilliant, rational, or imaginative—could possibly foresee the timing, the severity, or even the nature of all such precipitating events. Further, when these events did occur there might be neither enough time, resources, or information to undertake a full formal strategic analysis of all possible options and their consequences. Yet early decisions made under stress conditions often meant new thrusts, precedents, or lost opportunities that were difficult to reverse later.

AN INCREMENTAL LOGIC

Recognizing this, top executives usually consciously tried to deal with precipitating events in an incremental fashion. Early commitments were kept broadly formative, tentative, and subject to later review. In some cases neither the company nor the external players could understand the full implications of alternative actions. All parties wanted to test assumptions and have an opportunity to learn from and adapt to the others' responses. Such behavior clearly occurred during the 1973–1974 oil crisis; the ensuing interactions improved the quality of decisions for all. It also recurred frequently in other widely different contexts. For example:

- Neither the potential producer nor user of a completely new product or process (like xerography or float glass) could fully conceptualize its ramifications without interactive testing. All parties benefited from procedures that purposely delayed decisions and allowed mutual feedback. Some companies, like IBM or Xerox, have formalized this concept into "phase program planning" systems. They make concrete decisions only on individual phases (or stages) of new product developments, establish interactive testing procedures with customers, and postpone final configuration commitments until the latest possible moment.

    Similarly, even under pressure, most top executives were extremely sensitive to organizational and power relationships and consciously managed decision processes to improve these dynamics. They often purposely delayed initial decisions, or kept such decisions vague, in order to encourage lower-level participation, to gain more information from specialists, or to build commitment to solutions. Even when a crisis atmosphere tended to shorten time horizons and make decisions more goal oriented than political, perceptive executives consciously tried to keep their options open until they understood how the crisis would affect the power bases and needs of their key constituents. For example:

- General Motors's top management only incrementally restructured its various car lines as it understood, step by step, the way in which the oil crisis and environmental demands would affect the viability of each existing divisional and dealership structure. In the aggregate these amounted to the greatest shift in balance and positioning among GM's automobile lines since Alfred P. Sloan, and management was deeply concerned about the way its decisions would influence the power and prosperity of various groups.[17]

To improve both the informational content and the process aspects of decisions surrounding precipitating events, logic dictates and practice affirms that they should normally be handled on an incremental basis.

INCREMENTALISM IN STRATEGIC SUBSYSTEMS

One also finds that an incremental logic applies in attacking many of the critical subsystems of corporate strategy. Those subsystems for considering diversification moves, divestitures, major reorganizations, or government-external relations are typical and will be described here. In each case, conscious incrementalism helps to: cope with both the cognitive and process limits on each major decision; build the logical-analytical framework these decisions require; and create the personal and organizational awareness, understanding, acceptance, and commitment needed to implement the strategies effectively.

THE DIVERSIFICATION SUBSYSTEM

Strategies for diversification, either through R&D or acquisitions, provide excellent examples. The formal analytical steps needed for successful diversification are well documented.[18] However, the precise directions that R&D may project the company can only be understood step by step as scientists uncover new phenomena, make and amplify discoveries, build prototypes, reduce concepts to practice, and interact with users during product introductions. Similarly, only as each acquisition is sequentially identified, investigated, negotiated for, and integrated into the organization can one predict its ultimate impact on the total enterprise.

A step-by-step approach is clearly necessary to guide and assess the strategic fit of each internal or external diversification candidate. Incremental processes are also required to manage the crucial psychological and power shifts that ultimately determine the program's overall direction and consequences. These processes help unify both the analytical and behavioral aspects of diversification decisions. They create the broad conceptual consensus, the risk-taking attitudes, the organizational and resource flexibilties, and the adaptive dynamism that determine both the timing and direction of diversification strategies. Most important among these processes are:

- *Generating a genuine, top-level psychological commitment to diversification.* General Mills, Pillsbury,[19] and Xerox all started their major diversification programs with broad analytical studies and goal-setting exercises designed both to build top-level consensus around the need to diversify and to establish the general directions for diversification. Without such action, top-level bargaining for resources would have continued to support only more familiar (and hence apparently less risky) old lines, and doing this could delay or undermine the entire diversification endeavor.
- *Consciously preparing to move opportunistically.* Organizational and fiscal resources must be built up in advance to exploit candidates as they randomly appear. And a "credible activist" for ventures must be developed and backed by someone with commitment power. All successful acquirers created the potential for "profit centered" divisions within their organizational structures, strengthened their financial-controllership capabilities, created low-cost capital access, and maintained the shortest possible communication lines from the "acquisitions activist" to the resource-committing authority. All these actions integrally determined which diversifications actually could be made, the timing of their accession, and the pace at which they could be absorbed.
- *Building a "comfort factor" for risk taking.* Perceived risk is largely a function of one's knowledge about a field. Hence well-conceived diversification programs should anticipate a

trial-and-error period during which top managers reject early proposed fields or opportunities until they have analyzed enough trial candidates to "become comfortable with an initial selection. Early successes tend to be "sure things" close to the companies' past (real or supposed) expertise. After a few successful diversifications, managements tend to become more confident and accept other candidates—farther from traditional lines— at a faster rate. Again, the way this process is handled affects both the direction and the pace of the actual program.

- *Developing a new ethos.* If new divisions are more successful than the old—as they should be—they attract relatively more resources and their political power grows. Their most effective line managers move into corporate positions, and slowly the company's special competency and ethos change. Finally, the concepts and products that once dominated the company's culture may decline in importance or even disappear. Acknowledging these ultimate consequences to the organization at the beginning of a diversification program would clearly be impolitic, even if the manager both desired and could predict the probable new ethos. These factors must be handled adaptively, as opportunities present themselves and as individual leaders and power centers develop.

Each of the processes above interacts with all others (and with the random appearance of diversification candidates) to affect action sequences, elapsed time, and ultimate results in unexpected ways. Complexities are so great that few diversification programs end up as initially envisioned. Consequently, wise managers recognize the limits to systematic analysis in diversification and use formal planning to build the "comfort levels" executives need for risk taking and to guide the program's early directions and priorities. They then modify these flexibly, step by step, as new opportunities, power centers, and developed competencies merge to create new potentials.

THE DIVESTITURE SUBSYSTEM

Similar practices govern the handling of divestitures. Divisions often drag along in a less-than-desired condition for years before they can be strategically divested. In some cases, ailing divisions might have just enough yield or potential to offer hoped-for viability. In others, they might represent the company's vital core from earlier years, the creations of a powerful person nearing retirement, or the psychological touchstones of the company's past traditions.

Again, in designing divestiture strategies, top executives had to reinforce vaguely felt concerns with detailed data, build up managers' comfort levels about issues, achieve participation in and commitment to decisions, and move opportunistically to make actual changes. In many cases, the precise nature of the decision was not clear at the outset. Executives often made seemingly unrelated personnel shifts or appointments that changed the value set of critical groups, or started a series of staff studies that generated awareness or acceptance of a potential problem. They might then instigate goal assessment, business review, or "planning" programs to provide broader forums for discussion and a wider consensus for action. Even then they might wait for a crisis, a crucial retirement, or an attractive sale opportunity to determine the timing and conditions of divestiture. In some cases, decisions could be direct and analytical. But when divestitures involved the psychological centers of the organization, the process had to be much more oblique and carefully orchestrated. For example:

- When General Rawlings became president of General Mills, he had his newly developed Staff (Corporate Analysis) Department make informal presentations to top management on key issues. Later these were expanded to formal Management Operating Reviews (MORs) with all corporate and divisional top managers and controllers present. As problem operations were identified (many "generally known for a long time"), teams of corporate and divisional people were assigned to investigate them in depth. Once the necessary new data systems were built and studies came into place, they focused increasing attention on some hasty post–World War II acquisitions.

  First to go was a highly cyclical—and unprofitable—formula feeds business for which "there was no real heavy philosophical commitment." Then followed some other small divisions and the low-profit electronics business "which the directors didn't feel very comfortable with because it was so different. . . ." At the time, this business was headed by a recently appointed former Finance Department man "who had no strong attachments to electronics." Only then did the annual reports begin to refer to these conscious moves as ones designed "to concentrate on the company's major strengths." And only then, despite earlier concern, frustration, and discontent about its commodity aspects, could the traumatic divestiture of flour milling, the core of the company's traditions, be approached.

Careful incrementalism is essential in most divestitures to disguise intentions yet create the awareness, value changes, needed data, psychological acceptance, and managerial consensus required for such decisions. Early, openly acknowledged, formal plans would clearly be invitations to disaster.

THE MAJOR REORGANIZATION SUBSYSTEM

It is well recognized that major organizational changes are an integral part of strategy.[20] Sometimes they constitute a strategy themselves, sometimes they precede and/or precipitate a new strategy, and sometimes they help to implement a strategy. However, like many other important strategic decisions, macro-organizational moves are typically handled incrementally *and* outside of formal planning processes. Their effects on personal or power relationships preclude discussion in the open forums and reports of such processes.

In addition, major organizational changes have timing imperatives (or "process limits") of their own. In making any significant shifts, the executive must think through the new roles, capabilities, and probable individual reactions of the many principals affected. He may have to wait for the promotion or retirement of a valued colleague before consummating any change. He then frequently has to bring in, train, or test new people for substantial periods before he can staff key posts with confidence. During this testing period he may substantially modify his original concept of the reorganization, as he evaluates individuals' potentials, their performance in specific roles, their personal drives, and their relationships with other team members.

Because this chain of decisions affects the career development, power, affluence, and self-image of so many, the executive tends to keep close counsel in his discussions, negotiates individually with key people, and makes final commitments as late as possible in order to obtain the best matches between people's capabilities, personalities, and aspirations and their new roles. Typically, all these events do not come together at one convenient time, such as the moment annual plans are due. Instead the executive moves opportunistically, step by step, selectively moving people toward a broadly conceived organizational goal that is constantly modified and rarely articulated in detail until the last pieces fit together.

Major organizational moves may also define entirely new strategies the guiding executive cannot fully foresee. For example:

• When Exxon began its regional decentralization on a worldwide basis, the Executive Committee placed a senior officer and board member with a very responsive management style in a vaguely defined "coordinative role" vis-à-vis its powerful and successful European units. Over a period of two years this man sensed problems and experimented with voluntary coordinative possibilities on a pan-European basis. Only later, with greater understanding by both corporate and divisional officers, did Exxon move to a more formal "line" relationship for what became Exxon Europe. Even then the move had to be coordinated step by step with similar experimental shifts to regionalized consolidations in other areas of the world. All of these changes together led to an entirely new internal power balance toward regional and non-U.S. concerns and to a more responsive worldwide posture for Exxon.

• At General Mills, General Rawlings and his team of outside professional managers actively redefined the company's problems and opportunities in ways the preceding management could not have done. Once the divestitures noted above were made, the funds released were used for acquisitions, thus automatically increasing the visibility and power of the Controllership-Financial group. Similarly, with fewer large divisions competing for funds, the Consumer-Food groups rapidly increased in their importance. This ultimately led to a choice between these two groups' leaders for the next chairmanship of the company—and hence for control over the corporation's future strategy.

In such situations, executives may be able to predict the broad direction, but not the precise nature, of the ultimate strategy that will result. In some cases, such as Exxon, the rebalance of power and information relationships *becomes* the strategy, or at least its central element. In others, such as General Mills, organizational shifts are primarily means of triggering or implementing new strategic concepts and philosophies. But in all cases, major organizational changes create unexpected new stresses, opportunities, power bases, information centers, and credibility relationships that can affect both previous plans and future strategies in unanticipated ways. Effective reorganization decisions, therefore, allow for testing, flexibility, and feedback. Hence, they should, and usually do, evolve incrementally.

THE GOVERNMENT-EXTERNAL RELATIONS SUBSYSTEM

Almost all companies cited government and other external activist groups as among the most important forces causing significant changes in their strategic postures during the periods examined. However, when executives were asked, "How did your company arrive at its own strategy vis-à-vis these forces?" it became clear that few companies had cohesive strategies (integrated sets of goals, policies, and programs) for government-external relations, other than lobbying for or against specific legislative actions. To the extent that other strategies did exist, they were piecemeal, ad hoc, and had been derived in an evolutionary manner. Yet there seemed to be very good reasons for such incrementalism. The following are two of the best short explanations of the way these practices develop:

We are a very large company, and we understand that any massive overt action on our part could easily create more public antagonism than support for our viewpoint. It is also hard to say in advance exactly what public response any particular action might create. So we tend to test a number of different approaches on a small scale with only limited or local company identification. If one approach works, we'll test it further and amplify its use. If another bombs, we try to keep it from being used again. Slowly we find a series of advertising, public relations, community relations actions that seem to help. Then along comes another issue and we start all over again. Gradually the successful approaches merge into a pattern of actions that becomes our strategy. We certainly don't have an overall strategy on this, and frankly I don't think we devote enough [organizational and fiscal] resources to it. This may be our most important strategic issue.

I [the president] start conversations with a number of knowledgeable people. . . . I collect articles and talk to people about how things get done in Washington in this particular field. I collect data from any reasonable source. I begin wide-ranging discussions with people inside and outside the corporation. From these a pattern eventually emerges. It's like fitting together a jigsaw puzzle. At first the vague outline of an approach appears like the sail of a ship in a puzzle. Then suddenly the rest of the puzzle becomes quite clear. You wonder why you didn't see it all along. And once it's crystallized, it's not difficult to explain to others.

In this realm, uncontrollable forces dominate. Data is soft, can often be only subjectively sensed, and may be costly to quantify. The possible responses of individuals and groups to different stimuli are difficult to determine in advance. The number of potential opponents with power is high, and the diversity in their viewpoints and possible modes of attack is so substantial that it is physically impossible to lay out probabilistic decision diagrams that would have much meaning. Results are unpredictable and error costs extreme. Even the best intended and most rational-seeming strategies can be converted into disasters unless they are thoroughly and interactively tested. For example:

• In the 1960s General Motors found that technical discussions of cost versus benefit trade-offs were useless against demagogic slogans like "smog kills" or "GM is the worst polluter in the world." It publicly resisted some early attempts to impose pollution standards, stating that they were "beyond the state of the art." Then after successfully completing the costly and risky development of the catalytic converter, GM had its earlier concerns thrown in its face as "foot dragging" or "lying" about technical potentials. As one executive said, "You were damned if you did and damned if you didn't."

Only after prolonged interaction with regulators, legislators, and public interest groups did GM truly understand the needs and pressure potentials of its opponents. Area by area it learned to communicate better with various major interests. Only then could it identify effective *patterns* for dealing with all parties.

For such reasons, companies will probably always have to derive major portions of their government–external relations strategies in an experimental, iterative fashion. But such incrementalism could be much more proactive than it often has been in the past. Favorable public opinion and political action take a long time to mold. There is a body of knowledge about how to influence political action. There are also methods of informal and formal analyses that can help companies anticipate major political movements and adjust their goals or policies in a timely fashion. Once potential approaches are experimentally derived (without destroying needed flexibilities), more cohesive planning can ensure that the resources committed are sufficient to achieve the desired goals, that all important polities are included in the plans, and that rigorous and adaptive internal controls maintain those high performance, attitude, service, and image qualities that lend credibility to the strategy. But again, one sees logical incrementalism as the essential thread linking together information gathering, analysis, testing, and the behavioral and power considerations in this strategic subsystem.

FORMAL PLANNING IN CORPORATE STRATEGY

What role do classical formal planning techniques play in strategy formulation? All companies in the sample do have formal planning procedures embedded in their management direction and control systems. These serve certain essential functions. In a process sense, they do the following:

- provide a discipline forcing managers to take a careful look ahead periodically;
- require rigorous communications about goals, strategic issues, and resource allocations;
- stimulate longer-term analyses than would otherwise be made;
- generate a basis for evaluating and integrating short-term plans;
- lengthen time horizons and protect long-term investments such as R&D; and
- create a psychological backdrop and an information framework about the future against which managers can calibrate short-term or interim decisions.

In a decision-making sense, they do the following:

- fine-tune annual commitments;
- formalize cost reduction programs; and
- help implement strategic changes once decided on (for example, coordinating all elements of Exxon's decision to change its corporate name).
Finally, "special studies" had high impact at key junctures for specific decisions.

FORMAL PLANS ARE ALSO "INCREMENTAL"

Although individual staff planners were often effective in identifying potential problems and bringing them to top management's attention, the annual planning process itself was rarely (if ever) the initiating source of really new key issues or radical departures into new product/market realms. These almost always came from precipitating events, special studies, or conceptions implanted through the kinds of "logical incremental" processes described above.

In fact, formal planning practices actually institutionalize incrementalism. There are two reasons for this. First, in order to utilize specialized expertise and obtain executive involvement and commitment, most planning occurs "from the bottom up" in response to broadly defined assumptions or goals, many of which are long-standing or negotiated well in advance. Of necessity, lower-level groups have only a partial view of the corporation's total strategy and command only a fragment of its resources. Their power bases, identity, expertise, and rewards also usually depend on their existing products or processes. Hence, these products or processes, rather than entirely new departures, should and do receive their primary attention. Second, most managements purposely design their plans to be "living" or "ever green." They are intended only as "frameworks" to guide and provide consistency for future decisions made incrementally. To act otherwise would be to deny that further information could have a value. Thus properly formulated formal plans are also a part of an incremental logic.

SPECIAL STUDIES

Formal planning was most successful in stimulating significant change when it was set up as a "special study" on some important aspect of corporate strategy. For example:

- In 1958, when it became apparent that Pilkington's new float glass process would work, the company formed a Directors Flat Glass Committee consisting of all internal directors associated with float glass "to consider the broad issues of flat glass [strategy] in both the present and the future." The Committee did not attempt detailed plans. Instead, it tried to deal in broad concepts, identify alternate routes, and think through the potential consequences of each route some ten years ahead. Of some key strategic decisions Sir Alastair later said, "It would be difficult to identify an exact moment when the decision was made. . . . Nevertheless, over a period of time a consensus crystallized with great clarity."
- In the late 1960s, after the extraordinary success of the 914 copier, Xerox's chairman Wilson and president McColough began to worry about the positioning of their total product line. At their request, the company's engineers worked with the product planning department to evaluate a series of experimental products (that were then in development) from which top management could choose. These groups developed a series of strategies (from A through Q) concerning these alternative products—where to concentrate and where to deploy lesser resources. Top management chose Strategy Q, which led to the development of the product lines on which the company concentrated in the 1970s. Yet many of the initial targets for product positioning, timing, and price were adjusted as cost and market realities became clearer.

In each case there were also important precursor events, analyses, and political interactions, and each was followed by organizational, power, and behavioral changes. But interestingly, such special strategic studies also represent a "subsystem" of strategy formulation distinct from both annual planning activities and the other subsystems exemplified above. Each of these develops some important aspect of strategy, incrementally blending its conclusions with those of other subsystems, and it would be virtually impossible to force all these together to crystallize a completely articulated corporate strategy at any one instant.

TOTAL POSTURE PLANNING

Occasionally, however, managements do attempt very broad assessments of their companies' total posture. Two examples follow.

- Shortly after becoming CEO of General Mills, James McFarland decided that his job was "to take a very good company and move it to greatness," but that it was up to his management group, not himself alone, to decide what a great company was and how to get there. Consequently he took some thirty-five of the company's top managers away for a three-day management retreat. On the first day, after agreeing to broad financial goals, the group broke up into units of six to eight people. Each unit was to answer the question, "What is a great company?" from the viewpoints of stockholders, employees, suppliers, the public, and society. Each unit reported back at the end of the day, and the whole group tried to reach a consensus through discussion.

On the second day the groups, in the same format, assessed the company's strengths and weaknesses relative to the defined posture of "greatness." The third day focused on how to overcome the company's weaknesses and move it toward being a great company. This broad consensus led, over the next several years, to the surveys of fields for acquisition, the building of management's initial "comfort levels" with certain fields, and the acquisition-divestiture strategy that characterized the McFarland era at General Mills.

• Xerox Corporation used several such posture analyses between 1965 and 1974. The first of these was the Strategy Q analysis described above. In 1971, McColough formed another committee of top-line officers to define for the company how it should develop itself around a coalescing theme, "the architecture of information," which had seemed to catch the imagination of the company. This group produced a plan defining some eight business areas for the company. The plan was flexibly implemented through acquisition and internal development.

In 1974, McColough asked another group, with the full support of internal staffs and external consultants, to help define for the company what its posture should be vis-à-vis many of the great issues of the times (food shortages, energy, ecology, materials supplies, the world's poor, etc.). They were to "discard every taboo written, stated, or believed objective of the company." They were to "write strategies and comment on strategies in a broad frame" and report to the chairman and president on these matters. The committee was to use a full array of all the available formal strategic analysis techniques in arriving at its conclusions. These resulted in a series of discussions with the CEO and president.

Yet even such major endeavors were only portions of a total strategic process. Values that had been built up over decades stimulated or constrained alternatives. Precipitating events, acquisitions, divestitures, external relations, and organizational changes developed important segments of each strategy incrementally. Even the articulated strategies left key elements to be defined as new information became available, polities permitted, or particular opportunities appeared (like Pilkington's Electro-float invention or Xerox's Daconics acquisition). Major product thrusts (like Pilkington's TV tubes or Xerox's computers) proved unsuccessful. Actual strategies therefore evolved as each company overextended, consolidated, made errors, and rebalanced various thrusts over time. And it was both logical and expected that this would be the case.

LOGICAL INCREMENTALISM

All of the examples above suggest that strategic decisions do not lend themselves to aggregation into a single massive decision matrix where all factors can be treated relatively simultaneously in order to arrive at a holistic optimum. Many have spoken of the "cognitive limits"[21] that prevent this. Of equal importance are the "process limits"—i.e., the timing and sequencing imperatives necessary to create awareness, build comfort levels, develop consensus, select and train people, etc.—that constrain the system, yet ultimately determine the decision itself. Unlike the preparation of a fine banquet, it is virtually impossible for the manager to orchestrate all internal decisions, external environmental events, behavioral and power relationships, technical and informational needs, and actions of intelligent opponents so that they come together at any precise moment.

CAN THE PROCESS BE MANAGED?

Instead, executives usually deal with the logic of each "subsystem" of strategy formulation largely on its own merits and usually with a different subset of people. They try to develop or maintain in their own minds a consistent pattern among the decisions made in each subsystem. Knowing their own limitations and the unknowability of the events they face, they consciously try to tap the minds and psychic drives of others. They often purposely keep questions broad and decisions vague in early stages to avoid creating undue rigidities and to stimulate others' creativity. Logic, of course, dictates that they make final commitments *as late as possible* consistent with the information they have.

Consequently, many successful executives will initially set only broad goals and policies that can accommodate a variety of specific proposals from below, yet give a sense of guidance to the proposers.[22] As they come forward the proposals automatically and beneficially attract the support and identity of their sponsors. Being only proposals, executives can treat these at less politically charged levels, as specific projects rather than as larger goal or policy precedents. Therefore, they can encourage, discourage, or kill alternatives with considerably less political exposure. As events and opportunities emerge, they can incrementally guide the pattern of escalated or accepted proposals to suit their own purposes without getting prematurely committed to any rigid solution set that unpredictable events might prove wrong or that opponents find sufficiently threatening to coalesce against.

A STRATEGY EMERGES

Successful executives link together and bring order to a series of strategic processes and decisions spanning years. At the beginning of the process it is literally impossible to predict all the events and forces that will shape the future of the company. The best executives can do is to forecast the most likely forces that will impinge on the company's affairs and the ranges of their possible impact. They then attempt to build a resource base and a corporate *posture* so strong in selected areas that the enterprise can survive and prosper despite all but the most devastating events. They consciously select market/technological/product segments which the concern can "dominate" given its resource limits and place some "side bets" in order to decrease the risk of catastrophic failure or increase the company's flexibility for future options.[23]

They then proceed incrementally to handle urgent matters, start longer-term sequences whose specific future branches and consequences are perhaps murky, respond to unforeseen events as they occur, build on successes, and brace up or cut losses on failures. They constantly reassess the future, find new congruencies as events unfurl, and blend the organization's skills and resources into new balances of dominance and risk aversion as various forces intersect to suggest better—but never perfect—alignments. The process is dynamic, with neither a real beginning nor a real end. Pilkington Brothers Ltd. provides an excellent example.[24]

- After carefully formulating its broad float glass strategy in 1958, Pilkington Brothers Ltd. quickly developed a technical dominance in flat glass throughout the world. With its patents and established businesses it could control access to selected growth markets in specific countries. Float generated high growth and, after an initial investment period, high cash flows. These gave the company the resources to diversify geographically and into new product lines in order to decrease the risks inherent in the company's one product emphasis in a rapidly weakening British economy. It acquired, formed joint ventures, and expanded in selected product and geographical areas as opportunities became available. Meanwhile, socialism and modern communications combined to break down traditional dependencies among workers, employers, and communities. Growth and diversity required new professional managers and workers, and these executives created a new element in the lengthening gap between workers and owners. All these added to Pilkington's size and complexity.

  By 1965, the company had become too complex to manage with its old centralized organization. When a key executive retired, this opened a chain of promotional possibilities, and after a number of formal and informal studies, the organization was decentralized. The process went too far, however, and the company had to be tightened up through further planning, reorganization, and new controls. Meanwhile, float technology led to entirely new product possibilities, even higher profits, and increased credibility for its successful (nonfamily) inventor, knighted as Sir Alastair Pilkington. All of these elements reinforced a decision made broadly in the early 1960s to go public near the end of the decade in order to help with the family owners' death duties and to provide a more flexible capital base for the company. In 1970, just before the company was to go public, a strike convinced the owners to ask Lord Pilkington, who was about to retire as chairman, to stay on for three more years before Sir Alastair became chairman. The strike also speeded moves away from Pilkington's paternalistic management style to a more professional one. In the mid-1970s, the company's strategy and posture were still being shaped by the key personalities and decisions of the 1950s.

When the original float strategy was formulated, no one could have forecast or foreseen the interaction of all these events. Any rigid posture would have been doomed. Logic, therefore, dictated the kind of constantly adjusted incrementalism one sees in this vignette. The history of all other companies studied would lead to similar conclusions. Strategy deals with the unknowable, not the uncertain. It involves forces of such great number, strength, and combinatory powers that one cannot predict events in a probabilistic sense. Hence logic dictates that one proceed flexibly and experimentally from broad concepts toward specific commitments, making the latter concrete as late as possible in order to narrow the bands of uncertainty and to benefit from the best available information. This is the process of "logical incrementalism."

CONCLUSION

"Logical incrementalism" is not "muddling," as most people use that word. It is conscious, purposeful, proactive, good management. Properly managed, it allows the executive to bind together the contributions of rational systematic analyses, political and power theories, and organizational behavior concepts. It helps executives achieve cohesion and identity with new directions. It allows them to deal with power relationships and individual behavioral needs, and permits them to use the best possible informational and analytical inputs in choosing major courses of action. This article discusses the rationale behind "logical incrementalism" in strategy formulation.

RETROSPECTIVE COMMENTARY

Reviewing this article after a decade has been a challenge. It appeared as one of a trilogy in the *Sloan Management Review*; the three articles developed several aspects of proactive incremental management. The series provided the springboard for a later book, *Strategies for Change: Logical Incrementalism*.[25] Consequently, I have to look at it as a piece of a much larger project.

The article and its counterparts came into being because the prevalent theories of strategy formulation—although consistent and intellectually satisfying—did not seem to be working well in practice. Like others, I began to observe that the carefully designed strategic planning systems of major corporations were simply not performing well, and indeed not producing those companies' strategies. Instead of providing creative solutions, options, and a conceptual framework for major new moves, they had essentially become further extensions of the controllership function. Many had also become paperwork monstrosities and black holes for executives' time. As a researcher and consultant, I noted in company after company that while a quite cohesive strategy might indeed exist, the strategy generally seemed to come from someplace other than the formal planning process.

Somewhat perplexed by these ad hoc observations, I decided to seek out the real sources of large companies' important strategic changes. Ten large companies, each of which had just gone through such a change, agreed to cooperate extensively in a well-structured study. In all cases, as we unraveled the threads of history, the executives seemed genuinely intrigued—and often surprised—at how the enterprise had actually arrived at its final posture. In many cases, top executives who had agreed to give this "college professor" a valuable forty-five minutes for an interview flagged off other appointments, encroachments, and (on occasion) scheduled trips to extend the interview to two or three hours.

When the articles began to appear, I received the largest barrage of top executive write-ins in my publishing career. The usual message was essentially, "Thank goodness someone finally documented how and why real managers act in strategy formation." Other line executives seemed to appreciate the fact that there was a fragmented (but useful) theoretical literature, cited in the articles, that gave credence to practices they had based largely on their own intuition and experience. On the other hand, many staff planners and academics seemed genuinely bewildered, upset, or even angry, believing that their systems were under attack. The articles led to a wide-ranging series of studies and journal articles testing the degree of use and the effectiveness of incrementalism in different situations.

What seem to have been the problems, the confusions, and the contributions of the articles? Where do they fit into the generally nonlinear, sometimes murky, and usually incremental advance of management theory and practice?

INCREMENTALISM IS NOT ANTI-PLANNING

Probably the most disconcerting problem has been the tendency to pose incrementalism as the intellectual opposite of planning. While the articles and the book consciously tried to integrate the various rational-analytical, behavioral, psychological, and power theories of strategy into a broader context, this fact has often been overlooked. Hence our follow-up book—*The Strategy Process: Concepts, Contexts, and Cases*—which tried to better define and integrate the various major theories now prevalent.[26]

Managed or "logical" incrementalism is not the "disjointed incrementalism" of Lindblom,[27] or the "garbage can" approach of Cohen et al.,[28] or the "muddling" of Wrapp and others.[29] It demands conscious process management. It often involves a clear, thoroughly analyzed vision and set of purposes. But it also recognizes that the vision could be achieved by multiple means and that it may be politically unwise, motivationally counterproductive, or pragmatically misleading and wasteful to specify a particular set of means too early in the strategic process. It also recognizes that both the strategic program and the vision itself may be improved by incremental changes as new information becomes available. To believe or act otherwise is to deny the value of new information.

Within this framework, extensive formal planning is both possible and highly desirable. An innovation program provides the clearest example. Managers may well have a clear, even measurable, vision of the functions and performance characteristics a new device needs in order to be successful. But by definition, if innovation is required, no one has ever achieved that performance set in the same way before. Since innovation always involves the probability that a given approach will fail, an early commitment to a single option can lead to a completely incorrect choice. Similarly, a rigidly defined program can easily shut off valuable information, kill the commitment of key people, or waste resources by allowing work to continue for too long in a blind alley. New discoveries made outside or within the program can easily modify both critical dimensions of the ultimate goals that are achievable and the most fruitful means of achieving them. Yet one can *plan* to advantage; individual projects can be planned in detail, overall sequences can be planned broadly, and technical information, market scanning, and motivational and organizational support systems can be planned with professional thoroughness.

INCREMENTALISM SPEEDS STRATEGIC PROGRESS

A high degree of incrementalism has been apparent in virtually all the successful large-enterprise strategies I have observed since I began my study in the mid-1970s. This fact is not surprising, given the great ambiguities, radically changing environments, and largely unknowable range of competitive countermeasures present in any major company's strategic situation. And any serious study of the important national strategies of modern history—including those being played out at the present—would reach a similar conclusion. But is this situation simply descriptive, or is it prescriptive as well? For large organizations, it is both. Understanding the processes that have led to success for others can increase the probability of one's own success. Consciously managing informational, motivational, and political processes at the time a strategy is formulated also undoubtedly decreases the probability of catastrophic errors. Hence the right question is not whether strategy formulation in large organizations "should" be incremental, but rather the degree of incrementalism that is appropriate and the probable consequences of various possible degrees.

Incrementalism carried to one extreme is "reaction"; carried to another it is inaction. Unfortunately some managers have used the theory (wrongly) to justify such nonstrategic behavior. And many academics have labeled incrementalism as slow moving and bureaucratic. In the proper hands it is none of those things. Roosevelt would probably have created a completely destructive backlash had he overtly announced his strategy of rearming America and supporting its dawdling potential allies in 1939 and 1940. His incremental "cash and carry," lend lease, and "armed merchantship" programs made faster commitments to the war effort than a more open and thoroughly articulated strategy could have at that time.

Its potential for increasing the effectiveness of outcomes and decreasing times to implementation in business strategies is precisely why so many managers use incrementalism. Properly used, it speeds, rather than slows, decisions and commitments. In my studies and consulting practice, I often encounter executives who are frustrated when their clearly articulated, well-analyzed, and intellectually brilliant strategies are not implemented. When they shift to the kinds of incremental steps suggested in the *Sloan* series, movement suddenly occurs. In relatively short order, they begin to see positive strategic gains where few had appeared in the past. In retrospect I often wonder if I would have done better by naming the process "radical incrementalism." Given today's widely recognized need for greater speed in strategy development, the capacity of well-designed incrementalism to produce quicker and more effective decisions obviously deserves more thorough emphasis.

TESTING THEORY IN LARGE-SCALE SYSTEMS

Despite many elegant attempts to test the effectiveness of incremental strategy formulation, the nature of large-scale systems militates against any truly replicable test in the large-scale environments where it most applies. Almost by definition, a major strategy is a one-time event. Change the players, change the impinging environmental conditions, or change the competitors' responses, and you may expect a radically different outcome. Yet all of these factors would change markedly in any replicated experiment involving a large-scale strategic system.

If only one major event changes—often one outside the control of the strategist—outcomes can be radically altered. What would the Allies' World War II strategy have looked like if Hitler had gotten the atomic bomb first? What would the U.S. auto industry be like if the fundamentalist revolution in Iran had not suddenly ballooned oil prices? How successful would Apple be if IBM had decided to move a little sooner? Similarly, we can never know exactly what would have happened if failing analytical strategies like Ford's Edsel or IBM's FS system had been *more* incremental. Nor can we be sure how well the Energy Department's controlled fusion, General Motors's downsizing, or Continental Group's diversification strategies would have worked with *less* incrementalism. The determining experiment can never be performed.

We are therefore left with partial tests, and they usually exist in *much smaller systems*. This choice often ignores one of the important caveats about incrementalism—that it applies most clearly to large-scale systems. Small-scale systems often lack the inertia, the countervailing political powers, and the long history of prior commitments that make major strategy changes in large organizations so difficult to achieve. While the informational benefits of incrementalism generally hold in smaller organizations, the political, organizational, and motivational parameters are so different that lead times are substantially shorter. Thus the nature of strategy formulation often seems—and can be—more instantaneous and centrally controlled in smaller organizations.

On the other hand, there is a real question whether the centralized, top-down practices that may work well in small organizations can be equally effective in large companies. For illustration, one has only to look at the problems Roger Smith at General Motors and Frank Lorenzo at Eastern Airlines have had recently trying to use such techniques to redirect major enterprises. To these could be added examples of other large companies, *ad nauseam*, that have failed to make strategic changes with more structured centrist approaches.

In the last decade, I have repeatedly tried to warn other scholars that the theory was developed expressly for strategic changes in large companies that are in relatively good health at the time. Weekly, if not daily, I see its successful application in these situations. I am considerably more cautious about its validity in small company or crisis situations, although elements of incrementalism appear to be useful even in these circumstances. Like most theories and action patterns, the utility of incrementalism tends to be highly situational.

INCREMENTALISM VERSUS STRUCTURE IN MBA PROGRAMS

Teaching incrementalism has been interesting. Executive audiences tend to identify with the incremental approach, link it to cases with great sophistication, and move quickly to higher integrative levels of understanding. Teaching incremental thinking to MBAs or undergraduates, on the other hand, is a real challenge. Even professors who are devotees of the approach find it difficult to lead students with less high-level experience through the behavioral, informational, and political complexities of a major decision. The predominantly analytical MBA teaching approach, in particular, tends to emphasize evaluation of single-sequence alternatives, leading to closure on a particular action choice. The classic case analysis opening—"Bill Smith came into his office on Monday morning and wondered what he should do"—does not lend itself to working through the full chain of interactions that shape a complex strategy formulation even as it emerges. And asking MBA students to analyze a past decision process with questions about *why* Smith acted one way (and not another) in the sequence is less exciting and dynamic than posing the "What should he do?" question, especially if there are numbers to give inexperienced problem solvers a false sense of security.

Handling the softer, sequential, but often outcome-determining behavioral issues in a strategy situation will always be a problem in educational simulations. Yet ignoring them while concentrating on more quantitative factors is positively misleading. Avoiding mathematical analyses and dealing only with organizational or human issues is equally unrealistic. Unfortunately, however, the discipline orientation of university departments, Ph.D. education, and the research journals in which faculty members must publish often leads to just this result. Some business courses become essentially applied industrial economics courses (ignoring human factors) while others become advanced organizational behavior or organization design courses (ignoring hard financial, operations, or economic data). When either situation occurs, it diminishes students' understanding, as opposed to dealing with the full range of complexity in a strategic situation.

Another unfortunate segmentation (perhaps also caused by faculties' strong discipline orientations) is the breakdown of strategic management or business policy courses into "strategy formulation" and "strategy implementation" courses. In large organizations, if one delays beginning implementation until the strategy plan is complete, the strategy is generally doomed to failure. Similarly, if one attempts to implement a strategy without seriously considering the effects a particular implementation mode will have on the outcome, another type of disaster—one often encountered in industry and company histories—is likely to occur.

Incrementalism provides a useful vehicle for emphasizing the integration of the many valid (though individually incomplete) approaches to strategy analysis, formation, and implementation. It focuses on the reality that strategy development needs to be a continuous, evolving process. (In large organizations, formulation and implementation are usually simultaneous and overlapping.) It emphasizes that even major competitive analyses, industry analyses, and "critical factor" or "strength and weakness" tests are only temporary assessments; logic dictates that they must soon be updated. It underlines that the best-laid plans will prove fruitless without the human actions and commitments that can convert even less well-analyzed strategies into successes. (Conversely, if human factors are ignored, they can devastate the most brilliant conceptual framework.) The incremental framework demands that the full dynamics of strategy be considered holistically. Therein lies both its power and its primary limitation. Incrementalism recognizes that corporate strategy is so complex that no single person, analytical technique, or defined time period can deal with its totality.

The complexity of "logical," "proactive," or "radical" incrementalism makes the process itself difficult to explain and even more difficult to practice well. But, as we emphasize in *The Strategy Process*, strategy creation in large organizations is itself the most complex of management actions. As in understanding or teaching complex surgery, it does not pay to simplify models and training approaches too far. While one must appreciate and use the best techniques for each portion of the surgical procedure, the best results for the customer will come from dealing with the patient holistically and learning from future information about the patient's case as it becomes available. In dealing with the major reconstructive surgery of strategy change in large organizations, managed incrementalism still seems to provide a realistic and useful vehicle for the purpose—although, like my colleagues elsewhere, I continue to search for a more complete understanding of its full ramifications and for a better or simpler approach to replace it.

REFERENCES

[1] M. L. Mace, "The President and Corporate Planning," *Harvard Business Review,* January–February 1965, pp. 49–62; W. D. Guth, "Formulating Organizational Objectives and Strategy: A Systematic Approach," *Journal of Business Policy,* Fall 1971; K. J. Cohen and R. M. Cyert, "Strategy: Formulation, Implementation, and Monitoring," *Journal of Business* 46 (July 1973): 349–367; G. J. Skibbens, "Top Management Goal Appraisal," *International Management,* 1974; F. Goronzy and E. Gray, "Factors in Corporate Growth," *Management International Review* (1974): 75–90; W. E. Rothschild, *Putting It All Together: A Guide to Strategic Thinking* (New York: AMACOM, 1976).

[2] J. T. Cannon, *Business Strategy and Policy* (New York: Harcourt, Brace & Co. 1968); G. A. Steiner, *Top Management Planning* (New York: Macmillan, 1969); R. L. Katz, *Management of the Total Enterprise* (Englewood Cliffs, NJ: Prentice-Hall, 1970); E. K. Warren, *Long-Range Planning: The Executive Viewpoint* (Englewood Cliffs, NJ: Prentice-Hall, 1970); R. L. Ackoff, *A Concept of Corporate Planning* (New York: Wiley-Interscience, 1970); H. I. Ansoff, "Managerial Problem Solving," *Journal of Business Policy* (1971): 3–20; E. C. Miller, *Advanced Techniques for Strategic Planning* (New York: American Management Association, 1971); R .F. Vancil and P. Lorange, "Strategic Planning in Diversified Companies," *Harvard Business Review,* January–February 1975, pp. 81–90; R. F. Vancil, "Strategy Formulation in Complex Organizations," *Sloan Management Review,* Winter 1976, pp. 1–18.

[3] H.A. Simon, "On the Concept of Organization Goal," *Administrative Science Quarterly* 9 (June 1964): 1–22; P. Diesing, "Noneconomic Decision-Making," *Organizational Decision Making,* by M. Alexis and C. Z. Wilson (Englewood Cliffs, NJ: Prentice-Hall, 1967), pp. 185–200; C. Perrow,

"The Analysis of Goals in Complex Organizations," *American Sociological Review* 26 (February 1961): 854–866; P. Georgiou, "The Goal Paradigm and Notes towards a Counter Paradigm," *Administrative Science Quarterly* 18 (1973): 291–311.

4 R. M. Cyert, H. A. Simon, and D. B. Trow, "Observation of a Business Decision," *Journal of Business* 29 (October 1956): 237–248; J. M. Pfiffner, "Administrative Rationality," *Public Administration Review* (1960): 125–132; W. J. Gore, *Administrative Decision-Making: A Heuristic Model* (New York: John Wiley & Sons, 1964); J. L. Bower, "Planning within the Firm," *American Economic Review*, May 1970, pp. 186–194; A. Zaleznik, "Power and Politics in Organizational Life," *Harvard Business Review*, May–June 1970, pp. 47–58; R.A. Bauer and K. J. Gergen, eds., *The Study of Policy Formation* (New York: The Free Press, 1968); G. T. Allison, *Essence of Decision: Explaining the Cuban Missile Crisis* (Boston: Little, Brown & Co., 1971); A.M. Pettigrew, "Information Control as a Power Resource," *Sociology*, May 1972, pp. 187–204.

5 R. M. Cyert and J. G. March, *A Behavioral Theory of the Firm* (Englewood Cliffs, NJ: Prentice-Hall, 1963); L. R. Sayles, *Managerial Behavior: Administration in Complex Organizations* (New York: McGraw-Hill, 1964); Bower (May 1970); E. E. Carter, "The Behavioral Theory of the Firm and Top-Level Corporate Decisions," *Administrative Science Quarterly* 16 (1971): 413–428; H. Mintzberg, D. Raisinghani, and A. Théorêt"The Structure of 'Unstructured' Decision Processes," *Administrative Science Quarterly* 21 (June 1976): 246–275; J. Pfeffer, G. R. Salancik, and H. Leblebici, "The Effect of Uncertainty on the Use of Social Influence in Organizational Decision Making," *Administrative Science Quarterly* 21 (June 1976): 227–245; R. E. Miles and C. C. Snow, *Organizational Strategy: Structure and Process* (New York: McGraw-Hill, 1978).

6 Simon (June 1964); Cyert and March (1963).

7 W. H. Riker, *The Theory of Political Coalitions* (New Haven, CT: Yale University Press, 1962); Cyert and March (1963); W .D. Guth, "Toward a Social System Theory of Corporate Strategy," *Journal of Business* 49 (July 1976): 374–388.

8 C. E. Lindblom, "The Science of Muddling Through," *Public Administration Review* (Spring 1959); D. Braybrooke and C. E. Lindblom, *A Strategy of Decision: Policy Evaluation as a Social Process* (New York: The Free Press, 1963); H. E. Wrapp, "Good Managers Don't Make Policy Decisions," *Harvard Business Review*, September–October 1967, pp. 91–99; J. B. Quinn, "Strategic Goals: Process and Politics," *Sloan Management Review*, Fall 1977, pp. 21–37.

9 Cooperating companies included General Motors, Chrysler, Volvo (AB), General Mills, Pillsbury, Xerox, Texas Instruments, Exxon, Continental Group, and Pilkington Brothers.

10 C. I. Barnard, *The Function of the Executive* (Cambridge, MA: Harvard University Press, 1968); E. H. Bowman, "Epistemology, Corporate Strategy, and Academe," *Sloan Management Review*, Winter 1974, pp. 35–50; Mintzberg, Raisinghani, and Théorêt (June 1976).

11 For each company the author has attempted to create a background of secondary source data; interview at least ten of the executives most intimately associated with the strategic change process; cross-check viewpoints wherever possible; compare internal references with published materials; seek internal documentation if available; draw up a case history describing the process; submit each quotation or paraphrase used to the executive who was its source; clear the entire case for accuracy with an appropriate corporate authority. All quotations in this article have been released by their sources or are derived from secondary sources as noted.

12 For example, H. I. Ansoff, *Corporate Strategy: An Analytic Approach to Business Policy for Growth and Expansion* (New York: McGraw-Hill, 1965); R. L. Katz, *Cases and Concepts in Corporate Strategy* (Englewood Cliffs, NJ: Prentice-Hall, 1970); S. Schoeffler, R. D. Buzzell, and D. F. Heany, "Impact of Strategic Planning on Profit Performance," *Harvard Business Review*, March–April 1974, pp. 137–145.

[13] J. B. Quinn, "General Motors Corporation: The Downsizing Decision," in *The Strategy Process: Concepts, Contexts, and Cases,* Quinn et al. (Englewood Cliffs, NJ: Prentice-Hall, 1988).

[14] J. B. Quinn, "Xerox Corporation (A)" (Hanover, NH: Amos Tuck School, secondary source case, 1978).

[15] J. B. Quinn, "Pilkington Brothers P.L.C.," in Quinn et al. (1988).

[16] J. B. Quinn, "General Mills, Inc.," and "The Pillsbury Company," in Quinn et al. (1988).

[17] Quinn (General Motors case) in Quinn et al. (1988).

[18] These include: (1) clarifying the overall objectives of the corporation, (2) setting forth broad goals for the diversification program within these overall objectives, (3) defining specific criteria which acquisitions or developments should meet, (4) systematically searching out new product or acquisition candidates, (5) setting priorities for pursuing these, (6) evaluating specific candidates in technical, operational, and financial terms, (7) pricing acquisition deals or controlling R&D projects for adequate returns, (8) planning the integration of the new division or line into the enterprise, (9) implementing its integration and following up to see that intended yields are realized; M. L. Mace and G. G. Montgomery, *Management Problems of Corporate Acquisitions* (Cambridge, MA: Harvard University Press, 1962); J. B. Quinn and J. A. Mueller, "Transferring Research Results to Operations," *Harvard Business Review,* January–February 1963.

[19] Quinn (General Motors case) in Quinn et al. (1988).

[20] A. D. Chandler, *Strategy and Structure* (Cambridge, MA: MIT Press, 1962).

[21] J. G. March and H. A. Simon, *Organizations* (New York: John Wiley & Sons, 1958).

[22] For a more thorough explanation of goal-setting processes, see Quinn (Fall 1977).

[23] Ansoff (1965) details the need for internal and external flexibilities.

[24] Quinn (Pilkington Brothers case) in Quinn et al. (1988).

[25] J. B. Quinn, *Strategies for Change: Logical Incrementalism* (Homewood, IL: Richard D. Irwin, 1980).

[26] Quinn et al. (1988).

[27] C. E. Lindblom, *The Policy Making Process* (Englewood Cliffs, NJ: Prentice-Hall, 1968).

[28] M. D. Cohen and J. P. Olsen, "A Garbage Can Model of Organizational Change," *Administrative Science Quarterly,* 1972, pp. 1–25.

[29] Wrapp (September–October 1967).

An Effective Strategic Planning Approach for Public and Nonprofit Organizations*

JOHN M. BRYSON

I skate to where I think the puck will be.

WAYNE GRETZKY

Men, I want you to fight vigorously and then run. And as I am a little bit lame, I'm going to start running now.

GEN. GEORGE STEDMAN
U.S. ARMY (CIVIL WAR)

This chapter will present my preferred approach to strategic planning for public and non-profit organizations, functions, and communities. The process encompasses broad policy and direction setting, internal and external assessments, attention to key stakeholders, identification of key issues, development of strategies to deal with each issue, decision making, action, and continuous monitoring of results. The process draws on private sector approaches and applies them to public and nonprofit purposes.

First, however, let me emphasize that *any* strategic planning process is worthwhile only if it helps key decision makers *think* and *act* strategically. Strategic planning is not an end in itself, but merely a set of concepts to help leaders make important decisions and take important actions. Indeed, if any strategic planning process gets in the way of strategic thinking and acting, the process should be scrapped—not the thinking and acting!

The two quotes that begin this chapter help make the point that strategic thinking and acting are more important than any particular approach to strategic planning. Wayne Gretzky, one of the world's greatest ice hockey players, is talking about strategic thinking and acting when he says, "I skate to where I think the puck will be." He does not skate around with a thick strategic plan in his back pocket; hockey uniforms may not always *have* back pockets. What he does is think and act strategically every minute of the game, in keeping with a typically simple game plan worked out with his coaches in advance.

But let us explore Gretzky's statement further. Think about what one must know and be able to do in order to make, and deliver on, such a comment. One obviously would need to know the purposes and rules of the game, the strengths and weaknesses of one's own team, the opportunities and threats posed by the other team, the game plan, the arena, the officials, and so on. One would also have to be a well-equipped, well-conditioned, strong, and able hockey player. And it doesn't hurt to play for a very good team. In other words, those who can express confidently that they "skate to where they think the puck well be" know basically everything there is to know about strategic thinking and acting in hockey games.

Let us also consider the humorous statement of General George Stedman of the U.S. Army in the Civil War. At one point he and his men were badly outnumbered by Confederate soldiers. A hasty retreat was in order, but it made sense to give the lame and wounded, including the general, a chance to put some distance between themselves and the enemy before a full-scale retreat was called. They would then be in a position to fight another day. Stedman had no thick strategic plan in his back pocket, either, although we can assume he did *have* a back pocket. At most he probably had a fairly general battle plan worked out with his fellow officers and recorded in pencil on a map. Again, strategic thinking and acting were what mattered, not any particular planning process.

AN EIGHT-STEP STRATEGIC PLANNING PROCESS

Now, with that caution in mind let us proceed to a more detailed exploration of the eight-step process. The process, presented in Figure 1, is more orderly, deliberative, and participative than the process followed by Gretzky or Stedman while they are on the move. The steps are:

1. Initiating and agreeing on a strategic planning process.
2. Identifying organizational mandates.
3. Clarifying organizational mission and values.
4. Assessing the external environment: opportunities and threats.
5. Assessing the internal environment: strengths and weaknesses.
6. Identifying the strategic issues facing an organization.
7. Formulating strategies to manage the issues.
8. Establishing an effective organizational vision for the future.

These eight steps should lead to actions, results, and evaluation. I also emphasize that action, results, and evaluative judgments should emerge at each step in the process. In other words, implementation and evaluation should not wait until the end, but should be an integral and ongoing part of the process.

STEP 1. INITIATING AND AGREEING ON A STRATEGIC PLANNING PROCESS

The purpose of the first step is to negotiate agreement with key internal (and perhaps external) decision makers or opinion leaders about the overall strategic planning effort and the key planning steps. Their support and commitment are vital if strategic planning is to succeed (Olsen and Eadie, 1982). Also, involving key decision makers outside the organization usually is crucial to the success of public programs if implementation will involve multiple parties and organizations (McGowan and Stevens, 1983).

Obviously, some person or group must initiate the process. One of the initiators' first tasks is to identify exactly who the key decision makers are. The next task is to identify which persons, groups, units, or organizations should be involved in the effort. The initial agreement will be negotiated with at least some of these decision makers, groups, units, or organizations.

The agreement itself should cover the purpose of the effort; preferred steps in the process; the form and timing of reports; the role, functions, and membership of any group or committee empowered to oversee the effort; the role, functions, and membership of the strategic planning team; and commitments of necessary resources to proceed with the effort.

STEP 2. CLARIFYING ORGANIZATIONAL MANDATES

The formal and informal mandates placed on the organization are "the *musts*" it confronts. Actually, it is surprising how few organizations know precisely what they are mandated to do and not do. Typically, few members of any organization, for example, have ever read the relevant legislation, ordinances, charters, articles, and contracts that outline the organization's formal mandates. It may not be surprising, then, that many organizations make one or both of two fundamental mistakes. Either they believe they are more tightly constrained in their actions than they are; or they assume that if they are not explicitly told to do something, they are not allowed to do it.

STEP 3. CLARIFYING ORGANIZATIONAL MISSION AND VALUES

An organization's mission, in tandem with its mandates, provide its *raison d'être*, the social justification for its existence. For a government corporation or agency, or for a nonprofit organization, this means there must be identifiable social or political needs that the organization seeks to fill. Viewed in this light, organizations must always be considered a means to an end, not an end in and of themselves. Communities also should not be seen as an end in themselves, but must justify their existence based on how well they meet the social and political needs of their various stakeholders, including those stakeholders' needs for a "sense of community."

Identifying the mission, however, does more than merely justify the organization's existence. Clarifying purpose can eliminate a great deal of unnecessary conflict in an organization and can help channel discussion and activity productively. Agreement on purposes defines the arenas within which the organization will compete and, at least in broad outline, charts the future course. Moreover, an important and socially justifiable mission is a source of inspiration to key stakeholders, particularly employees. Indeed, it is doubtful that any organization ever achieved greatness or excellence without a basic consensus among its key stakeholders on an inspiring mission.

Before developing a mission statement, an organization should complete a stakeholder analysis. A *stakeholder* is defined as any person, group, or organization that can place a claim on an organization's attention, resources, or output, or is affected by that output. Examples of a government's stakeholders are citizens, taxpayers, service recipients, the governing body, employees, unions, interest groups, political parties, the financial community, and other governments. Examples of a nonprofit organization's stakeholders include clients or

FIGURE 1
Strategic Planning Process

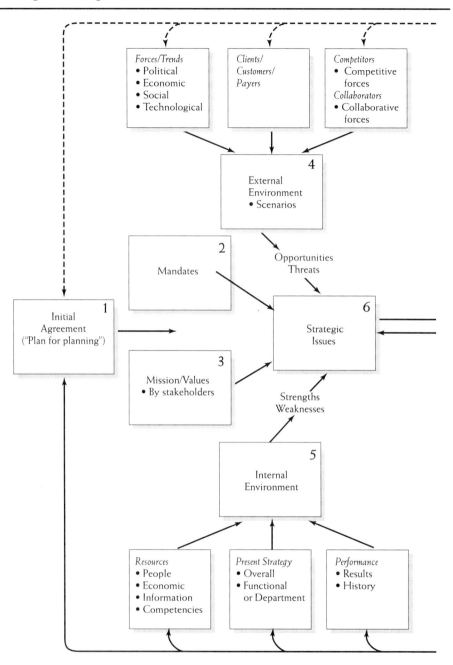

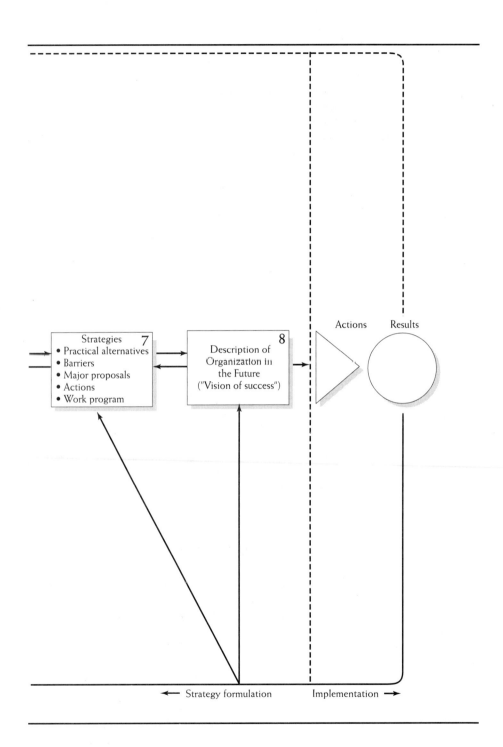

customers, third-party payers or funders, employees, the board of directors, other nonprofit organizations providing complementary services or involved as coventurers in projects, banks holding mortgages or notes, and suppliers. Attention to stakeholder concerns is crucial because *the key to success in public and nonprofit organizations is the satisfaction of key stakeholders.*

A complete stakeholder analysis will require the strategic planning team to identify the organization's stakeholders, their stake in the organization or its output, their criteria for judging the performance of the organization, how well the organization performs against those criteria, how the stakeholders influence the organization, and in general how important the various stakeholders are. A complete stakeholder analysis also should identify what the organization needs from its various stakeholders—for example, money, staff, or political support. A stakeholder analysis will help clarify whether the organization should have different missions and perhaps different strategies for different stakeholders.

After completing the stakeholder analysis, a strategic planning team can proceed to development of a mission statement by responding to six questions.

1. Who are we as an organization (or community)? This question can be surprisingly difficult for a strategic planning team to answer succinctly.
2. In general, what are the basic social or political needs we exist to fill, or the basic social or political problems we exist to address? Again, the answer to this question provides the justification for the organization's existence.
3. In general, what do we do to recognize or anticipate and respond to these needs or problems? This query should reveal whether the organization is active or passive, what it does to stay in touch with the needs it is supposed to fill, and in general what it does to make sure it does not become an end in itself. The answer to this question will also tell organizational members whether they will be praised or punished for bringing bad news to the organization about troubling events in the environment or critical evaluations by key stakeholders. Too many organizations shoot the messenger instead of attending to the message. Organizational members need to know they will not be punished for bringing back important but troubling information; otherwise, they will simply keep quiet and the organization will not have the benefit of useful feedback.
4. How should we respond to our key stakeholders?
5. What is our philosophy and what are our core values? Clarity about philosophy and core values will help an organization maintain its integrity. Furthermore, since only those strategies consistent with an organization's philosophy and values are likely to work, the response to this question also helps the organization choose effective strategies (Pfeiffer, Goodstein, and Nolan, 1986).
6. What makes us distinctive or unique? If there is nothing unique or distinctive about the organization, perhaps it should not exist. If it is a government corporation or agency, perhaps the private or nonprofit sectors should take over the organization's functions. If the private or nonprofit sectors fail to meet an important social or political need, perhaps a government corporation or agency should enter the field.

The mission statement itself might be very short, perhaps not more than a paragraph or a slogan. But development of the statement should grow out of lengthy discussions in response to these six questions. Complete answers to these questions actually may serve as a basic outline for a description of the organization in the future, its "vision of success," the last step in the process. But considerable intermediate work is necessary before a complete vision of success can be articulated.

STEP 4. ASSESSING THE EXTERNAL ENVIRONMENT

The planning team should explore the environment outside the organization to identify the opportunities and threats the organization faces. Basically, "inside" factors are those controlled by the organization and "outside" factors are those the organization does not control (Pfeffer and Salancik, 1978). Opportunities and threats can be discovered by monitoring a variety of political, economic, social, and technological forces and trends. PESTs is an appropriate acronym for these forces and trends, because organizations typically must change in response to them and the change can be quite painful. Unfortunately, organizations all too often focus only on the negative or threatening aspects of these changes, and not on the opportunities they present.

Besides monitoring PESTs, the strategic planning team also should monitor various stakeholder groups, including clients, customers, payers, competitors, or collaborators. The organization might construct various scenarios to explore alternative futures in the external environment, a practice typical of private sector strategic planning (Linneman and Klein, 1983).

Members of an organization's governing body, particularly if they are elected, often are better at identifying and assessing external threats and opportunities than the organization's employees. This is partly because a governing board is responsible for relating an organization to its external environment and vice versa (Thompson, 1967). Unfortunately, neither governing boards nor employees usually do a systematic or effective job of external scanning. As a result, most organizations are like ships trying to navigate treacherous waters without benefit of human lookouts or radar and sonar equipment.

Because of this, both employees and governing board members should rely on a relatively formal external assessment process. The technology of external assessment is fairly simple, and allows organizations—cheaply, pragmatically, and effectively—to keep tabs on what is happening in the larger world that is likely to have an effect on the organization and the pursuit of its mission.

STEP 5. ASSESSING THE INTERNAL ENVIRONMENT

To identify internal strengths and weaknesses, the organization might monitor resources (inputs), present strategy (process), and performance (outputs). Most organizations, in my experience, have volumes of information on their inputs, such as salaries, supplies, physical plant, and full-time equivalent (FTE) personnel. They tend to have a less clear idea of their present strategy, either overall or by function. And typically they can say little, if anything, about outputs, let alone the effects those outputs have on clients, customers, or payers. For example, while schools may be able to say how many students they graduate—an output—most cannot say how "educated" those students are. The recent movement toward standardized testing of school graduates is an attempt to measure outcomes in order to remedy this shortcoming (Flynn, 1986).

The relative absence of performance information presents problems both for the organization and for its stakeholders. Stakeholders will judge the worth of an organization according to how well it does against the criteria the stakeholders—not necessarily the organization—wish to use. For external stakeholders in particular, these criteria typically relate to performance. If the organization cannot demonstrate its effectiveness against the stakeholders' criteria, then regardless of any inherent worth of the organization, stakeholders are likely to withdraw their support.

The absence of performance information may also create, and harden, major organizational conflicts. This is because without performance criteria and information, there is no way to evaluate the relative effectiveness of alternative strategies, resource allocations, organizational designs, and distributions of power. As a result, organizational conflicts are likely to occur more often than they should, serve narrow partisan interests, and be resolved in ways that do not further the organization's mission.

The difficulties of measuring performance are well known (Flynn, 1986). But regardless of the difficulties, the organization will be continually challenged to demonstrate effective performance to its stakeholders. Government leaders and staff, for example, might interpret the recent willingness of the public to limit or even decrease taxation (as seen in Proposition 13 in California, Proposition 2½ in Massachusetts, and the 1981 and 1986 federal tax cuts) as pure selfishness on the public's part. One might also interpret these limitations on public expenditure as an unwillingness to support organizations that cannot demonstrate unequivocally effective performance.

STEP 6. IDENTIFYING THE STRATEGIC ISSUES FACING AN ORGANIZATION

Together the first five elements of the process lead to the sixth, the identification of strategic issues—the fundamental policy questions affecting the organization's mandates, mission and values, product or service level and mix, clients, users or payers, cost, financing, or management.

Strategic planning focuses on achievement of the best "fit" between an organization and its environment. Attention to mandates and the external environment, therefore, can be thought of as planning from the outside in. Attention to mission and values and the internal environment can be considered planning from the inside out. Usually, it is vital that strategic issues be dealt with expeditiously and effectively if the organization is to survive and prosper. An organization that does not respond to a strategic issue can expect undesirable results from a threat, a missed opportunity, or both.

The iterative nature of the strategic planning process often becomes apparent in this step when participants find that information created or discussed in earlier steps presents itself again as strategic issues. For example, many strategic planning teams begin their task with the belief that they know what their organization's mission is. They often find out in this step, however, that a key issue is lack of clarity on exactly what the mission should be. In other words, the organization's present mission is found to be inappropriate, given the team members' new understanding of the situation the organization faces, and a new mission must be created.

Strategic issues, virtually by definition, involve conflicts of one sort or another. The conflicts may involve ends (what); means (how); philosophy (why); location (where); timing (when); and the groups that might be advantaged or disadvantaged by different ways of resolving the issue (who). In order for the issues to be raised and resolved effectively, the organization must be prepared to deal with the almost inevitable conflicts that will occur.

A statement of a strategic issue should contain three elements. First, the issue should be described succinctly, preferably in a single paragraph. The issue itself should be framed as a question that the organization can do something about. If the organization cannot do anything about it, it is not an issue—at least for the organization (Wildavsky, 1979). An organization's attention is limited enough without wasting it on issues it cannot resolve.

Second, the factors that make the issue a fundamental policy question should be listed. In particular, what is it about mandates, mission, values, or internal strengths and weaknesses and external opportunities and threats that make this a strategic issue? Listing these factors will become useful in the next step, strategy development. Every effective strategy will build on strengths and take advantage of opportunities while it minimizes or overcomes weaknesses and threats. The framing of strategic issues therefore is very important because the framing will contain the basis for the issues' resolution.

Finally, the planning team should define the consequences of failure to address the issue. A review of the consequences will inform judgments of just how strategic, or important, various issues are. For instance, if no consequences will ensue from failure to address an issue, it is not an issue, at least not a strategic issue. At the other extreme, if the organization will be destroyed by failure to address an issue, or will miss a highly significant and valuable opportunity, the issue clearly is *very* strategic and should be dealt with immediately. The strategic issue identification step therefore is aimed at focusing organizational attention on what is truly important for the survival, prosperity, and effectiveness of the organization.

There are three basic approaches to identifying strategic issues: the direct approach, the goals approach, and the "vision of success" approach (Barry, 1986). The *direct approach* probably is the one that will work best for most governments and public agencies. It involves going straight from a review of mandates, mission, and SWOTs (strengths, weaknesses, opportunities, and threats) to the identification of strategic issues. The direct approach is best when there is no agreement on goals, or if the goals on which there is agreement are too abstract to be useful. In other words, it works best when there is no value congruence. It is best if there is no preexisting vision of success and developing a consensually based vision would be too difficult. This approach also works best when no hierarchical authority can impose goals on other actors. Finally, it is best when the environment is so turbulent that limited actions in response to issues seem preferable to development of goals and objectives or visions that may be rendered obsolete quickly. The direct approach, in other words, can work in the pluralistic, partisan, politicized, and relatively fragmented worlds of most public sector organizations (and communities), as long as there is a dominant coalition strong enough and interested enough to make it work.

The *goals approach* is more in line with conventional planning theory, which stipulates that an organization should establish goals and objectives for itself and then develop strategies to achieve them. This approach can work if there is fairly broad and deep agreement on the organization's goals and objectives, and if they are detailed and specific enough to guide the development of strategies. The approach also can be expected to work when there is a hierarchical authority structure with leaders at the top who can impose goals on the rest of the system. The strategic issues then will involve how best to translate goals and objectives into actions. This approach is more likely to work in a single-function public or nonprofit organization than in multi-organizational, multi-functional situations.

Finally, there is the *vision of success* approach, where the organization develops a "best" or "ideal" picture of itself in the future as it successfully fulfills its mission. The strategic issues then concern how the organization should move from the way it is now to how it would look and behave according to its vision. The vision of success approach is most useful if it will be difficult to identify strategic issues directly; if no detailed and specific agreed-upon goals and objectives exist and will be difficult to develop; and if drastic change is likely to be necessary. As conception precedes perception (May, 1969), development of a vision can provide the concepts to enable organizational members to see necessary changes. This approach also is more likely to work in a nonprofit organization than in a public sector organization.

The statement that there are three different approaches to the identification of strategic issues may raise the hackles of some planning theorists and practitioners who believe one should *always* start with either issues, or goals, or an idealized scenario for the organization. I argue that what will work best depends on the situation, and that the wise planner should assess the situational factors discussed above and choose an approach accordingly.

STEP 7. FORMULATING STRATEGIES TO MANAGE THE ISSUES

A strategy is defined as a pattern of purposes, policies, programs, actions, decisions, or resource allocations that define what an organization is, what it does, and why it does it. Strategies can vary by level, function, and time frame.

This definition is purposely broad, in order to focus attention on the creation of consistency across *rhetoric* (what people say), *choices* (what people decide and are willing to pay for), and *actions* (what people do). Effective strategy formulation and implementation processes will link rhetoric, choices, and actions into a coherent and consistent pattern across levels, functions, and time (Philip Bromiley, personal communication, 1986).

I favor a five-part strategy development process (to which I was first introduced by staff of the Institute of Cultural Affairs in Minneapolis). Strategy development begins with identification of practical alternatives, and dreams or visions for resolving the strategic issues. It is of course important to be practical, but if the organization is unwilling to entertain at least *some* dreams or visions for resolving its strategic issues, it probably should not be engaged in strategic planning. In other words, if the organization is willing to consider only minor variations on existing strategic themes, then it probably is wasting its time on strategic planning. After completing a strategic planning process, an organization may decide that minor variations are the best choice, but if it *begins* the process with that assumption, it is wasting its time with strategic planning.

Next, the planning team should enumerate the barriers to achieving those alternatives, dreams, or visions, and not focus directly on their achievement. A focus on barriers at this point is not typical of most strategic planning processes. But doing so is one way of assuring that any strategies developed deal with implementation difficulties directly rather than haphazardly.

Once alternatives, dreams, and visions, along with barriers to their realization, are listed, the team develops major proposals for achieving the alternatives, dreams, or visions either directly or indirectly, through overcoming the barriers. (Alternatively, the team might solicit proposals from key organizational units, various stakeholder groups, task forces, or selected individuals.) For example, a major Midwestern city government did not begin to work on strategies to achieve its major ambitions until it had overhauled its archaic civil service system. That system clearly was a barrier that had to be changed before the city government could have any hope of achieving its more important objectives.

After major proposals are submitted, two final tasks remain. Actions needed over the next two to three years to implement the major proposals must be identified. And finally, a detailed work program for the next six to twelve months must be spelled out to implement the actions.

An effective strategy must meet several criteria. It must be technically workable, politically acceptable to key stakeholders, and must accord with the organization's philosophy and core values. It should be ethical, moral, and legal. It must also deal with the strategic issue it was supposed to address. All too often I have seen strategies that were technically, politically, morally, ethically, and legally impeccable, but failed to deal with the issues they were developed to address. The strategies therefore were virtually useless.

STEP 8. ESTABLISHING AN EFFECTIVE ORGANIZATIONAL VISION FOR THE FUTURE

In the final step in the process, the organization develops a description of what it should look like as it successfully implements its strategies and achieves its full potential. This description is the organization's "vision of success" (Taylor, 1984). Few organizations have such a description or vision, yet the importance of such descriptions has long been recognized by well-managed companies (Ouchi, 1981; Peters and Waterman, 1982) and organizational psychologists (Locke, Shaw, Saari, and Latham, 1981). Typically included in such descriptions are the organization's mission, its basic strategies, its performance criteria, some important decision rules, and the ethical standards expected of all employees.

Such descriptions, to the extent that they are widely known and agreed to in the organization, allow organizational members to know what is expected of them without constant direct managerial oversight. Members are free to act on their own initiative on the organization's behalf to an extent not otherwise possible. The result should be a mobilization and direction of members' energy toward pursuit of the organization's purposes, and a reduced need for direct supervision.

Visions of success should be short—not more than several pages—and inspiring. People are inspired by a clear and forceful vision delivered with heartfelt conviction. Inspirational visions, such as Dr. Martin Luther King, Jr.'s "I Have a Dream" speech, have the following attributes: They focus on a better future, encourage hopes and dreams, appeal to common values, state positive outcomes, emphasize the strength of a unified group, use word pictures, images and metaphors, and communicate enthusiasm and excitement (Kouzes and Posner, 1987).

Some might question why development of a "vision of success" comes last in the process rather than much earlier. There are two basic answers. First, development of a vision does not have to come last. Some organizations are able to develop a fairly clearly articulated vision of success much earlier in the process.

However, most organizations will not be able to develop a vision of success until they have gone through several iterations of strategic planning—if they are able to develop a vision at all. A challenging yet achievable vision embodies the tension between what an organization *wants* and what it *can have*. Often several cycles of strategic planning are necessary before organizational members know what they want, what they can have, and how the two differ. A vision that motivates people will be challenging enough to spur action, yet not so impossible to achieve that it demotivates and demoralizes people. Most organizations, in other words, will find that their visions of success are likely to serve more as a guide for strategy implementation and less as a guide for strategy formulation.

Further, for most organizations, development of a vision of success is not *necessary* to produce marked improvements in performance. In my experience, most organizations could demonstrate a substantial improvement in effectiveness if they simply identified and resolved satisfactorily a few strategic issues. Most organizations most of the time simply do not address what is truly important; just gathering key decision makers to deal with a few important matters in a timely way would enhance organizational performance substantially.

APPLICATION ACROSS LEVELS AND FUNCTIONS

To return to Wayne Gretzky and George Stedman, one can easily imagine them zooming almost intuitively through the eight steps, while already on the move, in a rapid series of discussions, decisions, and actions. The eight steps merely make the process of strategic thinking and acting more orderly and allow more people to participate.

The process might be applied across levels and functions in an organization as outlined in Figure 2. The application is based on the system used by the 3M Corporation (Tita and Allio, 1984). The system's first cycle consists of "bottom up" development of strategic plans within a framework established at the top, followed by reviews and reconciliations at each succeeding level. In the second cycle, operating plans are developed to implement the strategic plans. Depending on the situation, decisions at the top of the organizational hierarchy may or may not require policy board approval, which explains why the line depicting the process flow diverges at the top.

A similar cyclic system is used by Hennepin County, Minnesota (the county that contains Minneapolis), to address fourteen areas of strategic concern (for example, finance, employment and economic development, transportation, program fragmentation and coordination). The system includes three cycles: strategic issue identification, strategy development, and strategy implementation (Eckhert, Haines, Delmont, and Pilaum, 1988).

CAVEATS

Although the steps are laid out in a linear, sequential manner, it must be emphasized that the process in practice is iterative. Participants typically rethink what they have done several times before they reach final decisions. Moreover, the process does not always begin at the beginning. Organizations typically find themselves confronted with a strategic issue that leads them to engage in strategic planning, but then they are likely to go back and begin at the beginning. In addition, implementation usually begins before all the planning is complete. As soon as useful actions are identified, they are taken—as long as they do not jeopardize future actions that might prove valuable.

In other words, in a linear, sequential process, the eight steps would be followed by decisions and actions to implement the strategies, and by evaluation of results. However, implementation typically does not, and should not, wait until the eight steps have been completed. For example, if the organization's mission needs to be redrafted, then it should be. If the SWOT analysis turns up weaknesses or threats that need to be addressed immediately, they should be. If an aspect of a strategy can be implemented without awaiting further developments, they should be. And so on. Both strategic thinking *and* acting are important, and all the thinking does not have to occur before any actions are taken.

The process is applicable to public and nonprofit organizations, functions, and communities. The only general requirements are a "dominant coalition" (Thompson, 1967) willing to sponsor and follow the process, and a process champion willing to push it.

Many organizational strategic planning teams that are familiar with and believe in the process should be able to complete it in a two- or three-day retreat, with an additional half-day meeting three to four weeks later to review the resulting strategic plan. Responsibility for preparing the plan can be delegated to a planner assigned to work with the team, or the organization's chief executive may choose to draft the plan personally. Additional time might be needed for further reviews and signoffs by key decision makers. Additional

FIGURE 2
Annual Strategic Planning Process

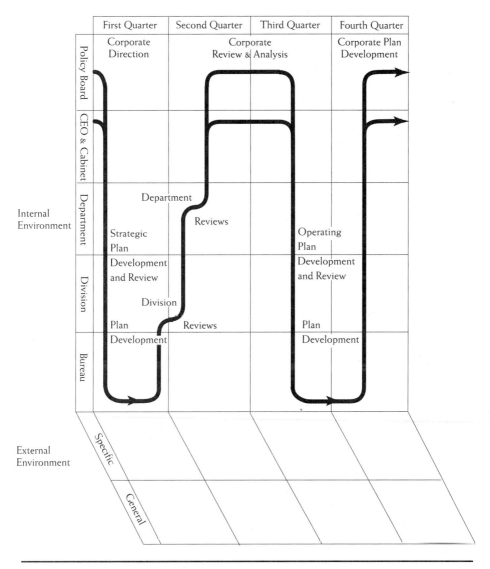

	First Quarter	Second Quarter	Third Quarter	Fourth Quarter

Source: Adapted from Bryson and Roering, 1987, p. 16.

time also might be necessary to secure information or advice for specific parts of the plan, especially recommended strategies.

If the organization is fairly large, then specific linkages will be necessary to join the process to different functions and levels so that the process can proceed in an orderly and integrated manner. One effective way to achieve such a linkage is to appoint the heads of all functional departments to the strategic planning team—indeed, to make *them* the strategic planning team. All department heads then can be sure that their departments' information and interests are represented in strategy formulation, and can oversee strategy implementation in their departments.

Indeed, the key decision makers might wish to form themselves into a permanent strategic planning committee or cabinet. I certainly would recommend this approach if it appears workable for the organization, for it emphasizes the role of policy makers and line managers as strategic planners and the role of strategic planners as facilitators of decision making by the policy makers and line managers. Pragmatic and effective strategies and plans are likely to result. Temporary task forces, strategic planning committees, or a cabinet can work, but whatever the arrangement, there is no substitute for the direct involvement of key decision makers in the process.

When applied to a function that crosses organizational boundaries or to a community, the process probably will need to be sponsored by a committee or task force of key decision makers, opinion leaders, "influentials," or "notables" representing important stakeholder groups. Additional working groups or task forces probably will need to be organized at various times to deal with specific strategic issues or to oversee the implementation of specific strategies. Because so many more groups will need to be involved, and because implementation will have to rely more on consent than authority, the process is likely to be much more time-consuming than strategic planning applied to an organization.

In addition, special efforts will be necessary to make sure that important connections are made, and incompatibilities resolved, between strategic plans and the community's comprehensive plan and the various devices used to implement it, such as the government's capital improvements program, subdivision controls, zoning ordinances, and the official map. The fact that these connections must be made, however, should not unduly hamper the process. Strategic planning and comprehensive planning can be complementary, and efforts should be made to assure they are, if the community's best interests and those of its various stakeholders are to be advanced (Rider, 1983; King and Johnson, 1988).

As we noted earlier, strategic planning is likely to embrace a far more comprehensive potential agenda than comprehensive planning, to be more broadly participative, to be more emphatic about the need to understand the community's strengths and weaknesses as well as the opportunities and threats it faces, to attend to other communities' competitive behavior, to be much more flexible in its design and output, to be less legalistic in its design and execution, and to be much more action-oriented. Strategic planning thus can infuse comprehensive planning with more strategic thought and action than ordinarily would occur. In addition, strategic planning can be used to develop practical strategies to implement the vision and policies likely to be found in comprehensive plans.

WHY STRATEGIC PLANNING IS HERE TO STAY

Many managers are likely to groan at the prospect of having yet another new management technique foisted upon them. They have seen cost-benefit analysis, planning-programming-budgeting systems, zero-based budgeting, management by objectives, and a host of other techniques trumpeted by their inventors, various authors, and cadres of management consultants. They have also seen the techniques all too often fall by the wayside after a burst of initial enthusiasm by their adopters. The managers frequently, and justifiably, feel as if they are the victims of some sort of perverse management hazing (Philip Eckhert, personal communication, 1985).

Strategic planning, however, is not just a passing fad, at least strategic planning of the sort proposed in this book. That is because the strategic planning process presented in this chapter builds on the nature of *political* decision making. So many of the other management techniques have failed because they have ignored, or tried to circumvent, or even tried to contradict the political nature of life in private, public, and nonprofit organizations. Too many planners and managers, at least in my experience, just do not understand that such a quest is almost guaranteed to be quixotic.

Most of these new management innovations have attempted to improve government decision making and operations by trying to impose a formal rationality on systems that are not rational, at least in the conventional meaning of that word. Political organizations are *politically rational*, and any technique that is likely to work well in such organizations must accept and build on the nature of political rationality (Wildavsky, 1979).

Let us pursue this point further by contrasting two different kinds of decision making: the "rational" planning model and political decision making (R.C. Einsweiler, personal communication, 1985). The rational planning model is presented in Figure 3. It is a rational-deductive approach to decision making that begins with goals, from which are deduced policies, programs, and actions to achieve the goals. If there is traditional planning theology, this model is one of its icons. Indeed, if there were a planning Moses, Figure 3 would have been etched on his tablets when he came down from the Mount.

But now let us examine a fundamental assumption of the rational planning model—that in the fragmented, shared-power settings that characterize many public and nonprofit organizations and communities, there will be a *consensus* on goals, policies, programs, and actions necessary to achieve organizational aims. The assumption just does not hold. Only in fairly centralized, authoritarian, and quasi-military bureaucracies will the assumption hold—maybe.

Now let us examine a model that contrasts sharply with the rational planning model, the political decision-making model presented in Figure 4. This model is inductive, not rational-deductive. It begins with issues, which by definition involve conflict, not consensus.

FIGURE 3
"Rational" Planning

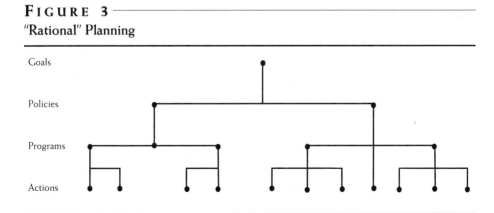

FIGURE 4
Political Decision Making

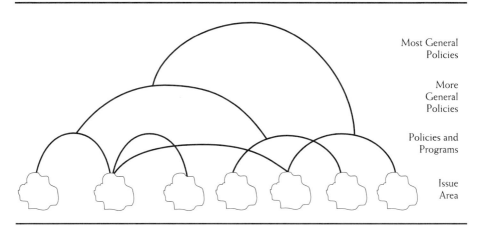

Most General
Policies

More
General
Policies

Policies and
Programs

Issue
Area

The conflicts may be over ends, means, timing, location, political advantage, and philosophy or reasons—and the conflicts may be severe. As efforts proceed to resolve the issues, policies and programs emerge that address the issues and that are politically rational, that is, they are politically acceptable to involved or affected parties. Over time, more general policies may be formulated to capture, frame, shape, guide, or interpret the policies and programs developed to deal with the issues. The various policies and programs are in effect treaties among the various stakeholder groups and, while they may not exactly record a consensus, at least they represent a reasonable level of agreement among stakeholders (Pfeffer and Salancik, 1978).

Now, recall that the heart of the strategic planning process discussed in this chapter is the identification and resolution of strategic—which is to say important—issues. The process, in other words, accepts political decision making's emphasis on issues and seeks to inform the formulation and resolution of those issues. Effective strategic planning therefore should make political decision makers more effective, and, if practiced consistently, might even make their professional lives easier. Since every key decision maker in a large public or nonprofit organization is, in effect, a political decision maker, strategic planning can help them and their organizations. Strategic planning therefore is an innovation that will last in government and nonprofit organizations. It will last because it accepts and builds on the nature of political decision making, and if done well actually improves political decisions, programs, and policies.

Now, having drawn a sharp distinction between the rational planning model and political decision making, I must emphasize that the two models are not inherently antithetical. They may simply need to be sequenced properly. The political decision-making model is necessary to work out a consensus on what programs and policies will best resolve key issues. The rational planning model can then be used to recast that consensus in the form of goals, policies, programs, and actions. While the planning and decision making that go into the formulation of a strategic plan may look fairly sloppy to an outsider, once a consensus is reached on what to do, the resulting strategic plan can be rewritten in a form that looks perfectly rational. The advantage of the strategic planning process outlined in this chapter is that it does not presume consensus where consensus does not exist.

SUMMARY

This reading has outlined an eight-step process for promoting strategic thinking and acting in governments, public agencies, nonprofit organizations, communities, or other entities. The steps are:

1. Initiating and agreeing on a strategic planning process.
2. Identifying organizational mandates.
3. Clarifying organizational mission and values.
4. Assessing the external environment: opportunities and threats.
5. Assessing the internal environment: strengths and weaknesses.
6. Identifying the strategic issues facing an organization.
7. Formulating strategies to manage the issues.
8. Establishing an effective organizational vision for the future, the "vision of success."

Following these eight steps come actions, results, and evaluation—all three of which should also emerge in each step of the process. Furthermore, while the process was presented in a linear, sequential fashion, typically it proceeds iteratively as groups continuously rethink connections among the various elements in the process on their way to formulating effective strategies. A set of sample strategic planning worksheets designed to help strategic planning teams work through the process is presented in Resource A.

Strategic planning is a management innovation that is likely to persist because, unlike many other recent innovations, it accepts and builds on the nature of *political* decision making. Raising and resolving important issues is the heart of political decision making, just as it is the heart of strategic planning. Strategic planning seeks to improve on the rawest forms of political decision making, however, by assuring that issues are raised and resolved in ways that benefit the organization and its key stakeholders.

REFERENCES

Barry, B. W. *Strategic Planning Workbook for Nonprofit Organizations.* St. Paul, Minn.: Amherst H. Wilder Foundation, 1986.

Eckhert, P., Haines, K., Delmont, T., and Pflaum, A. "Strategic Planning in Hennepin County, Minnesota: An Issues Management Approach." In J. M. Bryson and R. C. Einsweiler (eds.), *Strategic Planning—Threats and Opportunities for Planners.* Chicago and Washington: The Planners Press of the American Planning Association, 1988.

Einsweiler, R. C. "What the Top People Are Saying About Central City Planning." *Planning,* 1980, *46* (Oct.), 15–18.

Flynn, N. "Performance Measurement in Public Sector Services." *Policy and Politics,* 1986, 14(3), 389–404.

King, J., and Johnson, D. A. "The Oak Ridge, Tennessee Experience." In J.M. Bryson and R.C. Einsweiler (eds.), *Strategic Planning—Threats and Opportunities for Planners.* Chicago and Washington: The Planners Press of the American Planning Association, 1988.

Kouzes, J. M., and Posner, B. Z. *The Leadership Challenge: How to Get Extraordinary Things Done in Organizations.* San Francisco: Jossey-Bass, 1987.

Linneman, R. E., and Klein, H. E. "The Use of Multiple Scenarios by U.S. Industrial Companies: A Comparison Study, 1977–1981." *Long Range Planning*, 1983, *16*(6), 94–101.

Locke, E. A., Shaw, K. N., Saari, L. M., and Latham, G. P. "Goal Setting and Task Performance: 1969–1980." *Psychological Bulletin*, 1981, *90*, 125–152.

McGowan, R. P., And Stevens, J. M. "Local Government's Initiatives in a Climate of Uncertainty." *Public Administration Review*, 1983, *43*(2), 127–136.

May, R. *Love and Will.* New York: Norton, 1969.

Olsen, J. B., and Eadie, D. C. *The Game Plan: Governance with Foresight.* Washington: Council of State Planning Agencies, 1982.

Ouchi, W. *Theory Z: How Many American Businesses Can Meet the Japanese Challenge.* Reading, Mass.: Addison-Wesley, 1981.

Peters, T. J., and Waterman, R. H., Jr. *In Search of Excellence: Lessons from America's Best-Run Companies.* New York: Harper & Row, 1982.

Pfeffer, J., and Salancik, G. R. *The External Control of Organizations: A Resource Dependence Perspective.* New York: Harper & Row, 1978.

Pfeiffer, J. W., Goodstein, L. D., and Nolan, T.M. *Applied Strategic Planning: A How to Do It Guide.* San Diego, Calif.: University Associates, 1986.

Rider, R. W. "Making Strategic Planning Work in Local Government." *Long Range Planning*, 1983, *16*(3), 73–81.

Taylor, B. "Strategic Planning—Which Style Do You Need?" *Long Range Planning*, 1984, *17*, 51–62.

Thompson, J .D. *Organizations in Action.* New York: McGraw-Hill, 1967.

Tita, M. A., and Allio, R. J. "3M's Strategy System—Planning in an Innovative Organization." *Planning Review*, 1984 (September), *12*(5), 10–15.

Wildavsky, A. *Speaking Truth to Power.* Boston: Little, Brown, 1979.

PART 4

Political Strategy

Of Secretaries to Princes*

Thomas S. Axworthy
Executive Director of the CRB Foundation

INTRODUCTION

"The greatest trust between man and man," Francis Bacon advised, "is the trust of giving counsel."[1] If this is so, many current leaders have the right to feel abused. For example, on the eve of the 1996 Democratic convention, Dick Morris, President Clinton's longtime political strategist, was forced to resign because of personal peccadilloes. Morris later compounded his sin by signing a $2 million contract to write a tell-all book about the Clintons. As Juvenal asked in *The Sixteen Satires*, "But who is to keep guard over the guards themselves?"[2]

The recent spate of books on backroom advisers in the White House raises once again questions about leadership and democratic accountability. Do those in power—whether kings, presidents, or prime ministers—always require a loyal retinue? If so, what is the proper role of a leader's personal office? And what sort of qualities should he or she seek in a personal staff? Perhaps the most critical question of all is whether even a superbly advised leader can impose a pattern on events. Have our problems become too large, our systems too complex, our society too lacking in consensus for our politicians? They can preside but can anyone lead?

To help answer these questions, I will argue a three-part thesis:

- It is indeed possible to keep to a political agenda and to prevent the urgent from overwhelming the important. But to do so it is necessary to adopt a strategic approach to government. *Strategy necessitates choice.*
- To run a strategic presidency or prime ministership it is critical to recruit a highly competent personal staff. Nostalgia for simpler days is an inadequate response to the modern demands of government. A prime minister or president must make decisions on a host of matters about which he or she is not expert. *Choice necessitates advice.*
- In recruiting a personal staff a leader must distinguish between the demands of partisanship and the virtues of a professional civil service. Partisans bring creativity; public servants provide perspective. The political arm makes things move; bureaucratic routines prevent

*"Of Secretaries and Princes" by Thomas Axworthy. Reprinted by permission of the author.

errors. Both kinds of counsel are necessary, but in Canada we are now in danger of doing permanent damage to the concept of a neutral civil service. Paradoxically, a strongly partisan personal office is the best way to defend an apolitical public service. *Good advice necessitates different kinds of expertise.*

In making these arguments I will refer to episodes drawn from my decade (1974–1984) of service in the government of Canada, largely in the prime minister's office of Pierre Trudeau. Alert readers, therefore, should be ever wary of the danger of ex post facto self-justification. Dean Acheson, no mean chronicler himself, wisely cautioned that he had never read a report of a conversation in which the author came out second best.[3]

THE LAW OF ACCELERATION

Even the greatest of political leaders have often wearily agreed with Emerson that "things are in the saddle, and ride mankind."[4] Lincoln confessed that "I claim not to have controlled events, but confess plainly that events have controlled me."[5] Bismarck, no shrinking violet when it came to self-confidence, believed that "man cannot create the current of events. He can only float with it and steer."[6]

The pessimism of such great statesmen about their ability to master the forces transforming the 19th century is all the more striking because today the pace of change is accelerating at an exponential rate. Technology strides ahead. The number of actors on the global scene shoots upward. Interactions increase. Interdependence expands. No state, not even the most powerful, is any longer in complete control of its own destiny. Historian Arthur Schlesinger Jr., for example, has calculated that the past 2 lifetimes have seen more change than the planet's first 798 put together.[7]

The cumulative impact of such revolutions leaves one breathless. One part of us rejoices at the affluence and leisure that new technology brings. Another side of our soul hungers for stability. Politicians are caught in the middle, not knowing whether to welcome the new world or to defend the old ways. But as Henry Adams warned, "a law of acceleration, definite and constant as any law of mechanics, cannot be supposed to relax its energy to suit the conveniences of man."[8]

The demands placed on the time, energy, and physical resources of our leaders by this complex machinery are enormous. In 1983 Ian Clark, the deputy secretary to the cabinet, completed a study for the Organization for Economic Cooperation and Development (OECD) on Canada's central decision-making system.[9] Pressures on ministers were intense. In 1982–1983, for example, 300 meetings were held of full cabinet or cabinet committees, 900 cabinet memoranda circulated (how many read?), 750 policy decisions taken, 75 bills drafted, 4,000 order in council appointments made, and 6,000 Treasury Board spending decisions taken. As an additional example, a case study showed that the Department of Regional and Industrial Economic Expansion alone made a further 4,700 spending decisions, all of them theoretically under the purview of the minister. No human being could long keep up even with the press of this government business, let alone the equally heavy demands of constituents, party militants, media, and interest groups. To survive, one must choose. And to choose well one needs a strategic conception of the job.

A STRATEGIC PRIME MINISTERSHIP

In a healthy democracy, politics should mean more than a single-minded pursuit of office. Tyrants need seek only power. But leaders in a self-governing democracy must build a reciprocal relationship of trust and support with their fellow citizens. Democratic politics, therefore, is fundamentally a debate about conviction, whereas democratic leadership is the ability to educate, arouse, and energize citizens to work for goals that represent mutual values.

Put simply, a strategic approach to politics is the intelligent application of priorities to the complicated world of clashing values and interests. There is no magic to it: one decides on objectives, assesses the difficulties in achieving them, and calculates the resources available to throw into the contest. Yet, though easy to outline, strategic politics is excruciatingly difficult to implement. A leader must choose, from among a vast array of problems, which three or four issues will receive his or her individual attention. Once the choice is made events, or the competing priorities of colleagues, can too easily edge aside the top items of the agenda. With a plethora of ministries and a multiplicity of decision makers, even politicians with the best of intentions may not be able to coordinate action or concentrate sufficient resources to make headway.

In this endless battle to rescue an element of choice from the pressure of events, you may fail even with a strategic approach. But you are certain to fail without it. Recommending such a course, I once wrote Prime Minister Trudeau that the purpose of the prime minister's office (PMO) was "to join policy and politics, structure and process in a coherent plan that can change with events (but not too often) and that takes into account constraints and available resources."[10] To achieve this, four different components should interconnect:

Policy: Where do you want to go?

Politics: How do you get there?

Structure: How do you distribute authority?

Process: How do you run the system?

POLICY

Politicians are expected to have a five-point platform on every problem facing government. Although it is easy to design such a program, if a leader has not made a real intellectual and emotional commitment to the ideas, they remain only fodder for campaign speeches. A leader who has not identified those few policy themes most fundamental to his or her conception of the job before arriving in office will have difficulty putting an imprint on affairs while in office.

In a four-year term, a prime minister has the time to concentrate extensively on four or five issues at most. This is not to suggest that a prime minister can or should ignore the routine of government. Mistakes avoided are just as important as bills passed. It simply means that a leader can expend a significant amount of personal energy only on relatively few subjects. Since the most valuable resource in Ottawa is the time of the prime minister, to work intensively on four or five problems requires saying no to hundreds of other requests.

In a strategic prime ministership, it is the task of the PMO to deal with the disgruntled. In the 1980–1984 government, for example, the four priorities of constitutional reform, the national energy program, anti-inflation policy, and the peace initiative took up much of the prime minister's time. To allow Mr. Trudeau to concentrate on them our office systematically reduced the paper flow, spun out functions such as order in council appointments to other ministers, and took care that his luncheon guests included outsiders knowledgeable in the priority areas. Together with the reforms in the cabinet process initiated by the secretary to the cabinet Michael Pitfield (discussed later), these measures reduced the prime minister's involvement in administration and gave him time to manage personally his key concerns.

If prime ministers can at best immerse themselves in four or five key policy areas, the cabinet can devote substantial effort to only a further 25 or 30 problems. While Mr. Trudeau was working on the charter of rights or the peace initiative, for example, the minister of transport was engaged in negotiations over freight rates and the minister of finance was fighting unemployment. It is a sobering thought that the reputation and impact of a government rests on only the 25 issues that receive the top priority out of the 1,000 plus cabinet memoranda that will be produced by the bureaucracy in a four-year term. Thousands of issues must be managed but only 25 problems can receive full political attention. This basket of 25 priorities must meet the needs of the country, respond to the ideology of the party, and pass muster with the citizens of the policy. The success of a strategic prime ministership rests on which 25 issues are chosen.

POLITICS

Timing, organization, and communication are the very stuff of politics. Knowing when to proceed and when to delay, sensing when to be bold and when to be prudent, calculating the forces pro and con—these are the intuitive arts possessed by all great politicians. Timing makes or breaks a government. In 1974, for example, Mr. Trudeau's reelected government spent its first year debating issues in a model planning exercise; but by the time it was ready to move, economic events had overtaken it, wage and price controls had to be introduced, and the government never really recovered its balance. In 1980, by contrast, Mr. Trudeau moved quickly to use the results of the climactic Quebec referendum to spur the country to accept radical constitutional change.

Organizational politics is coalition building, pure and simple. Who can you bring onside and with what degree of intensity? Every government needs allies, especially those with media credibility. Over time, for example, the Trudeau government lost the support of business. No reform government can reasonably expect to have substantial support from this sector, but it was a serious weakness not to have a working, or even a civil, relationship with such a powerful interest. In his last government, Mr. Trudeau spent time trying to develop new allies—with the cooperative movement, for example—but the new friends gained never equalled the weight of the old friends lost.

The traditional cry of losing governments is that "our policies weren't wrong; they were simply not understood." More often than not, citizens understand their governments very well and that is exactly why the party in power loses, but the centrality of good communications can hardly be in doubt. Every great leader is a master of the communication medium of the age: Lincoln, the outdoor rally; Roosevelt, the radio; and Trudeau, the television set. It is no good decrying the age of the 30-second clip: one must simply master it, or disappear.

Policies that ignore politics quickly come to grief. Ukases that come down from on high with neither public support nor a plan to garner any are more commonly a failure of government than failure of an administration with few ideas. Politicians who become so convinced of the righteousness of their cause that they expect the public meekly to follow reflexively their banner forget that leadership in a democracy is reciprocal: the leader must first identify with the needs, aspirations, and values of the public before he or she can begin to educate. Moral leadership emerges from and always returns to the fundamental values of society, and party politics is the main venue for this debate over values.

A prime minister must lead a party before he or she leads a government. Parties represent a particular constellation of values, interests, blocs, and localities. Politics is a never-ending process of satisfying your supporters, disengaging the supporters of your opponents, and attracting the uninterested. The ideas that drive policy must somehow connect with the public. Thus, communicating the values inherent in a policy directive is just as important as writing a bill. Building a coalition to organize around an idea is just as important as passing a law. Ministering to a party, knowing the needs of the militants, and maintaining the sinews of organizational strength are crucial to a successful prime ministership. The party base should never be forgotten.

Policy and politics should intersect most dramatically at election time, but in Canada the conduct of modern campaigns is invariably a record of opportunities lost. The duty of the party is to define problems and find answers. In Great Britain political parties issue detailed manifestos outlining their visions of the future. In Canada personal image rather than policy substance drives the race. Policy announcements are too often viewed as tactical devices to be dropped whenever media attention is flagging. The press, which must be fed, is daily doled out a policy Gainsburger.

When politicians treat the party policy process so cavalierly, they fail the people. Trust, involvement, and ultimately faith in our system of self-government fade away if parties continually denigrate the intelligence of the citizenry. But such politicians also fool themselves: by starving their campaigns of a policy content, they are throwing away one of the most powerful instruments of reform. Elections bestow moral legitimacy; policy mandates give leaders the opportunity to overcome vested interests, to impart urgency to a sluggish public service, to demand sacrifices from a people, and to instill resolve within a cabinet and caucus. In 1962–1963 the Pearson Liberals, for example, made a major expansion of the welfare state a crucial part of their electoral appeal. Despite being a minority administration, the first Pearson government used this mandate to transform Canada's system of social security.

A strategic prime ministership, therefore, should begin to put down its roots in the campaign headquarters. The kind of campaign waged has a direct bearing on the nature of the government to follow. In the heat of an election it is difficult to have such discipline: one more promise to one more group may win one more seat. But by a curious process, the seeds of the next defeat are often sown in the moment of a seeming triumph.

STRUCTURE

The structure of decision making can determine whether a strategic prime ministership will work or not. While the pattern of authority must give the chief executive enough time to work on the central agenda, it must also allow the government as a whole to get on with its business. A prime minister may define a set of priorities, but his or her cabinet colleagues will have their own concerns and the routine of government involves hundreds of daily decisions. A prime minister who has a well-developed policy sense but whose government is continually blown off course by a series of minor crises is perilously neglecting structure.

In Mr. Trudeau's final term, Michael Pitfield, secretary of the cabinet, created a balanced structure that gave the prime minister overview responsibility while decentralizing major areas of decision making. The full cabinet and the priorities and planning committee, both chaired by the prime minister, concerned themselves largely with the central political objectives of the government. The strategic prime ministership was implemented through these two forms. Spending envelope decisions and sectoral strategies were delegated to cabinet committees on economic development and social policy. Removing spending fights and program auctions from the cabinet agenda freed important time for the discussion of central themes while the committee structure attended to specific needs.

PROCESS

Pierre Trudeau ran a collegial government and no apologies need be made for that style. He seldom reserved decisions for himself and loved instead to have his cabinet and caucus debate issues at length. The Trudeau style was undoubtedly time consuming and even frustrating to the ministers involved, but, as Bismarck once remarked, people with weak stomachs should not observe the manufacture either of sausages or of new laws. A collegial style of government gave ministers the right not only to run their departments but to question and to participate in the responsibilities of their colleagues. Critics point to the vast proliferation of paper, and several former ministers in the Trudeau cabinet have voiced their dissatisfaction with the consensual system.[11] Such a system is ponderous, but it is also fair. Ministers have to defend the policies of their colleagues. They should have some say in determining them.

One of the wisest maxims of public administration is "where you stand depends on where you sit."[12] Occasionally ministers define their role as implementing the government's priorities within their respective departments. But more commonly, ministers see themselves as being the spokespeople of their departmental interests to the prime minister and cabinet. Having 30 ministers in a room usually leads to 30 definitions of the public interest. A prime minister must bring order out of this babel and find the common thread that unites.

Discussion invites participation. Participation increases involvement. Involvement may lead to commitment. Such a progression is central to the concept of a strategic prime ministership. Ordering ministers or caucus members to toe a line is far less effective than winning their support through engagement. To persuade the 30 members of the cabinet or the 140 members of the caucus to put aside their parochial concerns to take up a central quest is the essence of parliamentary leadership. An engaged cabinet, caucus, or party can do wonders; a sullen group of colleagues simply sits on their hands. Prime ministers *must* seek to widen the circle of the committed.

THE GUARDIANS

Access to power, Plato advised, should be confined to men who are not in love with it.[13] Yet as with many of Plato's ideals, human nature keeps getting in the way. Every king has a court. People are attracted to power as moths are to a flame. Yet with examples like Oliver North, whose freelancing in the Iran-Contra affair seriously wounded President Reagan, or Dick Morris, who has recently embarrassed the Clintons, we should at least revisit Plato's critical question: What virtues should the city demand of its guardians?

Since every leader must constantly make decisions about matters in which he is not expert, the beginning of wisdom is to know what one does not know. Advisers should be recruited to fill the gaps in a leader's experience. The first rule of the office, therefore, is to recruit complementary skills. If the leader has spent a lifetime in the party but lacks policy depth, the staff should have a strong intellectual base. If a leader is relatively remote from party activists, assistants with extensive personal networks are needed. Balance should be sought not only between the leader and the staff but also within the office staff. Enthusiasm must be tempered with experience. The prime minister's office or the White House is not the best place for on-the-job training. Ignorance causes trouble. Robert Lovett, one of the wisest of President Truman's counselors, believed that "Good judgment is invariably the result of experience. And experience is frequently the result of bad judgment."[14] A sagacious leader will insist on a staff that has already learned from mistakes made elsewhere.

Loyalty is perhaps the virtue most praised and least practiced among politicians. Leaders hunger for loyalty because it is so rare. "Power is poison,"[15] wrote Henry Adams. He meant by that not only the corrosive effect authority has on the character of a leader, but also the predatory environment in which he or she must live. Everyone wants something. Supplicants want to use a leader's power for their ends; the leader wants to persuade them that his or her objectives should be their objectives. In this heated atmosphere having the support of people who genuinely want to promote your interest, as opposed to their own, is a valued commodity. Franklin D. Roosevelt explained his support of a controversial adviser in just such a way. To Wendell Willkie, his Republican opponent in the 1940 presidential election, he said, "Practically everybody who walks through that door wants something out of you. You'll learn what a lonely job this is and you'll discover the need for somebody like Harry Hopkins who wants nothing except to serve you."[16] Leaders need emotional succor. Staffs provide it.

But loyalty is not the same as sycophancy. As Cardinal Richelieu warned, "there is no plague more capable of ruining a state than the host of flatterers."[17] The best single test of loyalty is to tell the truth. Often the greatest service rendered to a leader is to force him or her to face unpalatable realities. To be able to do so requires a relationship of trust and respect.

Such a relationship usually rests on three building blocks. First, a leader has a right to demand high levels of performance. Mr. Trudeau's general standard was perfection, to be surpassed on special occasions! Second, a leader has the right to demand staff anonymity: it is the elected politicians who need publicity, not those who never have to face the voters. "The best way to stay out of trouble," President Kennedy told Theodore Sorenson, "is to stay out of sight."[18] Third, if a leader has the right to demand competence and anonymity, a staff should insist on a civilized norm of behavior. Some leaders, such as Lyndon Johnson, are prone to tantrums, abusive language, and lapses in decorum. In contrast, in Mr. Trudeau's office civility was the rule. Advisers who allow themselves to be abused eventually lose the respect of their masters. In the words of Walter Bagehot, "no man can argue on his knees."[19]

A PARTISAN OFFICE

In 1873 the new prime minister of Canada, Alexander Mackenzie, with not even a secretary to handle his mail, answered all letters himself, complaining "as letters come in bushels I have to answer them as fast as I can drive the pen."[20] In 1983 Mr. Trudeau received 9,000 pieces of mail a week, a volume that not even the industrious Mr. Mackenzie could have kept up with. Unsurprisingly, as the scope of government has expanded in Canada, so too has the size of the prime minister's personal office.

In 1968 Mr. Trudeau initiated one of the most significant structural changes in the history of Candian government. Before Mr. Trudeau, prime ministers' personal staffs were almost all seconded from the civil service. Sometimes the adviser was personally recruited by the prime minister, as was Arnold Heeney in 1938 or Tom Kent in 1963. On occasions an official who had entered the public service by the normal route of civil service examinations might show an aptitude for politics and, by close association with the prime minister, grow into a partisan. Such was the case with J.W. Pickersgill. Mr. Trudeau changed all that by making it clear that his personal staff would be openly partisan. Thus a new category of official was created—the political adviser. This was not new in the United States, where Roosevelt's advisers, such as Harry Hopkins, were explicitly partisan, but it was new in Canada. In the same period Harold Wilson's government in Great Britain also began to experiment with partisan advisers. The role of such individuals differed from that of the public service: they would advise on the interaction of policy and politics and not be subject to the formal rules of the public service. They could enter government without examination and they would leave government without the protection of the Public Service Act. Mr. Trudeau made the system honest by acknowledging what always had been the case—politics was part of the prime minister's office. It had been duplicitous to paper over this function with the screen of civil service impartiality.

In his last year as prime minister, 1983–1984, Mr. Trudeau's personal office employed 87 people and had an estimated budget of $4.2 million. The prime minister's civil service secretariat—the privy council office and federal provincial relations division—had 275 positions. These numbers pale in comparison to the United States. In the mid-1980s there were approximately 400 political staff members in the White House and 1,500 public servants in the executive branch. The prime minister's office has grown further under Prime Minister Mulroney: in 1985–1986 the PMO expanded to 117 with a budget of $6.6 million.

As is often pointed out in the literature, the Trudeau PMO was double the size of Mr. Pearson's. But these numbers can be deceiving, because three-quarters of the staff slots were taken up by secretarial or correspondence positions. Most people in the PMO simply answered the mail or the telephones. Only 20 or so persons were senior advisers. Although 20 is not a large number for such an office, my preference would be for an even smaller number.

In 1979 after the election defeat, as leader of the opposition Mr. Trudeau reduced his staff by 60 percent to only 30 with 12 senior people. Despite the obvious differences, that small staff functioned more cohesively with as much impact as the larger PMOs that preceded and followed it. A prime minister requires a few assistants, not another layer of bureaucracy. The purpose of the staff is to leave the leader more time, rather than less, to concentrate on major policy decisions. A large staff usually generates more work by taking up everyone's time in endless staff meetings. For the purposes of staffing a prime minister's office, the operative principle should be that less is more.

The personal office of the leader should make contributions to the four dimensions of the strategic prime ministership outlined earlier:

Policy: Knowing the trends

Politics: Promoting the party perspective

Structure: Knitting things together

Process: Keeping a grip during a crisis

POLICY INTELLIGENCE

Information is power. This may be a cliché but it is still a powerful insight. The PMO must connect daily with other assistants on the Hill, with the caucus, the party, and the media to keep abreast of events. My foremost objective—not often reached—was to avoid surprises. Part of the intelligence-gathering function should be to assess what the opposition is likely to do: on most issues my office spent considerable time on competitor analysis. Although personal networks are crucial for managing the information flow, polls provide the most reliable assessment of public opinion. Quarterly, the PMO in 1980–1984 prepared an assessment of public opinion and presented it to the cabinet. Every cabinet meeting, of course, gave ministers the opportunity to raise political issues under the regular agenda item of "Communications," but the quarterly "political" cabinet was the essential clearinghouse for the partisan agenda.

Party activists help create the climate of values to which decision makers respond. Individual members of the cabinet and the caucus bring regional perspectives to bear. The great departments of state have their own interests and are a vast reservoir of expertise. The prime minister's office must balance the competing priorities by assessing them against a standard of public acceptability. The PMO is more often a policy synthesizer than a policy initiator.

PARTISANSHIP

The PMO, along with party headquarters, is a central partisan agency. Just as the Finance Department brings economic expertise to a discussion and the Foreign Affairs Department advances international policy considerations, a role of the PMO is to promote a partisan perspective. Even though the partisan perspective does not always carry the day, it is essential that ministers understand the political implications of policy discussions. To that end, PMO advisers in Mr. Trudeau's office spent their time on major theme documents, such as the Speech from the Throne or the annual planning agenda meetings of the cabinet. Operational responsibilities were few; coordinating and goal-setting responsibilities were uppermost. Prior to the Speech from the Throne, for example, the PMO would research relevant Liberal party policy resolutions, work closely with the Liberal Party Policy Committee, and interview all ministers individually to get as complete a picture as possible of the political priorities. This role, however, was generally resented by the party militants rather than applauded. The feeling grew that the PMO was not transmitting party views so much as manipulating them. Such tensions, while perhaps inevitable, are ultimately self-defeating. Because the partisan perspective must compete with real power holders, such as those representing the Finance Department, a divided political wing simply means that bureaucratic priorities rather than political necessities will prevail.

COORDINATION

James Coutts, my predecessor as principal secretary, described the PMO as "a switchboard," and that metaphor is apt. As a central political agency it connects the party with the bureaucracy. More time in the PMO is spent on coordination than on any other activity. The romantic image (cultivated most assiduously by members of the PMO itself) portrays the staffer having long heart-to-heart talks with the prime minister, but in reality most members of the office spend their days with ministers, members of Parliament, and other assistants. Weeks may go by without a member of the PMO even seeing the prime minister.

With 30 government departments, 12 provincial party associations, and nearly 300 ridings, the job of meshing the various components of this huge machine is enormous. Even a simple task such as organizing the ministers' speaking engagements, so that Canada's outlying regions receive some attention, takes hundreds of phone calls. A strategic prime ministership must choose relatively few central themes, not only because of the time demands on the prime minister, but also because it takes a Herculean effort to coordinate the government machine.

CRISIS MANAGEMENT

Only crises came to the PMO; the easier problems got solved elsewhere. The critical clearinghouse of the PMO from 1981 through 1984 was a daily 8:30 A.M. meeting chaired by the principal secretary and including all senior staff. Here information was exchanged and tactics discussed. The operations, policy, and communications divisions of the office also attempted to have weekly planning meetings to anticipate future crises rather than reacting to daily concerns. Despite this heroic goal, such meetings often dissolved into tactical firefighting sessions. The only compensation in all this was knowing that the ability to defuse a crisis, promote calm, and instill confidence is among the most important characteristics of a central political staff. The only infallible rule is that crises are a true test of whether an office has the creativity and good humor to master events.

PRESERVING THE PUBLIC SERVICE

I believe in a strong partisan prime minister's office. If politics is a debate about values, there is a need for a contingent of value-driven people to influence the direction of the state. Commitment fosters creativity. It is the political dynamic of our system that brings about reform. But good government needs other virtues besides creativity. Impartiality, experience, and caution are equally important components to policy making. These virtues the public service provides. The Canadian system of government with its amalgam of partisan advisers and neutral public servants combines equal doses of commitment and consistency.

A close partnership between the principal secretary and the clerk of the privy council is crucial to the workings of a strategic prime ministership. Because both officers have equal access to the prime minister, it is essential that they establish between them an atmosphere of trust. I established with the two clerks with whom it was my privilege to work, Michael Pitfield and Gordon Osbaldeston, one overarching rule—no games. When we disagreed about the timing or substance of government policy, such arguments were to be made to the prime minister directly, most often at the daily 9:15 A.M. joint planning meeting. Briefing notes were equally shared. After the demise of the 1981 budget, I also made a special effort to share information with the deputy minister of finance. Prime ministers require both a partisan and a public service perspective. If either is systematically excluded or ignored, trouble will result.

Pierre Trudeau did the right thing in 1968. By creating the modern partisan PMO he made our system honest. It should be kept that way.

AN EVALUATION

Even if a strategic prime ministership is successfully implemented, there is, of course, a price to be paid. Donald Johnston, a senior minister in the Trudeau cabinets, laments, for example, that although in the 1970s Mr. Trudeau scrutinized every item on the cabinet agenda with zest, in his last term many issues were left to others: "After 1980 Trudeau no longer took home three binders of briefings for thorough study."[21] Johnston is right, but that was exactly the intent. Rather than the prime minister spending most of his time managing a great number of items, after 1980 Mr. Trudeau wanted to concentrate on a few big ones. Only with maximum prime ministerial involvement could the host of obstacles that stand in the way of reform be overcome. The crucial question in a strategic approach, then, is which big items?

In the 1980–1981 battle to repatriate the Constitution and entrench the Charter of Rights and Freedoms, all four components of the strategic approach were synchronized.[22] The policy was far reaching. The decision to have a parliamentary committee hold public hearings helped create a vast constituency in favor of the Charter of Rights, and by this device policy reform and organizational politics meshed as one. Structurally, the prime minister used the cabinet and the Planning and Priorities Committee to discuss fully the general terms while Justice Minister Jean Chretien employed his considerable skills in the day-to-day negotiations with the provinces. The Liberal party made constitutional reform central to its political appeal. Both the caucus and the cabinet believed that they had moved Mr. Trudeau to take even bolder steps than he had originally contemplated. The circle of commitment, therefore, was large and deep. And it had to be for, even with all this in place, provincial opposition to the charter was so intense that the battle for constitutional reform was, in the words of Wellington at Waterloo, "the nearest run thing you ever saw in your life."

By contrast, tax reform in 1981 was a major failure. In this, the outmoded process of budget making in Canada was the major culprit. In 1979 the Platform Committee of the Liberal party had recommended that tax loopholes be closed and income tax rates reduced. Finance Minister Allan MacEachen was thus implementing Liberal policy when he attempted such a reform in 1981. This fact was conveniently forgotten by many in the party and caucus when the debate turned sour.

But if the basic policy idea was good, almost every other canon of strategy was ignored. As senior political adviser to the prime minister at the time, I deserve my fair share of the blame. Like many I was so caught up in the constitutional and energy battles—which occurred at exactly the same time as Mr. MacEachen's budget planning—that the economic agenda was left solely to the Department of Finance. There were other errors and oversights. The Liberal party favored tax reform but had not campaigned on it. No public constituency had been created. Policy was divorced from politics. The tradition of budget secrecy has not changed since the era of Gladstone; because of this convention Mr. MacEachen did not benefit from the political and expert advice of his cabinet colleagues. The cabinet was surprised by the scope of the 1981 budget, and, when the attacks began, few defended it because none had a role in formulating it. Consultation with involved interest groups had also been minimal. In short, tax reform was a debacle for the Trudeau government. By contrast, in 1986 the Reagan administration made tax reform a hallmark of the president's second administration. James Baker did everything right, whereas we did everything wrong.

The sad history of the 1981 budget also suggests that whatever the four or five overall priorities of a government, the economy must always be one of them. Politically, the economy may be a no-win issue, but neglect will turn it into a clear loss. Living standards are nearly always the principal object of public concern, and no government can afford to ignore this reality.

Expectations will always exceed results, but the resulting dissatisfaction is simply a fact of 20th-century political life. Charles de Gaulle described this melancholy dilemma in his memoirs:

> At grips day after day with national and human realities in a sphere in which all is asperity, in which nothing is once and for all achieved, in which no one is ever remotely satisfied with what he gets, I was reminded that economic progress, like life itself, is a struggle whose course is never marked by a decisive victory. Even on the day of an Austerlitz the sun does not emerge to light up the battlefield.[23]

CONCLUSIONS

Government can make a difference only if there is true appreciation of how difficult and crucial it is to retain an element of choice from the welter of changing events. The urgent is always crowding out the important. A strategic approach and a strong partisan office, however, can help a leader master events. In summary, my recommendations are as follows:

- Have an agenda before you go in.
- Use the election campaign to seek a policy mandate.
- Concentrate on only a few themes, know the trade-offs, and never ignore the economy.
- Combine policy, politics, structure, and process into a coherent plan.
- Keep the personal staff small and give them thematic, not operational, responsibilities.
- Never forget that a political party is made up of volunteers.
- Never blur partisan and public service roles. Each has a different contribution to make.

Finally, despite the current attention focused on advisers and the back room, we should never forget that it is the elected politicians who make our system of self-government run. As Machiavelli recognized, "it is an infallible rule that a prince who is not wise himself cannot be well advised."[24]

NOTES

[1] Francis Bacon, *A Selection of His Works*, ed. Sidney Warhaft (Indianapolis, IN: Bobbs-Merrill, 1965), 97.

[2] Juvenal, *The Sixteen Satires*, trans. Peter Gneon (Harmondsworth, Middlesex: Penguin Books, 1967), 140.

[3] Quoted in Henry Kissinger, *White House Years* (Bantam: Little, Brown, 1979), xxii.

[4] Ralph Waldo Emerson, *The Selected Writings*, ed. Brooks Atkinson (New York: Modern Library, 1968), 770.

[5] Quoted in Arthur M. Schlesinger Jr., *The Cycles of American History* (Boston: Houghton McMillan, 1986), 168.

[6] A. J. P. Taylor, *Bismarck: The Man and the Statesman* (New York: Vintage Books, 1955), 70.

[7] Schlesinger, *Cycles*, xi.

[8] Henry Adams, *The Education of Henry Adams* (New York: The Modern Library, 1918), 493.

[9] Ian Clark, "A New Look into the Privy Council Office," December 30, 1983. Clark made his findings known through a series of public speeches to groups such as the chamber of commerce and the Ontario federal council.

[10] My 1981 memo to the prime minister on the need for a strategic approach drew heavily on a study of the Carter presidency by two former Carter assistants. See Benjamin W. Heineman Jr. and Curtis A. Hessler, *Memorandum for the President: A Strategic Approach to Domestic Affairs in the 1980's* (New York: Random House, 1980).

[11] See, for example, Donald Johnston, *Up the Hill* (Montreal: Optimum Publishing International, 1986), 53–73; Jean Chretien, *Straight from the Heart* (Toronto: Key Porter Books, 1985), 75–76; John Roberts, *Agenda for Canada: Towards a New Liberalism* (Toronto: Lester and Orpen Dennys, 1985), 47–50; and Eugene Whelan, *Whelan: The Man in the Green Hat* (Toronto: Irwin, 1986), 213–14. With so much firepower directed against the Trudeau planning system, a casual observer would naturally conclude that it must have been conceptually flawed. Mistakes were undoubtedly made. The frustrations expressed by the former ministers are evidently deeply felt. Yet many of the criticisms are remarkably similar to the broadsides Richard Crossman directed at the office of Harold Wilson in *The Diaries of a Cabinet Minister*, vols. I, II, and III (London: Hamish Hamilton and Jonathan Cape, 1975, 1976, and 1977). Frustration in a strong minister with central authority seems to be endemic. In that sense one begins to understand Charles C. Dawe's famous remark that "the Members of the Cabinet are a President's natural enemies" (quoted in Roger B. Porter, *Presidential Decision-Making: The Economic Policy Board* (New York: Cambridge University Press, 1980), 18. Good ministers have strong views about policy; they fight one another mercilessly to gain program resources; they believe that if only the prime minister would accept their point of view all would be sweetness and light. The problem is that in a cabinet of 30 or 40 individuals these views are often diametrically opposed. A prime minister must balance the opposing views while keeping the proponents within the nest. Ministers in a cabinet are always slightly disgruntled because no one ever gets their way completely.

The primary role of a central agency in such situations is to play fair. All sides should get a hearing. Cabinet agendas, time set aside for discussions, and private meetings with the prime minister must all be allocated impartially. One critic who disagrees that the Trudeau POM-PCO played fair is Donald Johnston. Mr. Johnston takes two incidents—the purchase of Petrofina by Petro Canada and the announcement of the Macdonald Commission—as evidence that ministers were excluded from key decisions. Petrofina was obviously a special case because it was a commercial transaction and the circle of insiders was kept very small (for what it is worth I was also excluded from those in the know), whereas the public announcement of the Macdonald

Commission was a quick response to a press leak. Two incidents out of the 300 issues annually brought to cabinet is not overwhelming evidence. Mr. Chretien, for example, has the opposite complaint. He wrote that Mr. Trudeau arranged too much discussion: "he was extraordinarily patient, he let everyone have a say, and he listened attentively, sometimes he was too patient, too generous . . . more often than not you wished that Trudeau would bring down the gavel" (p. 75). When the cabinet minutes are opened 30 years hence they will show that on issues such as the Constitution, energy, cruise missile testing, and the peace initiative, Mr. Trudeau returned again and again to his colleagues for advice and reflection. The Trudeau system of planning may have had many defects, but lack of ministerial involvement was not one of them.

[12] Richard E. Neustadt and Ernest R. May, *Thinking in Time: The Uses of History for Decision-Making* (New York: The Free Press, 1986), 157.

[13] Plato, *The Republic*, trans. B. Jowett (New York: Viking Books), chap. VII, 520–21.

[14] Quoted in Neustadt and May, *Thinking in Time*, 11.

[15] Adams, *The Education of Henry Adams*, 418.

[16] Quoted in Michael Medved, *The Shadow Presidents: The Secret History of the Chief Executives and Their Top Aides* (New York: Times Books, 1979), 198.

[17] Cardinal Richelieu, *The Political Testament*, trans. Henry Bertnan Hill (Madison, WI: The University of Wisconsin Press, 1961), 111.

[18] Medved, *The Shadow Presidents*, 355.

[19] Quoted in R. M. Punnett, *The Prime Minister in Canadian Government and Politics* (Toronto: Macmillan of Canada, 1977), 75.

[20] Ibid.

[21] Johnston, *Up the Hill*, 54.

[22] For my analysis of the constitutional debate, see Thomas S. Axworthy, "Colliding Visions: The Debate over the Charter of Rights and Freedoms 1980–81," in *The Journal of Commonwealth and Comparative Politics* 24 (November 1986): 239–53.

[23] Charles de Gaulle, *Memoirs of Hope: Renewal and Endeavour*, trans. Terence Kilmartin (New York: Simon and Schuster, 1971), 162.

[24] Niccolo Machiavelli, *The Prince and the Discourses* (New York: Modern Library, 1951), 88.

Toward a Methodology of Stakeholder Analysis*

THOMAS WELSH AND NOEL MCGINN

Stakeholder analysis is now widely accepted as an important method for increasing information for decision making and for increasing commitment to decisions once made. The concept is used in both business management and program evaluation even though there is no apparent communication among researchers in the two fields. Apparently the concept first appeared in a publication in 1965 (Ansoff 1965) but was first used in 1963 at the Stanford Research Institute (Freeman 1984). Stakeholder participation was featured in Ackoff's early work on strategy for corporate redesign (Ackoff 1974). Today many texts on corporate management recommend stakeholder analysis, especially for strategic management and planning (Alkhafaji 1989; Bryson 1990; Godet 1991; Hatten and Hatten 1988; Stoner and Freeman 1992). Information about stakeholders, who make up the environment of the organization, can enhance achievement of organizational goals. The active involvement of stakeholders in organizational planning and decision making increases the likelihood of successful action. More recently, the stakeholder concept has been used to critique the ethics of business practices (Collins 1989; Langtry 1994) and to propose a form of business organization controlled by stakeholders (Schlossberger 1994; Weiss 1994).

There is little cross-fertilization between business management writers and those who advocate stakeholder analysis for program evaluation. For example, a recent review of research on *participatory evaluation* (Cousins and Earl 1992) lists more than 80 references of which only two (Argyris and Schon 1978; Senge 1990) can be considered to be from business management. Neither of the two cited make important use of the stakeholder concept.

The concept of stakeholder analysis apparently was first used for program evaluation in the 1970s by the National Institute of Education in efforts to improve program design and management (Bryk 1983; Stake 1975). Enthusiasm for the involvement of stakeholders in evaluation design and program implementation has grown steadily. The concept now appears often in reports of change strategies for educational organizations and for technical assistance projects in developing countries (Bamberger 1991; Lawrence 1989; Salmen 1989; Thompson 1991).

The following arguments are given in support of stakeholder involvement. First, decision making can be improved by increasing information both about the range of concerns,

---

*"Toward a Methodology of Stakeholder Analysis" by Thomas Welsh and Noel McGinn. Reprinted by permission of the author.

objectives, and commitments of intended beneficiaries of programs and about alternative means to meet those objectives and concerns while sustaining the commitment. For example, the involvement of parents in the design of a new curriculum unit may alert planners to sensitive topics that should be avoided. Teachers may be able to suggest alternative ways to organize the unit. Second, the involvement of groups interested in the process and outcome of programs increases the understanding of those groups about the objectives and constraints, heightens the legitimacy of whatever policies are finally chosen, and contributes to mobilizing support for policy implementation. The benefits of involving stakeholders in the planning and decision process are recognized both by those who operate within the critical realist perspective and by constructivists (Maxwell and Lincoln 1990).

Most methodological work on stakeholders for educational organizations has focused on techniques for obtaining information from stakeholders (e.g., Brandon et al. 1993a; Brandon et al. 1993b; Hallett and Rogers 1994), rather than on their identification. Weiss (1983) developed one of the few lists of groups that should be included as stakeholders. In most publications, the selection of possible participants is ad hoc (that is, based on specific circumstances rather than derived from a formal method of identification). With few exceptions (Timar 1989), no attention has been given to what groups have been left out of the analysis and the consequences of this exclusion. For example, in one study participation in the development of an educational performance monitoring system was limited to superintendents, school board members, teachers, and representatives of professional education groups. The study results made no mention of who was left out (e.g., taxpayers who are not parents, evaluation professionals) and the possible impact of their absence (Henry et al. 1991). Many studies confuse beneficiaries with stakeholders, although the latter group is generally larger (Brandon et al. 1993b).

Most studies in the business field make no reference to how stakeholders were identified, although an early study (Rhenman 1968) suggested a stakeholder grid, a matrix that arranges stakeholders according to their source of power (formal or voting, economic, political) and the kind of stake they hold in an organization's decisions (equity, economic, influence). Various stakeholders are compared with each other in terms of the direction of their influence on economic, technological, political, social, and managerial dimensions. Another approach divides stakeholders into categories—supporters, uncommitted, and opposition—and then asks about the actions, beliefs, cooperative potential, and stakes of each group (Hatten and Hatten 1988). The central part of Godet's strategic planning approach is the use of a series of matrices to determine the relative power and relative concern of various stakeholders about critical issues (Godet 1991).

Some attention has been given to the stages or moments in which stakeholders should participate in the evaluation process (Ayers 1987). Evidently, however, no systematic attention has been given to the most appropriate moments for stakeholder involvement in policy formulation and planning processes, nor has attention yet been given to the most appropriate moments for different categories of stakeholders to participate.

The objective of this analysis is to propose a set of procedures for the comprehensive identification of stakeholders in educational organizations, their relative importance to the policy formulation, planning, and implementation processes, and the moments most appropriate for involvement by different groups. The case study that is presented with this discussion applies the method post hoc to a process of educational reform in Jamaica. The method was designed for use with national education systems but can be applied to smaller organizations.

A METHOD FOR IDENTIFICATION OF STAKEHOLDERS IN EDUCATION SYSTEMS

DEFINITION OF STAKEHOLDERS

Stakeholders are persons or groups with a common interest in a particular action and its consequences or who are affected by it. All actors in an institutional context are *potential* or *passive* stakeholders. In education this reservoir holds groups as diverse as parents, children, PTAs, educational faculties, taxpayers, teachers' unions, public service employees, public contractors, employers, and professional organizations, among others. All these groups have an interest in setting the educational agenda and shaping the organizations established to participate in the process of providing education.

In this process some actors are transformed from potential stakeholders to *kinetic* or *active* stakeholders. Kinetic stakeholders generally pursue their interests within the situation (context) of a particular organization within the institution. In this context stakeholders focus on particular issues that touch their interests. It is here that toes are stepped upon and dancing partners found as stakeholders enter into coalitions. The process can have transformational effects as coalitions see interests and possible consequences not recognized earlier. The transformations in turn lead to shifts in the organizational context. In all, little attention has been paid to the fact that stakeholders, chameleon like, change with the context and change the context because they are learning by the activity of participation.

CATEGORIES OF INTERESTS

The interests or effects of stakeholder action take three different forms and identify three categories of stakeholders. One set of interests focuses on the process of generating the decision, organizing a program, and managing a system. Often this involves the formation coalition, which will produce or stop something from being produced. The term *generation* is used to avoid the implication that, first, a tangible product always exists and, second, that there is a final product that is closed to further learning and change.

An example of generation in education is the process of developing a curriculum, printing textbooks, or constructing buildings. These stakeholders are known as producers, but they seek to accomplish their objectives by generating coalitions of interests, which produce a consensus that can be offered for general acceptance. The first broad category of stakeholders can, therefore, be called *generators* or *producers*.

A second set of interests focuses on the distribution of the product that is generated. In some cases this distribution involves an exchange of money, in which case the interest is in selling the product. Teachers may sometimes produce curriculum but more often are distributors. Education managers typically do not produce textbooks but are concerned about textbook distribution. In the same manner, teachers may be involved in the process of distributing students among different levels but are not involved in the resource decisions that make a particular pattern of distribution possible. For some, privatization of public education means private control over the distribution of a publicly produced curriculum. The second broad category of stakeholders is *distributors*.

A third set of interests in education focuses on the benefits to be derived from application of the product. Benefits come through use of the various products of educational activity. Students and their parents use knowledge and certification to enhance the student's life chances (as well as to improve the quality of his or her life). Employers are *users* of the human capital that is produced through education. Churches often are users of education, as are professional societies, the government, and a variety of other groups that expect education to contribute to the achievement of one of their objectives. It is important to note that it is the users who finance education systems, not the producers.

Any given person or group may occupy more than one of these stakeholder categories. For example, a person may be both a parent of a student (a user) and a provider of education (a generator and a distributor). The owner of a construction firm is a producer and may also be a user concerned with the quality of graduates that she or he can hire. The expression of these interests will occur in different moments of time, according to the process or cycle of policy formulation and implementation.

MOMENTS IN THE EXPRESSION OF INTERESTS

Our methodology defines six moments in the process of policy formulation and implementation. We refer to these as *moments* to indicate that they are transitory even though they may take place over days or weeks. Other schemes use fewer or more categories. Less important than the number of categories is the recognition that policy formulation and implementation is a complex, nonlinear, often recursive process that permits and attracts the participation of different persons and groups at different moments. The six moments are *manifesto, policy, program, project, application,* and *assessment.*

Manifesto

This refers to the result of discussions during that period of time in which institutional or organizational stakeholders identify a concern or set of concerns that require action. Depending on the weight of these concerns, other institutional stakeholders may become involved. The magnitude of this concern—its weight—progressively incorporates more institutional stakeholders, shifting them from a potential to kinetic position and so bringing their institutional interests to bear.

The kinetic stakeholders who participate in this moment regard themselves as having a right to define objectives for the education system. In general this is the largest group of stakeholders that gets involved in the policy formulation and implementation process.

Policy

A smaller group is for the most part self-selected from the larger pool of kinetic stakeholders who developed their manifesto, and this group is involved in the definition of specific goals to be pursued and the broad methods to be used in that pursuit. Not all potential stakeholders are familiar with the policy process or assign themselves competence in the definition of policies. Typically excluded from this process are groups that lack information about how education policy is formulated. Lower-level functionaries in the education system and most teachers are excluded from policy formulation, even though they are stakeholders. Officials of teacher unions, on the other hand, may be included in the process.

In many instances in education, initial policy choices touch off another round of public debate, which may result in a reformulation of the manifestos articulated by political parties or submitted to government by stakeholders. The debate, however, can draw more of the potential institutional stakeholders into the process. The manifesto, policy-choice debate process can enlarge the pool of organizational stakeholders who exercise the right to participate in formulating the policy choice.

Program

The process of translating policies into programs typically is carried out by staff members within the educational organization, occasionally with the participation of recognized experts and special-interest groups from the larger institution. The latter often represent different levels of contexts, namely the international, national, regional, and local levels. The allocation of the duty of program formulation activates potential stakeholders within the organization. The process of program design is iterative and may include reformulating the general policy statement that touched off the process.

Project

The specific sets of activities that take place during programs are called projects. The stakeholders that get involved at this stage generally are those groups immediately affected by each project. The balance of participation shifts from center to local, as specific groups of parents and teachers attempt to shape the decisions that will affect their lives.

Application

As in all organizations, the persons who make policy decisions (including the choice of schools to receive project funds) are not coterminous with those responsible for the use of those funds. Project descriptions and plans often leave considerable leeway for intervention by so-called implementors and local managers. The actions of these stakeholders are often not directly visible to many of the stakeholders who participated in decisions about the program or the policy. The stakeholders who participate in this moment tend to do so as individuals rather than as representatives of formal groups. For example, parents and teachers get involved to represent their individual interests. Application moment stakeholders deformalize the policy and program while tailoring the project to their organizational context. Even at this stage in the progress potential stakeholders are transformed into active or kinetic stakeholders. Sometimes they may have a more or less common set of interests and values with kinetic stakeholders who entered earlier, but this need not be the case.

Assessment

The best programs include procedures and instruments to assess the implementation of the project in terms of the specifications of the program and the goals of the policy. Assessments can focus on inputs, process, or outputs. Each kind of assessment affects a different set of stakeholders.

Assessments are inputs to discussions about the adequacy of policies, programs, and projects, which may lead to their reformulation. For that reason, program officials often attempt to control the design and execution of assessments and the dissemination of their findings. Assessments can also provide inputs for the debate that leads to a manifesto.

Who Is Dominant When? Users are most likely to be dominant in the manifesto moment and to be consulted in the assessment and policy moments. Producers have the most say in the policy, program, and assessment moments. Distributors in the education system have the most influence in the project and application moments. The focus and intensity of interest of each group changes according to moment of the policy formulation and implementation cycle. The overall interest, however, is defined by the *tasks* of the *system* that are affected by the policy in question.

CATEGORIES OF TASKS IN EDUCATION SYSTEMS

Education systems (schools and other organizations linked together with a common purpose) are designed to carry out four major categories of tasks. These tasks can be characterized as referring to access, retention, classification, and placement. Education systems do the following:

- Recruit, select, and admit students
- Attempt to keep students in the system long enough to experience a transforming effect
- Sort students into different tracks and levels
- Certify students for and place them in (institutions of) the larger society

The broad interests of stakeholders take a specific form according to the kind of task under discussion.

Educational organizations and their suppliers, together with the producers of education, benefit directly from the increase of access. In addition to those directly employed in education and owners of educational organizations, this group of stakeholders includes construction companies; companies that provide instructional materials, including textbooks; vendors of uniforms, food, and other consumables; insurance companies; universities and consulting firms that provide technical assistance services; companies that produce and apply tests; and domestic and international agencies that thrive on the health or illness of the educational establishment. Each of these groups can be mobilized to support the expansion of educational access.

Those involved in distribution are more interested in policies that affect the activities associated with retention and classification within the system. Teachers, for example, are primarily concerned with issues that affect the way they distribute education—that is, work with students. These concerns are often defined in terms of quality, but they primarily affect the work that teachers are expected to do. Most teacher unions are organized primarily to provide what are considered suitable working conditions and compensation for teachers and to protect their jobs. The managers of education systems also may be concerned with quality but again focus their attention on the way the work of education is carried out—that is, on the process of distribution.

Some groups that appear to be interested in distribution issues—for example, those who call for increased efficiency in education—are really primarily concerned about the production process. Although they give a nod to improving quality, they almost always back policies that involve doing the same with less rather than more with the same. Teachers, on the other hand, can be mobilized to do more with the same, as has been demonstrated in the ability of school-based management policies to increase teacher work and student learning with no increase in teacher pay. In effect, teachers are allowed to have a major say in the production of education, not just its distribution.

SPECIFIC MANAGEMENT ACTIVITIES OF THE EDUCATION SYSTEM

The management of every education system, and every organization that generates a product or provides a service, requires attention to five major activities: production, marketing, distribution, resource management, and research and development.

Generation/production is the most obvious activity, as was anticipated earlier. What we call "education" is a series of activities designed to transform persons individually and collectively. We "produce" learning in the sense that it occurs in part as a result of the generative activities of the educator. School managers and teachers are actively involved in the production process. Other stakeholders include those who believe themselves to have expert knowledge about production technologies, such as university professors, and groups that are affected by the kind of production technology used, such as vendors of computers or distance learning technologies.

Marketing is important because education systems require resources in order to carry out their activities. These resources are solicited from users of the benefits derived from the educational process. Marketing is addressed then to students and their parents, the local community, employers, religious groups, professional associations, politicians, and others who have an interest in the various products of the system. Public education is notorious for its lack of attention to marketing, except in time of financial retrenchment. Other stakeholders, however, may be actively promoting the benefits of public education. These would include political parties, manufacturers that seek a larger pool of trained labor, ethnic or language groups that want to promote a particular program, and especially schools and research centers whose fortunes vary directly with the level of overall interest in public education. Trade unions, which provide goods and services to education systems, must also be included in the reach of marketing.

Distribution is concerned with how the product and its generation are accessed by members of all levels of the community. Not only does this involve decisions about the location of school plants and facilities but also the direct and secondary employment generated. In addition, distribution involves the parents and teachers with the question as to who gets access to the different levels of education and the methodologies that will be used to implement the distribution decisions. Distribution obviously must reach as far back as the moment the manifesto was formulated and every subsequent moment. The central point is that distribution is not limited to the product.

A number of stakeholders also get involved in the management of resources. Groups concerned about the level and quality of outputs from education may focus on efficiency issues instead of production, seeking to maintain or boost outputs at the least possible additional cost. The stakeholders who focus on efficiency rather than production are likely to be those who have limited knowledge about the production process or lack means to obtain that knowledge. Some groups have more understanding of fiscal-finance issues, which are included under this rubric. These groups raise the question of effectiveness: Is the system doing the "right" thing with the resources? These groups are concerned with situations in which it is possible to do the wrong thing both well and badly!

A final set of stakeholders gets involved in issues that concern the improvement of the production process through research and development activities. Some (but not all) teachers are included in this category. Not all researchers are included because much research is diagnostic and relates to marketing and perhaps resource management but does not contribute to innovation in the areas of teaching and learning. Research and development activities could address all the relationships shown in Table 4 (presented later). Research and development also must be viewed from a wider perspective to include the full range of experiential to formal research. The former is conducted by parents and other community groups and is mostly a verbal, unwritten process. Although it is often anecdotal, it is valid.

PROCEDURES IDENTIFYING STAKEHOLDERS

The first step we recommend is to list all possible groups concerned with the inputs, process, and outputs of education. These can be listed under the three categories defined earlier: producers, distributors, and users. The objective in this stage is to list all possible stakeholders.

The second step in the process is to identify those moments in which each of the stakeholders listed is most likely to get involved in the policy formulation and implementation process. Or, if you wish, the task is to assign to the various moments those stakeholders that will be most active in attempting to influence the process. Table 1 can be used as a heuristic to suggest groups.

The objective of this step is to complete the task begun in the first step—identifying all stakeholder groups that might be interested in the educational institution and the organization in question across the range of issues that might be of concern. Inclusivity at this stage reduces the likelihood of leaving some stakeholder group out of consideration.

Attention has to be drawn to the fact that Third World nations have additional external stakeholders who play a major role in all aspects of educational choice and decisions. The World Bank, the International Development Bank, the African Development Bank, and a host of bilateral assistance agencies (e.g., the United States Agency for International Development, the Canadian International Development Agency, and the Swedish International Development Agency) assume the right and duty to intervene. They are often joined by nongovernmental organizations, such as foundations, and sometimes by transnational corporations who also seek to influence national education systems (McGinn 1994). These groups complicate the domestic stakeholder coalitions. For example, many Third World university education faculties are more ready to pursue the external agenda than the domestic. Although power corrupts, the lack of power corrupts more swiftly.

TABLE 1

Identification of Moments in which Various Stakeholders Are Likely to Get Involved

	DOMINANT INTEREST OF STAKEHOLDER		
MOMENTS	GENERATION	DISTRIBUTION	USE
Manifesto			
Policy			
Program			
Project			
Application			
Assessment			

TABLE 2

The Specific Interests of Stakeholders with Respect to Activities of the Organization

		ACTIVITIES OF THE ORGANIZATION			
STAKEHOLDER LEVELS	STAKEHOLDER CATEGORIES	ACCESS	RETENTION	CLASSIFICATION	PLACEMENT
International					
National					
Regional					
Local					

TABLE 3

The Specific Interests of Stakeholders with Respect to Management Activities

	MANAGEMENT ACTIVITIES			
STAKEHOLDERS	PRODUCTION	MARKETING	DISTRIBUTION	RESOURCE MANAGEMENT

The third step is to identify the particular issue that is the focus of attention and to determine where the organization is in the process of moving from concern about an issue to policy and eventually to implementation. The objective is to identify those stakeholders most likely to be involved in the immediate future. Although teachers may articulate great concern about policy, their representatives are likely to be most active around production and distribution issues that will affect the working conditions of their members.

The fourth step is to identify the specific interests of the stakeholders with respect to the kinds of activities the organization or system carries out. Table 2 provides a matrix for determining the level of influence each stakeholder has with respect to each task. In the next step, interests of the stakeholders are linked with the management activities of the organization. Table 3 provides a framework for completing this step.

The next step is to identify the priority of each stakeholder group by fitting each one into the most appropriate cell in the matrix presented in Table 4, which crosses the activities of education systems with specific management activities.

TABLE 4

The Priority Concern of Stakeholders

	MANAGEMENT ACTIVITIES			
TASKS OF ORGANIZATION	PRODUCTION	MARKETING	DISTRIBUTION	RESOURCE MANAGEMENT
Access				
Retention				
Classification				
Placement				

TABLE 5

The Identification of Issues by Moments and Organizational Tasks

	MOMENTS				
ORGANIZATIONAL TASKS	MANIFESTO	POLICY	PROGRAM	APPLICATION	ASSESSMENT
Access					
Retention					
Classification					
Placement					

The final step, as shown in Table 5, is to identify issues by moments and organizational activities. Changing the "message" or "product" in any of these cells may trigger further changes throughout the matrix. The importance of this matrix is, first, that it draws attention to the recursive nature of issue definition. Second, it can also prompt new coalitions and alliances as the reiteration occurs. Figure 1 illustrates this methodology.

This methodology for stakeholder analyses allows the comprehensive identification of stakeholders and their changing definitions and roles. The methodology links stakeholders to system tasks, management activities, and the best moments for intervention. It also assists in mapping the recursive patterns that occur when stakeholders move through the moments, and it highlights the fact that no particular moment is more critical than any other. The reiteration can be triggered at any cell in the matrix if the issue bears sufficient weight (that is, if it activates sufficient stakeholders).

REFERENCES

Ackoff, Russell. 1974. *Redesigning the future.* New York: John Wiley.
Alkhafaji, Abbass F. 1989. *A stakeholder approach to corporate governance: Managing in a dynamic environment.* New York: Quorum Books.

FIGURE 1

Sequence of Steps to Apply the Methodology

List all potential actors under categories of producer, distributor, user	Fill Table 1 with names of stakeholders categorized by interest and moments in which most likely to act
For each actor, decide whether and when will get involved, using categories of 5 moments	Fill Table 2 with stakeholders categorized by level and activities of most interest
Identify the issue that will be of most concern to each actor	Fill Table 3 with stakeholders categorized by management activities
Identify activities of organization of most interest to stakeholders, according to their level in society	Fill Table 4 with stakeholders categorized by task and by management activities
Decide how interests of stakeholders match activities of organization	Fill Table 5 with stakeholders categorized by moment and organizational tasks
Using classification of stakeholders by task in Table 2, decide how to relate tasks to management activities	
Using classification of stakeholders by moment in Table 1, decide how to relate tasks to moments	

Ansoff, I. 1965. *Corporate strategy*. New York: McGraw-Hill.

Argyris, Chris, and Donald A. Schon. 1978. *Organizational learning: A theory of action perspective*. Reading, MA: Addison-Wesley.

Ayers, T.D. 1987. Stakeholders as partners in evaluation: A stakeholder-collaborative approach. *Evaluation and Program Planning* 10: 263–71.

Bamberger, M. 1991. The politics of evaluation in developing countries. *Evaluation and Program Planning* 14, 4: 325–39.

Brandon, Paul R., Marlene A. Lindberg, and Zhigang Wang. 1993a. Enhancing validity through beneficiaries' equitable involvement in evaluation. *Evaluation and Program Planning* 16: 287–93.

Brandon, Paul R., Marlene A. Lindberg, and Zhigang Wang. 1993b. Involving program beneficiaries in the early stages of evaluation: Issues of consequential validity and influence. *Educational Evaluation and Policy Analysis* 15: 420–28.

THE **ROSE** PROGRAM IN JAMAICA

Secondary education in Jamaica as inherited from the British colonial days permits only a tiny fraction of graduates to be eligible for university admission. Examinations shunt students onto dead-end tracks at the end of the sixth grade and again at the ninth grade. Although high achievers can attend subsidized private or public senior high schools that prepare students for the university entrance examinations, for years the system has been criticized as inequitable and for not producing enough talented persons for Jamaica's economy.

In Jamaica all sectors of the society participate in some fashion in the discussion about problems in education. The more visible stakeholders concerned with generation are the ministry of education and the University of the West Indies. Those concerned with distribution are the Jamaica Teachers' Association and the various senior high schools that currently receive government support. Concerned with use are the two political parties, the Church of Jamaica and the Catholic Church, the various groups representing commerce and manufacturing (but not agriculture), the ministry of finance, and the Jamaica Planning Institute (ministry of planning). The issue appeared constantly in newspapers and on the radio, and it reached a crescendo during parliamentary election campaigns.

Finally, the number of groups demanding some solution pushed the government to act. The manifesto was composed of statements by several temporary coalitions. Their recommendations for a solution differed, but all demanded an expansion of access to secondary education.

The government's response to the manifesto was a policy decision to increase access to upper secondary education while leaving the established, elitist, senior high school system intact. The minister of education participated in the policy process, but the dominant actors were the Jamaica Planning Institute, the government's ministry of planning, and the minister of finance. It is likely that the government had contacted various international agencies to determine whether they would finance the expansion of secondary education.

Those who participated in designing the Reform of Secondary Education (ROSE) program involved World Bank officials, staff from the national planning office, university professors, representatives from some but not all senior high schools, and policy-level officials from the ministry of education. World Bank participation was preceded by an agreement (policy) that the World Bank would provide assistance to secondary schools while USAID and the InterAmerican Development Bank would provide assistance to primary schools.

The group of stakeholders that designed the ROSE program chose a strategy of improving the quality of lower secondary schools so that more students would pass the examination that determines entrance into upper secondary schools. ROSE provides funds for the improvement of existing lower secondary schools. Once the project was announced, senior high schools appeared to lose interest. Because they receive students directly from primary schools, and currently turn away most candidates, the policy had little to offer them. On the other hand, the curriculum unit of the ministry of education, previously inactive with regard to discussions of secondary education, became an important actor in design of the strategy to improve lower secondary education. The objective became to retain more students through dropout prevention activities and to raise scores on the ninth-grade examination for entrance into senior high school. The Teachers' Association continued to press for increased numbers of teachers and smaller class sizes.

The selection of which schools to improve is made by a small committee managed by the ministry of education but influenced by the Jamaica Planning Institute and by members of Parliament. Because the demand in Jamaica for entrance to upper secondary schools is much greater than can be satisfied, senior secondary officials in the ministry of education have not attempted to influence the choice of junior secondary schools to receive additional inputs. On the other hand, local officials who did not participate in the design of the ROSE program are now actively recruiting school improvement funds for institutions in their districts.

As with most other projects, what the ROSE program actually does at the moment of application is not totally what was expected. Program officials have been most concerned with whether inputs are being provided as planned, whereas those who participated in policy formulation have been most concerned with whether admissions to upper secondary schools have increased. Curriculum unit staff members are concerned primarily for the effects of the new curriculum on students. The administration and teachers in the participating junior secondary schools have, on the other hand, sometimes sought to apply ROSE funds to problems they consider more pressing.

As the program got under way, actual control seemed to shift from the project coordinator to the education officers who are responsible for the various schools and who often have close relationships with the headmasters and headmistresses. Although citizen groups had been vocal in the manifesto stage, once the program was under way they had no way to track what was going on and disappeared from the arena. The business stakeholders also ceased their involvement, as did the University of the West Indies. After several years, ROSE had been implemented on a much smaller number of schools than the World Bank had anticipated. The ministry of education continued to be enthusiastic about the program, especially as the first group of graduates did better on exams than had previous cohorts. But Jamaica has a serious debt crisis, and the government (planning and finance) seemed to have decided to slow down the rate of expenditure of the World Bank loan.

Bryk, Anthony S. 1983. *Stakeholder-based evaluation: New directions in program-based evaluation.* San Francisco: Jossey-Bass.

Bryson, John. 1990. *Strategic planning for public and nonprofit organizations.* San Francisco, CA: Jossey-Bass.

Collins, Dennis. 1989. Organizational harm, legal condemnation and stakeholder retaliation: A typology, research agenda and application. *Journal of Business Ethics* 8: 1–13.

Cousins, J. Bradley, and Lorna M. Earl. 1992. The case for participatory evaluation. *Educational Evaluation and Policy Analysis* 14: 397–418.

Freeman, R. Edward. 1984. *Strategic management: A stakeholder approach.* Boston: Pitman.

Godet, Michel. 1991. *From anticipation to action: A handbook of strategic prospective.* Paris: UNESCO Publishing.

Hallett, Michael A., and Robert Rogers. 1994. The push for "Truth in Sentencing": Evaluating competing stakeholders. *Evaluation and Program Planning* 17: 187–96.

Hatten, Kenneth, and Mary Louise Hatten. 1988. *Effective strategic management analysis and action.* Englewood Cliffs, NJ: Prentice-Hall.

Henry, Gary T., Kent C. Dickey, and Janet C. Areson. 1991. Stakeholder participation in educational performance monitoring systems. *Educational Evaluation and Policy Analysis* 13: 177–88.

Langtry, Bruce. 1994. Stakeholders and the moral responsibilities of business. *Business Ethics Quarterly* 4: 445–58.

Lawrence, John E.S. 1989. Engaging recipients in development evaluation: The stakeholder approach. *Evaluation Review* 13: 243–56.

McGinn, Noel. 1994. The impact of supranational organizations on public education. *International Journal of Educational Development* 14: 289–98.

Maxwell, Joseph A., and Yvonna S. Lincoln. 1990. Methodology and epistemology: A dialogue. *Harvard Educational Review* 60: 497–512.

Rhenman, Eric. 1968. *Industrial democracy and industrial management.* London: Tavistock Institute.

Salmen, Lawrence F. 1989. Beneficiary assessment: Improving the design and implementation of development projects. *Evaluation Review* 13: 273–91.

Schlossberger, Eugene. 1994. A new model of business: Dual-investor theory. *Business Ethics Quarterly* 4: 459–74.

Senge, Peter M. 1990. *The fifth discipline: The art and practice of organizational learning.* New York: Doubleday.

Stake, R. 1975. *Evaluating the art in education: A responsive approach.* Columbus, OH: Merrill.

Stoner, James A.F., and R. Edward Freeman. 1992. *Management.* Englewood Cliffs, NJ: Prentice-Hall.

Thompson, Randal Joy. 1991. Facilitating commitment, consensus, credibility, and visibility through collaborative foreign assistance project evaluations. *Evaluation and Program Planning* 14: 341–50.

Timar, Thomas B. 1989. The politics of school restructuring. *Phi Delta Kappan* 71: 165–75.

Weiss, Carol H. 1983. The stakeholder approach to evaluation: Origins and promise. In *Stakeholder-based evaluation: New directions in evaluation,* edited by Anthony S. Bryk. San Francisco: Jossey-Bass.

Weiss, Joseph W. 1994. *Business ethics: A managerial, stakeholder approach.* Belmont, CA: Wadsworth.

PART 5

Tools for Strategic Analysis and Planning

Benchmarking: How to Achieve Effective Goals and Objectives*

ROBERT C. CAMP

Traditional target setting methods have failed U.S. managers and blind sided them to competition. Only the approach of establishing operating targets and productivity programs based on industry best practices leads to superior performance. That process, being used increasingly in U.S. business, is known as *benchmarking*.

Two ancient truths convincingly illustrate why benchmarking is so vitally needed. One saying is over 2,500 years old and originates in China. It is hard to say how old the other is, but it originated in and is successfully practiced in Japan.

In the year 500 B.C., Sun Tzu, a Chinese general, wrote, "If you know your enemy and know yourself, you need not fear the result of a hundred battles." Sun Tzu's words could just as well show the way to success in all kinds of business situations. Solving ordinary business problems, conducting management battles, and surviving in the marketplace are all forms of war, fought by the same rules—Sun Tzu's rules.

The other truth is a simple word of unknown age. It is the Japanese word *dantotsu*, meaning striving to be the "best of the best." It is the very essence of benchmarking. We in America have no such word, perhaps because we always assumed we were the best. But world competitive events have smashed that notion forever. We cannot assume anything anymore. Benchmarking moves us past that assumption.

Benchmarking is a positive, proactive process to change operations in a structured fashion to achieve superior performance. The benefits of using benchmarking are that functions are forced to investigate external industry best practices and incorporate those practices into their operations. This leads to profitable, high-asset utilization businesses that meet customer needs and have a competitive advantage.

Benchmarking is firmly based on Sun Tzu's urging to view and understand not only the internal company world, but more importantly to assess the external constantly. Only coupled with the constant search for *dantotsu*, the "best of the best" methods and practices innovatively applied to business processes, will U.S. industry revitalize itself. The purpose of benchmarking is to ensure that probability of success.

The basic philosophical steps of benchmarking, listed as follows, are fundamental to success:

---

*"How to Achieve Effective Goals and Objectives" from *Benchmarking* by Robert C. Camp. Reprinted by permission of ASQC Press , 1989.

- *Know your operation.* You need to assess the strengths and weaknesses of the internal operation. That assessment must be based on the understanding that competitors will analyze your operation also to capitalize on the weaknesses they uncover. If you do not know the operation's strengths and weaknesses you will not be able to defend yourself. You will not know which operations to stress in the marketplace and which will require strengthening.
- *Know the industry leaders or competitors.* In a similar fashion you will only be prepared to differentiate your capabilities in the marketplace if you know the strength and weaknesses of the competition. More importantly, it will become clear that only the comparison to and understanding of the best practices of industry or functional leaders will ensure superiority.
- *Incorporate the best.* Learn from industry leaders and competition. If they are strong in given areas, uncover why they are and how they got that way. Find those best practices wherever they exist and do not hesitate to copy or modify and incorporate them in your own operation. Emulate their strengths.
- *Gain superiority.* If careful investigations of best practices have been performed, and if the best of those best practices have been installed, then you will have capitalized on existing strengths, brought weaknesses to match the marketplace, and gone beyond to incorporate the best of the best. This position is clearly a position of superiority.

Benchmarking is the formalized and more disciplined application of these very basic steps to operational improvement and the achievement of superiority. The generic benchmarking process is shown in Figure 1.

The generic benchmarking process makes several important points that will help early understanding of the process. First, benchmarking can be divided into two parts, practices and metrics. Practices are defined as the methods that are used; metrics are the quantified effect of installing the practices. Each can be investigated by the process. The tendency is for managers to work to determine the metrics or quantitative targets to quickly internalize the realization, good or bad, of what the organization will find from benchmarking against the external environment. This is a visceral approach to getting the bad news over quickly.

Benchmarking should be approached on the basis of investigating industry practices first. The metrics that quantify the effect of the practices can be obtained or synthesized later. One cannot determine why the gap exists from the metrics alone. Only the practices on which the metric is based will reveal why. The reverse is not always possible, and it could mislead or defeat the purpose of benchmarking.

Benchmarking is an understanding of practices. Once they are understood they can be quantified to show their numeric effect. Perhaps more important, once a metric is determined it will immediately beg the question "why?" Benchmarking is on soundest ground to have the practices understood to answer the question "why" up front. The contribution to the credibility of the findings is immeasurable.

The final point is that the benchmarking process and the benchmark findings must be understood by the organization to obtain commitment to take action to change. There are several ways to accomplish this. They will be described later.

Essential to the benchmarking process are both carefully designed communications to the organization and concerted management support. These are critical to such a radical

FIGURE 1
Generic Benchmarking Process

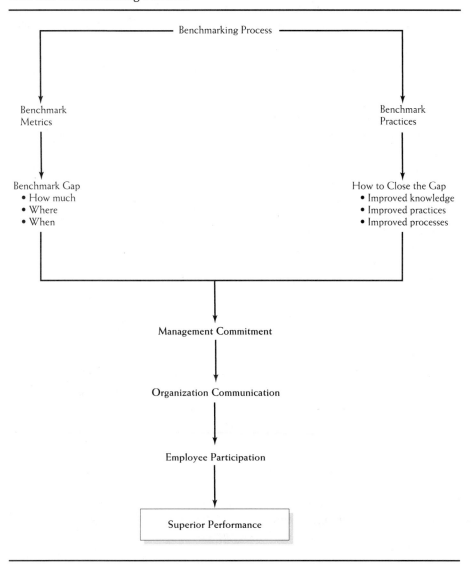

new way of doing business as benchmarking. There is also a definite place for employee involvement in benchmarking. The findings need to be implemented. What better way to do so smoothly than through the efforts of those closest to the work process. They are the most knowledgeable about how to adopt and implement the findings directly or adapt them to the work conditions.

The sum of these major actions is what leads to superior performance.

HISTORICAL PERSPECTIVE

The chronology of benchmarking mentioned here is that of Xerox Corporation. Xerox was fortunate to have discovered and applied benchmarking early in its drive to combat competition. It could just as well have been that of any other major industrial firm. The experience of Xerox, however, illustrates the need for and the promise of benchmarking.

In 1979, Xerox initiated a process called competitive benchmarking. Benchmarking was first started in Xerox Manufacturing Operations to examine its unit manufacturing costs. Selected product comparisons were made. Operating capabilities and features of competing copying machines were compared and mechanical components torn down for analysis. These early stages of benchmarking were called product quality and feature comparisons.

Comprehensive benchmarking was formalized with the analysis of copiers produced by the Xerox Japanese affiliate, Fuji-Xerox, and later other Japanese manufactured machines. These investigations confirmed the substantially higher U.S. manufacturing costs. When the manufacturing cost was completely analyzed it revealed that competitors were selling machines for what it cost Xerox to make them. U.S. manufacturing quickly shifted to adopt these externally set benchmark targets to drive its business plans.

Because of manufacturing's success in identifying competitor's new processes, new manufacturing components, and costs of manufacturing, senior management directed that benchmarking be performed by all business units and cost centers. At first only a few of the operating units used benchmarking, but by 1981 it was adopted as a corporate-wide effort. At the 1983 annual meeting of shareholders the chief operating officer announced that his number one priority was to achieve leadership through quality. Benchmarking was one of the three components of that effort. Benchmarking, along with employee involvement and the quality process, was seen as central to achieving quality in all products and processes. Benchmarking was visualized as the process of understanding customer requirements, and employee involvement was viewed as the process by which benchmarking would be implemented.

Prior to benchmarking, most unit cost and other targets for asset management and customer satisfaction were set internally by using standard budgeting procedures with adjustments for some assumed level of productivity and judgments about what would satisfy customer needs. This process was essentially a projection of past practices into the future. There was little concentration on targets established by the marketplace or by leadership firms with superior functional practices.

Most nonmanufacturing operations before 1981 made comparisons primarily with other internal operations. For example, managers compared the productivity of different regional distribution centers, or per pound transportation costs between regions. When directed to perform benchmarking, after-sale support functions—maintenance, repair service, distribution, invoicing, and collection—found it difficult to identify the analog to the successful product analyses performed in the benchmarking activities of manufacturing. That is to say, there was no machine or physical product to tear down. Therefore, these functions, as well as others, came to recognize that their product was incorporated and delivered through a process. The process was seen as that which needed to be detailed and later compared with the external environment. This later comparison would reveal methods and practice differences which could then be used to determine the benchmark.

Competitors' processes were therefore looked at operation-by-operation and step-by-step. In logistics, for example, that meant deciding on the major deliverables for transportation, warehousing, inventory management, and other processes. These were then compared to competitor functions to determine their key methods and practices. In the service organization the practices of dealers were examined; in the invoicing operations the practices of banks were investigated; in order entry the electronic transmission of orders from drugstores was considered.

While these early nonmanufacturing benchmarking efforts against direct product competitors were partially successful, it became clear that focusing on competitors' practices only could divert attention from the ultimate purpose; that is, superiority in each business function and, therefore, in the marketplace. Benchmarking solely against competitors may also uncover practices that are not optimal and not worthy of emulation. In addition, competitive benchmarking may lead to meeting the competitor's position, but it will not lead to creating practices superior to those of the competition. When these shortcomings are coupled with the obvious fact that getting information about competitors is difficult, other methods of benchmarking need to be pursued. This realization has led to the understanding that there are several ways to benchmark and that they each have their usefulness. What is fundamental is recognizing that benchmarking involves uncovering best practices wherever they exist.

MANAGERIAL PERSPECTIVE

In their continuing search for greater effectiveness, organizations have compared both overall performance and individual unit performance with that of others for many years. Comparisons are made most frequently within a company. These inward orientations tend to reinforce feelings of superiority and foster not-invented-here excuses. Comparisons with outsiders, however, may expose best industry practices and encourage the adoption of those practices. The practice of comparing performance between organizations, referred to as benchmarking, is a disciplined search for and establishment of a standard to which internal operations can be compared.

Benchmarking as discussed here is industrial research or intelligence gathering that allows a manager to compare his or her function's performance to the performance of the same function in other companies. Benchmarking identifies those management processes, practices, and methods the function or cost center would use if it existed in a competitive environment. Benchmarking is an indicator of what a business function's performance should or could be.

Although benchmarking should be an ongoing, continuous process, it is often only initiated when a business is losing market share, when profit levels are declining, or when customer dissatisfaction is high. This often happens because when a business is not in danger, there can be disincentives to improve operating costs and profits. Internal performance as opposed to competitive gain may be stressed to satisfy personal goals and ambitions. Rapid sales growth can mask inadequate performance in functions of the business.

Cost centers by their very nature leave a motivational void. They buffer the function from competition. Further, when performance to budget is stressed, time is often spent arguing about the size of the budget, not stressing improved performance. If profit generation was stressed, time would be spent generating revenue, controlling expenses, and anticipating the competitive environment. Benchmarking is the only way to overcome these deficiencies and force individual business functions to constantly test their ability to be competitive and profitable as measured by the external environment.

In benchmarking the manager's goal is to identify those companies, regardless of industry, which demonstrate superior performance in functions to be benchmarked so that their practices, processes, and methods can be studied and documented. A well-executed benchmarking investigation can provide a manager with detailed information about the best functional practices in the industry. These practices can then be used or modified to establish a long-term competitive advantage in the marketplace.

Benchmarking can benefit a company in several ways:

- It enables the best practices from any industry to be creatively incorporated into the processes of the benchmarked function.
- It can provide stimulation and motivation to the professionals whose creativity is required to perform and implement benchmark findings.
- Benchmarking breaks down ingrained reluctance of operations to change. It has been found that people are more receptive to new ideas and their creative adoption when those ideas did not necessarily originate in their own industry.
- Benchmarking may also identify a technological breakthrough that would not have been recognized, and thus not applied, in one's own industry for some time to come, such as bar coding, originally adopted and proven in the grocery industry. In these instances it is more important to uncover the industry best practices than to concentrate on obtaining comparative cost data. The business unit can determine for itself what cost levels could be achieved if it incorporated the benchmark practices in its own operations.
- Finally, those involved in the benchmarking process often find their professional contacts and interactions from benchmarking are invaluable for future professional growth. It permits the individuals to broaden their background and experience. It makes them more useful to the organization in future assignments.

BENCHMARKING DEFINED

There are several bases on which to define benchmarking as an activity. Benchmarking has a formal definition which has wide application to all business functions. Webster's definition is also informative. Perhaps even more important is the need for a working definition.

FORMAL DEFINITION

The formal definition was derived from experience and successes of the earliest days of applying benchmarking techniques in the manufacturing area:

> Benchmarking is the continuous process of measuring products, services, and practices against the toughest competitors or those companies recognized as industry leaders. (David T. Kearns, chief executive officer, Xerox Corporation)

There are several considerations in this definition requiring further description.

Continuous Process

Benchmarking is a self-improvement and management process that must be continuous to be effective. It cannot be performed once and disregarded thereafter on the belief that the task is done. It must be a continuous process because industry practices constantly change. Industry leaders constantly get stronger. Practices must be continually monitored to ensure that the best of them are uncovered. Only those firms that pursue benchmarking with discipline will successfully achieve superior performance. In an environment of constant change complacency is fatal.

Measuring

The term benchmarking implies measurement. Measurement can be accomplished in two forms. The internal and external practices can be compared and a statement of significant differences can be documented. This is a word statement measurement of the industry best practices that must be implemented to achieve superiority, although qualitative in nature. It describes the opportunity for change to best practices.

The practices can be quantified to show an analytical measurement of the gap between practices. It quantifies the size of the opportunity. This metric is often the single-minded measurement that most managers want. While it is important and traditional to strive to obtain analytically derived benchmark metrics, it will become apparent that both must be pursued. Practices on which the metrics are based should be pursued first. Benchmarking is not just an investigation of the metrics of the external business function, but an investigation to determine what practices are being used to ensure effectiveness and eventually superiority and which practices achieve the metrics. Benchmarking is not just a study of competition but a process of determining the effectiveness of industry leaders by measuring their results.

Products, Services, and Practices

Benchmarking can be applied to all facets of a business. It can be applied to the basic products and services. It can be applied to the processes that go into manufacturing those products. It can be applied to all process practices and methods that are in support of getting those products and services effectively to customers and meeting their needs. Benchmarking goes beyond the traditional competitive analysis to not only reveal what the industry best practices are, but to also obtain a clear understanding of how best practices are used.

It will be the view here that most business activities can be analyzed as processes. Most business activities have a beginning, an end, and a main activity. There is an output from the process that is what the next customer wants, whether that customer is internal or an external, end user or consumer of the output or product. A study of business processes and their methods and practices will be the main objective of the benchmarking approach.

Companies Renowned as Industry Leaders

Benchmarking should not be aimed solely at direct product competitors. In fact it could be a mistake to do so since they may have practices that are less than desirable. Benchmarking should be directed at those firms and business functions within firms that are recognized as the best or as industry leaders, such as banks for error-free document processing. The company serving as a benchmark partner is not always obvious. Careful investigation is needed to determine which firms to seek as benchmarking partners and why. Fortunately there are ways to uncover who and why they should be chosen.

In the formal sense benchmarking is an ongoing investigation and learning experience that ensures that best industry practices are uncovered, analyzed, adopted, and implemented. It focuses on what best practices are available. It ensures an understanding of how they are performed. And finally, it determines the worth of the practices or how well they are performed.

WEBSTER'S DEFINITION

The Webster's dictionary definition is also informative. It defines a benchmark as:

> A surveyor's mark . . . of previously determined *position* . . . and used as a reference point . . . standard by which something can be measured or judged.

Both definitions serve to reinforce the benchmark as being a standard for the comparison of other objects or activities. It is a reference point from which others are to be measured.

Outside of land surveying where a benchmark is well understood and accepted, there is only one other common use of the term. The computer industry has used the term to mean a standard process for measuring the performance capabilities of software and hardware systems from various vendors. The standard then serves as a basis of choice between the alternative offerings, each of which can have different features and functions, but meet the overall requirements by a different mix of capabilities.

Benchmarking used in the dictionary sense serves as a standard, but one which may change over time to reflect the real conditions of the business world, namely that business practices must change over time to remain competitive.

A WORKING DEFINITION

The definition of benchmarking, as seen from the perspective of one who has been involved in the process over a number of years and exercised the process many times, incorporates the previous definitions. But it goes beyond to emphasize some important considerations not included in these definitions. The working definition preferred for benchmarking is:

> Benchmarking is the search for industry best practices that lead to superior performance.

This definition is preferred because it is understandable by operationally oriented business units and functions. If they know their operations thoroughly, then the search to ensure that the best of proven practices are incorporated is a clear objective. The definition covers all possible business endeavors whether a product, service, or support process. It is not necessary to include them by specific reference.

The focus is on practices. It is only through change of current practices or methods of performing the business processes that overall effectiveness will be achieved. It stresses practices and the understanding of practices before deriving a benchmarking metric. Benchmarking metrics are seen as a result of understanding best practices, not something that can be quantified first and understood later.

The definition concentrates on achieving superior performance. In this regard it pursues *dantotsu*, the best of the best practices, best of class, or best of breed. That is, those best practices that are to be pursued regardless of where they exist—in one's own company, industry, or outside one's industry. It is only this view that will ensure superiority rather than parity.

The definition is proactive. It is a positive endeavor. It is one calculated to obtain cooperation of benchmarking partners. There should be few professionals who would object to constantly seeking best practices. There should be a constant sharing of ideas and debating about how the industry is going to constantly improve itself. This will only occur if the search is open and seen as benefiting both benchmark partners.

Benchmarking should be approached on a partnership basis in which both parties should expect to gain from the information sharing. The discussion of practices and methods, especially among noncompetitors, can only result in both parties gaining from the investigation and discussions. Even competitors can gain in discussions that appropriately skirt proprietary and sensitive topics. The concentration solely on best practices permits that objective to be achieved.

Benchmarking as a term should motivate managers because it is a positive activity, perceived as a mechanism for improving operations to proactively search for best practices. It will be only through the test of finding the best of the best in industry that any manager will be able to justify his or her own operation and assure that he or she has performed to the ultimate standard.

Benchmarking is the most credible of all justifications for operations. There can be little argument about a manager's position if he or she has sought the best in industry and incorporated it in his or her plans and processes.

WHAT IS BENCHMARKING?

There should be some understanding of what benchmarking is and is not, and its relationship to target setting. There are many misconceptions of what benchmarking is and these should be clearly understood and reinforced. What benchmarking is not should be quickly dispelled. Likewise, since benchmarking involves setting new directions, its relationship to targets should be understood also. These should give a better understanding of where benchmarking fits into the overall planning scheme.

WHAT IT IS, WHAT IT IS NOT

Benchmarking is not a mechanism for determining resource reductions. While that may occur because many operations do not emulate best industry practices, it does not necessarily mean a reduction. Resources will be redeployed to the most effective way of supporting customer requirements and obtaining customer satisfaction as a result of benchmarking activities. It may be that benchmarking will require a resource increase, both people and spending, as a result of more correctly determining true customer satisfaction levels and needs from benchmarking activities.

Benchmarking is not a panacea or program. It must be an ongoing management process that requires constant updating—the collection and sifting of external best practices and performance into the decision making and communications functions at all levels of the business. Benchmarking must have a structured methodology to ensure successful completion of thorough and accurate investigations. However, it must be flexible to incorporate new and innovative ways of assembling difficult-to-obtain information. The benchmarking process steps can be applied repetitively, yet be adaptable. The benchmarking process must keep those conducting the studies aware of new avenues of approach and information sources while accomplishing the basic task.

Benchmarking is not a cookbook process that requires only looking up ingredients and using them for success. Benchmarking is a discovery process and a learning experience. It requires observing what the best practices are and projecting what performance should be in the future. Through it, information can be gathered that will permit setting performance goals which are realistic in the context of the external business environment by ensuring that best, feasible, proven practices are incorporated into business operations.

Benchmarking is not a fad, but a winning business strategy. It assists managers in identifying practices that can be adapted to build winning, credible, defensible plans and strategies, and complement new initiatives to achieve the highest performance goals—namely, superior performance.

Benchmarking is a new way of doing business. It forces an external view to ensure correctness of objective setting. It is a new management approach. It forces constant testing of internal actions against external standards of industry practices. It promotes teamwork by directing attention on business practices to remain competitive rather than personal, individual interest. It removes the subjectivity from decision making.

BENCHMARKING AND TARGETS

Benchmarking is basically an objective-setting process. Benchmarks, when best practices are translated into operational units of measure, are a projection of a future state or endpoint. In that regard their achievement may take a number of years to attain. The benchmarks may most importantly indicate the direction that must be pursued rather than specific operationally quantifiable metrics that are immediately achievable. A benchmarking study may indicate that costs must be reduced and customer satisfaction levels increased or return on assets increased. In addition, the concentration on best practices supports the general direction that must be pursued with specific insights into how the benchmarks can or should be attained. The conversion of benchmarks to operational targets translates the long-term actions into specifics.

Targets are more precise although their quantification should be based on achievement of a benchmark. Furthermore, a target incorporates in it what realistically can be accomplished within a given time frame, usually one yearly budget cycle or business plan horizon. Considerations of available resources, business priorities, and other operational considerations convert benchmark findings to a target, yet steadily show progress toward benchmark practices and metrics. The significant difference between a complete benchmark definition and a target is that a carefully conducted benchmark investigation will not only show what the benchmark metric is but also how it will be achieved.

KEY PROCESS STEPS

The benchmarking process is displayed in Figure 2. . . .

It is important, however, to have a general understanding of the generic phases and some understanding of their rationale. The benchmarking process consists of five phases. The

FIGURE 2
Benchmarking Process Steps

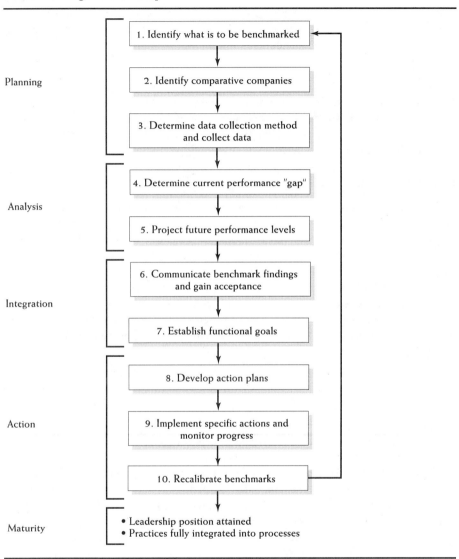

Planning

1. Identify what is to be benchmarked

2. Identify comparative companies

3. Determine data collection method and collect data

Analysis

4. Determine current performance "gap"

5. Project future performance levels

Integration

6. Communicate benchmark findings and gain acceptance

7. Establish functional goals

Action

8. Develop action plans

9. Implement specific actions and monitor progress

10. Recalibrate benchmarks

Maturity

• Leadership position attained
• Practices fully integrated into processes

process starts with a planning phase and proceeds through analysis, integration, action, and finally maturity.

PLANNING PHASE

The objective of this phase is to plan for the benchmarking investigations. The essential steps are those of any plan development—what, who, and how.

What Is to Be Benchmarked?

Every function of a business has or delivers a product. The product is the output of the business process of the function, whether a physical good, an order, a shipment, an invoice, a service, or a report. Benchmarking is appropriate for these and all other outputs. The products therefore must first be determined.

To Whom or What Will We Compare?

There are business to business, direct product competitors. These are certainly prime candidates to benchmark. But they are not enough. Benchmarking must be conducted against leadership companies and business functions regardless of where they exist. Only in this fashion will superiority be ensured.

How Will the Data Be Collected?

There is no one way to conduct benchmarking investigations. There is a process. There are an infinite variety of ways to obtain required data, and most data are readily and publicly available. A certain level of inquisitiveness and ingenuity is required, but a combination of methods that best meets the study needs will most often be productive. Sources of information are limited only by one's imagination.

What will be important is to recognize that benchmarking is a process not only to derive quantifiable metric goals and targets but more importantly to investigate and document those best industry practices which permit achievement of the goals and targets. A benchmarking study should concentrate on practices and methods. Their effect can always be quantified.

ANALYSIS PHASE

After determining what, how, and who is to be benchmarked, actual data gathering and analysis must be accomplished.

The analysis phase must involve a careful understanding of current process practices as well as those of benchmarking partners. The benchmarking process is, after all, a comparative analysis. What is desired is an understanding of internal performance on which to assess strengths and weaknesses. Is the benchmarking partner better? Why are they better? By how much? What best practices are being used now or anticipated? How can their practices be incorporated or adapted for implementation?

Answers to these questions will be the dimensions of any performance gap: negative, positive, or parity. The gap provides an objective basis on which to act—to close the gap or capitalize on a positive one. The gap, however, is a projection of performance and therefore will be one which changes as industry practices change. What is needed is not only an understanding of today's practices but where performance will be in the future. It is important that benchmarking be a continuing process so that performance is constantly recalibrated to ensure superiority.

INTEGRATION

Integration is the process of using benchmark findings to set operational targets for change. It involves careful planning to incorporate new practices in the operation and to ensure benchmark findings are incorporated in all formal planning processes.

The first step is to gain operational and management acceptance of benchmark findings. Findings must be clearly and convincingly demonstrated as being correct and based on substantive data. Credible data can be supported by deriving data and information from several sources to support the findings. Based on the findings action plans can then be developed.

Benchmark findings must be communicated to all organizational levels to obtain support, commitment, and ownership. This essential step can usually be accomplished through a variety of communications approaches. The key to the process will be the conversion of benchmark findings into a statement of operational principles to which the organization can subscribe and by which actions for change will be judged. These principles place the organization on notice that they are the rules by which the organization will improve itself to meet customer needs and eventually to attain superiority.

ACTION

Benchmarking findings and operational principles based on them must be converted to action. They must be converted to specific implementation actions and a periodic measurement and assessment of achievement must be put in place. People who actually perform the work tasks are most capable of determining how the findings can be incorporated into the work process. Their creative talents should be used to perform this essential step.

In addition, any plan for change should also contain milestones for updating the benchmark findings themselves, since the external practices are constantly changing. Therefore provision should be made for recalibration. Also, an ongoing reporting mechanism is needed. Progress toward benchmark findings must be reported to all employees. This feedback is especially necessary to those who assist with the implementation. They will want to know how they are doing.

MATURITY

Maturity will be reached when best industry practices are incorporated in all business processes, thus ensuring superiority. Superiority can be tested in several ways. In some instances services are sold to external customers in addition to serving the internal customer. If the now-changed process were to be made available to others would a knowledgeable businessperson prefer it? That becomes a powerful confirmation of a benchmark. Needless to say if other companies benchmark your own internal operations that also would be confirmation.

Maturity also is achieved when it becomes an ongoing, essential, and self-initiated facet of the management process. It becomes institutionalized. It is done at all appropriate levels of the organization, and not by specialists. While knowledgeable specialists may exist to consult on the most productive approaches for benchmarking, only when the focus on external practices becomes the responsibility of the entire organization will benchmarking truly have achieved its objectives of ensuring superiority through incorporation of best industry practices.

HOW TO GET STARTED IN BENCHMARKING

Those who initially are exposed to the subject of benchmarking often ask how they can get started. The author's preferred way is to have them read this text completely and implement and practice the 10-step benchmarking process. But for those who cannot spare the initial time and want a quick primer, [the] Quick Reference Guide is provided. It is broken down into two sections. The first section covers initial and somewhat general information gathering, but sound steps in the investigation process. The second section discusses information gathering in the unit's own functional area or area of interest.

To get started in the process of benchmarking there are some proven first steps. One must determine what to benchmark, assuming there is agreement that the next steps will be directed to gathering available data. This may come from library research and contacting internal personnel and sources. Those shown in [the] Quick Reference Guide are easily initiated approaches and should be done early in any benchmarking investigation. The guide gives initial target areas to turn to in these starting steps.

The focus of the second area of investigation is more external and on a specific function or area of interest. The information comes from periodicals about the function, associations that represent the function, service bureaus that offer services surrounding the function, and consultants who are knowledgeable about the function. Initial contact with these external sources starts the process of ensuring that all available public information is covered and relevant information is documented. These require a higher level of effort to get under way and should be approached based on sound planning and careful understanding of the scope of the investigations. It also includes two unique sources: industry experts and software vendors. . . .

While the guide is not to be inclusive, it does give quick reference to the initial steps found to be productive. A more thorough approach can be tailored following in-depth study of the text and time to define a careful benchmarking investigation. Starting with the guide will provide a faster start and nothing will be lost in the process. The guide is, however, only a guide. It cannot substitute for exercising the full 10-step process. *Caveat emptor* benchmarkers!

SUMMARY

Successful benchmarking is based on achieving several important factors and management behaviors. It requires management commitment to make tough decisions to base operational goals on a concerted view of the external environment. There must be a willingness on the part of those performing benchmarking to learn from others. They need to realize that internal operations cannot always have the best answer for every problem. They can and should learn from others and constantly measure themselves against the best in the industry. This text describes the necessary skills to conduct successful benchmarking activities. Creativity in extending the basic process will enhance what is covered here to achieve truly superior benchmarking results.

Benchmarking is a continuous process of measuring against the best. Goals are based on the benchmark findings to achieve superiority. Progress is measured periodically to update the organization's position toward achieving the benchmarks. Benchmarking results in process practices and measurable goals based on what the best in the industry is doing and is expected to do. The approach contrasts sharply with the rather imprecise, intuitive estimates of what needs to be done to characterize current searches for productivity. Benchmarking is the rational way of ensuring the organization is satisfying customer requirements and will continue to do so as customer requirements change over time. Benchmarking ultimately reflects an attitude to strive for excellence in every business endeavor.

Quick Reference Guide
How to Get Started in Benchmarking

A. Information Sources—Getting Started
   - Focus on an Area/Element That Needs to Be Pursued
     Examples:
     - (1) Order entry
     - (2) Service dispatching
     - (3) Warehouse storage
   - Contact a Business Library
     — Request a search of information produced in the last three to five years for your topic of interest
     — Library will identify articles/sources from
     - (1) External reports
     - (2) Public magazines
     - (3) Industry journals
     - (4) Annual reports
   - Contact Internal Experts
     — Market research
     — Competitive analysis
     — Functional experts
   - Survey Internal Reports/Studies
     — Special studies
     — Surveys
     — Market research
B. Information Sources—Specific/Functional
   - Subscribe/Monitor Trade Periodicals
   - Professional Associations
     — Newsletters
     — Seminars (especially speakers/tours)
     — Bibliographies
     — Special libraries
   - Service Agencies/Bureaus in the Business Function
     — Ask if they can share anonymous experiences from their client companies
     - (1) Industry practices or methods
     - (2) State-of-the-art methods/practices
   - Consulting Firms
     — Functional experts
     — Ask if they are aware of particular breakthroughs/practices in a specific area
   - Industry Experts
     — Department heads of noncompetitors
     — Teachers/professors at schools/universities
   - Systems Software Development and Hardware Vendors
     — Ask about their experiences working in your functional area

Strategic Tools and Techniques*

RICHARD KOCH

ANSOFF MATRIX

As shown in Illustration 1, this gives 4 options for increasing sales.

Box 1, selling more of existing products in existing markets, is a low risk, market share gain strategy. To be useful, this must specify how this objective is to be attained, for example by enlarging the salesforce, increasing advertising or cutting price.

Box 2 implies product development to sell new (or modified) products to existing customers: fine as long as the firm has a good track record of new product development and provided the new products share enough costs and skills with the existing products, and do not face a very strong incumbent competitor.

Box 3 takes existing products and sells them to new markets or customers. This is clearly sensible if the new markets can be cultivated at relatively little extra cost, but can be risky if a new market requires investment in fixed cost (for example, a new salesforce), if the customers have different requirements, or if there are entrenched competitors.

Box 4—new products to new markets—is the highest risk strategy: the segments being entered are not adjacent to the existing business and it is almost like starting a new business from scratch. The presumption is that Box 4 strategies are inherently unsound and should only be taken either in desperation or because there is a compelling short term opportunity not being exploited by others.

BCG MATRIX

The popular name for the Growth/Share Matrix, an abused but powerful tool encapsulating the most important insights into business of the past 50 years. See Growth/Share Matrix.

BPR (BUSINESS PROCESS RE-ENGINEERING)

A new way of rethinking what a company does and re-designing its processes from first principles in order to produce dramatic improvements in cost, quality, speed and service.

---

*"Strategic Tools and Techniques" from *The Financial Times Guide to Strategy* by Richard Koch, pp. 152–191, 1995. Reprinted by permission of Pitman Publishing.

ILLUSTRATION 1
The Ansoff Matrix for Business Development

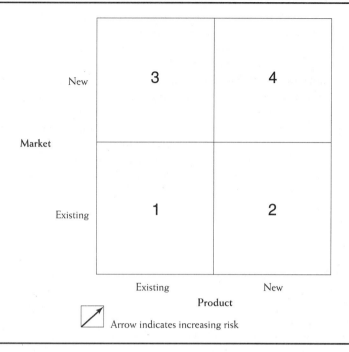

Arrow indicates increasing risk

BPR is the hottest management concept of the 1990s so far. Its advocates claim that Re-engineering (which they spell, incorrectly, without a hyphen) will be for the 1990s what Strategy was for the 1970s and Quality for the 1980s. This is certainly true as far as consulting revenues are concerned. But, BPR is not just a management fad and deserves to be taken seriously. Many leading U.S. companies (such as Eastman Kodak, Ford and Texas Instruments) have used BPR to change their way of doing business, leading to cost reductions in excess of 25 per cent, and in some specific areas of up to 90 per cent.

BPR claims to reinvent the way that companies do business, from first principles, by throwing out the view that firms should be organised into functions and departments to perform tasks, and paying attention instead to processes. A process here is a set of activities that in total produce a result of value to a customer, for example, developing a new product. Who is in charge of this? In the non-BPR-ed company the answer is 'no-one', despite the involvement of a large number of traditional functions such as R&D, marketing.

The essence of BPR is reversing the task specialisation built into most management thinking since Adam Smith's 1776 pin factory, and focussing instead on completing a total process with value to customers in one fell swoop. A good example is IBM Credit, which used to take 7 days to process applications for credit for people wishing to buy computers. Before BPR, there were five separate specialist stages through which an application progressed: logging the credit request; credit checking; modifying the standard loan covenant; pricing the loan; and compiling a quote letter. Experiments then proved that the actual work involved only took ninety minutes; the real delay was caused by having different departments that did the work in stages and had to pass it on to each other. The solution hit upon was to replace the specialists with generalists called deal structurers who handled all the steps in the process. The average turnaround time was reduced from seven days to four hours, and productivity was increased 100 times.

'Doing' BPR means taking a clean sheet of paper and asking fundamental questions like: Why do we do this at all? How does it help to meet customer needs? Could we eliminate the task or process if we changed something else? How can we get away from specialisation, so that several jobs are combined into one?

'BPR-ed' companies have thrown away their 'assembly lines', particularly in respect of clerical and overhead functions. One person, such as a 'customer service representative', may for example act as the single point of contact for a customer, taking care of selling, order taking, finding the equipment to be purchased, and delivering it personally. Performance improvement comes from eliminating the expense and misunderstandings implicit in 'handoffs' from one part of the organisation to another, as well as eliminating internal overheads necessary to manage the complexity brought on by task specialisation.

The process claims several benefits:

1. Customers can deal with a single point of contact (the 'case manager').
2. Several jobs can be combined into one, where the primary need to satisfy the customer is not lost in organisational complexity.
3. Workers make decisions, compressing work horizontally (that is, doing without supervisors and other overhead functions that are necessary as a result of specialisation), resulting in fewer delays, lower overhead costs, better customer response, and greater motivation of staff through empowerment.
4. The steps in the process are performed in a sensible order, and removing specialisation enables many more jobs to be done in parallel, as well as lowering the need for rework.
5. Processes can be easily adapted to cope with work of greater or lesser complexity, instead of forcing everything to go through the same lengthy work steps.
6. Work can be performed where it makes most sense, which is often not by specialists.
7. Checks and controls and reconciliations can be reduced without loss of quality.

Like all forms of radical change, BPR often fails: objective estimates are that this is so in almost 75 per cent of cases. The most frequent causes of failure are lack of top management commitment, an insufficiently broad canvass on which to operate (as when parts of the organisation refuse to take the effort seriously), and lack of readiness to adapt corporate culture. Nevertheless, BPR has achieved such stunning results in many documented cases that it cannot be ignored. In the most successful cases it is clear that BPR as a technique was the catalyst for more far reaching changes in culture and standards.

Two points about BPR are not sufficiently well made by its protagonists, for obvious reasons. One is that certain types of companies and businesses are more likely to benefit from BPR than others. The most susceptible companies are those where manufacturing is a relatively small part of the cost structure, where overheads are a large part, where customer needs have been neglected, and where the potential benefits of information technology (IT) have not yet been exploited.

The other point is that BPR is not a Do It Yourself technique: serious attempts at BPR nearly always involve help from consultants. As BPR has boomed, so too has the supply of consultant help, but often at the expense of quality. Many consultants reduce BPR to cost reduction techniques or re-badge their existing methodologies under the BPR banner, without having the imagination and creativity required for effective BPR. The likely result is that as most companies come to undertake some form of BPR, most will become disillusioned, and the technique itself may fall into disrepute.

BUSINESS ATTRACTIVENESS

An assessment of how attractive a business or market is, based on a number of criteria. Often a distinction is made between the attractiveness of the market, on the one hand, based on desiderata like market growth, average industry profitability, barriers to entry (which should be high), barriers to exit (preferably low), the bargaining power of customers and suppliers (ideally low), the predictability of technological change, the protection against substitutes, and on the other hand, the strength of the individual company's business within the market, based on relative market share, brand strength, cost position, technological expertise and other such assessments. One can then produce a matrix such as that shown in Illustration 2 and plot all a firm's businesses on the matrix to see where scarce corporate resources such as cash and good management should be allocated.

In [Illustration 2], the most obviously attractive businesses for investment would be D, followed by G, and then probably C or F. Business C could be a very good investment target, but only if the investment could drive it to a very strong position within the market (i.e. move it from the top left to the top right). If this is reckoned unlikely, it may be best to sell C for a high price. Businesses B and A are also disposal candidates if a reasonable price could be obtained.

The matrix is an alternative to the BCG Matrix and has the advantage that it can take into account several factors in evaluating the attractiveness of both business and market. On the other hand the lack of quantification of the axes can be a subjective trap, with management unwilling to admit that businesses are not attractive. For any overall corporate plan it is useful to position all businesses on both matrices, and see whether the prescriptions are at all different. If they are, you should carefully examine the assumptions leading to the difference.

COMB ANALYSIS

A very useful and simple technique for comparing customers' purchase criteria with their rating of suppliers. Let us assume that you are a textile manufacturer producing women's clothes and selling them to retailers who are fashion specialists. You want to find out what the most important reasons are for them to choose supply from one manufacturer rather than another. You also want to find out what the retailers think about you and your competitors on each of these purchase criteria.

You should then engage independent researchers to interview the retailers and ask them two questions. First, the researchers should ask the retailers to score on a 1–5 scale the importance of various purchase criteria. Let us assume that the average results are as shown in Illustration 3.

ILLUSTRATION 2
Business Attractiveness Matrix

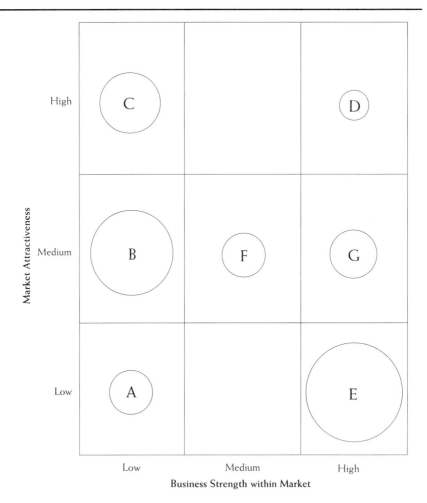

These results can now be displayed on the first part of the 'comb' chart (Illustration 4).

The second question the researchers ask is how each of the competing suppliers rates on each of these criteria, again on a 1–5 scale. Let us start by overlaying on the previous results (the retailers' purchase criteria) their rating of the company sponsoring the research, which we will call Gertrude Textiles (Illustration 5).

These results should be of great interest to Gertrude Textiles. Except on one criterion, Gertrude manages to score above the importance of the criterion to the retailer. Unfortunately, the one criterion on which Gertrude scores below market expectations is the most important one: the fashion appeal of its clothes. To increase market share, the one thing that Gertrude Textiles must focus on is improving its garments' fashion appeal. Of interest too is that on the last three criteria—willingness to deliver small quantities, price,

ILLUSTRATION 3 ────────────────────────────

Example of Comb Analysis

CRITERION	IMPORTANCE SCORE
Fashion appeal of garments	4.9
Strength of brand name	4.6
Service & speed of delivery	4.5
Willingness to deliver small orders	3.5
Price from manufacturer to them	3.0
Durability of garments	2.3

ILLUSTRATION 4 ────────────────────────────

Comb Chart: Retailers' Purchase Criteria

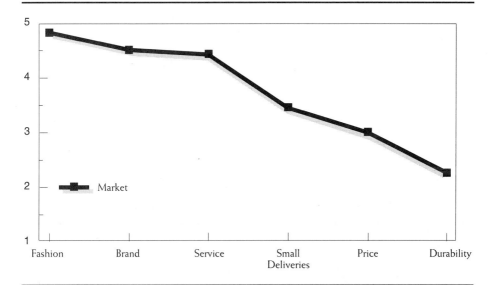

and the durability of its clothes—Gertrude scores *above* what the market requires. No doubt this is costing Gertrude a lot of money. This comb profile suggests that Gertrude could afford to not be so accommodating on small deliveries, could raise prices, and could stop building in long life to its clothes. The money saved should be invested in doing whatever is necessary to improve perceptions of its fashion appeal: perhaps by hiring away the top designer team from a rival.

This is where the rating of competitors adds to the picture. We can now overlay on the previous picture the ratings given by retailers to two of Gertrude's rivals: Fast Fashions and Sandy's Styles (Illustration 6).

From this we can make three important observations:

1. The only competitor that meets the market's very high fashion requirements is Sandy's Styles. This is the team for Gertrude Textiles to poach or beat.

ILLUSTRATION 5
Comb Chart: Retailers' Purchase Criteria and Their Rating of Gertrude Textiles on These Criteria

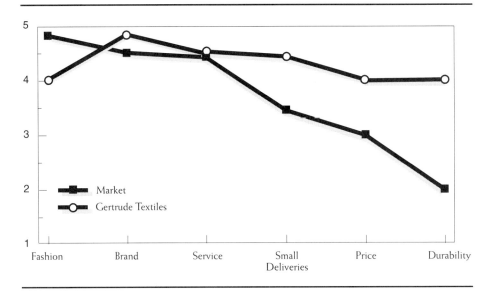

ILLUSTRATION 6
Comb Chart: Rating of Three Competitors against Market Criteria

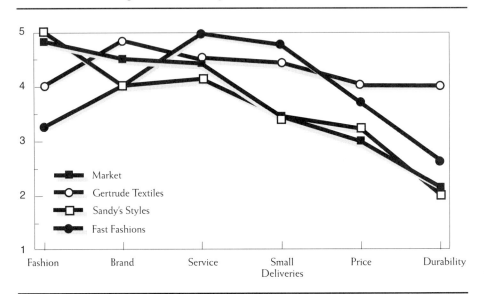

2. Gertrude has the best brand name, according to the retailers, and can meet all the other purchase criteria apart from fashion. If this criterion can be met, Gertrude will be in a very strong position to increase market share.

3. Only Gertrude is significantly over-performing on the price requirements of retailers. This helps to confirm that some price increases to retailers may be possible for Gertrude, particularly if the fashion element improves.

DECISION TREE

A flow chart that sets out possible future events and highlights the effects of decisions or chance occurrences in a sequential order. Can be very useful in estimating the probability that any event may happen, or simply in pinpointing the critical decisions that have to be made. For some peculiar reason decision trees are nearly always drawn from left to right, although I much prefer to draw them from top to bottom. Two examples are given in Illustration 7 and Illustration 8. In Illustration 7 a manufacturer is trying to decide whether to open a new factory, in the face of uncertainty about whether his main rival will decide to do the same thing and whether the economy will move into recession or boom. The decision tree helps him to lay out the possibilities and calculate the returns under all eight possible outcomes (Illustration 7).

So far the decision tree has helped by laying out the possibilities, although it does not yet tell Superior Sproggetts Limited (SSL) what to do. For this we need to overlay on the decision tree the *probabilities* of each of the four possible outcomes arising from (a) an investment by SSL and (b) a decision by SSL not to invest. Illustration 8 overlays these probabilities and therefore allows a calculation of the expected value (the weighted average value) in terms of ROCE (Return on Capital Employed) under both (a) and (b).

ILLUSTRATION 7
Decision Tree for Superior Sproggetts Limited

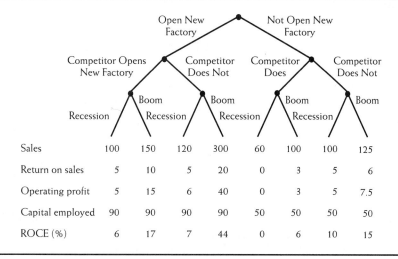

	Open New Factory				Not Open New Factory			
	Competitor Opens New Factory		Competitor Does Not		Competitor Does		Competitor Does Not	
	Recession	Boom Recession		Boom Recession		Boom Recession		Boom
Sales	100	150	120	300	60	100	100	125
Return on sales	5	10	5	20	0	3	5	6
Operating profit	5	15	6	40	0	3	5	7.5
Capital employed	90	90	90	90	50	50	50	50
ROCE (%)	6	17	7	44	0	6	10	15

ILLUSTRATION 8

Decision Tree with Probabilities and Expected Values

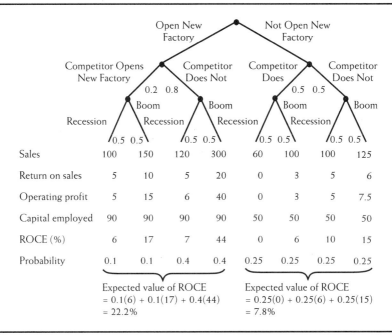

	Competitor Opens New Factory		Competitor Does Not		Competitor Does		Competitor Does Not	
	Recession	Boom	Recession	Boom	Recession	Boom	Recession	Boom
Sales	100	150	120	300	60	100	100	125
Return on sales	5	10	5	20	0	3	5	6
Operating profit	5	15	6	40	0	3	5	7.5
Capital employed	90	90	90	90	50	50	50	50
ROCE (%)	6	17	7	44	0	6	10	15
Probability	0.1	0.1	0.4	0.4	0.25	0.25	0.25	0.25

Expected value of ROCE
= 0.1(6) + 0.1(17) + 0.4(44)
= 22.2%

Expected value of ROCE
= 0.25(0) + 0.25(6) + 0.25(15)
= 7.8%

From this it can be seen that investment has a much higher expected return on capital, at 22 per cent, than the decision not to invest, which has an expected value of 8 per cent. One important reason for this is that the competitor is much less likely to invest if SSL does so first. Adding the probabilities helps to highlight the importance of this judgment.

Decision trees can be used for a wide variety of purposes and are a great help in clarifying what should be done when events are uncertain and outcomes depend to some degree on earlier uncertain events.

DELPHI TECHNIQUE

Forecasting technique using a number of experts (or managers) who each make estimates in round one, then receive everyone else's estimates and re-estimate in round two, and so on until consensus is reached.

EXPERIENCE CURVE

Along with the BCG Matrix, the greatest discovery of Bruce Henderson, although it started life in 1926 as the 'learning curve'. Briefly it states that when the accumulated production of any good or service doubles, unit costs in real terms (i.e. adjusted for inflation) have the potential to fall by 20 per cent. Accumulated production is not a concept much

ILLUSTRATION 9
Cost Experience Curve

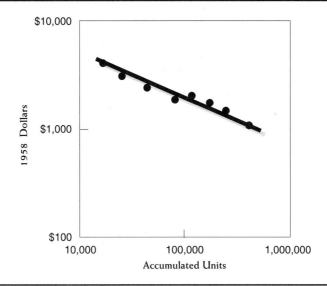

Source: Automobile Manufacturer's Association, BCG Analysis.

used, nor is it usually very easy to calculate: it is the total number of units of a product that have ever been made by a firm, or the total number of units of a product ever made by all participants in the market. It is not related to time, because accumulated production can double within one year for a new or very fast growth product, or take centuries for a very old or slow growth one.

BCG found and documented many exciting instances in the late 1960s and 1970s where accumulated production had increased rapidly and deflated (inflation adjusted) costs had fallen to 70–80 per cent of their previous level each time this happened. One of the most important examples is the decline in the cost of integrated circuits (ICs), which explains why the cost of calculators was able to plummet so dramatically. A typical example of a cost experience curve is shown in Illustration 9.

BCG used the experience tool both to identify cost reduction opportunities and as a dynamic tool for describing and influencing the battle between competitors in a particular product. If a particular firm was found *not* to have cut costs in line with the experience curve, this was held to be a cost reduction opportunity. The beauty of the method was that it described precisely the point that costs should have reached (although not how to get there), and therefore set a firm and seemingly objective target for management to meet. A great deal of cost reduction was actually achieved this way.

In terms of competitive strategy, BCG invented a second type of experience curve: related not to costs but to prices. For any market as a whole, but particularly for an individual firm, BCG would chart how real prices (after adjusting for inflation) had behaved in relation to accumulated production of the product. The price experience curve might or might not follow the shape of the cost experience curve. In Illustration 10 we show a cost experience

ILLUSTRATION 10 ———————————————————————————————

Price Experience Curve in Three Phases Compared to Cost Experience Curve

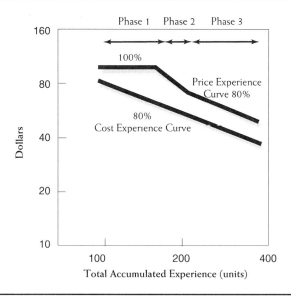

curve of 80 per cent (that is, costs behaved as they should, reducing by 20 per cent each time accumulated production doubled), but different cost behaviour in three phases. In the first phase, prices did not come down at all: in other words, the deflated price experience curve was 100 per cent (or in other words, prices were increased in line with inflation). In the second phase, prices come down very sharply, to compensate for the earlier failure to match cost reductions. In the third phase, prices fall in parallel with costs, that is, the price experience curve is also 80 per cent.

BCG explained the first phase as one of complacency and excess profits, where consumers are willing to continue paying a high price and where competitors all enjoy higher margins by not passing cost savings on to customers. Eventually, however, these high profits encourage new players into the marketplace, and at least one of these new players cuts costs to try to gain market share. The other players have to respond, and prices are therefore reduced until 'normal' margins obtain again.

BCG preached that it was doubly foolish to have a flatter price experience curve than cost experience curve (i.e. to widen margins in the first phase): firstly, because it would lead to loss of market share initially, and secondly because the player with the greater market share himself would have lower costs, so that a market leader who held market share (by having competitive prices, so that his price might be below new entrants' cost) would continually compound his competitive advantage of low cost and make it impossible for new players to enter unless they were willing to lose money initially. Prices should therefore be reduced by the market leader at least as fast as costs, in order to keep competitors out or unprofitable, and thus consolidate market leadership and compound the low cost position.

BCG was able to explain the success of Japanese companies such as Honda in motorcycles by reference to 'experience curve cost reduction' and 'experience curve pricing'.

Ultimately the experience curve effect was used to explain the incidence of short-termism in Western industry and the consequent loss of global market share.

The concepts behind the experience curve are wholly correct. It must be admitted that calculating accumulated volume was often a black art, and that BCG sometimes exaggerated the scientific and empirical nature of the experience curve. Since the late 1970s the experience curve as a practical management tool has fallen into disuse, though lone adherents still persist (and use it effectively). Experience curve thinking, even if no experience curves are drawn (and one suspects that very few Japanese executives ever drew such curves), should be an integral part of good management. The mysterious disappearance of the experience curve from Western boardrooms is much to be deplored, even though experience curve thinking is in part imbedded in the Quality Revolution of the 1980s and the BPR Revolution of the 1990s.

GROWTH/GROWTH MATRIX

Useful two-by-two chart (invented by BCG) which compares the growth of a firm's business in one product or business segment to the growth of the market as a whole, thus enabling one to see whether market share was being won or lost and by whom (Illustration 11).

Illustration 11 shows an example, using imaginary data, of three competitors in a particular market at a particular time (three, five or ten years are generally used). According to the (made up) data, the largest competitor is McKinsey, which is growing slower than the market as a whole (and therefore losing share); the next largest in BCG, which is growing at the same rate as the market; and the smallest but fastest growing competitor is Bain & Company. Note that companies on a growth/growth chart are always at the same vertical height, since this represents the overall market growth and must by definition be common for all.

Growth/growth charts are not much used nowadays but are very useful, especially if used in conjunction with the main BCG Matrix (the Growth/Share Matrix).

GROWTH/SHARE MATRIX

The Boston Consulting Group has invented several matrices, having consultants trained to think in terms of two-by-two displays, but this is the most famous and useful one (it is also sometimes called the BCG Matrix). Invented in the late 1960s and still of great importance today, it measures market growth and relative market share for all the business a particular firm has. An example is shown in Illustration 12.

It is important to define the axes properly. The horizontal axis is of fundamental importance and measures the market share that a firm has in a particular business *relative to the share enjoyed in that business by its largest competitor.* Thus if Engulf & Devour Plc has a 40 per cent market share in Business A and its nearest competitor has a 10 per cent market share, its relative market share ('RMS') is 400 per cent or 4 times (written as 4.0×). In Business B, Engulf & Devour may have a 5 per cent share and the leading competitor 10 per cent, in which case Engulf & Devour's relative market share is 50 per cent or 0.5×. Note that absolute market share (for example, 20 per cent of a market) means little, because it

ILLUSTRATION 11 ─────────────────────────────────

Examples of Growth/Growth Matrix with Competitors Arrayed

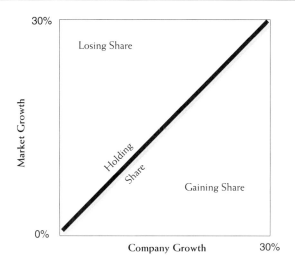

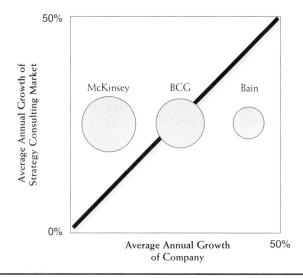

would mean a relative market share of 0.33 per cent (if the dominant competitor has 60 per cent market share), or of 10.0× (if the rest of the market is very fragmented and the next largest player only has 2 per cent).

The vertical axis is the growth rate of the market in which the business competes. Much confusion surrounds the precise definition of this market growth rate. The correct definition is the *expected future annual growth rate* (over the next five years) *in volume* (units of production) *of the market as a whole,* not of the particular Engulf & Devour business.

ILLUSTRATION 12

Engulf & Devour Plc, Growth/Share Matrix

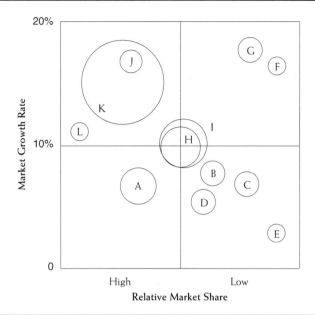

Before going on, it is important to understand the reasons why BCG and I think that the axes are significant. The relative market share is key because a business that is larger than its competitors (has a high relative market share, over 1.0✕) *ought to have lower costs, or higher prices, or both, and therefore higher profitability* than a competitor in that business with a lower share. This is generally, although not always, true, as confirmed by databases such as the PIMS studies.

It is also logical: a business with higher volume ought to be able to spread its fixed costs over more units, and therefore have lower fixed and overhead costs, as well as make better use of any expensive machinery or people that are the best for that particular business. The higher share business may also be able to charge a higher price, either because it has the best brand or because it has the best distribution or simply because it is the preferred choice of most people. Since price minus cost equals profit, the higher share competitor should have the highest margins, or be ploughing back his advantage in the form of extra customer benefits that will reinforce his market share advantage.

Note that we say that the higher share competitor *ought* to have lower costs or higher prices. It does not necessarily follow, since he may squander his potential advantage by inefficiency, sharing costs with unprofitable products, or by having poorer customer service than a rival. Where the higher share player does not have profits higher than competitors there is usually an unstable competitive relationship which can create both opportunity and vulnerability in that market (see the Opportunity/Vulnerability Index).

In some cases having a higher share of a business does not confer any benefit or potential benefit, for example where a one-man plumbing business faces a ten-man plumbing business, and the costs of labour are the same for everyone. Many people have claimed that the importance of market share, and the value of the Growth/Share Matrix, have been greatly overstated, and produce examples of cases where larger businesses are *less* profitable than smaller businesses, or where there is no systematic difference in profitability according to scale. On detailed examination, however, there are few individual business segments where it is not or cannot be a real advantage to be larger, all other things being equal. The qualification in the last phrase is absolutely crucial: relative market share is not the only influence on profitability, and it may be overwhelmed by different competitors' operating skills or strategies or random influences on profitability.

One of the major causes of confusion is that businesses are often not defined properly, in a sufficiently disaggregated way, before measuring market share. The niche player who focusses on a limited product range or customer base is playing in just one segment from the broad line supplier, who may be playing in several segments and may actually not be very large in any one segment despite appearing to have a high overall market share. For example, a national supermarket chain may be bigger than competitors who have regional chains, but the relevant basis of competition may be local scale and customer awareness. See Segmentation for the importance of correct business definition and some hints on how to do it.

If businesses are defined properly, the higher share competitor should have an advantage at least nine times out of ten. It therefore follows that the further to the left a business is on the BCG Matrix, the stronger it should be.

What about the vertical axis: the growth rate of the market? BCG claimed that there was a real difference between high growth businesses (where demand is growing at 10 per cent or more) and lower growth ones, because of greater fluidity in the former: that is, if the market is growing fast, there is more opportunity to gain market share. This is logical, both because more new business is up for grabs, and because competitors will react much more vigorously to defend their absolute share (to avoid a loss of turnover) than to defend loss of relative share, which they do not even notice in a fast changing market.

Having understood these points, we can go on to characterise the four quadrants of the BCG Matrix (see Illustration 13).

The bottom left-hand box contains the cash cows (also called gold mines in some early versions of the matrix: in many ways a better name). These businesses have high relative market share (they are by definition market leaders) and therefore ought to be profitable. They are very valuable and should be protected at all costs. They throw off a lot of cash, which can be reinvested in the business, used elsewhere in the business portfolio, used to buy other businesses, or paid out to shareholders.

The top left box comprises stars: high relative market share businesses in high growth markets. These are very profitable but may need a lot of cash to maintain their position. This cash should be made available. Whatever it takes to hold or gain share in star businesses should be undertaken. If they hold RMS, star businesses will become cash cows when the market growth slows down, and therefore hugely valuable over a long time. But if star businesses lose relative market share, as they are often allowed to do, they will end up as dogs and be of limited value.

The top right box holds question-marks (sometimes called wildcats): low RMS positions but in high growth markets. In this case 'question-mark' is a very good description of the business, since it has an uncertain future, and the decision on whether to invest in the business is both important and difficult. If a question-mark does not improve its relative market share—that is, if it remains a follower—it will end life as a dog. On the other hand, if

ILLUSTRATION 13
The Growth/Share Matrix Four Quadrants

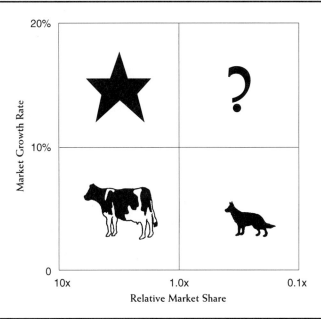

the volatility that market growth bestows is used and investment made in a question-mark to drive it into a leadership position, the business will migrate to being a star (profitable) and ends its days as a cash cow (very profitable and very cash positive). The problem is that question-mark businesses very often turn into cash traps, as money can be invested without any guarantee (and in some cases much chance) of attaining a leadership position. A business that is invested in heavily without ever attaining market leadership (like much of the British computer industry) will simply be an investment in failure and a gross waste of money.

The bottom right box is the dog kennel. Dogs are low relative market share positions in low growth businesses. The theory therefore says that they should not be very profitable and should not be able to gain share to migrate into cash cows. Given that the majority of most firm's businesses may be in this box, this is not a very cheerful notion.

In fact, the greatest weakness in the BCG theory relates to dogs, largely because of this fatalism. . . . Briefly, dogs *can* migrate into cash cows, by re-segmenting the business or simply by having greater customer responsiveness than the market leader. Even if leadership is not possible, it is usually worth while to improve market share position within the dog category. A business with a relative market share of 0.7✕ (70 per cent of the leader) may be quite profitable, highly cash positive, and quite different from a business with an RMS of only 0.3✕ (30 per cent of the leader).

Nevertheless, it may be true that there is limited room for manoeuvre with dog businesses, and they will generally be less attractive than stars or cash cows.

BCG super-imposed on the Growth/Share Matrix a theory of cash management (sometimes confusingly called portfolio management) which is intriguing and makes some

ILLUSTRATION 14

The Growth/Share Matrix Cash Characteristics

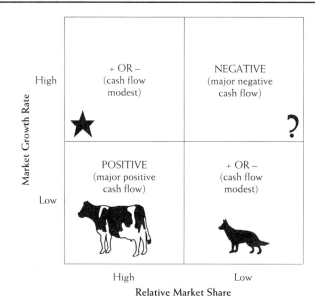

useful points, although it is also somewhat flawed. The theory looks at the cash characteristics of each of the quadrants (Illustration 14).

BCG's theory then came up with a hierarchy of uses of cash, numbered from 1 to 4 in their order of priority (Illustration 15).

1. The best use of cash, we can agree, is to defend cash cows. They should not need to use cash very often, but if investment in a new factory or technology is required, it should be made unstintingly.
2. We can also agree that the next call on cash should normally be in stars. These will need a great deal of investment to hold (or gain) relative market share.
3. The trouble begins here, with BCG's third priority, to take money from cash cows and invest in question-marks. The bastardised version of the theory stressed this cash flow in particular. BCG countered by stressing that investment in question-marks should be selective, confined to those cases where there was a real chance of attaining market leadership. With this qualification, BCG's point is sensible.
4. The lowest priority was investment in dogs, which BCG said should be minimal or even negative, if they were run for cash. This may be a sensible prescription, but the problem is that the dog kennel may contain a large range of breeds with different qualities, and a differentiated cash strategy is generally required within the dog kennel.

One real weakness of the BCG cash management theory, however, as BCG came to realise, was the assumption that the portfolio had to be in balance in respect of cash on an annual or three year basis. In fact, the cash invested in the overall business portfolio does

ILLUSTRATION 15 ───────────────────────
How to Use the Cash

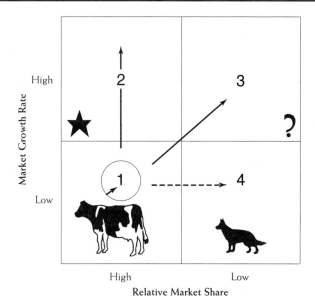

not have to equal the cash generated. Surplus cash can be invested outside of the existing portfolio, either by acquiring new businesses, by entering them from scratch, or by reducing debt or giving cash back to the shareholders. Conversely, if a business needs to invest more cash (for example, in an important and cash-guzzling star) than the business portfolio is generating, it should go out and raise the cash from bankers and/or shareholders to fund the cash gap. The business portfolio should not be thought of as a closed system.

The second major weakness of BCG views on cash, and one not fully realised until much later, was the implicit assumption that *all* businesses should be managed from the centre in a cashbox-plus-strategic-control way. See management styles for a refutation of this view. BCG's theory was immensely attractive to chairmen and chief executives seeking a sensible role for the Centre, and probably did a great deal more good than harm, but it is only a small minority of businesses that are actually run in this way. Indeed, the recent work by Goold and Campbell largely divides businesses into those that are run by financial control and those that follow strategic control or strategic planning. These are two very different approaches, the former decentralised, the latter more centralised, and it is difficult to combine the two styles, as BCG's approach assumed. Perhaps, in the future, someone will devise a method of control which does incorporate the strong points of both styles, but it will take much more than a two-by-two matrix to realise this vision.

The BCG Matrix marked a major contribution to management thinking. From the mid to late 1970s BCG tended to retreat too much under the weight of critical comment, and the matrix is not much used today. It is well overdue for a revival. Anyone who tries to apply it thoughtfully to his or her business will learn a lot during the process.

JUST-IN-TIME (JIT)

Valuable system developed first in Japan for production management aimed at minimising stock by having materials and work-in-progress delivered to the right place at the right time. As well as lowering costs, JIT can have other major benefits: the systematic identification of operational problems and their resolution by technology-based tools; higher levels of customer service and speeding up the time to market; higher quality standards by being 'right first time'; and higher standards of competence in the production function generally. To be most effective, JIT should be introduced as part of TQM (Total Quality Management), and it should be recognised at the outset that JIT is not just a technique, but a way of changing behaviour. A full JIT programme such as introduced by Toyota or Matsushita may take years to complete. But companies without JIT who compete against those with JIT will have a major handicap.

Properly conceived, JIT should be seen as a sychronising way of life: jobs must be completed quickly, but even more important is that they be completed just in time to fit in with the next step in the dance. This is a radically different concept from traditional assembly line thinking, which is sequential rather than synchronising. Charles Hampden-Turner and Fons Trompenaars point out that culturally, the U.S., U.K., Sweden and Holland are disposed towards trying to speed things up sequentially, whereas Japan, Germany and France are more geared towards synchronisation. This means that when installing JIT and other synchronising techniques in 'Anglo-Saxon' and similar countries, it should be realised that JIT can go against the cultural grain: people need to be re-trained to think and act in a synchronised way.

OPPORTUNITY/VULNERABILITY INDEX

An interesting outgrowth from the BCG Matrix, although not developed until the late 1970s/early 1980s (mainly by Bain & Company) and refined later that decade by The LEK Partnership, another strategy boutique. BCG had posited that high relative market share businesses (leaders) should be highly profitable, and the logic of the experience curve certainly suggested that the higher the market share, the higher the profitability (unless the firm was not using its potential advantages, or pricing to penetrate the market still further). It followed that it should be possible to construct a 'normative curve' to describe the profitability of the average business segment in a particular industry, or, with a wider band, all industries, according to a normal expectation given the segment's relative market share. This normative band is shown on the matrix in Illustration 16.

The parallel area between the two curved lines represents the normative curve: depending on the exact data used, perhaps 80 per cent of observations would fall between these broad limits, and it would be unusual (only 20 per cent of business segment positions) for businesses to fall outside the bands. (The normative band can be constructed based on actual data of business segment positions and profitability, but only correct segmentation: in practice such data can only be obtained with any degree of confidence after working within a client organisation, and building up an anonymous database of the relationships.) In fact empirical data did enable the normative band to be built up in this way. The band used to be shown coloured in yellow, hence the chart became known in some circles as a bananagram.

ILLUSTRATION 16
Opportunity/Vulnerability Matrix

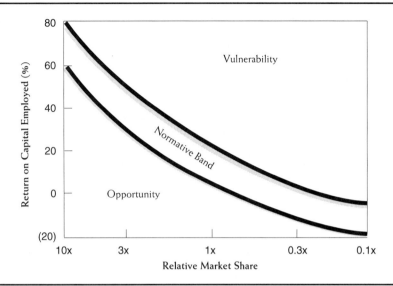

So what? Well, one implication is that high relative market share positions, correctly segmented, are as valuable as BCG said, whatever reservations one has about the experience curve. Managers should therefore strive to be in such businesses and cannot expect to have profitability above the required rate of return of investors unless a majority of their sales are in leaders or strong followers (at least .7× Relative Market Share, that is, at least 70 per cent as the leader in the segment). Another implication, not really made clearly by BCG, and in some ways obscured by the doctrine of the BCG matrix about dogs, was that it was useful to improve relative market share in a business segment *whatever the starting position*: useful to take a .3× RMS business and move it to a .6× RMS position, to take a .5× position and take it to 1.0×, to take a 2× position and move it to 4×, and so on. The chart enables one to calculate roughly what equilibrium profitability can be expected from any particular position, so that it is possible to state roughly the benefit of moving any particular segment position in this way and compare it to the expected short term cost of doing so (by extra marketing or service, product development or lower prices). In this way it can be seen (a) whether it is worth trying to raise RMS, and (b) which segments give the biggest bang for the buck.

But the most valuable use of the matrix lies not in the 80 per cent of positions that fall within the banana (normative curve), but rather in the 20 per cent that fall outside. Two examples of possible such positions are given in Illustration 17.

Business A is earning (say) 20 per cent Return On Capital Employed, a good return, but is in a weak Relative Market Share position (say .3×, or only 30 per cent the size of the segment leader). The theory and empirical data from the matrix suggest that the combination of these two positions is at best anomalous, and probably unsustainable. Business A is therefore in the 'vulnerability' part of the matrix. The expectation must be that in the medium term, either the business must improve its Relative Market Share position to

I L L U S T R A T I O N   1 7

Opportunity/Vulnerability Matrix Illustrative Positions of Business
Outside the Banana

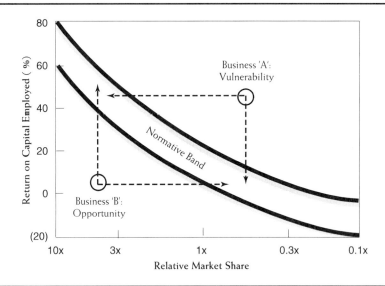

sustain its profitability (the dotted arrow moving left), or that it will decline in profitability (to about break even). Why should this happen? Well, the banana indicates that the market leader in this business may well be earning 40 per cent or even more ROCE in the
segment (the beauty of the method is that this can be investigated empirically). What may
be happening is that the leader is holding a price umbrella over the market: that is, is pricing unsustainably high, so that even the competitors with weak market share are protected
from normal competitive rainfall. What happens if the market leader suddenly cuts prices
by 20 per cent? He will still earn a good return, but the weaker competitors will not. (The
leader may not cut prices, but instead provide extra product benefits or service or other features, but the effect would still be a margin cut.) It is as well to know that business A is vulnerable. If relative market share cannot be improved, it is sensible to sell it before the
profitability degrades.

   Now let's look at Business B. This is a business in a strong relative market share position:
the leader in its segment, four times larger than its nearest rival. It is earning 8 per cent
ROCE. This is a wonderful business to find. The theory and practical data suggest that such
a business should be making 40 per cent ROCE, not 8 per cent. Nine times out of ten when
such businesses are found, it is possible to make them *very* much more profitable, usually
by radical cost reduction (often involving BPR), but sometimes through radical improvement of the service and product offering to the customer at low extra cost to the supplier,
but enabling a large price hike to be made. Managements of particular businesses very often
become complacent with historical returns and think it is impossible to raise profits in a
step function to three, four or five times their current level. The bananagram challenges
that thinking for leadership segment positions, and usually the bananagram is proved right.
After all, high relative market share implies huge potential advantages: but these must be
earned and exploited, as they do not automatically disgorge huge profits.

PORTER'S FIVE COMPETITIVE FORCES

Porter was an innovator in structural analysis of markets, which previously, even with BCG, tended to focus largely on direct competition in the industry, without looking systematically at the context in other stages of the industry value chain. Porter's five forces to analyse are:

1. Threat of potential new entrants
2. Threat from substitutes using different technology
3. Bargaining power of customers
4. Bargaining power of suppliers
5. Competition amongst existing suppliers.

The interactions amongst the five forces are shown in Illustration 18.

From this Porter builds a useful model of industry attractiveness and how this might change over time, both because of objective economic changes and also because of the ambitions of the players themselves.

ILLUSTRATION 18
Michael Porter's Five Competitive Forces

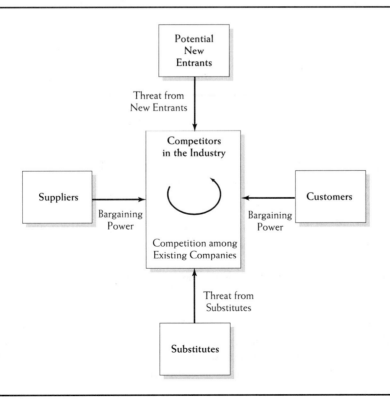

PRODUCT LINE PROFITABILITY

Much neglected, highly useful analysis of how much money a firm makes (fully costed) on each of its products or services. Usually throws up results that surprise managers, often showing that a majority of products lose money on a fully costed basis, and 100 per cent or more than 100 per cent of the profits are made by a small proportion of exceptional money spinners. No one has yet standardised a universally applicable way of conducting this analysis. Traditional accounting systems make it very difficult, and accurate product line profitability is nearly always supplied by outside consultants.

RCP (RELATIVE COST POSITION)

The cost position of a firm in a product relative to that of a competitor. For example, if it costs Heinz 10p to manufacture a can of beans, and it costs Crosse & Blackwell 11p for the same can, Heinz has an RCP advantage of about 10 per cent, or an RCP of 91 (C&B = 100). Classical economics assumes that firms in an industry will come to have the same cost position, but in the real world this is almost never true. RCP can be quite difficult to establish (usually requiring the use of specialist consultants) but it is often not what managers imagined, and the differences between competitors usually emerge as much greater than previously thought. It is useful (and necessary anyway, to arrive at the total answer) to look at RCP at each stage of the value chain: for example, X may have a 30 per cent cost advantage in production but have an inefficient salesforce, and be at a 10 per cent cost disadvantage in selling. Relative cost advantage is often, but by no means always, related to scale or experience advantages (expressed in RMS: Relative Market Share).

RCP analysis is not invalidated by differences in quality, or the fact that one supplier may have a better brand. The cost position can be looked at with the price realisation of each supplier indexed at 100, so that if Heinz receives 12p for its can of beans and C&B only 10p, Heinz's total and sub-divided costs can be looked at relative to the 12p, and C&B's relative to the 10p that they receive. On this basis, Heinz would have a total cost of 83 (10/12) and C&B a total cost of 110 (11/10): Heinz would be making a profit margin of 17 per cent but C&B would be losing 10 per cent. The real cost difference between the two firms (adjusted for price realisation) would be 27 per cent (110 minus 83). Heinz might be spending more on marketing, to help capture the extra price realisation, but the analysis would show this as well.

RCP analysis is expensive and only worth doing when there is a lot of turnover in the products being compared and there is a good chance that it will reveal things that can be acted upon, or help to set a competitive strategy in a battle worth winning. RCP analysis can lead to cost savings through imitation: for example, a competitor may miss out a process step altogether that the firm can also eliminate; or lead to a dramatic re-design of production to take out perhaps 30 per cent of cost.

RCP is little practised but where it has been used it has generally been extremely insightful and effective, saving tens of millions of pounds and giving a return of about 20–50 times the amount paid for the analysis (which will be several hundred thousand pounds). RCP cannot be conducted vis-à-vis most Japanese competitors, because it is impossible to discover their real costs, partly because of deliberate obfuscation, and partly because of the *keiretsu* system. See also RPP (Relative Price Position), and RMS.

RMS (RELATIVE MARKET SHARE)

The share of a firm in a business segment divided by the share of the largest competitor that the firm has. Much more important than market share as an absolute number. For example, if Sony's nearest competitor in making Walkman-type products is one tenth the size, Sony will have an RMS of 10 times (written as 10×, or 10.0×, or sometimes simply 10). The competitor, on the other hand, will have an RMS that is the reciprocal of this: it will have an RMS of 0.1×. One more example will suffice: if Coca-Cola in one national market has a market share of 60 per cent, and Pepsi-Cola, 30 per cent, then Coke has an RMS of 2×, and Pepsi 0.5×.

Relative market share should correlate with profitability. If it does not, one (or more) of five things is happening: either (1) the business segment has been defined incorrectly; or (2) the smaller competitor is much cleverer than the bigger: the leader is not using his potential advantage properly, and/or the follower has found a nifty way to lower costs or higher prices that has overcome the advantages of scale and experience; or (3) the leader is deliberately forfeiting profit now by expense reinvestment that will compound his advantage in the future, and lead to much higher profits then; or (4) there is over-capacity in the industry, so that the key concern is capacity utilisation, and the bigger competitors may simply have too much of the excess; or (5) it is a business not susceptible to normal scale, status and experience effects.

Let us take each of these in turn. (1) Incorrect business definition: more often than not, this is the reason. In most cases, the segment will not have been defined in a sufficiently disaggregated way. (2) A clever follower. This does happen, and is usually manifest in a refusal to play by the usual rules of the game. (3) Long term compounding strategy by the leader. May be true if it is Japanese or Korean, almost certainly not otherwise. (4) Excess capacity: yes, sometimes. (5) Industry and business not susceptible to scale, experience or status: very rare. Even service businesses generally are skewed in favour of the bigger players, who have greater advantages in terms of branding, reputation, lower marketing and selling costs, and greater expertise and ability to attract the best recruits.

One of the most useful charts to draw for any business, if the data can be collected, is shown in Illustration 19, which looks at the profitability (in terms of ROS or ROCE) of different competitors in a business segment.

The chart shows a typical pattern, but the beauty of the method is that empirical data can be displayed to see whether and how far the expected pattern applies. If there is deviance from the normal pattern, the reasons given in (1) to (5) above can be systematically investigated.

The chart stops at 2× (two times) RMS only because in this case the leader was here. In other examples the relationship has been observed to continue working over whatever range of RMS applies: businesses with a 10× RMS really do make very high ROCE: normally in the 60–90 per cent range.

Observation of this relationship led to the development of a very useful tool—the Opportunity/Vulnerability Matrix. . . . See also RCP.

ILLUSTRATION 19
Typical Pattern of Profitability by RMS

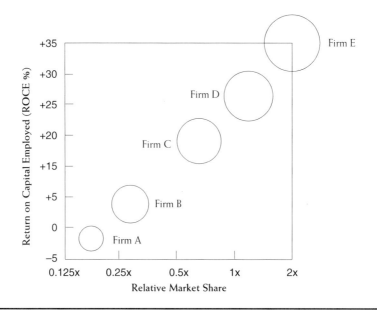

RPP (RELATIVE PRICE POSITION)

A complement to RCP (Relative Cost Position). RPP looks at the price realisation for two or more competitors in the same product or service. If two identical packets of crisps are sold in the same outlet, one under the KP brand, and one a retailer's private label, and the former is 20p and the latter 18p, then the KP RPP is 20/18 = 111 and the RPP of the retailer's brand is 18/20 = 90. RPP shows how far there is a brand, quality or distribution advantage. See also RCP.

S-CURVE

The growth pattern resembling an S: slow to pick up, followed by a period of maximum growth, then a point of inflection leading to gradually slower growth. Study of the 1665 Plague in England led to the conclusion that the spread of disease followed a mathematically predictable path, and the same methodology has been used with some success to predict the rate at which a new product will penetrate into any given population, given the early experience. If, for example, you knew that the penetration of dishwashers into Korea was 1 per cent in the first year, 2 per cent in the second year and 4.5 per cent in the third year, you could calculate a prediction for future years.

The formula to be used to calculate each year's observation is f/1 − f, where:

f = the penetration (expressed as a fraction: e.g. 1 per cent = 0.01), and
1 – f = one minus the penetration fraction (e.g. 1 – 0.01 = 0.99)
f/1 – f = 0.0101 in this case, or for the 2 per cent observation
      = 0.02/0.98
      = 0.0204

If the observations are plotted on semi-log paper and a straight line is drawn through the observations, predictions for future years emerge in the form of the 'answer' above (e.g. 0.0204), which can then be converted by algebra into the percentage prediction. A simple computer program will perform the calculations without the need to resort to plotting on semi-log paper.

The same procedure can be used in modified form where you know that there will be a saturation level at a given point. In dishwashers in Korea, for example, you may know from similar cases that no-one below a certain income level will ever own a dishwasher. Let us assume that this cuts out 40 per cent of the population: the saturation level is therefore 60 per cent. Instead of using 1.0 as the maximum point, therefore, we would use 0.6, the saturation point(s). The calculation would then be f/s – f, and the first observation (at 1 per cent) would become:

$$0.01/.6 - 0.01 = 0.1695.$$

Many people are sceptical of the power of this methodology until they actually use it. It is not, of course, a magic predictor, but it does enable you to calculate what the answer would be if the current momentum persists. It will work out when the growth will slow because there is a diminishing pool of people to be 'converted' to the new product.

SEGMENTATION

Most usefully, the process of analysing customers, costs and competitors in order to decide where and how to wage the competitive battle; or a description of the competitive map according to the contours of the business segments. Sadly, segmentation is often used to describe a more limited (and often misleading) exercise in dividing up customer groups. Proper segmentation only takes place at the level of identifying the business segments: this is at the root of any firm's business strategy. Segmentation in this most useful sense is what is discussed below.

It is crucial for any firm to know which segments it is operating in, to know its relative market share in those segments, and to focus on those segments where it has or can build a leadership position. A segment is a competitive system, or arena, where it is possible to build barriers against other firms, by having lower costs or customer-satisfying differentiation (which will be expressed in higher prices, and/or in higher customer volume which itself will lead to lower costs). A segment can be a particular product, or a particular customer group being sold a standard product, or a particular customer group being sold a special product or provided with a special service, or a particular distribution channel or region, or any combination of the above. What matters is that the following conditions for a genuine segment are *all* satisfied:

1. The segment must be capable of clear distinction, so that there is no doubt which customers and products fall inside and outside the segment.
2. The segment must have a clear and limited set of competitors that serve it.
3. It must be possible to organise supply of a product or service to the segment in a way that represents some specialisation, and is differentiated from supply to another or other segments.
4. The segment must have purchase criteria that are different in important ways from other segments.
5. The segment must be one where competitors specialise, and where there is a characteristic market share ranking that can be described.
6. The segment must be capable of giving at least one competitor a profitability advantage, either by having lower costs, or higher prices, than other competitors, or both.
7. It must be possible to build barriers around the segment to deter new entrants.

Segmentation may change over time. To take the example of the motor car, Henry Ford created his own segment around the black model-T Ford: the mass produced, standard automobile. Initially, he had 100 per cent of this segment, and it satisfied all of the rules above. Then it became possible to provide other colours at relatively low cost, and General Motors changed the mass automobile market to include any colour, standard car: the 'black car' segment ceased to exist and became part of a wider competitive arena. Subsequently new segments emerged, based on sports/high performance criteria, and later on 'compact' low fuel consumption cars.

Geography is a fascinating and changing dimension of segmentation. Most products and services start out by having a very limited geographical reach: one region or one country. The U.K. crisp (what Americans call potato chips) market is an interesting example. At one time the market was dominated by Smiths, then by Golden Wonder (who innovated with a range of flavours), both national competitors. But slowly but surely a new regional competitor, Walkers, emerged, based on superior quality. Initially the segment boundaries of Walkers were very restricted, based around the Midlands where the company was based. Within these regions the national segmentation did not rule: Walkers was the number one supplier by a long way, although nationally very small. Gradually, with greater production and improved distribution, Walkers became a national competitor, and for a time market leader, again causing the segmentation to revert to a national level.

An increasing number of markets are global: the battle between Pepsi and Coke is fought out beyond the boundaries of individual countries. Nevertheless, segment relative market share positions often vary significantly in different countries: if Pepsi outsells Coke in one national market, against the global trend, that national market is today a separate segment. If, on the other hand, relative market shares around the world converge, the whole world can become one segment for cola drinks. Economics comes into this as well. To take one far-fetched example, assume that Coke came to have a two to one advantage over Pepsi everywhere in the world except New Zealand, where Pepsi was by far the leader, it would be correct to speak of New Zealand as a separate segment, but the rest of the world would be one segment and the marketing scale advantage enjoyed by Coke everywhere else would make New Zealand a barely tenable separate segment for Pepsi: at some point, the most interesting segmentation would have become global, even if national segment enclaves temporarily continued to exist.

Similarly, segments can be carved out or relinquished within a product range. At one time, British motorcycles were the market leaders throughout the world whatever type or power of bike was being considered: motorcycles were one global segment. Then the Japanese began to develop bikes, based around the low-powered bikes for which there was greatest domestic demand. What happened first was that this low c.c. market became a separate segment in Japan, because the market leaders (Honda and Yamaha) were different from the leaders in the rest of the world market (and in Japan in mid and high performance bikes). Then the Japanese companies, by trial and error, managed to develop a market for these low c.c. bikes in America, and later throughout the world, so that low c.c. bikes became a separate global segment. Later, using modular designs and high cost sharing, the Japanese suppliers entered mid size bikes, became market leaders in these, thus changing the segmentation around the world by annexing the mid market, so that there were two global segments: the low-to-mid segment (dominated by the Japanese), and the high performance segment, still dominated by Norton and BSA. Then, in the early 1970s, the Japanese began to edge their way into the high performance segment, and BMW created a separate high-comfort, high-safety segment, so that the world motorcycle market had two major segments: the `BMW' segment, and the rest (the majority) of the market, served largely by Japanese competitors.

In diagnosing what segments you are in today—whether the market is one big segment or several small ones—the best way is to set up hypotheses that X market is a separate segment from Y market, and then test according to the following rules. The short set of rules, that will give you the correct answer 95 per cent of the time, is to ask just two questions:

1. Are there separate competitors, with significant market share, in segment X that do not participate in segment Y? If so, it is a separate segment.
2. Are the relative market share positions in market X different from those in market Y, even if the same competitors compete? If so, it is a separate segment. For example, Heinz and HP compete in both the red sauce (ketchup) and thick brown sauce markets in the U.K., but in the first Heinz is miles ahead of HP, and in the latter HP is way ahead: so they are separate segments.

To be absolutely sure, apply the following additional rules:

3. Is your firm's profitability different in market X from market Y? If so, even if it is the same product being supplied to different customers, it may be a separate segment.
4. Are the cost structures different in the two markets?
5. Are there technological barriers between the two markets that only some competitors can surmount?
6. Are prices different (for the same product or service) in the different markets?
7. Is it possible to gain an economic advantage by specialising in one of the markets, by gaining lower costs or higher prices in that market?

Because segmentation changes over time, it is interesting to look both at the empirical segmentation today, which is defined particularly by the first two questions above, and also at potential segmentation based on the economics of the business: what is called economic segmentation. Economic segmentation applies questions (3) to (7) above to ask, not just whether the segmentation is distinct today, but whether it could be distinct. Economic segmentation can be used as a technique to re-segment a market, either by creating a new, smaller segment out of an existing segment (as with the initial Japanese move to create a below-250 c.c. motorcycle segment), or to merge two segments together (as with the later annexation of first the mid and then the high performance motorcycle segments) in order to realise economies of scale. Economic segmentation asks: could we obtain lower costs or higher prices or both by redefining the segment and changing the rules of the game?

SEVEN SS, 7S FRAMEWORK

A framework for thinking about a firm's personality; a diagnostic tool for describing any company, developed by Peters & Waterman and their then colleagues in McKinsey around 1980. Seven elements of an organisation, all beginning with S—strategy, structure, systems, style, skills, staff and shared values—can be used as a checklist. Do the Ss fit well together, or are they inconsistent or unclear? When the Ss fit well together and reinforce each other, the organisation is likely to be moving forward purposefully; where the Ss are in conflict, it is likely to lack unity and momentum. The Seven Ss are shown in Illustration 20.

Note, however, that an organisation with seven consistent Ss will be much harder to change than one where the Ss are visibly in disarray.

ILLUSTRATION 20
The Seven Ss

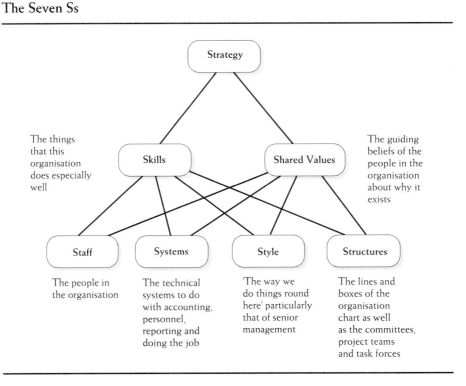

SUSTAINABLE GROWTH RATE (SGR)

Concept invented by BCG in the early 1970s to measure and demonstrate the effects of leverage and the proportion of earnings retained on the rate at which a company could grow. The point was that a firm could be constrained from growing (in the absence of new equity) if it had too little debt or retained too low a proportion of its earnings (that is, if dividends were too high a proportion of earnings). Since BCG believed (correctly) that the successful firm should aim to grow market share in its major markets, it tended to use the SGR to urge firms to become high debt, low dividend corporations, channelling as much money as possible back into investment. For the algebraicly inclined, the SGR formula is:

$$SGR = D/E \ (R - i)p + Rp$$

where:

$$D/E = \text{Debt/Equity}$$
$$R = \text{return on assets, after tax}$$
$$i = \text{interest rate, after tax}$$
$$p = \text{percentage of earnings retained.}$$

The SGR is more an interesting curiosity than a useful management tool, except where firms are competing pretty much head to head in a single segment business. The flaw in the thinking is that very few firms are that: there are usually a very large number of businesses and funds for one can come from one or more other businesses, or from the sale of one or more businesses. It is rarely the case that financial policy constrains growth.

TIME-BASED COMPETITION

Concept invented by BCG which holds that the time it takes a firm to get a product from conception to the customer, or to complete its tasks and provide goods or services to market can be the key to competitive advantage. Time is a crucial factor in the internal and external chain of customers-and-suppliers. At each internal or external customer/supplier interface there is not just a risk, but a near-certainty, that time will be wasted. And time really is money, as well as being service to boot. The total time taken through the chain—throughput time—determines not only the firm's costs, but is also a litmus test of the firm's responsiveness to customers. Concentration of time to market therefore kills two birds with one concept: service and cost. If quality is free, reducing the time to market has negative costs as well as customer benefits. Notwithstanding its importance, time-based competition is basically a package of earlier discoveries, and it in turn has been repackaged as just a part of BPR (business process re-engineering).

It has been long realised that most of the time taken to make a product or provide a service is generally not 'productive' time but the gaps between different stages of the process. An example is given in the entry on BPR of IBM Credit, which at one time took 7 days to process a credit application for a would-be computer buyer: but the actual work involved took only 90 minutes. By cutting out the gaps and giving responsibility to one person, costs can be cut, customer satisfaction and retention increased, and profits dramatically increased.

Another example, this time quoted in the 'bible' of time-based competition (*Competing Against Time: How Time-Based Competition is Reshaping Global Markets*, by George Stalk, Jr., and Thomas M. Hout), is the 'H-Y War' in the early 1980s between Honda and Yamaha. This revolved around the speed with which new motorcycles could be produced. Honda won the war by producing first 60 new motorcycle models in a year, and then another 113 new models in 18 months, speed that Yamaha could not match.

Most organisations, even well run ones like Yamaha, soak up time like a sponge. Stalk and Hout invented the '0.05 to 5 rule', which says that most products are receiving value for between one-half of one per cent and five per cent of the time that they are in the value delivery system of the firm. In other words, over 95 per cent of the time products spend in their companies is wasted; eliminate the wasted time, and time to market can be increased between 20 and 200 times!

The time to market a product can be calculated and compared to that of several competitors; the idea behind time-based competition is to become the shortest time-to-market competitor. It is worth stopping to think through the implications for your own business.

TIME ELASTICITY OF PROFITABILITY

BCG's term for the relationship between a supplier's profit and the speed with which the product is supplied (the elapsed time between the customer's decision to buy and his receipt of the product or service). Short elapsed time equals high profit; long elapsed time equals low profit. This is because the customer will pay top whack if he can obtain the product at once, but if he has to wait he will shop around and may lower the price he will pay. Customers made to wait may also cancel their orders.

The firm's value-delivery system therefore needs to be changed to speed up time to market. Any extra costs will be more than compensated for by higher prices and greater market share.

Decision and Planning Tools[†]

GLEN D. HOFFHERR AND NORMAN W. YOUNG[*]

In our daily business we face many situations for which we do not have detailed factual information. We are forced to make decisions on what we think rather than on what we know. We then apply the accumulation of our experiences, knowledge, and possibly the recommendations of our associates to make the decision. We are generally thought to have good judgment if the results of our decisions are good for the organization. Decisions that do not bring about the desired results may cause our judgment to be called into question. The tools in this article will help you make better decisions by focusing on the information you have.

There is a group of tools often called the 7 *New QC tools*, or the 7 *Management and Planning tools*. These names do not describe the power of these tools or who should use them. They would more accurately be called decision and planning tools. This article lists and describes the authors' favorite decision and planning tools. They are used most effectively to make decisions and plans when you do not have hard data or facts. There is no right or wrong way to use any of these tools. Remember that the purpose of any tool is to enable you to make a better decision. These tools are powerful vehicles for gathering, organizing, examining, and presenting the collective judgment(s) of you and your coworkers. They will improve the quality of the decisions you make and increase your success at solving problems and achieving goals.

Many of these tools can be used in multiple ways. Some have facets that predispose them to certain situations. As you work with the tools, you will find that you use some every day and others infrequently. You will develop comfort and expertise with the tools you use most often.

In our zeal to develop the science of leadership and decision making, we often over-use tools and techniques. The result is that we lose sight of the goal that we are trying to accomplish, or miss an opportunity through analysis paralysis. Thus, it is most important to know when not to use tools. When the proper decision is clear to all concerned, when you have

[*] Source: Much of the information contained in this article is taken from *The Toolbook: Decision Making and Planning for Optimum Results* and the courseware that is associated with it. The authors gratefully acknowledge the publisher, Markon Inc., for granting permission to use excerpts from these two works.

[†]"Decision and Planning Tools" by Glen D. Hoffherr and Norman W. Young, 1995. Reprinted by permission of the authors.

adequate resources and everyone is in agreement—ACT! You will, however, want to employ the tools when:

- you are having difficulty analyzing complex alternatives,
- you disagree with coworkers and must find a way to come to consensus,
- you need to organize large volumes of data,
- you have limited resources and must set priorities, or
- you want to develop a complete plan including priorities, schedules, and contingency plans.

These tools organize judgmental or soft data into clear pictures that promote effective decision making. Successful decision making begins with the proper mindset. In traditional organizations, we have assumed that one person, the manager, has all the answers. As our world has become more complex, so have the decisions we face. Today everyone in the organization must be able to make good decisions; they must have the appropriate tools to be able to function adequately in their jobs.

Today good decisions involve the consideration of many alternatives. Through the participation of others, we search for every possible option. We try to consider what could go wrong. Our attitudes towards others and the process we use will affect the value we receive. To receive the most benefit from these tools:

- value the differences of others; they can offer a different point of view,
- value the ideas of others; this will keep creative ideas flowing,
- embrace ambiguity; it promotes creativity,
- be flexible; this will lead to more effective planning,
- trust your (and others') initial reactions; it may prevent making fundamental mistakes, and
- use them only when they are needed, not because you think you should.

Each tool is different, but there are some common guidelines that make all the tools more effective.

- Get the right people to form the group—diverse, willing, and skilled.
- Empower the group by defining operating limits, granting the authority to make changes, providing protection, support, and resources, and defining measures of accountability.
- Clearly define the opportunity or goal.
- Allow time to complete the process.
- Include new ideas at any time.
- Make decisions only by consensus. Majority vote creates winners and losers. The time required to reach consensus will be offset by the speed of implementation.
- *Make the tool work for you, do not work for the tool.*

These tools are known by many different names. The name listed first is the authors' choice. The tools that will be covered in this article are brainstorming, forced choice, card sort (affinity diagram), cause & effect map (relationship diagram, ID), selection window, tree diagram, force field analysis, matrices, problem prevention plan (contingency plan, PDPC), and PERT chart (CPM, arrow diagram).

BRAINSTORMING

Brainstorming is the most commonly used method for the generation of a large number of ideas in a group setting. Despite its widespread usage, there remains a body of empirical data that indicates that its use by individuals or nominal groups (groups that never physically meet) may be more effective than its use by people in a meeting-type setting. We think brainstorming is most effective when used by a group of four to nine people.

Like many commonly used tools, there is some confusion regarding the source of brainstorming. Mizuno in the *7 New QC Tools* (1979) indicated that it was introduced to Japan in 1952. Donelson Forsyth in *An Introduction To Group Dynamics* (1983) cites the following version.

> Brainstorming was developed in 1957 by Alex F. Osborne, an advertising executive. He defined four traits which contributed to the generation of new alternatives or ideas. Virtually all brainstorming work today is based on the traits of expressiveness, non-evaluative, quantity, and building as described below.
>
> Osborne recommended:
>
> - recording all of the ideas in full view of participants,
> - stimulating ideas by asking open-ended questions,
> - utilizing a turn-taking procedure if interaction becomes unequal,
> - evaluating ideas at a later session.
>
> In 1974, Rickards added the idea of warm up exercises to 'break the ice' and get discussion started.
>
> Experience has shown that training in brainstorming procedures, practicing brainstorming, and allowing the participants to record their ideas after the brainstorming session improves the group's proficiency.

The cornerstone of judgmental decision making is the generation of creative alternatives. Virtually every decision and planning tool requires such alternatives. As a freewheeling vehicle for getting new ideas, brainstorming can help a group break through existing patterns of thought and generate new options. Often, however, we fail to get the results we need by omitting one of the few *but critical* rules of brainstorming. Remember, creativity is the result of productive controversy. The following rules apply to any type of group creative process, including brainstorming.

1. *Expressiveness.* Each individual in the group must have complete freedom to express any idea that comes to mind, no matter how strange, wild, or fanciful. Freewheeling ideas are encouraged, and constraint is avoided.
2. *Non-evaluative.* Ideas are not to be evaluated in any way during the generation phase. All ideas are valuable, and criticizing another's viewpoint is not allowed. A negative comment can stifle the energy and creativity of a group so that the exercise becomes useless.
3. *Quantity.* The goal of the generation process is to create as many ideas as possible. Even the most unrealistic idea can provide the stimulus or basis for a totally new and valuable idea. Having many new ideas increases the possibility of generating excellent solutions.

FIGURE 1

Results of Brainstorming

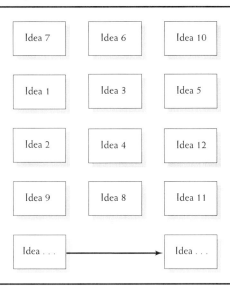

4. *Building.* Brainstorming is conducted in a group so that participants can draw from one another. We draw from each other by modifying and adding to our ideas. This will create mental bridges to new opportunities.

To complete a brainstorming session, first select a purpose. Be as specific as possible, but consider the resources available to the group. Be sure everyone in the group fully understands and agrees with the purpose. Next, organize your group. Decide who will write, and where the ideas will be placed for best visibility. Be sure to place only one idea on a card and write clearly so that everyone can read the cards. Be wild! Impossible ideas can stimulate spontaneity and help to suspend critical judgment. Finally, set a time limit. The pressure of a time limit helps to put evaluation on hold. It is the creative, right side of the brain that has the ability to react, while the evaluative left brain requires time to think through any new idea. The output of a typical brainstorming session is shown in Figure 1.

FORCED CHOICE

Forced choice is an adaptation of a forced choice matrix from a training course taught by M.B. Bryce Associates in the late 1960s. It relies on a basic pairwise comparison to aid the user in sorting large lists, or lists where there is little difference between the options presented. In its matrix form, the forced choice was cumbersome to use and required the use of special preprinted matrix forms.

The free form adaptation described here was developed by N.W. Young in 1981 when he created a list-based pairwise comparison in a basic language computer program. It was further refined for use in a facilitated group setting to aid the group in reaching consensus on the priority of options in a list.

The forced choice requires a list of items or alternatives to be sorted against an agreed-upon standard. Each alternative is measured against the standard. It also requires a method of marking the choices made during a sort. Completing the forced choice can help you make choices in complex situations, as well as to help defuse difficult political situations by helping a group make choices together. It is most effective in defining areas of inconsistency in logic and is easily completed individually or in a group.

To complete a forced choice, select a list to be sorted or ranked. This list can be the product of a creative effort, such as brainstorming or any other situation that produces alternatives to be sorted. Write the list where everyone can see it. Leave a blank area or column to the right. Draw a line to separate the area on the right from the list and additional lines to separate each of the alternatives. This is not required, but it will simplify the necessary record keeping. Now define a standard for the sort. When selecting standards, consider customer impact, satisfaction, time, cost, level of quality, and so on. The standard must be clearly voiced.

Then perform a pairwise comparison to isolate a single choice among many choices. The comparison will focus all resources on the single choice and simplify the process of selection. Since the number of comparisons required to sort or rank a list grows rapidly as the list gets longer, the use of the pairwise comparison is limited only by time. Begin the pairwise comparison of each item in the list with every other item in the list. Form a sentence using the items being compared and the standard of comparison. Make a mark in the right-hand column for the item that wins the comparison. Continue using the same comparison until each possible pairwise comparison has been made once. To ensure that no possible comparisons are missed and none are performed more than once, use the following methodology.

(a) Compare the *1st* item with each item below it in the list, that is, compare item 1 with item 2, compare item 1 with item 3, compare item 1 with item 4, and so on until you reach the end of the list.

(b) Compare the *2nd* item with each item below it in the list, that is, compare item 2 with item 3, compare item 2 with item 4, and so on until you reach the end.

(c) Compare the *nth* item with each item below it in the list, that is, compare item n with item n + 1, compare item n with item n + 2, and so on.

(d) The last comparison will be the next to last item with the last item.

After you have completed all comparisons, summarize and analyze the results by adding the number of marks each item received and writing that number at the end of the row. The item, or option, with the highest number has best met the standard. Those with lower numbers have met the standard to a lesser degree. Understanding of the results will be improved for larger lists by rewriting the list in numerical order from the top to the bottom.

Beware of items that have the same numerical value. This points out areas where the results of your comparisons were inconsistent or circular reasoning was used. Such inconsistencies near the bottom of your list (after reordering) will have little effect on your future efforts. Inconsistencies at or near the top of the reordered list suggest fuzzy comprehension of the most important items. Further discussion and more research may be necessary before you are ready to take action, based on the results of the forced choice. Figure 2 shows how to complete a forced choice.

FIGURE 2

Forced Choice Using Brainstormed List

Greatest Impact on Reduced Sales

Out of control processes	///	3
Flexibility to customer needs	//	2
Customer communication difficulties	////	(4)
Product quality is lacking	/	1
Product shipping problems		0

CARD SORT (AFFINITY DIAGRAM)

The card sort is a generic name for a tool that uses the creativity of a group to organize large amounts of information or complex situations into manageable order. It begins with a clearly defined purpose to keep the group on track. It then uses creative techniques, such as brainstorming or mind mapping, to generate a large volume of ideas. Finally, silent sorting promotes group interaction without criticism.

The card sort has a long history and is known by several other names and variations including the following:

The *person card sort* was used in anthropological work in the 1930s to sort information about artifacts. It was also used to some advantage during the Watergate investigations and to plan the Apollo moon landings.

The *KJ Method®* is the registered trademark of Jiro Kawakita who is credited with creating the card sort as we know it today. In the 1960s this Japanese anthropologist developed the rules that allow us to sift efficiently through large amounts of data and to allow new patterns of information to rise to the surface.

The *affinity diagram* is a variation of the KJ Method first documented in *The 7 New QC Tools* by Shigeru Mizuno.

The *Shiba method* is a creation of Shobi Shiba, a Japanese consultant who was a student of Dr. Kawakita. He uses a new rule set, popularized at the Center for Quality in Boston, Massachusetts, based on logical rather that intuitive methods.

The *whole brain affinity model* was developed by Glen Hoffherr, John Moran, and Richard Talbot and published in GOAL/QPC's *Competitive Times Newsletter*. The whole brain affinity takes the power and strength of the traditional card sort and adds Ned Herrmann's brain dominance model. The Herrmann brain dominance model is a metaphorical interpretation of how we think. This seminal work on problem solving combines the two into a colorful implementation of the card sort that shows the cognitive styles of the participant group.

The card sort combines techniques from the variations to produce an integrated tool that performs the task in a straightforward manner.

The card sort is a technique to bring order and structure to a large number of ideas. It helps a group reach consensus. Its primary strength is that it promotes interaction without criticism and facilitates building a plan. It can provide the synergy to break through old paradigms that might have prevented progress in the past as well as unite a group that has been divided on an issue. The card sort works best with a diverse group of four to nine people that contains at least one content expert. It begins with a clear statement of purpose to focus the group's energy. Materials such as 3" × 5" cards or Post-it® notes to facilitate the gathering and movement of ideas are a must.

To complete a card sort, first select a purpose. Be as specific as possible, but consider the resources available to the group. The purpose may be assigned, result from the use of some other tool or method, or evolve from your current discussion. Be sure the purpose is worded clearly and everyone in the group fully understands and agrees. Write the purpose where it can be clearly seen by the entire group. The more important the purpose, the easier it is to motivate the group to generate ideas.

Headline the purpose and record ideas, leaving ample space to list more ideas. Generate a list of ideas, typically through brainstorming. There are a number of other creative techniques, including mind mapping and dialogue, that can help generate the list. (The list may already exist from some other source, in which case simply transfer it to the card sort medium.)

Each idea should be expressed in at least three words, including a noun and a verb. Place only one idea on a card and write clearly. As each idea is placed where everyone can see it, someone should read it aloud. When the group has posted all of the ideas, it is time to begin sorting.

The sorting process is a group activity. The idea cards must be accessible to all members of the group. Sort the cards by picking up a card and placing it next to another card that you feel is related. Cards can be moved several times and put in a new cluster. The sorting is done in silence by all members of the group at the same time. Continue sorting in silence until the sorting visibly slows down. This will normally require about 15 to 20 minutes. Each cluster of cards should contain no more than nine.

The next step is to develop headers. During this part of the card sort, there is opportunity for much interaction and discussion. The group must generate a header for each cluster. The header ideally summarizes and compresses all the ideas of the cards in the cluster. Any card that does not fit within a cluster should be set to the side for later consideration. Each header statement needs at least three words, including a noun and a verb. Headers should be as specific as possible to reduce the chance for misinterpretation. The group

FIGURE 3 —————————————————————————————
Card Sort Using Brainstormed List

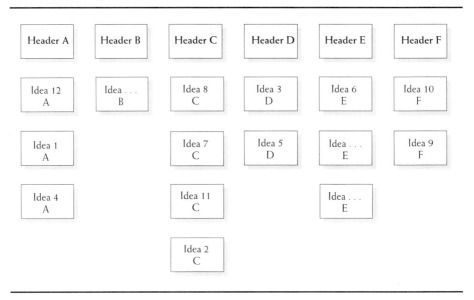

reaches consensus on the theme and wording of each header. When a header has been defined and accepted, place it above the cards in the cluster. This header card should be clearly marked to distinguish it from the idea cards. The group may choose to use an idea card as a header. If this is done, be sure it is clearly marked as a header. Each card in a cluster should also be marked with the identification of the header. This can be a letter, number, color, or even a word if the cards are large enough. Figure 3 shows how a completed card sort would appear.

CAUSE & EFFECT MAP (RELATIONSHIP DIAGRAM, ID)

In *The 7 New QC Tools* Shigeru Mizuno describes the "Relations Diagram Method" as having been developed by The Society for QC Technique Development in 1979. It was based on the work of T. Brown in a 1977 paper titled, "Inquiry into the Relation of Cause and Effect," Delmar, New York: Scholar's Facsimiles & Reprints. The method was created to:

• analyze problems with a complex network of causes and effects, and
• view the whole problem from a broad perspective.

Another name for the tool is *interrelationship digraph* or *ID*. The authors have not been able to find any reason for this choice of name and no adequate definition of digraph has been unearthed.

Cause and effect relationships exist when the action of one item determines or creates conditions (effects) in another item. Understanding cause and effect relationships allows groups to focus resources where they are most likely to produce results. They also provide a beginning point for developing the order of tasks and process steps, balancing resource distribution to prevent overloading, and isolating root causes to focus continuous improvement efforts in any planning process. Cause and effect networks are complex sets of relationships.

The cause and effect map is a technique to display graphically this type of relationship, invoking the intuitive right side of the brain. This method helps determine cause and effect relationships by providing a way to visually identify key driving forces as root causes, as well as point out key bottlenecks (major effects). The cause and effect map can help a group effectively analyze situations with a complex network of cause and effect relationships by providing a broad perspective. Key drivers are primary, or root causes, that are having the greatest impact on the network. They are often the most effective place to concentrate efforts to resolve the entire situation. Bottlenecks are the restraints in a network. They are affected by the most causes and usually cannot be resolved by themselves. The cause and effect map requires a set of interrelated options, ideas, or issues to be analyzed. It is best completed by a group of four to nine people, drawing the map where everyone can see it.

To complete the cause and effect map, begin by identifying the topic or purpose for the map and putting it at the top of the work area. Now write the options, ideas, or issues to be analyzed in a circular pattern. Write large enough that everyone can read the options. After placing the options around a circular pattern, number them to make the process of comparison easier to track. Numbering is particularly important with larger option lists.

When the options have been placed on the map, it is time to begin the process of pairwise comparisons. Each option must be compared just once with each of the other options to determine if there is a cause and effect relationship. When such a relationship is found, draw a line with an arrow pointing to the effect. If no relationship is found, simply proceed to the next pair. (To keep track of the comparisons, it helps to proceed in an orderly fashion. Compare option one with option two, then option one with option three, and so on until you have traversed the entire circle of options.)

When option one has been compared to each of the others, then start with option two and compare it with option three and all of the other options except option one. The cause and effect relationship between option two and option one was already examined. After completing the option two comparisons, continue around the circle comparing each option with every other option just once until you have a map of options connected by their relationships.

Analyze the map by counting the number of incoming arrows and outgoing arrows for each option and note the numbers for in and out beside the option as shown in Figure 4. The option or options with the highest number of outgoing arrows are the primary drivers or root causes. Changes in these options will affect the majority of the other options. Therefore, resources applied to these areas can produce pronounced change.

The option or options that are receiving the most incoming arrows are key bottlenecks. These outcomes are affected by many other options and may even be inhibiting other options from proceeding as they should. Mark visibly the key drivers and bottlenecks to further clarify your map in complex networks.

Be certain to examine only cause and effect relationships. If the group stays with this criteria, it is probable that only about 50 percent of the relationships will have arrows. In addition, this tool forces a group to make a decision since it does not allow for two-way arrows. Figure 4 shows a completed cause and effect map.

FIGURE 4
Cause & Effect Map Using Card Sort Headers

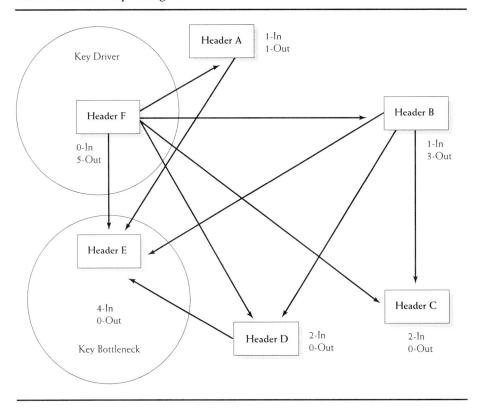

SELECTION WINDOW

A bit of wisdom from a book by Peter Drucker, *The Effective Executive,* taught that effectiveness comes not from doing things well but from "doing the right things." The selection window is a helpful vehicle for choosing the right thing to do. Apart from *The Toolbook,* the authors are unaware of any other sources for this tool. In his national best-seller, *The Seven Habits of Highly Effective People,* Stephen Covey describes a tool he calls "The Time Management Matrix." Using scales of importance and urgency, he teaches us to create the habit of putting first things first, or doing the right thing. The selection window uses a similar rationale but uses the scales of importance and effort. It is designed to integrate your resources and purposes and help you to decide what is the right thing to do.

The selection window is a simple technique to select the right things to do, integrating effort and importance with your purpose. It is a method for deciding when to use groups, as well as a way to evaluate and understand the importance and effort (resources) needed. It requires a clearly defined high-level purpose, a list of options or alternatives to accomplish the purpose, and the time to provide a careful consideration of each option. The selection window can keep you focused on your purpose and aid in short- and long-term projects.

To complete the selection window, begin by identifying your purpose. It helps to write your purpose where it can be a constant reminder. Generate a list of options, alternatives, or opportunities that can help you accomplish your purpose. One list that often benefits by this type of analysis is the "To Do" list.

Begin the selection window by drawing a square containing four equal boxes. The boxes must be large enough to write the opportunities inside. Mark the square with effort on the left and importance on the bottom. Use a numerical scale from a low of 1 to a high of 10. Evaluate each option against the criteria of effort and importance. Now review the selection window and take appropriate action.

Do now. Items of high importance, and low effort should be done immediately. These are the "right" things that you have the resources and time to do now. Each will have significant impact on achieving your purpose.

To do. Items of low importance and low effort should be placed on a "To Do" list. Use these items as fillers. Although they are of low importance (we did not say no importance), they are possibly important enough to justify a small expenditure of resources. Be careful! It may seem unimportant to determine priorities, but these areas can dominate our time to the exclusion of our most important items.

Forget. Items of low importance and high effort do not justify the expenditure of the high level of resources required to complete them.

Groups. Items of high importance and high effort should be the focus of groups. They are important enough to deserve the attention that only a skilled group of people working together effectively can supply. They will determine whether or not you accomplish your purpose.

Figure 5 shows a completed selection window on things that could be done to satisfy a customer in a small office supply company.

TREE DIAGRAM

The concept of using a *tree* or subdividing a subject like branches of a tree is not new. We have all seen tree-type diagrams used to portray the structure and relationships within an organization. The traditional organization chart is a vertical tree. Saaty points out in *Decision Making for Leaders* that hierarchies or trees are the mechanism the brain uses to structure and store complex information.

In *The 7 New QC Tools*, Mizuno introduces the systematic diagram with the alternate name of *dendrogram* from the Greek word for tree. The dendrogram is used "to find the most appropriate option." Mizuno then goes on to describe the wide variety of uses for the tree diagram, including:

- Functional analysis (from value engineering)
- Correlation tree
- Reverse PERT chart
- Decision tree

FIGURE 5

Selection Window Using Card Sort Headers

- Fault tree analysis
- YS technique (Yabiki Seiichiro)

The tree diagram is designed to expand a purpose into the tasks required to accomplish it. In this form it is also called an *outline diagram*. The tree diagram starts with a stated purpose and enables you to view the full range of details required to accomplish your purpose. It is also a method to expand your purpose into tasks to be performed. It can be used by individuals or a group of people focused on the purpose. The tree diagram is one method for viewing a complete hierarchy of tasks and their linkages. It provides the structure to ensure a complete plan.

Begin the tree diagram by reviewing your purpose to be accomplished. Be sure everyone in the group clearly understands the purpose. A review of your criteria for success at this point can further clarify planning. Write the purpose at the top or the left of your work area. The tree diagram can be expanded in any direction, but the left-to-right format lends itself to using other tools after completing the tree diagram.

The diagram will be easy to read if you enclose the purpose and the other elements of the tree diagram in boxes. Using cards or Post-it® notes can make it easier to reorganize the tree if it grows in an unexpected direction. You cannot predict the number of branches that will be formed, or the number of divisions for each branch.

Generate all the high-level tasks, or "targets" that must be completed to accomplish the purpose. Targets are those things that combined together accomplish the purpose and can be developed by applying brainstorming to the purpose. Another method is to use the headers or idea cards developed in a card sort performed on the purpose. A tree diagram cannot be completed by simply turning a card sort on its side.

Place each of the targets in a box, lined up to the right of the purpose. Leave plenty of space between each target to allow for growth of the tree diagram. Connect the targets to the purpose to form the first branches of the tree diagram. Expand each target to define the subordinate tasks that are necessary to accomplish each target. Use group dialogue, or any creative process, to define tasks. When the subordinate tasks have been defined and recorded for each target, draw the lines that will connect them to the target.

Each subordinate task should then be subdivided into further levels of subtasks until the final level is achievable. Each subtask should be broken down until it can be given to a person or group to be completed. This expansion may add more levels to your tree. Levels of detail may be added unevenly, causing one branch to grow larger than others.

The final step in making a tree diagram is to test the validity of the work. This is done by reviewing each task and level on the tree diagram to see if it logically connects to the tasks above and below it. You might consider expanding to a larger group that includes the people who will actually perform the tasks. Their knowledge and experience may help you see gaps or unnecessary tasks. When this is complete, review each subtask to ensure its necessity to the completion of the task. Expect this questioning process to cause change in the tree diagram. A tree diagram is shown in Figure 6.

FORCE FIELD ANALYSIS

Stephen R. Covey mentions the force field analysis in his book *The Seven Habits of Highly Effective People*, Simon & Schuster (1989). He credits sociologist Kurt Lewin as the developer of this model that shows the driving forces as rising and restraining forces as pushing down. Lewin's focus on the dynamics at work in any change process began over 40 years ago. During World War II, our government tried to change the beef-buying habits of housewives to expand use of internal organs and to limit the use of muscle cuts to aid the war effort. Women were unwilling to change at first because they did not know enough about selecting and preparing the recommended meats. However, when the president's wife got involved in the problem and began to understand the benefits, change began to happen. Lewin learned:

> *When people become involved in a problem, they become significantly and sincerely committed to coming up with solutions to the problem.*
>
> LEWIN

Moran, Talbot, and Benson in *A Guide to Graphical Problem-Solving Processes* (1990) described the procedural steps for the force field analysis as it is more typically shown and used.

FIGURE 6

Tree Diagram Using Card Sort Headers and Ideas

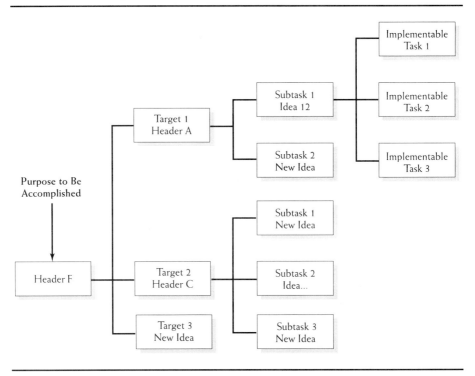

The force field analysis is a technique to visually identify the forces affecting accomplishment of your purpose. It is a way to show supporting and resisting forces. Force field analysis can help you analyze the depths of your resources to overcome the resistance by providing a clear picture of the situation to share with others. It can be completed by one person, but it is most effective when applied by a diverse group with a clearly defined purpose and a method to accomplish it.

Begin by drawing vertical and horizontal lines. Make the spaces large enough that there is plenty of room to write. At the extreme right, under the horizontal line, print your purpose. This is to provide focus for the generation of supporting and resisting forces. It may further help to add an arrow to the horizontal line to indicate the direction of positive accomplishment. Further clarity can be added by marking the left side as driving forces and those on the right as resisting.

List the forces driving toward your purpose on the left side of the vertical line and those resisting your efforts on the right. These lists could be created by using brainstorming or simply by carefully examining your initial plan. When each list is complete, go over the lists again and assign a strength to each force. A scale from high to low provides a good initial view of the situation. Now draw an arrow under each force pointing to the vertical line. The arrow's length indicates the strength of the force.

Evaluate the results. Force field analysis provides a clear visualization of the forces with which you are dealing. Examine both the driving and resisting forces for opportunities for improvement. Your goals are first to seek ways to reduce or eliminate resisting forces. This

FIGURE 7

Force Field Analysis on Implementable Task from Tree Diagram

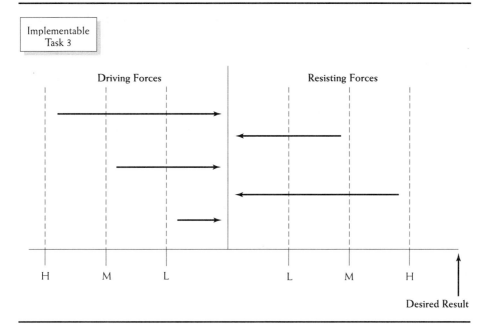

action serves to conserve resources and reduce the effort required to accomplish your goal. If necessary, you should seek additional resources to aid in overcoming the resisting forces.

A completed force field analysis is shown in Figure 7. As shown, there is not always a resisting force for every driving force. By adding the strength of the force, it is easier to see which driving forces can be added to and which resisting forces can be decreased.

MATRICES

The matrix format of rows and columns has long been used to guide the gathering and organization of large amounts of information. Matrices are created manually or through a variety of semi-automated and automated vehicles including the computer spreadsheet. The number of rows varies widely, based on the application. The number and width of the columns varies based on the size and type of the data contained. The value of a matrix is defined by its contents. Two major types of matrices are the most common. The first type contains information and the second contains correlations between two sets of variables. Examples of both types of matrices follow.

S.M.A.R.T. PLAN

The S.M.A.R.T. plan is defined by the information it contains. This matrix provides the key information that is necessary to build a successful plan. The S.M.A.R.T. plan requires a set of tasks to accomplish your purpose. It can be a vehicle for guiding a group in the development of a working plan that defines clear accountability and goals. It is a technique for structuring task details, which includes a measure of completion, assignment of responsibility, resources required, time to complete, and predecessor tasks. It is a way to plan the implementation of the tasks necessary to accomplish your purpose.

Like all decision making and planning tools, the S.M.A.R.T. plan begins with a clearly defined purpose. Write this purpose at the top of your work area. List the tasks or specifics necessary to accomplish your purpose. These can be created as part of the process of building the S.M.A.R.T. plan, or they may be transferred from a completed tree diagram. The process of selecting the implementation details of each specific provides an additional test of the work performed in a tree diagram. If you find a specific or task is not sufficiently detailed, do not hesitate to return to the tree and modify it before continuing.

Now that the S.M.A.R.T. plan is set up, the work of defining the implementation details begins by identifying the measure of completion for each specific. A measure is a clearly visible indicator that the specific is complete. Measures can include dates, quantities, or performance levels. There must be no doubt when the measure has been reached. A good measure can also show progress. Measures are agreed upon by consensus.

Each specific must be assigned to a person or a group to assure its completion. Assignment is one of the keys to success in any plan. Assignment provides accountability. It must be very specific. In addition, it must provide opportunity for participation. No assignment should ever be made without at least the agreement of the assignee. The ideal situation is one in that qualified groups or group members have sufficient motivation or interest to volunteer.

Completion of each specific requires the availability of resources. Resources include time sufficient to create quality results as well as capital, capital equipment, raw materials, and supplies. Personnel with appropriate skill, knowledge, experience, and commitment are also essential.

Any form of planning requires an understanding of a desired endpoint. In more advanced planning techniques, the duration of each task is also included. The S.M.A.R.T. plan assumes that the group has considered project time as one of the resources. Timing provides a target for task or specific completion, a guide for planning the details of task implementation and acquiring resources, and an early start date for any task dependent on, or succeeding, this task.

Putting the proper priority and sequence on specifics requires an understanding of the linkages between them. A predecessor defines what must be done before this task can be accomplished. Predecessors provide an outline of the order in which tasks must be done as a guide for planning the implementation details and utilization of resources. A specific may have one, many, or even no predecessors.

For short specific lists, write the specific in the predecessor column. For longer lists, number the list of specifics and use the number of the predecessor. Figure 8 shows a S.M.A.R.T. plan type of matrix.

CORRELATION MATRIX

The second type of matrix is a correlation matrix. In this form of matrix, one list of variables is compared to a second list of variables. They are often compared with numbers or symbols. The most common symbols are ◎ for a strong relationship, ○ for a medium relationship, and △ for a weak relationship. The number 9 is often substituted for the strong

FIGURE 8

S.M.A.R.T. Plan Matrix on Implementable Task from Tree Diagram

Specific	Measurable	Assignment	Resources	Time	Predecessors
Implementable Task 3	Deliverable	GH	8 Person Hours	1 Week	Target 1 Subtask 2 Implementable 4

relationship symbol, the number 3 for the medium, and the number 1 for the weak. These numbers are based on experience and are not numerically valid. The reason for the multiple is that it surfaces the most important items. These symbols come from the Japanese symbols for win, place, and show at the horse racetrack. The first translations contained these symbols, and they have become common in U.S. quality documentation. An example of a correlation matrix is shown in Figure 9.

FIGURE 9

Correlation Matrix

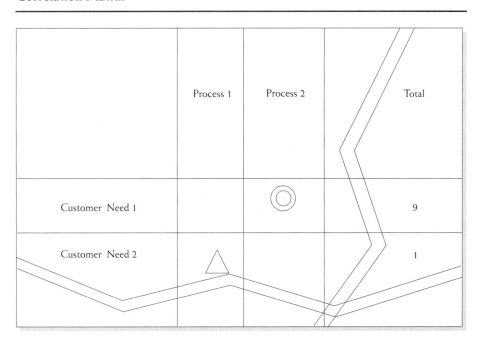

PROBLEM PREVENTION PLAN
(CONTINGENCY PLAN, PDPC)

What could go wrong? This question is an essential part of planning. Unfortunately, we often do little other than worry. The problem prevention plan is a method for planning around contingencies and creating alternatives or solutions for every foreseeable contingency.

The earliest reference to a contingency planning method that formulates the same questions is the process decision program chart (PDPC) described in *The 7 New QC Tools* by Shigeru Mizuno. This tool structures the implementation steps of a plan, and then asks "what if?" and prompts for possible countermeasures.

The two common methods used to implement the PDPC often cause confusion. The first is a modified tree diagram where each level of questioning is exploded downward. The second is a "book" outline format where process steps, their contingencies, and possible countermeasures are related by outline numbers like the chapters in a book.

The problem prevention plan is a much easier, more thorough method of contingency planning. It is also easier to understand. It is an enhanced implementation more closely related to the potential problem analysis used by J.D. James in the quality leadership process. In addition to defining the "what ifs?," now called *potential problems*, the tool defines potential causes to allow a more specific focus on feasible countermeasures, or preventions. The last enhancement is the ranking of the levels of the plan based on achievement of the goal.

The problem prevention plan is a technique to determine what can go wrong with your plan before it does. It is a method for rating the seriousness and likelihood of potential problems, a vehicle for investigating the causes of potential problems, a way to identify actions that can prevent problems from occurring, and a tool to trigger implementation of preventive action. The power in this tool is the structured "worrying" process that yields precise actions to keep our plans on track and helps us accomplish our purposes.

The problem prevention plan requires a purpose to be accomplished and a plan to accomplish it. It can be especially valuable when uncertainty exists or risk is high because it provides a comprehensive strategy before a major plan is implemented. This type of planning can help you identify and remove roadblocks to your success.

Begin the problem prevention plan by defining a list of what could go wrong with your plan. Write the purpose to be accomplished at the top of the page, board, or chart pad. Consider using a creative tool, such as brainstorming, to develop the list. Look for potential problems that could get in the way (perhaps from a force field analysis). A potential problem is something that can prevent a plan or process step from occurring or producing the planned output. It can alter the quality of the resulting output or cause delays.

To construct the problem prevention plan, place the list to the left of a board or sheet of paper and create columns for probability and seriousness. For each of the potential problems, rank both the probability of its occurrence and the seriousness. Probability is the likelihood that the potential problem will happen. Seriousness is the impact on the accomplishment of the purpose if it does happen, ranked high to low.

Identify the potential problem with the highest probability of occurrence and of a most serious nature, marking them for further analysis. For each identified potential problem (high probability and seriousness), develop a list of potential causes. List the potential problem at the top of a page. Search for potential causes using dialogue, brainstorming, or some other creative process. Rate the probability of occurrence of each of the potential causes on a scale

FIGURE 10
Problem Prevention Plan

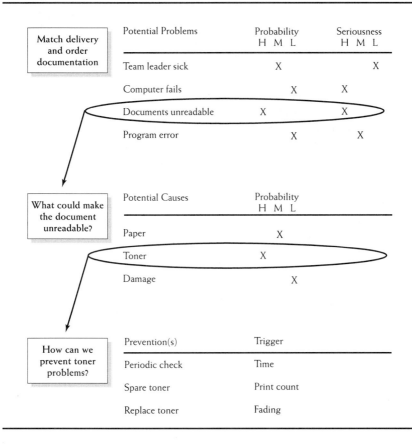

ranked high to low. Select the potential causes that are most likely to happen. Further analyze them to attempt to prevent them from happening.

For the highest probability, discuss and select actions that can prevent a future problem. List the potential cause at the top. Search for preventions using dialogue, brainstorming, or some other creative process. For each prevention, define a trigger that will signal the beginning of the prevention. A trigger can be an event, a time, or a measure.

In this planning stage, solutions are changes in our plans to prevent the possibility of a problem. Alternatives are actions that can be taken to minimize or eliminate the problem if it occurs. Figure 10 shows a problem prevention plan on matching delivery and order documentation.

PERT CHART (CPM, ARROW DIAGRAM)

Some useful project planning and tracking methods have come from the work of Henry Gantt. The best known of these is PERT, or program evaluation and review technique, and the PERT planning method.

A PERT chart is also called an *activity network diagram. Project Management with CPM, PERT and Precedence Diagramming* by Moder, Phillips and Davis, Van Nostrand Reinhold (1983) places the origin of the PERT chart in the work of a Polish scientist, Karol Adamiecki, in the early 1930s. Adamiecki created the "Harmony Graph" matrix with a time scale on the vertical axis and activities on the horizontal axis. Movable strips under each activity indicated the duration of the activity, and the horizontal axis contained a reference to inter-task dependencies.

The PERT Planning Method as we know it today was formed in 1958 by a research team from Lockheed Aircraft Corporation, the Navy Special Projects Office, and Booz, Allen, and Hamilton in their plan to develop the Polaris Missile System. The critical path method (CPM) was created concurrently by a team from DuPont and Remington Rand Univac. Their method identified the shortest, or critical, path through a project.

Today's PERT planning method has three variations based on the display and duration of activities. These include activity on arrow, activity on node, and precedence diagram. The full PERT planning method is extremely complex and can be confusing. The PERT chart contained in this article is a simplified activity on node diagram that includes the identification of a critical path. It is our goal to provide the benefits of PERT planning through a simplified charting technique designed to be used following the tree diagram and S.M.A.R.T. plan.

The PERT chart is a technique to organize tasks or activities into a schedule, a visual method for identifying predecessor activities, and a means of identifying the minimum time required to complete the project. It can identify gaps or missing tasks in your project plan, show the critical path through your project plan, and track your project to completion. The PERT chart requires a clear understanding of your purpose to be accomplished and a knowledge of the tasks or activities necessary to accomplish the purpose. Most often, computer planning programs are used to facilitate completing and updating PERT charts.

As with any decision-making or planning tool, the most important place to start is with a clear understanding of the purpose to be accomplished. A concise purpose statement can improve substantially your ability to plan. Once you have defined your purpose, establish a list of the tasks that must be performed. The PERT chart depends on other tools, such as the card sort, a tree diagram, or a S.M.A.R.T. plan, to define the tasks necessary to accomplish your purpose.

Record the predecessors for each task. These are the tasks that must be completed before the current task can be started. This information from the S.M.A.R.T. plan is recorded in the first blank column. For each task, define the task duration. This is the total time required to perform the task with the assigned resources. Use the same unit of time for each task, that is, hours or days. Assigning duration requires knowledge of the manner in which the work will be performed. The assistance of those who will perform the work can be invaluable. If the task is not sufficiently detailed, you will have difficulty. This can be an indication that the task needs to be subdivided.

The second key to defining duration is a knowledge of the resources available. Often an unacceptable duration can be shortened through the application of more resources. Warning: There are some operations that by their nature are sequential and cannot be done in parallel. Ensure that the availability of additional resources will help and not hinder or waste.

The PERT planning method works backward from the purpose to be accomplished to build a linked, time-driven plan that identifies each task and its starting point in order to meet a desired completion date. The reality of PERT is that it is often worked both ways several times to gain understanding and to help all the tasks fit together in the best possible manner.

The original PERT did not have the array of judgmental tools that we have today, nor was it assisted by today's computer technology. With the use of other judgmental tools, such as the S.M.A.R.T. plan and the tree diagram, it becomes possible to work forward from the earliest possible start to determine the actual completion of the purpose.

To use a PERT chart, create a temporary calendar scale that covers the time from a starting time to the date when it should be complete. Working forward or backward requires an initial calendar scale to facilitate the location of tasks on the chart. The final calendar scale is defined by the creation of the PERT diagram on the chart and can be placed only after the diagram is completed.

Working from the first task to be accomplished, place the tasks to be completed on the chart. Each task should be enclosed in a circle or ellipse with its required completion date written clearly above or below it. Remember this comes from the S.M.A.R.T. plan. Add the task number to the task. On large or complex charts, the task number will be vital to maintaining order and conserving space. Draw an arrow from the task to the next task to be accomplished. For the last task to be done, the arrow is drawn to the purpose. Place the task duration, or time required to complete the task, on the arrow as shown in Figure 11.

The completed PERT chart will provide a network of tasks that must be completed to accomplish your purpose. The total time to get from the start to a completed purpose will

FIGURE 11
PERT Chart on Implementable Tasks from S.M.A.R.T. Plan

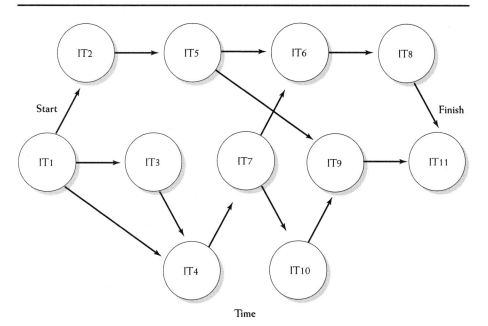

depend on how many tasks can be accomplished in parallel. The more things you can do at the same time, the sooner you will be done, but there is a limit. That limit is the critical path through your network of tasks. The critical path is the longest path of predecessor/successor tasks in the network. It is discovered by adding the duration of tasks together for each of the possible paths through the network. The path with the longest duration defines the minimum time required to accomplish your purpose. Clearly mark the critical path with double lines or color for all to see. The critical path will also determine the time or length of your calendar scale. At this point, redraw the calendar scale and PERT network to assure harmony between the network and scale and to ensure coherency of task placement.

Considerable development work has been performed on the PERT chart since it was created. Entire courses exist to teach the PERT/CPM (critical path method) planning method. There are also a number of computer programs on the market that implement this process. In a more intensive study, you will encounter some of the following terms:

Activity   The task to be done (or specific).
Node   The circle or ellipse in which the task to be done is written (or event).
Predecessor   A task that must be completed before the current task can be started.
Successor   A task that cannot be started until the current task is completed.
Duration   The time required to complete a task.
Early start   The soonest a task can be started.
Late start   The latest a task can be started and still stay on schedule.
Early finish   The soonest or most optimistic time a task can be finished.
Late finish   The latest a task can be finished and still not delay the following tasks.
Slack   The difference between the time a task should start and when it must start.

When used on a PERT, these terms are often abbreviated, such as EF for early finish and LS for late start. Figure 11 shows a completed PERT chart.

Reengineering: Process Redesign*

Terence T. Burton

Process redesign is the first element of a reengineering framework. The objective of process redesign is to reinvent, reposition, restructure, and de-departmentalize critical business processes in a manner that creates a renewed focus on customer need, not business as usual with a few added enhancements. Process redesign demands that we abandon the parochial rules about business and adopt a start-over mind-set.

Ultimately, our goal is to reengineer what is typically a homogeneous business into several stand-alone focused value centers. This is typically accomplished by a complete overhaul of the company's infrastructure, including such processes as:

- Physical
- Business
- Technical
- Information
- People

Some of the activities characteristic of process redesign include:

- Linking business processes together to decrease product and informational movement, defective business process queues, work-in-process, material or information handling, time, complexity, and associated costs.
- Reducing cycle times by overlapping business process activities, such as processing a customer order, developing a new product, purchasing raw materials, or preparing compliance documentation.
- Creating the conditions for an immediate exposure and solution to business process problems and opportunities achieved by the entire workforce.
- Providing real-time feedback mechanisms to business process and subprocess owners. This supports the creation of self-management, self-measurement, and self-adjustment.

---

*Selected text and illustrations from *The Reengineering Toolbox* by The Center for Excellence in Operations, Inc. (CEO), Nashua, New Hampshire, Terence T. Burton, President. Reprinted by permission.

- Process redesign has focused traditionally on making the "as-is" incrementally better. Reengineering causes individuals to work from a much broader definition of process redesign than occurs with traditional continuous improvement methods. Process redesign in a reengineering sense depends largely upon an organization's distance from its desired, or "ultimate," state.

In our implementation experiences, we have found that process redesign evolves to a new level of breakthrough improvement. Every organization performs at different levels, from excellent to poor, depending on the process and goal. Therefore, it is logical that the next generation of process redesign include concurrent activities focused on the following analyses:

1. Some business processes currently meet or exceed customer needs, and the proper activity to support process redesign is reinforcement of current practices. This usually includes the soft aspects of traditional continuous improvement, such as team building and improving facilitation and leadership skills.
2. Other business processes fall short of meeting customer needs and require small, incremental improvements. The proper activity to support process redesign is continuous improvement of the "as-is." This usually includes the soft aspects of continuous improvement as previously described, plus the traditional TQM problem solving tools (for example, The 7 Old Tools, The 7 New Tools, SPC, charting and measurement techniques, and so on).
3. Every organization has business processes that, no matter how much reinforcement or incremental improvement is pursued, will never meet the customer's need within the customer's time window. These are the candidates to be reinvented or rediscovered. One of the largest causes of reengineering failures has been the lack of tools to deal with reinvention needs.

Unfortunately, many reengineering initiatives are nothing more than slash and burn downsizing efforts, recycled TQM or continuous improvement activities, in vogue movements, or a new list of MIS projects. The major causes of reengineering failure include overreliance on technology as a solution and application of old tools that focus on continuous improvements of the "as-is." *Old* tools focus on competencies (for example, how to make current conditions better). *Reengineering* tools focus on antecedents (for example, what needs to be done) and encourage entrepreneurial thinking and invention of new business processes. Anything else results in what actually is downsizing, TQM, continuous improvement, created activities, or a new list of MIS projects.

CEO's Breakthrough! Reengineering™ framework addresses the full spectrum of inventing, managing, and implementing breakthrough improvement. The purpose of *The Reengineering Toolbox* is to share our implementation methodology and "out-of-box" tools because we feel these are critical to achieving real breakthrough results. Successful implementation makes the difference with reengineering separate organizations that "wish" or "think" things will automatically change simply because they have launched a reengineering initiative.

The Breakthrough! Reengineering™ BPR tools presented in this article are from CEO's book, *The Reengineering Toolbox*. These tools are much more difficult to apply in real life than, for example, the seven standard TQM tools because they must be applied by entrepreneurial process redesigners. We have learned from our implementation experiences that there are many reasons for this fact. The most pronounced difference in reengineering is that in many situations, the process forces you to start in the abstract to create a new reality. There may not be a process because it may not yet exist. Additionally, many of these tools are applied to knowledge-based activities, in which definitions of customers, products, processes, quality, performance, and success are often unclear.

Applying Pareto charts, run diagrams, and check sheets to real-life situations on the shop floor is a structured, linear problem-solving process. The operator typically is provided with quality and workmanship standards, process/routing, work instructions, set-up sheets, quality measurement criteria, and tooling/gauges. The operator has the benefit of a defined product and process and can measure physical results against a predetermined standard. Imagine how much success this operator would have if he or she were sent to an empty space to apply these tools! This is the challenge of reengineering. Application of these new reengineering tools for process redesign requires a totally new thinking process characterized by out-of-box thinking and business as unusual.

PROCESS REDESIGN

TEN P BUSINESS REENGINEERING CHECKLIST

The 10 P Business Reengineering Checklist (Figure 1) is used in conjunction with business process mapping. The 10 P checklist adds dimensional value for each activity that is a business, technical, or administrative process. It also helps in rationalizing the real needs of a business process and to remove any unnecessary activities.

Business processes in most organizations have evolved over decades. As a consequence, many of the activities that are routinely performed in organizations do not stand up to the test of the 10 P checklist. Often, activities are identified that produce unnecessary or incorrect product or have no customer. In practice, it is not unusual to find that some of the 10 P checklist items have no answer.

BPR Methodology:

1. Decide and describe the business segment or process to be analyzed.
2. For each of the checklist categories, fill in the answer to the category in as much detail as possible.
3. For each answer provided, check off whether it is a complete, partial, or missing answer.
4. Total the number of check marks in each of the rating columns.
5. If you have 80 percent or more of the check marks in the "complete" rating column, you understand your business segment or process very well. Experience has shown that most organizations usually have most of the check marks in the partial or missing columns, indicating that much work is required.
6. Identify the data required to complete the answers to the categories, determine the data sources, and decide who will obtain the data and when.
7. Collect the data.

F I G U R E   1

Ten P Business Reengineering Checklist

Process Description: Date:

Category	Answer	Answer Rating			Data Collection				
		Complete	Partial	Missing	Source	Data	Required	Who	When
Purpose									
Procedure									
Practice									
Participants									
Pace									
Place									
Period frequency									
Product									
Purchaser									
Performance									
	Total Check Marks								

BPR Results:

- Clear understanding of a business segment or reason for a process's existence.
- Compelling reason to eliminate the business segment or process where no clear answer can be found.

BUSINESS PROCESS MAPPING

Business process mapping (Figure 2) is a scoping tool used to document and diagnose the standard internal business processes that deliver products and/or services to the customer. This tool helps the enterprise understand the sequence of activities, relationships, process element cycle times, resources consumed, process cost, information and physical activity flows, and process participants.

Business process mapping is a flexible process that can be adapted to the preferences of the organization. Business process mapping can be accomplished through Post-it® notes, brown paper analysis, computer-generated flowcharts, freehand drawings, flip charts, and the like. The approach we choose is not as important as the purpose and results achieved.

FIGURE 2

Business Process Mapping

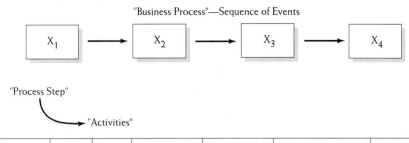

"Business Process"—Sequence of Events

Activities	Time	Cost	Resources	Performance	Value		Comments
					Add	Consume	

BPR Methodology:

1. Chart the major cross-functional process steps and the sequence of events in a business process.
2. Document the specific activities and elements of each process step.
3. Determine critical descriptive data to analyze and assess the activities that are required to complete each process step.
4. Apply the 10 P Business Reengineering Checklist to each activity in the process.
5. Segment value-adding and value-consuming efforts in the process and begin identifying opportunities to eliminate, combine, or streamline process activities.

BPR Results:

- Cross-functional business process maps.
- Process dynamics, redundancies, disconnects, waste.
- A solid foundation for breakthrough change.

THROW IT AWAY (TIA) ANALYSIS

Throw It Away Analysis (Figure 3) is a tool designed to stimulate innovation and reinvention. Throw It Away Analysis is conducted as a structured small group exercise made up of process participants and those who might be helpful who come from outside the business process. These forward-thinking individuals usually ask tough questions, such as "Why is this done and is it necessary?" The objective of this exercise is to get the process owners to think out-of-box and raise possibilities that may seem crazy, unthinkable, impossible,

F I G U R E 3 ――――――――――――――――――――――――――――――
Throw It Away Analysis

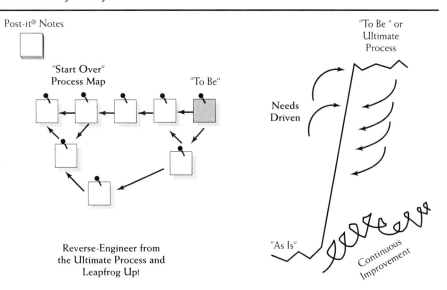

Business Segment of Process: _____   Date: _____

Sequential Process Steps	Throw It Away or Rearrange it	What Could Happen	Potential Impact	Potential New Process Flow

and ridiculous. Be aware that some of the results of Throw It Away Analysis may well be impossible or ridiculous but often one leads to the creation of a process breakthrough.

BPR Methodology:

1. Assemble a small team of six to eight process and non-process owners.
2. List out the sequential steps on a flip chart using Post-it® notes.
3. Have the participants explore what would happen if one of the process steps were removed. The facilitator removes the process step Post-it® note from the flip chart so it is viewed as being thrown away. The facilitator should remove one Post-it® note at a time and encourage the team to rearrange the process flow without that step.
4. Record the results of the exploration on the Throw It Away Matrix.
5. Stop the exercise after each of the process steps has been subjected to the Throw It Away Analysis.

BPR Results:

- A detailed analysis of each process step's worth and contribution.
- A potentially new flow or simplified one.
- Development of an attitude favorable to change.

TOUCH VERSUS ELAPSED ANALYSIS

Touch versus Elapsed Analysis (Figure 4) is an opportunity identification tool designed to define the ultimate potential improvement in an "As-is" business process. This tool compares the elapsed time documented from the business process mapping with the cumulative actual work time. This comparison is made through a pilot exercise where a subassembly, product, or document is walked through each of the process elements without any delays. Process participants are made aware that this exercise will happen and must give their immediate attention to it. They are instructed to drop whatever they are doing and complete their aspect of the business process as fast as possible. Once the exercise is completed, each participant is asked to analyze what is preventing him/her from continuous processing all of the time.

BPR Methodology:

1. Record the sequential process steps from the business process mapping tool and the documented elapsed time.
2. Inform all those involved in the pilot exercise of their roles and responsibilities.
3. Run the pilot exercise and record the actual work time.
4. Calculate the Reengineering Improvement Ratio.
5. Identify the process steps for reengineering or elimination.

BPR Results:

- A calculated ratio of actual work to total elapsed time.
- Targets of process reinvention to greatly reduce cycle time.

FIGURE 4
Touch versus Elapsed Analysis

Start

Finish
3 Weeks Later
(7,200 Minutes)

"I just walked it
through in 60
minutes."

EE:AA = 7200:60
          = 120:1

Business Segment of Process: _____   Date: _____

Sequential Process Steps	Documented Elapsed Time	Actual Work Time	Reengineering Improvement Ratio	Focus of the Reengineering Effort
Total			Elapsed/Actual, Expressed as an EE:AA Ratio (for example, 100:1)	

TOTAL ENTERPRISE QUALITY MANAGEMENT

ADAPT PROBLEM-SOLVING NETWORK

ADAPT (Figure 5) is an analytical network to support reengineering that is similar to the PDCA cycle for TQM. Solving business problems via the reengineering ideology requires out-of-box thinking. This type of problem solving is unstructured, nonlinear, and random in nature. The ADAPT network is used to encourage entrepreneurial behavior and risk.

FIGURE 5
ADAPT™ (Out-of-Box PDCA)

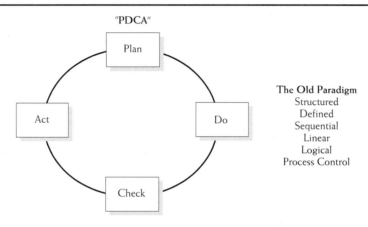

"PDCA"

The Old Paradigm
Structured
Defined
Sequential
Linear
Logical
Process Control

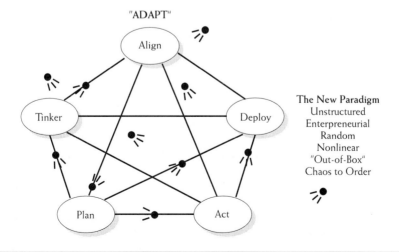

"ADAPT"

The New Paradigm
Unstructured
Enterpreneurial
Random
Nonlinear
"Out-of-Box"
Chaos to Order

PDCA is a repetitive sequential process, and ADAPT is a network of conceptual activities connected by tightropes. Imagine the spatial masses moving on and off the page on a Z-axis. You might be in the Deploy space and determine that the next step is Plan. However, because of real circumstances (for example, the tightropes intersect and lead you on a new course of action), there is not enough time for planning. The importance of ADAPT is to help us to recognize which space we are in, to determine the next space of the reengineering process, and to adjust if you land in a different destination. Reengineering is forced (but well managed) chaos and disequilibrium followed by order at a higher performance level.

BPR Methodology:

1. *Align* resources toward a common set of reengineering goals and objectives that will generate new organizational orders, such as agility, seamlessness, self-management, and the best possible performance.
2. *Deploy* resources to work toward the achievement of reengineering goals.
3. *Act* or try something new. Keep in mind that with reengineering it is difficult to plan until you take action first (that is, unplug the existing PC-based 3 week quotation system and start from scratch).
4. *Plan* the next set of actions and the definitions of success.
5. *Tinker,* or check and adjust your progress based on the latest information.

BPR Results:

• A new awareness of managed chaos and development of individual thinking capabilities.

SUPPLY CHAIN MANAGEMENT

SUPPLY CHAIN ACTIVITY NETWORK (SCAN)

SCAN (Figure 6) is a method for diagramming the elements of a company's supply chain. This tool provides a generic framework for baselining the "as-is" supply chain, its execution steps and cycle times, and its performance criteria. SCAN also provides the foundation for out-of-box process redesign to eliminate or simplify the supply chain.

BPR Methodology:

1. Expand the framework of SCAN to reflect the specific operational elements of the company's supply chain (that is, create the detailed supply chain map of your company).
2. Detail other descriptive elements of the supply chain, such as process elements, cycle times, methods deployed, and so on. Note: Detailing can be accomplished through the use of other tools such as Purpose and Process Mapping, Touch versus Walk-through, 10P, Journeys between Charting, Bill of Resources, and the like.
3. Analyze the completed SCAN of your company for redundancies, duplicate efforts, waste, or non-value-added activities.
4. Brainstorm, discussing how to break the homogeneous SCAN into multiple purpose value centers with fault tolerant logistics characteristics.
5. Reengineer and simplify the SCAN. Define the implementation steps, resources, and organizational implications of the SCAN after reengineering.

FIGURE 6
Supply Chain Activity Network

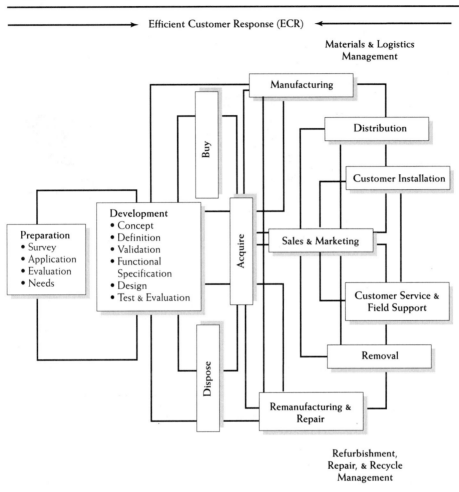

BPR Results:

• An "as-is" SCAN.
• A "to-be" SCAN.

SERVICE COST VALUE MATRIX

The Service Cost Value Matrix (Figure 7) is based on activity-based costing and management approaches. Its objective is to analyze a business process in terms of values added versus values consumed.

BPR Methodology:

1. Define the services provided to the organization and the level of resources consumed to provide these services.

FIGURE 7 —————————————————————————

Service Cost Value Matrix

Analysis of Traditional
Chart of Accounts

Business Process
Chart of Accounts

Product/Service	% of Resource Consumption	Cost of Product/Service	Value of Product/Service

2. Identify an individual chart of account costs directly related to the business process and accumulate costs into a business process cost bucket.
3. Calculate ratios of total resource consumption based on services provided by the business process (this is used as the statistical base for allocating costs).
4. Allocate total costs to services provided based on the level of resource consumption.
5. Compare the value added with the value consumed and determine activities any future reengineering or continuous improvement efforts will focus on.

BPR Results:

• An analysis of value of service versus cost of service for major elements of a business process.
• Definition of cost drivers.

ORGANIZATIONAL ROBUSTNESS

ORGANIZATIONAL INVOLVEMENT MAPPING

The Organizational Involvement Mapping tool (Figure 8) is a process to understand better the core business or technical processes that deliver a valued product or service to your

FIGURE 8

Organizational Involvement Mapping

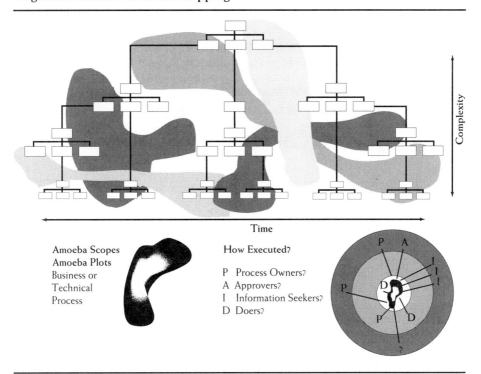

Time

Amoeba Scopes
Amoeba Plots
Business or
Technical
Process

How Executed?

P   Process Owners?
A   Approvers?
I   Information Seekers?
D   Doers?

customer. Most organizations have between five to eight core business or technical processes that should not be confused with business functions. A few parts of many business functions are included in a business process. Organizations are arranged in a vertical hierarchy, but business processes flow in horizontal and diagonal directions and do not necessarily follow the formal structure. Organizational Involvement Mapping depicts visually the business and technical process flows, and who is involved in their execution.

BPR Methodology:

1. Construct a detailed organization chart of the company or division under study.
2. Develop a listing of the core business or technical processes that deliver a valued product or service to the customer. Most organizations have between five to eight core business or technical processes.
3. Plot on the organization chart how each of the business or technical processes is accomplished. Connect the plotted points with a freehand amoeba figure that embodies all functions that make this process a reality.
4. Develop an execution plot that shows the level of involvement of each person who is identified in a function that contributes to this process. Identify each person as either a doer, a process owner, an approver, or an information seeker.
5. Determine if any of the work being performed in the rings can be eliminated or transferred to the doer ring. Most of the outer rings cause the majority of delays that the doer ring experiences.

BPR Results:

- Identified core business or technical processes.
- Visualization of how these business or technical processes interact and are accomplished.
- Classification of those involved in these processes.
- Identification of work that can be moved to doers or eliminated.

SPEED-TO-CUSTOMER

DEVELOPMENT PROCESS MAPPING

Development Process Mapping (Figure 9) is a reengineering tool used to define the structured, logical steps and the elapsed cycle times an organization deploys to develop new products. This tool can be used in conjunction with other reengineering tools (that is, touch

FIGURE 9

Development Process Mapping

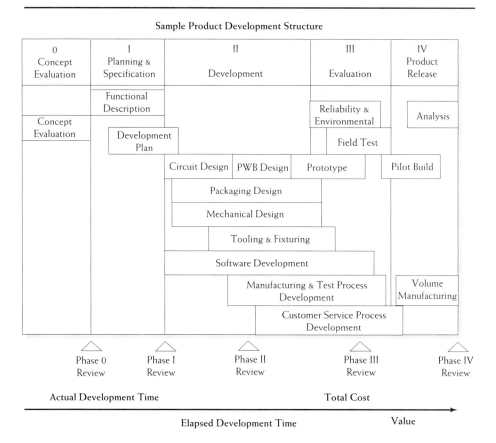

Sample Product Development Structure

development time versus elapsed development time, Development Process Capability, 10 P Checklist, Journeys between Charting, Organizational Involvement Mapping, and so on). This tool pinpoints areas and practices of the existing product development process that can be examined to reduce cycle times and improve development product and process quality. It can also be used as a basis for developing "fast lane" development rules that bypass normal development practices for certain exceptional situations.

BPR Methodology:

1. Define the current product development phases, guidelines, check sheet items, and formal approval requirements.
2. Determine organizations, functions, departments, and specific activity skills involved in the current development process.
3. Develop "as-is" Development Process Maps for those new product development efforts that are known (for products currently being developed, or for products already released for commercialization).
4. Supplement Development Process Maps with descriptive or performance information, such as cycle times, development costs, time-to-market performance, organizational involvement, budgets, and so on.
5. Develop "to-be" Development Process Maps based on questions, such as, "How would you develop this new product all over again knowing what we know today?, What would you have done differently?, How could we have saved 50 percent of the time?, How could we have reduced product cost by 20 percent?, What changes will produce breakthroughs in product development?" Note: These maps can be developed in focus groups or brainstorming sessions.
6. Reengineer the Product Development Process, including Phase Definitions, Roles and Responsibilities, Phase Review and Gatekeeping, Design Review Procedures, Project/Resource Management Methodologies, and Success Measurement.

BPR Results:

• Directions and requirements for developing a flexible, agile, rapid-response development process.

DEVELOPMENT PROJECT MAPPING

Development Project Mapping (Figure 10) is a reengineering tool used to take an inventory of development projects-in-process. This tool can be used in conjunction with MVP Filtering to reconcile product/technology strategy and product development. In the majority of cases, organizations can "purge" their open development projects and thus regain focus and resource capacity for programs that are strategically important.

Development Project Mapping is typically an emotional and political exercise similar to reducing work-in-process on the plant floor. The philosophy is to avoid being caught up in developing faster processes to execute what you should not be doing in the first place.

BPR Methodology:

1. Create an inventory of Product Development Efforts based on the following classifications:

FIGURE 10

Development Project Mapping

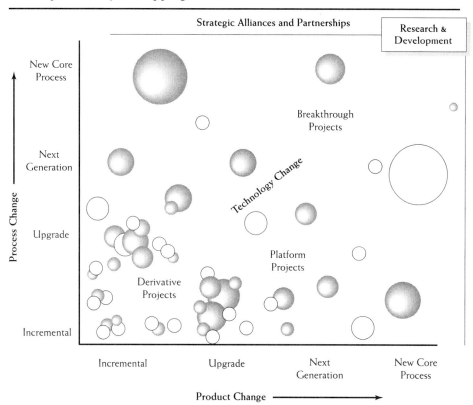

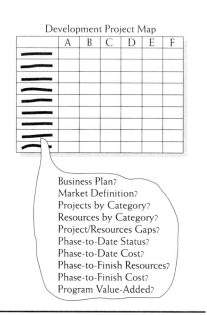

Problems
Too Many Projects (50%–75%)
Wrong Mix of Projects
Incorrect Execution Sequence
Misuse of Resources
Loss of Focus
Missed Market Windows
Products without Customers
Technologies without Markets

Development Project Map

Business Plan?
Market Definition?
Projects by Category?
Resources by Category?
Project/Resources Gaps?
Phase-to-Date Status?
Phase-to-Date Cost?
Phase-to-Finish Resources?
Phase-to-Finish Cost?
Program Value-Added?

- *Derivatives:* Projects that are cost-reduced versions or enhancements of existing products.
- *Platforms:* Fundamental improvements in cost, quality, functionality, or performance over previous generations.
- *Breakthroughs:* Significant developments of existing products and processes.
- *Research & Development:* Creation of new technologies that eventually translate into commercial development.
- *Strategic Alliances:* Activities outside the boundaries of the map that fit one of the categories previously mentioned.

2. Develop a descriptive profile for each project (for example, resources, costs, priorities, market potential, risk, and so on).
3. Determine Phase-To-Date and Phase-To-Finish facts, such as cost, cycle time, financial impact, resource constraints, trade-offs, and so on.
4. Purge the development workload based on short-term criteria and particular time-to-market needs.
5. Repeat the process monthly to manage development resources, program work flows, resource gaps, budget overruns, and development velocity.

BPR Results:

- An effective Product Development Management tool to prevent overload conditions.

PART 6

Sources of Competitive Advantage

The Resource-Based Theory of Competitive Advantage: Implications for Strategy Formulation*

Robert M. Grant

Strategy has been defined as "the match an organization makes between its internal resources and skills . . . and the opportunities and risks created by its external environment."[1] During the 1980s, the principal developments in strategy analysis focussed upon the link between strategy and the external environment. Prominent examples of this focus are Michael Porter's analysis of industry structure and competitive positioning and the empirical studies undertaken by the PIMS project.[2] By contrast, the link between strategy and the firm's resources and skills has suffered comparative neglect. Most research into the strategic implications of the firm's internal environment has been concerned with issues of strategy implementation and analysis of the organizational processes through which strategies emerge.[3]

Recently there has been a resurgence of interest in the role of the firm's resources as the foundation for firm strategy. This interest reflects dissatisfaction with the static, equilibrium framework of industrial organization economics that has dominated much contemporary thinking about business strategy and has renewed interest in older theories of profit and competition associated with the writings of David Ricardo, Joseph Schumpeter, and Edith Penrose.[4] Advances have occurred on several fronts. At the corporate strategy level, theoretical interest in economies of scope and transaction costs have focussed attention on the role of corporate resources in determining the industrial and geographical boundaries of the firm's activities.[5] At the business strategy level, explorations of the relationships between resources, competition, and profitability include the analysis of competitive imitation,[6] the appropriability of returns to innovations,[7] the role of imperfect information in creating profitability differences between competing firms,[8] and the means by which the process of resource accumulation can sustain competitive advantage.[9]

Together, these contributions amount to what has been termed "the resource-based view of the firm." As yet, however, the implications of this "resource-based theory" for strategic management are unclear for two reasons. First, the various contributions lack a single integrating framework. Second, little effort has been made to develop the practical

FIGURE 1 ───
A Resource-Based Approach to Strategy Analysis: A Practical Framework

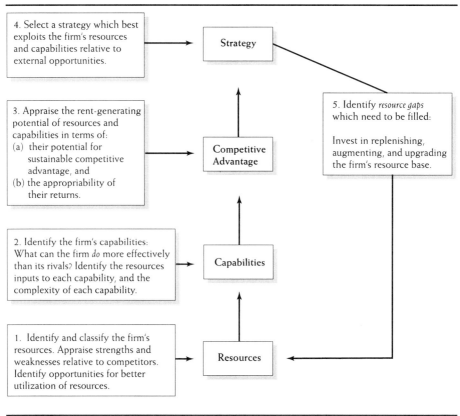

implications of this theory. The purpose of this article is to make progress on both these fronts by proposing a framework for a resource-based approach to strategy formulation which integrates a number of the key themes arising from this stream of literature. The organizing framework for the article is a five-stage procedure for strategy formulation: analyzing the firm's resource-base; appraising the firm's capabilities; analyzing the profit-earning potential of firm's resources and capabilities; selecting a strategy; and extending and upgrading the firm's pool of resources and capabilities. Figure 1 outlines this framework.

RESOURCES AND CAPABILITIES
AS THE FOUNDATION FOR STRATEGY

The case for making the resources and capabilities of the firm the foundation for its long-term strategy rests upon two premises: first, internal resources and capabilities provide the basic direction for a firm's strategy; second, resources and capabilities are the primary source of profit for the firm.

RESOURCES AND CAPABILITIES AS A SOURCE OF DIRECTION

The starting point for the formulation of strategy must be some statement of the firm's identity and purpose—conventionally this takes the form of a mission statement which answers the question: "What is our business?" Typically the definition of the business is in terms of the served market of the firm: e.g., "Who are our customers?" and "Which of their needs are we seeking to serve?" But in a world where customer preferences are volatile, the identity of customers is changing, and the technologies for serving customer requirements are continually evolving, an externally focused orientation does not provide a secure foundation for formulating long-term strategy. When the external environment is in a state of flux, the firm's own resources and capabilities may be a much more stable basis on which to define its identity. Hence, a definition of a business in terms of what it is capable of doing may offer a more durable basis for strategy than a definition based upon the needs which the business seeks to satisfy.

Theodore Levitt's solution to the problem of external change was that companies should define their served markets broadly rather than narrowly: railroads should have perceived themselves to be in the transportation business, not the railroad business. But such broadening of the target market is of little value if the company cannot easily develop the capabilities required for serving customer requirements across a wide front. Was it feasible for the railroads to have developed successful trucking, airline, and car rental businesses? Perhaps the resources and capabilities of the railroad companies were better suited to real estate development, or the building and managing of oil and gas pipelines. Evidence suggests that serving broadly defined customer needs is a difficult task. The attempts by Merrill Lynch, American Express, Sears, Citicorp, and, most recently, Prudential-Bache to "serve the full range of our customers' financial needs" created serious management problems. Allegis Corporation's goal of "serving the needs of the traveller" through combining United Airlines, Hertz car rental, and Westin Hotels was a costly failure. By contrast, several companies whose strategies have been based upon developing and exploiting clearly defined internal capabilities have been adept at adjusting to and exploiting external change. Honda's focus upon the technical excellence of 4-cycle engines carried it successfully from motorcycles to automobiles to a broad range of gasoline-engine products. 3M Corporation's expertise in applying adhesive and coating technologies to new product development has permitted profitable growth over an ever-widening product range.

RESOURCES AS THE BASIS FOR CORPORATE PROFITABILITY

A firm's ability to earn a rate of profit in excess of its cost of capital depends upon two factors: the attractiveness of the industry in which it is located, and its establishment of competitive advantage over rivals. Industrial organization economics emphasizes industry attractiveness as the primary basis for superior profitability, the implication being that strategic management is concerned primarily with seeking favorable industry environments, locating attractive segments and strategic groups within industries, and moderating competitive pressures by influencing industry structure and competitors' behavior. Yet empirical investigation has failed to support the link between industry structure and profitability. Most studies show that differences in profitability within industries are much more important than differences between industries.[10] The reasons are not difficult to find: international competition, technological change, and diversification by firms across industry boundaries have meant that industries which were once cozy havens for making easy profits are now subject to vigorous competition.

The finding that competitive advantage rather than external environments is the primary source of inter-firm profit differentials between firms focuses attention upon the sources of competitive advantage. Although the competitive strategy literature has tended to emphasize issues of strategic positioning in terms of the choice between cost and differentiation advantage, and between broad and narrow market scope, fundamental to these choices is the resource position of the firm. For example, the ability to establish a cost advantage requires possession of scale-efficient plants, superior process technology, ownership of low-cost sources of raw materials, or access to low-wage labor. Similarly, differentiation advantage is conferred by brand reputation, proprietary technology, or an extensive sales and service network.

This may be summed up as follows: business strategy should be viewed less as a quest for monopoly rents (the returns to market power) and more as a quest for Ricardian rents (the returns to the resources which confer competitive advantage over and above the real costs of these resources). Once these resources depreciate, become obsolescent, or are replicated by other firms, the rents they generate tend to disappear.[11]

We can go further. A closer look at market power and the monopoly rent it offers suggests that it too has its basis in the resources of firms. The fundamental prerequisite for market power is the presence of barriers to entry.[12] Barriers to entry are based upon scale economies, patents, experience advantages, brand reputation, or some other resource which incumbent firms possess but which entrants can acquire only slowly or at disproportionate expense. Other structural sources of market power are similarly based upon firms' resources: monopolistic price-setting power depends upon market share which is a consequence of cost efficiency, financial strength, or some other resource. The resources which confer market power may be owned individually by firms, others may be owned jointly. An industry standard (which raises costs of entry), or a cartel, is a resource which is owned collectively by the industry members.[13] Figure 2 summarizes the relationships between resources and profitability.

TAKING STOCK OF THE FIRM'S RESOURCES

There is a key distinction between resources and capabilities. Resources are inputs into the production process—they are the basic units of analysis. The individual resources of the firm include items of capital equipment, skills of individual employees, patents, brand names, finance, and so on. But, on their own, few resources are productive. Productive activity requires the cooperation and coordination of teams of resources. A capability is the capacity for a team of resources to perform some task or activity. While resources are the source of a firm's capabilities, capabilities are the main source of its competitive advantage.

IDENTIFYING RESOURCES

A major handicap in identifying and appraising a firm's resources is that management information systems typically provide only a fragmented and incomplete picture of the firm's resource base. Financial balance sheets are notoriously inadequate because they disregard

FIGURE 2
Resources as the Basis for Profitability

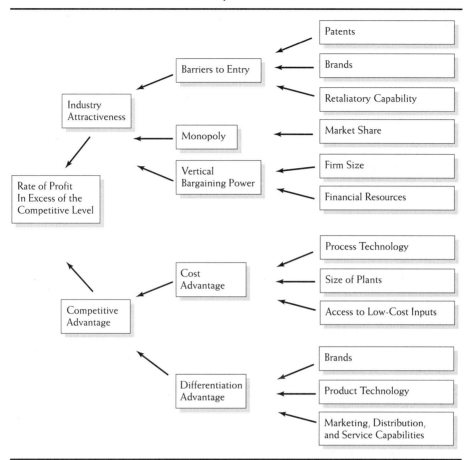

intangible resources and people-based skills—probably the most strategically important resources of the firm.[14] Classification can provide a useful starting point. Six major categories of resource have been suggested: financial resources, physical resources, human resources, technological resources, reputation, and organizational resources.[15] The reluctance of accountants to extend the boundaries of corporate balance sheets beyond tangible assets partly reflects difficulties of valuation. The heterogeneity and imperfect transferability of most intangible resources precludes the use of market prices. One approach to valuing intangible resources is to take the difference between the stock market value of the firm and the replacement value of its tangible assets.[16] On a similar basis, valuation ratios provide some indication of the importance of firms' intangible resources. Table 1 shows that the highest valuation ratios are found among companies with valuable patents and technology assets (notably drug companies) and brand-rich consumer-product companies.

The primary task of a resource-based approach to strategy formulation is maximizing rents over time. For this purpose we need to investigate the relationship between resources

TABLE 1

Twenty Companies among the U.S. Top 100 Companies with the Highest Ratios of Stock Price to Book Value on March 16, 1990

COMPANY	INDUSTRY	VALUATION RATIO
Coca-Cola	Beverages	8.77
Microsoft	Computer software	8.67
Merck	Pharmaceuticals	8.39
American Home Products	Pharmaceuticals	8.00
Wal-Mart Stores	Retailing	7.51
Limited	Retailing	6.65
Warner Lambert	Pharmaceuticals	6.34
Waste Management	Pollution control	6.18
Marrion Merrell Dow	Pharmaceuticals	6.10
McCaw Cellular Communications	Telecom equipment	5.90
Bristol Myers Squibb	Pharmaceuticals	5.48
Toys 'R' Us	Retailing	5.27
Abbot Laboratories	Pharmaceuticals	5.26
Walt Disney	Entertainment	4.90
Johnson & Johnson	Health care products	4.85
MCI Communications	Telecommunications	4.80
Eli Lilly	Pharmaceuticals	4.70
Kellogg	Food products	4.58
H.J. Heinz	Food products	4.38
Pepsico	Beverages	4.33

Source: *The 1990 Business Week Top 1000.*

and organizational capabilities. However, there are also direct links between resources and profitability which raise issues for the strategic management of resources:

- *What opportunities exist for economizing on the use of resources?* The ability to maximize productivity is particularly important in the case of tangible resources such as plant and machinery, finance, and people. It may involve using fewer resources to support the same level of business, or using the existing resources to support a larger volume of business. The success of aggressive acquirors, such as ConAgra in the U.S. and Hanson in Britain, is based upon expertise in rigorously pruning the financial, physical, and human assets needed to support the volume of business in acquired companies.
- *What are the possibilities for using existing assets more intensely and in more profitable employment?* A large proportion of corporate acquisitions are motivated by the belief that the resources of the acquired company can be put to more profitable use. The returns from transferring existing assets into more productive employment can be substantial. The remarkable turnaround in the performance of the Walt Disney Company between 1985 and 1987 owed much to the vigorous exploitation of Disney's considerable and unique assets: accelerated development of Disney's vast landholdings (for residential development as well as entertainment purposes); exploitation of Disney's huge film library through cable TV,

videos, and syndication; fuller utilization of Disney's studios through the formation of Touchstone Films; increased marketing to improve capacity utilization at Disney theme parks.

IDENTIFYING AND APPRAISING CAPABILITIES

The capabilities of a firm are what it can do as a result of teams of resources working together. A firm's capabilities can be identified and appraised using a standard functional classification of the firm's activities. For example, Snow and Hrebiniak examined capabilities (in their terminology, "distinctive competencies") in relation to ten functional areas.[17] For most firms, however, the most important capabilities are likely to be those which arise from an integration of individual functional capabilities. For example, McDonald's possesses outstanding functional capabilities within product development, market research, human resource management, financial control, and operations management. However, critical to McDonald's success is the integration of these functional capabilities to create McDonald's remarkable consistency of products and services in thousands of restaurants spread across most of the globe. Hamel and Prahalad use the term "core competencies" to describe these central, strategic capabilities. They are "the collective learning in the organization, especially how to coordinate diverse production skills and integrate multiple streams of technology."[18] Examples of core competencies include:

- NEC's integration of computer and telecommunications technology
- Philips' optical-media expertise
- Casio's harmonization of know-how in miniaturization, microprocessor design, material science, and ultrathin precision casting
- Canon's integration of optical, microelectronic, and precision-mechanical technologies which forms the basis of its success in cameras, copiers, and facsimile machines
- Black and Decker's competence in the design and manufacture of small electric motors

A key problem in appraising capabilities is maintaining objectivity. Howard Stevenson observed a wide variation in senior managers' perceptions of their organizations' distinctive competencies.[19] Organizations frequently fall victim to past glories, hopes for the future, and wishful thinking. Among the failed industrial companies of both America and Britain are many which believed themselves world leaders with superior products and customer loyalty. During the 1960s, the CEOs of both Harley-Davidson and BSA-Triumph scorned the idea that Honda threatened their supremacy in the market for "serious motorcycles."[20] The failure of the U.S. steel companies to respond to increasing import competition during the 1970s was similarly founded upon misplaced confidence in their quality and technological leadership.[21]

The critical task is to assess capabilities relative to those of competitors. In the same way that national prosperity is enhanced through specialization on the basis of comparative advantages, so for the firm, a successful strategy is one which exploits relative strengths. Federal Express's primary capabilities are those which permit it to operate a national delivery system that can guarantee next day delivery; for the British retailer Marks and Spencer, it is the ability to manage supplier relations to ensure a high and consistent level of product quality; for General Electric, it is a system of corporate management that reconciles control, coordination, flexibility, and innovation in one of the world's largest and most diversified corporations. Conversely, failure is often due to strategies which extend the firm's activities beyond the scope of its capabilities.

CAPABILITIES AS ORGANIZATIONAL ROUTINES

Creating capabilities is not simply a matter of assembling a team of resources: capabilities involve complex patterns of coordination between people and between people and other resources. Perfecting such coordination requires learning through repetition. To understand the anatomy of a firm's capabilities, Nelson and Winter's concept of "organizational routine" is illuminating. Organizational routines are regular and predictable patterns of activity which are made up of a sequence of coordinated actions by individuals. A capability is, in essence, a routine, or a number of interacting routines. The organization itself is a huge network of routines. These include the sequence of routines which govern the passage of raw material and components through the production process, and top management routines which include routines for monitoring business unit performance, for capital budgeting, and for strategy formulation.

The concept of organizational routines offers illuminating insights into the relationships between resources, capabilities, and competitive advantage:

- *The relationship between resources and capabilities.* There is no predetermined functional relationship between the resources of a firm and its capabilities. The types, the amounts, and the qualities of the resources available to the firm have an important bearing on what the firm can do since they place constraints upon the range of organizational routines that can be performed and the standard to which they are performed. However, a key ingredient in the relationship between resources and capabilities is the ability of an organization to achieve cooperation and coordination within teams. This requires that an organization motivate and socialize its members in a manner conducive to the development of smooth-functioning routines. The organization's style, values, traditions, and leadership are critical encouragements to the cooperation and commitment of its members. These can be viewed as intangible resources which are common ingredients of the whole range of a corporation's organizational routines.
- *The trade-off between efficiency and flexibility.* Routines are to the organization what skills are to the individual. Just as the individual's skills are carried out semi-automatically, without conscious coordination, so organizational routines involve a large component of tacit knowledge, which implies limits on the extent to which the organization's capabilities can be articulated. Just as individual skills become rusty when not exercised, so it is difficult for organizations to retain coordinated responses to contingencies that arise only rarely. Hence there may be a trade-off between efficiency and flexibility. A limited repertoire of routines can be performed highly efficiently with near-perfect coordination— all in the absence of significant intervention by top management. The same organization may find it extremely difficult to respond to novel situations.
- *Economics of experience.* Just as individual skills are acquired through practice over time, so the skills of an organization are developed and sustained only through experience. The advantage of an established firm over a newcomer is primarily in the organizational routines that it has perfected over time. The Boston Consulting Group's "experience curve"

represents a naive, yet valuable attempt to relate the experience of the firm to its performance. However, in industries where technological change is rapid, new firms may possess an advantage over established firms through their potential for faster learning of new routines because they are less committed to old routines.

- *The complexity of capabilities.* Organizational capabilities differ in their complexity. Some capabilities may derive from the contribution of a single resource. DuPont's successful development of several cardiovascular drugs during the late 1980s owed much to the research leadership of its leading pharmacologist Pieter Timmermans.[22] Drexel Burnham Lambert's capability in junk bond underwriting during the 1980s resided almost entirely in the skills of Michael Millken. Other routines require highly complex interactions involving the cooperation of many different resources. Walt Disney's "imagineering" capability involves the integration of ideas, skills, and knowledge drawn from movie making, engineering, psychology, and a wide variety of technical disciplines. As we shall see, complexity is particularly relevant to the sustainability of competitive advantage.

EVALUATING THE RENT-EARNING POTENTIAL: SUSTAINABILITY

The returns to a firm's resources and capabilities depend upon two key factors: first, the sustainability of the competitive advantage which resources and capabilities confer upon the firm; and, second, the ability of the firm to appropriate the rents earned from its resources and capabilities.

Over the long-term, competitive advantage and the returns associated with it are eroded both through the depreciation of the advantaged firm's resources and capabilities and through imitation by rivals. The speed of erosion depends critically upon the characteristics of the resources and capabilities. Consider markets where competitive advantage is unsustainable: in "efficient" markets (most closely approximated by the markets for securities, commodities, and foreign exchange) competitive advantage is absent; market prices reflect all available information, prices adjust instantaneously to new information, and traders can only expect normal returns. The absence of competitive advantage is a consequence of the resources required to compete in these markets. To trade in financial markets, the basic requirements are finance and information. If both are available on equal terms to all participants, competitive advantage cannot exist. Even if privileged information is assumed to exist ("weakly efficient" markers), competitive advantage is not sustainable. Once a trader acts upon privileged information, transactions volume and price movements signal insider activity, and other traders are likely to rush in seeking a piece of the action.

The essential difference between industrial markets and financial markets lies in the resource requirements of each. In industrial markets, resources are specialized, immobile, and long-lasting. As a result, according to Richard Caves, a key feature of industrial markets is the existence of "committed competition—rivalrous moves among incumbent producers that involve resource commitments that are irrevocable for non-trivial periods of time."[23] The difficulties involved in acquiring the resources required to compete and the need to commit resources long before a competitive move can be initiated also implies that competitive advantage is much more sustainable than it is in financial markets. Resource-based approaches to the theory of competitive advantage point towards four characteristics of resources and capabilities which are likely to be particularly important determinants of the sustainability of competitive advantage: *durability, transparency, transferability,* and *replicability*.

DURABILITY

In the absence of competition, the longevity of a firm's competitive advantage depends upon the rate at which the underlying resources and capabilities depreciate or become obsolete. The durability of resources varies considerably: the increasing pace of technological change is shortening the useful life spans of most capital equipment and technological resources. On the other hand, reputation (both brand and corporate) appears to depreciate relatively slowly, and these assets can normally be maintained by modest rates of replacement investment. Many of the consumer brands which command the strongest loyalties today (e.g., Heinz sauces, Kellogg's cereals, Campbell's soup, Hoover vacuum cleaners) have been market leaders for close to a century. Corporate reputation displays similar longevity: the reputations of GE, IBM, DuPont, and Procter & Gamble as well-managed, socially responsible, financially sound companies which produce reliable products and treat their employees well has been established over several decades. While increasing environmental turbulence shortens the life spans of many resources, it is possible that it may have the effects of bolstering brand and corporate reputations.

Firm capabilities have the potential to be more durable than the resources upon which they are based because of the firm's ability to maintain capabilities through replacing individual resources (including people) as they wear out or move on. Rolls Royce's capability in the craft-based manufacture of luxury cars and 3M's capability in new product introduction have been maintained over several generations of employees. Such longevity depends critically upon the management of these capabilities to ensure their maintenance and renewal. One of the most important roles that organizational culture plays in sustaining competitive advantage may be through its maintenance support for capabilities through the socialization of new employees.[24]

TRANSPARENCY

The firm's ability to sustain its competitive advantage over time depends upon the speed with which other firms can imitate its strategy. Imitation requires that a competitor overcomes two problems. First is the information problem: What is the competitive advantage of the successful rival, and how is it being achieved? Second is the strategy duplication problem: How can the would-be competitor amass the resources and capabilities required to imitate the successful strategy of the rival? The information problem is a consequence of imperfect information on two sets of relationships. If a firm wishes to imitate the strategy of a rival, it must first establish the capabilities which underlie the rival's competitive advantage, and then it must determine what resources are required to replicate these capabilities. I refer to this as the "transparency" of competitive advantage. With regard to the first transparency problem, a competitive advantage which is the consequence of superior capability in relation to a single performance variable is more easy to identify and comprehend than a competitive advantage that involves multiple capabilities conferring superior performance across several variables. Cray Research's success in the computer industry rests primarily upon its technological capability in relation to large, ultra-powerful computers. IBM's superior performance is multidimensional and is more difficult to understand. It is extremely difficult to distinguish and appraise the relative contributions to 3M's success of research capability, scale economies in product development and manufacturing, self-sufficiency through backward integration, and superior customer service through excellence in sales, service, and technical support.

With regard to the second transparency problem, a capability which requires a complex pattern of coordination between large numbers of diverse resources is more difficult to comprehend than a capability which rests upon the exploitation of a single dominant resource. For example, Federal Express's next-day delivery capability requires close cooperation between numerous employees, aircraft, delivery vans, computerized tracking facilities, and automated sorting equipment, all coordinated into a single system. By contrast, Atlantic Richfield's low-cost position in the supply of gasoline to the California market rests simply on its access to Alaskan crude oil. Imperfect transparency is the basis for Lippman and Rumelt's theory of "uncertain imitability": the greater the uncertainty within a market over how successful companies "do it," the more inhibited are potential entrants, and the higher the level of profit that established firms can maintain within that market.[25]

TRANSFERABILITY

Once the established firm or potential entrant has established the sources of the superior performance, imitation then requires amassing the resources and capabilities necessary for a competitive challenge. The primary source of resources and capabilities is likely to be the markets for these inputs. If firms can acquire (on similar terms) the resources required for imitating the competitive advantage of a successful rival, then that rival's competitive advantage will be short lived. As we have seen, in financial markets the easy access by traders to finance and information causes competitive advantage to be fleeting. However, most resources and capabilities are not freely transferable between firms; hence, would-be competitors are unable to acquire (on equal terms) the resources needed to replicate the competitive advantage of an incumbent firm. Imperfections in transferability arise from several sources:

- *Geographical immobility.* The costs of relocating large items of capital equipment and highly specialized employees puts firms which are acquiring these resources at a disadvantage to firms which already possess them.
- *Imperfect information.* Assessing the value of a resource is made difficult by the heterogeneity of resources (particularly human resources) and by imperfect knowledge of the potential productivity of individual resources.[26] The established firm's ability to build up information over time about the productivity of its resources gives it superior knowledge to that of any prospective purchaser of the resources in question.[27] The resulting imperfection of the markets for productive resources can then result in resources being either underpriced or overpriced, thus giving rise to differences in profitability between firms.[28]
- *Firm-specific resources.* Apart from the transactions costs arising from immobility and imperfect information, the value of a resource may fall on transfer due to a decline in its productivity. To the extent that brand reputation is associated with the company which created the brand reputation, a change in ownership of the brand name erodes its value. Once Rover, MG, Triumph, and Jaguar were merged into British Leyland, the values of these brands in differentiating automobiles declined substantially. Employees can suffer a similar decline in productivity in the process of inter-firm transfer. To the extent

that an employee's productivity is influenced by situational and motivational factors, then it is unreasonable to expect that a highly successful employee in one company can replicate his/her performance when hired away by another company. Some resources may be almost entirely firm specific—corporate reputation can only be transferred by acquiring the company as a whole, and even then the reputation of the acquired company normally depreciates during the change in ownership.[29]

- *The immobility of capabilities.* Capabilities, because they require interactive teams of resources, are far more immobile than individual resources—they require the transfer of the whole team. Such transfers can occur (e.g., the defection of 16 of First Boston's mergers and acquisitions staff to Wasserstein, Perella and Company).[30] However, even if the resources that constitute the team are transferred, the nature of organizational routines—in particular, the role of tacit knowledge and unconscious coordination—makes the recreation of capabilities within a new corporate environment uncertain.

REPLICABILITY

Imperfect transferability of resources and capabilities limits the ability of a firm to buy in the means to imitate success. The second route by which a firm can acquire a resource or capability is by internal investment. Some resources and capabilities can be easily imitated through replication. In retailing, competitive advantages which derive from electronic point-of-sale systems, retailer charge cards, and extended hours of opening can be copied fairly easily by competitors. In financial services, new product innovations (such as interest rate swaps, stripped bonds, money market accounts, and the like) are notorious for their easy imitation by competitors.

　　Much less easily replicable are capabilities based upon highly complex organizational routines. IBM's ability to motivate its people and Nucor's outstanding efficiency and flexibility in steel manufacture are combinations of complex routines that are based upon tacit rather than codified knowledge and are fused into the respective corporate cultures. Some capabilities appear simple but prove exceptionally difficult to replicate. Two of the simplest and best-known Japanese manufacturing practices are just-in-time scheduling and quality circles. Despite the fact that neither require sophisticated knowledge or complex operating systems, the cooperation and attitudinal changes required for their effective operation are such that few American and European firms have introduced either with the same degree of success as Japanese companies. If apparently simple practices such as these are deceptively difficult to imitate, it is easy to see how firms that develop highly complex capabilities can maintain their competitive advantage over very long periods of time. Xerox's commitment to customer service is a capability that is not located in any particular department, but it permeates the whole corporation and is built into the fabric and culture of the corporation.

　　Even where replication is possible, the dynamics of stock-flow relationships may still offer an advantage to incumbent firms. Competitive advantage depends upon the stock of resources and capabilities that a firm possesses. Dierickx and Cool show that firms which possess the initial stocks of the resources required for competitive advantage may be able to sustain their advantages over time.[31] Among the stock-flow relationships they identify as sustaining advantage are: "asset mass efficiencies"—the initial amount of the resource which the firm possesses influences the pace at which the resource can be accumulated; and "time compression diseconomies"—firms which rapidly accumulate a resource incur disproportionate costs ("crash programs" of R&D and "blitz" advertising campaigns tend to be less productive than similar expenditures made over a longer period).

EVALUATING RENT-EARNING POTENTIAL: APPROPRIABILITY

The returns to a firm from its resources and capabilities depend not only on sustaining its competitive position over time, but also on the firm's ability to appropriate these returns. The issue of appropriability concerns the allocation of rents where property rights are not fully defined. Once we go beyond the financial and physical assets valued in a company's balance sheet, ownership becomes ambiguous. The firm owns intangible assets such as patents, copyrights, brand names, and trade secrets, but the scope of property rights may lack precise definition. In the case of employee skills, two major problems arise: the lack of clear distinction between the technology of the firm and the human capital of the individual; and the limited control which employment contracts offer over the services provided by employees. Employee mobility means that it is risky for a firm's strategy to be dependent upon the specific skills of a few key employees. Also, such employees can bargain with the firm to appropriate the major part of their contribution to value added.

The degree of control exercised by a firm and the balance of power between the firm and an individual employee depends crucially on the relationship between the individual's skills and organizational routines. The more deeply embedded are organizational routines within groups of individuals and the more are they supported by the contributions of other resources, then the greater is the control that the firm's management can exercise. The ability of IBM to utilize its advanced semiconductor research as an instrument of competitive advantage depends, in part, upon the extent to which the research capability is a team asset rather than a reflection of the contribution of brilliant individuals. A firm's dependence upon skills possessed by highly trained and highly mobile key employees is particularly important in the case of professional service companies where employee skills are the overwhelmingly important resource.[32] Many of the problems that have arisen in acquisitions of human-capital-intensive companies arise from conflicts over property rights between the acquiring company and employees of the acquired company. An interesting example is the protracted dispute which followed the acquisition of the New York advertising agency Lord, Geller, Fredrico, Einstein by WPP Group in 1988. Most of the senior executives of the acquired company left to form a new advertising agency taking several former clients with them.[33] Similar conflicts have arisen over technology ownership in high-tech start-ups founded by former employees of established companies.[34]

Where ownership is ambiguous, relative bargaining power is the primary determinant of the allocation of the rents between the firm and its employees where. If the individual employee's contribution to productivity is clearly identifiable, if the employee is mobile, and the employee's skills offer similar productivity to other firms, then the employee is well placed to bargain for that contribution. If the increased gate receipts of the L.A. Kings ice hockey team can be attributed primarily to the presence of Wayne Gretzky on the team and if Gretzky can offer a similar performance enhancement to other teams, then he is in a strong position to appropriate (as salary and bonuses) most of the increased contribution. The less identifiable is the individual's contribution, and the more firm-specific are the skills being applied, the greater is the proportion of the return which accrues to the firm. Declining profitability among investment banks encouraged several to reassert their bargaining power vis-à-vis their individual stars and in-house gurus by engineering a transfer of reputation from these key employees to the company as a whole. At Citibank, Salomon Brothers, Merrill Lynch, and First Boston, this resulted in bitter conflicts between top management and some senior employees.[35]

FORMULATING STRATEGY

Although the foregoing discussion of the links between resources, capabilities, and profitability has been strongly theoretical in nature, the implications for strategy formulation are straightforward. The analysis of the rent-generating potential of resources and capabilities concludes that the firm's most important resources and capabilities are those which are durable, difficult to identify and understand, imperfectly transferable, not easily replicated, and in which the firm possesses clear ownership and control. These are the firm's "crown jewels" that need to be protected and play a pivotal role in the competitive strategy which the firm pursues. The essence of strategy formulation, then, is to design a strategy that makes the most effective use of these core resources and capabilities. Consider, for example, the remarkable turnaround of Harley-Davidson between 1984 and 1988. Fundamental was top management's recognition that the company's sole durable, nontransferable, irreplicable asset was the Harley-Davidson image and the loyalty that accompanied that image. In virtually every other area of competitive performance—production costs, quality, product and process technology, and global market scope—Harley was greatly inferior to its Japanese rivals. Harley's only opportunity for survival was to pursue a strategy founded upon Harley's image advantage, while simultaneously minimizing Harley's disadvantages in other capabilities. Harley-Davidson's new models introduced during this period were all based around traditional design features, while Harley's marketing strategy involved extending the appeal of the Harley image of individuality and toughness from its traditional customer group to more affluent professional types. Protection of the Harley-Davidson name by means of tougher controls over dealers was matched by wider exploitation of the Harley name through extensive licensing. While radical improvements in manufacturing efficiency and quality were essential components of the turnaround strategy, it was the enhancing and broadening of Harley's market appeal which was the primary driver of Harley's rise from 27 to 44 percent of the U.S. heavyweight motorcycle market between 1984 and 1988, accompanied by an increase in net income from $6.5 million to $29.8 million.

Conversely, a failure to recognize and exploit the strategic importance of durable, untransferable, and irreplicable resources almost inevitably has dire consequences. The troubles of BankAmerica Corporation during the mid-1980s can be attributed to a strategy that became increasingly dissociated from the bank's most important assets: its reputation and market position in retail banking in the Western United States. The disastrous outcome of U.S. Air Group's acquisition of the Californian carrier, PSA, is similarly attributable to U.S. Air's disregard for PSA's most important asset—its reputation in the Californian market for a friendly, laid-back style of service.

Designing strategy around the most critically important resources and capabilities may imply that the firm limits its strategic scope to those activities where it possesses a clear competitive advantage. The principal capabilities of Lotus, the specialist manufacturer of sports cars, are in design and engineering development; it lacked both the manufacturing capabilities or the sales volume to compete effectively in the world's auto market. Lotus's turnaround during the 1980s followed its decision to specialize upon design and development consulting for other auto manufacturers, and to limit its own manufacturing primarily to formula one racing cars.

The ability of a firm's resources and capabilities to support a sustainable competitive advantage is essential to the time frame of a firm's strategic planning process. If a company's resources and capabilities lack durability or are easily transferred or replicated, then the company must either adopt a strategy of short-term harvesting or it must invest in developing new sources of competitive advantage. These considerations are critical for small technological start-ups where the speed of technological change may mean that innovations offer only temporary competitive advantage. The company must seek either to exploit its initial innovation before it is challenged by stronger, established rivals or other start-ups, or it must establish the technological capability for a continuing stream of innovations. A fundamental flaw in EMI's exploitation of its invention of the CT scanner was a strategy that failed to exploit EMI's five-year technical lead in the development and marketing of the X-ray scanner and failed to establish the breadth of technological and manufacturing capability required to establish a fully fledged medical electronics business.

Where a company's resources and capabilities are easily transferable or replicable, sustaining a competitive advantage is only feasible if the company's market is unattractively small or if it can obscure the existence of its competitive advantage. Filofax, the long-established British manufacturer of personal organizers, was able to dominate the market for its products so long as that market remained small. The boom in demand for Filofaxes during the mid-1980s was, paradoxically, a disaster for the company. Filofax's product was easily imitated and yuppie-driven demand growth spawned a host of imitators. By 1989, the company was suffering falling sales and mounting losses.[36] In industries where competitive advantages based upon differentiation and innovation can be imitated (such as financial services, retailing, fashion clothing, and toys), firms have a brief window of opportunity during which to exploit their advantage before imitators erode it away. Under such circumstances, firms must be concerned not with sustaining the existing advantages, but also with creating the flexibility and responsiveness that permits them to create new advantages at a faster rate than the old advantages are being eroded by competition.

Transferability and replicability of resources and capabilities is also a key issue in the strategic management of joint ventures. Studies of the international joint ventures point to the transferability of each party's capabilities as a critical determinant of the allocation of benefits from the venture. For example, Western companies' strengths in distribution channels and product technology have been easily exploited by Japanese joint venture partners, while Japanese manufacturing excellence and new product development capabilities have proved exceptionally difficult for Western companies to learn.[37]

IDENTIFYING RESOURCE GAPS AND DEVELOPING THE RESOURCE BASE

The analysis so far has regarded the firm's resource base as predetermined, with the primary task of organizational strategy being the deployment of these resources so as to maximize rents over time. However, a resource-based approach to strategy is concerned not only with the deployment of existing resources, but also with the development of the firm's resource base. This includes replacement investment to maintain the firm's stock of resources and to augment resources in order to buttress and extend positions of competitive advantage as well as broaden the firm's strategic opportunity set. This task is known in the strategy literature as filling "resource gaps."[38]

Sustaining advantage in the face of competition and evolving customer requirements also requires that firms constantly develop their resources bases. Such "upgrading" of competitive advantage occupies a central position in Michael Porter's analysis of the competitive advantage of nations.[39] Porter's analysis of the ability of firms and nations to establish and maintain international competitive success depends critically upon the ability to continually innovate and to shift the basis of competitive advantage from "basic" to "advanced" factors of production. An important feature of these "advanced" factors of production is that they offer a more sustainable competitive advantage because they are more specialized (therefore less mobile through market transfer) and less easy to replicate.

Commitment to upgrading the firm's pool of resources and capabilities requires strategic direction in terms of the capabilities that will form the basis of the firm's future competitive advantage. Thus, Prahalad and Hamel's notion of "core competencies" is less an identification of a company's current capabilities than a commitment to a path of future development. For example, NEC's strategic focus on computing and communications in the mid-1970s was not so much a statement of the core strengths of the company as it was a long-term commitment to a particular path of technological development.

Harmonizing the exploitation of existing resources with the development of the resources and capabilities for competitive advantage in the future is a subtle task. To the extent that capabilities are learned and perfected through repetition, capabilities develop automatically through the pursuit of a particular strategy. The essential task, then, is to ensure that strategy constantly pushes slightly beyond the limits of the firm's capabilities at any point of time. This ensures not only the perfection of capabilities required by the current strategy, but also the development of the capabilities required to meet the challenges of the future. The idea that, through pursuing its present strategy, a firm develops the expertise required for its future strategy is referred to by Hiroyuki Itami as "dynamic resource fit":

> Effective strategy in the present builds invisible assets, and the expanded stock enables the firm to plan its future strategy to be carried out. And the future strategy must make effective use of the resources that have been amassed.[40]

Matsushita is a notable exponent of this principle of parallel and sequential development of strategy and capabilities. For example, in developing production in a foreign country, Matsushita typically began with the production of simple products, such as batteries, then moved on the production of products requiring greater manufacturing and marketing sophistication:

> In every country batteries are a necessity, so they sell well. As long as we bring a few advanced automated pieces of equipment for the processes vital to final product quality, even unskilled labor can produce good products. As they work on this rather simple product, the workers get trained, and this increased skill level then permits us to gradually expand production to items with increasingly higher technology level, first radios, then televisions.[41]

The development of capabilities which can then be used as the basis for broadening a firm's product range is a common feature of successful strategies of related diversification. Sequential product addition to accompany the development of technological, manufacturing, and marketing expertise was a feature of Honda's diversification from motorcycles to cars, generators, lawn mowers, and boat engines; and of 3M's expansion from abrasives to adhesives, videotape, and computer disks.

In order both to fully exploit a firm's existing stock of resources, and to develop competitive advantages for the future, the external acquisition of complementary resources may be necessary. Consider the Walt Disney Company's turnaround between 1984 and 1988. In order for the new management to exploit more effectively Disney's vast, under-utilized stock of unique resources, new resources were required. Achieving better utilization of Disney's film studios and expertise in animation required the acquisition of creative talent in the form of directors, actors, scriptwriters, and cartoonists. Putting Disney's vast real estate holdings to work was assisted by the acquisition of the property development expertise of the Arvida Corporation. Building a new marketing team was instrumental in increasing capacity utilization at Disneyland and Disney World.

CONCLUSION

The resources and capabilities of a firm are the central considerations in formulating its strategy: they are the primary constants upon which a firm can establish its identity and frame its strategy, and they are the primary sources of the firm's profitability. The key to a resource-based approach to strategy formulation is understanding the relationships between resources, capabilities, competitive advantage, and profitability—in particular, an understanding of the mechanisms through which competitive advantage can be sustained over time. This requires the design of strategies which exploit to maximum effect each firm's unique characteristics.

REFERENCES

[1] Charles W. Hofer and Dan Schendel, *Strategy Formulation: Analytic Concepts* (St. Paul, MN: West, 1978), p. 12.

[2] Robert D. Buzzell and Bradley T. Gale, *The PIMS Principles: Linking Strategy to Performance* (New York, NY: Free Press, 1987).

[3] See, for example, Henry Mintzberg, "Of Strategies, Deliberate and Emergent," *Strategic Management Journal*, 6 (1985): 257–272; Andrew M. Pettigrew, "Strategy Formulation as a Political Process," *International Studies of Management and Organization*, 7 (1977): 78–87; J.B. Quinn, *Strategies for Change: Logical Incrementalism* (Homewood, IL: Irwin, 1980).

[4] David Ricardo, *Principles of Political Economy and Taxation* (London: G. Bell, 1891); Joseph A. Schumpeter, *The Theory of Economic Development* (Cambridge, MA: Harvard University Press, 1934); Edith Penrose, *The Theory of the Growth of the Firm* (New York, NY: John Wiley and Sons, 1959).

[5] David J. Teece, "Economies of Scope and the Scope of the Enterprise," *Journal of Economic Behavior and Organization*, 1 (1980): 223–247; S. Chatterjee and B. Wernerfelt, "The Link between Resources and Types of Diversification: Theory and Evidence," *Strategic Management Journal*, 12 (1991): 33–48.

[6] R.P. Rumelt, "Towards a Strategic Theory of the Firm," in R.B. Lamb, ed., *Competitive Strategic Management* (Englewood Cliffs, NJ: Prentice Hall, 1984); S.A. Lippman and R.P. Rumelt, "Uncertain Imitability: An Analysis of Interfirm Differences in Efficiency under Competition," *Bell Journal of Economics*, 23 (1982): 418–438; Richard Reed and R.J. DeFillippi, "Causal Ambiguity, Barriers to Imitation, and Sustainable Competitive Advantage," *Academy of Management Review*, 15 (January 1990): 88–102.

[7] David J. Teece, "Capturing Value from Technological Innovation: Integration, Strategic Partnering, and Licensing Decisions," *Interfaces*, 18/3 (1988): 46–61.

[8] Jay B. Barney, "Strategic Factor Markets: Expectations, Luck and Business Strategy," *Management Science*, 32/10 (October 1986): 1231–1241.

[9] Ingemar Dierickx and Karel Cool, "Asset Stock Accumulation and the Sustainability of Competitive Advantage," *Management Science*, 35/12 (December 1989): 1504–1513.

[10] R. Schmalensee, "Industrial Economics: An Overview," *Economic Journal*, 98 (1988): 643–681; R.D. Buzzell and B. T. Gale, *The PIMS Principles* (New York, NY: Free Press, 1987).

[11] Because of the ambiguity associated with accounting definitions of profit, the academic literature increasingly uses the term "rent" to refer to "economic profit." "Rent" is the surplus of revenue over the "real" or "opportunity" cost of the resources used in generating that revenue. The "real" or "opportunity" cost of a resource is the revenue it can generate when put to an alternative use in the firm or the price which it can be sold for.

[12] W.J. Baumol, J.C. Panzer, and R.D. Willig, *Contestable Markets and the Theory of Industrial Structure* (New York, NY: Harcourt Brace Jovanovitch, 1982).

[13] In economist's jargon, such jointly owned resources are "public goods"—their benefits can be extended to additional firms at negligible marginal cost.

[14] Hiroyuki Itami [*Mobilizing Invisible Assets* (Cambridge, MA: Harvard University Press, 1986)] refers to these as "invisible assets."

[15] Based upon Hofer and Schendel, op. cit., pp. 145–148.

[16] See, for example, Iain Cockburn and Zvi Griliches, "Industry Effects and the Appropriability Measures in the Stock Market's Valuation of R&D and Patents," *American Economic Review*, 78 (1988): 419–423.

[17] General management, financial management, marketing and selling, market research, product R&D, engineering, production, distribution, legal affairs, and personnel. See Charles C. Snow and Lawrence G. Hrebiniak, "Strategy, Distinctive Competence, and Organizational Performance," *Administrative Science Quarterly*, 25 (1980): 317–336.

[18] C.K. Prahalad and Gary Hamel, "The Core Competence of the Corporation," *Harvard Business Review* (May/June 1990), pp. 79–91.

[19] Howard H. Stevenson, "Defining Corporate Strengths and Weaknesses," *Sloan Management Review* (Spring 1976), pp. 51–68.

[20] Richard T. Pascale, "Honda (A)," Harvard Business School, Case no. 9-384-049, 1983.

[21] Paul R. Lawrence and Davis Dyer, *Renewing American Industry* (New York, NY: Free Press, 1983), pp. 60–83.

[22] "Du Pont's 'Drug Hunter' Stalks His Next Big Trophy," *Business Week*, November 27, 1989, pp. 174–182.

[23] Richard E. Caves, "Economic Analysis and the Quest for Competitive Advantage," *American Economic Review*, 74 (1984): 127–128.

[24] Jay B. Barney, "Organizational Culture: Can It Be a Source of Sustained Competitive Advantage?" *Academy of Management Review*, 11 (1986): 656–665.

[25] Lippman and Rumelt, op. cit.

[26] This information problem is a consequence of the fact that resources work together in teams and their individual productivity is not observable. See A.A. Alchian and H. Demsetz, "Production, Information Costs, and Economic Organization," *American Economic Review,* 62 (1972): 777–795.

[27] Such asymmetric information gives rise to a "lemons" problem. See G. Akerlof, "The Market for Lemons: Qualitative Uncertainty and the Market Mechanism," *Quarterly Journal of Economics,* 84 (1970): 488–500.

[28] Barney, op. cit.

[29] The definition of resource specificity in this article corresponds to the definition of "specific assets" by Richard Caves ("International Corporations: The Industrial Economics of Foreign Investment," *Economica,* 38 (1971): 1–27); it differs from that used by O.E. Williamson [*The Economic Institutions of Capitalism* (New York, NY: Free Press, 1985), pp. 52–56]. Williamson refers to assets which are specific to particular transactions rather than to particular firms.

[30] "Catch a Falling Star," *The Economist,* April 23, 1988, pp. 88–90.

[31] Dierickx and Cool, op. cit.

[32] The key advantage of partnerships as an organizational form for such businesses is in averting conflict over control and rent allocation between employees and owners.

[33] "Ad World Is Abuzz as Top Brass Leaves Lord Geller Agency," *Wall Street Journal,* March 23, 1988, p. A1.

[34] Charles Ferguson ["From the People Who Brought You Voodoo Economics," *Harvard Business Review* (May/June 1988), pp. 55–63] has claimed that these start-ups involve the individual exploitation of technical knowledge which rightfully belongs to the former employers of these new entrepreneurs.

[35] "The Decline of the Superstar," *Business Week,* August 17, 1987, pp. 90–96.

[36] "Faded Fad," *The Economist,* September 30, 1989, p. 68.

[37] Gary Hamel, Yves Doz, and C.K. Prahalad, "Collaborate with Your Competitors—and Win," *Harvard Business Review* (January/February 1989), pp. 133–139.

[38] Stevenson (1985), op. cit.

[39] Michael E. Porter, *The Competitive Advantage of Nations* (New York, NY: Free Press, 1990).

[40] Itami, op. cit., p. 125.

[41] Arataroh Takahashi, *What I learned from Konosuke Matsushita* (Tokyo: Jitsugyo no Nihonsha, 1980) [in Japanese]. Quoted by Itami, op. cit., p. 25.

Time—The Next Source of Competitive Advantage*

GEORGE STALK, JR.

Like competition itself, competitive advantage is a constantly moving target. For any company in any industry, the key is not to get stuck with a single simple notion of its source of advantage. The best competitors, the most successful ones, know how to keep moving and always stay on the cutting edge.

Today, *time* is on the cutting edge. The ways leading companies manage time—in production, in new product development and introduction, in sales and distribution—represent the most powerful new sources of competitive advantage. Though certain Western companies are pursuing these advantages, Japanese experience and practice provide the most instructive examples—not because they are necessarily unique but because they best illustrate the evolutionary stages through which leading companies have advanced.

In the period immediately following World War II, Japanese companies used their low labor costs to gain entry to various industries. As wage rates rose and technology became more significant, the Japanese shifted first to scale-based strategies and then to focused factories to achieve advantage. The advent of just-in-time production brought with it a move to flexible factories, as leading Japanese companies sought both low cost and great variety in the market. Cutting-edge Japanese companies today are capitalizing on time as a critical source of competitive advantage: shortening the planning loop in the product development cycle and trimming process time in the factory—managing time the way most companies manage costs, quality, or inventory.

In fact, as a strategic weapon, time is the equivalent of money, productivity, quality, even innovation. Managing time has enabled top Japanese companies not only to reduce their costs but also to offer broad product lines, cover more market segments, and upgrade the technological sophistication of their products. These companies are time-based competitors.

FROM LOW WAGES TO VARIETY WARS

Since 1945, Japanese competitors have shifted their strategic focus at least four times. These early adaptations were straightforward; the shift to time-based competitive advantage is not nearly so obvious. It does, however, represent a logical evolution from the earlier stages.

In the immediate aftermath of World War II, with their economy devastated and the world around them in a shambles, the Japanese concentrated on achieving competitive advantage through low labor costs. Since Japan's workers were still productive and the yen was devalued by 98.8% against the dollar, its labor costs were extraordinarily competitive with those of the West's developed economies.

Hungry for foreign exchange, the Japanese government encouraged companies to make the most of their one edge by targeting industries with high labor content: textiles, shipbuilding, and steel—businesses where the low labor rates more than offset low productivity rates. As a result, Japanese companies took market share from their Western competition.

But this situation did not last long. Rising wages, caused by high inflation, combined with fixed exchange rates to erode the advantage. In many industries, manufacturers could not improve their productivity fast enough to offset escalating labor costs. By the early 1960s, for instance, the textile companies—comprising Japan's largest industry—were hard-pressed. Having lost their competitive edge in world markets, they spiraled downward, first losing share, then volume, then profits, and finally position and prestige. While the problem was most severe for the textile business, the rest of Japanese industry suffered as well.

The only course was adaptation: in the early 1960s, the Japanese shifted their strategy, using capital investment to boost work-force productivity. They inaugurated the era of scale-based strategies, achieving high productivity and low costs by building the largest and most capital-intensive facilities that were technologically feasible. Japanese shipbuilders, for example, revolutionized the industry in their effort to raise labor productivity. Adapting fabrication techniques from mass production processes and using automatic and semiautomatic equipment, they constructed vessels in modules. The approach produced two advantages for the Japanese. It drove up their own productivity and simultaneously erected a high capital-investment barrier to others looking to compete in the business.

The search for ways to achieve even higher productivity and lower costs continued, however. And in the mid-1960s, it led top Japanese companies to a new source of competitive advantage—the focused factory. Focused competitors manufactured products either made nowhere else in the world or located in the high-volume segment of a market, often in the heart of their Western competitors' product lines. Focusing of production allowed the Japanese to remain smaller than established broad-line producers, while still achieving higher productivity and lower costs—giving them great competitive power.

Factory costs are very sensitive to the variety of goods a plant produces. Reduction of the product-line variety by half, for example, raises productivity by 30%, cuts costs 17%, and substantially lowers the break-even point. Cutting the product line in half again boosts productivity by 75%, slashes costs 30%, and diminishes the break-even point to below 50%. (See "The Benefits of Focus.")

In industries like bearings, where competition was fierce in the late 1960s, the Japanese fielded product lines with one-half to one-quarter the variety of their Western competitors. Targeting the high-volume segments of the bearing business—bearings for automobile applications was one—the Japanese used the low costs of their highly productive focused factories to undercut the prices of Western competitors.

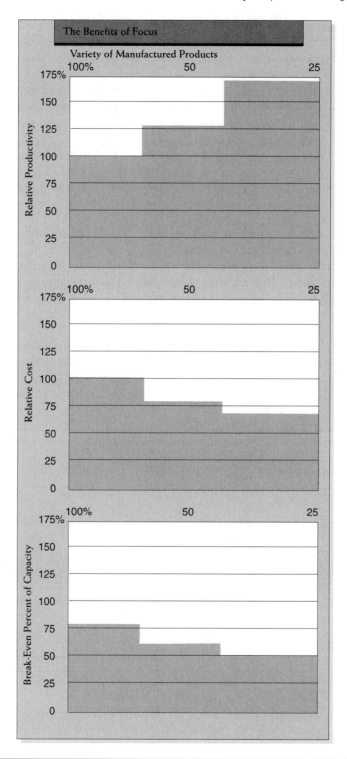

Cutting variety yields higher productivity, lower costs, and reduced break-even points.

SKF was one victim. With factories scattered throughout Europe, each geared to a broad product line for the local market, the Swedish company was a big target for the Japanese. SKF reacted by trying to avoid direct competition with the Japanese: it added higher margin products to serve specialized applications. But SKF did not simultaneously drop any low-margin products, thereby complicating its plant operations and adding to production costs. In effect, SKF provided a cost umbrella for the Japanese. As long as they operated beneath it, the Japanese could expand their product line and move into more varied applications.

Avoiding price competition by moving into higher margin products is called margin retreat—a common response to stepped-up competition that eventually leads to corporate suicide. As a company retreats, its costs rise as do its prices, thus "subsidizing" an aggressive competitor's expansion into the vacated position. The retreating company's revenue base stops growing and may eventually shrink to the point where it can no longer support the fixed cost of the operation. Retrenchment, restructuring, and further shrinkage follow in a cycle that leads to inevitable extinction.

SKF avoided this fate by adopting the Japanese strategy. After a review of its factories, the company focused each on those products it was best suited to manufacture. If a product did not fit a particular factory, it was either placed in another, more suitable plant or dropped altogether. This strategy not only halted SKF's retreat but also beat back the Japanese advance.

At the same time, however, leading Japanese manufacturers began to move toward a new source of competitive advantage—the flexible factory. Two developments drove this move. First, as they expanded and penetrated more markets, their narrow product lines began to pinch, limiting their ability to grow. Second, with growth limited, the economics of the focus strategy presented them with an unattractive choice: either reduce variety further or accept the higher costs of broader product lines.

In manufacturing, costs fall into two categories: those that respond to volume or scale and those that are driven by variety. Scale-related costs decline as volume increases, usually falling 15% to 25% per unit each time volume doubles. Variety-related costs, on the other hand, reflect the costs of complexity in manufacturing: setup, materials handling, inventory, and many of the overhead costs of a factory. In most cases, as variety increases, costs increase, usually at a rate of 20% to 35% per unit each time variety doubles.

The sum of the scale- and variety-related costs represents the total cost of manufacturing. With effort, managers can determine the optimum cost point for their factories—the point where the combination of volume and variety yields the lowest total manufacturing cost for a particular plant. When markets are good, companies tend to edge toward increased variety in search of higher volumes, even though this will mean increased costs. When times are tough, companies pare their product lines, cutting variety to reduce costs.

In a flexible factory system, variety-driven costs start lower and increase more slowly as variety grows. Scale costs remain unchanged. Thus the optimum cost point for a flexible factory occurs at a higher volume and with greater variety than for a traditional factory. A gap emerges between the costs of the flexible and the traditional factory—a cost/variety gap that represents the competitive advantage of flexible production. Very simply, a flexible factory enjoys more variety with lower total costs than traditional factories, which are still forced to make the trade-off between scale and variety. (See "The Advantage of Flexible Manufacturing.")

Yanmar Diesel illustrates how this process works. In 1973, with the Japanese economy in recession, Yanmar Diesel was mired in red ink. Worse, there was no promise that once

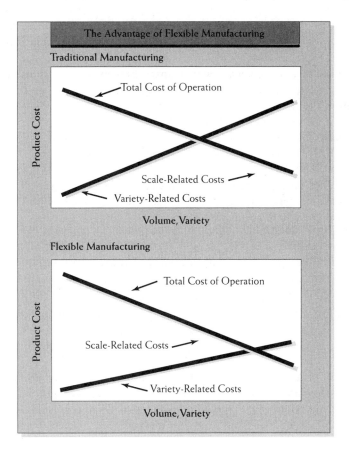

For flexible factories, the optimum cost points occur at a higher volume and with higher variety than for traditional factories.

the recession had passed, the existing strategy and program would guarantee real improvement in the company's condition.

As a Toyota supplier, Yanmar was familiar with the automaker's flexible manufacturing system. Moreover, Yanmar was impressed with the automaker's ability to weather the recession without losing money. Yanmar decided to install the Toyota procedure in its own two factories. The changeover took less than five years and produced dramatic results: manufacturing costs declined 40% to 60%, depending on the product; factory break-even points dropped 80% to 50%; total manufacturing labor productivity improved by more than 100%.

But it was Yanmar's newfound capability in product variety that signaled the arrival of a unique strategic edge: during the restructuring Yanmar more than quadrupled its product line. With focused factories, Yanmar could have doubled productivity in such a short time only by reducing the breadth of the product line by 75%. The Toyota system made Yanmar's factories more flexible, reducing costs and producing a greater variety of products.

As its inventor, Taiichi Ohno, said, the Toyota production system was "born of the need to make many types of automobiles, in small quantities with the same manufacturing process."

With its emphasis on just-in-time production, total quality control, employee decision making on the factory floor, and close supplier relations, the Toyota system gave the many Japanese manufacturers who adopted it in the mid-1970s a distinct competitive advantage.

A comparison of a U.S. company with a Japanese competitor in the manufacture of a particular automotive suspension component illustrates the nature and extent of the Japanese advantage. The U.S. company bases its strategy on scale and focus: it produces 10 million units per year—making it the world's largest producer—and offers only 11 types of finished parts. The Japanese company's strategy, on the other hand, is to exploit flexibility. It is both smaller and less focused: it manufactures only 3.5 million units per year but has 38 types of finished parts.

With one-third the scale and more than three times the product variety, the Japanese company also boasts total labor productivity that is half again that of its American competitor. Moreover, the unit cost of the Japanese manufacturer is less than half that of the U.S. company. But interestingly, the productivity of the Japanese direct laborers is not as high as that of the U.S. workers, a reflection of the difference in scale. The Japanese advantage comes from the productivity of the overhead employees: with one-third the volume and three times the variety, the Japanese company has only one-eighteenth the overhead employees. (See "Flexible Manufacturing's Productivity Edge.")

In the late 1970s, Japanese companies exploited flexible manufacturing to the point that a new competitive thrust emerged—the variety war. A classic example of a variety war was the battle that erupted between Honda and Yamaha for supremacy in the motorcycle market, a struggle popularly known in Japanese business circles as the H-Y War. Yamaha ignited the H-Y War in 1981 when it announced the opening of a new factory which would make it the world's largest motorcycle manufacturer, a prestigious position held by Honda. But Honda had been concentrating its corporate resources on the automobile business and away from its motorcycle operation. Now, faced with Yamaha's overt and public challenge, Honda chose to counterattack.

Honda launched its response with the war cry, "Yamaha wo tsubusu!" ("We will crush, squash, slaughter Yamaha!") In the no-holds-barred battle that ensued, Honda cut prices, flooded distribution channels, and boosted advertising expenditures. Most important—and

Flexible Manufacturing's Productivity Edge
(Automobile Suspension Component)

	U.S. COMPETITOR	JAPANESE COMPETITOR
Annual volume	10M	3.5M
Employees		
Direct	107	50
Indirect	135	7
Total	242	57
Annual units/Employee	43,100	61,400
Types of finished parts	11	38
Unit cost for comparable part (index)	$100	$49

(1987 figures)

most impressive to consumers—Honda also rapidly increased the rate of change in its product line, using variety to bury Yamaha. At the start of the war, Honda had 60 models of motorcycles. Over the next 18 months, Honda introduced or replaced 113 models, effectively turning over its entire product line twice. Yamaha also began the war with 60 models; it was able to manage only 37 changes in its product line during those 18 months.

Honda's new product introductions devastated Yamaha. First, Honda succeeded in making motorcycle design a matter of fashion, where newness and freshness were important attributes for consumers. Second, Honda raised the technological sophistication of its products, introducing four-valve engines, composites, direct drive, and other new features. Next to a Honda, Yamaha products looked old, unattractive, and out of date. Demand for Yamaha products dried up; in a desperate effort to move them, dealers were forced to price them below cost. But even that didn't work. At the most intense point in the H-Y War, Yamaha had more than 12 months of inventory in its dealers' showrooms. Finally Yamaha surrendered. In a public statement, Yamaha President Eguchi announced, "We want to end the H-Y War. It is our fault. Of course there will be competition in the future but it will be based on a mutual recognition of our respective positions."

Honda didn't go unscathed either. The company's sales and service network was severely disrupted, requiring additional investment before it returned to a stable footing. However, so decisive was its victory that Honda effectively had as much time as it wanted to recover. It had emphatically defended its title as the world's largest motorcycle producer and done so in a way that warned Suzuki and Kawasaki not to challenge that leadership. Variety had won the war.

TIME-BASED COMPETITIVE ADVANTAGE

The strength of variety as a competitive weapon raises an interesting question. How could Japanese companies accommodate such rapid rates of change? In Honda's case, there could be only three possible answers. The company did one of the following:

1. Began the development of more than 100 new models 10 to 15 years before the attack.
2. Authorized a sudden, massive spending surge to develop and manufacture products on a crash basis.
3. Used structurally different methods to develop, manufacture, and introduce new products.

In fact, what Honda and other variety-driven competitors pioneered was time-based competitiveness. They managed structural changes that enabled their operations to execute their processes much faster. As a consequence, time became their new source of competitive advantage.

While time is a basic business performance variable, management seldom monitors its consumption explicitly—almost never with the same precision accorded sales and costs. Yet time is a more critical competitive yardstick than traditional financial measurements.

Today's new-generation companies compete with flexible manufacturing and rapid-response systems, expanding variety and increasing innovation. A company that builds its strategy on this cycle is a more powerful competitor than one with a traditional strategy based on low wages, scale, or focus. These older, cost-based strategies require managers to do whatever is necessary to drive down costs: move production to or source from a low-wage country; build new facilities or consolidate old plants to gain economies of scale; or focus operations down to the most economic subset of activities. These tactics reduce costs but at the expense of responsiveness.

In contrast, strategies based on the cycle of flexible manufacturing, rapid response, expanding variety, and increasing innovation are time based. Factories are close to the customers they serve. Organization structures enable fast responses rather than low costs and control. Companies concentrate on reducing if not eliminating delays and using their response advantages to attract the most profitable customers.

Many—but certainly not all—of today's time-based competitors are Japanese. Some of them are Sony, Matsushita, Sharp, Toyota, Hitachi, NEC, Toshiba, Honda, and Hino; time-based Western companies include Benetton, The Limited, Federal Express, Domino's Pizza, Wilson Art, and McDonald's. For these leading competitors, time has become the overarching measurement of performance. By reducing the consumption of time in every aspect of the business, these companies also reduce costs, improve quality, and stay close to their customers.

BREAKING THE PLANNING LOOP

Companies are systems; time connects all the parts. The most powerful competitors understand this axiom and are breaking the debilitating loop that strangles much of traditional manufacturing planning.

Traditional manufacturing requires long lead times to resolve conflicts between various jobs or activities that require the same resources. The long lead times, in turn, require sales forecasts to guide planning. But sales forecasts are inevitably wrong; by definition they are guesses, however informed. Naturally, as lead times lengthen, the accuracy of sales forecasts declines. With more forecasting errors, inventories balloon and the need for safety stocks at all levels increases. Errors in forecasting also mean more unscheduled jobs that have to be expedited, thereby crowding out scheduled jobs. The need for longer lead times grows even greater and the planning loop expands even more, driving up costs, increasing delays, and creating system inefficiencies.

Managers who find themselves trapped in the planning loop often respond by asking for better forecasts and longer lead times. In other words, they treat the symptoms and worsen the problem. The only way to break the planning loop is to reduce the consumption of time throughout the system; that will, in turn, cut the need for lead time, for estimates, for safety stocks, and all the rest. After all, if a company could ever drive its lead time all the way to zero, it would have to forecast only the next day's sales. While that idea of course is unrealistic, successful time-based competitors in Japan and in the West have kept their lead times from growing and some have even reduced them, thereby diminishing the planning loop's damaging effects.

Thirty years ago, Jay W. Forrester of MIT published a pioneering article in HBR, "Industrial Dynamics: A Major Breakthrough for Decision Makers" (July–August 1958), which established a model of time's impact on an organization's performance. Using "industrial dynamics"—a concept originally developed for shipboard fire control systems—Forrester tracked the effects of time delays and decision rates within a simple busi-

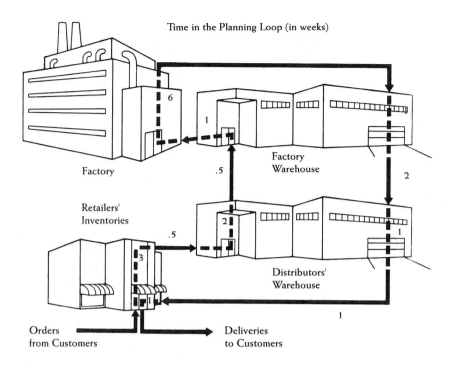

Time in the Planning Loop (in weeks)

ness system consisting of a factory, a factory warehouse, a distributors' inventory, and retailers' inventories. The numbers in the illustration "Time in the Planning Loop" are the delays in the flow of information or product, measured in weeks. In this example, the orders accumulate at the retailer for three weeks, are in the mail for half a week, are delayed at the distributor for two weeks, go back into the mail for another half a week, and need eight weeks for processing at the factory and its warehouse. Then the finished product begins its journey back to the retailer. The cycle takes 19 weeks.

The system in this example is very stable—as long as retail demand is stable or as long as forecasts are accurate 19 weeks into the future. But if unexpected changes occur, the system must respond. The chart, also taken from the Forrester article, shows what happens to this system when a simple change takes place: demand goes up 10%, then flattens. Acting on new forecasts and seeking to cut delivery delays, the factory first responds by ramping up production 40%. When management realizes—too late—that it has overshot the mark, it cuts production 30%. Too late again it learns that is has overcorrected. This ramping up and cutting back continue until finally the system stabilizes, more than a year after the initial 10% increase.

What distorts the system so badly is time: the lengthy delay between the event that creates the new demand and the time when the factory finally receives the information. The longer that delay, the more distorted is the view of the market. Those distortions reverberate throughout the system, producing disruption, waste, and inefficiency.

These distortions plague business today. To escape them, companies have a choice: they can produce to forecast or they can reduce the time delays in the flow of information and product through the system. The traditional solution is to produce to forecast. The new approach is to reduce time consumption.

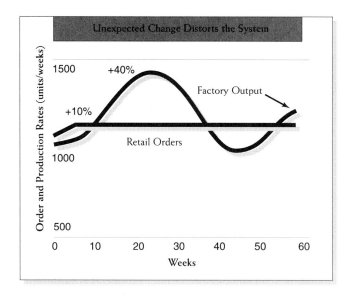

Because time flows throughout the system, focusing on time-based competitive performance results in improvements across the board. Companies generally become time-based competitors by first correcting their manufacturing techniques, then fixing sales and distribution, and finally adjusting their approach to innovation. Ultimately, it becomes the basis for a company's overall strategy.

TIME-BASED MANUFACTURING

In general, time-based manufacturing policies and practices differ from those of traditional manufacturers along three key dimensions: length of production runs, organization of process components, and complexity of scheduling procedures.

When it comes to lot size, for instance, traditional factories attempt to maximize production runs while time-based manufacturers try to shorten their production runs as much as possible. In fact, many Japanese companies aim for run lengths of a single unit. The thinking behind this is as simple as it is fundamental to competitive success: reduced run lengths mean more frequent production of the complete mix of products and faster response to customers' demands.

Factory layout also contributes to time-based competitive advantage. Traditional factories are usually organized by process technology centers. For example, metal goods manufacturers organize their factories into shearing, punching, and braking departments; electronic assemblers have stuffing, wave soldering, assembly, testing, and packing departments. Parts move from one process technology center to the next. Each step consumes valuable time: parts sit, waiting to move; then move; then wait to be used in the next step. In a traditional manufacturing system, products usually receive value for only .05% to 2.5% of the time that they are in the factory. The rest of the time products sit waiting for something to happen.

Time-based factories, however, are organized by product. To minimize handling and moving of parts, the manufacturing functions for a component or a product are as close together as possible. Parts move from one activity to the next with little or no delay. Because the production process eliminates the need to pile and repile parts, they flow quickly and efficiently through the factory.

In traditional factories, scheduling is also a source of delay and waste. Most traditional factories use central scheduling that requires sophisticated materials resource planning and shop-floor control systems. Even though these systems are advanced, they still waste time: work orders usually flow to the factory floor on a monthly or weekly basis. In the meantime, parts can sit idle.

In time-based factories, local scheduling enables employees to make more production control decisions on the factory floor, without the time-consuming loop back to management for approval. Moreover, the combination of the product-oriented layout of the factory and local scheduling makes the total production process run more smoothly. Once a part starts through the production run, many of the requirements between manufacturing steps are purely automatic and require no intermediate scheduling.

These differences between traditional and time-based factories add up. Flexible factories enjoy big advantages in both productivity and time: labor productivity in time-based factories can be as much as 200% higher than in conventional plants; time-based factories can respond eight to ten times faster than traditional factories. Flexible production means significant improvements in labor and net-asset productivity. These, in turn, yield reductions of up to 20% in overall costs and increases in growth for much less investment.

Toyota offers a dramatic example of the kinds of improvements that leading time-based competitors are making. Dissatisfied with the response time of a supplier, Toyota went to work. It took the supplier 15 days to turn out a component after arrival of the raw materials at its factory. The first step was to cut lot sizes, reducing response time to 6 days. Next Toyota streamlined the factory layout, reducing the number of inventory holding points. The response time fell to 3 days. Finally Toyota eliminated all work-in-progress inventories at the supplier's plant. New response time: 1 day.

Toyota, of course, is not alone in improving manufacturing response times. Matsushita cut the time needed to make washing machines from 360 hours to just 2; Honda slashed its motorcycle fabricating time by 80%; in North America, companies making motor controllers and electrical components for unit air conditioners have improved their manufacturing response times by 90%.

TIME-BASED SALES AND DISTRIBUTION

A manufacturer's next challenge is to avoid dissipation of factory performance improvements in other parts of the organization. In Jay Forrester's example of the planning loop, the factory and its warehouse accounted for roughly one-half of the system's time. In actuality today, the factory accounts for one-third to one-half of the total time—often the most "visible" portion of time. But other parts of the system are just as important, if less apparent. For example, in the Forrester system, sales and distribution consume as much or more time than manufacturing.

What Forrester modeled, the Japanese experienced. By the late 1970s, leading Japanese companies were finding that inefficient sales and distribution operations undercut the benefits of their flexible manufacturing systems. Toyota, which at that time was divided into two separate companies, Toyota Motor Manufacturing and Toyota Motor Sales, again makes this point. Toyota Motor Manufacturing could manufacture a car in less than 2 days. But Toyota Motor Sales needed from 15 to 26 days to close the sale, transmit the order to the factory, get the order scheduled, and deliver the car to the customer. By the late 1970s, the cost-conscious, competition-minded engineers at Toyota Manufacturing were angry at their counterparts at Toyota Motor Sales, who were frittering away the advantage gained in the production process. The sales and distribution function was generating 20% to 30% of a car's cost to the customer—more than it cost Toyota to manufacture the car!

Finally, in 1982 Toyota moved decisively to remedy the problem. The company merged Toyota Motor Manufacturing and Toyota Motor Sales. The company announced that it wanted to become "more marketing driven." While Toyota assured the public that the reorganization only returned it to its configuration in the 1950s, within 18 months all the Toyota Motor Sales directors retired. Their jobs were left vacant or filled by executives from Toyota Motor Manufacturing.

The company wasted no time in implementing a plan to cut delays in sales and distribution, reduce costs, and improve customer service. The old system, Toyota found, had handled customer orders in batches. Orders and other crucial information would accumulate at one step of the sales and distribution process before dispatch to the next level, which wasted time and generated extra costs.

To speed the flow of information, Toyota had to reduce the size of the information batches. The solution came from a company-developed computer system that tied its salespeople directly to the factory scheduling operation. This link bypassed several levels of the sales and distribution function and enabled the modified system to operate with very small batches of orders.

Toyota expected this new approach to cut the sales and distribution cycle time in half—from four to six weeks to just two to three weeks across Japan. (For the Tokyo and Osaka regions, which account for roughly two-thirds of Japan's population, the goal was to reduce cycle time to just two days.) But by 1987 Toyota had reduced system responsiveness to eight days, including the time required to make the car. In the Forrester example, this achievement is equivalent to cutting the 19-week cycle to 6 weeks. The results were predictable: shorter sales forecasts, lower costs, happier customers.

TIME-BASED INNOVATION

A company that can bring out new products three times faster than its competitors enjoys a huge advantage. Today, in one industry after another, Japanese manufacturers are doing just that to their Western competition:

- In projection television, Japanese producers can develop a new television in one-third the time required by U.S. manufacturers.
- In custom plastic injection molds, Japanese companies can develop the molds in one-third the time of U.S. competitors and at one-third the cost.
- In autos, Japanese companies can develop new products in half the time—and with half as many people—as the U.S. and German competition.

To accomplish their fast-paced innovations, leading Japanese manufacturers have introduced a series of organizational techniques that precisely parallel their approach to flexible manufacturing:

- In manufacturing, the Japanese stress short production runs and small lot sizes. In innovation, they favor smaller increments of improvement in new products, but introduce them more often—versus the Western approach of more significant improvements made less often.
- In the organization of product development work, the Japanese use factory cells that are cross-functional teams. Most Western new product development activity is carried out by functional centers.
- In the scheduling of work, Japanese factories stress local responsibility, just as product development scheduling is decentralized. The Western approach to both requires plodding centralized scheduling, plotting, and tracking.

The effects of this time-based advantage are devastating; quite simply, American companies are losing leadership of technology and innovation—supposedly this country's source of long-term advantage. Unless U.S. companies reduce their new product development and introduction cycles from 36–48 months to 12–18 months, Japanese manufacturers will easily out-innovate and outperform them. Taking the initiative in innovation will require even faster cycle times.

Residential air conditioners illustrate the Japanese ability to introduce more technological innovation in smaller increments—and how in just a few years these improvements add up to remarkably superior products. The Japanese introduce innovations in air conditioners four times faster than their American competitors; in technological sophistication the Japanese products are seven to ten years ahead of U.S. products.

Look at the changes in Mitsubishi Electric's three-horsepower heat pump between 1975 and 1985. From 1975 to 1979, the company did nothing to the product except change the sheet metal work, partly to improve efficiency but mostly to reduce materials costs. In 1979, the technological sophistication of the product was roughly equal to that of the U.S. competition. From this point on, the Japanese first established, and then widened the lead.

In 1980, Mitsubishi introduced its first major improvement: a new product that used integrated circuits to control the air-conditioning cycle. One year later, the company replaced the integrated circuits with microprocessors and added two important innovations to increase consumer demand. The first was "quick connect" freon lines. On the old product (and on the U.S. product), freon lines were made from copper tubing and cut to length, bent, soldered together, purged, and filled with freon—an operation requiring great skill to produce a reliable air conditioner. The Japanese substituted quick-connect freon lines—precharged hoses that simply clicked together. The second innovation was simplified wiring. On the old product (and still today on the U.S. product) the unit had six color-coded wires to connect. The advent of microprocessors made possible a two-wire connection with neutral polarity.

These two changes did not improve the energy-efficiency ratio of the product; nor were they intended to. Rather, the point was to fabricate a unit that would be simpler to install and more reliable, thereby broadening distribution and increasing demand. Because of these innovations, white-goods outlets could sell the new product, and local contractors could easily install it.

In 1982, Mitsubishi introduced a new version of the air conditioner featuring techno-logical advances related to performance. A high-efficiency rotary compressor replaced the outdated reciprocating compressor. The condensing unit had louvered fins and inner fin tubes for better heat transfer. Because the balance of the system changed, all the electronics had to change. As a result, the energy-efficiency ratio improved markedly.

In 1983, Mitsubishi added sensors to the unit and more computing power, expanding the electronic control of the cycle and again improving the energy-efficiency ratio.

In 1984, Mitsubishi came out with another version of the product, this time with an inverter that made possible an even higher energy-efficiency ratio. The inverter, which requires additional electronics for the unit, allows unparalleled control over the speed of the electric motor, dramatically boosting the appliance's efficiency.

Using time-based innovation, Mitsubishi transformed its air conditioner. The changes came incrementally and steadily. Overall they gave Mitsubishi—and other Japanese com-panies on the same track—the position of technological leadership in the global residen-tial air-conditioning industry.

In 1985, a U.S. air-conditioner manufacturer was just debating whether to use integrated circuits in its residential heap pump. In view of its four- to five-year product development cycle, it could not have introduced the innovation until 1989 or 1990—putting the American company ten years behind the Japanese. Faced with this situation, the U.S. air-conditioner company followed the example of many U.S. manufacturers that have lost the lead in technology and innovation: it decided to source its air conditioners and components from its Japanese competition.

TIME-BASED STRATEGY

The possibility of establishing a response time advantage opens new avenues for constructing winning competitive strategies. At most companies, strategic choices are limited to three options:

1. Seeking coexistence with competitors. This choice is seldom stable, since competitors refuse to cooperate and stay put.
2. Retreating in the face of competitors. Many companies choose this course; the business press fills its pages with accounts of companies retreating by consolidating plants, focus-ing their operations, outsourcing, divesting businesses, pulling out of markets, or mov-ing upscale.
3. Attacking, either directly or indirectly. The direct attack involves the classic con-frontation—cut price and add capacity, creating head-on competition. Indirect attack requires surprise. Competitors either do not understand the strategies being used against them or they do understand but cannot respond—sometimes because of the speed of the attack, sometimes because of their inability to mount a response.

Of the three options, only an attack creates the opportunity for real growth. Direct attack demands superior resources; it is always expensive and potentially disastrous. Indirect attack promises the most gain for the least cost. Time-based strategy offers a powerful new approach for successful indirect attacks against larger, established competitors.

Consider the remarkable example of Atlas Door, a ten-year-old U.S. company. It has grown at an average annual rate of 15% in an industry with an overall annual growth rate of less than 5%. In recent years, its pretax earnings were 20% of sales, about five times the industry average. Atlas is debt free. In its tenth year the company achieved the number one competitive position in its industry.

The company's product: industrial doors. It is a product with almost infinite variety, involving limitless choices of width and height and material. Because of the importance of variety, inventory is almost useless in meeting customer orders; most doors can be manufactured only after the order has been placed.

Historically, the industry had needed almost four months to respond to an order for a door that was out of stock or customized. Atlas's strategic advantage was time: it could respond in weeks to any order. It had structured its order-entry, engineering, manufacturing, and logistics systems to move information and products quickly and reliably.

First, Atlas built just-in-time factories. These are fairly simple in concept. They require extra tooling and machinery to reduce changeover times and a fabrication process organized by product and scheduled to start and complete all of the parts at the same time. But even the performance of the factory—critical to the company's overall responsiveness—still only accounted for $2\frac{1}{2}$ weeks of the completed product delivery cycle.

Second, Atlas compressed time at the front end of the system, where the order first entered and was processed. Traditionally, when customers, distributors, or salespeople called a door manufacturer with a request for price and delivery, they would have to wait more than one week for a response. If the desired door was not in stock, not in the schedule, or not engineered, the supplier's organization would waste even more time, pushing the search for an answer around the system.

Recognizing the opportunity to cut deeply into the time expenditure in this part of the system, Atlas first streamlined, then automated its entire order-entry, engineering, pricing, and scheduling processes. Today Atlas can price and schedule 95% of its incoming orders while the callers are still on the telephone. It can quickly engineer new special orders because it has preserved on computer the design and production data of all previous special orders—which drastically reduces the amount of re-engineering necessary.

Third, Atlas tightly controlled logistics so that it always shipped only fully complete orders to construction sites. Orders require many components. Gathering all of them at the factory and making sure that they are with the correct order can be a time-consuming task. It is even more time-consuming, however, to get the correct parts to the job site *after* they have missed the initial shipment. Atlas developed a system to track the parts in production and the purchased parts for each order, ensuring arrival of all necessary parts at the shipping dock in time—a just-in-time logistics operation.

When Atlas started operations, distributors were uninterested in its product. The established distributors already carried the door line of a larger competitor; they saw no reason to switch suppliers except, perhaps, for a major price concession. But as a start-up, Atlas was too small to compete on price alone. Instead, it positioned itself as the door supplier of last resort, the company people came to if the established supplier could not deliver or missed a key date.

Of course, with industry lead times of almost four months, some calls inevitably came to Atlas. And when it did get a call, Atlas commanded a higher price because of its faster delivery. Atlas not only got a higher price but its time-based processes also yielded lower costs: it thus enjoyed the best of both worlds.

In ten short years, the company replaced the leading door suppliers in 80% of the distributors in the country. With its strategic advantage the company could be selective, becoming the house supplier for only the strongest distributors.

In the wake of this indirect attack, the established competitors have not responded effectively. The conventional view is that Atlas is a "garage shop operator" that cannot sustain its growth: competitors expect the company's performance to degrade to the industry average as it grows larger. But this response—or nonresponse—only reflects a fundamental lack of understanding of time as the source of competitive advantage. The extra delay in responding only adds to the insurmountable lead the indirect time-based attack has created. While the traditional companies track costs and size, the new competitor derives advantage from time, staying on the cutting edge, leaving its rivals behind.

PART 7

Global Strategies and the Future

International Business Strategies and Multinational Corporations*

KIP BECKER

SECTION I: MNC GLOBAL BUSINESS ENVIRONMENT ISSUES

THE IMPORTANCE OF INTERNATIONAL BUSINESS TO THE LARGE FIRM

Strategy requires identifying the relationship between a firm's resources and the competitive environment. It signifies a plan of action for maximizing the firm's strength against the forces at work in the business environment.[1] International business strategies differ in scope from domestic ones. The playing field is larger; the players often are bigger and have more resources to bring to bear. There has been some recent discussion concerning multinational behavior. Yao-Su Hu, an ex–World Bank economist, believes that few multinational national corporations (MNCs) actually exist.** He states that companies such as the British company ICI (Table 1), DuPont, General Motors, and U.S. General Electric have the majority of their employees in their domestic country, where ownership and control is also maintained. Each company is exposed to many jurisdictions around the world but normally has a home government and a home tax authority. Hu additionally states that the primary source of a company's international competitive advantage lies with the home nation. Even Nestlé, with 95 percent of its assets and employees outside Switzerland, gains considerable advantage from being perceived as a Swiss company.[2] Although Hu's observations should be recognized, it is equally important to understand that what has gone on before does not necessarily dictate the future; the global business environment is compelling all large firms to participate in it. For the MNC the choice no longer is whether to be in or out but how best to participate.

---

*"International Business Strategies and Multinational Corporations" by Kip Becker. Reprinted by permission of the author.

**Multinational national corporations (MNCs) are large corporations with assets ranging from more than $500 million to billions. Many MNCs have assets exceeding the GDP of countries. MNCs operate in multiple nations, have operations distributed worldwide, and derive a significant percentage of their revenues from foreign sales.

T ABLE 1

ICI: The True Multinational (1991)

	% TOTAL NET OPERATING ASSETS	% TOTAL EMPLOYEES	% TOTAL TURNOVER
United Kingdom (home base)	43.9	40.1	20.8
Foreign operations	56.1	59.9	79.2
Continental Europe	16.6	14.0	25.6
Americas	23.4	24.1	30.7
Asia/Pacific	13.5	12.8	17.2
Other	2.4	9.0	5.8

Source: C. Lorenz, "The Multinational Myth Explodes," *Financial Times*, March 4, 1992, 7.

Today the competition for products, services, and ideas pays no respect to national borders, and many whole industries (such as automobiles, carbonated drinks, and consumer electronics) can be classified as global. Many new industries, such as video- and audio-cassettes, compact discs, satellite networks, robots, and fiber optics, have had globally standardized products from their inception.[3] As with many MNCs, IBM Digital and Gillette's sales from overseas operations have made up over half of their total sales for quite some time. Table 2 presents the top 50 multinational firms.

INFRASTRUCTURE AND GLOBAL BUSINESS

As manufacturers go global, so must such support systems as raw material sources, advertising agencies, and bankers. Advances in transportation and communication have further aided the revolutionary expansion in trade and travel, and information flow has been reduced from months to days and can be instantaneous. Millions of viewers around the world, for example, watched the same live broadcasts of the afternoon briefings of the Iraqi-UN war. Within minutes the same viewers saw the discussions on CNN about the effects of the war on world business. By 1990 there were 1 billion telephones in the world that could dial each other directly.[4] Compare this level of communication with that experienced by shipping companies years ago, which knew that their sailing clippers had made the trading trip to Japan only when the ships returned to the home port months after their departure.

Almost all the major industries have global markets, competitors, and suppliers. Rapid technological advances in transportation and communications, the convertibility of the world's major currencies, the liberalization of credit policies, the tariff and nontariff reductions sponsored by the General Agreement on Tariffs and Trade (GATT), and the integration of capital markets have collectively made the world richer and more interdependent. Not all of the world, however, shares equally in infrastructure development. One of the problems MNCs have to address when engaging in international business is the differential level of the world's commercial infrastructure. Multinational corporations are much better suited to deal with this problem than small firms, however, and many multinational corporations can, in fact, create their own infrastructure by laying their own phone lines and setting up private systems to deliver mail, provide training, and staff offices. Smaller firms must normally adjust to the business environment as it exists, suffering the consequences of any inadequacies.

TABLE 2

50 Largest Public Companies

RANK 1997/1996		COMPANY (COUNTRY)	MARKET VALUE	FISCAL 1996 SALES	PERCENT CHANGE FROM 1995	FISCAL 1996 PROFIT	PERCENT CHANGE FROM 1995
1	1	General Electric (U.S.)	$214,454	$79,179	13%	$7,280	11%
2	2	Royal Dutch/Shell (Netherlands/U.K.)	177,537	131,020	21	9,434	39
3	3	Coca-Cola (U.S.)	167,334	18,546	3	3,492	17
4	4	Nippon Telegraph & Telephone (Japan)	152,784	54,799	2	1,544	−16
5	5	Exxon (U.S.)	152,706	134,357	8	7,510	16
6	12	Microsoft (U.S.)	151,438	11,358	31	3,454	57
7	10	Merck (U.S.)	124,936	19,829	19	3,881	16
8	14	Intel (U.S.)	116,144	20,847	29	5,157	45
9	7	Toyota Motor (Japan)	111,924	105,297	14	3,319	50
10	8	Philip Morris (U.S.)	107,778	69,204	5	6,303	16
11	34/52	Novartis (Switzerland)	99,031	26,986	1	1,716	−45
12	15	Procter & Gamble (U.S.)	95,677	35,764	· 1	3,415	12
13	6	Bank of Tokyo-Mitsubishi (Japan)	93,712	752,318	N.A.	352	N.A.
14	16	International Business Machines (U.S.)	89,570	75,947	6	5,429	30
15	13	Johnson & Johnson (U.S.)	85,740	21,620	15	2,887	20
16	11	Roche Holding (Switzerland)	85,403	11,891	8	2,904	16
17	31	Bristol-Myers Squibb (U.S.)	80,989	15,065	9	2,850	57
18	29	Pfizer (U.S.)	77,152	11,306	13	1,929	23
19	19	Wal-Mart Stores (U.S.)	76,603	106,146	12	3,056	12
20	25	Glaxo Wellcome (U.K.)	73,574	14,274	9	3,417	17
21	26	Dupont (U.S.)	70,983	43,810	4	3,636	10
22	22	British Petroleum (U.K.)	70,710	76,548	37	3,639	18
23	30	American International Group (U.S.)	70,139	28,205	9	2,897	15
24	–	Deutshe Telekom (Germany)	66,041	40,946	6	1,038	−70
25	59	Eli Lilly (U.S.)	60,710	7,347	9	1,524	−34
26	28	Hewlett-Packard (U.S.)	58,218	38,420	22	2,586	6
27	–	Berkshire Hathaway (U.S.)	58,162	10,500	37	2,489	198
28	24	PepsiCo (U.S.)	57,901	31,645	4	1,149	−28
29	40	Unilever (Netherlands/U.K.)	57,160	108,120	10	5,173	13
30	9	AT&T (U.S.)	56,968	52,184	3	5,908	7
31	64	SBC Communications (U.S.)	56,444	13,898	10	2,101	N.A.
32	38	Citicorp (U.S.)	55,846	277,653	10	3,788	9
33	70	Lloyds TSB Group (U.K.)	55,251	252,303	0	2,697	64
34	32	Mobil (U.S.)	54,976	80,782	7	2,964	25
35	39	Walt Disney (U.S.)	54,176	18,739	54	1,214	−12
36	33	HSBC Holdings (U.K.)	54,093	405,037	4	5,330	26
37	27	Nestle (Switzerland)	53,159	45,053	7	2,533	17
38	69	Gillette (U.S.)	52,789	9,698	10	949	−11
39	50	Abbott Laboratories (U.S.)	51,632	11,013	10	1,882	11
40	17	Sumitomo Bank (Japan)	51,552	513,781	8	294	−10
41	66	Smithkline Beecham Group (U.K.)	50,827	13,562	13	1,922	21
42	47	American Home Products (U.S.)	49,245	14,088	5	1,883	12
43	35	Allianz Holding (Germany)	48,396	41,899	6	1,428	45
44	42	Chevron (U.S.)	48,315	43,893	18	2,607	180
45	–	DDI (Japan)	48,220	8,738	52	−225	N.A.
46	48	British Telecom (U.K.)	47,273	25,558	3	3,554	5
47	78	NationsBank (U.S.)	47,085	184,936	−1	2,375	22
48	49	Fannie mae (U.S.)	46,286	350,496	11	2,725	26
49	91	Lucent Technologies (U.S.)	46,114	23,286	9	224	−77
50	36	BellSouth (U.S.)	46,030	19,040	6	2,863	N.A.

Source: *Wall Street Journal*, September 18, 1997, p. R25.

THE NEED FOR FLEXIBILITY

In an ever more integrated global economy, the ability of any nation's industries to maintain significant market share will increasingly be determined by how well it manages its overseas investments, development, and technology. Two trends in government policy making offer help. One is the stretching of trade borders. The European Community (EC) and the recent U.S.-Canada-Mexico Free Trade Agreement are examples. The second is changing the approach to industrial cooperation from an antitrust perspective to an improvement in overall industry competitive power in foreign markets.

Some have suggested that MNCs adopt a Protean approach to enterprise. In Greek mythology the god Proteus was able to change form instantly, could see the future, and was endowed with vast stores of information and knowledge.[5] MNCs driven by global competition must also develop flexible, multidimensional decision-making processes capable of responding to a rapidly changing environment.

The role of business and government has also seen change. Today governments and MNCs acknowledge more of their mutual interests. During the 1970s MNCs were under heavy attack. The media highlighted stories such as Lockheed's unauthorized payments to Japanese officials and ITT's alleged attempts to overthrow the elected Allende government in Chile. Acting collectively, nation-states have heightened their involvement with global companies. The following are some indicators:

- The Organization for Economic Cooperation and Development (OECD) approved codes of conduct for MNCs in 1976.
- The UN created a Center on Transnational Corporations to monitor the global enterprise.
- Decision 24 of the Andean Pact countries required systematic divestment by MNCs.
- The U.S. Foreign Corrupt Practices Act of 1977 was established.

Regulation alone has not seemed sufficient. Many countries formed public-sector MNCs with an "if you can't beat them, join them" type of attitude, and by the end of the 1970s state-controlled MNCs actually represented approximately one-fifth of the 500 largest companies headquartered outside the United States.

By the 1980s the nation-states' distrust of private-sector MNCs had moderated. In addition, many less developed countries (LDCs) witnessed slower growth, state-owned MNCs did not fair well, and many nations began to sell off uncompetitive state MNCs. With the growth of Asian business, a new role for the Third World private-sector MNCs has arrived. Table 3 lists the 30 largest emerging market companies. Recent data show that 40 of *Fortune's* "overseas 500" companies were headquartered in newly industrialized countries (NICs). Daewoo, Hyundai, and Samsung are some notables. Of the 500, Japan accounted for the most (195), followed by the United Kingdom (82), France (48), and Germany (37). The largest foreign company, Sumitomo Corporation, is a trading company that in reality is made up of earnings from many smaller 500 firms. It is nevertheless interesting to compare Sumitomo, which has revenues of $158 billion and 13,000 employees, with the largest U.S. firm, General Motors, which has revenues of $127 billion and 775,000 employees.

In order to broaden corporate horizons, private-sector MNCs are altering ethnocentric viewpoints. For example, an Italian, Albert Vitale, is running Doubleday & Co., the U.S. publishing affiliate of the West German media conglomerate Bertelmann A.G.[6] A global broadening of MNC ownership also is taking place. More than 500 U.S. companies now list their shares on more than one exchange worldwide. All this presents a greater range of strategies and alternatives for MNCs.

TABLE 3

Top 30 Companies from Emerging Market (1994)

Market Capitalization, End June 1994
(in billions of dollars)

Company	Country	0	10	20	30
Telefonos de Mexico	Mexico				
Korea Electric Power	South Korea				
Tenaga Nasional	Malaysia				
Cathay Life Insurance	Taiwan				
Telekom Malaysia	Malaysia				
Eletrobras	Brazil				
Telebras	Brazil				
Hua Nan Bank	Taiwan				
Grupo Financiero Banacci	Mexico				
YPF	Argentina				
Grupo Carso	Mexico				
First Bank	Taiwan				
Petrobras	Brazil				
Grupo Televisa	Mexico				
Cifra	Mexico				
Pohang Iron & Steel	South Korea				
Chang Hwa Bank	Taiwan				
Bangkok Bank	Thailand				
Telecomasia	Thailand				
Telefonica de Argentina	Argentina				
Cemex	Mexico				
China Steel	Taiwan				
Samsung Electronics	South Korea				
Malayan Banking	Malaysia				
Resorts World	Malaysia				
Endesa	Chile				
San Miguel	Philippines				
Genting	Malaysia				
Siam Cement	Thailand				
Telecomunicacoes de Sao Paulo	Brazil				

Source: Morgan Stanley Capital International.

Section II: Global versus International Strategies

Part 1: The Global and International Dimensions

Whereas environmental factors are largely externally determined, the decision to develop global or international strategies is determined internally. Table 4 lists five global strategy issues and the positions they display when comparing the "pure" multidomestic strategy (international business in which locations are viewed as profit centers and stand-alone operations) with the "pure" global strategy.

Maximization of worldwide performance through a multidomestic strategy seeks to maximize the local competitive advantage, revenues, or profits. A global strategy seeks to maximize through concentration, standardization, and integration. A multidomestic strategy essentially adopts a diversification mode. Countries are selected on the basis of their stand-alone potential for revenues and profits. Products and the marketing programs in each of these countries are tailored to local needs. All or most of the value chain is reproduced in each country, except that under the exporting option much of the value chain is kept in one country. Also, managers in each country make competitive moves without considering what happens elsewhere. In contrast, those using a global strategy may enter a country market, which is unattractive but may have global strategic significance. The home market of a global competitor could be such a market.

A global strategy often embodies the concentration mode, in which major shares in major markets, core product standardization, and a uniform marketing approach tend to be the objectives. Unilever, for example, achieved great success with a fabric softener that used a common positioning advertising theme in many countries and a symbol (a teddy bear) in other countries. A key feature of the global strategy is that value chain activity occurs in different countries resulting in a total costs reduction. Furthermore, competitive moves are integrated across countries of operation so that competitors are kept at bay or even beaten down.[7]

TABLE 4

Globalization and International Dimensions

DIMENSION	PURE MULTIDOMESTIC STRATEGY	PURE GLOBAL STRATEGY
Market offering	No particular pattern	Significant share in major markets
Product offering	Fully customized in each country	Fully standardized worldwide
Location of value-added activities	All activities in each country	Concentrated one activity in each (different) country
Marketing approach	Local	Uniform worldwide
Competitive moves	Stand-alone by country	Integrated across countries

Source: George S. Yip, "Global Strategy, in a World of Nations," *Sloan Management Review* 31 (fall 1989), 31.

General Electric's early strategy for becoming a major player in the European appliance market was arrived at through a joint venture with the United Kingdom's GEC Plc. This was in response to Whirlpool and Maytag having established global strategic alliances. Electrolux, in an attempt to be the first global appliance maker, took over Zanussi Industries (1986) to become the top producer of appliances in Western Europe. Later that year Electrolux acquired White Consolidated Industries, the third largest U.S. appliance maker.

Advantages and Disadvantages of a Global MNC Strategy

Table 5 provides an overview of factors that favor a global strategy; Table 6 provides an overview of some of the arguments against it.

The global strategy can provide cost reductions through economies of scale as a result of obtaining production volumes and by pooling production activities. Sony Corporation, for example, has concentrated its compact disc production in Terre Haute, Indiana, and Salzburg, Austria. Cost reductions also can result from moving production activities to lower-cost countries, such as the U.S.-owned production maquiladora plants in Mexico. A third way to reduce costs is by exploiting the flexibility to move production to whichever plant has lower costs at any given time. Dow Chemical uses a linear programming model to arrive at the lowest cost mix of production volume by location for each planning period. The capability of switching production can further reduce costs by enhancing the MNC's bargaining power vis-à-vis suppliers, workers, and host governments. A global strategy increases competitive leverage because the MNC integrates its moves to contain competition. Becton Dickenson of the United States entered Hong Kong, the Philippines, and Singapore in an attempt to prevent the further expansion of a Japanese competitor.[8]

TABLE 5
Advantages of the Global Strategy

EXTERNAL ADVANTAGES

The globalization of customer markets grows.
  —People's wants homogenize.
  —People are more willing to sacrifice specific preferences in product features, functions, design, and the like for a better price-quality ratio, resulting in lower prices and higher standard quality.
Mobility of target market across countries increases.
Foreign competition at home and abroad increases.
Global transportation and communications become speedier, more varied, and cheaper.
Resource markets are globalized.
A supporting infrastructure, such as global financial systems, emerges.

FIRM-SPECIFIC ADVANTAGES

Costs are reduced through scale economies in production and, increasingly, in R&D and marketing.
The number of multinational cooperative ventures increases.
Competitive leverage increases.

TABLE 6
Disadvantages of the Global Strategy

EXTERNAL DISADVANTAGES

Most evidence suggests increased heterogeneity of market segments within each
 country, but there is an increase in the number of global market segments.

There is no evidence that consumers are becoming universally more price sensitive.

Countries differ significantly with respect to some key factors, which prevents an MNC
 from following a global strategy.

Governments often impose restrictions that limit the MNC's ability to follow a
 standardized global strategy.

Technological development in flexible factory automation allows for the production of
 nonstandardized products at substantial cost savings.

FIRM-SPECIFIC DISADVANTAGES

Cost of production is only one component—and often not the critical one—in
 determining the total cost of operations.

Standardized product lines tend to be overdesigned for some markets, underdesigned
 for others; similarly they can be underpriced in some markets and overpriced in
 others.

Most MNCs have established operations in various countries, and it is not easy to
 ignore the variety in many of these operations—exporting, joint ventures and wholly
 owned subsidiaries—and to design a single global strategy.

It is difficult to implement a global strategy in an MNC with a decentralized
 organizational structure, because it reduces the autonomy and responsibility of
 country managers; it is also contrary to the desirable movement toward
 entrepreneurship and greater responsibilities to decentralized units.

Integrated global competitive moves can mean incurring expenses in markets that do
 not have the potential to pay back; it can also mean sacrificing revenues, profits, or
 competitive position in some countries in order to encourage a competitor to divert
 resources from another country.

Companies may raise the potential for globalization by matching or preempting the
moves of individual competitors. When Unilever launched a hostile takeover bid for
Richardson Vicks Inc. of the United States, Procter & Gamble decided to outbid Unilever
and greatly strengthened its European position by utilizing Richardson Vick's European system. Government regulations, or lack of them, can also create or inhibit industry global-
ization/regionalization conditions. The nations of the EU, for example, are attempting to
create "one-market" conditions, which should certainly encourage many firms to consider
the formation of single regionalization strategies. The North America Free Trade Agreement
(NAFTA) should encourage globalization activities in North America.

Which Is the Best Strategy? The ideal strategy is the one that matches the degree of
globalization to the potential of the industry (firm). Whatever the push toward globalization
may be, the most successful strategies are those that find the delicate balance between international and global dimensions which make optimal use of a firm's resources and interests.

PART 2: MNCs AND STRATEGY DESIGN

Seeking the Right Blend of Globalized Strategies

Without doubt, the market battles for the larger firms will involve global settings and include partnerships with firms who are now competitors. Certainly many new alliances will be established, such as the formation of Computer Technology Corporation, in which 21 leading companies are jointly financing technological research efforts. The Department of Justice approved the corporation on the condition that it disband when its research generated a marketable product. The EU has major technological cooperative projects among a large number of companies. L'Esprit and Eureka are two of the best known.[9] Japan is even further ahead in the formation of such cooperatives.

The search for an appropriate balance between a global and a national strategy is an ongoing exercise. Large corporations that are taking part in world markets have evolved from using mainly multidomestic strategies—which were designed to serve the multiple needs of national markets through relatively independent local subsidiaries—to using global strategies by supplying standardized products to world markets through global-scale operations. This requires that the MNC shift to what has been termed a *transnational strategy*,* which maximizes global economies while being responsive to the restrictions imposed by various countries. The transnational firm

- Builds and legitimizes multiple and diverse internal perspectives able to sense the complex environmental demands and opportunities
- Has physical assets and management capabilities, which are distributed internationally but are interdependent
- Requires a robust and flexible international integrative process[10]

Global Competitiveness and Alliances   The global competitiveness of the firm in a global context will be determined by two major factors: (1) the company's ability to obtain and commercialize innovations in products and technological processes and (2) the company's managerial ability to develop and implement the optimum strategy. Optimizing the use of high technologies requires substantial changes in a firm's managerial infrastructure and strategies to allow for alliances, networking, and flexibility.[11] Philips, for example, cooperated openly with Sony and Matsushita for product development of compact discs and digital cassettes until the final product specifications were written. From then on, the three companies competed aggressively. The initial cooperation and subsequent competition brought advantages to all three manufacturers.

In an effort to grasp a larger piece of the world marketplace, even the largest of companies have turned to alliances. In 1991 the biggest telephone companies in Britain (British Telecommunications), Japan (Nippon Telegraph & Telephone), and Germany (Deutsche Bundespost Telekom) began talks aimed at establishing a joint venture that would offer a form of one-stop telecommunications shopping and provide internal telecommunications systems. Other examples of competitors forming alliances are Airbus Industries

---

*Transnational firms supply standardized products to world markets through global-scale operations. A transnational strategy maximizes global economies while being responsive to the restrictions imposed by various countries.

with Lockheed, Chrysler with Mitsubishi, and Johnson & Johnson with Merck. In its publication "The Global Corporation—Obsolete So Soon?" Booz, Allen & Hamilton predicts that current economic and political developments that stress nationalism and regionalism over international free markets mean that today's global firms will be superseded by "relationship enterprises." These will be networks of strategic alliances among huge firms that span industries and countries and are held together by common goals. This goal encourages them to act almost as a single company. According to Booz, Allen & Hamilton, these corporate juggernauts will have revenues nearing $1 trillion by early next century, which is larger than all but the world's six largest economies.[12] The concept of international alliances as a major MNC survival strategy appears to be valid even today. Consider that Boeing, members of the Airbus consortium, McDonnell Douglas, Mitsubishi, Kawasaki, and Fuji are already talking about jointly developing a new super-jumbo jet. In addition, the world's big telecoms have united to provide a worldwide network of fiber-optic submarine cables. IBM alone has more than 400 strategic alliances around the world, such as its efforts with Siemens and Toshiba to develop a costly new generation of DRAM computer chips. Since 1985 the rate of growth for joint ventures between the United States and foreign partners has been 27 percent.[13]

Others point to the fact that even though the sales for MNCs are international, the firms really remain national. In 1991, for example, only 2 percent of the board members of U.S. MNCs were foreign. Foreign board members are, for the most part, nonexistent in the large Japanese companies. In addition to internal constraints, external ones such as antitrust laws that limit global takeovers and nationalism keep firms from being truly global. It seems that nobody likes to think of "their" nation's companies managed by "foreigners" and certainly foreign ownership is unpopular. This was clearly demonstrated when the U.S. government blocked what seemed to be a fairly reasonable attempt of U.S. Air and British Air to merge. Not all alliances work out. McKinsey Consulting Company's data have shown that the most successful alliances change dramatically during their first years. Markets keep evolving and so must partnerships. GE aircraft engines isolated one common source of stress: If when one company is improving, its partner must improve as well. When alliances can't adapt, they fail. One such failure was among TRW and Fujitsu. When TRW could not sell Fujitsu's point-of-sale terminals, it blamed the Japanese company for failing to adapt rapidly to consumer needs. Fujitsu complained that it did not have sufficient input into decisions. After two years the relationship ended with Fujitsu buying out TRW's interest.[14]

The Development of a Global Business Strategy

The five major components of the strategic planning process involve stages of interrelated decisions. (1) The first component defines the business that the firm is in, (2) the second determines the firm's goals and objectives, (3) the third determines specific performance objectives, (4) the fourth formulates strategies, and (5) the fifth forms a relationship between resource allocation and the required budget.

Defining the business that the firm is in includes an assessment of the firm's resources, comparative advantages, product/services, and market scope. It also includes a discussion of which customers are to be served, which needs are to be satisfied, and what technologies are to be used to satisfy those needs. This discussion should clarify which products/services would be appropriate in specific market segments. Determining the mission, goals, and objectives for international business is accomplished across the international business sectors and markets in which the firm operates. This usually involves trade-offs among the potentially conflicting objectives of international business growth and market share gains.

The development of a global business strategy requires that an MNC define its business, determine its mission, define its goals and objectives, assess its resources, evaluate its comparative advantages, and consider the needs and wants of its worldwide customers. A clever strategy, additionally, focuses on enhancing value for customers rather than simply beating competition. As the great Sun Tzu observed 500 years before Christ, "The smartest strategy in war is the one that allows you to achieve your objectives without having to fight."[15]

In the late 1960s and early 1970s, most Japanese companies concentrated on reducing costs through programs such as quality circles, value engineering, and zero defects. Then, as these companies went global, they concentrated on the value conscious middle-class U.S. and EC markets. The strategy sought product differentiation through more models and features. Today, a number of the largest and most successful Japanese MNCs face the common problems of attack from low-cost NIC manufacturers and difficulty in capturing upper-scale market segments. The only low-cost strategies left for the Japanese MNCs to pursue are either to take the labor content out of manufacturing through automation, unstaffed operations, and flexible manufacturing systems or to make direct investments in manufacturing in the NICs. Therefore it was not surprising when Honda announced in 1992 it was entering a motorcycle venture with the Chinese government to produce motorcycles for the Chinese market, which is quickly becoming one of the world's most lucrative markets, but not without risk. This was clear when in 1989 the Communist party limited sales after motorcyclists played an active role in demonstrations. The partners were producing 500,000 bikes by 1995.[16]

The Development of a Winning Business Strategy

By the early 1980s, criticisms of MNC strategies emerged. Many felt that European and American MNCs did not focus on the important determinants of corporate success and pointed out that Japanese companies were concentrating on quality, productivity, and teamwork. In addition, new competitors using advanced technology often spearheaded powerful attacks against even the most established MNCs. What was to follow was a decade of restructuring, eliminating unprofitable product lines, lowering costs, and attempting to achieve a sustainable competitive advantage.

While many MNCs were complaining that the foreign markets in Japan were inaccessible, others were developing strategies to build market share. Schick Razors, for example, was able to take 69.5 percent of the Japanese market (30.3 percent of the U.S. share), and Coca-Cola maintains a strong 33 percent (41 percent of U.S. and 42 percent of European shares). With a careful and well-studied entrance into Japanese markets, Toys 'R' Us found strong demand for its stores. Inflexible MNC giants such as GM (35 percent of U.S. and 11 percent of European shares) and Ford (24 percent of U.S. and 11 percent of European shares), which had been unwilling to even modify their product's steering wheel to meet the "they drive on the other side of the road" driving needs of Japan, have continually been unable to gain additional market share (3 percent and 1 percent, respectively).

The concept of global strategy has bloomed, but its many facets have made it difficult for companies to obtain a clear direction. Global strategy was introduced more than 20 years ago by the distinction between an ethnocentric, polycentric, regiocentric, or geocentric approach by MNCs to multinational management.[17] The starting point for this categorization was seen as the driving force behind the way the firm structured its worldwide activities. In much of the current writings the focus has been narrowed and the concept has been linked almost exclusively with how an MNC structures the flow of tasks within its worldwide, value-adding system. The more the flow of tasks are integrated and rationalized, the more global the MNC's strategy is assumed to be.[18] Different tasks offer different degrees of advantages from global integration and national differentiation. Optimally an MNC must configure its value chain to obtain the best possible advantages.[19] The large corporation has to add value above and beyond what could be achieved if its business units were independent by developing synergetic links between business units.[20]

The perspectives regarding global strategy are varied, as the following four viewpoints illustrate:

1. The core of a winning global strategy lies in developing standardized world-class products to be marketed throughout the world in the same way.[21]
2. MNCs must develop a wide product portfolio with many product varieties so that investments in technology and distribution channels can be shared. Such cross-subsidization and a strong worldwide distribution system are the ways to success.[22]
3. A winning global strategy must exploit economies of scale producing global volumes, take preemptive positions through quick and large investments, and manage interdependently to achieve synergies across different activities.[23]
4. A winning global strategy must concentrate on arbitrage, flexibility, and options to use the volatile global economy to advantage. Multiple sourcing, production shifting to realize benefits from changing factor costs and exchange rates, and arbitrage in financial and information markets are necessary.[24]

Entering and Maintaining Foreign Markets

The MNC must not only design strategies to enter foreign markets but must recognize the importance of having strategies designed to maintain one's position.

Strategies for Entering Markets

Entering where your product may be ignored. The initial strategic task for the MNC is to identify opportunities worldwide and identify entry points that might have weak or complacent competitors. Take, for example, the entry decisions of Japanese firms during the 1960s. Knowing that the U.S. market was vast but highly competitive, the majority of firms chose to enter markets where defenses were weakest and chose to export small products such as motorcycles, cars, TVs, and copiers. These products were largely ignored as they were not in direct competition with existing U.S. companies.

Creating entry opportunity. When markets are highly competitive, MNCs can create opportunities that do not currently exist to avoid direct competition. Take, for example, the entrance of Japanese firms into the watch—or time—industry. Japanese MNCs understood that their products could not compete with the perceived quality of products made by the Swiss, who dominated the world timepiece market with their jeweled movement accuracy. As a result, the Japanese entered the market with inexpensive quartz watches of equal—or greater—accuracy than Swiss watches. As the Sony Walkman and the compact disc have proved, creating opportunities through creativity—although expensive in terms of R&D—can often help a company to avoid costly and dangerous head-on competition in foreign markets.

Market Maintenance   Even once the MNC is established in foreign markets, there is little time to rest. Products must be continually adapted both to stay ahead of the competition and to meet ever-changing consumer preferences. Shortly after entering the home movie market, for example, Japanese firms switched from the 20-year-old 8mm format to the now-popular video format and reduced the camera size from what might be considered small luggage to a self-focusing unit with audio that would fit in the palm of a hand.

Strategic Progression

It is important to appreciate that strategy must be viewed not as a one-time assessment of the international environment but as an evolving plan. It is necessary for the strategies to remain flexible and adapt to the continually changing market conditions. Frequently, an MNC will find that in spite of its intensive planning, the environment may choose not to cooperate with its vision of the future. Nissan in 1993, for example, was forced to rethink its strategy in Barcelona, Spain. Nissan Motor Iberica, the majority-owned Spanish subsidiary, had plunged into a 1992 loss of $121 million. Nissan's ambitious expansion program had run into problems due to a failing European economy, rising company indebtedness, and heavy competition. By increasing the number of Spanish-built Terrano II four-wheel drives that the company exported to Japan from 10,000 to 12,000, Nissan was able to remain profitable while waiting for the European market to recover.[25]

Three Stages of Development That Strategies Must Address   It is essential that strategies address the progressive stages of (1) opportunity identification, (2) entry plans, and (3) market maintenance schemes (Table 7).

T A B L E   7
Three Progressive Stages That Strategies Must Address

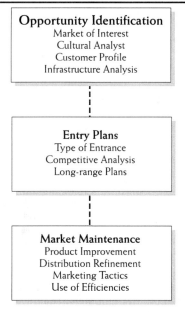

Opportunity Identification
Market of Interest
Cultural Analyst
Customer Profile
Infrastructure Analysis

Entry Plans
Type of Entrance
Competitive Analysis
Long-range Plans

Market Maintenance
Product Improvement
Distribution Refinement
Marketing Tactics
Use of Efficiencies

SECTION III: STRATEGIC OBJECTIVES OF AN MNC

DEVELOPING AN ORGANIZING FRAMEWORK

A framework for the development of a global strategy should include the three important strategic MNC objectives of (1) efficiency, (2) management of risk, and (3) development of learning capabilities in order to innovate and adapt to changes (Table 8). Sources of competitive advantage can be obtained by (1) utilizing national differences in input and output markets, (2) gaining from scale economies in different activities, and (3) obtaining synergies or economies of scope from the diversity of activities and organizational economies of scale. An overall competitive position in world markets is developed by taking strategic actions that optimize resources and bring about the achievement of these, at

TABLE 8

Global Strategy: An Organizing Framework

STRATEGIC OBJECTIVES	SOURCES OF COMPETITIVE ADVANTAGE		
	NATIONAL DIFFERENCES	SCALE ECONOMIES	SCOPE ECONOMIES
Achieving efficiency in current operations	Benefiting from differences in factor costs-wages and cost of capital	Expanding and exploiting potential scale economies in each activity	Sharing investments and costs across products, markets, and businesses
Managing risks	Managing different kinds of risks arising from market or policy-induced changes in comparative advantages of different countries	Balancing scale with strategic and operational flexibility	Developing portfolio diversification of risks and creating options and side-bets
Innovation, learning, and adaption	Learning from societal differences in organizational and managerial processes and systems	Benefiting from experience-cost reduction and innovation	Establishing shared learning across organizational components in different products, markets, or businesses

Source: S. Ghoshal, "Global Strategy: An Organizing Framework," *Strategic Management Journal 8* (1987), 428.

times, conflicting objectives. This checklist can be used when reviewing the strategic alternatives available to both the MNC and its competition.

STRATEGIC OBJECTIVES

Efficiency Objective

The overall efficiency of the MNC can be defined as the ratio of output values to input costs. Products can be differentiated to raise the exchange value of output, or a firm can produce in lower-cost countries to minimize the costs of its input. The efficiency perspective has dominated the field of strategic management for some time and is termed the integration-responsiveness framework or analysis. This analysis defines the cost advantages associated with the global integration of tasks compared to the benefits of responding to national differences. Toyota provides an example of a firm whose strategy was based on integration advantages arising from centralized production and decision making. Although efficiency is an important strategic objective, the actual overall strategic goal is to create value in an efficient manner, not efficiency.[26]

The Management-of-Risk Objective

MNCs face domestic risks as well as the unique difficulties that are associated with operating across national boundaries. International risks tend to fall into four categories. The first category comprises macroeconomic or political risks, such as wars and movements in exchange rates. The MNC normally can exert only limited influence against this type of risk and in most cases the risk is fairly uncontrollable. The second category relates to the policy actions of different national governments that affect the business climate for the foreign firm. To some extent, depending on the amount of foreign taxes paid and the number of nationals the MNC hires, the corporation may be able to influence these actions. The third area of risk focuses on the actions of competitors. In the global arena the range and depth of competitive response is often greater than it is on the national level, because the resources and technological base of competitors can be extensive. The final type of international risk for the MNC is internal and involves the resource risks arising from the possibility that the MNC may be unable to obtain all the resources required to remain competitive as its strategy progresses.

The strategic task for the MNC is to consider the impact of the four types of risks as part of strategy development. Some risks can be diversified, shifted, or shared through routine market transactions, but those that cannot should be of particular concern.

Innovation and the Learning Curve Objective

Through its world operations, an MNC can increase its profits by exploiting its technology, brand name, or management capabilities. An important additional asset of the MNC may well be the organizational and technological learning that results from operating in diverse environments. The exposure to multiple cultures and markets leads to the development of diverse capabilities and resources. This synergetic interaction may be a key explanation for the ongoing success of the MNC.[27]

Liquid Tide, a Procter & Gamble Company product, for example, has ingredients that were developed by P&G's research and development centers in three countries. The U.S. center contributed the ingredient that helps suspend dirt in wash water. From the Japan center came the surfactants, or cleaning agents (the Japanese wash their clothes in cold water and as a result the surfactants must have a higher cleaning ability). The Brussels center produced the antiuniversal salt ingredient (water in Europe contains twice the universal salt level of that in the United States).[28] The multinational nature of P&G led to the development of a superior product that could be marketed worldwide.

The MNC has a significant opportunity to learn, but to maximize the opportunity the organization must be structured appropriately. If R&D is centralized and national subsidiaries are used primarily for value adding, global learning benefits may not occur to any meaningful extent. If, however, national subsidiaries are too autonomous, then their local loyalties and turf protection may inhibit the flow of knowledge to the global systems. Information flows from all parts of the organization must be encouraged, and there must be an active attempt to synthesize knowledge flows for the greater benefit of the total MNC.

SOURCES OF COMPETITIVE ADVANTAGES

Three significant areas of competitive advantages are available to the firm: (1) utilizing national differences in input and output markets, (2) economies of scale, and (3) economies of scope.[29]

Utilizing National Differences

Because nations are at different economic levels of development, they have different factor costs. In the short term, MNCs can gain by locating their facilities where the cost is lowest. This strategy works better for purchasing finished goods than it does for determining plant location. Nations tend to move toward higher-wage scales over time and efficiencies can be lost. Japan, for example, now purchases from Korea and Malaysia many of the items it produced only a decade ago. It will not be long before many goods manufactured in Korea are replaced by ones produced in new manufacturing sites in China.

Nations also differ in output markets as consumers' tastes, preferences, and behavioral responses to advertising and promotion differ across nations. An MNC can also gain through the appropriate differentiation of national/regional output markets. Other sources of national differences that can be utilized are in human resources areas that arise from educational systems, and organizational and managerial know-how.[30]

It is important to recognize that national differences are not static; dynamic changes are occurring, and the speed of change varies significantly among nations. An MNC has to anticipate and strategically respond to such changes.

Economies of Scale

Economies of scale help MNCs to gain lower costs through expanded volumes. The concept of the value-added chain helps the MNC to analyze the extent of scale for each value-creating activity. In some cases production must be great to offset research and development costs. Industries such as chemicals and telecommunications sales must be international and production costs low in order to recover initial development costs. Building huge plants with worldwide capability has the drawback of creating inflexibility. It is important that the size be balanced against the requirement of retaining flexibility. This is becoming increasingly possible with the use of newer technologies such as computer-aided design, computer-aided manufacturing, and robotics. In many industries, such as clothing, MNCs are trading

TABLE 9

Scope Economies in Product and Market Diversification

	SOURCES OF SCOPE ECONOMIES	
	PRODUCT DIVERSIFICATION	MARKET DIVERSIFICATION
Shared Assets	Using factory automation with flexibility to produce multiple products (Ford)	Establishing a global brand name (Coca-Cola)
Shared External Agents	Using a common distribution channel for multiple products (Matsushita)	Servicing multinational customers worldwide (Citibank)
Shared Learning	Sharing R&D in computer and communications businesses (NEC)	Pooling knowledge developed in different markets (Procter & Gamble)

Source: Adapted from S. Ghoshal, "Global Strategy: An Organizing Framework," *Strategic Management Journal* 8 (1987), 435.

the flexibility to alter sizes, styles, and colors over more massive, but more rigid, production facilities. Some companies, such as the Gap, are now changing clothing styles monthly in an effort to stimulate sales to younger, fashion-conscious consumers.

Economies of Scope

Scope economies arise from the ability to share costs, investments, and R&D across products or markets. Table 9 provides an illustration of selected MNCs that are known to gain from economies-of-scope activities.

Scope Activities Can Overcome Some Scale Problems   To overcome the inflexibility associated with large plants, Ford has developed some automated plants that have the flexibility to produce multiple products. Coca-Cola gains scope economies from having a global brand name. Matsushita can use selected distribution channels to carry its diverse product line. NEC obtains scope economies in R&D through its global strategy of being in both the computer and communications industries. By having two technologies in-house, NEC can achieve scope economies in new product development. The attempt to achieve greater scope economies, however, has often resulted in a trade-off of increased organizational complexity and higher management requirements.[31]

STRATEGIC TRADE-OFFS BETWEEN OBJECTIVES AND ADVANTAGES

The MNC operates in a global environment with multiple options and ever present trade-offs between its strategic objectives and the sources of competitive advantage. A global strategy directed toward efficiency implies that each value element occurs at the cheapest cost location where scale economies can be obtained. This might yield a configuration in which R&D centers are concentrated in developed countries, assembly plants are in large markets/regions (including LDCs), and components are made exclusively in LDCs. Therefore R&D costs occur in high-cost countries, whereas revenues accrue in a variety of countries, ranging from rich to poor. If R&D costs are a substantial percentage of sales, then this may well increase the exchange rate exposure of that MNC. In general, a global strategy tends to require centralization of decision making and a high degree of coordination. This naturally shifts organizational power from the subsidiaries/affiliates to headquarters.

Conversely, global strategies designed to optimize risk may sacrifice some efficiency. For instance, R&D may be spread over a number of countries where the MNC has subsidiaries in order to offset any risk of pressure from host governments. Operational risk can be further decreased by having standby plants that are not working at full capacity in some countries. Trade-offs also are ever present between the sources of competitive advantages. Scope economies gained through product diversification may limit the possibilities of scale economies in each product's output.

Developing an MNC strategy is truly a complex undertaking.[32] An MNC must evaluate its resources and differential advantages as well as its competitors and the many environments in which it functions. It must then determine its dominant strategic objective, analyze the trade-offs entailed by adopting a primary strategic objective, and adopt an adjusted strategy based on the primary objective and its ensuing trade-offs. To make matters even more confusing, MNC managers are often responsible for implementing a strategy for which a portion of the design was based on uncertain environmental conditions.

APPROACHES TO UNCERTAINTY AND THE STRATEGIC PLAN

Strategic planning, as it is usually practiced, follows the predict-and-prepare philosophy, whereby it serves as a road map by providing a defined destination with steps to reach it. This form of strategic planning has yielded questionable benefits, however, because, unlike a road map, where locations and paths to them remain fixed, the competitive environment is always changing. Imagine following a familiar highway that should take you to a favorite beach location only to find out at the end of your trip that the beach has been moved. This would be confusing, time and resource consuming, and quite frustrating, to say the least. Now consider the trip to be a competitive race to the beach. Now that you know the beach can move, you will continually exchange maps for updated ones and attempt to learn which direction the beach could be headed, while paying close attention to your gas gauge so that any delays or detours do not cause you to run out of fuel. You do all this while carefully watching the others in the race, so as not to collide with competitors. This is more like the world of MNC planning and strategy!

Change, and the uncertainty which accompanies it, is the Achilles' heel of strategic planning. For strategic planning to be truly useful in the international business environment, it must include approaches to cope with uncertainty.[33] Three such approaches follow:

1. The predict and prepare approach: The conventional approach.
2. The power approach—attempting to dominate or eliminate sources of uncertainty.
3. The structural approach—building an internal capacity for flexible response and adaptation.

The Predict and Prepare Approach

The predict and prepare approach has a major shortcoming—contingency plans are too often precapsuled programs designed to respond to preconceived situations that never occur as expected.[34] Because the anticipated future events never quite occur as forecast, companies tend to react to the slightly different outcomes with "shoot from the hip" management styles that tend to be individualistic and unpredictable and can differ from country to country depending on local management's response.

Appreciating the shortcoming of the predict and prepare approach, MNCs have historically attempted to deal with the issue of uncertainty by using either the power or the structural approach. The power approach is an attempt by the MNC to directly influence external issues, whereas the structural approach attempts to position the MNC for environmental changes by reducing the time needed to adjust to changing conditions or even redesigning major portions of the corporate system. These types of alternatives do not flow normally out of the strategic planning process. In spite of the care, resources, and technologies applied to forecasting, however, unforeseen global events quite often surprise even the most astute international business manager.

The Power Approach

The power response is a direct attempt by the MNC to control its environment through such actions as lobbying for changes in government regulations, obtaining government funds or grants for R&D or capital investments, using the political process to block entry of competitors, and acting to shape and dominate the competitive environment. IBM and Boeing aircraft are examples of companies that are extremely active in government lobbying.

Competitive environments can also be dominated through the process of acquisitions and divestiture. For example, General Electric consolidated its position in medical diagnostic imaging equipment by buying Johnson & Johnson's division and trading its consumer electronics division for Thomson S.A.'s medical equipment business. Power actions also can reduce competitive vulnerability. Weaker players often use the courts to shape industry structure and keep stronger competitors in check. The reverse also is true. IBM does not hesitate to sue competitors anywhere in the world for any alleged patent infringement. Traditional strategic planning often ignores employing aggressive power resources to shape the competitive environment to most suit the firm.

The Structural Approach

The structural response is typified by the Boy Scout slogan "Be prepared"; the MNC should prepare for uncertainty and expect the future to vary from predictions. There are a number of ways to do this. One is to broaden the product and market scope of the MNC as the diversity created by being in more countries and having more products tends to give the MNC stability and durability. Another structural mechanism is to set up strategic alliances and joint ventures. At a more fundamental level, structural coping means that an MNC must be designed to absorb uncertainties over which it cannot exert control. Strategic planning should push international business managers to build the MNC's flexibility by evaluating its value chain cost configuration and operating technologies. Managers should consider the following areas:

- *The large MNC as a collection of smaller firms.* If future markets, products, and technology are relatively unpredictable, the firm should be designed to flow with entrepreneurial market development.
- *Loose coupling and partial integration.* This refers to various interfirm arrangements whereby most of the benefits of close coordination are obtained but outright ownership with its economic risk and reduction in flexibility is avoided. Most global franchising systems can be demonstrated to be coupling. An example of partial integration consists of integrating the information flow across independent businesses throughout a global supply chain. Toyota's just-in-time inventory system is an early application of this principle. The Japanese automakers are trying to integrate the information flow from showrooms to supplies of components and raw materials. The objective is to reduce the waiting time from order to delivery. Benetton, the Italian clothing designer, has created a strategic system of feeder production operations that has resulted in sales of more than $1 billion with only 1,200 direct employees. Amstrad, the British computer firm, contracts out the manufacturing process to a network of Far Eastern firms and directly employs a relatively small number of employees.
- *Building and inventorying strategic resources.* The Canon Corporation exemplifies this method. Its way of dealing with uncertainty is to hire a large number of new engineers each year and to develop capability in selected hybrid generic technologies that may be combined in different ways to take advantage of emerging opportunities. The R&D plus the abundance of engineers ensures a steady stream of new products.

SECTION IV: THE IMPORTANCE OF SERVICES IN GLOBAL MNC STRATEGY

CUSTOMER SERVICE AS AN MNC COMPETITIVE STRATEGY

Customer service has emerged as a viable strategic weapon for the multinational corporation and, in some cases, can actually provide important international competitive advantages. John Deere, the American heavy-equipment manufacturer, competes in global markets by claiming to provide 24-hour service anywhere in the world. This promise provides a product differentiation; that is, it differentiates Deere's company from those that attempt to compete with price. The IBM personal computer is an example of a global product that is marketed at a premium price sustained by service. IBM's emphasis and sales orientation has been to sell at top price and support the product with superior service. Through its international dealer system, IBM can support its MNC PC customers throughout the world, providing for consistency in each country the customer has an office.[35]

Services that include all the activities (beyond assembly and sale) that are necessary can be linked to products in order to attract and hold customers. These services are normally intangible and inseparable and cannot be inventoried. One problem with them being intangible is that it is difficult to demonstrate the services in advance of the product purchase. Consider the U.S. computer disaster-recovery company of Sun Guard Data, Inc. Sun Guard sold contracts to companies for many years before a major computer disaster in Chicago demonstrated that its product could actually get firms up and running within hours, even firms that used huge databases that demanded continual on-line interaction.

FIGURE 1

Framework for Global Markets

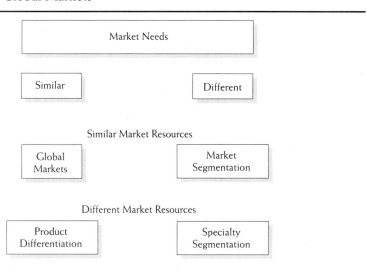

Source: Richard Lankan and Myroslaw J. Kyj, "Is a Global Customer Service Policy Desirable?" *Asia-Pacific International Journal of Business Logistics* 2, no. 2 (1989), 12.

Customer service is usually inseparable from the tangible product. As such, the total actual value of the product is a combination of both the product and the services that support it.

A Global or Local Customer Service Strategy?

The MNC must decide whether it should have a global customer service strategy or a strategy tailored to each foreign market. It is useful to compare market needs to market resources, as diagrammed in Figure 1.

RESTRUCTURING THE COMPETITIVE POSITION

Service technologies are restructuring the entire competitive posture of industries and nations. The term *service technologies* includes not only information technologies but all other systems operations, hardware, or software developed specifically for service functions. Examples are diagnostic techniques, advanced cargo handling or passenger movement equipment for transportation, specialized food distribution/preparation systems for chain restaurants, satellite communication systems for banking, and even frabic-cutting software that allows companies, such as the Gap, to change clothing designs whenever desired.

Apple Computer and IBM established themselves early as "intellectual holding" companies by outsourcing manufacturing and making as little of the product internally as possible. The value-added component in most products comes not from direct production or conversion processes but from the technological improvements, styling design, quality, marketing, timing, and financial contributions of service activities. Because these knowledge-based intangibles can be relocated globally, relatively cost-free MNCs are able to tap the best sources available to obtain a competitive advantage. The capacity to command and coordinate service activities, supplier networks, and contract relations internationally has become an extremely important strategic weapon.

Competing with the "Service Core"

Few MNCs can profitably own all needed service activities, so they tend to form coalitions with partners through information, communication, and contract arrangements. A new form of international enterprise is emerging with a limited set of core strategic activities, which enables the firm to coordinate a changing network of the world's best production and service suppliers. This network acts much like the Japanese *Kieretsu* concept of linked networks of banks, manufacturers, suppliers, and distributors, long credited as the heart of Japan's trading success. Because it would be quite difficult for an MNC such as IBM or Xerox to produce all elements of its value chains internally, what has evolved is a development of wide-ranging, changing coalitions with outside service and support groups. Such coalitions, along with a service core plus other international coalition networks, compete against one another. AT&T and NEC joined forces to provide such a network, and IBM has joint ventures or partial ownership in Network Equipment Technologies, MCI Communications, Sears/MCI, Open Software Foundation, PCO Fiber Optics, Intel, Nippon Tel & Tel, Ericcson, Bell Atlantic, Credit Agricole, and Banque Paribas. Internally, both IBM and Xerox generate about one-third of their revenues from direct sales of software and services and at least a third from sale of the value-added design as well as embodied system, software, and marketing services.[36]

Managing Systems to Lower Risks

Many MNCs lower their risks and leverage their assets substantially by managing systems instead of managing workers and machines. This happens for several reasons:

- Outsourcing can make the world's best talent available.
- Risk is lowered when the MNC links with a new unit if a provider does not perform well.
- If new technologies emerge, it is easier to switch sources.
- If demand falls, the coordinating MNC is not stuck with idle capacity and inventory.
- The system offers the added motivation, flexibility, and lower overhead cost of relative decentralization.

An emerging strategy is for the MNC to do in-house the core system activities that contribute to competitive advantage and to source the remaining activities from the world's best suppliers. A truly maintainable advantage derives from service activities such as skill sets, experience factors, know-how, market understanding, databases, and distribution capabilities that others cannot reproduce and that have demonstrable value for the customer. The Honda multiple product strategy developed naturally out of its dominant skills in three key areas:

1. Design of small efficient engines
2. Management of small-scale assembly with extensive outsourcing of fabricated parts
3. Creative management of different distribution channels[37]

Honda's growth focused on a natural extension to products that required similar skills, as opposed to similar products. Honda's advertisement "Six Hondas in a Two-Car Garage," which refers to a car, a snow blower, a lawn mower, a motorcycle, a boat, and outdoor power tools, illustrates this growth process.

TECHNOLOGY AND MNC STRATEGY

Transferring Technology

A strategy for transferring or selling technology abroad requires a clear understanding of both the technological process and the consumer needs that are to be satisfied. What is to be transferred may be any combination of product-oriented, process-oriented, or management-oriented technologies, and the mode of transfer may be through subsidiaries, joint ventures, licensing agreements, turnkey operations, engineering consulting/contractor services, or exports. Table 10 outlines some reasons that a multinational may have for selling technology.

Ability to Absorb Technology   The absorptive capability of the firm receiving technology is important in the transfer process. Absorption is a function of the amount of technological know-how internalized by the recipient organization's employees and the employees' learning curve. The selection of a mode of a transfer, as seen from the technology service/product viewpoint, depends on the nature of the technology to be transferred. When the technology to be transferred consists of unorganized or unmodified knowledge, a joint venture becomes more appropriate; when the technology consists of a higher level of knowledge, however, codification of arm's-length arrangements such as licensing can be used. An increasingly popular transfer channel between MNCs is reciprocal or cross-licensing. Such formal or tacit understanding gives each participating enterprise access to new information and is a means of preserving stability in established oligopolistic product markets. Payments are generally netted out, and duplication of the research effort is avoided.[38]

TABLE 10
Reasons for Selling Technology

- *Mission mismatch.* The technology does not fit with the firm's corporate mission.
- *No access to capital.* The firm has insufficient financial resources to exploit the technology.
- *Narrow market window of opportunity.* The firm may be unable to exploit the technology quickly enough.
- *Insufficient size.* The potential business is smaller than expected.
- *Resources needed elsewhere.* Pressing financial requirements elsewhere in the firm must be fulfilled.
- *Unprofitable.* The technology cannot be made profitable by the firm.
- *Technological irrelevance.* The firm has a new technology that supersedes the one for sale.
- *Strategic imperative.* Allowing other firms access is the most appropriate strategic action (e.g., franchising).

Source: Noel Capon and Rashi Glazer, "Marketing and Technology: A Strategic Co-alignment," Working Paper Report No. 86-106, Cambridge, Massachusetts, Marketing Science Institute, July 1986, 18.

Technology Transfer as a Process   The formulation of international strategies for technology transfer can be viewed as a four-step process. (1) First, the firm must assess the internal and external technological environment. (2) It must then analyze the technologies employed by each of its business units compared to that of its competitors in each relevant technological market. (3) Third, the MNC must evaluate its technological profile in terms of a technology portfolio. (4) Finally, managers must determine the importance of the technology in terms of the firm's position in regard to current technology, value-added components, rate of technological change, and attractive potential markets.[39]

The firm must then match the technology-based and product-based portfolios to ensure the complementarity and synchronization of technological and business strategies. Only after these steps have been completed can the company develop a technology strategy that reflects its technology investment priorities.

TECHNOLOGY AND MNC INTERNATIONAL EXPANSION

The once typical pattern of systematic expansion abroad from a basis of strength in a set of products or markets is now considered a luxury few modern MNCs can afford. Markets and products are less proprietary and entry barriers once relied on to protect positions are decreasing. Due to rapidly changing technologies and unstable product/market structures, even technology is becoming less proprietary. As such, an obsession with technology is less important to the MNC than access and use. Sustainable long-term MNC growth is increasingly being gained from a policy based on broad valuation, continual development, and the exploitation of technology. The essence of a coherent technology strategy is that the MNC should

- View technology as an asset
- Try to maximize returns on this asset
- View its total technological asset base as a portfolio of technologies, whose elements change over time as some technologies enter and others exit
- Recognize that technological change will require new strategies and different resources

Figure 2 offers one formulation of the technology portfolio. Its eight-cell matrix builds on the four-cell product portfolio growth/market-share matrix, though the entries are technologies rather than products. In the premarket phase all technologies are cash users so the circles are shaded. In the market phase the horizontal axis indicates the competitive position of the firm. The placement of the circles indicates the high- and low-growth stages of the product life cycle and their shading reflects cash generation.[40]

A topology of technological strategies helps the MNC to develop its overall strategy. The proposed set is as follows:

- Only intra-MNC transfers to its own subsidiaries in order to retain the technological know-how
- Release of technology through negotiated relationships such as joint ventures, cross-licensing, or licensing agreements
- Sale of technology no longer considered crucial in light of the MNC's changing business objectives
- Sale of obsolete technology

FIGURE 2

The Technology Portfolio

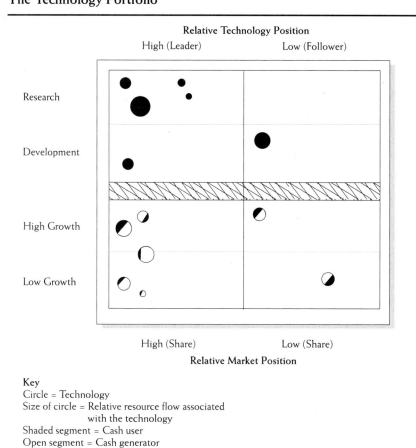

Relative Technology Position
High (Leader)   Low (Follower)

Research

Development

High Growth

Low Growth

High (Share)   Low (Share)
Relative Market Position

Key
Circle = Technology
Size of circle = Relative resource flow associated
                with the technology
Shaded segment = Cash user
Open segment = Cash generator

Source: Noel Capon and Rashi Glazer, "Marketing and Technology: A Strategic Co-Alignment," Working Paper Report No. 86-106, Cambridge, Massachusetts, Marketing Science Institute, July 1986, 27.

This topology integrates the concepts underlying the product life cycle (in which products eventually decline) and the knowledge diffusion process (which represents the flow of knowledge or technology through time and space). This generates a much broader conceptualization than that offered by classifications based exclusively on the nature of the technology or the transfer channel. (Note that in the international product life cycle the innovating MNC initially exports but often later seeks lower-cost production bases abroad as markets develop and the technology becomes standardized.)

An MNC has good reasons for simultaneously exploiting and selling technology. Sale to a competitor also acts as a disincentive for competitive invention, and the competitor may share the expense of market development. MNCs find that LDC markets may close unless the MNCs are willing to sell technology. As a result, it is incumbent on MNCs, as global competitors, to develop a technology service/product strategy that provides for transfer when appropriate, while protecting the MNC throughout the process.

SECTION V: EUROPE: AN EXAMPLE OF MNC INTERESTS AND STRATEGIES

MNC INVOLVEMENT IN EUROPE'S MARKETS

The three most important markets—North America, Europe, and the Asian Pacific—are developing distinctive features and are becoming more exclusive unto themselves. The current European experience provides an excellent example of multinational behavior in world markets and is worth reviewing.

The European Environment

The region is experiencing explosive change, and the development of a strategy for increased EU involvement is a priority for European, Pacific Basin, and American MNCs as this market comprises 30 percent of the world's GNP.

To maintain market share, European MNCs are coming together to form bigger international champions that can compete against the intrusive American and Japanese giants (Table 11). Some examples are as follows:

- *Semiconductors.* The Thomson group of France has merged this part of its business with SGS of Italy. Together they rank 12th by sales in the world chip market.
- *Household durables.* Thomson also is buying Ferguson, Thorn EMI's "brown goods" division. Then Thomson and Philips will control more than half of Europe's production of electronic home-entertainment goods.
- *Copper.* Pechiney of France is merging its copper business with Societa Metallurgica Italiana to form Europe's biggest copper group.
- *Publishing.* West Germany's Bertlesmann, the world's biggest publisher, owns France's largest book club.

Many MNC mergers across European national boundaries have proven unsuccessful. A study done some years ago suggested that half the mergers were successful, one-fifth were not worth doing, and the rest were failures.[41] Some well-publicized failures were Unidata, the French-German-Dutch computer group that was supposed to combat IBM in Europe; the Dunlop-Pirelli linkage which broke up in 1980; and VFW of West Germany and Fokker of Holland, the aircraft makers who also broke up in 1980. Still, the merger mania continues and recently has been especially powerful in the $27 billion publishing industry. Elsevier, the large Dutch publisher, has joined Pearson PLC, the U.K. publisher of the *Financial Times* and owner of *Les Echos*, the premier business daily in France. The Elsevier-Pearson Group is potentially one of the most powerful international book, newspaper, and magazine combines.

Japanese Strategy for Europe

The Japanese strategy for a unified European market was to initiate plant and R&D investments prior to the 1992 unification date. In early 1989, 411 Japanese plants were

TABLE 11
European Community Cross-Border Deals (January 1988–June 1992)

Buyer	Target	Industry	Year	U.S. Dollars (in millions)
Hong Kong & Shanghai Bank	Midland Bank (U.K.)	Banking	1992	7,366
Grand Metropolitan (U.K.)	Pillsbury (U.S.)	Food	1988	5,750
BAT (U.K.)	Farmers Group (U.S.)	Insurance	1988	5,200
Volkswagen (Germany)	Skoda (Czech) (33% stake)	Auto manufacture	1990	5,039
Nestlé (Switzerland)	Rowntree (U.K.)	Food	1988	4,917
Victoire (France)	Colonia (Germany)	Insurance	1989	4,885
Pechiney (France)	American National Can (U.S.)	Packaging	1988	4,000
French group led by Credit Lyonnais	Executive Life (U.S.)	Insurance	1991	3,750
Alcatel Alsthom (France)	Alcatel NV (Netherlands)	Telecommunications	1992	3,700
Allianz (Germany)	Firemans Fund (U.S.)	Insurance	1990	3,300
Rhone Poulenc (France)	Rorer (U.S.)	Pharmaceuticals	1990	3,200
Elf Aquitaine (France), Thyssen and Deutsche SB Kauf (Germany)	Minol and Leuna oil refinery (Germany)	Petroleum filling stations and oil refinery	1992	3,086
Telefonica (Spain) and Citibank (U.S.)	Entel South (Argentina)	Telecommunications	1990	2,830
Nestlé (Switzerland)	Source Perrier (France)	Mineral water	1992	2,760
Northern Telecom (Canada)	STC (U.K.)	Telecommunications	1990	2,600
Maxwell Communication (U.K.)	Macmillan (U.S.)	Publishing	1988	2,600
Ford (U.S.)	Jaguar (U.K.)	Auto manufacture	1989	2,458
France Telecom, Stet (Italy) and JP Morgan (U.S.)	Entel North (Argentina)	Telecommunications	1990	2,412
Stora (Sweden)	Feldmuhle Nobel (Germany)	Paper and board products	1990	2,400
Seibu Saison (Japan)	Inter-Continental Hotels (U.K.)	Hotels	1988	2,268
Schneider (France)	Square D (U.S.)	Electrical products	1991	2,230
CGE (France)	Telettra (Italy)	Telecommunications	1990	2,228
Siemens (Germany), GEC (U.K.)	Plessey (U.K.)	Electronics	1989	2,038*
Fiat (Italy)	FSM (Poland)	Auto manufacture	1992	2,000
St. Gobain (France)	Norton (U.S.)	Abrasives	1990	2,000
Bass (U.K.)	Holiday Inns (U.S.)	Hotels	1989	2,000

*Siemens share only.

Source: KPMG tables, 1992.

Cross-Border Deals Involving EC Companies

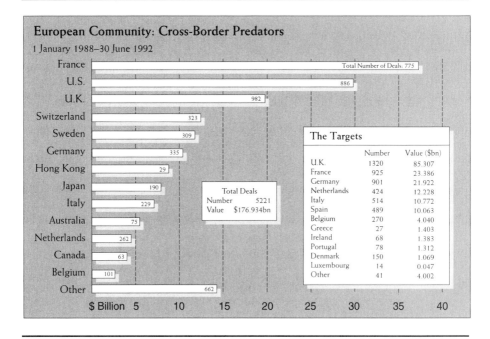

European Community: Cross-Border Predators

1 January 1988–30 June 1992

France — Total Number of Deals: 775
U.S. — 886
U.K. — 982
Switzerland — 323
Sweden — 309
Germany — 335
Hong Kong — 29
Japan — 190
Italy — 229
Australia — 75
Netherlands — 262
Canada — 63
Belgium — 101
Other — 662

Total Deals
Number   5221
Value $176.934bn

The Targets

	Number	Value ($bn)
U.K.	1320	85.307
France	925	23.386
Germany	901	21.922
Netherlands	424	12.228
Italy	514	10.772
Spain	489	10.063
Belgium	270	4.040
Greece	27	1.403
Ireland	68	1.383
Portugal	78	1.312
Denmark	150	1.069
Luxembourg	14	0.047
Other	41	4.002

Source: T. Dickson, "Euro Skepticism Slows an Inevitable Process," *Financial Times* (October 19, 1992), 28.

operating in Europe, double the number in 1983 and almost 25 percent more than in early 1988. This provided a network of small to medium-sized subsidiaries; the preferred locations (in rank order) were the United Kingdom, France, West Germany, and Spain. Research and development efforts have favored Germany. Fujitsu, NEC, Nissan, and Toshiba plants have often been sized to supply the whole EU. The Japanese want to exploit the opportunity of serving one large market and want to be inside Europe in case a protectionist "Fortress Europe" emerges.[42]

Gaining a Foothold in Europe

Many other non-EC firms also are entering Europe before new restrictions arise. IBM has subsidiaries in all EC countries with advertising that stresses the regional "Germanness," "Britishness," and so on of each local subsidiary. In contrast, AT&T has a different strategy. It has not tried to create a European image but has formed alliances with local partners such as Philips of Holland, Italtel and Olivetti of Italy, Marconi of Spain, and Telefonica of Spain.

EUROPEAN MNC STRATEGIES

It appears that there will clearly be a redefinition of the European value chain given the changes in EU cost structures and a movement toward uniform infrastructure regulations. Attempts will be made to eliminate duplication in distribution systems, standardize product lines, and move manufacturing to large plants at a few cost-advantageous locations. EC firms such as Philips and Unilever have already made such moves. Unilever will make all its dishwasher powders for Europe at one plant in Lyons and all its toilet soap at another in Port Sunlight. In instances where a standardized product line is not warranted and the optimal size of final product plants is relatively small, the strategy will favor economies of scale in large plants that make standardized components. Electrolux is doing this with its washing machine components, where the final product is different from country to country (in this case the difference occurs because the French load from the top, Britons load from the front, West Germans insist on powerful machines that can spin most the dampness out of their wash load, and Italians prefer a slower spin as they use the sun to help speed up the drying).[43] Avery International Europe has instrumented the service-oriented strategy of delivering its product to the customer anywhere in Europe within 24 hours. Further, the company has reorganized its logistics operations by cutting its warehouses from one per country to five regional warehouses.[44] IBM may create cross-country groups specializing in manufacturing, distribution, and financial services. Many firms will follow predictable generic strategies of product differentiation and cost reduction. 3M, for example, has begun to rationalize by concentrating production in fewer plants.

In Such an Important Market No MNC Is Complacent

Multinationals in Europe will need high levels of innovation to differentiate their products, and they will need to cut costs in new ways if they are to remain competitive. Coca-Cola and Colgate-Palmolive have created new management groups to be responsible for Europe as a region, which will provide a Euro-marketing perspective and greater efficiency in all areas. Ford Motor Company Europe is the most vertically integrated automobile manufacturer in Europe and is well positioned, but it is taking substantial additional strategic actions. Ford purchased the British firm of Jaguar in 1991 and plans to invest $7.5 billion for plant modernization and equipment throughout the EU while redesigning its European product line to fit local tastes and standard components. General Electric, less entrenched than Ford, has invested $1.7 billion in Spain and, in addition, formed a $580 million joint venture with the United Kingdom's GEC Plc, which gives General Electric 50 percent of GEC's profitable $1 billion European appliance business, a 50 percent share in its electrical distribution equipment business, and a 10 percent share in its venture with France's Alsthom. Furthermore, General Electric has acquired Borg Warner's European chemical operation. Even food producers—such as HJ Heinz, which is spending $1 billion on plant modernization, marketing, and acquisitions—have eyes on the European market. Heinz states two major objectives: (1) to push its frozen Weight Watchers meals across Europe against Nestlé's Lean Cuisine and (2) to expand its ketchup market share. Not to be outspent by manufacturing companies, service companies are actively engaged in European expansion as well. Federal Express, for example, spent more than $250 million to acquire courier companies in West Germany, Italy, and the Netherlands, and Grey Advertising acquired complementary companies across Europe, which doubled billings to $1.4 billion.[45]

SECTION VI: SUMMARY

Strategy requires managers to identify the firm's resources and its competitive environment and to recognize the relationship between them. Strategy should provide business with a focus on the long-term future goals of the firm as opposed to short-term operational objectives. This temporal aspect interjects a degree of ambiguity into the process, which has important management implications.

Manufacturing MNCs must assure that support systems such as raw materials sources, advertising agencies, and bankers are available in locations of expansion. Such services can be obtained by having current providers follow the MNC's international moves or they can be acquired locally. The global competitiveness of the firm will be determined by two major management factors. The first is the ability to obtain and commercialize innovations in products and technological processes. The second is to possess the managerial capabilities to develop and implement the optimum strategy. Managers of MNCs must develop flexible multidimensional decision-making processes capable of responding to a rapidly changing environment.

An MNC's decision-making process can be centralized or decentralized depending on company philosophy and organizational structure. Managers must decide between establishing globalized positions or pursuing different strategies for each product in the firm's portfolio depending on its market share, the segment growth rate, and the nature of the product. Only a global view of products and markets, combined with favorable cost-volume relationships, can truly lead to a portfolio that can confront global competition.

MNCs must realize that a successful international business strategy should focus on enhancing value for customers rather than on simply beating competition. An important management insight is borrowed from the great Sun Tzu who observed 500 years before Christ that the smartest strategy in war is the one that allows you to achieve your objectives without having to fight.

A relatively new management responsibility has been to direct the service aspects of the firm's production. Customer service has emerged as a viable strategic weapon for the multinational corporation. In some cases it has become a major international competitive strategy. The value-added component in most products comes not from direct production or conversion processes but from the technological improvements, styling design, quality, marketing, timing, and financial contributions of service activities. One of management's major challenges for the coming decade will be developing new alliances since no MNC can afford to profitably own all needed service activities. Alliances, while often problematic, can be formidable competitive assets as they are difficult for competitors to rapidly imitate. The outcome of MNC management cooperation can be shorter product development cycles, new products with superior attributes, and lower costs resulting from designs that facilitate production and service.

Though many managers see the importance of domestic market dominance, it is essential they understand the importance of world market share and grasp the key strategic objectives of efficiency, management of risk, and development of learning capabilities in order to innovate and adapt to future changes. MNCs will find that competitive advantage is developed by taking strategic actions that optimize achievement of, at times, conflicting objectives. Business normally has three goals available for such development:

- To exploit the differences in the markets of both input and output countries
- To gain from scale economies in its different activities
- To obtain synergies or economies of scope from the diversity of its activities and organization

The manager's strategic responsibility is to use all three tools to simultaneously optimize the company's goals while considering the impact of the four types of risks. Risks can be diversified, shifted, or shared through routine market transactions.

The MNC has the advantage over smaller firms as its exposure to multiple cultures and markets leads management to develop diverse capabilities and resources. This synergetic interaction may be a key explanation for the ongoing success of the MNC. One of the drawbacks of the MNC's large size is possible inflexibility. It is important that bigness be balanced with flexibility. The overall competitiveness of the MNC is strongly linked to its ability to respond to rapid changes in the competitive environment. This is becoming increasingly possible through the use of newer technologies and advanced communications. However, attempts to achieve greater scope economies often involve trade-offs of increased organizational complexity and higher management requirements. In addition, global strategies directed at optimizing risk may sacrifice efficiency. To the extent that control is not possible, structural responses must be implemented to reduce the MNC's vulnerability.

In today's world, sustainable, long-term MNC corporate growth comes increasingly from a policy based on broad valuation, continual development, and exploitation of technology. It is incumbent on MNC managers, who intend their firms to be global competitors, to develop a technology service/product strategy that allows the MNC to transfer to alliance firms when appropriate and protects the MNC throughout the process. The essence of a coherent technology strategy is that management

- Views technology as an asset
- Tries to maximize returns on this asset
- Views its total technological asset base as a portfolio of technologies, whose elements change over time as some technologies enter and others exit
- Recognizes that technological change will require new strategies and different resources

All strategies will have some factors that favor globalization and some factors that favor multinational approaches. Managers must analyze the conditions that support both approaches and be able to recognize which is the most appropriate choice. The ideal strategy matches the degree of globalization to the potential of the industry (firm). Whatever the push toward global may be, it is important for the MNC to recognize that the most successful strategies are those that find the delicate balance between international and global that is unique to each firm's interest.

REFERENCES

[1] Kenichi Ohmae, *The Mind of the Strategist* (Bergenfield, NJ: Penguin Books, 1983), 248.

[2] Christopher Lorenz, "The Multinational Myth Explodes," *Financial Times* (March 4, 1992), 7.

[3] H. Takenchi and M. E. Porter, "Three Roles of International Marketing in Global Strategy," in *Competition in Global Industries*, ed. M. E. Porter (Boston: Harvard Business School Press, 1986), 111–46.

[4] K. R. Whitmore, "A Common Agenda for an Uncommon Future," *MIT Management* (formerly *Sloan*) (summer 1987), 5–9.

[5] Thomas R. Horton, "Tomorrow's Protean Enterprise," *Management Review* (September 1989), 5–6.

[6] David A. Heenan, "A Different Outlook for Multinational Companies," *The Journal of Business Strategy* (July/August 1988), 51–54.

[7] George S. Yip, "Global Strategy, in a World of Nations," *Sloan Management Review* 31, no. 1 (fall 1989), 29–41.

[8] M. R. Cvar, "Case Studies in Global Competition," in *Competition in Global Industries*, ed. M. E. Porter (Boston: Harvard Business School Press, 1986).

9 P. Nueno and V. Oosterveld, "The Staus of Strategy in Europe," in *Technology in the Modern Corporation*," ed. M. Horwich (New York: Pergamon Press, 1986).

10 C. A. Barlett, "Building and Managing the Transnational: The New Organizational Challenge," in *Competition in Global Industries*," ed. M. E. Porter (Boston: Harvard Business School Press, 1986).

11 Arnaldo C. Hax, "Building the Firm of the Future," *Sloan Management Review* 30, no. 3 (spring 1989), 75–82.

12 "The Global Firm R.I.P.," *The Economist* (February 6, 1993), 69.

13 Stratford Sherman, "Are Strategic Alliances Working?" *Fortune* (September 21, 1992), 77.

14 Stratford Sherman, "Are Strategic Alliances Working?" *Fortune* (September 21, 1992), 78.

15 Kenichi Ohmae, "Getting Back to Strategy," *Harvard Business Review* (November/December 1988), 149–56.

16 R. Thomson, "Honda Announces First Motorcycle Venture in China," *Financial Times* (May 27, 1992), 3.

17 H. V. Perlmutter, "The Tortuous Evolution of the Multinational Corporation," *Columbia Journal of World Business* (January/February 1969), 9–18.

18 J. Leontiades, "Market Share and Corporate Strategy in International Industries," *Journal of Business Strategy* 78+ (March 1984), 30–37.

19 M. E. Porter, "Competition in Global Industries: A Conceptual Framework," paper presented to the Colloquium on Competition in Global Industries, Harvard Business School, Boston, 1984.

20 "The State of Strategic Thinking," *The Economist* (May 23, 1987), 17–21.

21 T. Levitt, "The Globalization of Markets," *Harvard Business Review* (May/June 1983), 92–102.

22 G. Hamel and C. K. Prahalad, "Do You Really Have a Global Strategy?" *Harvard Business Review* (July/August 1985), 139–48.

23 T. Hout, M. E. Porter, and E. Rudden, "How Global Companies Win Out," *Harvard Business Review* (September/October 1982), 98–108.

24 B. Kogut, "Designing Global Strategies: Profiling from Operational Flexibility," *Sloan Management Review* (fall 1985), 27–38.

25 Kevin Done, "Nissan to Export Spanish 4WD Vehicles to Japan," *Financial Times* (March 3, 1993), 7.

26 C. Y. Woo and K. O. Cool, "The Impact of Strategic Management and Strategic Risk," Mimeo, Krannert Graduate School of Management, Purdue University, West Lafayette, Indiana, 1985.

27 A. L. Calvet, "A Synthesis of Foreign Direct Investment Theories and Theories of the Multinational Firm," *Journal of International Business Studies* (spring/summer 1981), 43–60.

28 C. A. Barlett and S. Ghoshal, "The New Global Organization: Differentiated Roles and Dispersed Responsibilities," Working Paper No. 9-786-013, Harvard Business School, Boston, October 1985.

29 M. E. Porter, *Competitive Advantage* (New York: The Free Press, 1985).

30 D. E. Westney, "International Dimensions of Information and Communications Technology," unpublished manuscript (Boston: MIT, Sloan School of Management, 1985).

31 P. Lorange, M. S. Scott Morton, and S. Ghoshal, *Strategic Control* (St. Paul, MN: West Publishing, 1986).

32 The concepts presented above draw heavily from S. Ghoshal, "Global Strategy: An Organizing Framework," *Strategic Management Journal* 8 (1987), 425–40.

33 Yvan Allaire and Milaela E. Firsirotu, "Coping with Strategic Uncertainty," *Sloan Management Review* 30, no. 3 (spring 1989), 7–16.

34 M. E. Naylor, "Planning for Uncertainty: The Scenario—Strategy Matrix," in *The Strategic Management Handbook*, ed. K. J. Albert (New York: McGraw-Hill, 1983).

35 Ian Gillespie, "The IBM Story," quoted in Hanns Ostmeier, Summary of Conference on Standardizing International Entry Positioning and Distribution Strategies, cosponsored by The Marketing Science Institute and the European Institute for Advanced Studies in Management, Brussels, October 27 and 28, 1986.

36 James Brian Quinn, Thomas L. Doorley, and Penny C. Paquette, "Technology in Services: Rethinking Strategic Focus," *Sloan Management Review* 31, no. 2 (winter 1990), 79–87.

37 J. B. Quinn, *Honda Motor Company* (Hanover, NH: The Tuck School at Dartmouth, 1986).

38 Piero Telesio, "Foreign Licensing in Multinational Enterprises," in *Technology Crossing Borders: The Choice, Transfer and Management of International Technology Flows*, ed. Robert Stobaugh and Louis T. Wells, Jr. (Boston, MA: Harvard Business School Press, 1984).

39 Narendra K. Sethi, Bert Movsesian, and Kirk D. Hickey, "Can Technology Be Managed Strategically?" *Long Range Planning* 18, no. 4 (1985), 96.

40 Noel Capon and Rashi Glazer, "Marketing and Technology: A Strategic Co-alignment," Working Paper Report No. 86-106, Marketing Science Institute, Cambridge, Massachusetts, July 1986.

41 "Are Europe's Companies Becoming More European?" *The Economist* (June 27, 1987), 65–66.

42 "Japanese in Europe: Circle the Quality," *The Economist* (April 15, 1989), 74.

43 "The Stubborn Stains of Nationalism," *The Economist* (October 22, 1988), 69–70.

44 James M. Higgins and Tuico Santalainen, "Strategies for Europe 1992," *Business Horizons* (July/August 1989), 54–58.

45 Thomas F. Gross, "Europe 1992: American Firms Blaze the Hottest Frontier," *Management Review* (September 1989), 24–29.

Winning in Global Markets*

ROSABETH MOSS KANTER

Whenever you fly on an airplane, you are experiencing the world's most globalized environment—even if you never leave your own country.

Consider the components of the airline industry: a world fleet of aircraft whose numbers and exact locations are almost always known. Manufactured by a handful of giants such as Boeing, Lockheed, or Airbus. Financed by one of the few world leasing groups such as Guinness Peat Aviation in Ireland. Virtually identical interiors, regardless of the carrier's name on the exterior. World safety standards and a world air traffic control system using English as the common language. A work force with universal training determined by the technology of the plane that can deploy its knowledge over many employers of many nationalities. International agreements covering everything from route structures to baggage liabilities. Reservations and ticketing by computer, making it possible to go nearly anywhere on nearly any combination of carriers on a single ticket.

Air travel also stirs chauvinistic political sentiments, reflecting another aspect of globalization: the anxiety it arouses. National pride, concerns about sovereignty, and local economic interests encourage countries to subsidize flagship airlines or set rules that favor their own carriers.

What the automobile did to promote suburbanization, the jet airplane did to promote globalization. It makes places more similar as they become more accessible. From 1960 to 1988 the real cost of international travel dropped nearly 60 percent. In the United States alone during the same period, the number of foreigners entering on business rose by 2,800 percent.[1] In early 1995, the World Travel and Tourism Council, a global coalition of CEOs of seventy leading travel-related companies—from aircraft manufacturers to hotels—claimed that this industry cluster, including products for travel and services purchased by travelers, would produce 10.5 percent of 1995's total U.S. GDP.

The airport duty-free shopping area was the first global shopping center. Featuring brand-name items known around the world as well as a few local products, it is almost a prototype for today's enclosed shopping mall. Indeed, the British Airport Authority has developed Pittsburgh Airport into a shopping area so attractive that local nontravelers come to spend the day.

Is the world becoming a global shopping mall? For more affluent economic groups a similar array of choices is becoming available. Take teenage boys as a world consumer segment. My teenage son, Matthew, has gone on outings with peers in Rome, São Paulo, Manila, and Jakarta to experience local culture. In each city he visited a local shopping mall, where the boys—all wearing Levi's—played video games and ate a McDonald's hamburger.

Whether or not the world is becoming a global shopping mall, many believe that it *should* be. Some Americans fervently proclaim their desire to put quality first in their purchases and products from anywhere available without restriction, arguing against "Buy American" marketing campaigns as though the "right to shop" is one of the freedoms guaranteed by the Constitution. Political shifts toward democracy and free market systems throughout the world can be understood as choice-led revolutions in a search for the best of competing goods and services. A Hungarian economic minister's wife impressed a group of American leaders at a dinner I attended by giving a better explanation than her husband for the fall of communism in Eastern Europe. While he invoked oil prices, trade relations, and monetary policy, she said simply, "My friends and I wanted to go shopping." Transformations in Eastern Europe seem to have been fueled by people's desire to buy rather than their desire to vote, by dreams of purchasing rather than dreams of participating.

Actual cross-border shopping is common only in certain border towns, such as Bellingham, Washington, just north of Seattle, whose biggest industry is retailing, serving Canadian shoppers. Or at world crossroads, such as Miami. The big shopping centers of Miami report that between 35 and 45 percent of purchases are made by foreign visitors who come with empty bags and leave with full ones, according to Miami airport officials. Dadeland Shopping Center across from a large hotel earns almost half its revenues from Latin American visitors who come to see their doctor, visit their kids in American schools, and buy consumer goods. In California, Japanese tourists can be found buying Japanese electronic devices because they are cheaper in the United States. Business travelers also shop across borders, such as the Scottish executive I met in Glasgow who lives down the road from the distillery making his favorite Scotch whiskey but buys it in airport duty-free shops.

The global shopping mall is becoming a reality because people everywhere want to purchase the world's best without leaving home. They are demanding that producers for the home market meet higher standards, using their knowledge of what's available elsewhere and their theoretical access to it to push for more choices.

THE FOUR PROCESSES OF GLOBALIZATION

Globalization is a process of change stemming from a combination of increasing cross-border activity and information technology enabling virtually instantaneous communication worldwide. And it promises to give everyone everywhere access to the world's best.

Four broad processes are associated with globalization: mobility, simultaneity, bypass, and pluralism. Together they help put more choices in the hands of individual consumers and organizational customers, which, in turn, generates a "globalization cascade"—mutually reinforcing feedback loops that strengthen and accelerate globalizing forces. Two phenomena occur simultaneously: the regulated are getting deregulated (which loosens political control), while the unorganized are getting organized (which increases industry coordination).

PROCESS #1: MOBILITY—CAPITAL, PEOPLE, IDEAS

Key business ingredients such as capital, labor, and ideas are increasingly mobile. Not only do investors have the world to choose from, but information technology makes it

"Bypass" first referred to the rise of private switching networks that went around American regional telephone operating companies' wires. Now wireless networks such as cellular and satellite systems bypass land-wire systems altogether. Companies establish their own networks more easily. By 1994 the number of leased international telephone lines for private communication networks more than doubled from 17,000 in 1988. Texas Instruments' fifty worldwide facilities can beam messages to each other via eight leased satellite channels.[9]

Bypass implies numerous alternative routes to reach and serve customers. As these routes multiply and customers are able to choose among them, dominating particular channels is no longer a long-term advantage. For example, the rise of world overnight package delivery services bypasses government postal services. So does the fax machine. Some electronic funds transfers bypass central banks. In transactions never appearing on balance of trade reports, Texas Instruments "imports" software used to design semiconductors via satellite from its Bangalore, India, software facility.[10] Japanese subscribers to mail-order catalogs find an increasing number of brochures mailed from Hong Kong; Japanese companies save 20–30 percent on postage costs by sending bulk mail outside for remailing back to Japan, bypassing Japan's expensive postal service monopoly.[11]

Consider the literal multiplication of television channels: from the original 3 national broadcast networks in the United States to over 62 national and 9 regional cable networks—and still more programming originating from 1,100 local cable systems. Or the development of alternatives for buying computers: from dealing directly with a company's in-house sales force to computer stores to direct mail, when Dell Computer bypassed even the stores by selling computers by catalog. Retail trade in general is also evolving channels, from small neighborhood shops to large department stores to discounters to warehouse clubs to catalogs to home shopping.

Entrepreneurs change the nature of industries through bypass, finding or creating new routes outside of established channels. Ruth Owades founded Calyx & Corolla to sell fresh flowers by catalog, thereby going around Florists Telegraph Delivery, the network that permitted local florists to fulfill orders for one another around the United States. Calyx & Corolla is an attractive alternative built around an alternative network, a partnership between Owades's company, a score of leading growers, and Federal Express (itself a classic example of bypass), which guarantees overnight delivery of flowers picked to order.

The wealthy have always had ways to bypass inadequate or inconvenient public systems, such as private schools, private transportation (their own planes), or discreet private banks in other countries. When regulations are loosened or affluence grows, some private systems become more widely accessible. An air charter service on Martha's Vineyard and Nantucket became a scheduled short-hop airline; some private schools are becoming "charter schools," receiving Massachusetts education funds to experiment with alternatives on behalf of the public.

Newer channels are not run by old-style government-backed monopolies. They are more universal, less place specific; they can be tapped into from anywhere. And many of them coexist.

PROCESS #4: PLURALISM—"THE CENTER CANNOT HOLD"

The fourth process associated with globalization is the relative decline of monopolistic "centers" once activities concentrated in few places disperse to multiple centers of expertise and influence.

"The center cannot hold," predicted Irish poet William Butler Yeats. Throughout the world, centers are being decentralized. While Hollywood is still the film capital, there are now important studios for MGM, Disney, and Universal in Orlando, Florida, and Miami is taking film business from Orlando. Detroit, once the most powerful determinant of automotive standards in the world, housing the three American giants that had emerged after industry consolidation following World War II, had to learn to share power with Japan. The U.S. portion of world car production dropped from 18.4 percent in 1982 to 15.3 percent in 1992, bouncing back to 16.9 percent in 1993; within the United States, Michigan now shares the distinction of housing North American headquarters for auto companies with Tennessee, Ohio, and South Carolina. New York City as a world financial capital has been joined by Tokyo and London, and Boston is a leader in new financial services such as mutual funds. High-tech research and innovation has spread from Northern California and Boston's Route 128 to many other U.S. and world locations. And the share of U.S. patents issued to foreigners increased from 38 percent in 1980 to 47 percent in 1990, although U.S. companies are on the comeback trail, with the foreign share decreasing to 45 percent in 1993.

Traditional centers often still thrive as directors of the action and its main beneficiaries, even while activities disperse elsewhere. But their automatic dominance or power to shape events declines when expertise and influence spread. As President Clinton discovered, the role of "Superpower" is difficult to sustain when other nations have become strong in their own right, pursue independent paths, and recognize that they have alternatives. European allies felt no compulsion to follow America's lead on Bosnia. China could refuse to bend to U.S. pressure on human rights because Japan and Europe are alternative sources of foreign investment and technology.

Within countries, giants that enjoyed favored and protected status as "national champions," especially government-owned enterprises, are being privatized, broken up, or opened to competition. In the United States, AT&T, broken up in 1983, is joined as a telecommunications giant not only by new rivals in long-distance service, but by its seven former children, which are now powerful industry forces in their own right. AT&T is still strong, with excellent performance and a bright future. But it is no longer virtually alone.

"The center cannot hold" with respect to corporate headquarters, too. Pluralism is reflected in the breakup and dispersion of corporate headquarters functions and the creation of centers of excellence in many parts of the world. In 1990 IBM broke up Armonk's monopoly by transferring 120 executives and the headquarters of its $10 billion communications business from suburban New York to Europe. Hewlett-Packard, whose strong performance made it the world's third largest computer company by 1993, has its corporate headquarters in Palo Alto, California, but its world center for medical equipment in Boston; for personal computer business in Grenoble, France; for fiber-optic research in Germany; for computer-aided engineering software development in Australia; and for laser printers in Singapore. Asea Brown Boveri, a $25 billion company that competes effectively with General Electric and is often heralded as the model for the new "federated" organization, has a small headquarters with one hundred people in Zurich and runs the rest of its worldwide business and staff functions from wherever key executives are located, reporting results in U.S. dollars and using English as its official language. CEO Percy Barnevik calls his office at headquarters the place "where my mail arrives before the important letters are faxed to wherever I happen to be."[12]

Products increasingly reflect linkages among many organizations in many parts of the world. Take Jhane Barnes, a New York menswear designer. The collection one season was designed in New York; wool from Australian sheep was woven into suit fabric in a Japanese textile factory using a spinning technique invented in Italy; cotton from Brazil and Peru and special fabrics from Finland were found for shirts; buttons and linings were made in Italy; the final items were tailored in Hong Kong and Italy; and the advertising campaign was directed from New York.[13] Similarly, Mazda's MX-5 Miata was designed in California, financed from Tokyo and New York, created in prototype in Worthing, England, and assembled in Michigan and Mexico using advanced electronic components invented in New Jersey and fabricated in Japan. To catalog part of the Helsinki Library, the information service company Saztec microfilmed the card catalog in Helsinki, then did partial data entry in Manila, computer formatting in Sydney, Australia, database searching for full entries in Toronto, conversion to the Finnish catalog system in Dayton, Ohio, and final checking in London.[14]

THINK LIKE THE CUSTOMER: THE GLOBAL BUSINESS LOGIC

Among many now discredited ideas of the industrial economy is the theory that power comes from control over the means of production. In the global information economy, power comes from influence over consumption. As mobility and alternatives give customers more choices, power shifts from those producing goods and services to those buying them.

Pick an industry. Computers? Manufacturers once told customers what to buy and charged a premium for it. Now hardware is a commodity, and the hot growth area is software, an industry in which customers tell producers what to make. Pharmaceuticals? Drug companies were once darlings of the American stock market for surefire profits, with "detail men" telling physicians what to prescribe and hospital pharmacies carrying out the orders. Now hospital chains, hospital purchasing cooperatives, and health maintenance organizations tell the drug industry what prices they are willing to pay and how they want products delivered. Retailing? Food manufacturers in North America once told grocery stores when they needed to reorder the brands their advertising made consumers crave. Now supermarkets equipped with scanners have real-time information about consumer preferences and tell manufacturers when to produce and ship.

Customer power derives from industry consolidation and networking, which join smaller players to create big clout. It stems from increased competition and channel proliferation, which give customers the power of choice. It is based on easily accessible information, which increases customer knowledge and sophistication. World standard setters and databases give customers information to compare suppliers across regions and countries. ISO 9000, a European process assurance standard from the International Organization for Standardization, is a de facto world minimum standard, sometimes called an international visa for quality. America's Baldrige Award criteria for business excellence are used in many countries.

As globalization of markets increases customers' choices, those who supply them must move from thinking like producers to thinking like customers. "Producer" logic differs from "customer" logic in fundamental ways.

Producers think they are making products. Customers think they are buying services. From a customer's standpoint, a product is nothing more than a tangible means for getting a service performed.

In addition to the primary use, customers want more services delivered along with particular goods.

In a customer-centered world, industries are defined by patterns of consumption or similarities of use, not by patterns of production. Visionary companies are reaching across industry lines to create future technology: C&C (computers and communication) for NEC of Japan; IM&M (information movement and management) for AT&T. Competing in the computer systems integration business are hardware manufacturers (like IBM), software developers (such as Oracle), and spinoffs of accounting firms (Andersen Consulting).

Producers want to maximize return on the resources they own. Customers care about whether resources are applied for their benefit, not who owns them. By most financial measures, producers are successful when they can extend the value of their investment in tools, capabilities, facilities, people, or products they already possess. They want to sell more of what they already have the capacity to make. But customers do not necessarily care about the ownership of particular resources; they want the best resources pulled together from any source that will meet their needs.

If company A's widget works better in combination with company B's gasket, why should customers be forced to take only what company A offers? If company A wants to keep its widget customers, it might be compelled to stop pushing its own gaskets and form an alliance with company B to offer customers a joint system. This shift of logic leads companies toward greater flexibility: less ownership of fixed capacity, including its own captive parts and service suppliers, and more partnering with other companies to meet the needs of particular customers.

Producers worry about visible mistakes. Customers are lost because of invisible mistakes. Producers want smooth, error-free processes. Customers want to have their problems solved and dreams fulfilled.

Some companies worship at the quality altar, hoping that zero defects will guarantee business salvation. But during the past decade, quality programs have been criticized for being too narrowly producer oriented, focusing merely on reducing the costs of visible mistakes. Farsighted managers now worry more about invisible mistakes—failing to take risks, failing to innovate to create new value for customers.

In a sense, every business today, not just those in the garment trade, is a "fashion" business. To compete effectively, companies must innovate continually and in ever shorter cycles. Keeping customers as well as attracting new ones requires constantly offering new and better products, with design innovations based on new technologies. To be truly customer oriented, managers must be concerned about what they do not yet see. Where there is a customer wish but no way yet to fulfill it, there is an opportunity for innovation. Fulfill it yourself, or someone else will. Surrounding every business are both invisible opportunities—customers' hopes and dreams—and invisible enemies—new companies outside the country or outside the industry possessing capabilities better able to fulfill those hopes.

Producers think their technologies create products. Customers think their needs create products. Producers believe they are market oriented when they ask customers their opinions of products that already exist. Customers think companies are market oriented when they themselves set priorities for design.

Companies sometimes find it hard to take customer needs seriously even when they try. In a leading computer company trying to move from pushing specific products to offering total system solutions, a senior executive said, "If customers don't like our solutions, they must have the wrong problems." In contrast, successful technology companies increasingly let customer needs and desires guide product design, turning customer questions into immediate improvements and agendas for the next innovation.

Some companies try to get everyone involved in customer-centered innovation. Because Ocean Spray asked its employees to be idea scouts, inviting them to regular product development forums, the company scored several important wins with customers. It was the first juice producer in the United States to use innovative packaging technology—the paper bottle—from Tetrapak of Sweden.

Producers organize for internal managerial convenience. Customers want their convenience to come first. In producer logic, managerial considerations are paramount: organizing functions, describing jobs, or controlling systems. What makes a company manageable, however, might detract from serving the customer. For example, from a producer standpoint, uniformity and standardization are easiest to manage. But customers want variety and customization. When a company serving world markets from London closes its switchboards at five o'clock Greenwich mean time, international customers cannot ask questions or make appointments during their own workday. Whose needs are being met, the customers' or the company's? After all, if every product is really a service, then every contact or communication with customers is also the product.

Thinking like the customer requires companies to develop an abundant stock of the three primary assets for global success: *concepts*—the guiding premises behind the company's work, including leading-edge ideas, designs, or formulations for products or services that create value for their customers; *competence*—the ability to execute to the highest-quality standards, to run routine production effectively, as ideas are translated into applications for customers; and *connections*—close relationships with partners that can augment resources, join in creating still more value for customers, or simply open doors and widen horizons. Possession of these three C's make companies and people world class. They are the basis for business excellence.[15]

Unlike tangible assets tied to particular places—facilities, equipment, product inventory—these intangible resources are portable and fluid. They decline in value rapidly if not replenished constantly. Therefore world class companies are more *entrepreneurial*, continuously seeking even better concepts, investing in customer-driven innovation. They are more *learning oriented*, searching for ideas and experience through informal inquisitiveness as well as formal education, holding their staffs to a high performance standard, and investing in their people's knowledge and skills. And they are more *collaborative*, valuing relationships and willing to work closely with other companies as their partners in achieving a common objective.

PROGRAMMING SUCCESS THROUGH CONCEPTS, COMPETENCE, AND CONNECTIONS: THE POWERSOFT CASE

Information technology is one of the prime movers of the global economy, helping to create the global shopping mall. And computer software is one of the fastest-growing occupations for the future. Software is also one of those boundary-blurring categories: classified with service industries yet manufacturing packaged products. It is no surprise, then, that a Boston-area software company illustrates how companies respond to the new global logic by embedding the three C's in their business practice.

Powersoft's roots are in a computer programming service bureau started in the 1970s by Mitchell Kertzman, a Brandeis University dropout and radio disc jockey. But its blossoming is more recent, stemming from the decoupling of software from hardware that created explosive growth in the American software industry. Kertzman transformed his service bureau in the 1980s into a producer of manufacturing automation software. It received its first $150,000 state venture capital investment in 1983 when sales were still under $1 million.

Kertzman soon saw that mainframe computers would be bypassed and that networking tools were the wave of the future. In 1987 Powersoft researched the requirements of its manufacturing customers and saw that they shared the same need Powersoft had: for tools for developing and managing software. Kertzman found David Litwack, former head of R&D for Cullinet, a large mainframe software company in the area, who had a business plan to try to develop the software. Both had grown up in the same part of Boston. Powersoft funded the development of Litwack's tools and then rebuilt its own product using them. Litwack is now Powersoft's president, Kertzman chairman and CEO. Kertzman also chairs the Massachusetts Software Council.

Powersoft has grown rapidly since the 1990 launch of its PowerBuilder client/server software tools that allow programmers to link independent computers. In 1993 Powersoft introduced PowerViewer and PowerMaker; issued its first public stock offering; and earned $8 million on sales of $51 million, up from $3.5 million on $20 million in sales in 1992. In 1994 Powersoft outgrew its facility in Burlington, Massachusetts, one of the "edge cities" near Boston housing high-technology firms, moving into a former Digital Equipment building a few stops away on Route 128. This move was fraught with symbolism: a small software innovator replacing a downsizing hardware giant. Then, in November 1994, Powersoft announced its intention to merge with Sybase, forming the world's seventh-largest software company and one of the largest in the client/server field.

CONCEPTS: SETTING WORLD STANDARDS

Powersoft's goal is innovation on a world scale derived from the understanding of customer needs. Ever shorter lead times in the software industry mean that only the best survive; Powersoft's competitive edge comes from setting world standards for its category. "Technology is a global business," Kertzman said. "We must get critical mass around the world faster and faster to become a standard. Competitive leads last a very short time. The minute you poke your head out in the leadership position, everybody is after you."

Having a significant amount of international business is thus a necessity even to sell products at home. Leadership in software must be world leadership, and corporate customers using Powersoft tools must be supported wherever they are. Powersoft sold overseas as soon as PowerBuilder was ready. Four years later Powersoft had distribution joint ventures in forty-four countries and had just released the Kanji edition of PowerBuilder in Japan. Early in 1994 Powersoft acquired Watcom International Corporation of Waterloo, Ontario, Canada. Powersoft's European headquarters is in Berkshire, England. In 1992 it opened a customer service and support center in London, then in June 1994 acquired some of its European distributorships, established service and support centers in Paris and Brussels, and planned Pacific Rim offices.

But success today, gone tomorrow. In an industry characterized by cutthroat competition and a blinding speed of change, the company needs constant innovation. "This is war, make no mistake about it," a Powersoft executive observed. Formidable competitors include Gupta, Oracle, Sybase, Knowledgware, Microsoft, and "the competition du jour"—emerging companies going after Powersoft's niches. American companies dominate software now, but Kertzman watches the rest of the world; Japan has targeted the software industry.

Powersoft has to be entrepreneurial, innovating constantly. Its leaders wanted to be the first to bring manufacturing systems to a new platform. Kertzman still seeks the "next bench"—something new that will be needed in the future. "Every time we do a new release," he said, "we must redefine the category."

Innovation comes from listening to customers and empowering associates to act on what they hear. A senior manager reported: "Our developers are dedicated to developing a product which is exactly what our customers want. The customer service organization is one of the things that differentiates us from our main competition and makes us head and shoulders above the rest: how we leverage technology to make things easier for our customer and get them the information they need to be successful." Customer relations specialists listen to customer questions, make spot changes for those customers, and then incorporate the ideas into long-term technical plans. At "Q review" sessions they tear apart customers' questions and give the findings to management and product designers as the basis for further innovation.

Powersoft tools are customer friendly. PowerBuilder, for example, is easily understood by traditional mainframe MIS programmers. They do not have to learn a new language; Powersoft software is graphical and intuitive. The benefit for customers is that they can use their existing programmers, who were generally hired to manage a system, not create a new one. "The artists coming out of graduate schools who can create new systems are very good, very smart, but they cost a lot of money and they take a lot of time to get things done," Kertzman says. "Our tools let mainstream banks and corporations get productivity out of the programmers they have."

COMPETENCE: INVESTING IN LEARNING

Rapid technological change poses a challenge: how to ensure that new knowledge constantly enters the organization and that people have skills for both today's and tomorrow's work. Without new knowledge, the company falls behind. Without encouragement for the current work force to learn, employees become obsolete with each new technological wave.

A low attrition rate at Powersoft is attributed to hiring "only the best" through a rigorous process including interviews by at least six people and family visits to the company. One professional previously with a computer hardware company claimed that Powersoft's strength as a place to work is its "interesting, motivated, highly intelligent people. Hopefully I'm interesting, intelligent, and highly motivated myself!" Human resource vice president Traci Weaver urges managers not to hire out of desperation when rapid growth makes them hungry for people, but to maintain standards for excellence. Powersoft's training commitments include about three weeks a year of technical training for everyone and extra courses for managers; additional learning is encouraged by a full tuition reimbursement program. "Training is part of the culture," Weaver said. So is cosmopolitanism. Powersoft hires engineers of diverse national origins, the older ones with international experience; participants in my focus groups say they have their pick of the world's best places but chose the Boston area and Powersoft.

Coleman Sisson, vice president of customer services, sees a direct connection between Powersoft's culture of caring for people and its ability to satisfy customers. "A lot of companies say that customer satisfaction is their number one goal. Of course it is. Can you imagine 'customer dissatisfaction' being the number one goal? That's obvious. But I think if you want to achieve satisfaction, you should focus on satisfying your employees. Because if you do that, they are the ones who are going to talk to the customers anyway. I'm not. Not five thousand customers a day." Employees report that Sisson responds to comments and criticisms about Powersoft products on the Internet, giving people his direct call-in number.

Similarly, Kertzman and other top executives are lauded by workers for their friendliness, accessibility, and interest in their ideas, which encourages initiative. "If you have an idea and they like it," one associate said, "they'll suggest that you write it up so you get credit." Rewarding enterprising employees with the chance to move their ideas into action, and get recognized for this, is characteristic of high-innovation, learning-oriented companies.

Powersoft gives people abundant information and the tools to succeed at their jobs. Education is a daily process, as folders of competitive intelligence are passed around the company. An engineer praised the support he gets. "Our computers are top of the line, the fastest available," he said. "If we need CD-ROM drives, we get CD-ROM drives; it's never a question. If you need it, you get it. Whenever we're exploring problems, if it involves a third-party software package, we just go get it. You don't have the excuse of not having the tool to get the job done."

Powersoft people have to become multiskilled experts who understand all their customers' needs, supporting customers that use other multiple-application software. High-innovation companies are known for giving people broad jobs that cut across territories. "It is not sufficient to be able to service just your own product; you must be able to help customers with all of their interfacing products," a systems engineer said. "When customers call our support line and the problem involves another piece of software or includes hardware, we don't say it's not our problem. We help them solve it."

CONNECTIONS: CASUAL COLLABORATIONS TO THE LOTUS KEIRETSU

With under eight hundred people, Powersoft is far from a giant, but its reach is vast. Powersoft's partnership network mushrooms to include tens of thousands of people working in its interest; for example, thirteen thousand developers received PowerBuilder training in 1993 and serve as extended family. In an industry characterized by dense ties, Powersoft's emphasis on relationships stands out; it has a department to manage relationships, guided by an executive for alliances.

Multiple advantages come from a major relationship with Lotus Development, one of the world's major software companies, a short drive away in Cambridge. Powersoft has enough Lotus connections for Kertzman to dub Powersoft part of the "Lotus keiretsu," in a comparison with Japanese business networks. A former Lotus marketing head serves on Powersoft's board, and Powersoft shares manufacturing space with Lotus.

Having consolidated manufacturing just outside of Boston, closing a facility in Puerto Rico, Lotus had some downtime in the local facility. A new Powersoft employee formerly with Lotus told operations director Peter Barker about this. Coincidentally, Powersoft was not happy with the company it used to duplicate, package, and ship its software. Barker made a call to Lotus mostly as a courtesy but discovered a significant opportunity. Lotus liked the idea of converting manufacturing to a profit center earning revenues from outside; the Powersoft deal would also help ensure that the facility could produce steadily.

Now Powersoft gets cost savings, access to innovation, and a set of relationships that lead to still other opportunities. Combining Lotus and Powersoft raw material purchasing provides savings to both companies. Powersoft reduces other costs by piggybacking on Lotus relationships. Lotus is the second-largest regional user of Federal Express shipping after L. L. Bean, and Powersoft gets the benefits of Lotus's high-volume discount with Federal Express. Powersoft uses Lotus packaging advances, because it is easier for Lotus to manufacture more of its own boxes than to change setups for Powersoft. The industry standard is cardboard packaging that costs from $11 to $13 per software box. Lotus developed a different kind of packaging out of corrugated paper, more functional and only $.85 a box. Powersoft saves over $10 a package because of the Lotus connection.

Barker calls the relationship synergistic: each company teaches the other. For example, Powersoft is developing the PowerBuilder Library for Lotus Notes, extending the reach of Lotus databases into mainstream corporate and commercial application development. But the Lotus product development agreement is only one example among hundreds. External collaboration is rampant at Powersoft. Powersoft's products are more appealing when they can interact with others' products, and Powersoft's reach is greater when it can tap into many distribution and support networks. As users want more services and applications, it becomes less likely that any one company can provide all of them.

For *development*, Powersoft has two hundred CODE partnerships ("client/server open development environment") with complementary companies to integrate its tools with other programs. The biggest names in computing—IBM, Digital, Novell, Hewlett-Packard, Microsoft, Oracle, and Knowledgware—are partners as well as competitors; Sybase is a development partner, competitor, and Powersoft's new corporate parent. Other CODE partners range from Texas Instruments to a former Burlington neighbor, Bachman.

Relationships are both cooperative and wary. "Microsoft in Utah and Sybase and Oracle in California helped make us famous" as tools vendors, according to Bill Critch, director of alliances and business development. "We were small and neutral, the Switzerland of our field. But as we get larger we're a competitive threat."

For *marketing*, Powersoft has partnerships with almost one hundred resellers, companies affectionately known as "power channels"—consultants, systems integrators, and project developers in the client server industry, which together account for 55 percent of its North American sales. Marketing partners include large systems integrators such as the Big Six accounting firms, the consulting organizations of IBM, Digital, EDS, and Perot Systems, and independent software vendors such as Dun & Bradstreet, which has six hundred developers working on PowerBuilder applications. AT&T includes PowerBuilder with other tools to its customers. Thirty of sixty customer training partners also sell Powersoft products.

Some relationships have multiple dimensions, such as Powersoft's international technology and marketing alliance with Attachmate, a leader in networking software and a neighbor of Microsoft in the Seattle area with 1994 revenues of $391 million. Attachmate launched a cooperatively developed product, EXTRA! Tools for PowerBuilder, which enables corporate developers using mainframes to integrate data quickly and easily into applications created with PowerBuilder, opening a large new market for Powersoft tools.

These relationships are delicate balancing acts. To work with so many competing companies, Powersoft has to help each feel it is gaining an edge against other competitors by investing in Powersoft programs. To avoid conflicts between resellers and Powersoft's own sales force, Powersoft representatives are considered territory managers, compensated in terms of total sales even if resellers close the deal. And particular relationships wax and wane in importance as technology changes. But Powersoft's connections are one of its major assets; the company could not succeed without them.

INNOVATORS FOR THE GLOBAL SHOPPING MALL

The processes of globalization come to life in companies of the future like Powersoft: mobile people and ideas, technologies for simultaneous use worldwide, new information channels that bypass stand-alone mainframes and offer tools for new computer links to form, and a flexible network of pluralistic partnerships instead of a single powerful hierarchy.

Companies fit to win in global markets share an emphasis on innovation, learning, and collaboration. They

- *organize around customer logic:* rapidly feed customer needs and desires into new product and service concepts and transform the overall concept of the business when technologies and markets shift;
- *set high goals:* try to be the world standard setter in the niches they pursue and seek to "re-define the category" with each new offering;
- *select people who are broad, creative thinkers:* define their jobs broadly rather than narrowly, encourage them to become multiskilled at working across territories, and give them the best tools for those jobs;
- *encourage enterprise:* empower people to seek new product and service concepts, let them act on their ideas, and provide abundant recognition for initiative;
- *support constant learning:* circulate information widely, track competitors and innovators throughout the world, measure themselves against world quality standards, and offer continual training to keep everyone's knowledge current;
- *collaborate with partners:* combine the best of their own and their partners' expertise for customized customer applications.

Their cultures combine apparent opposites: tough standards with caring for people, an emphasis on proprietary innovations with an ability to share with partners. And their principal assets are the three C's: concepts, competence, and connections, which they continually nurture and replenish.

Companies like these are creating the global shopping mall of the future. And in the process of globalization, they become world class: focused outward rather than inward, steeped in the latest knowledge, and comfortable operating across the boundaries of function, industry, company, community, or country.

In addition to direct interviews and the references, statistics have been compiled from industry associations such as the Food Marketing Institute and cable television trade associations, company records, automotive industry tracking services such as *Ward's*, and United Nations and U.S. government publications that regularly report industry statistics, such as *Statistical Abstracts of the United States*.

References

[1] William B. Johnston, "Global Work Force 2000: The New World Labor Market," *Harvard Business Review*, vol. 69, March–April 1991, pp. 115–27.

[2] Joel Kurtzman, *The Death of Money*, New York: Simon & Schuster, 1993.

[3] Josh Hyatt, "DEC pays $45,000 in wages, fines," *Boston Globe*, January 11, 1994.

[4] Johnston, "Global Work Force 2000."

[5] *Chronicle of Higher Education Almanac* for 1993.

[6] John Maxwell Hamilton, "Keeping Up with Information: On Line in the Philippines and London," in Rosabeth Moss Kanter, Barry A. Stein, and Todd D. Jick, *The Challenge of Organizational Change*, New York: Free Press, 1992, pp. 108–24.

[7] Kenichi Ohmae, "Managing in a Borderless World," *Harvard Business Review*, vol. 67, May–June 1989.

[8] The Food Marketing Institute referred us to several research services in the United States and Britain that confirmed this impression and offered to go shopping in a few dozen countries for a hefty fee in order to prove it.

[9] Hamilton, "Keeping Up with Information."

[10] *Ibid.*

[11] Emiko Terazono, "Hong Kong Stamps on Japan's Postal Pride," *Financial Times*, November 2, 1994, p. 7.

[12] William Taylor, "The Logic of Global Business: An Interview with ABB's Barnevik," *Harvard Business Review*, vol. 69, March–April 1991, pp. 90–105, and in Kanter, Stein, and Jick, *The Challenge of Organizational Change*.

[13] "The Global Suit," *Harvard Business Review*, vol. 69, March–April 1991.

[14] Hamilton, "Keeping Up with Information."

[15] The three C's, and the practices behind them, reflect the underlying vision of business excellence conveyed by the criteria for the U.S. Baldrige National Quality Award. The Baldrige has added considerably to the conventional definition of quality as process assurance, which is only one aspect of operational competence; the award now emphasizes work-force skills and human resource development along with organizational processes. Innovation in customer-driven product and service concepts is stressed in the strategic planning section. Customer and supplier collaboration are highlighted. See *The Malcolm Baldrige National Quality Award 1995 Criteria*, Gaithersburg, Maryland: National Institute of Standards and Technology, 1995.

How Competition for the Future Is Different*

GARY HAMEL AND C. K. PRAHALAD

TOWARD THE FUTURE

We are standing on the verge, and for some it will be the precipice, of a revolution as profound as that which gave birth to modern industry. It will be the environmental revolution, the genetic revolution, the materials revolution, the digital revolution, and, most of all, the information revolution. Entirely new industries, now in their gestation phase, will soon be born. Such prenatal industries include microrobotics—miniature robots built from atomic particles that could, among other things, unclog sclerotic arteries; machine translation—telephone switches and other devices that will provide real-time translation between people conversing in different languages; digital highways into the home that will offer instant access to the world's store of knowledge and entertainment; urban underground automated distribution systems that will reduce traffic congestion; "virtual" meeting rooms that will save people the wear and tear of air travel; biomimetic materials that will duplicate the wondrous properties of materials found in the living world; satellite-based personal communicators that will allow one to "phone home" from anywhere on the planet; machines capable of emotion, inference, and learning that will interact with human beings in entirely new ways; and bioremediation—custom designed organisms—that will help clean up the earth's environment.

Existing industries—education, health care, transportation, banking, publishing, telecommunications, pharmaceuticals, retailing, and others—will be profoundly transformed. Cars with on-board navigation and collision avoidance systems, electronic books and personally tailored multimedia educational curricula, surgeries performed in isolated locales by a remote controlled robot, and disease prevention via gene replacement therapy are just some of the opportunities that are emerging to reshape existing products, services, and industries.

Many of these mega-opportunities represent billions of dollars in potential future revenues. One company has estimated the potential market for information services in the home, via interactive TV, to be worth at least $120 billion per year in 1992 dollars—home video ($11 billion), home catalog shopping ($51 billion), video games ($4 billion), broadcast advertising ($27 billion), other information services ($9 billion), and more.[1] Many of these mega-opportunities have the potential to fundamentally transform the way we live and work, in much the same way that the telephone, car, and airplane transformed twentieth-century lifestyles.

Each of these opportunities is also inherently global. No single nation or region is likely to control all the technologies and skills required to turn these opportunities into reality. Markets will emerge at different speeds around the world, and any firm hoping to establish a leadership role will have to collaborate with and learn from leading-edge customers, technology providers, and suppliers, wherever they're located. Global distribution reach will be necessary to capture the rewards of leadership and fully amortize associated investments.

The future is now. The short term and the long term don't abut one another with a clear line of demarcation five years from now. The short term and long term are tightly intertwined. Although many of tomorrow's mega-opportunities are still in their infancy, companies around the world are, at this moment, competing for the privilege of parenting them. Alliances are being formed, competencies are being assembled, and experiments are being conducted in nascent markets—all in hopes of capturing a share of the world's future opportunities. In this race to the future there are drivers, passengers, and road kill. (*Road kill*, an American turn of phrase, is what becomes of little creatures who cross the highway in the path of an oncoming vehicle.) Passengers will get to the future, but their fate will not be in their own hands. Their profits from the future will be modest at best. Those who drive industry revolution—companies that have a clear, premeditated view of where they want to take their industry and are capable of orchestrating resources inside and outside the company to get there first—will be handsomely rewarded.

Thus, the question of which companies and countries create the future is far from academic. The stakes are high. The wealth of a firm, and of each nation in which it operates, largely depends on its role in creating tomorrow's markets and its ability to capture a disproportionate share of associated revenues and profits.

Perhaps you have visited the Henry Ford Museum at Greenfield Village in Dearborn, Michigan. Although the home of Ford Motor Co.'s world headquarters, Dearborn's additional claim to fame is Greenfield Village and the museum where you can see the industrial history of the United States. The exhibits are a testimony to pioneers who created new industries and revolutionized old ones: Deere, Eastman, Firestone, Bell, Edison, Watson, the Wright brothers, and, of course, Ford. It was the foresight of these pioneers that created the industries that created the unprecedented prosperity that created the American lifestyle. Any visitor strolling through the museum who has enjoyed the material comforts of a middle-class American lifestyle can't help but recognize the enormous debt he or she owes to these industrial pioneers. Similarly, any German citizen owes much to the pioneers who built that country's innovative, globe-spanning chemical companies, world-class machine tool industry, and automakers that set the benchmarks for excellence for nearly a century. The success of Japanese firms in redefining standards of innovation and performance in the electronics and automobile industries propelled Japan from an industrial also-ran into a world economic superpower and paid for all those Waikiki holidays and Louis Vuitton handbags.

Failure to anticipate and participate in the opportunities of the future impoverishes both firms and nations. Witness Europe's concern over its abysmal performance in creating high-wage jobs in new information technology-related businesses, or Japan's worry over the inability of its financial institutions to capture the high ground of innovation and new business creation, or America's anxiety that Japanese companies may steal a march in the commercialization of superconductivity. Even protectionist-minded politicians realize that a nation that can do little more than protect the industries of the past will lose its economic standing to countries that help create the industries of the future.

The future is not an extrapolation of the past. New industrial structures will supersede old industrial structures. Opportunities that at first blush seem evolutionary will prove to be revolutionary. Today's new niche markets will turn out to be tomorrow's mass markets. Today's leading edge science will become tomorrow's household appliance. At one time IBM described the personal computer as an "entry system"—the expectation was that anyone buying a PC would move up to more powerful computers, and that PCs could happily coexist with mainframes. Ten years later, desktop workstations and local client-server computers were displacing mainframes from more and more applications. Although today's wireless telephones—both cellular and cordless—may seem no more than an adjunct to traditional tethered telephones, in ten years all wired phones will likely seem anachronistic. Twenty years ago few observers expected mutual funds to significantly erode the "share of savings" captured by banks and savings and loans. But savers became investors and by 1992, mutual funds in the United States represented 96% of the money that private investors put into the stock market. Mutual funds accounted for 11.4% of total financial assets in the United States, up from only 2.0% in 1975, whereas the share taken by commercial banks and savings and loans fell from 56.2% in 1975 to 37.3% in 1992.[2] Again, there is no way to create the future, no way to profit from the future, if one cannot imagine it.

To compete successfully for the future, senior managers must first understand just how competition for the future is different from competition for the present. The differences are profound. They challenge the traditional perspectives on strategy and competition. We will see that competing for the future requires not only a redefinition of strategy, but also a redefinition of top management's role in creating strategy.

COMPETITION FOR TODAY VERSUS COMPETITION FOR TOMORROW

Pick up a strategy textbook or marketing handbook and the focus will almost certainly be on competition within extant markets. The tools of segmentation analysis, industry structure analysis, and value chain analysis are eminently useful in the context of a clearly defined market, but what help are they when the market doesn't yet exist? Within an existing market most of the rules of competition have already been established: what price-performance trade-offs customers are willing to make, which channels have proved most efficient, the ways in which products or services can be differentiated, and what is the optimal degree of vertical integration. Yet in emerging opportunity arenas like genetically engineered drugs, multimedia publishing, and interactive television, the rules are waiting to be written. (In existing industries, the rules are waiting to be rewritten.) This vastly complicates the business of making strategic choices. So how is the context for strategy-making different when the focus is on tomorrow rather than today, and when there is little or no clarity about industry structure and customer preferences?

MARKET SHARE VERSUS OPPORTUNITY SHARE

Strategy researchers and practitioners have focused much attention on the problem of getting and keeping market share. For most companies, market share is the primary criterion for measuring the strength of a business's strategic position. But what is the meaning of market share in markets that barely exist? How can one maximize market share in an industry where the product or service concept is still underdefined, where customer segments have yet to solidify, and customer preferences are still poorly understood?

Competition for the future is competition for *opportunity share* rather than market share. It is competition to maximize the share of future opportunities a company could potentially access within a broad *opportunity arena*, be that home information systems, genetically engineered drugs, financial services, advanced materials, or something else.

The question that must be answered by every company is, given our current skills, or *competencies* as we will call them, what share of future opportunities are we likely to capture? This question leads to others: Which new competencies would we have to build, and how would our definition of our "served market" have to change, for us to capture a larger share of future opportunities? Whether for a country or a company, the issue is much the same: how to attract and strengthen the skills that form the competencies (e.g., optoelectronics, biomimetics, genetics, systems integration, financial engineering) that provide a gateway to future opportunities.

To gain a disproportionate share of future profits it is necessary to possess a disproportionate share of the requisite competencies. Because such competencies represent the patient and persistent accumulation of intellectual capital rather than a God-given endowment, governments can legitimately play a role in strengthening such competencies (through educational policy, tax incentives, recruitment of inward investment, government-sanctioned private-sector joint ventures, etc.).[3] Singapore, for example, has employed just such means to enhance the range and quality of nationally resident competencies. But to know which competencies to build, policy-makers and corporate strategists must be prescient about the broad shape of tomorrow's opportunities. Top management must be just as obsessed with maximizing opportunity share as with maximizing market share. As we will see, this means a commitment to build competence leadership in new areas, long before the precise form and structure of future markets comes completely into view.

Business Units versus Corporate Competencies

Competition for the future is not product versus product or business versus business, but company versus company—what we term "interfirm competition." This is true for several reasons. First, because future opportunities are unlikely to fit neatly within existing SBU boundaries, competing for the future must be a corporate responsibility, and not just the responsibility of individual business unit heads. (This responsibility may be exercised by a group of corporate officers or, preferably, a cohort of SBU heads working horizontally across the organization.) Second, the competencies needed to access the new opportunity arena may well be spread across a number of business units, and it is up to the corporation to bring these competencies together at the appropriate point within the organization. Third, the investment and timeframe required to build the new competencies necessary to access tomorrow's markets may well tax the resources and patience of a single business unit.

It is important that top managers view the firm as a portfolio of competencies, for they must ask, "Given our particular portfolio of competencies, what opportunities are we uniquely positioned to exploit?" The answer points to opportunity arenas that other firms, with different competence endowments, may find difficult to access. For example, it would be hard to imagine any other firm than Eastman Kodak creating a product like Photo-CD, which required an in-depth understanding of both chemical film and electronic imaging competencies. Canon may understand electronic imaging and Fuji may understand film, but only Kodak had a deep understanding of both.

So the question for top managers is, "How do we orchestrate *all* the resources of the firm to create the future?" This was the question George Fisher faced when he left Motorola to become Kodak's new chief executive. At IBM, Lou Gerstner put together a top team to look for transcendent opportunities. Given IBM's still impressive set of competencies, the question was, "What can we do that other companies might find difficult to do?" Companies like Matsushita and Hewlett-Packard, long champions of bottom-up innovation and business unit autonomy, have recently been searching for opportunities that blend the skills of multiple business units. Even Sony, which has traditionally granted near total autonomy to individual product development teams, has realized that more and more of its products must function as part of complex systems. It has therefore moved to restructure its audio, video, and computer groups for better coordination of new product development.[4]

Creating the future often requires that a company build new core competencies, competencies that typically transcend a single business unit—both in terms of the investment required and the range of potential applications. Within Sharp, for example, it is not up to each business unit to decide how much to invest in perfecting flat screen displays. Sharp competes as a corporation against Toshiba, Casio, and Sony to build world leadership in this area.

The sheer size, scope, and complexity of future opportunities may also require a corporate rather than an individual unit perspective. Mega-opportunities don't yield easily to "skunk works" or undirected entrepreneurship. A lone employee with a bit of free time and access to a small slush fund may create Post-it Notes but is unlikely to bring the interpreting telephone from conception to reality or make much progress on creating a new computing architecture. Consistent, focused competence-building requires something more than "thriving on chaos."

STAND-ALONE VERSUS INTEGRATED SYSTEMS

Most textbooks on the management of innovation and new product development assume that the company controls most of the resources needed for the commercialization of that innovation. Such an assumption is increasingly likely to be wrong. Many of the most exciting new opportunities require the integration of complex systems rather than innovation around a stand-alone product. Not only does no single business unit have all the necessary capabilities, neither does a single company or country. Few companies can create the future single-handedly; most need a helping hand. Motorola, IBM, and Apple banded together to create a new semiconductor-based computer architecture. Hoping to take advantage of the potential convergence between the videogame industry and the telecommunications industry, AT&T has formed partnerships with, or taken small equity stakes in, a number of computer game makers. Even Boeing has often found it necessary to reach out to foreign partners for the development of its next-generation aircraft.

The need to bring together and harmonize widely disparate technologies, to manage a drawn-out standards-setting process, to conclude alliances with the suppliers of complementary products, to co-opt potential rivals, and to access the widest possible array of distribution channels, means that competition is as much a battle between competing and often overlapping coalitions as it is a battle between individual firms. Competition for the future is both intercorporate and intercoalition. As we will see, an understanding of how to put such a coalition together and keep it pointed toward a common future are central to the task of competing for the future.

SPEED VERSUS PERSEVERANCE

Yet another way in which competition for the future is different from competition for the present is the timeframe. Today, speed is of the essence.[5] Product life cycles are getting shorter, development times are getting tighter, and customers expect almost instantaneous service. Yet the relevant timeframe for exploring and conquering a new opportunity arena may be ten years, twenty years, or even longer. AT&T first built a prototype of a videophone in its labs in 1939, first demonstrated a videophone to the public at the New York World's Fair in 1964, and finally introduced a model for home use in 1992, 53 years after its first prototype. And even now, video telephony has yet to become a mass market product. Marc Porat, president and CEO of General Magic, a company that is developing the software for tomorrow's personal communication devices, believes it may take a decade or more to turn his company's vision of intelligent, ubiquitous, mobile personal communications into a reality.[6] Leadership in fundamentally new industries is seldom built in anything less than 10 or 15 years, suggesting that perseverance may be just as important as speed in the battle for the future.

Obviously, no company is likely to persevere for 20 years unless it has a deep, visceral commitment to the particular opportunity. JVC, a subsidiary of Matsushita and the world leader in VCRs, began developing videotape competencies in the late 1950s and early 1960s, yet it wasn't until the late 1970s, nearly 20 years later, that JVC hit the jackpot with its VHS-standard machines. What keeps a company going for this length of time? Just what did JVC see in the VCR, or AT&T in the video telephone, or Apple Computer in the Lisa and then the Macintosh, that compelled them to pick themselves up time and time again when they stumbled on the inevitable hurdles, and keep pressing on toward the finish line? What they saw was the potential to deliver new and profound customer benefits. For JVC, it was the desire to "take control [of program scheduling] away from the broadcasters and give it back to the viewers." An engineer would term this "time-shift," but a technical description of the opportunity dramatically underplays its potential impact on lifestyles. Such commitment was also evident at Apple (making computers user friendly), at Ford in its early years (putting a car in every garage), at Boeing (bringing air travel to the masses), at CNN (providing the news around the clock), and at Wal-Mart (offering friendly service and rock-bottom prices to rural Americans).

Organizational commitment and perseverance are driven by the desire to make a difference in people's lives—the bigger the difference, the deeper the commitment. This suggests another difference between competition for the future and competition for the present, namely, the prospect of making an impact, rather than the certitude of immediate financial returns. In contrast, strategic moves within the confines of existing markets are likely to be predicated on traditional financial analysis. But this is not possible in the early stages of competition for the future. No one in the early 1960s could have produced a meaningful set of pro-formas around the VCR opportunity. By the early 1970s, when one might have legitimately made a stab at developing a business case, it was too late for anyone who had not been working on videotape competencies since the early 1960s to catch up without help from one of the pioneers.

This is not to say that commitment to a new opportunity arena is based solely on gut feeling, or that companies at work to create the future are not hoping for substantial financial rewards. A commitment substantial enough to beget the perseverance required to create the future must be based on something more than a hunch. There are ways of judging the potential impact of a market-creating innovation that may still be many years in the future. Questions to consider might include: How many people will be affected by this innovation? How valuable will they find this innovation? What is the potential scope for the application of this innovation? In the case of the VCR, there were a host of specific indicators one might have considered: How many people had televisions? How fast was the penetration of televisions in the home growing? How many hours did the average person watch television? How often were they away when some potentially interesting program was being broadcast? How often were they forced to choose between two appealing shows broadcast simultaneously? Were there programs they would like to watch more than once? Would they find it more convenient to watch movies at home than at the cinema? Would movie studios and other software providers be willing to release movies not shown on TV as prerecorded software? Might videocameras be attractive to consumers? and so on.

There should be no mushy-headed wishfulness involved in competing for the future. The absence of a business case does not mean that one commits to a whopping great investment in some hair-brained scheme. As we will see, the investment commitments in the early stages of competition for the future may be quite modest; small as they may be, however, the emotional and intellectual commitment to the future needs to be near absolute. Steve Jobs and Steve Wozniak had virtually no money, but their commitment to creating a computer for every "man, woman, and child" was unshakable.

One of President Reagan's favorite stories provides an illustration. Waking up to her tenth birthday, a young farm girl rises before the sun and runs out to the barn, hoping her parents have bought her a pony. She flings open the barn door, but in the dim light can see no pony, just mounds of horse manure. Being an optimist she declares, "With all this manure around, there must be a pony in here somewhere." Similarly, companies that create the future say to themselves, "With all this potential customer benefit, there must be a way to make some money in here somewhere." A company that cannot commit emotionally and intellectually to creating the future, even in the absence of a financially indisputable business case, will almost certainly end up as a follower.

Think of the people who left Europe in the nineteenth century or Asia in the twentieth century to start a new life in the United States. At the outset of their journeys, few immigrants could have foretold exactly when and how they would achieve economic success in the new world, yet they set out for the "land of opportunity" nevertheless. More than that, many of them willingly accepted great hardship during the journey itself. The important point is that the commitment to be a pioneer precedes an exact calculation of financial gain. A company that waits around for the numbers to "add up" will be left flat-footed in the race to the future. Without a clear-eyed view of the ultimate prize, a company is all too likely to abandon the race when unexpected hazards are encountered en route. Nevertheless, as we will emphasize again and again, a company must ultimately find a profitable route to the future.

STRUCTURED VERSUS UNSTRUCTURED ARENAS

We now come to what are the two most important ways in which competition for the future is different from competition for the present: (1) It often takes place in "unstructured" arenas where the rules of competition have yet to be written, and (2) it is more like a triathlon than a 100-meter sprint. We will see that these differences demand a very different way of thinking about strategy and the role of senior management.

Some industries are more "structured" than others, in that the rules of competition are more clear-cut, product concepts better defined, industry boundaries more stable, technology change more predictable, and customer needs more precisely measurable. Unpredictable and turbulent change can come to any industry today (think of how long the three big U.S. television networks dominated their cozy little industry), and new opportunity arenas like genetic engineering are almost universally unstructured. More and more industries, by their very nature, seem to be perpetually underdefined, or even undefinable.

Take the "digital industry." It is not one industry, but a collection of industries that are simultaneously converging and disintegrating.[7] It is an industry that has been around since the invention of the transistor, but is now, more than ever, underdefined. Figure 1 depicts the digital industry, circa 1990. While some firms like AT&T spanned several industry groupings, the industry could be broadly partitioned into seven more or less-distinct components: (1) computer system suppliers (from Compaq to IBM, and Apple to Hewlett-Packard), (2) information technology service companies (EDS, Cap Gemini, Andersen Consulting), (3) companies whose primary interest was in operating systems and application software for computers (Microsoft and Lotus, most notably, but also Novell, Computer Associates, Oracle, and a myriad of smaller companies focused on specific "vertical" markets), (4) the owners and operators of the digital networks that transmit data and voice

F IGURE 1

The Evolving Digital Space

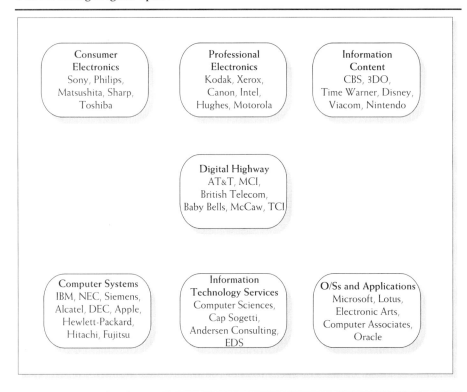

(including AT&T, McCaw, MCI, cable television companies, television and radio broadcasters, and regional telephone operating companies), (5) the providers of information content (Time Warner, Bertelesmann, MCA, Bloomberg Financial Markets, Polygram, Columbia Pictures, Dow-Jones, Reed International, and McGraw-Hill to name a few), (6) the manufacturers of professional electronics gear (Xerox, Canon, Kodak, and Motorola; defense electronics companies like Rockwell; and factory automation equipment manufacturers), and (7) the familiar consumer electronics producers (Sony, Philips, Matsushita, and Samsung among others). In the early 1990s, industry observers, corporate strategists, trade journals, and consultants mapped the digital industry more or less along these lines.

The problem, for any company intent on getting to the future first, is that this is a map of the past and not of the future. For companies looking forward, it had become clear by the early 1990s that the labels used to distinguish among the different components of the digital industry were fast losing their descriptive power. It seemed unlikely that the future digital industry would be usefully partitioned into software versus hardware, computing versus communications, professional versus consumer, content versus conduit, services versus products, and horizontal markets versus vertical markets. Was the Macintosh a hardware or software innovation? How could one call Sharp's Personal Organizer a hardware product when software accounted for the biggest part of its development budget? What about all those hardware companies—Sony, Matsushita, and Toshiba—buying their way into the entertainment software industry? Did it make sense to distinguish between computing and communications when more and more personal computers were using the local telephone network to hook up to Prodigy or CompuServe, or when corporate customers demanded integrated networking of data, voice, and video? What was the distinction between professional versus consumer electronics when Motorola, because of the success of its cellular phones, was compelled to admit that it had become, de facto, a consumer electronics company? And when Time Warner wired homes in Orlando for two-way, interactive video and information services, just where was the dividing line between content and conduit? Pummeled by regulatory changes, advances in digital technology, changes in lifestyles, the raw ambition of companies intent on getting to the future first and those paranoid at the prospect of being left behind, the digital industry seemed to be in a state of permanent turmoil.

The digital industry may be more complex and variegated than most, but it is certainly not unique in the challenges it poses to the traditional tools and methods of strategy analysis. Deregulation, globalization, fundamental breakthroughs in science, and the strategic importance of information technology are blurring boundaries in a wide variety of industries. The boundaries between ethical and over-the-counter drugs have been blurring, as have been the boundaries between pharmaceuticals and cosmetics. Industry borders have been blurring between commercial banking, investment banking, and brokerages; between computer hardware and software vendors; and between publishers, broadcasters, telecommunication companies, and film studios. Adding to this stew is a trend toward disintermediation—whether that be Wal-Mart dealing directly with manufacturers or corporate borrowers bypassing banks—and a trend toward corporate confederacies and away from pervasive vertical and horizontal integration, like Toyota and its suppliers. The result, in all these cases, is an industry "structure" that is exceedingly complex and almost indeterminate.

In an environment of turbulent and seemingly unpredictable change, being "adaptive" is not good enough. A rudderless ship in gale force winds will simply go round in circles.

Neither is it enough to adopt a "wait-and-see" attitude. A company that pulls in its sails and waits for the calmer seas will find itself becalmed in an industry backwater. However tumultuous the industry, executives still have to make strategic choices. On the other hand, how can a company, possessing only a map of the past, make an intelligent decision about which technologies to pursue, which core competencies to build, which product or service concepts to back, which alliances to form, and what kind of people to hire?

Strategy, as taught in many business schools and practiced in most companies, seems to be more concerned with how to position products and businesses within the existing industry structure than how to create tomorrow's industries. Of what use are the traditional tools of industry and competitor analysis to executives caught up in the melee to create the world's digital future, or to managers trying to understand the opportunities presented by the collapsing boundaries of the financial services industry or the genetics revolution? Of what use are the principles of competitive interaction, drilled into the heads of countless MBA students as they worked their way through the comparatively simple cases of Coca-Cola versus Pepsi, the chain saw industry, DuPont in titanium dioxide, and Procter & Gamble versus Kimberly-Clark in the disposable diaper business? At least in these cases one could easily determine where the industry began and ended. It's not that difficult to determine who is making soft drinks, for example, and who is not. But where does the digital industry begin and end? Or the genetics industry? Or the entertainment industry? Or the retail financial services industry? On any given day, for example, AT&T might find Motorola to be a supplier, a buyer, a competitor, *and* a partner. In well-established industries it is easy to identify product and customer segments. With no preexisting "value chain," how can one anticipate where and how money can be made in the industry, decide which activities to "control," and know how vertically or horizontally integrated to be?

Traditional industry structure analysis, of the kind that is the subject of strategy textbooks, is of little help to executives competing in unstructured industries. On the other hand, simply doing away with existing industry boundaries, as we have done in Figure 2, provides no more help to companies trying to make sense of such a tumultuous industry.

Strategic planning typically takes, as its point of departure, the extant industry structure. Traditional planning seeks to position the firm optimally within the existing structure by identifying which segments, channels, price points, product differentiators, selling propositions, and value chain configurations will yield the highest profits. Although a view of strategy as a positioning problem is certainly legitimate, it is insufficient if the goal is to occupy the high ground in tomorrow's industries. If strategy is seen only as a positioning game, it will be difficult for a company to avoid becoming trapped in an endless game of catch-up with farsighted competitors.

Usually, the current industry structure and the rules of competitive engagement therein have been defined by the industry leader. Although it may be possible to find a profitable niche within the present industry terrain—as Japanese mainframe computer makers did for a while, mimicking IBM—there is typically little growth and prosperity to be found in the shadow of the industry leader. Companies that see strategy as primarily a positioning exercise are industry rule-takers rather than rule-breakers and rule-makers; they are unlikely to be the defining entity in their industry, now or ever.

In short, strategy is as much about competing *for* tomorrow's industry structure as it is about competing *within* today's industry structure. Competition within today's industry structure raises issues such as: What new features should be added to a product? How can we get better channel coverage? Should we price for maximum market share or maximum prof-

FIGURE 2

The Digital Industry Space without Boundaries

Baby Bells	Andersen Consulting	McCaw
3DO		
NEC		
Microsoft	Kodak	Nintendo
Motorola	Canon	
Philips	Sony	British Telecom
Xerox	Lotus Alcatel Toshiba	
Sharp		Hitachi
TCI	Fujitsu Intel Hughes	
EDS		
CBS	AT&T	Hewlett-Packard
Oracle		
IBM	DEC	MCI
Computer Sciences		
Time Warner	Siemens	Matsushita
Cap Sogetti		Disney
Apple	Electronic Arts	
Computer Associates		

its? Competition for tomorrow's industry structure raises deeper questions such as: Whose product concepts will ultimately win out? Which standards will be adopted? How will coalitions form and what will determine each member's share of the power? And, most critically, how do we increase our ability to influence the emerging shape of a nascent industry?

What is up for grabs in an unstructured industry is the future structure of the industry. Sooner or later, to one degree or another, and however briefly, new structures will emerge. Conceiving of strategy as a quest to proactively configure nascent industries, or fundamentally reconfigure existing industries to one's own advantage, is a very different perspective than a view of strategy as positioning individual businesses and products within today's competitive environment. If the goal is competing for the future, we need a view of strategy that addresses more than the problem of maximizing profits in today's markets.

SINGLE-STAGE VERSUS MULTISTAGE COMPETITION

While much attention has been lavished by managers and business consultants on the product development process and the competition between rival products or services in the marketplace, this really represents only the last 100 meters of a much longer race. Product development is a 100-yard dash, while industry development and transformation is a triathlon, where contestants cycle for 100 miles, swim a mile or two, and then run a marathon. Each event represents a distinct challenge to the triathlete.

Competition for the future of the digital industry is still in its early stages, but by reviewing one particular race, the race to develop the VCR, we can observe the distinct stages of competition for the future. We use the VCR as an example both because enough time has passed so that objective judgments can be made about who won and why, and because the VCR was the first major innovation in consumer electronics that was commercialized first in mass markets by Japanese, rather than U.S. or European companies. And although companies like Motorola and Apple today are attempting to resurrect a consumer electronics industry led by U.S. firms, it was the VCR that established the unequivocal dominance of Japanese companies in consumer electronics. The VCR also added billions of largely uncontested profits to the coffers of its Japanese pioneers. Like many other industry development marathons, the race to commercialize the VCR spanned decades, rather than years. The first videotape recorder was produced by a California company, Ampex, in 1959, but it wasn't until the late 1970s that Matsushita introduced its VHS standard and broke the tape at the finish line.

The first hurdle for any would-be pioneer was to commit to the videotape opportunity arena. Three companies saw clearly the potential for videotape—Philips, Sony, and Matsushita (JVC)—and each worked diligently for close to two decades to produce a VCR for home use. At JVC, what was initially the commitment of a small team to the videotape opportunity soon became a corporatewide commitment. Neither RCA, the color television pioneer, nor Ampex, the inventor of videotape, ever demonstrated the same unflinching commitment to the VCR, although both companies made aborted attempts to produce a home machine.

The second hurdle was to acquire the competencies that would be necessary to shape and profit from the future. The challenge of creating a compact videocassette that would pack two, four, or six hours of color recording onto a tape that was a fraction of the length and width of tapes used to produce a half hour of black and white recording time on reel-to-reel videorecorders was a daunting one—what engineers call a "nontrivial technical problem." For more than 15 years Philips, Sony, and Matsushita raced to perfect their videotape competencies. Learning how to manufacture the extremely precise, revolving video-recording heads presented a major competence-building challenge to all comers. An executive at JVC believed that making a VCR was at least ten times more complex than making a television set.

The third hurdle was to discover what configuration of price, features, size, and software was necessary to unlock the mass market. After all, consumers had never seen a VCR before. They could hardly be relied on to provide manufacturers with precise product development specs. How much record time did consumers want? Would they pay as much as $2,500 for a machine? Was slow motion an important feature? The only way to answer those questions was to go into the market again and again, each time improving the product, and coming that little bit closer to the demands of the consumer.

Matsushita launched several VCR models into the market before the company struck gold with VHS. Sony's U-matic VCR, which ultimately became a standard-setter in the professional VCR market, was originally introduced as a "consumer video." But the machine's size and price made it unattractive to home users. The more rapid the pace of market experimentation, the quicker the learning about what customers really want in a product. While Japanese competitors were experimenting in the marketplace, RCA was experimenting only in the lab. RCA didn't launch its consumer videoplayer until 1980. Therefore, it was not surprising that RCA's product, which lacked a record capability, missed the mark badly with consumers.

A fourth hurdle was to establish one's own technical approach to video recording as the industry standard. The battle here was among Sony's Beta, JVC's VHS, and Philips's

V2000, each incompatible with the other. It was clear that whoever won the standards battle would reap great benefits in terms of software availability, licensing income, and economies of scale in component production. The losers would find themselves, millions of R&D dollars later, in a technological cul-de-sac that they could escape only by switching to a competitor's standard. Sony took an early lead, and had 85% of the U.S. VCR market by the end of 1976. But when JVC introduced a machine with a two-hour record time, compared to Sony's one-hour, Sony's lead began to evaporate. The coup de grace came when JVC succeeded in co-opting a number of key partners into its battle with Sony. Telefunken in Germany, Thomson in France, Thorn in Great Britain, and RCA and GE in the United States were all early VHS licensees, initially sourcing components and finished VCRs from JVC and Matsushita.

The wide selection of VHS brands and models, relative to Beta, soon convinced software suppliers to put their money behind VHS, and within two years the market battle between Beta and VHS was over. Philips's V2000, launched in Europe some 18 months after VHS, was dead on arrival despite the fact that Philips had more or less kept pace with its Japanese competitors over the 15-year competence acquisition phase. But in the 18-month gap between the launch of VHS and the launch of V2000, Matsushita managed to sell several million VCRs around the world, making it almost impossible for Philips to catch up with Matsushita's blistering pace of cost reduction and feature improvement. Thus, although the VCR marathon was a full 26 miles, the winner didn't emerge until the last mad scramble for the finish line. But in a marathon, winning by a nose is often as good as winning by a mile. Indeed, attempting to far outdistance a competitor too early in the race may well lead a company into spending too much too soon or running out of resources before the future arrives—the fate that befell Ampex (even though Ampex and Sony were roughly the same size in 1959 when Ampex invented videotape recorders). Although JVC won only by a yard or two, no one who wasn't in the race at the beginning was anywhere near the finish line when it ended.

The final challenge was to keep up in the battle for market share (as opposed to the battle for standards share). The weapons were fast-paced feature enhancement and cost reduction. Sony and Philips ultimately converted to the VHS camp, but Matsushita's early volume advantage gave it an edge in the race to steadily improve price and performance. In 1993, more than 15 years after the launch of VHS and more than 30 years after Matsushita began its pursuit of the videotape opportunity, Matsushita retained its title as the world leader in VCRs.

Whether the race to shift the pharmaceutical industry toward gene-engineered drugs, to allow customers to bank and shop via their PCs or televisions, or to produce cars with noncombustion engines, the race to the future occurs in three distinct, overlapping stages: competition for *industry foresight* and *intellectual leadership*, competition to *foreshorten migration paths*, and competition for *market position and market share*. We will introduce these themes briefly now, and then return to them in later chapters.

Competition for Industry Foresight and Intellectual Leadership

This is competition to gain a deeper understanding than competitors of the trends and discontinuities—technological, demographic, regulatory, or lifestyle—that could be used to transform industry boundaries and create new competitive space. This is competition to be prescient about the size and shape of tomorrow's opportunities. This is competition to conceive fundamentally new types of customer benefits, or to conceive radically new ways of delivering existing customer benefits. In short, it is competition to imagine the future.

Competition to Foreshorten Migration Paths

In between the battle for intellectual leadership and the battle for market share is typically a battle to influence the direction of industry development (the battle to control and foreshorten migration paths). Many years may elapse between the conception of a radically transformed industry future and the emergence of a real and substantial market. Dreams don't come true overnight, and the path between today's reality and tomorrow's opportunities is often long and tortuous.

In the second stage of competition there is a race to accumulate necessary competencies (and overcome technical hurdles), to test and prove out alternate product and service concepts (by progressively discovering what customers really want), to attract coalition partners who have critical complementary resources, to construct whatever product or service delivery infrastructure may be required, and to get agreement around standards, if necessary. If competition in the first stage is competition to *imagine* a new opportunity arena, competition in the second stage is competition to actively *shape* the emergence of that future industry structure to one's own advantage.

Competition for Market Position and Market Share

Finally, one gets to the last stage of competition. By this stage, competition between alternate technological approaches, rival product or service concepts, and competing channel strategies has largely been settled. Competition shifts to a battle for market share and market position within fairly well-defined parameters of value, cost, price, and service. Innovation is focused on product line extensions, efficiency improvement, and what are usually marginal gains in product or service differentiation. (Figure 3 shows the three stages of competition for the future.)

Competition for the future can be likened to pregnancy. Like competition for the future, pregnancy has three stages—conception, gestation, and labor and delivery. These three stages correspond to competition for foresight and intellectual leadership, competition to foreshorten migration paths, and competition for market position and share. It is the third phase of competition that is the focus of attention in most strategy textbooks and strategic planning exercises. Typically, the assumption is that the product or service concept is well established, the dimensions of competition are well-defined, and the boundaries of the industry have stabilized. But focusing on the last stage of market-based competition, without a deep understanding of premarket competition, is like trying to make sense of the process of childbirth without any insight into conception and gestation.

The question for managers to ask themselves at this point is which stage receives the bulk of our time and attention: conception, gestation, or labor and delivery? Our experience suggests that most managers spend a disproportionate amount of time in the delivery room, waiting for the miracle of birth. But as we all know, the miracle of birth is most unlikely, unless there's been some activity nine months previously. Again, we believe that managers are spending too much time managing the present, and not enough creating the future. But to create the future, a company must first be able to forget some of its past.

FIGURE 3

Three Phases of Competition for the Future

INTELLECTUAL LEADERSHIP	MANAGEMENT OF MIGRATION PATHS	COMPETITION FOR MARKET SHARE
Gaining industry foresight by probing deeply into industry drivers.	Preemptively building core competencies, exploring alternate product concepts, and reconfiguring the customer interface.	Building a worldwide supplier network.
Developing a creative point of view about the potential evolution of: • Functionality • Core competencies • Customer interface	Assembling and managing the necessary coalition of industry participants.	Crafting an appropriate market positioning strategy. Preempting competitors in critical markets. Maximizing efficiency and productivity.
Summarizing this point of view in a "strategic architecture."	Forcing competitors onto longer and more expensive migration paths.	Managing competitive interaction.

REFERENCES

[1] "Next big thing: Age of Interactive TV May Be Near as IBM and Warner Talk Deal," *The Wall Street Journal Europe*, 21 May 1992, p. B1+.

[2] J.M. Laderman and G. Smith, "The Power of Mutual Funds," *Business Week International*, 18 January 1993, pp. 43–40.

[3] However, it should be noted that when governments have lavished protection on a single firm or two, in hopes of producing national or regional champions, the results have typically been less than hoped for. The most successful model seems to be one where government policy-makers and industrialists have a broad consensus about a new opportunity arena, say high-definition television, where government then puts in place a set of modest incentives to encourage development of the technology, brokers to some degree collaboration between several fiercely competing local contenders, and lets the marketplace decide the winner. This was the approach taken by the FCC in the U.S. HDTV standards battle, where several consortia of two, three, or more firms each raced to get its technology accepted as the standard, and worked with the other coalitions to minimize the risks of getting left out in the cold if their standard was not chosen. This approach is in marked contrast to the less-successful approach of the European HDTV strategy, which was a thinly disguised attempt to prop up Philips, or the Japanese approach in which there was an attempt to force a single, predetermined standard onto the rest of the world.

[4] Brenton R. Schlender, "How Sony Keeps the Magic Going," *Fortune*, 24 February 1992, p.27.

[5] See, for example, George Stalk, Jr., and Thomas M. Hout, *Competing Against Time: How Time-Based Competition Is Reshaping Global Markets* (New York: The Free Press, 1990).

[6] Louise Kehone, "Rebels Turned Diplomats," *Financial Times*, 8 February 1993, p. 8.

[7] Because of a widespread familiarity with the "digital" opportunity arena we've chosen it for our illustration here. One could, of course, produce a similar map of the genetic opportunity arena, encompassing pharmaceutical, chemical, agricultural, and food products firms, or of the financial services opportunity, or new materials opportunity arena, *ad infinitum*.

Managing for the Future: The 1990s and Beyond*

PETER DRUCKER

THE CHANGING WORLD ECONOMY

I begin with the remark that 1992 is after all not a terribly important date. Many things will be decided between now and then, but the important event has already happened, and it has nothing to do with governments. Governments are, alas, no longer performance centers, as they were in the nineteenth century. The main event is that the businessmen of Europe have already decided that there is a European economy. Has there ever been a precedent to guide us? Yes; and not so long ago, either.

When I first went to the U.S.A. as correspondent for five British newspapers in the late 1930s, it was just becoming a national market. It had been a political unit for 150 years, but there were very few national U.S. businesses: none of the big banks, none of the big insurance companies, only 3 of the then 10–12 automobile companies, and a few of the steel companies (and then only because the U.S. navy required it) had national scale or coverage. All the rest were local or regional. Most of them were unfamiliar with other parts of the country—after all, it took six uncomfortable days in the train, without air conditioning, to reach Los Angeles from New York or Washington. Few people went there from the east except film stars.

Then, suddenly, in the mid-1930s every business had to learn to think national. Very few actually acted national. Contrary to what most foreigners think, the U.S.A. still has a tiny minority of companies that are fully national. The majority remain regionally based on the East Coast, West Coast, or in the Midwest to this day. Nevertheless, U.S. companies had to learn quickly to think and act in contemplation of the national market. This is what is happening in Europe.

Looking at this example will not, however, tell any business what to do in its own particular circumstances. Beware of prescriptions. A company must make up its own mind by examining its own business, its own market, its own competition and deciding where the new competition may arise—even though the CEO may never have been to Spain except

---

on holiday, any more than many Americans have visited the West Coast. In any case, it must rethink strategy in contemplation of a fundamental change: location of markets, the need for expansion, alignment, and structure. This has to happen anyhow. Once it has been done, 1992 ceases to be a major event.

But New International Dynamics Do Matter

The European single market is, however, symptomatic of a capital change in the way the world economy functions. Whether you like it or not (and I for one do not), the world is very rapidly changing its form of economic integration. We are moving toward a world economy that is integrated not by free trade or protectionism, as in the past, but increasingly through a hybrid of the two which we can call reciprocity. What do I mean by reciprocity? International trade has evolved from a complementary exchange of goods and services to an adversarial exchange. In an adversarial trade relationship, if an attacking country excludes foreign competition and imports, as the Japanese did, in effect the defender is unable to counterattack. It cannot win; so what can it do?

One answer is to form an economic bloc or region, such as the European Economic Community scheduled for 1992. This gives smaller economies the larger market they need for competitive scale. At the same time, regionalism creates an entity that can deploy an effective trade policy transcending both protectionism and free trade. Thus reciprocity—in which, in principle, each bloc's businesses would have the same degree of access to the other blocs' markets—is rapidly emerging as the new guiding principle for the world economy. It may be the only way of preventing it from slipping into extreme protectionism.

We do not yet know exactly what reciprocity will entail in practice. Does it mean that European banks can do business in the U.S.A. on the same terms as U.S. banks, or on the same terms as those on which they do business in Europe? That is still up in the air. Questions such as these will be decided *ad hoc*, with endless friction and compromise, and in every case the answer will be slightly different. What is certain is that the EEC will adopt it as its main trade policy—and that is already having an effect elsewhere.

For example, the prospect of the European single market was the direct cause of the free trade agreement between the U.S.A. and Canada. In Europe it is impossible to comprehend the unlikeliness of this venture without the threat of the single market. It flies in the face of everything that Canada has ever felt important. Even now, Canadians are not enthusiastic; they simply had no choice but to throw in their economic lot with their dominating neighbor. After Canada, there is now an even bigger question: Does Mexico in its turn have any choice? There is no deeper cultural dividing line in the world than this unmarked border between two totally different civilizations and value systems. For 150 years the lodestar of Mexico's policy was to keep as far away as possible from the huge and dangerous monster next door. Yet suddenly, despite tremendous politico-cultural tensions, the possibility of Mexico being forced to integrate itself into the North American economy is better than 50 percent. It is no longer absurd to contemplate it.

In the East Too

There are other emerging regions. In China, the pressure of enormous unemployment on one hand and the disparity between the energy of the coast and the lethargy of the interior on the other is beginning to split the country into rival economic warlordships once again. If, as is distinctly possible, a coastal belt containing all the commercial energy develops along a stretch from Tientsin to Canton, then very soon we shall see a new Far Eastern bloc organized around Japan. The Chinese cities are already in their economic orientation (although not yet politically or socially) pointing toward this new superstar and center, despite the tremendous Chinese fear and distrust of the foreigner, particularly the Asiatic foreigner. A Japan-centered Pacific Rim region is probably in the process of being formed.

A NEW INTERNATIONAL ECONOMIC ORDER IS EMERGING

In the newly emerging world economic order—transnational, regionally integrated, and information intensive—two changes already stand out. First, tomorrow's transnationals are unlikely to be manufacturing companies. The service economy is going transnational. Most of 256 public hospitals in Japan are today maintained and managed by a Chicago-based maintenance company. Virtually every big office building in Manhattan is maintained and managed by a maintenance company based in Aarhus, Denmark. Since Japan lacks business and engineering teachers, it is bringing the students to the faculty; and, inconceivable just a few years ago, three leading nongovernmental universities in Tokyo are building campuses on the West Coast of the U.S.A. for Japanese students. Banking and finance are more advanced still in transnational development. In large part because governmental politics are still focused on the concerns of the blue-collar factory worker, the service economy is going transnational much faster than manufacturing.

Second, in the new world economy investment is growing much faster than trade. Classic economic theory says that investment follows trade. In the nineteenth century that was true. In the twentieth century it is the other way around. To take a topical case, look at the Japanese automobile companies and their suppliers in the U.K. No sooner does Honda, Nissan, or Toyota establish a factory in the U.K than it imports its own suppliers as well to provide it with components. This is in part because the Japanese do not find it natural to buy from an independent supplier. In Japan a company is either a master or a servant, and the supplier which sells to more than one master is not to be trusted. But consider a less obvious example of the same phenomenon. Why did U.S. exports not collapse in the years of the overvalued dollar in the mid-1980s? For a similar reason: in spite of the price penalty, Japanese subsidiaries of U.S. companies kept on buying machinery, spare parts, and materials from their tried and trusted suppliers back in the U.S.A.

Yet in an investment-led world economy, a strategy based on exports is out of date. One of the factors that lost the U.K. its economic leadership in the nineteenth century was, ironically, its mastery of exporting. This meant that in every port in the world, the main importer was a Scot, and a Scot who bought almost exclusively from Manchester and Glasgow. Since they could not penetrate their key markets by the traditional route of exports, U.S. and West German companies were obliged to establish factories there instead. They had to invest before they could trade. In this kind of world, proximity to and feel for markets have become decisive, and these require market presence and market standing. So now, one of the accepted facts that economic history (rather than the economic textbook) teaches is that a company cannot hold a leadership position in a key market unless it manufactures there. The Japanese have taken 20 percent of the U.S. automobile market, compared with the 30 percent captured by foreign manufacturers in all. Yet only half of the Japanese share has been taken from the U.S. Big Four. The rest has been stolen from the Europeans, notably Volkswagen, which had no less than 12 percent of the market in 1969. Alas, the unions barred Volkswagen from manufacturing in the U.S.A. the first time round. In 1973, when the oil shock struck, VW was not in the market as a manufacturer, and it misread the signs. When it did try to come back and manufacture, it was too late.

Once again, investment is the economic driver. The real economy of goods and services no longer dominates the transnational economy. The London interbank market daily turns over 10–15 times the amount of eurodollars, euromarks, or euroyen which are needed to finance world trade in goods and services. No figures exist for the foreign exchange markets, but they are certainly bigger still; far greater than needed for commercial trading purposes. These flows finance capital movements and investments. If the corporation does not maintain its investments in its key markets, it will have no sales.

In the transition, of course, these arrangements hold some difficulties for the wealth-creating sectors of national markets. We still hold the nineteenth-century assumption that there is a shortage of liquid funds. The reality today is that there is a surplus. One reason is that the economies of the developed world are becoming steadily more knowledge intensive and less capital and labor intensive. Another is the enormous amounts of money accumulated in small savings accounts and large pension funds. So instead of rationing, their traditional function, now the large investors are looking for places to put their money. The results are not necessarily always economically optimal, except in the very short run.

Look at junk bonds. In effect, junk bonds are simply another form of equity financing, the main purpose of which is to give industry and the takeover specialists very cheap money (because it is debt and the interest is tax-free) at a high yield to the lender. Not surprisingly, the banks have rushed to participate in a miraculous market that gives them 15 percent at a cost to the borrower of 6 or 7 percent. It is doubtful whether this is in the interests of the economy. Where there is excess liquidity there is a risk of making investments guided by short-term speculation, whether it is lending money to Zaire or to the latest takeover artist.

FINANCE, A MODEL FOR THE FUTURE: ADAPT OR DIE

As this suggests, of all the changes so far, the fastest and most extensive are those which have transformed the world financial system. Money, like information, knows no fatherland, with the practical consequence that financial systems in countries at similar stages of economic development are strikingly similar irrespective of legislation or social habits. We can therefore look at what happens in one part of the developed world and see what it tells us about where the rest of the world is going. The U.S.A. has gone the furthest: partly because it was most severely regulated and partly because the markets, less dominated by a few very big units, were most flexible.

When the financial revolution began around 1960, we all predicted the imminent triumph of the financial supermarket: a money continuum, from total liquidity and minimum risk at one end, to minimum liquidity with very high risk at the other, all at a suitably graded price. We were wrong for two reasons. First, to most people money is not a commodity. U.S. retailer Sears Roebuck has always prided itself on being the buyer for the U.S. family. It looked at the investment demand on the part of the masses and bought a major brokerage house. For many years it was a total disaster. Very few of us are willing to buy our investments, even in government bonds, next to where we buy our children's underwear. It is not right. It is not becoming. Money is, if not sacred, at least different.

The second reason for the failure of the financial supermarket is that in every developed country there are two separate markets with entirely different characters: retail and institutional. Whether one institution can serve both of them is still unclear. The retail market is a strange beast. When I worked in the City of London more than 50 years ago, my very wise boss said to me: "Mr. Drucker, never forget that in the richest country in the world only one family out of every 20 can lay aside more money than is needed for the funeral of the head of the family." Today probably at least half the families in all developed countries lay more aside than is required for a funeral. Not enormous sums: most people only spend less than they make once they are past the age of 50. Except in Japan, where compensation follows the life curve, income patterns are skewed so that rewards really begin to climb when the children are grown up and the spending needs begin to go down. At that stage people are too old to change. Suddenly they have a little money individually— and those small individual sums collectively add up to an almost unbelievable total.

Almost everyone has radically underestimated these amounts, as companies have found that dared to bring out new financial products. The U.S. saving rates are some of the lowest in the world, yet sales of mutual funds boomed in 1983–87, in two years actually exceeding the official total savings. And all this without affecting other forms of saving. Clearly, something is wrong with the figures. However, for companies the great challenge is how to service this formidable reservoir of money. For a start, do the big life insurance companies have the right distribution system? To be sure, there are several life insurance agents in every little town. They have their lists of customers, some of whom are the right age, 50+, which is where the money is. Yet most life insurance companies still stubbornly insist on selling the one product that is guaranteed not to survive this century, the whole life policy. In an affluent economy, whole life makes absolutely no sense. For anyone who is not poor, it is the worst buy on the financial market. Term insurance or group life provides more protection for one-sixth of the premium, but even that is a hopeless investment. If it can be unbundled, the same sum will provide twice as much life insurance and 50 percent more investment. And yet in Europe, at least, these terrible buys still flourish. But they will not survive even a mild bout of inflation. People are not that stupid. So far not one life insurance company has succeeded using agency channels. The agency system has not responded to the great challenge of serving the retail finance market.

INSTITUTIONAL FINANCE MUST CHANGE TOO

On the other side of the financial markets are the enormous institutions of capital, the pension funds, which in every developed country will soon be the only true capitalists left. How will we organize them for constructive investment? Currently by their constitution the interests of the pension funds are purely financial. If they can make money by buying or selling, then they have no choice but to do it. The trouble is that, as any businessman knows, the short-term financial view is not enough to build a business. How therefore can we get the pension funds to be owners, and thus business builders, rather than investors? What tools shall we need? What instruments? These are crucial questions.

The final critical question about the financial system is whether the commercial banks can survive when they can no longer make a living out of interest differentials. The public has become too sophisticated, the costs of capital are much too high, and borrowers have so many different ways of raising money that the traditional commercial loan is the least attractive alternative. One bank, Citicorp, already makes 60 percent of its money in fees, compared with 20 percent at the most for the majority. Can banks switch from being paid for money to being paid for information? Assets in a bank are increasingly a liability. The bank of tomorrow will have no assets. It will be a market arbitrageur rather than an interest arbitrageur. This challenge is particularly acute for the European banks that bestride the Netherlands, Belgium, Austria, and Spain like giants, but which are pygmies on the world scene. In terms of serving their countries, these have been the best banks of all, successfully building their domestic economies precisely because they were big enough to do everything and small enough to know what was required. Can they survive, and in what form?

These are some of the questions thrown up by the changing world economy. Nineteen ninety-two has caused them to be directly posed, but they were there all along. They will all be answered, by my best guess, before 1993, not by the process of thinking them through, but by acting on events.

THE KNOWLEDGE SOCIETY

INFORMATION MATTERS

Just as modern money penetrated the whole world within less than a century and totally changed people's lives and aspirations, we can safely assume that information now penetrates everywhere. On my last and longest trip to China, I spent almost three weeks looking at factories and cotton plantations in the interior. The biggest cotton plantations are in the most remote province, near the Mongolian border in the extreme north. It was hard to get there, and the plantations were very poor and primitive: only the meeting halls had electric light, for example. At one site we held a meeting, and at 6 o'clock the 22 plantation managers got up, asked to be excused for a short period, and disappeared. After half an hour they came back, and we resumed the discussion. Why the interruption, I inquired, another meeting or a party of visitors? "No," they replied. "It was *Dallas* on television."

INFORMATION MEANS A NEW TYPE OF MANAGEMENT

Thus information moves everywhere. And its effects are everywhere pervasive. In the case of the corporation, any business that has tried to organize itself around information has rapidly reduced its number of management levels by at least half, and usually by 60 percent. The first and most spectacular case was Massey Ferguson. Virtually bankrupt, the world's largest farm equipment and diesel manufacturer required radical surgery. It was a complex business in organizational terms, with headquarters in Canada, production primarily in Europe, and 60 percent of its markets in the U.S.A. Because it was managed by people who had previously worked at General Motors and Ford, it was organized like a U.S. automobile company, with 14 layers of management. Today it has 6 and the number is still coming down.

Massey Ferguson thought about the information it needed to run its business. The moment it did so, it discovered a great truth: many levels of management in fact manage nothing. They make no decisions. In reality they are only boosters, amplifying the very faint signals that come up and down through the organization. If a company can organize itself around its information needs, these layers become redundant.

There are good reasons why large organizations will have to become information-based. Demographics is one. The knowledge workers who increasingly make up the work force are not amenable to the command-and-control methods of the past. Another reason is the need to systematize innovation and entrepreneurship, quintessentially knowledge work. And a third is the requirement to come to terms with information technology. Computers turn out data—vast amounts of it. But data is not information. Information is data endowed with relevance and purpose. A company must decide what information it needs to operate its affairs, otherwise it will drown in data.

To organize in this way requires a new structure. Although it is perhaps too early to draw an organization chart of the information-based organization, we can set out some broad considerations.

One hundred and twenty-five years ago, when large enterprises first came into being, the only organizational structure they had to model themselves on was the army: hierarchical, command-and-control, line and staff. Tomorrow's model is the symphony orchestra or the football team or the hospital. Mahler's symphonies require the presence of 385 instrumentalists on stage, never mind the singers. If it were to organize itself the way we organize our big companies today, a modern orchestra would have a chief executive officer plus a chairman conductor flanked by two nonexecutive conductors, six vice-chairman conductors, and countless vice-president conductors. Instead of which there is one conductor to whom every specialist instrumentalist plays directly, because everyone has the same score. In other words, there are no intermediaries between the specialists and the top manager, and they are organized as a gigantic task force. The organization is totally flat.

There is a famous 1920s joke about the then-new discipline of industrial engineering which takes on fresh meaning today. The story concerns a (needless to say) German engineer who attends a symphony concert on which he writes a report. He points out that most of the musicians sit around doing nothing most of the time: Would it not be more efficient if they played the Rossini, Beethoven, and Brahms simultaneously rather than in sequence, thus occupying the players all the time? Well, the orchestra still functions by playing one work at a time. Indeed, one of the lessons of organizing around information is the importance of concentration to prevent people from becoming fatally confused. The orchestra can perform precisely because all the players know they are playing Mozart, not Haydn. A medical team performing an operation also has a score, although an unwritten one. But the performance of a business or a government agency creates its own score, or many scores, as it goes along. An information-based organization must therefore structure itself around goals that clearly state expectations and objectives both for the enterprise and for each specialist. There must be strongly organized feedback so that every member can exercise self-control by comparing expectations with the actual outcome.

I believe, therefore, that we are moving toward more concentrated organizations and units of organizations, based on much clearer business and individual goals, on self-discipline and on systematic feedback. If this is truly the case, businesses will have to learn that they must build their communications system on information up rather than information down. Information becomes communication only if the recipient understands and accepts it. If information only moves down, that cannot happen. The structure must be based on the upward communication of information that enables those at the top to know what goes on at the bottom, at the sharp end.

CHANGING SOCIETY: THE DECLINE OF THE SERVANT . . .

Some of the greatest changes in social structure in the history of the human race have taken place this century. These changes have been nonviolent, which is perhaps why few people pay them any attention. Yet had any of the great economists or sociologists of the last century been apprised of them, they would have laughed in disbelief. Consider the cases of the domestic servant and the farmer. The first scientific census, the British census of 1910, famously defined lower middle class as the family that could not afford more than three servants. How many people have spotted even one servant lately, other than at Madame Tussaud's? Servants antedate history by millennia, and in 1913 they were the largest single employee group in any developed country. Thirty percent of all wage earners were domestic servants. They are all gone.

. . . THE FARMER . . .

So, almost, are farmers. There is now no developed country in the world in which farmers form more than 8 percent of the population. The political power of the farmer has evaporated. In the 1988 U.S. election the farmer became a nonperson. Both candidates went to Iowa for two hours, but that was all. They could not care less how the 3 percent of the U.S. population who are still farmers cast their vote. Politicians have good antennae. They know that the farmers' power has become the smile on the face of the Cheshire cat. In Japan, there is one farm vote for seven city votes; but one-third of all the money for the war chest of the Japanese politicians comes from the Farmers' Cooperative Bank. This power is likely to be broken as a result of the Recruit scandal. Farmers' power will soon be over, even in Japan.

. . . AND THE WORKER

The blue-collar industrial worker is going the same way. No century has seen anything like his rise and his decline. A very short time ago it seemed that this group was ineluctably controlling society, politics, and markets. To test market a new product in the U.S.A. in the 1950s, a company went to the solid blue-collar communities that would make or break it. Not today; not even in the U.K. By the end of the century in every developed country, blue-collar workers will be no more important or numerous than farmers. Their numbers have declined by a full third in the past 20 years.

It is not only the numbers that have fallen, however. There are now few manufacturing companies where blue-collar labor costs rise above 15 percent. A country such as Spain has five to seven years during which its reservoir of highly trained, cheap labor will remain an asset. By the end of the century, if its manufacturing has not evolved to the point where labor costs are below 15 percent, that labor force will have become a liability. No Western country can compete with Shanghai, where $1 a day is an excellent wage, and only the top 10 percent of the work force makes even $1.

The answer for Western manufacturing is not necessarily automation. Information is not the same as automation, or even information technology, and no firm should start by buying a machine. Rather, the first step is to rationalize the process in order to identify what machines are necessary. A company that begins by buying robots or automating its existing process will almost certainly waste monstrous amounts of money and become less productive in the process. General Motors proves the point. GM spent the not inconsiderable sum of $30 billion on robots, with the result that labor costs went up, not down. GM's blue-collar labor costs are now 28 percent compared with Ford's 15 percent and Toyota's 16 percent (in the U.S.A.). At the new Honda plant, built in a high-wage area, the figure will come down to 11.5 percent. Cars, remember, are a relatively ancient industry. In the new industries labor costs should be even lower.

Most people believe that the favorite child of capitalism was the owner of capital: the capitalist. A better candidate is the blue-collar industrial worker. In 1850 he was still a laborer hired by the hour, paid a few pennies, without social standing or political power. He was neglected and despised. By 1950 he belonged to the dominant social class. He enjoyed health insurance, pensions, job security, and political power that would have seemed unthinkable only two generations before. He still has the benefits, of course. But the brief moment of dominance is suddenly over. And all this without real social convulsions.

THE LEARNING SOCIETY IS TAKING OVER

In the place of the blue-collar world is a society in which access to good jobs no longer depends on the union card, but on the school certificate. Between, say, 1950 and 1980 it was economically irrational for a young American male to stay at school. In three months a 16-year-old school leaver with a job at a unionized steel plant could be taking home more money than his university-educated cost accountant brother would make in his life. Those days are over. From now on the key is knowledge. The world is becoming not labor intensive, not materials intensive, not energy intensive, but knowledge intensive.

Japan today produces two and a half times the quantity of manufactured goods as 25 years ago with the same amount of energy and less raw material. In large part this is due to the shift to knowledge-intensive work. The representative product of the 1920s, the automobile, at the time had a raw material and energy content of 60 percent. The representative product of the 1980s is the semiconductor chip, which has a raw material and energy content of less than 2 percent. The 1990s equivalent will be biotechnology, also with a content of about 2 percent in materials and energy, but with a much higher knowledge content. Assembling microchips is still fairly labor intensive (10 percent). Biotechnology will have practically no labor content at all. Moreover, fermentation plants generate energy rather than consume it. The world is becoming knowledge intensive not just in the labor force, but in process.

Knowledge is always specialized. The oboist in the London Philharmonic Orchestra has no ambition to become first violinist. In the last 100 years only one instrumentalist, Toscanini, has become a conductor of the first rank. Specialists remain specialists, becoming ever more skillful at interpreting the score. Yet specialism carries dangers, too. Truly knowledgeable people tend by themselves to overspecialize, because there is always so much more to know. As part of the orchestra, that oboist alone does not make music. He or she makes noise. Only the orchestra playing a joint score makes music. For both soloist and conductor, getting music from an orchestra means not only knowing the score, but learning how to manage knowledge. And knowledge carries with it powerful responsibility, too. In the past, the holders of knowledge have often used (abused) it to curb thinking and dissent, and to inculcate blind obedience to authority. Knowledge and knowledge people have to assume their responsibilities.

MOST EDUCATION DOES NOT DELIVER KNOWLEDGE . . .

The advent of the knowledge society has far-ranging implications for education. Schools will change more in the next 30 years than they have since the invention of the printed book. One reason is modern learning theory. We know how people learn, and that learning is not at all the same thing as teaching. We know, for instance, that no two human beings learn in the same way. The printed book set off the greatest explosion in learning and the love of learning the world had ever seen. But book learning was for adults. The printed book is basically adult-friendly. In contrast, the new learning tools are child-friendly, as anyone with a computer-using eight- or nine-year-old child will know. By the age of eleven most children except the freaks begin to be bored with the computer; for them it is just a tool. But up to that age, children treat computers as extensions of themselves. The advent of such powerful tools alone will force the schools to change.

. . . So Organizations Must Do It Themselves

But there is another consideration. For the first time in human history it really matters whether or not people learn. When the Prince Regent asked Marshal Blücher if he found it a great disadvantage not to be able to read and write, the man who won the battle of Waterloo for Wellington replied: "Your Royal Highness, that is what I have a chaplain for." Until 1914 most people could do perfectly well without such accomplishments. Now, however, learning matters. The knowledge society requires that all its members be literate, not just in reading, writing, and arithmetic, but also in (for example) basic computer skills and political, social, and historical systems. And because of the vastly expanding corpus of knowledge, it also requires that its members learn how to learn.

There will—and should—be serious discussion of the social purpose of school education in the context of the knowledge society. That will certainly help to change the schools. In the meantime, however, the most urgent learning and training must reach out to the adults. Thus, the focus of learning will shift from schools to employers. Every employing institution will have to become a teacher. Large numbers of American and Japanese employers and some Europeans already recognize this. But what kind of learning? In the orchestra the score tells the employees what to do; all orchestra playing is team playing. In the information-based business, what is the equivalent of this reciprocal learning and teaching process? One way of educating people to a view of the whole, of course, is through work in cross-functional task forces. But to what extent do we rotate specialists out of their specialties and into new ones? And who will the managers, particularly top managers, of the information-based organization be? Brilliant oboists, or people who have been in enough positions to be able to understand the team, or even young conductors from smaller orchestras? We do not yet know. Above all, how do we make this terribly expensive knowledge, this new capital, productive?

The world's largest bank reports that it has invested $1.5 billion in information and communications systems. Banks are now more capital intensive than the biggest manufacturing company. So are hospitals. Only 50 years ago a hospital consisted of a bed and a sister. Today a fair-sized U.S. hospital of 400 beds has several hundred attending physicians and a staff of up to 1,500 paramedics divided among some 60 specialties, with specialized equipment and labs to match. None, or very few, of these specialisms even existed 50 years ago. But we do not yet know how to get productivity out of them; we do not yet know in this context what productivity means. In knowledge-intensive areas we are pretty much where we were in manufacturing in the early nineteenth century. When Robert Owen built his cotton mills in Scotland in the 1820s, he tried to measure their productivity. He never managed it. It took 50 more years until productivity as we understand it could be satisfactorily defined. We are currently at about the Robert Owen stage in relation to the new organizations. We are beginning to ask about productivity, output, and performance in relation to knowledge. We cannot measure it. We cannot yet even judge it, although we do have an idea of some of the things that are needed.

How, for instance, do famous conductors build a first-rate orchestra? They tell me that the first job is to get the clarinetist to keep on improving as a clarinetist. She or he must have pride in the instrument. The players must be craftsmen first. The second task is to create in the individuals a pride in their common enterprise, the orchestra: "I play for Cleveland, or Chicago, or the London Philharmonic, and that is one of the best orchestras in the world." Third, and this is what distinguishes a competent conductor from a great one, is to get the orchestra to hear and play that Haydn symphony in exactly the way the conductor hears it. In other words, there must be a clear vision at the top. This orchestra focus is the model for the leader of any knowledge-based organization.

INNOVATION AND ENTREPRENEURSHIP

I turn now to crucial issues for managers in the knowledge society: innovation and entrepreneurship.

It is not a coincidence that these necessary concepts are back in fashion. For a long period they were neglected, to the point where for all intents and purposes they vanished from the list of corporate concerns. Only in the last 15–20 years have these two practices—for that is what they are, neither science nor art—come to the fore again.

On neither side of the Atlantic is the record of the new entrepreneurial companies exemplary. It is probably better than those of the nineteenth century, but it is still not nearly good enough. By now we know pretty much what is needed for those companies to survive and to prosper: the practice of entrepreneurship, like the practice of management, has its rules and knowledge base. But to confine the focus of innovation and entrepreneurship to the new individual entrepreneur is too narrow. If start-ups and new businesses were the main or only locus of innovation, our societies could probably not survive.

LESSONS FROM THE NINETEENTH CENTURY'S INNOVATIVE CLIMATE

There is one great difference between the innovative climate of the last 20 years and the late nineteenth century. Our rate of innovation (social as well as technical, that is just as important) is equally rapid. But practically all the institutions, business or other, of the nineteenth century were new: they emerged in the 50 or so years between 1865 (the year of Perkins's first aniline dye, Siemens's first dynamo) and 1914, when the First World War paralyzed the entrepreneurial energies of the West. During that period a new institution, a major invention or innovation emerged on average more often than once a year. Some of them led to the founding of new industries. But they did not displace existing institutions. They emerged, as it were, into a vacuum. Thus, the Home Office set up British local government in 1856 from scratch. In the same decade the first modern U.S. university was founded. Today the task is different: we have to learn to make existing institutions capable of innovation. We know what is needed, and it is relatively uncomplicated, although that does not mean it is easy. But if existing institutions cannot learn to innovate, the social consequences will be almost unbearably severe.

INNOVATION MATTERS BECAUSE OURS IS A KNOWLEDGE-BASED SOCIETY

Knowledge changes extremely fast. But that in itself is not new; knowledge has always changed fast. What is new is that knowledge matters. In a crafts society, which ours essentially was until late in the nineteenth century, major changes occurred perhaps every

80 years. In military technology, between the disappearance of the longbow in the reign of Elizabeth I and the launching of the *Dreadnought* in 1906, a significant innovation took place every 60 years. Today, courtesy of the Pentagon, it is probably every 60 days. We have learned to innovate because we cannot expect that the accumulated competence, skill, knowledge, product, services, and structure of the present will be adequate for very long. The change is not so much that the pace of accumulation is so much more rapid. It is rather that the center of gravity of knowledge is constantly on the move.

I have talked about institutions rather than businesses. This is intentional. In a market economy, innovation comes easier to businesses. In fact it is equally important in every other field of endeavor. But although the principles of innovation and entrepreneurship apply just as well to government institutions or universities, the practice is different. There is nothing more reactionary than a liberal faculty in a university. It is the ultimate in reaction. It is the motto of the U.S. universities that when a subject becomes totally obsolete, then a required course should be built around it. To survive and be useful, they must learn how to innovate.

INNOVATION MEANS ABANDONING THE OLD

What do we know about innovation? First, it has very little to do with genius. It has very little or nothing to do with inspiration. It is hard, systematic work. The myth is that an owner-entrepreneur can depend on a flash of genius. I have been working with owner-entrepreneurs for 40 years: the ones who depend on the flash of genius also go out like one.

Innovation depends rather on what we might call "organized abandonment." When the French economist J. B. Say coined the word *entrepreneur* 200 years ago, he meant it as a manifesto and a declaration of intent: the entrepreneur in his scheme was someone who upsets and disorganizes. Later Joseph Schumpeter, the only modern economist to take entrepreneurship seriously, described the process as "creative destruction." To get at the new and better, you have to throw out the old, outworn, obsolete, no longer productive, as well as the mistakes, failure, and misdirections of effort of the past. To put it another way, think of the old medical saying: "As long as the patient eliminates there is a chance. But once the bowels and the bladder stop, death does not take long." If organizations cannot get rid of their waste products, they poison themselves. They must organize abandonment, a most difficult thing to do, because most organizations develop a strong emotional attachment to the products they make.

Take a typical case. He is the head of a company that makes writing instruments. When he was 25 years old, he had an idea for a mechanical pencil. Everybody ridiculed the notion, but he put his job on the line and fought for it, and it turned out to be a successful product. He is now the head of the company that makes it, and as a consequence he has seen much more of it than he saw of his wife and children and is deeply emotionally involved with this company and this object. And then some eager young whippersnapper comes along as he did 30 years ago with an idea which makes the old product obsolete. He has very little love for that young man and he will not encourage him to persist with his idea, unless he builds organized abandonment into the company.

Innovation is not genius, nor is it necessarily, or even primarily, technical. There was not much technology involved in moving a lorry body off its wheels and putting it on a ship. But containerization roughly quadrupled the productivity of the oceangoing freighter and made possible the colossal expansion of world trade over the last 40 years. Similarly, few technical innovations can compete for impact with the humble textbook, newspapers, or insurance. Installment buying, invented by a U.S. maker of farm implements to enable poorly off farmers to buy his equipment, literally transforms economies. And so the list goes on. For all its visibility and glamour, science-based innovation is actually less reliable, less predictable, and probably less likely to lead to company profits than almost any other sort.

THE ZERO-BASED AUDIT

So now we know what innovation is not. More positively, we also know what is needed to put it into action. The key to innovation is to sit down every three years and systematically put every aspect of the company on trial for its life: every product, service, technology, market, and distribution channel.

Here is a clue: nothing is changing quite so fast today as distributive channels. Very few economists or newspaper commentators seem to realize that the service economy, which is expanding so fast, does not operate in contradiction to, or grow at the expense of, the goods economy. It is a distributive channel for the goods economy. And the fastest-growing segment of the channel is leisure. There is no developed country in which people now work more than half the hours they worked in 1910. Economists may not consider leisure part of the economy, but it is responsible for a huge amount of goods distribution. The same sort of growth is visible in other service institutions such as hospitals and schools. Sixty years ago, health care took less than 1 percent of developed GNP or consumer spending. Now, health care, and especially hospitals, account for 7–11 percent of enormously expanded national products. To repeat: the service economy is a distribution channel for goods, economically speaking, and distribution channels change faster than goods or services themselves. So examine them closely.

The zero-budgeting exercise also demands that managers look at every process and procedure, not to mention every staff activity, inside the organization and ask, " If we did not do this already, given what we now know, would we do it the same way?" If the answer is no, do not say, "Let us call in a management consultant to make a study." Say, "What do we do?" Sometimes the right thing to do is to make minor changes, sometimes to reposition the company entirely. Sometimes the answer is to simplify. Where there are six product lines, perhaps they should be cut to one or two. Sometimes they should be abandoned altogether. But the important thing is to do something. At that point the organization is open to innovation. Dr. Johnson said that nothing so concentrates a man's mind as the knowledge that he is to be hanged in a fortnight. Nothing quite so sharpens a manager's mind as the knowledge that his mechanical pencil will be taken away from him—then he starts to innovate.

INNOVATION MEANS LOOKING ON CHANGE
AS AN OPPORTUNITY

Systematic innovation requires a willingness to look on change as an opportunity. Innovations do not create change. That is very rare. They may if successful make an enormous difference, but most of the innovations that aim at changing society, or markets, or customers, fail. Innovations that succeed do so by exploiting change, not attempting to force it.

In *Innovation and Entrepreneurship* (1985) I wrote that "systematic innovation…consists in the purposeful and organized search for changes, and in the systematic analysis of the opportunities such changes might offer for economic or social innovation." I went on to identify seven sources to look out for as signs and sources of a chance to innovate. Four of these sources are within the enterprise (business or otherwise) or the industry in which they operate. They are basically symptoms of change. They are: the unexpected success or failure; the incongruity (the discrepancy between reality as it is and reality as it is assumed to be); innovation based on process need; and changes in industry or market structure that take people unawares. The other three sources involve changes outside the industry or enterprise, namely, demographics; changing tastes, perceptions, and meanings; and new knowledge, both scientific and nonscientific.

The most useful of the seven "windows" of innovation (which is why I list it first) is always the unexpected, especially the unexpected success. It is the least risky and the least arduous. Yet it is almost totally neglected. What is even worse, managers often actively reject it.

Consider for a moment that prime product of modern accounting: the monthly or weekly report. This was a tremendous eye-opener. Nobody had ever had systematic figures before. Most people see the first page that shows them they are over budget, but how many receive the other "first" page that shows where they are ahead of budget? They should order their accountants to produce it immediately. Without this information an organization becomes fixated on its problems. However, it is usually the case that the first indication of an opportunity is where a company is faring better than expected. Most of the figures and variations turn out to be not significant, of course, and managers can explain them immediately. But one out of every 20 might mean something. It might be pointing to something we did not know.

A leading hospital supplier launched a new line of instruments for clinical tests. The new products did quite well. Then suddenly orders started appearing from a quite different spectrum of customers: university, industry, and government laboratories. No one noticed that the company had tripped over a new and better market. It did not even send a sales person to visit the new customers. The result: a competitor has not only recognized and captured the industrial laboratory market; exploiting the scale of the new segment, it has seized the hospital market, too. This is a very typical story. The first firm had failed to understand the significance of an unexpected success. It has now been bought out by a pharmaceutical company.

Of the other sources of innovation, scientific and technical research is listed last because, although undeniably important, it is also the most difficult, has the longest lead time, and is the most risky. We know quite a bit about how to manage research. But, as with other change opportunities, the important part is systematically to look out of the window and ask, is this an opportunity for the company? And if so, what kind of an opportunity? Most changes for most companies are not. Changes in population structure are very important for some businesses and totally unimportant for others. For a steel mill, except in so far as it affects the labor supply, there is almost no interest in demographics. On the other hand, changes in environmental awareness are of tremendous importance to a steel mill.

INNOVATION IS WORK ABOVE ALL

Everyone knows the second law of thermodynamics: all work degenerates into heat and friction. Drucker's first law is that everything degenerates into work, and if it does not degenerate into work, nothing gets done. A lot of it then becomes heat and friction, but first it has to be work. How we organize for work on innovation is a matter for the individual company. Very big and bureaucratic firms can be as innovative as small and nonbureaucratic ones. I am not actively proposing bureaucracy; the point is that it is a matter of systematic organization, clear strategy, and (again) hard work.

Du Pont, a notably bureaucratic company, has an enviable record as a successful and rapid innovator. 3M is not bureaucratic, but it is a very large company which has institutionalized innovation to the extent of incorporating it into the company's goals: at any period, no less than 25 percent of its turnover must come from products invented in the last five years. It always meets this target. And the goals are internalized. At 3M nobody gets into upper middle management who has not innovated, and everyone knows it. Forty years ago we were not so sure how to do these things. Now there is no excuse. The common pretext of waiting for the genius with the flash of inspiration will no longer wash. Any enterprise, no matter what its function, can today organize itself to undertake systematic entrepreneurship and purposeful innovation.

PERSONAL EFFECTIVENESS

We now come to the fourth and final part of our survey. In the light of the changing world economy, the advent of the information-based organization, and the need to systematize innovation and entrepreneurship, what skills and abilities will an executive need to be effective in the next years? The old skills are, of course, required, but there are some new ones which are likely to become increasingly important. I can think of three.

SKILL 1: MANAGEMENT BY GOING OUTSIDE

All managers are now *In Search of Excellence*. In that book Tom Peters preaches that managers should walk around. Walking around within the company is still to be recommended, but I believe that the emphasis has changed. The important thing now is to be enough on the outside of the company to be able to stand back and draw the right conclusions.

When everything around the company—markets, technologies, distributive channels, and values—is in a ferment of change, to wait in the office until the reports arrive on an executive's desk may be too long. One paramount piece of advice to senior managers: the next time a salesman goes on vacation, go out and take his or her place. Ignore the returning salesman's complaint that the customers are up in arms about the incompetent who took his place. The point of the exercise is that it forces you outside, into the marketplace, where results are. Remember that there are no results inside the firm. Up to the point where the customer reorders, there are only costs.

The external perspective might, for example, profitably prod companies to look at those who are not their customers but ought to be. A firm with a 22 percent market share is the market leader in most industries. Yet the more significant figure is that 78 percent of potential customers buy elsewhere. Why? That is usually the first indication of opportunities.

For several years I worked with the joint management and labor committees of our two largest automobile companies, General Motors and Ford. I could not persuade either unions or managements that what they mean by the word *quality* is not what customers mean. Ford and GM are very proud of the fact that when their cars come off the line they are "better" in quality terms than the Japanese. The trouble is that management and union people alike define quality as what is in the car when they deliver it. But it is the customer who defines quality, not the manufacturer. For example, I have a summer house in the Colorado Rockies, a 1,200-mile drive from my home in California. When something goes wrong with my car, I expect the local dealer in the next small town to have the part and fix the car. Yet GM and Ford have a compensation structure that rewards dealers for sales of new cars, not for service, and certainly not for keeping spare parts, so I have to wait a week for a spare part to arrive from a warehouse. Toyota, on the other hand, rewards service, so the dealer has the part in inventory and can replace it at once. Why can I not persuade Ford and GM that I am right? Because when I tell them to go outside, they simply talk to their own dealers.

So the first imperative is to learn to be outside, where the results of the business take place. And the only way to be on the outside is to work, not to visit. Nothing is more wasteful than a visit to the Barcelona subsidiary. But work for two days, standing behind the counter, and it is surprising how much the manager will learn about that company.

SKILL 2: FIND OUT THE INFORMATION YOU NEED TO DO YOUR JOB

Second, people must learn to take responsibility for their own information needs. Information responsibility to others is increasingly understood. But everyone in the information-based organization needs constantly to be thinking through what information he or she needs to make a valuable contribution in his or her own job. This may well be the most radical break with the present conventions of work. Even in the most highly computerized companies, perhaps especially in these companies, very few people have information. What they actually have is data, in such quantities that it causes information overload or blackout.

Information responsibility addresses another key problem. Most managers still believe that they need an information specialist to tell them what information they should have. But information specialists are providers of tools. They can tell us to use a hammer to bash an upholstery nail into a chair. But they cannot tell us whether we should be upholstering a chair in the first place. It is the manager's job to figure out what information he needs to identify:

1. what he is doing now;
2. what he should be doing; and
3. how he can get from (1) to (2).

This is by no means an easy task. But only if it is carried out will information begin to be the servant and the tool, and MIS departments results centers rather than the cost centers which they are now.

Until very recently there was no such thing as information. There were only experience and anecdotes. Now, for the first time, there are data. To convert those data into information means asking what you need, from whom, when, and in what form, and making sure that those who can provide the information also know and understand their responsibilities. A manager must ask, too, what information others require from him or her.

In the information-based organization of tomorrow, people will very largely have to control themselves. This does not mean we shall all be working in free-form organizations. That is nonsense. A land animal on this earth cannot be more than six inches in size without having a skeleton. Companies are the same. Above a very small size, every company needs the skeleton of a formal command structure. But an animal does not perform work or feel through the skeleton. It has a nervous system and a musculature for that. In the same way, information systems enable a person to organize and integrate his or her own work. They are also what someone takes control of and responsibility for. At that point the apparently insurmountable task of operating in a form that requires an *ad hoc* team looms much less large. The cross-functional team is the key. No one begins with pure research, applied research, engineering, development, manufacturing, or marketing any more. It takes much too long and results in wonderful products that nobody buys.

FOCUS FOR EFFECTIVENESS

In the same vein, managers should spend a little time thinking through what their company should hold them accountable for by way of contribution and results over the next 18 months. "What is the one thing that I, and only I, can do that if done well will make a difference?" A clear priority is essential. Do not diversify, do not splinter, do not try to do too many things at once. Without priorities, managers will be pulled in 5,000 directions at the same time. This applies particularly to top managers. Textbooks dwell, quite rightly, on the need to delegate down. What they fail to mention is that the real delegation is always up. In the end, the problem always comes to rest on the boss's desk. The buck stops there. That is his job, of course. But he above all needs to have time to do his own work; and he above all needs to know what his one, or two at most, contributions are to be.

As managers, we are not effective enough because we try to do too many things. The other great bane of organizations is that we believe that what we are trying to achieve is so obvious that we do not need to tell the person next door. Modern psychology began when Bishop Berkeley stated that because no two bodies can occupy the same space, nobody else could see what was obvious to one person. The people on whom you depend must understand what it is you are trying to accomplish, and you must communicate your priorities to them.

SKILL 3: BUILD LEARNING INTO THE SYSTEM

The third element of effectiveness is building learning into the system.

One of the great puzzles of history has always been the sixteenth century. By 1560 Europe was dominated by two institutions which 25 years earlier did not even exist: the north by the Calvinist church and the south by the Jesuit order. Both came into being in 1535, and by the seventh decade of the century they had become dominant institutions. Most of their members worked by themselves, in considerable danger and under great pressure. What was their secret? With the benefit of modern learning theory, we can begin to see what happened. Calvin and Loyola applied the most important principle in learning: that of feedback. In any key activity area, the first step is to set down what you expect will happen. Nine months later, the actual results are examined and compared with original expectations.

As Loyola and Calvin discovered, feedback is the primary key to learning. Crucially, since no one is productive by putting weaknesses to work, feedback identifies the strengths. Learners need to know their strengths in order to find out where to improve. What bad habits inhibit those strengths? In what areas has the Good Lord simply not provided any ability at all? Most schools and most education are problem-focused; they concentrate on correcting weakness. Up to a point, that is necessary. Every student needs the basic skills.

But real world-beating performance, like learning, is built on strengths. When it is so organized, learning is astonishingly rapid, for the simple reason that is has focus.

Learning, moreover, must be continuous. We have to recognize the unwelcome fact that the knowledge of those who are five years out of school is by definition obsolescent. The U.S. authorities now require physicians to take refresher courses and sit requalifying exams every five years. This caused initial grumbles from the examinees, which almost without exception gave way to wonderment at how much had changed and how much they had forgotten. The same principle should apply for engineers, and even more so for marketing. It should therefore be part of every manager's practice to go back to school every so often for a week at a time. Many big companies are currently building their own in-house education facilities. I advise caution here. The greatest danger to the big company is the belief that there is a right way, a wrong way, and our way. In-house training tends to emphasize and strengthen that view. Skills, yes; teach them in-house. But for purposes of broadening the horizon, questioning established beliefs, and for organized abandonment, it is better to be confronted with diversity and challenge. For these, managers should be exposed to people who work for different companies and do things in different ways.

Those are some of the key things for an individual to know and do about making and keeping himself or herself effective as an executive in a challenging world. There are enormous opportunities, because change *is* opportunity. But there is no predictability. Turbulence—for those who still remember a little mathematics—is characterized by having no predictability. It is certain that the unexpected will happen; but it is impossible to predict where, when, or how. We live in a very turbulent time, not because there is so much change, but because it moves in so many different directions. In this situation, the effective executive has to be able to recognize and run with opportunity, to learn, and constantly to refresh the knowledge base.

INDEX